SHŌBŌGENZŌ
THE TRUE DHARMA-EYE TREASURY
VOLUME I

BDK English Tripiṭaka Series

SHŌBŌGENZŌ
THE TRUE DHARMA-EYE TREASURY
Volume I

(Taishō Volume 82, Number 2582)

Translated from the Japanese

by

Gudo Wafu Nishijima
and
Chodo Cross

Numata Center
for Buddhist Translation and Research
2007

Gudo Nishijima was born in Yokohama, Japan, in 1919, and graduated from Tokyo University in 1946. In 1940 he first met Master Kōdō Sawaki, whose teaching he received until the master's death in 1965. During this time he combined the daily practice of zazen and study of the Shōbōgenzō *with a career at the Japanese Ministry of Finance and at a securities financing company. In 1973 he became a priest under the late Master Renpo Niwa, and in 1977 he received transmission of the Dharma from Master Niwa (who subsequently became abbot of Eiheiji). Shortly thereafter Nishijima became a consultant to the Ida Ryogokudo company, and in 1987 established the Ida Ryogokudo Zazen Dōjō in Ichikawa City near Tokyo. He continues to give instruction in zazen and lectures, in Japanese and in English, on Master Dōgen's works in Tokyo and Osaka and at the Tokei-in Temple in Shizuoka Prefecture.*

Chodo Cross was born in Birmingham, England, in 1959. He went to Japan in 1982, after graduating from Sheffield University, met Nishijima Roshi in June 1982, and received the Buddhist precepts in May 1983. In 1994 he returned to England to train as a teacher of the FM Alexander Technique. He formally received the Dharma in 1998 and in the following year established the Middle Way Re-education Centre (www.the-middle-way.org).

Second Printing, 2009
ISBN: 978-1-886439-35-1
Library of Congress Catalog Card Number: 2007938225

Published by
Numata Center for Buddhist Translation and Research
2620 Warring Street
Berkeley, California 94704

Printed in the United States of America

A Message on the Publication of the English Tripiṭaka

The Buddhist canon is said to contain eighty-four thousand different teachings. I believe that this is because the Buddha's basic approach was to prescribe a different treatment for every spiritual ailment, much as a doctor prescribes a different medicine for every medical ailment. Thus his teachings were always appropriate for the particular suffering individual and for the time at which the teaching was given, and over the ages not one of his prescriptions has failed to relieve the suffering to which it was addressed.

Ever since the Buddha's Great Demise over twenty-five hundred years ago, his message of wisdom and compassion has spread throughout the world. Yet no one has ever attempted to translate the entire Buddhist canon into English throughout the history of Japan. It is my greatest wish to see this done and to make the translations available to the many English-speaking people who have never had the opportunity to learn about the Buddha's teachings.

Of course, it would be impossible to translate all of the Buddha's eighty-four thousand teachings in a few years. I have, therefore, had one hundred thirty-nine of the scriptural texts in the prodigious Taishō edition of the Chinese Buddhist canon selected for inclusion in the First Series of this translation project.

It is in the nature of this undertaking that the results are bound to be criticized. Nonetheless, I am convinced that unless someone takes it upon himself or herself to initiate this project, it will never be done. At the same time, I hope that an improved, revised edition will appear in the future.

It is most gratifying that, thanks to the efforts of more than a hundred Buddhist scholars from the East and the West, this monumental project has finally gotten off the ground. May the rays of the Wisdom of the Compassionate One reach each and every person in the world.

NUMATA Yehan
Founder of the English
Tripiṭaka Project

August 7, 1991

Editorial Foreword

In January 1982, Dr. NUMATA Yehan, the founder of Bukkyō Dendō Kyōkai (Society for the Promotion of Buddhism), decided to begin the monumental task of translating the complete Taishō edition of the Chinese Tripiṭaka (Buddhist canon) into the English language. Under his leadership, a special preparatory committee was organized in April 1982. By July of the same year, the Translation Committee of the English Tripiṭaka was officially convened.

The initial Committee consisted of the following members: (late) HANAYAMA Shōyū (Chairperson), (late) BANDŌ Shōjun, ISHIGAMI Zennō, (late) KAMATA Shigeo, KANAOKA Shūyū, MAYEDA Sengaku, NARA Yasuaki, (late) SAYEKI Shinkō, (late) SHIOIRI Ryōtatsu, TAMARU Noriyoshi, (late) TAMURA Kwansei, URYŪZU Ryūshin, and YUYAMA Akira. Assistant members of the Committee were as follows: KANAZAWA Atsushi, WATANABE Shōgo, Rolf Giebel of New Zealand, and Rudy Smet of Belgium.

After holding planning meetings on a monthly basis, the Committee selected one hundred thirty-nine texts for the First Series of translations, an estimated one hundred printed volumes in all. The texts selected are not necessarily limited to those originally written in India but also include works written or composed in China and Japan. While the publication of the First Series proceeds, the texts for the Second Series will be selected from among the remaining works; this process will continue until all the texts, in Japanese as well as in Chinese, have been published.

Frankly speaking, it will take perhaps one hundred years or more to accomplish the English translation of the complete Chinese and Japanese texts, for they consist of thousands of works. Nevertheless, as Dr. NUMATA wished, it is the sincere hope of the Committee that this project will continue unto completion, even after all its present members have passed away.

Dr. NUMATA passed away on May 5, 1994, at the age of ninety-seven, entrusting his son, Mr. NUMATA Toshihide, with the continuation and completion of the Translation Project. The Committee also lost its able and devoted Chairperson,

Professor HANAYAMA Shōyū, on June 16, 1995, at the age of sixty-three. After these severe blows, the Committee elected me, then Vice President of Musashino Women's College, to be the Chair in October 1995. The Committee has renewed its determination to carry out the noble intention of Dr. NUMATA, under the leadership of Mr. NUMATA Toshihide.

The present members of the Committee are MAYEDA Sengaku (Chairperson), ISHIGAMI Zennō, ICHISHIMA Shōshin, KANAOKA Shūyū, NARA Yasuaki, TAMARU Noriyoshi, Kenneth K. Tanaka, URYŪZU Ryūshin, YUYAMA Akira, WATANABE Shōgo, and assistant member YONEZAWA Yoshiyasu.

The Numata Center for Buddhist Translation and Research was established in November 1984, in Berkeley, California, U.S.A., to assist in the publication of the BDK English Tripiṭaka First Series. The Publication Committee was organized at the Numata Center in December 1991. Since then the publication of all the volumes has been and will continue to be conducted under the supervision of this Committee in close cooperation with the Editorial Committee in Tokyo.

MAYEDA Sengaku
Chairperson
Editorial Committee of
the BDK English Tripiṭaka

Publisher's Foreword

On behalf of the Publication Committee, I am happy to present this contribution to the BDK English Tripiṭaka Series. The initial translation and editing of the Buddhist scripture found here were performed under the direction of the Editorial Committee in Tokyo, Japan, chaired by Professor Sengaku Mayeda, Professor Emeritus of Musashino University. The Publication Committee members then put this volume through a rigorous succession of editorial and bookmaking efforts.

Both the Editorial Committee in Tokyo and the Publication Committee in Berkeley are dedicated to the production of clear, readable English texts of the Buddhist canon. The members of both committees and associated staff work to honor the deep faith, spirit, and concern of the late Reverend Dr. Yehan Numata, who founded the BDK English Tripiṭaka Series in order to disseminate Buddhist teachings throughout the world.

The long-term goal of our project is the translation and publication of the one hundred-volume Taishō edition of the Chinese Buddhist canon, plus a few influential extracanonical Japanese Buddhist texts. The list of texts selected for the First Series of this translation project is given at the end of each volume.

As Chair of the Publication Committee, I am deeply honored to serve in the post formerly held by the late Dr. Philip B. Yampolsky, who was so good to me during his lifetime; the esteemed Dr. Kenneth K. Inada, who has had such a great impact on Buddhist studies in the United States; and the beloved late Dr. Francis H. Cook, a dear friend and colleague.

In conclusion, let me thank the members of the Publication Committee for the efforts they have undertaken in preparing this volume for publication: Senior Editor Marianne Dresser, Dr. Hudaya Kandahjaya, Dr. Eisho Nasu, Reverend Kiyoshi Yamashita, and Reverend Brian Nagata, President of the Numata Center for Buddhist Translation and Research.

John R. McRae
Chairperson
Publication Committee

Note on the BDK English Tripiṭaka Series Reprint Edition

After due consideration, the Editorial Committee of the BDK English Tripiṭaka Series chose to reprint the translation of Dōgen's *Shōbōgenzō* by Gudo Wafu Nishijima and Chodo Cross (originally published under the title *Master Dogen's Shobogenzo, Books 1–4,* by Windbell Publications, 1996–1999) in order to make more widely available this exemplary translation of this important text. The remaining volumes II, III, and IV of this edition of *Shōbōgenzō: The True Dharma-eye Treasury* will appear in the forthcoming year.

Aside from the minor stylistic changes and the romanization of all Chinese and Japanese characters in adherence to the publishing guidelines of the BDK English Tripiṭaka Series, this edition reproduces as closely as possible the original translation.

Contents

A Message on the Publication of the English Tripiṭaka
NUMATA Yehan v

Editorial Foreword *MAYEDA Sengaku* vii

Publisher's Foreword *John R. McRae* ix

Note on the BDK English Tripiṭaka Series Reprint Edition xi

Translators' Introduction *Gudo Wafu Nishijima and Chodo Cross* xv

Shōbōgenzō: The True Dharma-eye Treasury, Volume I

Chapter One. *Bendōwa:* A Talk about Pursuing the Truth 3
Chapter Two. *Maka-hannya-haramitsu: Mahāprajñāpāramitā* 31
Chapter Three. *Genjō-kōan:* The Realized Universe 41
Chapter Four. *Ikka-no-myōju:* One Bright Pearl 49
Chapter Five. *Jū-undō-shiki:* Rules for the Hall of Accumulated Cloud 59
Chapter Six. *Soku-shin-ze-butsu:* Mind Here and Now Is Buddha 65
Chapter Seven. *Senjō:* Washing 75
Chapter Eight. *Raihai-tokuzui:* Prostrating to the Marrow of Attainment 89
Chapter Nine. *Keisei-sanshiki:* The Voices of the River Valley and the Form of the Mountains 109
Chapter Ten. *Shoaku-makusa:* Not Doing Wrongs 127
Chapter Eleven. *Uji:* Existence-time 143
Chapter Twelve. *Kesa-kudoku:* The Merit of the *Kaṣāya* 157
Chapter Thirteen. *Den-e:* The Transmission of the Robe 195
Chapter Fourteen. *Sansuigyō:* The Sutra of Mountains and Water 217
Chapter Fifteen. *Busso:* The Buddhist Patriarchs 235
Chapter Sixteen. *Shisho:* The Certificate of Succession 245
Chapter Seventeen. *Hokke-ten-hokke:* The Flower of Dharma Turns the Flower of Dharma 263

Chapter Eighteen. *Shin-fukatoku:* Mind Cannot Be Grasped (The Former) 289
Chapter Nineteen. *Shin-fukatoku:* Mind Cannot Be Grasped (The Latter) 297
Chapter Twenty. *Kokyō:* The Eternal Mirror 313
Chapter Twenty-one. *Kankin:* Reading Sutras 341

Appendix I. Chinese Masters 359

Appendix II. *Fukanzazengi: Universal Guide to the Standard Method of Zazen* (*Rufubon*—The Popular Edition) 363

Appendix III. *Busso:* The Buddhist Patriarchs 371

Appendix IV. The *Kaṣāya* 373

Appendix V. Traditional Temple Layout 375

Appendix VI. *Lotus Sutra* References 381

Glossary of Sanskrit Terms 413

Bibliography 447

Index 455

A List of the Volumes of the BDK English Tripiṭaka (First Series) 487

Translators' Introduction

Preface
by Gudo Wafu Nishijima

The *Shōbōgenzō* was written by Dōgen in the thirteenth century. I think that reading the *Shōbōgenzō* is the best way to come to an exact understanding of Buddhist theory, for Dōgen was outstanding in his ability to understand and explain Buddhism rationally.

Of course, Dōgen did not depart from traditional Buddhist thought. However at the same time, his thought as expressed in the *Shōbōgenzō* follows his own unique method of presentation. If we understand this method, the *Shōbōgenzō* would not be difficult to read. But unless we understand his method of thinking, it would be impossible for us to understand what Dōgen is trying to say in the *Shōbōgenzō*.

Buddhists revere the Buddha, Dharma, and Sangha. Buddha means Gautama Buddha. Sangha means those people who pursue Gautama Buddha's truth. Dharma means reality. Dōgen's unique method of thought was his way of explaining the Dharma.

Basically, he looks at a problem from two sides, and then tries to synthesize the two viewpoints into a middle way. This method has similarities with the dialectic method in Western philosophy, particularly as used by Hegel and Marx. Hegel's dialectic, however, is based on belief in spirit, and Marx's dialectic is based on belief in matter. Dōgen, through the Buddhist dialectic, wants to lead us away from thoughts based on belief in spirit and matter.

Dōgen recognized the existence of something that is different from thought; that is, reality in action. Action is completely different from intellectual thought and completely different from the perceptions of our senses. So Dōgen's method of thinking is based on action and, because of that, it has some unique characteristics.

First, Dōgen recognized that things we usually separate in our minds are, in action, one reality. To express this oneness of subject and object Dōgen says, for example:

> If a human being, even for a single moment, manifests the Buddha's posture in the three forms of conduct, while [that person] sits up straight in *samādhi,* the entire world of Dharma assumes the Buddha's posture and the whole of space becomes the state of realization.

This sentence, taken from the *Bendōwa* chapter (Chapter One), is not illogical but it reflects a new kind of logic.

Secondly, Dōgen recognized that in action, the only time that really exists is the moment of the present, and the only place that really exists is this place. So the present moment and this place—the here and now—are very important concepts in Dōgen's philosophy of action.

The philosophy of action is not unique to Dōgen; this idea was also the center of Gautama Buddha's thought. All the Buddhist patriarchs of ancient India and China relied upon this theory and realized Buddhism itself. They also recognized the oneness of reality, the importance of the present moment, and the importance of this place.

But explanations of reality are only explanations. In the *Shōbōgenzō,* after he had explained a problem on the basis of action, Dōgen wanted to point the reader into the realm of action itself. To do this, he sometimes used poems, he sometimes used old Buddhist stories that suggest reality, and he sometimes used symbolic expressions.

So the chapters of the *Shōbōgenzō* usually follow a four-phased pattern. First Dōgen picks up and outlines a Buddhist idea. In the second phase, he examines the idea very objectively or concretely, in order to defeat idealistic or intellectual interpretations of it. In the third phase, Dōgen's expression becomes even more concrete, practical, and realistic, relying on the philosophy of action. And in the fourth phase, Dōgen tries to suggest reality with words. Ultimately, these trials are only trials. But we can feel something that can be called reality in his sincere trials when we reach the end of each chapter.

I think this four-phased pattern is related with the Four Noble Truths preached by Gautama Buddha in his first lecture. By realizing Dōgen's method of thinking, we can come to realize the true meaning of Gautama Buddha's Four Noble Truths. This is why we persevere in studying the *Shōbōgenzō.*

Notes on the Translation
by Chodo Cross

Source Text

The source text for Chapters One to Twenty-one is contained in the first three volumes of Nishijima Roshi's twelve-volume *Gendaigo-yaku-shōbōgenzō* (*Shōbōgenzō in Modern Japanese*). The *Gendaigo-yaku-shōbōgenzō* contains Dōgen's original text, notes on the text, and the text rendered into modern Japanese. Reference numbers enclosed in brackets at the beginning of some paragraphs of this translation refer to corresponding page numbers in the *Gendaigo-yaku-shōbōgenzō,* and much of the material reproduced in the notes comes from the *Gendaigo-yaku-shōbōgenzō.*

The *Gendaigo-yaku-shōbōgenzō* is based upon the ninety-five–chapter edition of the *Shōbōgenzō,* which was arranged in chronological order by Master Hangyō Kōzen sometime between 1688 and 1703. The ninety-five–chapter edition is the most comprehensive single edition, including important chapters such as *Bendōwa* (Chapter One) and *Hokke-ten-hokke* (Chapter Seventeen) that do not appear in other editions. Furthermore, it was the first edition to be printed with woodblocks, in the Bunka era (1804–1818), and so the content was fixed at that time. The original woodblocks are still preserved at Eiheiji, the temple in Fukui prefecture that Dōgen founded.

Sanskrit Terms

As a rule, Sanskrit words such as *samādhi* (the balanced state), *prajñā* (real wisdom), and *bhikṣu* (monk), which Dōgen reproduces phonetically with Chinese characters, read in Japanese as *zanmai, hannya,* and *biku,* have been retained in Sanskrit form.

In addition, some Chinese characters representing the meaning of Sanskrit terms that will already be familiar to readers (or which will become familiar in the course of reading the *Shōbōgenzō*) have been returned to Sanskrit. Examples are *hō* ("reality," "law," "method," "things and phenomena"), usually translated as "Dharma" or "*dharma*s"; *nyorai* ("Thus-come"), always translated as "Tathāgata"; and *shōmon* ("voice-hearer"), always translated as *"śrāvaka."*

There are places in the *Shōbōgenzō* where Dōgen himself, relying on his wide familiarity with Chinese sutras, traces the origin of Chinese characters back to Sanskrit words. A prominent example is *dō* ("way," "truth"), which, in the opening paragraph of Chapter Seventy (Vol. III), *Hotsu-bodaishin,* Dōgen explicitly identifies with the Sanskrit term *bodhi.*

Even in translating Chinese terms whose Sanskrit derivation Dōgen does not explicitly recognize, knowledge of the Sanskrit can still be very helpful. An early example is the adjective *mui* used in the opening sentence of Chapter One, *Bendōwa,* to describe zazen. Japanese dictionaries define *mui* as "idle" or "inactive," but Nishijima Roshi originally translated it as "natural." In Buddhist sutras, *mui* represents the Sanskrit *asaṃskṛta,* which is defined in the Monier-Williams *Sanskrit-English Dictionary* as "not prepared, not consecrated; unadorned; unpolished, rude (as speech)." The Sanskrit dictionary definition, while by no means an absolute criterion, supports Nishijima Roshi's interpretation that *mui* describes zazen as natural, or without intention; something as it is.

Another example: The character *ro,* "leakage," appears in the opening sentences of the *Lotus Sutra,* where it represents the Sanskrit *āsrava.* The *Sanskrit-English Dictionary* defines *āsrava* as "the foam on boiling rice; a door opening into water and allowing the stream to descend through it; (with Jainas) the action of the senses which impels the soul towards external objects; distress, affliction, pain." Thus, in the second paragraph of Chapter Ten, *Shoaku-makusa,* the noun *muro,* "no leakage," appears to describe the state without emotional distress, that is, the balanced and satisfied state of body-and-mind. This does not mean that *muro* should be translated as "the state without emotional distress" or as "the balanced and satisfied state of body-and-mind," but such meaning will hopefully be conveyed by a literal translation such as "[the state] without excess" or "[the state] without the superfluous," supported by a note and a cross-reference to the Glossary of Sanskrit Terms.

Chinese Proper Nouns

In general Chinese proper nouns have been romanized according to their Japanese pronunciation—as Dōgen would have pronounced them for a Japanese audience. Thus, we have let the romanization of all names of Chinese masters follow the Japanese pronunciation, while also adding an appendix showing the Chinese romanization of Chinese masters' names. For other Chinese proper names, we have used Chinese romanization only for terms such as the Shaolin Temple (in Japanese romanization Shōrinji), whose Chinese romanization may already be familiar to most readers.

Chinese Text

Dōgen wrote the *Shōbōgenzō* in Japanese, that is to say, using a combination of Chinese characters (squared ideograms usually consisting of many strokes) and the Japanese phonetic alphabet which is more abbreviated. Chinese of course is written in Chinese characters only. Therefore when Dōgen quotes a passage, or borrows a phrase, from a Chinese text—as he very often does—it is readily apparent to the eye as a string of Chinese ideograms uninterrupted by Japanese squiggles. We attempted to mirror this effect, to some degree, by using italics for such passages and phrases. (Editorial Note: In this BDK English Tripiṭaka Series edition, all such passages appear in quotemarks.)

A pattern that occurs frequently in the *Shōbōgenzō* is a quotation of Chinese characters from a conversation between Zen masters, or from a sutra, followed by Dōgen's commentary, in which each Chinese character takes on new meaning. An early example is in the second paragraph of Chapter Two, *Maka-hannya-haramitsu,* where Dōgen quotes the *Great Wisdom Sutra* (*Mahāprajñāpāramitā-sūtra*). The sutra says *setsu sa ze nen,* literally, "[the monk] secretly makes this thought." As a conventional phrase, this just means "[the monk] secretly thinks." However, individually, the character *setsu* (secret) suggests something beyond thinking and sense perception, that is, something real; the character *sa* (make or work) suggests action; the character *ze* (this) suggests concrete reality; and the character *nen* (thought, idea, mindfulness) suggests not only thought but the monk's real state of mind. So Dōgen's commentary says that the monk's *setsu sa ze nen* ("secretly working concrete mind") is real wisdom itself.

In this way, Dōgen emphasizes that the words of the sutras and masters whom he reveres are not meant to convey only conceptual meaning. Those words are trying to bring us back to the reality that is prior to words. This is particularly true with respect to the *Lotus Sutra.* The *Lotus Sutra* contains the characters *zekyō,* "this sutra." In several chapters of the *Shōbōgenzō* (specifically Chapter Fifty-two [Vol. III], *Bukkyō,* but see also Chapter Seventeen, *Hokke-ten-hokke*) the fact emerges that, in Dōgen's mind, this sutra and the real universe in which we live are identified. That being so, Dōgen, in his commentaries, seems to treat the characters of the *Lotus Sutra* not as a stream of concepts but rather as a series of momentary mirrors, or independent blocks, of real form—to be brought in and rearranged as Dōgen sees fit.

In such instances, readers will want to refer to the Chinese characters in question. Fortunately, due to the generosity of Mr. Tadashi Nakamae (who provided the computer) and the industriousness of Michael and Yoko Luetchford (who installed the software and created and input unavailable characters), we were able to reproduce the Chinese characters in the notes and in an appendix of *Lotus Sutra* references. (Editorial Note: In adherence to the publishing guidelines of the BDK English Tripiṭaka Series, all Chinese characters have been omitted in this reprint edition. Interested readers may consult the original Windbell Publications edition, *Master Dogen's Shobogenzo,* Books 1–4.)

The Meaning of *Shōbogenzō,* "True Dharma-eye Treasury"

Shō means "right" or "true." *Hō,* "law," represents the Sanskrit "Dharma." All of us belong to something that, prior to our naming it or thinking about it, is already there. And it already belongs to us. "Dharma" is one name for what is already there.

Hōgen, "Dharma-eye," represents the direct experience of what is already there. Because the Dharma is prior to thinking, it must be directly experienced by a faculty that is other than thinking. *Gen,* "eye," represents this direct experience that is other than thinking.

Shōbōgen, "true Dharma-eye," therefore describes the right experience of what is already there.

Zō, "storehouse" or "treasury," suggests something that contains and preserves the right experience of what is already there. Thus, Nishijima Roshi has interpreted *Shōbōgenzō,* "true Dharma-eye treasury," as an expression of zazen itself.

All who benefit from this translation, myself included, should be profoundly grateful to Nishijima Roshi for his unceasing effort to clarify the real meaning of *Shōbōgenzō.*

SHŌBŌGENZŌ
THE TRUE DHARMA-EYE TREASURY
VOLUME I

by

Dōgen

[Chapter One]

Bendōwa

A Talk about Pursuing the Truth

Translator's Note: Ben *means "to make an effort" or "to pursue,"* dō *means "the truth," and* wa *means "a talk" or "story." Master Dōgen usually used the word* bendō *to indicate the practice of zazen, so* Bendōwa *means a talk about pursuing the truth, or a talk about the practice of zazen. This volume was not included in the first edition of the* Shōbōgenzō. *It was found in Kyoto in the Kanbun era (1661–1673), and added to the* Shōbōgenzō *when the ninety-five–chapter edition was edited by Master Hangyō Kōzen in the Genroku era (1688–1704).*

[11] When the buddha-tathāgatas,[1] each having received the one-to-one transmission of the splendid Dharma, experience the supreme state of *bodhi,*[2] they possess a subtle method that is supreme and without intention. The reason this [method] is transmitted only from buddha to buddha, without deviation, is that the *samādhi* of receiving and using the self[3] is its standard. For enjoyment of this *samādhi,* the practice of [za]zen, in the erect sitting posture, has been established as the authentic gate. This Dharma[4] is abundantly present in each human being, but if we do not practice it, it does not manifest itself, and if we do not experience it, it cannot be realized. When we let go, it has already filled the hands; how could it be defined as one or many? When we speak, it fills the mouth; it has no restriction in any direction. When buddhas are constantly dwelling in and maintaining this state, they do not leave recognitions and perceptions in separate aspects [of reality]; and when living beings are eternally functioning in this state, aspects [of reality] do not appear to them in separate recognitions and perceptions.[5] The effort in pursuing the truth[6] that I am now teaching makes the myriad *dharma*s[7] real in experience; it enacts the oneness of reality on the path of liberation.[8] At that moment of clearing barriers and getting free, how could this paragraph be relevant? 15a13

15b [14] After I established the will to pursue the Dharma, I visited [good] counselors[9] in every quarter of our land. I met Myōzen[10] of Kennin [Temple]. Nine seasons of frosts and of flowers[11] swiftly passed while I followed him, learning a little of the customs of the Rinzai lineage. Only Myōzen had received the authentic transmission of the supreme Buddha-Dharma, as the most excellent disciple of the founding master, Master Eisai[12]—the other students could never compare with him. I then went to the great kingdom of Song, visiting [good] counselors in the east and west of Chekiang[13] and hearing of the tradition through the gates of the five lineages.[14] At last I visited Zen Master Nyojō[15] of Daibyakuhō Mountain,[16] and there I was able to complete the great task of a lifetime of practice. After that, at the beginning of the great Song era of Shōjō,[17] I came home determined to spread the Dharma and to save living beings—it was as if a heavy burden had been placed on my shoulders. Nevertheless, in order to wait for an upsurge during which I might discharge my sense of mission, I thought I would spend some time wandering like a cloud, calling here and there like a water weed, in the style of the ancient sages. Yet if there were any true practitioners who put the will to the truth first, being naturally unconcerned with fame and profit, they might be fruitlessly misled by false teachers and might needlessly throw a veil over right understanding. They might idly become drunk with self-deception, and sink forever into the state of delusion. How would they be able to promote the right seeds of *prajñā,*[18] or have the opportunity to attain the truth? If I were now absorbed in drifting like a cloud or a water weed, which mountains and rivers ought they to visit?[19] Feeling that this would be a pitiful situation, I decided to compile a record of the customs and standards that I experienced firsthand in the Zen monasteries of the great kingdom of Song, together with a record of profound instruction from a [good] counselor which I have received and maintained. I will leave this record to people who learn in practice and are easy in the truth, so that they can know the right Dharma of the Buddha's lineage. This may be a true mission.

15c [17] [The sutras] say: Great Master Śākyamuni at the order on Vulture Peak[20] transmitted the Dharma to Mahākāśyapa.[21] [The Dharma] was authentically transmitted from patriarch to patriarch and it reached Venerable Bodhidharma.[22] The Venerable One himself went to China and transmitted the Dharma to Great Master Eka.[23] This was the first transmission of the Buddha-

Dharma in the Eastern Lands.[24] Transmitted one-to-one in this manner, [the Dharma] arrived naturally at Zen Master Daikan,[25] the Sixth Patriarch. At that time, as the real Buddha-Dharma spread through the Eastern [Land of] China, it became clear that [the Dharma] is beyond literary expression. The Sixth Patriarch had two excellent disciples, Ejō of Nangaku[26] and Gyōshi of Seigen.[27] Both of them, having received and maintained the posture of Buddha,[28] were guiding teachers of human beings and gods alike. [The Dharma] flowed and spread in these two streams, and five lineages were established. These are the so-called Hōgen sect, Igyō sect, Sōtō sect, Unmon sect, and Rinzai sect. In great Song [China] today the Rinzai sect alone holds sway throughout the country. Although there are differences between the five traditions, the posture with the stamp of the Buddha's mind[29] is only one. Even in the great kingdom of Song, although from the Later Han dynasty[30] onward philosophical texts had been disseminated through the country, and had left some impression, no one could decide which were inferior and which were superior. After the ancestral master came from the west, he directly cut to the source of the confusion,[31] and spread the unadulterated Buddha-Dharma. We should hope that the same thing will happen in our country. [The sutras] say that the many patriarchs and the many buddhas, who dwelled in and maintained the Buddha-Dharma, all relied on the practice of sitting erect in the *samādhi* of receiving and using the self,[32] and esteemed [this practice] as the right way to disclose the state of realization. Human beings who attained the truth in the Western Heavens and Eastern Lands followed this style of practice. This [practice] relies on the mystical and authentic transmission of the subtle method from master to disciple, and the [disciple's] reception and maintenance of the true essence of the teachings.

[20] In the authentic transmission of [our] religion, it is said that this Buddha-Dharma,[33] which has been authentically and directly transmitted one-to-one, is supreme among the supreme. After the initial meeting with a [good] counselor we never again need to burn incense, to do prostrations, to recite Buddha's name, to practice confession, or to read sutras. Just sit and 16a
get the state that is free of body and mind. If a human being, even for a single moment, manifests the Buddha's posture in the three forms of conduct,[34] while [that person] sits up straight in *samādhi,* the entire world of Dharma assumes the Buddha's posture and the whole of space becomes the state of

realization. [The practice] thus increases the Dharma joy that is the original state of the buddha-tathāgatas, and renews the splendor of their realization of the truth. Furthermore, throughout the Dharma worlds in ten directions, ordinary beings of the three states and the six states[35] all become clear and pure in body and mind at once; they experience the state of great liberation,[36] and their original features appear. Then all *dharma*s experience and understand right realization and myriad things each put their Buddhist body into practice; in an instant, they totally transcend the limits of experience and understanding; they sit erect as kings of the *bodhi* tree;[37] in one moment, they turn the great Dharma wheel[38] which is in the unequaled state of equilibrium;[39] and they expound the ultimate, unadorned, and profound state of *prajñā*. These balanced and right states of realization also work the other way,[40] following paths of intimate and mystical cooperation, so that this person who sits in zazen steadfastly gets free of body and mind, cuts away miscellaneous impure views and thoughts [accumulated] from the past, and thus experiences and understands the natural and pure Buddha-Dharma. Throughout each of the infinitesimal, innumerable seats of truth of the buddha-tathāgatas, [the practitioner] promotes the Buddha's work and spreads its influence far and wide over those who have the ascendant makings of a buddha, thus vividly uplifting the ascendant real state of a buddha. At this time, everything in the universe in ten directions—soil, earth, grass, and trees; fences, walls, tiles, and pebbles—performs the Buddha's work. The people that receive the benefit thus produced by wind and water are all mystically helped by the fine and unthinkable influence of the Buddha, and they exhibit the immediate state of realization. All beings who receive and utilize this water and fire spread the influence of the Buddha in the original state of experience, so that those who live and talk with them, also, are all reciprocally endowed with the limitless buddha-virtue. Expanding and promoting their activity far and wide, they permeate the inside and the outside of the entire
16b universe with the limitless, unceasing, unthinkable, and incalculable Buddha-Dharma. [The state] is not dimmed by the views of these individuals themselves, however, because the state in the quietness, without intentional activity, is direct experience. If we divide practice-and-experience into two stages, as in the thoughts of common folk, each part can be perceived and understood separately. [But] if perception and understanding are mixed in, that is

not the standard state of experience, because the standard state of experience is beyond deluded emotion. Although, in the quietness, mind and external world enter together into the state of experience and pass together out of the state of realization, [those movements] are the state of receiving and using the self.[41] Therefore, [movements of mind and the external world] neither stir a single molecule nor disturb a single form, but they accomplish the vast and great work of Buddha and the profound and fine influence of Buddha. The grass, trees, soil, and earth reached by this guiding influence all radiate great brightness, and their preaching of the deep and fine Dharma is without end. Grass, trees, fences, and walls become able to preach for all souls, [both] common people and saints; and conversely, all souls, [both] common people and saints, preach for grass, trees, fences, and walls. The world of self-consciousness, and [the world] of consciousness of external objects, lack nothing—they are already furnished with the concrete form of real experience. The standard state of real experience, when activated, allows no idle moment. Zazen, even if it is only one human being sitting for one moment, thus enters into mystical cooperation with all *dharma*s, and completely penetrates all times; and it therefore performs, within the limitless universe, the eternal work of the Buddha's guiding influence in the past, future, and present. For everyone it is completely the same practice and the same experience. The practice is not confined to the sitting itself; it strikes space and resonates, [like] ringing that continues before and after a bell. How could [the practice] be limited to this place? All concrete things[42] possess original practice as their original features; it is beyond comprehension. Remember, even 16c
if the countless buddhas in ten directions, as numerous as the sands of the Ganges, tried with all their power and all their buddha-wisdom to calculate or comprehend the merit of one person's zazen, they could not even get close.

[26] Now we have heard how high and great is the merit of this zazen. [But] some stupid person might doubtingly ask, "There are many gates to the Buddha-Dharma. Why do you solely recommend sitting in zazen?"[43]

I say: Because it is the authentic gate to the Buddha-Dharma.

[26] [Someone] asks, "Why do you see it as the only authentic gate?"

I say: Great Master Śākyamuni exactly transmitted, as the authentic tradition, this subtle method of grasping the state of truth, and the tathāgatas of the three times[44] all attained the truth through zazen. Thus the fact that [zazen] is the authentic gate has been transmitted and received. Furthermore, the patriarchs of the Western Heavens and the Eastern Lands all attained the truth through zazen. Therefore I am now preaching [zazen] to human beings and gods as the authentic gate.

[27] [Someone] asks, "That which relies upon receiving the authentic transmission of the subtle method of the Tathāgata, or upon following the traces of the ancestral masters, is surely beyond the intellect of the common person. Reading sutras and reciting the names of buddhas, however, may naturally become the causes and conditions of enlightenment. But as for just idly sitting without doing anything, how can that be the means of getting enlightenment?"

I say: If you now think that the *samādhi* of the buddhas, the supreme and great Dharma, is idle sitting without doing anything, you are a person who insults the Great Vehicle.[45] [Such] delusion is so deep that it is like being in the ocean and saying there is no water. [In zazen] we are already seated,
17a stably and thankfully, in the buddhas' *samādhi* of receiving and using the self. Is this not the accomplishment of vast and great virtue? It is pitiful that your eyes are not yet open and your mind remains in a drunken stupor. In general, the state of the buddhas is unthinkable: intelligence cannot reach it. How much less could disbelief or inferior wisdom know the state? Only people of great makings and right belief can enter into it. For people of disbelief, even if taught, it is difficult to receive the teaching—even on Vulture Peak there were people [about whom the Buddha said,] "That they withdraw also is fine."[46] As a general rule, when right belief emerges in our mind, we should do training and learn in practice. Otherwise, we should rest for a while. Regret the fact if you will, but from ancient times the Dharma has been dry. Further, do you know for yourself any virtue that is gained from practices such as reading sutras and reciting names of buddhas? It is very unreliable to think that only to wag the tongue and to raise the voice has the virtue of the Buddha's work. When we compare [such practices] with the Buddha-Dharma, they fade further and further into the distance. Moreover, we open sutras to clarify the criteria that the Buddha taught of instantaneous and gradual practice,[47] and those who practice according to the teaching are invariably caused to attain the state of real experience. This is completely different from aspiring to the virtue of attainment of *bodhi* by vainly exhausting the intellect.

Trying to arrive at the Buddha's state of truth [only] through action of the mouth, stupidly chanting thousands or tens of thousands of times, is like hoping to reach [the south country of] Etsu by pointing a carriage toward the north. Or it is like trying to put a square peg into a round hole. Reading sentences while remaining ignorant of how to practice [is like] a student of medicine forgetting how to compound medications. What use is that? Those 17b
who chant endlessly are like frogs in a spring paddy field, croaking day and night. In the end it is all useless. It is still more difficult for people who are deeply disturbed by fame and gain to abandon these things. The mind that craves gain is very deep, and so it must have been present in the ancient past. How could it not be present in the world today? It is most pitiful. Just remember, when a practitioner directly follows a master who has attained the truth and clarified the mind, and when the practitioner matches that mind and experiences and understands it, and thus receives the authentic transmission of the subtle Dharma of the Seven Buddhas,[48] then the exact teaching appears clearly and is received and maintained. This is beyond the comprehension of Dharma teachers who study words.[49] So stop this doubting and delusion and, following the teaching of a true master, attain in experience the buddhas' *samādhi* of receiving and using the self, by sitting in zazen and pursuing the truth.

[32] [Someone] asks, "The Flower of Dharma[50] and the teaching of the *Garland* [*Sutra*],[51] which have now been transmitted into this country, are both ultimate expressions of the Great Vehicle. Moreover, in the case of the Shingon sect,[52] [the transmission] passed directly from Tathāgata Vairocana to Vajrasattva, and so [the transmission from] master to disciple is not at random. Quoting the principles which it discusses, that "Mind here and now is buddha" and "This mind becomes buddha,"[53] [the Shingon sect] proclaims that we realize the right realization of the five buddhas[54] in one sitting, without undergoing many *kalpa*s[55] of training. We can say that this is the ultimate refinement of the Buddha's Dharma. What is so excellent then about the practice which you now solely recommend, to the exclusion of these other [practices]?"

I say: Remember, among Buddhists we do not argue about superiority and inferiority of philosophies, or choose between shallowness and profundity in the Dharma; we need only know whether the practice is genuine or artificial. Some have entered into the stream of the Buddha's truth at the invitation of

grass, flowers, mountains, and rivers. Some have received and maintained
17c the stamp of Buddha by grasping soil, stones, sand, and pebbles. Furthermore, the vast and great word[56] is even more abundant than the myriad phenomena. And the turning of the great Dharma wheel is contained in every molecule. This being so, the words "Mind here and now is buddha" are only the moon in water,[57] and the idea "Just to sit is to become buddha" is also a reflection in a mirror. We should not be caught by the skillfulness of the words. Now, in recommending the practice in which *bodhi* is directly experienced, I hope to demonstrate the subtle truth that the Buddhist patriarchs have transmitted one-to-one, and thus to make you into people of the real state of truth. Moreover, for transmission of the Buddha-Dharma, we must always take as a teacher a person who has experienced the [Buddha's] state. It is never enough to take as our guiding teacher a scholar who counts words; that would be like the blind leading the blind. In this, the lineage of the authentic transmission of the Buddhist patriarchs, we all revere wise masters who have attained the truth and experienced the state, and we cause them to dwell in and to maintain the Buddha-Dharma. This is why, when Shintōists of [the lineages of] *yin* and *yang*[58] come to devote themselves, and when arhats who have experienced the fruit[59] come to ask for Dharma, we give each of them, without fail, the means of clarifying the mental state. This is something that has never been heard in other lineages. Disciples of the Buddha should just learn the Buddha-Dharma. Furthermore, we should remember that from the beginning we have never lacked the supreme state of *bodhi,* and we will receive it and use it forever. At the same time, because we cannot perceive it directly,[60] we are prone to beget random intellectual ideas, and because we chase after these as if they were real things, we vainly pass by the great state of truth. From these intellectual ideas emerge all sorts of flowers in space:[61] we think about the twelvefold cycle[62] and the twenty-five spheres of existence; and ideas of the three vehicles and the five vehicles[63] or of having buddha[-nature] and not having buddha[-nature] are endless. We should not think that the learn-
18a ing of these intellectual ideas is the right path of Buddhist practice. When we solely sit in zazen, on the other hand, relying now on exactly the same posture as the Buddha, and letting go of the myriad things, then we go beyond the areas of delusion, realization, emotion, and consideration, and we are not concerned with the ways of the common and the sacred. At once we are roaming

outside the [intellectual] frame, receiving and using the great state of *bodhi.* How could those caught in the trap of words compare [with this]?

[37] [Someone] asks, "Among the three kinds of training[64] there is training in the balanced state, and among the six *pāramitās*[65] there is the *dhyāna pāramitā,* both of which all bodhisattvas learn from the outset and all bodhisattvas practice, regardless of whether they are clever or stupid. The zazen [that you are discussing] now is surely [only] one of these. Why do you say that the Tathāgata's right Dharma is concentrated in this [practice of zazen]?"

I say: The question arises because this right Dharma-eye treasury, the supreme and great method, which is the one great matter[66] of the Tathāgata, has been called the "Zen sect." Remember that this title "Zen sect" was established in China and the east; it is not heard in India. When Great Master Bodhidharma first stayed at Shaolin Temple in the Songshan Mountains,[67] and faced the wall for nine years, monks and laymen were still ignorant of the Buddha's right Dharma, so they called [Master Bodhidharma] a brahman who made a religion of zazen. Thereafter, the patriarchs of successive generations all constantly devoted themselves to zazen. Stupid secular people who saw this, not knowing the reality, talked at random of a zazen sect. Nowadays, dropping the word *"za,"* they talk of just the Zen sect.[68] This interpretation is clear from records of the patriarchs.[69] [Zazen] should not be discussed as the balanced state of *dhyāna* in the six *pāramitā*s and the three kinds of training. That this Buddha-Dharma is the legitimate intention of the one-to-one transmission has never been concealed through the ages. In the order on Vulture Peak in ancient times, when the Tathāgata gave the Dharma to Venerable Mahākāśyapa, transmitting the right Dharma-eye treasury and the fine mind of nirvana, the supreme and great method, only to him, the cer- 18b
emony was witnessed directly by beings among the celestial throng which are present in the world above, so it must never be doubted. It is a universal rule that those celestial beings will guard and maintain the Buddha-Dharma eternally; their efforts have never faded. Just remember that this [transmission of zazen] is the whole truth of the Buddha's Dharma; nothing can be compared with it.

[40] [Someone] asks, "Why, in discussing entry into the state of experience, do Buddhists recommend us to practice the balanced state of *dhyāna* solely by sitting, which is [only] one of the four forms of conduct?"[70]

I say: It is difficult to calculate all the ways that buddhas have successively practiced since ancient times to enter the state of real experience. If we want to find a reason, we should remember that what Buddhists practice is reason in itself. We should not look for [a reason] besides this. But an ancestral master has praised [sitting] by saying, "Sitting in zazen is the peaceful and joyful gate of Dharma."[71] So in conclusion the reason may be that, of the four forms of conduct, [sitting is the most] peaceful and joyful. Furthermore, [sitting] is not the way practiced by one or two buddhas; all the buddhas and all the patriarchs possess this way.

[41] [Someone] asks, "In regard to this practice of zazen, a person who has not yet experienced and understood the Buddha-Dharma may be able to acquire that experience by pursuing the truth in zazen. [But] what can a person who has already clarified the Buddha's right Dharma expect to gain from zazen?"

I say: We do not tell our dreams before a fool, and it is difficult to put oars into the hands of a mountaineer; nevertheless I must bestow the teaching. The thought that practice and experience are not one thing is just the idea of non-Buddhists. In the Buddha-Dharma practice and experience are completely the same. [Practice] now is also practice in the state of experi-
18c ence; therefore, a beginner's pursuit of the truth is just the whole body of the original state of experience. This is why [the Buddhist patriarchs] teach, in the practical cautions they have handed down to us, not to expect any experience outside of practice. And the reason may be that [practice itself] is the directly accessible original state of experience. Because practice is just experience, the experience is endless; and because experience is practice, the practice has no beginning. This is how both Tathāgata Śākyamuni and Venerable Patriarch Mahākāśyapa were received and used by the practice that exists in the state of experience. Great Master Bodhidharma and the Founding Patriarch Daikan[72] were similarly pulled and driven by the practice that exists in the state of experience. The examples of all those who dwelled in and maintained the Buddha-Dharma are like this. The practice that is never separate from experience exists already: having fortunately received the one-to-one transmission of a share of the subtle practice, we who are beginners in pursuing the truth directly possess, in the state without intention, a share of original experience. Remember, in order to prevent

us from tainting the experience that is never separate from practice, the Buddhist patriarchs have repeatedly taught us not to be lax in practice. When we forget the subtle practice, original experience has filled our hands; when the body leaves original experience behind, the subtle practice is operating throughout the body. Moreover, as I saw with my own eyes in great Song China, the Zen monasteries of many districts had all built zazen halls accommodating five or six hundred, or even one or two thousand monks, who were encouraged to sit in zazen day and night. The leader of one such order[73] was a true master who had received the Buddha's mind-seal. When I asked him the great intent of the Buddha-Dharma, I was able to hear the principle that practice and experience are never two stages. Therefore, in accordance with the teaching of the Buddhist patriarchs, and following the way of a true master, he encouraged [everyone] to pursue the truth in zazen; [he encouraged] not only the practitioners in his order but [all] noble friends who sought the Dharma, [all] people who hoped to find true reality in the Buddha-Dharma, without choosing between beginners and late learners, without distinction between common people and sacred people. Have you not heard the words of the ancestral master[74] who said, "It is not that there is no practice-and-experience, but it cannot be tainted." Another [master] said, "Someone who 19a
sees the way practices the way."[75] Remember that even in the state of attainment of the truth, we should practice.

[44] [Someone] asks, "The masters who spread the teachings through our country in previous ages had all entered Tang China and received the transmission of Dharma. Why, at that time, did they neglect this principle, and transmit only philosophical teaching?"

I say: The reason that past teachers of human beings did not transmit this method was that the time had not come.

[45] [Someone] asks, "Did those masters of former ages understand this method?"

I say: If they had understood it, they would have made it known to all.

[45] [Someone] asks, "It has been said that we should not regret our life and death,[76] for there is a very quick way to get free of life and death. That is, to know the truth that the mental essence is eternal. In other words, this physical body, having been born, necessarily moves toward death; but this mental essence never dies at all. Once we have been able to recognize that

the mental essence which is unmoved by birth and decay[77] exists in our own body, we see this as the original essence. Therefore the body is just a temporary form; it dies here and is born there, never remaining constant. [But] the mind is eternal; it is unchangeable in the past, future, or present. To know this is called 'to have become free of life and death.' Those who know this principle stop the past [cycle of] life and death forever and, when this body passes, they enter the spirit world. When they present themselves in the spirit world,[78] they gain wondrous virtues like those of the buddha-tathāgatas. Even if we know [this principle] now, [our body] is still the body that has been shaped
19b by deluded behavior in past ages, and so we are not the same as the saints. Those who do not know this principle will forever turn in the cycle of life and death. Therefore we should just hasten to understand the principle that the mental essence is eternal. Even if we passed our whole life in idle sitting, what could we expect to gain? The doctrine I have expressed like this is truly in accord with the truth of the buddhas and the patriarchs, is it not?"

I say: The view expressed now is absolutely not the Buddha's Dharma; it is the view of the non-Buddhist Senika.[79] According to that non-Buddhist view, there is one spiritual intelligence existing within our body. When this intelligence meets conditions, it can discriminate between pleasant and unpleasant and discriminate between right and wrong, and it can know pain and irritation and know suffering and pleasure—all [these] are abilities of the spiritual intelligence. When this body dies, however, the spirit casts off the skin and is reborn on the other side; so even though it seems to die here it lives on there. Therefore we call it immortal and eternal. The view of that non-Buddhist is like this. But if we learn this view as the Buddha's Dharma, we are even more foolish than the person who grasps a tile or a pebble thinking it to be a golden treasure; the delusion would be too shameful for comparison. National Master Echū[80] of great Tang China strongly cautioned against [such thinking]. If we equate the present wrong view that "mind is eternal but forms perish" with the splendid Dharma of the buddhas, thinking that we have escaped life and death when we are promoting the original cause of life and death, are we not being stupid? That would be most pitiful. Knowing that this [wrong view] is just the wrong view of non-Buddhists, we should not touch it with our ears. Nevertheless, I cannot help wanting to
19c save you from this wrong view and it is only compassionate [for me] now

[to try]. So remember, in the Buddha-Dharma, because the body and mind are originally one reality, the saying that essence and form are not two has been understood equally in the Western Heavens and the Eastern Lands, and we should never dare to go against it. Further, in the lineages that discuss eternal existence, the myriad *dharmas* are all eternal existence: body and mind are not divided.[81] And in the lineages that discuss extinction, all *dharmas* are extinction: essence and form are not divided.[82] How could we say, on the contrary, that the body is mortal but the mind is eternal? Does that not violate right reason? Furthermore, we should realize that living-and-dying is just nirvana;[83] [Buddhists] have never discussed nirvana outside of living-and-dying. Moreover, even if we wrongly imagine the understanding that "mind becomes eternal by getting free of the body" to be the same as the buddha-wisdom that is free of life and death, the mind that is conscious of this understanding still appears and disappears momentarily, and so it is not eternal at all. Then isn't [this understanding] unreliable? We should taste and reflect. The principle that body and mind are one reality is being constantly spoken by the Buddha-Dharma. So how could it be, on the contrary, that while this body appears and disappears, the mind independently leaves the body and does not appear or disappear? If there is a time when [body and mind] are one reality, and another time when they are not one reality, then it might naturally follow that the Buddha's preaching has been false. Further, if we think that life and death are something to get rid of, we will commit the sin of hating the Buddha-Dharma. How could we not guard against this? Remember, the lineage of the Dharma which [asserts that] "in the Buddha-Dharma the essential state of mind universally includes all forms," describes the whole great world of Dharma inclusively, without dividing essence and form, and without discussing appearance and disappearance. There is no [state]—not even *bodhi* or nirvana—that is different from the essential state of mind. All *dharmas*, myriad phenomena and accumulated things, are totally just the one mind, without exclusion or disunion. All these 20a
various lineages of the Dharma assert that [myriad things and phenomena] are the even and balanced undivided mind, other than which there is nothing; and this is just how Buddhists have understood the essence of mind. That being so, how could we divide this one reality into body and mind, or into life-and-death and nirvana? We are already the Buddha's disciples. Let

us not touch with our ears those noises from the tongues of madmen who speak non-Buddhist views.

[51] [Someone] asks, "Must a person who is devoted to this zazen always adhere spotlessly to the precepts?"

I say: Keeping the precepts, and pure conduct,[84] are the standard of the Zen lineages and the usual habit of Buddhist patriarchs. [But] those who have not yet received the precepts, or who have broken the precepts, are not without their share [of the benefit of zazen].

[51] [Someone] asks, "Is there nothing to prevent a person who practices this zazen from also performing mantra and quiet-reflection practices?"[85]

I say: When I was in China, I heard the true essence of the teachings from a true master; he said that he had never heard that any of the patriarchs who received the authentic transmission of the Buddha-seal ever performed such practices additionally, in the Western Heavens or in the Eastern Lands, in the past or in the present. Certainly, unless we devote ourselves to one thing, we will not attain complete wisdom.

[52] [Someone] asks, "Should this practice also be undertaken by laymen and laywomen, or is it performed only by people who have left home?"

I say: An ancestral master has been heard to say that, with respect to understanding of the Buddha-Dharma, we must not choose between men and women, high or low.

[52] [Someone] asks, "People who leave home get free of all involvements at once, so they have no hindrances in practicing zazen and pursuing the truth. How can a busy layperson devotedly do training and be at one with the unintentional state of Buddhist truth?"

20b I say: In general, the Buddhist Patriarch,[86] overfilled with pity, left open a wide and great gate of compassion so that all living beings could experience and enter [the state of truth]; what human being or god could not want to enter? Thus, when we study the past and the present, there are many confirmations of such [experience and entry]. For instance, Taisō[87] and Junsō[88] were, as emperors, very busy with affairs of state [but] they pursued the truth by sitting in zazen and realized the Buddhist Patriarch's great truth. Both Minister Ri (Ch. Li) and Minister Bō (Ch. Fang), serving as [the emperor's] lieutenants, were the arms and legs of the whole nation [but] they pursued the truth by sitting in zazen and experienced and entered the Buddhist Patriarch's truth. This [practice-and-experience] rests only upon whether or not the will is present; it does not relate to whether the body stays at home or leaves home. Moreover, any person who profoundly discerns the superiority or inferiority of things will naturally have belief. Still more, those who think that worldly affairs hinder the Buddha-Dharma only know that there is no Buddha-Dharma in the world; they do not know that there are no worldly *dharma*s in the state of Buddha. Recently in great Song [China] there was [a man] called Minister Hyō (Ch. Feng), a high-ranking official who was accomplished in the Patriarch's truth. In his later years he made a poem in which he expressed himself as follows:

> When official business allows, I like to sit in zazen.
> I have seldom slept with my side touching a bed.
> Though I have now become prime minister,
> My fame as a veteran practitioner has spread across the four seas.

This was somebody with no time free from official duties but, because his will to the Buddha's truth was deep, he was able to attain the truth. We should reflect on ourselves [in comparison] with him, and we should reflect on the present [in comparison] with those days. In the great kingdom of Song, the present generation of kings and ministers, officials and commoners, men and women, all apply their mind to the Patriarch's truth, without exception. Both the military and literary classes are resolved to practice [za]zen and to learn the truth. Those who resolve it will, in many cases, undoubtedly clarify the mental state. Thus, it can naturally be inferred that worldly affairs do 20c
not hinder the Buddha-Dharma. When the real Buddha-Dharma spreads throughout a nation the buddhas and the gods guard [that nation] ceaselessly, so the reign is peaceful. When the imperial reign is peaceful, the Buddha-Dharma comes into its own. Furthermore, when Śākyamuni was in the world, [even] people of heavy sins and wrong views were able to get the truth, and in the orders of the ancestral masters, [even] hunters and old woodcutters entered the state of realization, to say nothing of other people. We need only study the teaching and the state of truth of a true teacher.

[56] [Someone] asks, "Even in the present corrupt world in this latter age,[89] is it still possible to realize the state of real experience when we perform this practice?"

I say: Philosophers have occupied themselves with such concepts and forms, but in the real teaching of the Great Vehicle, without discriminating between "right," "imitative," and "latter" Dharma, we say that all those who practice attain the state of truth. Furthermore, in this directly transmitted right Dharma, both in entering the Dharma and getting the body out, we receive and use the treasure of ourselves. Those who are practicing can naturally know whether they have got the state of real experience or not, just as people who are using water can tell by themselves whether it is cold or warm.

[57] [Someone] asks, "It is said that in the Buddha-Dharma once we have clearly understood the principle that mind here and now is buddha, even if our mouth does not recite the sutras and our body does not practice the Buddha Way, we are not lacking in the Buddha-Dharma at all. Just to know that the Buddha-Dharma originally resides in each of us is the whole of the attainment of the truth. There is no need to seek anything else from other people. How much less need we bother about pursuing the truth in zazen?"

I say: These words are extremely unreliable. If it is as you say, how could any intelligent person fail to understand this principle once it had been
21a explained to them? Remember, we learn the Buddha-Dharma just when we give up views of subject and object. If knowing that "we ourselves are just buddha" could be called the attainment of the truth, Śākyamuni would not have bothered to teach the moral way in the past. I would like now to prove this through the subtle criteria of the ancient patriarchs:

Long ago, there was a monk called Prior Sokkō[90] in the order of Zen Master Hōgen.[91] Zen Master Hōgen asks him, "Prior Sokkō, how long have you been in my order?"

Sokkō says, "I have served in the master's order for three years already."

The Zen master says, "You are a recent member of the order. Why do you never ask me about the Buddha-Dharma?"

Sokkō says, "I must not deceive you, master. Before, when I was in the order of Zen Master Seihō, I realized the state of peace and joy in the Buddha-Dharma."

The Zen master says, "Relying upon what words were you able to enter?"

Sokkō says, "I once asked Seihō: Just what is the student that is I?[92] Seihō said: The children of fire[93] come looking for fire."

Hōgen says, "Nice words. But I am afraid that you may not have understood."

Sokkō says, "The children of fire belong to fire. [So] I understood that their being fire yet looking for fire represented my being myself yet looking for myself."

The Zen master says, "I have become sure that you did not understand. If the Buddha-Dharma were like that, it could never have been transmitted until today."

At this Sokkō became embarrassed and distressed, and he stood up [to leave]. [But] on the road he thought, "The Zen master is [respected] throughout the country [as] a good counselor, and he is a great guiding master to 21b
five hundred people. There must surely have been some merit in his criticism of my wrongness."

[Sokkō] goes back to the Zen master to confess and to prostrate himself in apology. Then he asks, "Just what is the student that is I?"

The Zen master says, "The children of fire come looking for fire."

Under the influence of these words, Sokkō grandly realized the Buddha-Dharma.

Clearly, the Buddha-Dharma is never known with the intellectual understanding that "we ourselves are just buddha." If the intellectual understanding that "we ourselves are just buddha" were the Buddha-Dharma, the Zen master could not have guided [Sokkō] by using the former words, and he would not have admonished [Sokkō] as he did. Solely and directly, from our first meeting with a good counselor, we should ask the standards of practice, and we should singlemindedly pursue the truth by sitting in zazen, without allowing a single recognition or half an understanding to remain in our minds. Then the subtle method of the Buddha-Dharma will not be [practiced] in vain.

[61] [Someone] asks, "When we hear of India and China in the past and present, there are those who realized the state of truth on hearing the voice of a bamboo, or who clarified the mind on seeing the colors of the flowers.[94] Furthermore, the Great Teacher Śākyamuni experienced the truth when he saw the bright star, Venerable Ānanda[95] realized the Dharma when a temple flagpole fell, and not only that: among the five lineages following from the Sixth Patriarch[96] many people have clarified the mental state under the

influence of a single word or half a line of verse. Had they all, without exception, pursued the truth by sitting in zazen?"

I say: We should know that these people of the past and present who clarified the mind on seeing forms and who realized the truth on hearing sounds, were all without intellectual doubt in pursuing the truth, and just in the moment of the present there was no second person.

[62] [Someone] asks, "In India and China, the people are originally unaffected and straight. Being at the center of the civilized world makes them
21c so. As a result, when they are taught the Buddha-Dharma they understand and enter very quickly. In our country, from ancient times the people have had little benevolence and wisdom, and it is difficult for us to accumulate the seeds of rightness. Being the savages and barbarians[97] [of the southeast] makes us so. How could we not regret it? Furthermore, people who have left home in this country are inferior even to the laypeople of the great nations; our whole society is stupid, and our minds are narrow and small. We are deeply attached to the results of intentional effort, and we like superficial quality. Can people like this expect to experience the Buddha-Dharma straight away, even if they sit in zazen?"

I say: As you say, the people of our country are not yet universally benevolent and wise, and some people are indeed crooked. Even if we preach right and straight Dharma to them, they will turn nectar into poison. They easily tend toward fame and gain, and it is hard for them to dissolve their delusions and attachments. On the other hand, to experience and enter the Buddha-Dharma, one need not always use the worldly wisdom of human beings and gods as a vessel for transcendence of the world.[98] When the Buddha was in [the] world, [an old monk] experienced the fourth effect [when hit] by a ball,[99] and [a prostitute] clarified the great state of truth after putting on a *kaṣāya;*[100] both were dull people, stupid and silly creatures. But aided by right belief, they had the means to escape their delusion. Another case was the devout woman preparing a midday meal who disclosed the state of realization when she saw a stupid old *bhikṣu*[101] sitting in quietness. This did not derive from her wisdom, did not derive from writings, did not depend on words, and did not depend on talk; she was aided only by her right belief. Furthermore, Śākyamuni's teachings have been spreading through the three-thousand-world only for around two thousand or so years. Countries are of

many kinds; not all are nations of benevolence and wisdom. How could all people, moreover, possess only intelligence and wisdom, keenness [of ear] and clarity [of eye]? But the right Dharma of the Tathāgata is originally fur- 22a
nished with unthinkably great virtue and power, and so when the time comes it will spread through those countries. When people just practice with right belief, the clever and the stupid alike will attain the truth. Just because our country is not a nation of benevolence or wisdom and the people are dull-witted, do not think that it is impossible for us to grasp the Buddha-Dharma. Still more, all human beings have the right seeds of *prajñā* in abundance. It may simply be that few of us have experienced the state directly, and so we are immature in receiving and using it.

[65] The above questions and answers have come and gone, and the alternation between audience and speaker has been untidy. How many times have I caused flowers to exist in flowerless space?[102] On the other hand, the fundamental principle of pursuing the truth by sitting in zazen has never been transmitted to this country; anyone who hoped to know it would have been disappointed. This is why I intend to gather together the few experiences I had abroad, and to record the secrets of an enlightened teacher,[103] so that they may be heard by any practitioner who desires to hear them. In addition, there are standards and conventions for monasteries and temples but there is not enough time to teach them now, and they must not be [taught] in haste.

[66] In general, it was very fortunate for the people of our country that, even though we are situated east of the Dragon Sea and are far separated by clouds and mist, from around the reigns of Kinmei[104] and Yōmei,[105] the Buddha-Dharma of the west spread to us in the east. However, confusion has multiplied over concepts and forms, and facts and circumstances, disturbing the situation of practice. Now, because we make do with tattered robes and mended bowls, tying thatch so that we can sit and train by the blue cliffs and white rocks, the matter of the ascendant state of buddha becomes apparent at once, and we swiftly master the great matter of a lifetime of practice. This is just 22b
the decree of Ryūge [Mountain],[106] and the legacy of Kukkuṭapāda [Mountain].[107] The forms and standards for sitting in zazen may be practiced following the *Fukanzazengi* which I compiled in the Karoku era.[108]

[68] Now, in spreading the Buddha's teaching throughout a nation, on the one hand, we should wait for the king's decree, but on the other hand,

when we recall the bequest of Vulture Peak, the kings, nobles, ministers, and generals now manifested in hundred myriad *koṭi*s of realms all have gratefully accepted the Buddha's decree and, not forgetting the original aim of earlier lives to guard and maintain the Buddha's teaching, they have been born. [Within] the frontiers of the spread of that teaching, what place could not be a buddha land? Therefore, when we want to disseminate the truth of the Buddhist patriarchs, it is not always necessary to select a [particular] place or to wait for [favorable] circumstances. Shall we just consider today to be the starting point? So I have put this together and I will leave it for wise masters who aspire to the Buddha-Dharma and for the true stream of practitioners who wish, like wandering clouds or transient water weeds, to explore the state of truth.

Mid-autumn day, [in the third year of] Kanki.[109]

Written by the *śramaṇa*[110] Dōgen, who entered Song [China] and received the transmission of the Dharma.

Shōbōgenzō Bendōwa

Notes

1 *Shobutsu nyorai.* The expression derives from the *Lotus Sutra* (see LS 1.88). *Nyorai* represents the Sanskrit word *tathāgata,* which means "one who has arrived in the state of reality." It is the highest epithet of a buddha. See Glossary of Sanskrit Terms.

2 *Anoku-bodai,* short for *anokutara-sanmyaku-sanbodai,* which is a transliteration of the Sanskrit phrase *anuttara samyaksaṃbodhi. Bodhi* means "perfect wisdom," "the truth," or "the state of truth." See Glossary of Sanskrit Terms.

3 *Jijuyō-zanmai. Ji* means "self," *ju* means "to receive," and *yō* means "to use." *Zanmai* represents the Sanskrit word *samādhi* (see Glossary of Sanskrit Terms). *Samādhi* is explained from many viewpoints in the *Shōbōgenzō,* for example as *jishō-zanmai, samādhi* as self-experience; as *hosshō-zanmai, samādhi* as Dharma-nature; as *kai-in-zanmai, samādhi* as the state like the sea; and as *zanmai-ō-zanmai,* the *samādhi* that is king of *samādhi*s. *Jijuyō-zanmai* suggests the state of natural balance that we experience when making effort without an intentional aim.

4 *Hō* has a wide range of meanings: Dharma, *dharma*s (see Glossary of Sanskrit Terms), law, things and phenomena, method, reality, etc. "This Dharma" suggests the method of zazen and at the same time the reality of zazen.

5 In the state of zazen, our consciousness is whole.

6 "Effort" is *kufu;* "pursuing the truth" is *bendō,* as in the chapter title *Bendōwa.* Master Dōgen used the words *kufu-bendō* to express zazen itself.

7 *Banpō,* lit., ten thousand *dharma*s; in other words, all things and phenomena. See note 4.

8 *Shutsuro. Shutsu* means "to get out" and *ro* means "path" or "road." The *Fukanzazengi* contains the phrase *shusshin no katsuro,* "the vigorous road of the body getting out," that is, the state of vigorous action in which our body gets free from intellectual worries and sensory attachments.

9 *Chishiki,* short for *zenchishiki,* from the Sanskrit *kalyāṇamitra* (see Glossary of Sanskrit Terms).

10 Zenkō. Zen stands for Myōzen; *kō* is an honorific. Master Myōzen and Master Dōgen set off together in 1223 to investigate Buddhism in China. Master Myōzen died on May 5, 1225, at the age of forty-one, in the Ryōnenryō Dormitory at Tendōzan. Before

becoming the disciple of Master Eisai, Master Myōzen had learned the teachings of the Tendai sect on Mount Hiei.

11 The seasons of autumn and spring, respectively.

12 Master Eisai (1141–1215), who went to China and introduced the transmission of the Rinzai sect into Japan.

13 A province in eastern China, bordering the East China Sea.

14 The so-called Sōtō, Rinzai, Hōgen, Igyō, and Unmon sects. See Chapter Forty-nine (Vol. III), *Butsudō.*

15 Jō Zenji, Master Tendō Nyojō (1163–1228), successor of Master Setchō Chikan. Usually referred to in the *Shōbōgenzō* as Senshi, "my late master."

16 Daibyakuhō, lit., "Great White Peak," is another name for Tendōzan, where Master Tendō Nyojō led the order from 1224 until his death.

17 The Shōjō era was from 1228 to 1233.

18 Real wisdom. See Chapter Two, *Maka-hannya-haramitsu.*

19 In order to find a true teacher.

20 Vulture Peak (Skt. Gṛdhrakūṭa) is so called because the silhouette of the mountain resembles a vulture. The Buddha often preached there.

21 Master Mahākāśyapa, the first patriarch in India.

22 Master Bodhidharma (sixth century), the twenty-eighth patriarch in India and the First Patriarch in China.

23 Master Taiso Eka, the Second Patriarch in China.

24 *Tōchi* (Eastern Lands): China. Master Dōgen commonly referred to India and China as *saiten-tōchi,* "the Western Heavens and the Eastern Lands."

25 Master Daikan Enō (638–713), the Sixth Patriarch in China.

26 Master Nangaku Ejō (677–744).

27 Master Seigen Gyōshi (d. 740), the Seventh Chinese Patriarch in Master Dōgen's lineage.

28 *Butsu-in,* lit., "Buddha-seal." *In* can be interpreted as a seal of approval, that is, certification. Or it can be interpreted as concrete form, or posture.

29 *Butsu-shin-in,* lit., "Buddha-mind–seal." In Chapter Seventy-two (Vol. III), *Zanmai-ō-zanmai,* Master Dōgen says that the Buddha-mind–seal is the full lotus posture itself.

30 The Later Han dynasty was from 25 to 221 C.E.

[31] Literally, "cut the roots of the arrowroot and wisteria." These two vines symbolize something confused or complicated. See Chapter Forty-six (Vol. III), *Kattō.*

[32] *Jijuyō-zanmai;* the state of natural balance, see note 3.

[33] *Buppō,* "Buddha-Dharma," or "Buddhist method," in this case means zazen itself.

[34] *Sangō,* the three kinds of conduct or behavior; that is, behavior of body, speech, and mind.

[35] *Sanzu,* lit., "three courses," or the three miserable states or worlds, are hell, the world of hungry ghosts (*preta*s), and the world of animals. *Rokudō,* lit., "six ways" or the six human states, are the three miserable worlds plus the worlds of demons (*asura*s), human beings, and gods (*deva*s). See Glossary of Sanskrit Terms.

[36] *Dai-gedatsu-chi. Dai* means great. *Gedatsu* represents the Sanskrit *vimukti,* which means to get free of all hindrances. *Chi* means state.

[37] The Sanskrit *bodhi* means the state of truth. The Buddha attained the truth sitting under a pipal tree (*Ficus religiosa*). In Buddhist countries this tree is called the *bodhi* tree.

[38] *Tenbōrin,* turning of the Dharma wheel, symbolizes Buddhist preaching. See Chapter Seventy-four (Vol. IV), *Tenbōrin.*

[39] *Mutōdō,* lit., "equality without equal," from the Sanskrit *asamasama.* The expression appears in the *Heart Sutra* (see Chapter Two, *Maka-hannya-haramitsu*), and in the *Lotus Sutra* (LS 3.270).

[40] Toward the practitioner—the practice influences both object and subject.

[41] *Jijuyō no kyōgai,* lit., "the area of receiving and using self," that is, the state of natural balance. See note 3.

[42] *Hyakutō,* lit., "hundreds of heads," suggesting miscellaneous concrete things.

[43] Questions and answers are not separated in the source text. They have been separated here for ease of reading.

[44] *Sanze,* the past, present, and future; eternity.

[45] *Daijō,* Mahayana Buddhism. See Glossary of Sanskrit Terms, Mahayana.

[46] *Taiyakukei.* See LS 1.86–88.

[47] *Tonzen-shugyō. Tonzen* stands for *tongo,* "instantaneous realization," and *zengo,* "gradual realization." These represent two views of realization—as occurring just in the moment of practice, and as a process continuing over a long line of moments—based on the two views of time.

[48] The seven ancient buddhas were Vipaśyin, Śikhin, Viśvabhū, Krakucchanda, Kanakamuni, Kāśyapa, and Śākyamuni (see Chapter Fifteen, *Busso*). Belief in the Seven

Buddhas reflects the belief that the Dharma is eternal, predating the historical Buddha, Śākyamuni.

49 *Hōsshi.* In Master Dōgen's time some priests in the Tendai sect had this title.

50 *Hokkeshū. Hokke* stands for *Hokkekyō, "Sutra of the Flower of Dharma,"* the *Lotus Sutra. Shū* means religion or sect. *Hokkeshū* was the name formerly used for the Tendai sect, which was established in China by Master Tendai Chigi based on the *Lotus Sutra.* It was introduced into Japan by Master Saichō (767–822).

51 *Kegonkyō,* lit., "Kegon teaching," means the teaching of the Kegon sect, which was also established in China, based on the *Avataṃsaka-sūtra* (Jp. *Kegonkyō; Garland Sutra*), see note 79. It was introduced into Japan in 736.

52 *Shingonshū.* The Shingon sect is derived from Vajrayana Buddhism. Master Kūkai went to China and brought the teachings of the Shingon sect back to Japan in 806. Vajrayana Buddhism reveres Vajrasattva, the Diamond Buddha, who is said to have received the transmission from Vairocana, the Sun Buddha.

53 "Mind here and now is buddha" is *soku-shin-ze-butsu*—the title of Chapter Six. "This mind becomes buddha" is *ze-shin-sa-butsu.*

54 That is, the five buddhas in the mandala used in the esoteric Buddhism of the Shingon sect. A mandala is a pictorial representation with Vairocana Buddha in the middle surrounded by buddhas to his north, south, east, and west.

55 *Go,* or *kō,* represents the sound of the Sanskrit *kalpa,* which means an infinitely long time. A *kalpa* was explained, for example, as the time it would take to wear away a large boulder if a heavenly being brushed it once every three years with its sleeve.

56 *Kōdai no monji,* lit., "the wide and great characters," suggests Dharma as not only the accumulation of material phenomena but also something that has meaning.

57 An image of the moon, not the moon itself.

58 *Meiyō no shintō. Meiyō* means "*yin* and *yang.*" Shintō, lit., "Way of the Gods," is the ethnic spiritual religion of Japan. The idea of two lineages of Shintō, the *yin* and the *yang,* seems to have originated with attempts of the Shingon sect to reconcile its teachings with indigenous Japanese beliefs.

59 An arhat is a person who has attained the ultimate state (the fourth effect) of a *śrāvaka* (see Glossary of Sanskrit Terms), that is, the ultimate level of abstract Buddhist learning. The arhat is the subject of Chapter Thirty-four (Vol. II), *Arakan.*

60 "Perceive it directly" is *jōtō,* short for *jōju-gattō,* lit., "receiving a hit." Generally, *jōtō* means to be struck by reality directly in momentary experience. In the last section of his independent work *Gakudōyōjinshū* (*Collection of Concerns in Learning the Truth*), Master Dōgen explains *jōtō,* or "receiving a hit," as follows: "Using this body and mind, we directly experience the state of buddha. This is to receive a hit."

[61] *Kūge,* "flowers in space," symbolizes images. See Chapter Forty-three (Vol. III), *Kūge.*

[62] *Jūni-rinden,* the twelvefold cycle of cause and effect, from the Sanskrit *dvādaśānga pratītyasamutpāda* (see Glossary of Sanskrit Terms). See, for example, LS 2.56.

[63] *Sanjō,* "three vehicles," or the three kinds of Buddhists, are explained in Chapter Twenty-four (Vol. II), *Bukkyō.* They are the *śrāvaka,* who relies on the theory of four philosophies; the *pratyekabuddha,* who relies on the theory of dependent origination (the twelvefold cycle of cause and effect); and the bodhisattva, who relies on the six *pāramitā*s (the six accomplishments). The five vehicles are these three, plus human beings and gods.

[64] *Sangaku,* from the Sanskrit *tisraḥ śikṣāḥ,* are the precepts (*śīla*), the balanced state (*dhyāna,* usually translated as "meditation"), and wisdom (*prajñā*). See Glossary of Sanskrit Terms.

[65] The Sanskrit word *pāramitā* means that which has arrived at the opposite shore, an accomplishment. *Rokudō,* the six *pāramitā*s, are giving (*dāna*), keeping the precepts (*śīla*), patience (*kṣānti*), diligence (*vīrya*), the practice of meditation (*dhyāna*), and real wisdom (*prajñā*). The Sanskrit *dhyāna* was rendered into Chinese and Japanese as *chan* or *zen.*

[66] *Ichidaiji* appears in the *Lotus Sutra.* See LS 1.88–90 and Chapter Seventeen, *Hokke-ten-hokke.*

[67] The Songshan Mountains consist of two main peaks, Taishitsu to the east, and Shōshitsu to the west. These mountains contained many Buddhist temples; Shaolin Temple was on Shōshitsu Peak.

[68] The zazen sect is *zazenshū,* lit., "sitting *dhyāna* sect." Dropping the *za* gives *zenshū,* lit., "*dhyāna* sect," or Zen sect.

[69] *Kōroku,* "broad records," and *goroku,* "record of the words." See Bibliography.

[70] *Shigi,* walking, standing, sitting, and lying down.

[71] *Zazen wa sunawachi anraku no homon nari.* These words may originate with Master Chōro Sōsaku, who was the editor of the *Zenenshingi* (*Pure Criteria for Zen Monasteries*). Master Dōgen quotes the same words in the *Fukanzazengi* (see Appendix II). The word *anraku,* "peaceful and joyful" or "stable and comfortable," is contained in the title of the fourteenth chapter of the *Lotus Sutra, "Anrakugyō"* ("Peaceful and Joyful Practice").

[72] Master Daikan Enō. See note 25.

[73] Master Tendō Nyojō.

[74] Master Nangaku Ejō. The conversation between Master Daikan Enō and Master Nangaku Ejō is recorded in *Shinji-shōbōgenzō,* pt. 2, no. 1. See also Chapter Seven, *Senjō;* Chapter Twenty-nine (Vol. II), *Inmo;* and Chapter Sixty-two (Vol. III), *Hensan.*

[75] *Keitokudentōroku,* chapter 5, in the section on Master Honjō.

[76] *Shōji,* lit., "life and death" or "living-and-dying," is the title of Chapter Ninety-two (Vol. IV).

[77] *Shōmetsu. Shō* means not only "life" but also "birth" and "appearance." In this paragraph *shōmetsu* has also been translated as "appearance and disappearance."

[78] *Shōkai,* lit., "essence-ocean."

[79] The *Avataṃsaka-sūtra* (Jp. *Kegonkyō; Garland Sutra*) records many questions put to the Buddha by a brahman called Senika. See Chapter Six, *Soku-shin-ze-butsu.*

[80] Master Nan'yō Echū (675?–775), successor of Master Daikan Enō. "National Master" was his title as teacher of the emperor. See for example Chapters Six, Eighteen, Nineteen, and Forty-four (Vol. III).

[81] For example, the Sarvāstivāda school, rendered as *setsu-issai-u-bu,* or "the school that preaches the existence of all things," held that *dharma*s have a real existence in the past, present, and future. This school flourished in India for many centuries and was widely studied in China and Japan.

[82] "Extinction" is *jakumetsu,* which was sometimes used as a translation of the Sanskrit nirvana, but which here is opposed to *jōjū,* "eternal existence." Thus, "lineages that discuss extinction" roughly correspond to the Śūnyatā school, or *kūmon,* i.e., the school that stressed the teachings of *śūnyatā,* which deny that there can be any static existence.

[83] The Sanskrit word *nirvāṇa* literally means the extinction of a flame. See Glossary of Sanskrit Terms, nirvana.

[84] *Jikai-bongyō. Bongyō* represents the Sanskrit *brahmacarya* (see Glossary of Sanskrit Terms). *Gyōji,* lit., "conduct and keeping" or "practice and continuance," is the title of Chapter Twenty-nine (Vol. II).

[85] *Shingon-shikan no gyo. Shingon,* lit., "truth-word," means mantra. The use of mantras is characteristic of the esoteric Buddhism of the Shingon sect. *Shikan,* lit., "ceasing and reflecting," representing the Sanskrit words *śamatha* (quietness) and *vipaśyanā* (insight, reflection), is a practice of the Tendai sect: the method of practice is almost the same as the practice of zazen explained by Master Dōgen, but in the Tendai sect the practice is not regarded as sufficient in itself.

[86] *Busso* is the title of Chapter Fifteen. Translated as "Buddhist patriarchs," it refers to the Buddhist patriarchs in general; when capitalized, as "the Buddhist Patriarch," it usually refers to the Buddha or to Master Bodhidharma.

[87] Taisō, a Tang emperor who reigned from 763 to 779, and a student of Master Nan'yō Echū.

[88] Junsō, another Tang emperor, who reigned from 805 to 806.

[89] *Matsudai. Ma* stands for *mappō,* "latter Dharma." The years after the Buddha's death were divided into three periods: *shōbō,* "right Dharma," the first five hundred years during which the Dharma would flourish; *zōbō,* "imitative Dharma," the next one thousand years during which the Dharma begins to pale; and *mappō,* "latter Dharma," the next ten thousand years during which the Dharma degenerates. See Glossary of Sanskrit Terms, under *saddharma.*

[90] *Sokkō-kan-in.* Sokkō is the monk's name; *kō* is an honorific used for both priests and laymen, approximately equivalent to *san* in modern Japanese. *Kanin* or *kansu* is one of the six main officers of a large temple.

[91] Master Hōgen Bun'eki (885–958), successor of Master Rakan Keichin and founder of the Hōgen sect.

[92] *Gakunin no jiko. Gakunin,* student, was used by a student to refer to himself. *Jiko* means "self." So Sokkō's question was "What am I?"

[93] *Byōjō-dōji. Byō* or *hei* is the third calendar sign, read as *hinoe,* or "older brother of fire." *Jō* or *tei* is the fourth calendar sign, read as *hinoto,* or "younger brother of fire." *Dōji* means child. The words "The children of fire come looking for fire" suggest the real effort of a practitioner to pursue what is already there.

[94] These examples of Buddhist masters realizing the truth are recorded in detail in Chapter Nine, *Keisei-sanshiki.*

[95] Master Ānanda was the second patriarch in India, the successor of Master Mahākāśyapa.

[96] Master Daikan Enō.

[97] *Ban-i.* As the center of civilization, the Chinese supposed the existence of four groups of barbarians surrounding them. These included the *nan-ban,* the savages of the south and the *tō-i,* the barbarians of the east. So the words "savages and barbarians" suggest people living to the south and east of China, including the Japanese.

[98] *Shusse* can be interpreted either as "to transcend the secular world" or as "to manifest oneself in the world." In the latter usage, the words usually mean to become the master of a large temple.

[99] A young monk wanted to play a joke on a stupid old monk who lived in the Buddha's order. So he led the old monk into a dark room and hit him with a ball, saying, "You have got the first effect." He hit him again and said, "You have got the second effect." Then he hit him a third time and said, "You have got the third effect." Finally he hit him one last time and said, "You have got the fourth effect." Strangely, when the old monk came out of the dark room he had actually experienced the fourth effect. *Shika,* the fourth effect, refers to the state of an arhat, that is, the ultimate state of Hinayana Buddhism.

[100] The story of the prostitute who put on a *kaṣāya* (Buddhist robe) as a joke is recorded in Chapter Twelve, *Kesa-kudoku.*

[101] A Buddhist monk (see Glossary of Sanskrit Terms).

[102] Here *kūge,* "flowers in space," represents abstract images as opposed to reality. (In Chapter Forty-two [Vol. III], *Kūge,* flowers in space and real flowers are identified.)

[103] Master Tendō Nyojō.

[104] 539–571.

[105] 585–587.

[106] Master Ryūge Kodon (835–923), successor of Master Tōzan Ryōkai, lived on Ryūge Mountain and made many poems praising the beautiful scenery of nature.

[107] Master Mahākāśyapa, successor of the Buddha, is said to have died on Kukkuṭapāda Mountain in Magadha.

[108] The Karoku era was from 1225 to 1227. Master Dōgen returned to Japan in the late summer of 1227 and wrote his first draft of the *Fukanzazengi* (*Universal Guide to the Standard Method of Zazen*) shortly thereafter. The initial version is called *Shinpitsubon,* " Original Edition." After revising this edition, Master Dōgen finally arrived at the *Rufubon,* "Popular Edition." See Appendix II.

[109] The fifteenth day of the eighth lunar month, 1231.

[110] Monk (see Glossary of Sanskrit Terms).

[Chapter Two]

Maka-hannya-haramitsu

Mahāprajñāpāramitā

Translator's Note: Maka *is a phonetic rendering of the Sanskrit word* mahā, *which means "great."* Hannya *is a phonetic rendering of the Sanskrit word* prajñā, *which can be translated as "real wisdom" or "intuitive reflection."* Haramitsu *is a phonetic rendering of the Sanskrit word* pāramitā, *which literally means "to have arrived at the opposite shore," that is, to have accomplished the truth. So* maka-hannya-haramitsu *means the accomplishment that is great real wisdom. In this chapter, Master Dōgen wrote his interpretation of the* Mahāprajñāpāramitāhṛdaya-sūtra. Hṛdaya *means heart. This short sutra, usually called the* Heart Sutra, *represents the heart of the six hundred volumes of the* Mahāprajñāpāramitā-sūtra. *Even though it is very short, the* Heart Sutra *contains the most fundamental principle of Buddhism. What is the most fundamental principle?* Prajñā. *What is* prajñā? Prajñā, *or real wisdom, is a kind of intuitive ability that occurs in our body and mind, when our body and mind are in the state of balance and harmony. We normally think that wisdom is something based on the intellect, but Buddhists believe that wisdom, on which our decisions are based, is not intellectual but intuitive. The right decision comes from the right state of body and mind, and the right state of body and mind comes when our body and mind are balanced and harmonized. So* mahāprajñāpāramitā *is wisdom that we have when our body and mind are balanced and harmonized. And zazen is the practice by which our body and mind enter the state of balance and harmony.* Mahāprajñāpāramitā, *then, is the essence of zazen.*

[71] "When Bodhisattva Avalokiteśvara[1] practices the profound *prajñāpāramitā,* the whole body[2] reflects that the five aggregates[3] are totally empty."[4] The five aggregates are form, feeling, perception, volition, and consciousness. They are five instances of *prajñā*. Reflection is *prajñā* itself. When this principle is preached and realized, it is said that "matter is just the immaterial"[5] and the immaterial is just matter. Matter is matter, the immaterial is the 22c

immaterial.[6] They are hundreds of things,[7] and myriad phenomena. Twelve instances of *prajñāpāramitā* are the twelve entrances [of sense perception].[8] There are also eighteen instances of *prajñā.*[9] They are eyes, ears, nose, tongue, body, and mind;[10] sights, sounds, smells, tastes, sensations, and properties;[11] plus the consciousnesses of eyes, ears, nose, tongue, body, and mind. There are a further four instances of *prajñā.* They are suffering, accumulation, cessation, and the Way.[12] There are a further six instances of *prajñā.* They are giving, pure [observance of] precepts, patience, diligence, meditation, and *prajñā* [itself].[13] One further instance of *prajñāpāramitā* is realized as the present moment. It is the state of *anuttara samyaksaṃbodhi.*[14] There are three further instances of *prajñāpāramitā.* They are past, present, and future.[15] There are six further instances of *prajñā.* They are earth, water, fire, wind, space, and consciousness.[16] And there are a further four instances of *prajñā* that are constantly practiced in everyday life: they are walking, standing, sitting, and lying down.[17]

[74] In the order of Śākyamuni Tathāgata there is a *bhikṣu*[18] who secretly thinks, "I shall bow in veneration of the profound *prajñāpāramitā.* Although in this state there is no appearance and disappearance of real *dharma*s,[19] there are still understandable explanations of all precepts, all balanced states, all kinds of wisdom, all kinds of liberation, and all views. There are also understandable explanations of the fruit of one who has entered the stream, the fruit of [being subject to] one return, the fruit of [not being subject to] returning, and the fruit of the arhat.[20] There are also understandable explanations of [people of] independent awakening,[21] and [people of] *bodhi.*[22] There are also understandable explanations of the supreme right and balanced state of *bodhi.* There are also understandable explanations of the treasures of Buddha, Dharma, and Sangha. There are also understandable explanations of turning the wonderful Dharma wheel[23] to save sentient beings." The Buddha, knowing the *bhikṣu*'s mind, tells him, "This is how it is. This is how it is. The profound *prajñāpāramitā* is too subtle and fine to fathom."[24]

The *bhikṣu*'s "secretly working concrete mind"[25] at this moment is, in the state of bowing in veneration of real *dharma*s, *prajñā* itself—whether or not [real *dharma*s] are without appearance and disappearance—and this is a "venerative bow" itself. Just at this moment of bowing in veneration, *prajñā* is realized as explanations that can be understood: [explanations] from "precepts, balance, and wisdom,"[26] to "saving sentient beings," and so on. This state is described as being without.[27] Explanations of the state of "being without" can thus be understood. Such is the profound, subtle, unfathomable *prajñāpāramitā.*

[76] The god Indra[28] asks the venerable monk Subhūti,[29] "Virtuous One! When bodhisattva *mahāsattvas*[30] want to study[31] the profound *prajñāpāramitā,* how should they study it?"

Subhūti replies, "Kauśika![32] When bodhisattva *mahāsattva*s want to 23a
study the profound *prajñāpāramitā,* they should study it as space."[33]

So studying *prajñā* is space itself. Space is the study of *prajñā.*

[77] The god Indra subsequently addresses the Buddha, "World-honored One! When good sons and daughters receive and retain, read and recite, think reasonably about, and expound to others this profound *prajñāpāramitā* that you have preached, how should I guard it? My only desire, World-honored One, is that you will show me compassion and teach me."

Then the venerable monk Subhūti says to the god Indra, "Kauśika! Do you see something that you must guard, or not?"

The god Indra says, "No, Virtuous One, I do not see anything here that I must guard."

Subhūti says, "Kauśika! When good sons and daughters abide in the profound *prajñāpāramitā* as thus preached, they are just guarding it. When good sons and daughters abide in the profound *prajñāpāramitā* as thus preached, they never stray. Remember, even if all human and nonhuman beings were looking for an opportunity to harm them, in the end it would be impossible. Kauśika! If you want to guard the bodhisattvas who abide in the profound *prajñāpāramitā* as thus preached, it is no different from wanting to guard space."[34]

Remember, to receive and retain, to read and recite, and to think reasonably about [*prajñā*] are just to guard *prajñā.* And to want to guard it is to receive and retain it, to read and recite it, and so on.

[78] My late master, the eternal buddha, says:

> Whole body like a mouth, hanging in space;
> Not asking if the wind is east, west, south, or north,
> For all others equally, it speaks *prajñā.*
> *Chin ten ton ryan chin ten ton.*[35]

This is the speech of *prajñā* [transmitted] by Buddhist patriarchs from rightful successor to rightful successor. It is *prajñā* as the whole body, it is *prajñā* as the whole of others,[36] it is *prajñā* as the whole self, and it is *prajñā* as the whole east, west, south, and north.

[79] Śākyamuni Buddha says, "Śāriputra![37] These many sentient beings should abide in this *prajñāpāramitā* as buddhas. When they serve offerings
23b to, bow in veneration of, and consider the *prajñāpāramitā,* they should be as if serving offerings to and bowing in veneration of the buddha-bhagavats.[38] Why? [Because] the *prajñāpāramitā* is no different from the buddha-bhagavats, and the buddha-bhagavats are no different from the *prajñāpāramitā.* The *prajñāpāramitā* is just the buddha-bhagavats themselves, and the buddha-bhagavats are just the *prajñāpāramitā* itself. Wherefore? Because, Śāriputra, the apt, right, and balanced state of truth, which all the tathāgatas have, is always realized by virtue of the *prajñāpāramitā*. Because, Śāriputra, all bodhisattva *mahāsattva*s, the independently awakened, arhats, those beyond returning, those who will return once, those received into the stream, and so on, always attain realization by virtue of *prajñāpāramitā*. And because, Śāriputra, all of the ten virtuous paths of action[39] in the world, the four states of meditation,[40] the four immaterial balanced states,[41] and the five mystical powers[42] are always realized by virtue of the *prajñāpāramitā.*"

[80] So buddha-bhagavats are the *prajñāpāramitā,* and the *prajñāpāramitā* is "these real *dharma*s." These "real *dharma*s" are "bare manifestations": they are "neither appearing nor disappearing, neither dirty nor pure, neither increasing nor decreasing." The realization of this *prajñāpāramitā* is the realization of buddha-bhagavats. We should inquire into it, and we should experience it. To serve offerings to it and to bow in veneration is just to serve and to attend buddha-bhagavats, and it is buddha-bhagavats in service and attendance.

Shōbōgenzō Maka-hannya-haramitsu

Preached to the assembly at Kannondōri-in Temple on a day of the summer retreat in the first year of Tenpuku.[43]

Copied in the attendant monks' quarters at Kippō Temple in Etsu[44] on the twenty-first day of the third lunar month in spring of the second year of Kangen.[45]

The Heart Sutra of Mahāprajñāpāramitā

Bodhisattva Avalokiteśvara, when practicing the profound *prajñāpāramitā,* reflects that the five aggregates are totally empty, and overcomes all pain and wrongdoing. Śāriputra, matter is no different from the immaterial, and the immaterial is no different from matter. Matter is just the immaterial, and the immaterial is just matter. Feeling, perception, volition, and consciousness are also like this. Śāriputra, these real *dharma*s are bare manifestations. They are neither appearing nor disappearing, neither tainted nor pure, neither increasing nor decreasing. Therefore, in the state of emptiness, there is no form, no feeling, no perception, no volition, no consciousness. There are no eyes, ears, nose, tongue, body, or mind; no sights, sounds, smells, tastes, sensations, properties. There is no realm of eyes, nor any other [elementary realm]: there is no realm of mind-consciousness. There is no ignorance, and no ending of ignorance, nor any other [causal process]: there is no old age and death, and no ending of old age and death. There is no suffering, accumulation, cessation, or path. There is no wisdom, and no attaining—because [the state] is nonattainment. Bodhisattvas rely upon *prajñāpāramitā,* and therefore their minds have no hindrance. They have no hindrance, and therefore they are without fear. They leave all confused dream-images far behind, and realize the ultimate state of nirvana. Buddhas of the three times rely upon *prajñāpāramitā,* and therefore they attain *anuttara samyaksaṃbodhi.* So remember: *prajñāpāramitā* is a great and mystical mantra; it is a great and luminous mantra; it is the supreme mantra; it is a mantra in the unequaled state of equilibrium. It can clear away all suffering. It is real, not empty. Therefore we invoke the mantra of *prajñāpāramitā.* We invoke the mantra as follows:

Gate, gate, pāragate, pārasamgate. Bodhi, svāhā.

The Heart Sutra of Prajñā

Notes

1 Kanjizai Bosatsu, lit., "Bodhisattva of Free Reflection," is one of the Chinese renderings of Avalokiteśvara Bodhisattva (see Chapter Thirty-three [Vol. II], *Kannon,* and the *Lotus Sutra,* chapter 25, *Kanzeon-bosatsu-fumon*). This paragraph begins with the same words as the *Heart Sutra.*

2 Master Dōgen added to the first line of the *Heart Sutra* the word *konshin,* "whole body," as the subject of *shoken,* "to reflect."

3 *Go-un,* from the Sanskrit *pañca-skandha.* See Glossary of Sanskrit Terms, *skandha.*

4 "Empty," *kū,* which represents the Sanskrit *śūnyatā* (see Glossary of Sanskrit Terms). As an adjective, *kū* means bare, bald, naked, empty, as it is.

5 "The immaterial" is also *kū,* this time used as a noun. In this case, *kū* means the immaterial, that which is empty, or devoid of physical substance; that is, the spiritual or mental face of reality as opposed to matter. In other cases, the noun *kū* means the empty state, that is, the state in which reality is as it is. See Chapter Twenty-two (Vol. II), *Busshō.*

6 The sutra says *shiki-soku-ze-kū,* "matter is just the immaterial," and *kū-soku-ze-shiki,* "the immaterial is just matter." Master Dōgen added *shiki-ze-shiki,* matter is matter, and *kū-ze-kū,* the immaterial is the immaterial.

7 *Hyakusō,* lit., "hundreds of weeds."

8 *Jūni-ju,* "twelve entrances," from the Sanskrit *dvādaśāyatanāni,* are the six sense organs and their objects.

9 *Juhachi-kai,* lit., "eighteen realms," from the Sanskrit *aśṭādaśa dhātavaḥ,* are the senses, their objects, and the six corresponding kinds of consciousness. See Glossary of Sanskrit Terms under *dhātu-loka.*

10 *Shin,* "body," from the Sanskrit *kāya,* means the body, or the skin, as the organ of touch. *I,* "mind," from the Sanskrit *manas,* means the mind as the center of thought, which is placed on the same level as the senses, below *prajñā.*

11 *Shoku, hō,* "sensations and properties" from the Sanskrit *sparśa* and *dharma,* represent the objects of body and mind as sense organs.

12 *Shitai,* the four philosophies, or the Four [Noble] Truths, are *ku, shu, metsu, dō.* These words derive from the Sanskrit *duḥkha-satya* (truth of suffering), *samudaya-satya*

(truth of accumulation), *nirodha-satya* (truth of dissolution), and *mārga-satya* (truth of the right way).

13 *Rokudō,* the six *pāramitā*s. In Sanskrit they are as follows: Giving is *dāna,* explained in detail in Chapter Forty-five (Vol. III), *Bodaisatta-shishōbō.* Pure [observance of] precepts is *śīla.* Patience is *kṣānti.* Diligence is *vīrya.* Meditation is *dhyāna.* (*Dhyāna* is sometimes represented phonetically in the *Shōbōgenzō* by the Chinese characters *zen-na,* but in this case *dhyāna* is expressed as *jō-ryo,* lit., "quiet thought.") The sixth *pāramitā,* real wisdom, is *prajñā.*

14 The Sanskrit *anuttara samyaksaṃbodhi* (see Chapter One, note 2) is rendered into Chinese in the second paragraph of this chapter as *mujō-shōtō-bodai,* "the supreme right and balanced state of *bodhi.*" Alternative renderings into Chinese are *mujō-shōtō-gaku,* "the supreme right and balanced state of truth," and *mujō-tōshō-gaku,* "the supreme balanced and right state of truth."

15 *Sanze,* the three times.

16 *Rokudai,* the six elements. In Sanskrit, *saḍ dhātavaḥ.* See Glossary of Sanskrit Terms under *dhātu.*

17 *Shigi,* the four forms of conduct.

18 The Sanskrit word *bhikṣu* (originally "mendicant") means a Buddhist monk.

19 *Mu-shohō-shōmetsu,* or *shohō no shōmetsu nashi.* The *Heart Sutra* says *ze-shohō-kūsō . . . Fushō-fumetsu:* "These real *dharma*s are bare manifestations. They neither appear nor disappear."

20 The *śrāvaka* ("auditor") passes through these four stages. In Sanskrit, the first is *srotāpanna,* the second is *sakṛdāgāmin,* the third is *anāgāmin,* and the fourth is arhat.

21 *Doku-kaku,* lit., "independently awakened," means *pratyekabuddha*, a naturalistic Buddhist. The distinction between *śrāvaka*s, *pratyekabuddha*s, bodhisattvas, and buddhas, which the Buddha explains in the *Lotus Sutra,* is described in Chapter Twenty-four (Vol. II), *Bukkyō.*

22 *Bodai,* in this case, seems to suggest a person who has the state of *bodhi,* that is, a bodhisattva.

23 *Tenmyōhōrin,* "turning the wonderful Dharma wheel," means Buddhist preaching. See Chapter Seventy-four (Vol. IV), *Tenbōrin.*

24 This passage is quoted from the *Daihannyakyō,* chapter 291, "Attachment and Nonattachment to Form."

25 *Setsu-sa-ze-nen.* In the sutra, these characters literally mean "secretly made this thought." But *sa,* "make," also means "to act," or "to function"; *ze,* "this," also means "concrete"; and *nen,* "thought," or "image in the mind," also means "mindfulness," or "state of mind." Master Dōgen interpreted *nen* not as a thought but as the monk's state of mind, which is *prajñā* itself, which is the state of action itself.

[26] Precepts, balance, and wisdom are *sangaku,* the three kinds of training. See Glossary of Sanskrit Terms under *tisraḥ śikṣāḥ.*

[27] *Mu, nashi,* expresses absence. In this paragraph, *mu-shometsu* is translated as "there is no appearance and disappearance" (see note 19), and "without appearance and disappearance." As a noun, *mu* means "the state of being without," i.e., the state that is free. This usage is explained in detail in Chapter Twenty-two (Vol. II), *Busshō.* The character *mu* appears over twenty times in the *Heart Sutra.*

[28] *Tentai-shaku. Tentai* is literally "god-emperor" and *shaku* stands for Śakra-devānām-indra, which is the Sanskrit name of the god Indra. This figure was incorporated into Buddhism as a guardian of Buddhist teachings. See Glossary of Sanskrit Terms.

[29] *Guju-zengen. Guju,* or "venerable monk," is derived from the Sanskrit *āyuṣmat,* a term of reverence. Zengen, lit., "Good Manifestation," is the Chinese rendering of Subhūti, one of the Buddha's disciples.

[30] *Mahāsattva* literally means "great being." Both bodhisattva and *mahāsattva* describe a Buddhist practitioner.

[31] *Gaku* includes both the meaning of "learn" and of "practice." Study of *prajñā* as space suggests the concrete practice of zazen.

[32] Kauśika is another name of Indra. See Glossary of Sanskrit Terms.

[33] *Kokū,* "empty space," or "space," from the Sanskrit *ākāśa,* is the title of Chapter Seventy-seven (Vol. IV), *Kokū.*

[34] This story is also from the *Daihannyakyō,* chapter 291.

[35] This poem about a windbell is from the *Nyojōoshōgoroku* (*Record of the Words of Master* [*Tendō*] *Nyojō*). The last line of the poem, *"chin ten ton ryan chin ten ton,"* represents onomatapoeically the sound of the windbell. The original Chinese characters can be read in several ways in Japanese; for example, *teki chō tō ryō teki chō tō.* The original Chinese pronunciation is not known.

[36] "Others" is *ta,* which sometimes means "others" and sometimes means "the external world." In Master Dōgen's commentary it suggests the latter meaning.

[37] Śāriputra was one of the Buddha's ten great disciples, and said to be foremost in wisdom. He died while the Buddha was still alive. Much of the *Mahāprajñāpāramitā-sūtra* is addressed to Śāriputra.

[38] Bhagavat is a Sanskrit term of veneration. See Glossary of Sanskrit Terms.

[39] *Jū-zengōdō,* or the ten paths of good action, are followed by refraining from doing the ten kinds of bad conduct, namely: killing, stealing, committing adultery, telling lies, two-faced speech, abusive slander, useless gossip, greed, anger, and devotion to wrong views.

[40] *Shi-jōryo,* or the "four *dhyāna*s." See Chapter Ninety (Vol. IV), *Shizen-biku.*

[41] *Shi-mushiki-jō,* or "the four balanced states that transcend the world of matter," are as follows: 1) *kū-muhen-sho-jō,* "balance in infinite space"; 2) *shiki-muhen-sho-jō,* "balance in infinite consciousness"; 3) *mu-shō-u-sho-jō,* "balance in not having anything"; and 4) *hisō-hihisō-sho-jō,* "balance in transcendence of thinking and not-thinking." Such enumeration of concepts is characteristic of Theravāda Buddhism.

[42] *Go-jinzū.* The five mystical powers are discussed in Chapter Twenty-five (Vol. II), *Jinzū.*

[43] 1233.

[44] Corresponds to present-day Fukui prefecture.

[45] 1244.

[Chapter Three]

Genjō-kōan

The Realized Universe

Translator's Note: Genjō *means "realized," and* kōan *is an abbreviation of* kofu-no-antoku, *which was a notice board on which a new law was announced to the public in ancient China. So* kōan *expresses a law, or a universal principle. In the* Shōbōgenzō, genjō-kōan *means the realized law of the universe, that is, Dharma or the real universe itself. The fundamental basis of Buddhism is belief in this real universe, and in* Genjō-kōan *Master Dōgen preaches to us the realized Dharma, or the real universe itself. When the seventy-five–chapter edition of the* Shōbōgenzō *was compiled, this chapter was placed first, and from this fact we can recognize its importance.*

[83] When all *dharma*s are [seen as] the Buddha-Dharma, then there is delusion and realization, there is practice, there is life and there is death, there are buddhas and there are ordinary beings. When the myriad *dharma*s are 23c
each not of the self, there is no delusion and no realization, no buddhas and no ordinary beings, no life and no death. The Buddha's truth is originally transcendent over abundance and scarcity, and so there is life and death, there is delusion and realization, there are beings and buddhas. And though it is like this, it is only that flowers, while loved, fall; and weeds while hated, flourish.

[84] Driving ourselves to practice and experience the myriad *dharma*s is delusion. When the myriad *dharma*s actively practice and experience ourselves, that is the state of realization. Those who greatly realize[1] delusion are buddhas. Those who are greatly deluded about realization are ordinary beings. There are people who further attain realization on the basis of realization. There are people who increase their delusion in the midst of delusion. When buddhas are really buddhas, they do not need to recognize themselves as buddhas. Nevertheless, they are buddhas in the state of experience, and they go on experiencing the state of buddha.

[85] When we use the whole body and mind to look at forms, and when we use the whole body and mind to listen to sounds, even though we are sensing them directly, it is not like a mirror's reflection[2] of an image, and not like water and the moon. While we are experiencing one side, we are blind to the other side.

[86] To learn the Buddha's truth is to learn ourselves. To learn ourselves is to forget ourselves. To forget ourselves is to be experienced by the myriad *dharma*s. To be experienced by the myriad *dharma*s is to let our own body and mind, and the body and mind of the external world, fall away. There is a state in which the traces of realization are forgotten; and it manifests the traces of forgotten realization for a long, long time.

[87] When people first seek the Dharma, we are far removed from the borders of Dharma. [But] as soon as the Dharma is authentically transmitted to us, we are a human being in [our] original element. When a man is
24a sailing along in a boat and he moves his eyes to the shore, he misapprehends that the shore is moving. If he keeps his eyes fixed on the boat, he knows that it is the boat that is moving forward. Similarly, when we try to understand the myriad *dharma*s on the basis of confused assumptions about body and mind, we misapprehend that our own mind or our own essence may be permanent. If we become familiar with action and come back to this concrete place, the truth is evident that the myriad *dharma*s are not self. Firewood becomes ash; it can never go back to being firewood. Nevertheless, we should not take the view that ash is its future and firewood is its past. Remember, firewood abides in the place of firewood in the Dharma. It has a past and it has a future. Although it has a past and a future, the past and the future are cut off. Ash exists in the place of ash in the Dharma. It has a past and it has a future. The firewood, after becoming ash, does not again become firewood. Similarly, human beings, after death, do not live again. At the same time, it is an established custom in the Buddha-Dharma not to say that life turns into death. This is why we speak of "no appearance." And it is the Buddha's preaching established in [the turning of] the Dharma wheel that death does not turn into life. This is why we speak of "no disappearance."[3] Life is an instantaneous situation, and death is also an instantaneous situation. It is the same, for example, with winter and spring. We do not think that winter becomes spring, and we do not say that spring becomes summer.

[89] A person getting realization is like the moon being reflected[4] in water: the moon does not get wet, and the water is not broken. Though the light [of the moon] is wide and great, it is reflected in a foot or an inch of water. The whole moon and the whole sky are reflected in a dewdrop on a blade of grass and are reflected in a single drop of water. Realization does not break the individual, just as the moon does not pierce the water. The individual does not hinder the state of realization, just as a dewdrop does not 24b
hinder the sky and moon. The depth [of realization] may be as the concrete height [of the moon]. The length of its moment should be investigated in large [bodies of] water and small [bodies of] water, and observed in the breadth of the sky and the moon.[5]

[90] When the Dharma has not yet satisfied the body and mind we feel already replete with Dharma. When the Dharma fills the body and mind we feel one side to be lacking. For example, sailing out beyond the mountains and into the ocean, when we look around in the four directions, [the ocean] appears only to be round; it does not appear to have any other form at all. Nevertheless, this great ocean is not round, and it is not square. Other qualities of the ocean are inexhaustibly many: [to fishes] it is like a palace and [to gods] it is like a string of pearls.[6] But as far as our eyes can see, it just seems to be round. As it is for [the ocean], so it is for the myriad *dharma*s. In dust and out of the frame,[7] [the myriad *dharma*s] encompass numerous situations, but we see and understand only as far as our eyes of learning in practice are able to reach. If we wish to hear how the myriad *dharma*s naturally are,[8] we should remember that besides their appearance of squareness or roundness, the qualities of the oceans and qualities of the mountains are numerous and endless; and that there are worlds in the four directions. Not only the periphery is like this: remember, the immediate present, and a single drop [of water] are also like this.

[91] When fish move through water, however they move, there is no end to the water. When birds fly through the sky, however they fly, there is no end to the sky. At the same time, fish and birds have never, since antiquity, left the water or the sky. Simply, when activity is great, usage is great, and when necessity is small, usage is small. Acting in this state, none fails 24c
to realize its limitations at every moment, and none fails to somersault freely at every place; but if a bird leaves the sky it will die at once, and if a fish

leaves the water it will die at once. So we can understand that water is life and can understand that sky is life. Birds are life, and fish are life. It may be that life is birds and that life is fish. And beyond this, there may still be further progress. The existence of [their] practice-and-experience, and the existence of their lifetime and their life, are like this. This being so, a bird or fish that aimed to move through the water or the sky [only] after getting to the bottom of water or utterly penetrating the sky, could never find its way or find its place in the water or in the sky. When we find this place, this action is inevitably realized as the universe. When we find this way, this action is inevitably the realized universe [itself].[9] This way and this place are neither great nor small; they are neither subjective nor objective; neither have they existed since the past nor do they appear in the present; and so they are present like this. When a human being is practicing and experiencing the Buddha's truth in this state, to get one *dharma* is to penetrate one *dharma,* and to meet one act is to perform one act. In this state the place exists and the way is mastered, and therefore the area to be known is not conspicuous. The reason it is so is that this knowing and the perfect realization of the Buddha-Dharma appear together and are experienced together. Do not assume that what is attained will inevitably become self-conscious and be recognized by the intellect. The experience of the ultimate state is realized at once. At the same time, its mysterious existence is not necessarily a manifest realization.[10] Realization is the state of ambiguity itself.[11]

25a [94] Zen Master Hōtetsu[12] of Mayokuzan is using a fan. A monk comes by and asks, "The nature of air is to be ever-present, and there is no place that [air] cannot reach. Why then does the master use a fan?"

The master says, "You have only understood that the nature of air is to be ever-present, but you do not yet know the truth[13] that there is no place [air] cannot reach."

The monk says, "What is the truth of there being no place [air] cannot reach?"

At this, the master just [carries on] using the fan. The monk does prostrations.[14] The real experience of the Buddha-Dharma, the vigorous road of the authentic transmission, is like this. Someone who says that because [the air] is ever-present we need not use a fan, or that even when we do not use [a fan] we can still feel the air, does not know ever-presence, and does not know the nature of air. Because the nature of air is to be ever-present, the behavior[15] of Buddhists has made the earth manifest itself as gold and has ripened the Long River into curds and whey.[16]

Shōbōgenzō Genjō-kōan

This was written in mid-autumn[17] in the first year of Tenpuku,[18] and was presented to the lay disciple Yō Kōshu of Chinzei.[19]

Edited in [the fourth] year of Kenchō.[20]

Notes

1 *Daigo,* "great realization," is the title of Chapter Twenty-six (Vol. II). Here it is used as a verb, *daigo suru,* "greatly realize."

2 *Yadosu* literally means "to accommodate."

3 "No appearance" is *fushō.* "No disappearance" is *fumetsu.* The words *fushō-fumetsu*—which appear for example in the *Heart Sutra,* quoted in Chapter Two, *Maka-hannya-haramitsu*—express the instantaneousness of the universe.

4 Throughout this paragraph, "to be reflected in" is originally *yadoru,* lit., "to dwell in."

5 We should investigate realization as concrete facts.

6 This sentence alludes to a traditional Buddhist teaching that different subjects see the same ocean in different ways: to fish it is a palace, to gods it is a string of pearls, to humans it is water, and to demons it is blood or pus. *Yōraku,* "string of pearls," represents the Sanskrit *muktāhāra,* a name for a string of pearls or jewels worn by royalty and nobility in ancient India.

7 *Jinchū-kakuge,* "inside dust, outside the frame," means the secular world and the world experienced in the Buddhist state.

8 *Banpo no kafu,* lit., "the family customs of the myriad *dharmas*." *Ka* means house, home, or family. *Fu* means wind, air, style, behavior, custom.

9 *Genjō-kōan* is used first as a verb, *genjō-kōan su,* and second as a noun, *genjō-kōan.*

10 "Manifest realization" and "realization" (in the next sentence) are originally the same characters: *genjō.*

11 "The state of ambiguity" is *kahitsu.* A Chinese sentence beginning with these characters would ask the question, "Why should it necessarily be that. . . ?" or "How can it conclusively be decided that. . . ?"

12 A successor of Master Baso Dōitsu.

13 *Dōri* means truth, principle, or fact. The monk was interested in philosophical theory, but the master recommended him to notice concrete facts.

14 *Shinji-shōbōgenzō,* pt. 2, no. 23. According to the story in the *Shinji-shōbōgenzō,* after the monk's prostration, the master says, "Useless master of monks! If you got a thousand students, what gain would there be?"

[15] *Fū.* Two meanings of *fū* are relevant in this section. The first is "wind" or "air," as in the story. The second is "customs," "manners," or "behavior," as in this usage. See also note 8.

[16] Master Goso Hōen said in his formal preaching, "To change the Earth into gold, and to churn the Long River into a milky whey." *Soraku,* or "curds and whey," was some kind of edible dairy product, like yogurt or cheese. Chōga, lit., "Long River," is the Chinese name for the galaxy we call the Milky Way.

[17] In the lunar calendar, autumn is the seventh, eighth, and ninth lunar months. As the autumn sky is usually very clear, this is a good time to view the moon. Several chapters of the *Shōbōgenzō* were written around the time of the autumn equinox on the fifteenth day of the eighth lunar month.

[18] 1233.

[19] Corresponds to present-day Kyushu.

[20] 1252.

[Chapter Four]

Ikka-no-myōju

One Bright Pearl

Translator's Note: Ikka *means "one,"* myō *means "bright" or "clear," and* ju *means "pearl." So* ikka-no-myōju *means one bright pearl. This chapter is a commentary on Master Gensha Shibi's words that the whole universe in all directions is as splendid as a bright pearl. Master Dōgen loved these words, so he wrote about them in this chapter.*

[97] In [this] *sahā* world,[1] in the great kingdom of Song, in Fuzhou province, at Genshazan, [there lived] Great Master Shūitsu, whose Dharma name [as a monk] was Shibi and whose secular surname was Sha.[2] While still a layman he loved fishing, and he would float down the Nantai River on his boat, following the other fishermen. It may have been that he was not waiting even for the fish with golden scales that lands itself without being fished.[3] At the beginning of the Kantsū[4] era of the Tang dynasty, suddenly he desires to leave secular society; he leaves his boat and enters the mountains. He is 25b
already thirty years old, [but] he has realized the precariousness of the floating world and has recognized the nobility of the Buddha's Way. At last he climbs Seppōzan, enters the order of Great Master Shinkaku,[5] and pursues the truth[6] day and night. One day, in order to explore widely the surrounding districts, he leaves the mountain, carrying a [traveling] bag. But as he does so, he stubs his toe on a stone. Bleeding and in great pain, [Master Gensha] all at once seriously reflects as follows: "[They say] this body is not real existence. Where does the pain come from?" He thereupon returns to Seppō. Seppō asks him, "What is it, Bi of the *dhūta*?"[7] Gensha says, "In the end I just cannot be deceived by others."[8] Seppō, loving these words very much, says, "Is there anyone who does not have these words [inside them]? [But] is there anyone who can speak these words?" Seppō asks further, "Bi of the *dhūta,* why do you not go exploring?"[9] Master [Gensha] says, "Bodhidharma did not come to the Eastern Lands; the Second Patriarch did not go to the

Western Heavens."[10] Seppō praised this very much. In his usual life as a fisherman [Master Gensha] had never seen sutras and texts even in a dream. Nevertheless, profundity of will being foremost, his outstanding resolve made itself apparent. Seppō himself considered [Gensha] to be outstanding among the sangha; he praised [Gensha] as the preeminent member of the order. [Gensha] used vegetable cloth for his one robe, which he never replaced, but patched hundreds of times. Next to his skin he wore clothes of paper, or wore moxa.[11] Apart from serving in Seppō's order, he never visited another [good] counselor. Nevertheless, he definitely realized the power to succeed to the master's Dharma. After he had attained the truth at last, he taught people with the words that the whole universe in ten directions is one bright
25c pearl. One day a monk asks him, "I have heard the master's words that the whole universe in ten directions is one bright pearl. How should the student understand [this]?" The master says, "The whole universe in ten directions is one bright pearl. What use is understanding?" On a later day the master asks the question back to the monk, "The whole universe in ten directions is one bright pearl. How do you understand [this]?" The monk says, "The whole universe in ten directions is one bright pearl. What use is understanding?" The master says, "I see that you are struggling to get inside a demon's cave in a black mountain."[12]

[101] The present expression "the whole universe in ten directions is one bright pearl" originates with Gensha. The point is that the whole universe in ten directions is not vast and great, not meager and small, not square or round, not centered or straight, not in a state of vigorous activity, and not disclosed in perfect clarity. Because it is utterly beyond living-and-dying, going-and-coming,[13] it is living-and-dying, going-and-coming. And because it is like this, the past has gone from this place, and the present comes from this place. When we are pursuing the ultimate, who can see it utterly as separate moments? And who can hold it up for examination as a state of total stillness? "The whole of the ten directions" describes the ceaseless [process] of pursuing things to make them into self, and of pursuing self to make it into something. The arising of emotion and the distinctions of the intellect, which we describe as separation, are themselves [as real as] turning the head and changing the face, or developing things and throwing [oneself] into the moment. Because we pursue self to make it into something, the whole of the

ten directions is in the ceaseless state. And because [the whole of the ten directions] is a fact before the moment, it sometimes overflows beyond [our] regulating ability which is the pivot of the moment.[14] "The one pearl" is not yet famous, but it is an expression of the truth. It will be famously recognized. "The one pearl" goes directly through ten thousand years: the eternal past has not ended, but the eternal present has arrived. The body exists now, and the mind exists now. Even so, [the whole universe] is a bright pearl. It is not grass and trees there and here, it is not mountains and rivers at all points of the compass; it is a bright pearl. "How should the student understand it?" Even though it seems that the monk is playing with his conditioned intellect[15] in speaking these words, they are the clear manifestation of the great activity, which is 26a
just the great standard itself. Progressing further, we should make it strikingly obvious that a foot of water is a one-foot wave: in other words, a yard of the pearl is a yard of brightness. To voice this expression of the truth, Gensha says, "The whole universe in ten directions is one bright pearl. What use is understanding?" This expression is the expression of truth to which buddha succeeds buddha, patriarch succeeds patriarch, and Gensha succeeds Gensha. If he wants to avoid this succession—while it is not true that no opportunity for avoidance exists—just when he is ardently trying to avoid it, [the moment] in which he speaks and lives is the total moment, conspicuously manifest before him. Gensha, on a subsequent day asks the monk, "The whole universe in ten directions is one bright pearl. How do you understand [this]?" This says that yesterday [Master Gensha] was preaching the established rule, but his exhalations today rely upon the second phase: today he is preaching an exception to the established rule. Having pushed yesterday aside, he is nodding and laughing. The monk says, "The whole universe in ten directions is one bright pearl. What use is understanding?" We might tell him: "You are riding your adversary's horse to chase your adversary. When the eternal buddha preaches for you, he is going among different kinds of beings."[16] We should turn [back] light and reflect[17] for a while: How many cases and examples of "What use is understanding?" are there? We can tentatively say that while teaching and practice are seven dairy cakes and five vegetable cakes, they are also "south of the Shō [River]" and "north of the Tan [River]."[18]

[105] Gensha says, "I see that you are struggling to get inside a demon's cave in a black mountain." Remember, the face of the sun and the face of

the moon have never changed places since the eternal past. The sun's face appears together with the sun's face, and the moon's face appears together with the moon's face. For this reason, [Master Yakusan Igen said,] "Even if I say that the sixth moon[19] is a very nice time of year, I should not say that my surname is Hot."[20] Thus, this bright pearl's possession of reality and lack of beginning are limitless, and the whole universe in ten directions is one bright pearl. Without being discussed as two pearls or three pearls, the whole body[21] is one right Dharma-eye, the whole body is real substance, the whole
26b body is one phrase, the whole body is brightness, and the whole body is the whole body itself. When it is the whole body it is free of the hindrance of the whole body; it is perfect roundness,[22] and roundly it rolls along.[23] Because the virtue of the bright pearl exists in realization like this, there are Avalokiteśvaras[24] and Maitreyas[25] in the present, seeing sights and hearing sounds; and there are old buddhas and new buddhas manifesting their bodies and preaching the Dharma.[26] Just at the moment of the present, whether suspended in space or hanging inside a garment,[27] whether kept under a [dragon's] chin[28] or kept in a topknot,[29] [the one bright pearl,] in all cases, is one bright pearl throughout the whole universe in ten directions. To hang inside a garment is its situation, so do not say that it will be dangling on the surface. To hang inside a topknot or under a chin is its situation, so do not expect to play with it on the surface of the topknot or on the surface of the chin. When we are intoxicated, there are close friends[30] who give us a pearl; and we should always give a pearl to a close friend. When the pearl is hung upon us we are always intoxicated. That which "already is like this"[31] is the one bright pearl which is the universe in ten directions. So even though it seems to be continually changing the outward appearance of its turning and not turning, it is just the bright pearl. The very recognition that the pearl has been existing like this is just the bright pearl itself. The bright pearl has sounds and forms that can be heard like this. Already "having got the state like this,"[32] those who surmise that "I cannot be the bright pearl," should not doubt that they are the pearl. Artificial and nonartificial states of surmising and doubting, attaching and rejecting, are just the small view. They are nothing more than trying to make [the bright pearl] match the narrow intellect. How could we not love the bright pearl? Its colors and light, as they are, are endless. Each color and every ray of light at each moment and in every situation is the

virtue of the whole universe in ten directions; who would want to plunder it?[33] No one would throw a tile into a street market. Do not worry about falling or not falling[34] into the six states of cause and effect.[35] They are the original state of being right from head to tail, which is never unclear, and the bright pearl is its features and the bright pearl is its eyes. Still, neither I nor you know what the bright pearl is or what the bright pearl is not. Hundreds of thoughts and hundreds of negations of thought have combined to form a very clear idea.[36] At the same time, by virtue of Gensha's words of Dharma, we have heard, recognized, and clarified the situation of a body and mind which has already become the bright pearl. Thereafter, the mind is not personal; why should we be worried by attachment to whether it is a bright pearl or is not a bright pearl, as if what arises and passes were some person?[37] Even surmising and worry is not different from the bright pearl. No action nor any thought has ever been caused by anything other than the bright pearl. Therefore, forward steps and backward steps in a demon's black-mountain cave are just the one bright pearl itself. 26c

Shōbōgenzō Ikka-no-myōju

Preached to the assembly at Kannondōrikōshōhōrinji in the Uji district of Yōshū[38] on the eighteenth day of the fourth lunar month in the fourth year of Katei.[39]

Copied in the prior's quarters of Kippōji in Shibi county, in the Yoshida district of Esshū,[40] on the twenty-third day of the intercalary seventh lunar month in the first year of Kangen,[41] attendant *bhikṣu* Ejō.

Notes

1 *Shaba-sekai. Shaba* represents the Sanskrit *sahālokadhātu,* which means the world of human beings.

2 Master Gensha Shibi (835–907), successor of Master Seppō Gison. When monks died they were not referred to by the name used in their lifetime. "Great Master Shūitsu" is Master Gensha's posthumous title. Shibi is his *hōki,* or "Dharma [name] to be avoided." See also Chapter Sixteen, *Shisho,* note 32.

3 Even as a layman Master Gensha led a relaxed and peaceful life, without worrying about the results of his efforts.

4 860 to 873.

5 Master Seppō Gison (822–907), successor of Master Tokusan Senkan. Great Master Shinkaku is his posthumous title.

6 *Bendō* expresses the practice of zazen.

7 Bizuda. *Bi* is from the name Shibi. *Zuda* is from the Sanskrit word *dhūta,* which means ascetic practice. Master Gensha was known for his hard practice, so he got the nickname of Bizuda. The twelve *dhūta* are listed in Chapter Thirty (Vol. II), *Gyōji.* See also LS 2.310.

8 The expression is ironic. Master Gensha makes it sound as if he would like to be able to learn from others, but in the end it is impossible: he can be satisfied not with secondhand knowledge but only by experiencing things for himself.

9 *A hensan,* or "thorough exploration," is the title of Chapter Sixty-two (Vol. III). Here it is used as a verb, *a hensan suru.*

10 Master Bodhidharma actually did come to the Eastern Lands (China), but "Master Bodhidharma did not come to the Eastern Lands" suggests that he came to China naturally, rather than out of personal intention. The Second Patriarch, Master Taiso Eka, did not go to the Western Heavens (India), and "The Second Patriarch did not go to the Western Heavens," suggests similarly that it was natural for him not to go.

11 Coarse vegetable fiber.

12 *Shinji-shōbōgenzō,* pt. 1, no. 15.

13 *Shōji-korai,* or "living-and-dying, going-and-coming," is an expression of everyday life that appears frequently in the *Shōbōgenzō.*

[14] *Kiyō no kantoku. Kiyō* means the central part of a mechanism; at the same time, *ki* suggests the moment of the present. *Kantoku* means "being able to control."

[15] *Gosshiki,* or "karmic consciousness." The term is discussed in Chapter Twenty-two (Vol. II), *Busshō.*

[16] *Irui-chū-gyō,* "going among different kinds of beings" (in the five or six destinies), is a common expression in the *Shōbōgenzō*. In this case it suggests the absolute difference between the real understanding of Master Gensha and the intellectual understanding of the monk.

[17] *E-kō-hen-shō* describes the state in zazen. The expression appears in the *Fukanzazengi* (Appendix II).

[18] The Shō River flows north of the Tan River, and the Tan River flows south of the Shō River. In China the area between the two rivers was used as a symbol of one thing that can be expressed in two ways. In this sentence, cakes symbolize concrete things, and "south of the Shō River" and "north of the Tan River" represent subjective views. In Buddhist teaching and practice, recognition of concrete facts and theoretical understanding are both important.

[19] *Rokugatsu,* or "the sixth lunar month," was an uncomfortably hot time in the south of China.

[20] Buddhist monks would customarily avoid giving their family name, and reply instead, "It is a nice time of year."

[21] *Zenshin,* "whole body," sometimes suggests the universe as the Buddha's whole body. See Chapter Seventy-one (Vol. III), *Nyorai-zenshin.*

[22] "Perfect roundness" is *en-da-da-chi,* lit., "circle diagonal-diagonal state." *En* means circular or perfect. *Da,* repeated for emphasis, means diagonal; at the same time, it suggests the absence of corners, i.e., roundness. *Chi* means "state."

[23] *Ten-roku-roku. Ten* means "to turn" or "to roll." *Roku-roku* is onomatopoeic for a round object rolling.

[24] Bodhisattva Avalokiteśvara is the subject of Chapter Thirty-three (Vol. II), *Kannon.* See also the *Lotus Sutra,* chapter 25, *Kanzeon-bosatsu-fumon.*

[25] Bodhisattva Maitreya is expected to be born five thousand six hundred and seventy million years in the future, to save all living beings who were left unsaved by the Buddha. See, for example, LS 1.62. In this sentence the bodhisattvas Avalokiteśvara and Maitreya symbolize Buddhist practitioners today.

[26] Alludes to the description of Avalokiteśvara ("Hearer of the Sounds of the World") in the *Lotus Sutra*. See LS 3.252.

[27] See LS 2.114.

[28] Black dragons keep a pearl under their chins. The black dragon's pearl is a symbol of the truth.

[29] See LS 2.276.

[30] See LS 2.114.

[31] *Kize-inmo.* At the beginning of Chapter Twenty-nine (Vol. II), *Inmo,* Master Ungo Dōyō discusses *kize-inmo-nin,* or "a person in the state of already being like this."

[32] *Toku-inmo.* These characters also appear in Chapter Twenty-nine (Vol. II), *Inmo.*

[33] Master Gensha said, "It is forbidden for anyone to plunder a street market." See *Shinji-shōbōgenzō,* pt. 1, no. 38.

[34] *Furaku,* "not falling," and *fumai,* "not being unclear," represent opposing views of cause and effect. See, for example, Chapter Seventy-six (Vol. IV), *Dai-shugyō.*

[35] *Rokudō no inga* are the six states through which we pass according to the law of cause and effect: the state of beings in hell, the state of hungry ghosts, the state of animals, the state of angry demons, the state of human beings, and the state of gods.

[36] *Mei-mei no sōryō. Sōryō* means "idea" or "thinking." In this sentence, Master Dōgen substituted *sō,* "weeds" (symbolizing concrete things), for *sō,* "idea," in order to allude to the traditional saying *mei-mei-taru hyaku-sō-tō,* "clear-clear are hundreds of weeds" (see Chapter Twenty-two [Vol. II], *Busshō*).

[37] The original word for "some person" is *tare,* which means "who?"

[38] Corresponds to present-day Kyoto prefecture.

[39] 1238.

[40] Corresponds to present-day Fukui prefecture.

[41] 1243.

[Chapter Five]

Jū-undō-shiki 27a3

Rules for the Hall of Accumulated Cloud

Translator's Note: Jū-undō *or "hall of accumulated cloud" was the name of the zazen hall of Kannondōrikōshōhōrinji.* Shiki *means rules. So* Jū-undō-shiki *means "Rules for the Hall of Accumulated Cloud." Kannondōrikōshōhōrinji was the first temple established by Master Dōgen. He built it in Kyoto prefecture in 1233, several years after coming back from China.* Jū-undō *was the first zazen hall to be built in Japan. Master Dōgen made these rules for the hall, and titled them. The chapter was not included in the* Shōbōgenzō *when the seventy-five–chapter edition was compiled, but was added when the ninety-five–chapter edition was compiled at the end of the seventeenth century. The inclusion of this chapter is very useful in understanding the* Shōbōgenzō, *because what is written here represents in a concrete way Master Dōgen's sincere attitude in pursuing the truth.*

[111] People who have the will to the truth and who discard fame and gain may enter. We should not randomly admit those who might be insincere. If someone is admitted by mistake, we should, after consideration, make them leave. Remember, when the will to the truth has secretly arisen, fame and gain evaporate at once. Generally, in [all] the great-thousandfold world,[1] there are very few examples of the right and traditional transmission. In our country, this will be seen as the original source. Feeling compassion for future ages, we should value the present.

[112] The members of the hall should harmonize like milk and water, and should wholeheartedly promote each other's practice of the truth. Now we are for the present [as] guests and hosts,[2] but in future we will forever be Buddhist patriarchs. So now that each of us is meeting what is hard to meet, and is practicing what is hard to practice, we must not lose our sincerity. This [sincerity] is called "the body and mind of the Buddhist patriarchs"; it inevitably becomes buddha and becomes a patriarch. We have already left

our families and left our hometowns; we rely on clouds and rely on waters.[3] The benevolence of [the members of] this sangha, in promoting [each other's] health and in promoting [each other's] practice, surpasses even that of a father and mother. A father and mother are only parents for the short span between life and death, but [the members of] this sangha will be friends in the Buddha's truth forever.

[113] We should not be fond of going out. If absolutely necessary, once in one month is permissible. People of old lived in distant mountains or practiced in remote forests. They not only had few human dealings but also totally
27b discarded myriad involvements. We should learn their state of mind in shrouding their light and covering their tracks. Now is just the time to [practice as if to] put out a fire on our head. How could we not regret idly devoting this time to worldly involvements? How could we not regret this? It is hard to rely on what has no constancy, and we never know where, on the grass by the path, our dewdrop life will fall. [To waste this time] would be truly pitiful.

[114] While we are in the hall we should not read the words of even Zen texts. In the hall we should realize the principles and pursue the state of truth. When we are before a bright window,[4] we can enlighten the mind with the teachings of the ancients. Do not waste a moment of time. Singlemindedly make effort.[5]

[115] We should make it a general rule to inform the leader of the hall[6] where we are going, whether it is night or day. Do not ramble around at will. That might infringe the discipline of the sangha. We never know when this life will finish. If life were to end during an idle excursion, that would certainly be something to regret afterward.

[115] We should not strike other people for their mistakes. We should not look on people's mistakes with hatred. In the words of an ancient,[7] "When we do not see others' wrongness or our own rightness, we are naturally respected by seniors and admired by juniors." At the same time, we should not imitate the wrongs of others. We should practice our own virtue. The Buddha prevented wrongdoing, but not out of hatred.

[116] Any task, big or small, we should do only after informing the leader of the hall. People who do things without informing the leader of the hall should be expelled from the hall. When formalities between members and leaders are disrupted, it is hard to tell right from wrong.

[116] In and around the hall, we should not raise the voice or gather 27c
heads to converse. The leader of the hall should stop this.

[117] In the hall we should not practice ceremonial walking.[8]

[117] In the hall we should not hold counting beads.[9] And we should not come and go with the hands hanging down.[10]

[118] In the hall we should not chant, or read sutras. If a donor[11] requests the reading of sutras by the whole order, then it is permissible.

[118] In the hall we should not loudly blow the nose, or loudly hack and spit. We should regret the fact that our moral behavior is still [so] imperfect. And we should begrudge the fact that time is stealing away, robbing us of life with which to practice the truth. It might be natural for us to have minds like fish in a dwindling stream.

[119] Members of the hall should not wear brocade. We should wear [clothes of] paper, cotton, and so forth. Since ancient times, all the people who clarified the truth have been like this.

[119] Do not come into the hall drunk. If someone forgetfully [enters] by mistake, they should do prostrations and confess. Also, alcohol should not be brought into [the hall]. Do not enter the hall flushed and inebriated.[12]

[120] If two people quarrel, both should be sent back to their quarters, because they not only hinder their own practice of the truth but also hinder others. Those who see the quarrel coming but do not prevent it are equally at fault.

[120] Anyone who is indifferent toward the instructions for [life] in the hall should be expelled by the common consent of all members. Anyone whose mind is in sympathy with the transgression is [also] at fault.

[121] Do not disturb the other members by inviting guests, whether monks 28a
or laypeople, into the hall. When talking with guests in the vicinity [of the hall], do not raise the voice. Do not deliberately boast about your own training, greedily hoping for offerings. [A guest] who has long had the will to participate in practice, and who is determined to tour the hall and do prostrations,[13] may enter. In this case also, the leader of the hall must be informed.

[121] Zazen should be practiced as in the monks' halls [of China].[14] Never be even slightly lazy in attending and requesting [formal and informal teaching], morning and evening.

[122] During the midday meal and morning gruel, a person who drops the accessories for the *pātra*[15] on the ground should be penalized[16] according to the monastery rules.

[122] In general, we should staunchly guard the prohibitions and precepts of the Buddhist patriarchs. The pure criteria of monasteries should be engraved on our bones, and should be engraved on our minds.

[123] We should pray that our whole life will be peaceful, and that our pursuit of the truth will abide in the state without intent.

[123] These few rules [listed] above are the body and mind of eternal buddhas. We should revere them and follow them.

The twenty-fifth day of the fourth lunar month in the second year of Rekinin.[17] Set forth by the founder of Kannondōrikōshōgokokuji, *śramaṇa* Dōgen.

Notes

[1] *Daisenkai* is short for *sanzen-daisen-sekai,* or "the three-thousand-great-thousand-fold world." This expression, which derives from the ancient Indian belief that the world comprises many groups of thousands of worlds, occurs frequently in the *Lotus Sutra.* See for example, LS 2.218–220.

[2] *Hinju,* translated in paragraph 116 as "members and leaders."

[3] In China and Japan monks are commonly referred to as *unsui,* which means "clouds and water."

[4] Suggests a place, other than the zazen hall, suitable for reading.

[5] *Sen-itsu ni kufu su.* These words also appear in the *Fukanzazengi.*

[6] *Dōshu,* "leader of the hall," would have been the head monk (not Master Dōgen himself).

[7] Master Hakuyō Hōjun. See *Zokudentōroku,* chapter 29.

[8] *Gyōdō,* ceremonial walking, is a way of serving offerings to the buddha image, in which the practitioner circles the buddha image three times, walking around clockwise so that the buddha image remains to the practitioner's right.

[9] Some people use a kind of rosary, usually with one hundred and eight beads, to count the recitations of Buddha's name, and so on. The Sanskrit term for a rosary is *akṣa-sūtra.* See Glossary of Sanskrit Terms.

[10] In other words, we should hold the hands in front of the chest in *shashu,* with the right hand covering the left fist.

[11] "Donor" is originally *dāna* (giving), the first of the six *pāramitās*. In this case *dāna* stands for *dānapati,* the Sanskrit word for a person who supports a Buddhist order. The reading of sutras at a donor's request is explained in detail in Chapter Twenty-one, *Kankin.*

[12] "Flushed and inebriated" is originally *niragi nokashi te.* Being written in *hiragana,* the Japanese phonetic alphabet, this allows alternative interpretations. The interpretation used here is that *niragu* means to temper steel, or to redden; and *nokashi te* means emboldened, or inebriated. The traditional interpretation in Japan has been that *nira* means leeks, *gi* means onions, and *no ka shi te* means smelling, so the sentence would mean "Do not enter the hall smelling of leeks and onions."

[13] *Junrei* stands for *jundō-raihai,* or "to go round the hall and do prostrations." The method is explained in Chapter Twenty-one, *Kankin.*

[14] In large temples in China the zazen hall was called the *sōdō,* or "monks' hall," because the monks would live in the hall, not only sitting but also eating and sleeping there.

[15] *Pātra* is the Sanskrit word for the Buddhist food bowl. See Chapter Seventy-eight (Vol. IV), *Hatsu-u.*

[16] "Penalized" is *batsu-yu,* lit., "penalty of oil." In the temples of China oil for lamps was scarce, so it is likely that monks were penalized by paying oil from their ration.

[17] 1239.

[Chapter Six]

Soku-shin-ze-butsu

Mind Here and Now Is Buddha

Translator's Note: Soku *means "here and now."* Shin *means "mind."* Ze *means "is."* Butsu *means "buddha." The principle of* soku-shin-ze-butsu, *or "mind here and now is buddha" is very famous in Buddhism, but many people have interpreted the principle to support the beliefs of naturalism. They say if our mind here and now is just buddha, our conduct must always be right, and, in that case, we need not make any effort to understand or to realize Buddhism. However, this interpretation is a serious mistake. The principle* soku-shin-ze-butsu, *"mind here and now is buddha," must be understood not from the standpoint of the intellect but from the standpoint of practice. In other words, the principle does not mean belief in something spiritual called "mind" but it affirms the time "now" and the place "here" as reality itself. This time and place must always be absolute and right, and so we can call them the truth or "buddha." In this chapter, Master Dōgen explained this meaning of* soku-shin-ze-butsu, *"mind here and now is buddha."*

[125] What every buddha and every patriarch has maintained and relied upon, without exception, is just "mind here and now is buddha." Many students, however, misunderstand that "mind here and now is buddha" did not exist in India but was first heard in China. As a result, they do not recognize their mistake as a mistake. Because they do not recognize the mistake as a mistake, many fall down into non-Buddhism. When stupid people hear talk of "mind here and now is buddha," they interpret that ordinary beings' intellect and sense perception, which have never established the *bodhi*-mind, are just buddha. This derives from never having met a true teacher. The reason I say that they become non-Buddhists is that there was a non-Buddhist in India, called Senika, whose viewpoint is expressed as follows:

> The great truth exists in our own body now, so we can easily recognize its situation. In other words, [a spiritual intelligence] distinguishes

between pain and pleasure, naturally senses cold and warmth, and recognizes discomfort and irritation. [The spiritual intelligence] is neither restricted by myriad things nor connected with circumstances: things come and go and circumstances arise and pass, but the spiritual intelligence always remains, unchanging. This spiritual intelligence is all around, pervading all souls—common and sacred—without distinction. In its midst, illusory flowers in space exist for the time being, but when momentary insight has appeared, and things have vanished and circumstances have disappeared, then the spiritual intelligence, the original essence, alone is clearly recognizable, peaceful, and eternal. Though the physical form may be broken, the spiritual intelligence departs unbroken; just as, when a house burns down in a fire, the master of the house leaves. This perfectly clear and truly spiritual pres-
28b ence is called "the essence of perception and intelligence." It is also described as "buddha," and called "enlightenment." It includes both the subject and the object, and it permeates both delusion and enlightenment. [So] let the myriad *dharma*s and all circumstances be as they are. The spiritual intelligence does not coexist with circumstances and it is not the same as things. It abides constantly through passing *kalpa*s. We might also call the circumstances that exist in the present "real," insofar as they derive from the existence of the spiritual intelligence: because they are conditions arising from the original essence, they are real things. Even so, they are not eternal as the spiritual intelligence is, for they exist and then vanish. [The spiritual intelligence] is unrelated to brightness and darkness, because it knows spiritually. We call this "the spiritual intelligence," we also call it "the true self," we call it "the basis of awakening," we call it "original essence," and we call it "original substance." Someone who realizes this original essence is said to have returned to eternity and is called a great man who has come back to the truth. After this, he no longer wanders through the cycle of life and death; he experiences and enters the essential ocean[1] where there is neither appearance nor disappearance. There is no reality other than this, but as long as this essence has not emerged, the three worlds[2] and the six states[3] are said to arise in competition.

This then is the view of the non-Buddhist Senika.

[129] Master Echū, National Master Daishō,[4] of the great kingdom of Tang, asks a monk, "From which direction have you come?"

The monk says, "I have come from the south."

The master says, "What [good] counselors are there in the south?"

The monk says, "[Good] counselors are very numerous."

The master says, "How do they teach people?"

The monk says, "The [good] counselors of that quarter teach students directly that mind here and now is buddha. Buddha means consciousness itself. You now are fully endowed with the essence of seeing, hearing, awareness, and recognition. This essence is able to raise the eyebrows and to wink, to come and go, and to move and act. It pervades the body, so that when [something] touches the head, the head knows it, and when something touches the foot, the foot knows it. Therefore it is called 'the true all-pervading intelligence.' Apart from this there is no buddha at all. This body must appear and disappear, but the mental essence has never appeared or disappeared since the limitless past. The appearance and disappearance of the body is like a dragon changing its bones, a snake shedding its skin, or a person moving out of an old house. This body is inconstant; the essence is constant. 29a
What they teach in the south is, for the most part, like this."

The master says, "If it is so, they are no different from the non-Buddhist Senika. He said, 'In our body there is a single spiritual essence. This essence can recognize pain and irritation. When the body decays the spirit departs; just as when a house is burning the master of the house departs. The house is inconstant; the master of the house is constant.' When I examine people like this, they do not know the false from the true. How can they decide what is right? When I was on my travels, I often saw this kind. Recently they are very popular. They gather assemblies of three or five hundred people and, eyes gazing toward the heavens, they say 'This is the fundamental teaching of the south.'[5] They take the *Platform Sutra*[6] and change it, mixing in folk stories, and erasing its sacred meaning. They delude and disturb recent students. How could [theirs] be called the oral teaching?[7] How painful it is, that our religion is being lost. If seeing, hearing, awareness, and recognition could be equated with the buddha-nature, Vimalakīrti[8] would not have said, 'The

Dharma is transcendent over seeing, hearing, awareness, and recognition. When we use seeing, hearing, awareness, and recognition, it is only seeing, hearing, awareness, and recognition; it is not pursuit of the Dharma.'"

[131] National Master Daishō is an excellent disciple of the eternal buddha of Sōkei.[9] He is a great good counselor in heaven above and in the human world. We should clarify the fundamental teaching set forth by the National Master, and regard it as a criterion[10] for learning in practice. Do not follow what you know to be the viewpoint of the non-Buddhist Senika. Among those of recent generations who subsist as masters of mountains in the great kingdom of Song, there may be no one like the National Master. From the ancient past, no counselors to equal the National Master have ever manifested themselves in the world. Nevertheless, people of the world mistakenly think that even Rinzai[11] and Tokusan[12] might equal the National Master. Only people [who think] like this are great in number. It is a pity that there are no teachers with clear eyes. This "mind here and now is buddha" that the Buddhist patriarchs maintain and rely upon is not seen by non-Buddhists and [people of] the two vehicles, even in their dreams. Buddhist patriarchs alone, together with Buddhist patriarchs,[13] possess hearing, action, and experience that have enacted and that have perfectly realized "mind here and now is buddha." Buddhas[14] have continued to pick up and to throw away
29b hundreds of weeds, but they have never represented themselves as a sixteen-foot golden body.[15] "The immediate"[16] universe[17] exists; it is not awaiting realization,[18] and it is not avoiding destruction. "This concrete"[19] triple world[20] exists; it is neither receding nor appearing, and it is not just mind.[21] "Mind"[22] exists as fences and walls; it never gets muddy or wet, and it is never artificially constructed. We realize in practice that "mind here and now is buddha,"[23] we realize in practice that "the mind which is buddha is this,"[24] we realize in practice that "buddha actually is just the mind,"[25] we realize in practice that "mind-and-buddha here and now is right,"[26] and we realize in practice that "this buddha-mind is here and now."[27]

[134] Realization in practice like this is just "mind here and now is buddha" picking itself up and authentically transmitting itself to "mind here and now is buddha." Authentically transmitted like this, it has arrived at the present day. "The mind that has been authentically transmitted" means one mind as all *dharma*s, and all *dharma*s as one mind. For this reason, a man

of old[28] said, "When a person becomes conscious of the mind, there is not an inch of soil on the earth." Remember, when we become conscious of the mind, the whole of heaven falls down and the whole ground is torn apart. Or in other words, when we become conscious of the mind, the earth grows three inches thicker. An ancient patriarch said,[29] "What is fine, pure, and bright mind? It is mountains, rivers, and the earth, the sun, the moon, and the stars." Clearly, "mind" is mountains, rivers, and the earth, the sun, the moon, and the stars. But what these words say is, when we are moving forward, not enough, and when we are drawing back, too much. Mind as mountains, rivers, and the earth is nothing other than mountains, rivers, and the earth. There are no additional waves or surf, no wind or smoke. Mind as the sun, the moon, and the stars is nothing other than the sun, the moon, and the stars. There is no additional fog or mist. Mind as living-and-dying, coming-and-going, is nothing other than living-and-dying, coming-and-going. There is no additional delusion or realization. Mind as fences, walls, tiles, and pebbles is nothing other than fences, walls, tiles, and pebbles. There is no additional mud or water. Mind as the four elements and five aggregates is nothing other than the four elements and five aggregates. There is no additional horse or monkey.[30] Mind as a chair or a whisk[31] is nothing other than a chair
or a whisk. There is no additional bamboo or wood. Because the state is like 29c
this, "mind here and now is buddha" is untainted "mind here and now is buddha." All buddhas are untainted buddhas. This being so, "mind here and now is buddha" is the buddhas [themselves] who establish the will, undergo training, [realize] *bodhi,* and [experience] nirvana. If we have never established the will, undergone training, [realized] *bodhi,* and [experienced] nirvana, then [the state] is not "mind here and now is buddha." If we establish the mind and do practice-and-experience even in a single *kṣaṇa,*[32] this is "mind here and now is buddha." If we establish the will and do practice-and-experience in a single molecule, this is "mind here and now is buddha." If we establish the will and do practice-and-experience in countless *kalpa*s, this is "mind here and now is buddha." If we establish the will and do practice-and-experience in one instant of consciousness, this is "mind here and now is buddha." If we establish the will and do practice-and-experience inside half a fist, this is mind here and now is buddha. To say, on the contrary, that undergoing training to become buddha for long *kalpa*s is not "mind

here and now is buddha" is never to have seen, never to have known, and never to have learned "mind here and now is buddha." It is never to have met a true teacher who proclaims "mind here and now is buddha." The term "buddhas" means Śākyamuni Buddha. Śākyamuni Buddha is just "mind here and now is buddha." When all the buddhas of the past, present, and future become buddha, they inevitably become Śākyamuni Buddha, that is, "mind here and now is buddha."

Shōbōgenzō Soku-shin-ze-butsu

Preached to the assembly at Kannondōrikōshōhōrinji in the Uji district of Yōshū,[33] on the twenty-fifth day of the fifth lunar month in the first year of Enō.[34]

Notes

1 *Shōkai.* See Chapter One, *Bendōwa.*

2 *Sangai,* "three worlds" or "triple world," are the worlds of volition, matter, and the immaterial. See Chapter Forty-seven (Vol. III), *Sangai-yuishin.*

3 *Rokudō,* the six [miserable] states, are the state of beings in hell, the state of hungry ghosts, the state of animals, the state of angry demons, the state of human beings, and the state of gods.

4 Master Nan'yō Echū (675?–775), successor of Master Daikan Enō. "National Master Daishō" was his title as a teacher of the emperor. Master Dōgen often refers to Master Nan'yō Echū simply as the National Master.

5 Master Nan'yō Echū lived in the north of China which was the center of Chinese civilization at the time of the Tang dynasty (619–858), so Buddhist philosophy was strong in the north. However, the Buddhism of southern China was thought to be very practical. The government moved south in the Song dynasty (960–1279) in response to invasion from the north.

6 The *Rokusodaishihōbōdangyō* (*Platform Sutra of the Sixth Patriarch's Dharma Treasure*) is a collection of the teachings of Master Daikan Enō, the Sixth Patriarch in China and the master of Master Nan'yō Echū.

7 *Gonkyō,* "oral teaching," suggests the original teaching of the Buddha, which was not recorded in writing until the first century B.C.E., when the Pāli canon was written on palm leaves in the monasteries of Sri Lanka.

8 Jōmyō, lit., "Pure Name," is a Chinese rendering of Vimalakīrti, a layman of the Buddha's time who was excellent in Buddhist philosophy. Many questions and answers between Vimalakīrti and the Buddha are recorded in the *Vimalakīrti Sutra* (Skt. *Vimalakīrtinirdeśa-sūtra*).

9 Master Daikan Enō.

10 "Criterion" is *kikan,* lit., "turtle mirror." In ancient China, fortune-tellers would sometimes heat a turtle shell and divine an appropriate course of action by looking at the crack. Thus, a turtle shell was used like a mirror, as a criterion for making decisions.

11 Master Rinzai Gigen (d. 867), founder of the Rinzai sect, successor of Master Ōbaku Kiun. See Chapter Forty-nine (Vol. III), *Butsudō.*

12 Master Tokusan Senkan (780–865), successor of Master Ryūtan Sōshin. See Chapter Eighteen, *Shin-fukatoku.*

13 *Yui-busso-yo-busso* is a variation of *yui-butsu-yo-butsu,* "buddhas alone, together with buddhas." The *Lotus Sutra* says, "Buddhas alone, together with buddhas, can perfectly realize that all *dharma*s are real form." See LS 1.68.

14 *Butsu* means "buddha." The following four sentences begin with *butsu,* "buddha"; *soku,* "here and now"; *ze,* "is"; and *shin,* "mind," respectively.

15 The sixteen-foot golden body is the idealized image of the Buddha.

16 *Soku* can function as an adjective ("here and now," "immediate," "actual"); it can function as a copula, i.e., a linking verb, to express the oneness of two factors (A *soku* B = "A, that is, B"); it can function as an adverb ("here and now," "just," "immediately," "directly," "actually"); and it can also function as a conjunction expressing temporal contingency (A *soku* B = "A, immediately followed by B").

17 *Soku-kōan,* "the immediate universe" or "the here-and-now universe." Here *soku* is used as an adjective.

18 *Genjō. Genjō* and *kōan* are often associated, as in the title of Chapter Three, *Genjō-kōan.*

19 *Ze* can function as an adjective ("this," "concrete," "this concrete"; or "right," "correct"); it can function as a copula in the same way as *soku* ("is," "are," "is just the same as"); it can function as an adverb ("here and now," "actually"); and it can function as a pronoun ("this").

20 *Zesangai,* "this triple world" or "this concrete triple world." Here *ze* is used as an adjective.

21 *Yuishin. Sangai yuishin,* "the triple world is just mind," is the title of Chapter Forty-seven (Vol. III), *Sangai-yuishin.*

22 *Shin* means mind.

23 *Soku-shin ze butsu,* as in the title of this chapter. In this case, *soku* (here and now) is an adjective and *ze* (is) is a copula. The four expressions following this expression represent further combinations of the four characters *soku-shin-ze-butsu.* See following notes.

24 *Shin-soku-butsu ze.* In this case, *soku* (which is) is a copula and *ze* (this) is a pronoun.

25 *Butsu soku ze shin.* In this case, *soku* (actually) is an adverb and *ze* (is just) is a copula.

26 *Soku-shin-butsu ze.* In this case, *soku* (here and now) and *ze* (right) are both adjectives.

27 *Ze-butsu-shin soku.* In this case also, *ze* (this) and *soku* (here and now) are both adjectives.

[28] Master Chōrei Shutaku. His words mean that to know the mind is just to know reality, in which an inch of soil cannot be separated from the whole earth.

[29] Master Isan Reiyū asked the question to his disciple Master Kyōzan Ejaku. See *Shinji-shōbōgenzō,* pt. 2, no. 68.

[30] Horse and monkey allude to the phrase *i-ba shen-en,* or "horse-will, monkey-mind." The horse represents the restless will and the monkey represents the mischievous intellect.

[31] *Hossu* is a ceremonial fly whisk—a wooden stick with a long plume of animal hair—held by a master during a Buddhist lecture.

[32] *Setsuna* represents the Sanskrit *kṣāṇa,* "moment." Sixty-five *kṣāṇa*s are said to pass in the clicking of the fingers.

[33] Corresponds to present-day Kyoto prefecture.

[34] 1239.

[Chapter Seven]

Senjō 30a

Washing

Translator's Note: Sen *means "to wash," and* jō *means "to purify." So* senjō *means "washing." Buddhism is neither idealism nor materialism but belief in reality, which has both a spiritual side and a material side. So Buddhism insists that to clean our physical body is to purify our mind. Therefore, in Buddhism, cutting our fingernails, shaving our head, and washing our body are all very important religious practices. In this chapter Master Dōgen expounds the religious meaning of such daily behavior, and preaches the importance in Buddhism of cleansing our physical body.*

[139] There is practice-and-experience that Buddhist patriarchs have guarded and maintained; it is called "not being tainted."

[140] The Sixth Patriarch[1] asks Zen Master Daie[2] of Kannon-in Temple on Nangakuzan, "Do you rely on practice and experience or not?"

Daie says, "It is not that there is no practice and experience, but the state can never be tainted."

The Sixth Patriarch says, "Just this untainted state is that which buddhas guard and desire. You are also like this. I am also like this. And the ancestral masters of India[3] were also like this. . . ."[4]

[140] The *Sutra of Three Thousand Dignified Forms for Ordained Monks*[5] says, "Purifying the body means washing the anus and the urethra,[6] and cutting the nails of the ten fingers." So even though the body and mind is not tainted, there are Dharma practices of purifying the body and there are Dharma practices of purifying the mind. Not only do we clean body and mind; we also clean the nation and clean beneath trees.[7] To clean the nation, even though it has never become dirty, is "that which buddhas guard and desire"; and even when they have arrived at the Buddhist fruit, they still do not draw back or cease. It is hard to fathom this point. To enact the Dharma is the point. To attain the state of truth is to enact the Dharma.

[141] The "Pure Conduct" chapter of the *Garland Sutra*[8] says, "When we relieve ourselves, we should pray that living beings will get rid of impurity and will be free of greed, anger, and delusion. Then, having arrived at the water, we should pray that living beings will progress toward the supreme state of truth and attain the Dharma that transcends the secular world. While we are washing away impurity with the water, we should pray that living beings will have pure endurance, and will ultimately be free of dirt."

[142] Water is not always originally pure or originally impure. The body is not always originally pure or originally impure. All *dharma*s are also like this. Water is never sentient or nonsentient, the body is never sentient or nonsentient, and all *dharma*s are also like this. The preaching of the Buddha,
30b the World-honored One, is like this. At the same time, [to wash] is not to use water to clean the body; [rather,] when we are maintaining and relying upon the Buddha-Dharma in accordance with the Buddha-Dharma, we have this form of behavior, and we call it "washing." It is to receive the authentic transmission of a body and mind of the Buddhist Patriarch immediately; it is to see and to hear a phrase of the Buddhist Patriarch intimately; and it is to abide in and to retain a state of brightness of the Buddhist Patriarch clearly. In sum, it is to realize countless and limitless virtues. At just the moment when we dignify body and mind with training, eternal original practice is completely and roundly realized. Thus the body and mind of training manifests itself in the original state.

[144] We should cut the nails of [all] ten fingers. Of ["all] ten fingers" means the fingernails of both left and right hands. We should also cut the toenails. A sutra says, "If the nails grow to the length of a grain of wheat, we acquire demerit." So we should not let the nails grow long. Long nails are naturally a precursor of non-Buddhism. We should make a point of cutting the nails. Nevertheless, among the priests of the great kingdom of Song today, many who are not equipped with eyes of learning in practice grow their nails long. Some have [nails] one or two inches long, and even three or four inches long. This goes against the Dharma. It is not the body and mind of the Buddha-Dharma. People are like this because they are without reverence for the old traditions[9] of Buddhists; venerable patriarchs who possess the state of truth are never like this. There are others who grow their hair long. This also goes against the Dharma. Do not mistakenly suppose

that because these are the habits of priests in a great nation, they might be right Dharma.

[145] My late master, the eternal buddha, spoke stern words of warning to priests throughout the country who had long hair or long nails. He said, "Those who do not understand [the importance of] shaving the head[10] 30c are not secular people and are not monks; they are just animals. Since ancient times, was there any Buddhist patriarch who did not shave the head? Those today who do not understand [the importance of] shaving the head are truly animals." When he preached to the assembly like this, many people who had not shaved their heads for years shaved their heads. In formal preaching in the Dharma hall or in his informal preaching, [the master] would click his fingers loudly as he scolded them.[11] "Not knowing what the truth is, they randomly grow long hair and long nails; it is pitiful that they devote a body and mind in the south [continent] of Jambudvīpa[12] to wrong ways. For the last two or three hundred years, because the truth of the Founding Patriarch has died out, there have been many people like these. People like these become the leaders of temples and, signing their names with the title of 'master,' they create the appearance of acting for the sake of the many, [but] they are without benefit to human beings and gods. Nowadays, on all the mountains throughout the country, there is no one at all who has the will to the truth. The ones who attained the truth are long extinct. Only groups of the corrupt and the degenerate [remain]." When he spoke like this in his informal preaching, people from many districts who had arbitrarily assumed the title of "veteran master" bore no grudge against him and had nothing to say for themselves. Remember, growing the hair long is something that Buddhist patriarchs remonstrate against, and growing the nails long is something that non-Buddhists do. As the children and grandchildren of Buddhist patriarchs, we should not be fond of such violations of the Dharma. We should clean the body and mind, and we should cut the nails and shave the head.

[147] "Wash the anus and the urethra": Do not neglect this. There was an episode in which, through this practice, Śāriputra[13] caused a non-Buddhist to submit himself. This was neither the original expectation of the non-Buddhist nor the premeditated hope of Śāriputra, but when the dignified behavior of the Buddhist patriarchs is realized, false teaching naturally succumbs. When [monks] practice beneath a tree or on open ground,[14] they have

no constructed toilets; they rely on conveniently located river valleys, streams, and so on, and they clean themselves with pieces of soil. This is [when] there is no ash. They just use two lots of seven balls of soil. The method of using
31a the two lots of seven balls of soil is as follows: First they take off the Dharma robe and fold it, then they pick up some soil—not black but yellowish soil—and divide it into balls, each about the size of a large soy bean. They arrange these into rows of seven balls, on a stone or some other convenient place, making two rows of seven balls each. After that they prepare a stone to be used as a rubstone. And after that they defecate. After defecating they use a stick, or sometimes they use paper. Then they go to the waterside to clean themselves, first carrying three balls of soil to clean with. They take each individual ball of soil in the palm of the hand and add just a little water so that, when mixed with the water, [the soil] dissolves to a consistency thinner than mud—about the consistency of thin rice gruel. They wash the urethra first. Next, they use one ball of soil, in the same way as before, to wash the anus. And next, they use one ball of soil, in the same way as before, briefly to wash the impure hand.[15]

[149] Ever since [monks] started living in temples, they have built toilet buildings. These are called *tōsu* (east office), or sometimes *sei* (toilet), and sometimes *shi* (side building).[16] They are buildings that should be present wherever monks are living. The rule in going to the toilet is always to take the long towel.[17] The method is to fold the towel in two, and then place it over the left elbow so that it hangs down from above the sleeve of your jacket. Having arrived at the toilet, hang the towel over the clothes pole.[18] The way to hang it is as it has been hanging from your arm. If you have come wearing a *kaṣāya* of nine stripes, seven stripes, and so on, hang [the *kaṣāya*] alongside the towel. Arrange [the *kaṣāya*] evenly so that it will not fall down. Do not throw it over [the pole] hastily. Be careful to remember the mark [on
31b the pole]. "Remembering the mark" refers to the characters written along the clothes pole; these are written inside moon-shaped circles on sheets of white paper, which are then attached in a line along the pole. So remembering the mark means not forgetting by which character you have put your own gown,[19] and not getting [the places] mixed up. When many monks are present do not confuse your own place on the pole with that of others. During this time, when [other] monks have arrived and are standing in lines, bow

to them with the hands folded.[20] In bowing, it is not necessary to face each other directly and bend the body; it is just a token bow of salutation with the folded hands placed in front of the chest. At the toilet, even if you are not wearing a gown, still bow to and salute [other] monks. If neither hand has become impure, and neither hand is holding anything, fold both hands and bow. If one hand is already soiled, or when one hand is holding something, make the bow with the other hand. To make the bow with one hand, turn the hand palm upward, curl the fingertips slightly as if preparing to scoop up water, and bow as if just lowering the head slightly. If someone else [bows] like this, you should do likewise. And if you [bow] like this, others should do likewise. When you take off the jacket[21] and the gown, hang them next to the towel. The way to hang them is as follows: Remove the gown and bring the sleeves together at the back, then bring together the armpits and lift them up so that the sleeves are one over the other. Then, take the inside of the back of the collar of the gown with the left hand, pull up the shoulders with the right hand, and fold the sleeves and the left and right lapels
over each other. Having folded the sleeves and lapels over each other, make 31c
another fold, down the middle from top to bottom, and then throw the collar of the gown over the top of the pole. The hem of the gown and the ends of the sleeves will be hanging on the near side of the pole. For example, the gown will be hanging from the pole by the join at the waist. Next, cross over the ends of the towel which are hanging down on the near and far sides of the pole, and pull them across to the other side of the gown. [There,] on the side of the gown where the towel is not hanging, cross over [the ends] again and make a knot. Go round two or three times, crossing over [the ends] and making a knot, to ensure that the gown does not fall from the pole to the ground. Facing the gown, join the palms of your hands.[22] Next, take the cord and use it to tuck in the sleeves.[23] Next, go to the washstand and fill a bucket with water and then, holding [the bucket] in the right hand, walk up to the toilet. The way to put water into the bucket is not to fill it completely, but to make ninety percent the standard. In front of the toilet entrance, change slippers. Changing slippers means taking off your own slippers in front of the toilet entrance and putting on the straw [toilet] slippers.[24]

[153] The *Zenenshingi*[25] says, "When we want to go to the toilet, we should go there ahead of time. Do not get into a state of anxiety and haste

by arriving just in time. At this time, fold the *kaṣāya*, and place it on the desk in your quarters, or over the clothes pole."

[154] Having entered the toilet, close the door with the left hand. Next, pour just a little water from the bucket into the bowl of the toilet. Then put the bucket in its place directly in front of the hole. Then, while standing facing the toilet bowl, click the fingers three times. When clicking the fingers, make a fist with the left hand and hold it against the left hip. Then put the hem of your skirt and the edges of your clothes in order, face the entrance,
32a position the feet either side of the rim of the toilet bowl, squat down, and defecate. Do not get either side of the bowl dirty, and do not soil the front or back of the bowl. During this time, keep quiet. Do not chat or joke with the person on the other side of the wall, and do not sing songs or recite verses in a loud voice. Do not make a mess by weeping and dribbling, and do not be angry or hasty. Do not write characters on the walls, and do not draw lines in the earth with the shit-stick. The stick is to be used after you have relieved yourself. Another way is to use paper; old paper should not be used, and paper with characters written on it should not be used. Distinguish between clean sticks and dirty sticks. The sticks are eight *sun*[26] long, of triangular section, and the thickness of a thumb. Some are lacquered and some are not lacquered. Dirty [sticks] are thrown into the stick box. Clean [sticks] originally belong in the stick rack. The stick rack is placed near the board [that screens] the front of the toilet bowl. After using the stick or using paper, the method of washing is as follows: Holding the bucket in the right hand, dip the left hand well [into the water] and then, making the left hand into a dipper, scoop up the water; first rinsing the urethra three times and then washing the anus. Make yourself pure and clean by washing according to the method. During this time, do not tip the bucket so suddenly that water spills out of the hand or splashes down, causing the water to be used up quickly. After you have finished washing put the bucket in its place, and then, taking [another] stick, wipe yourself dry. Or you can use paper. Both places, the urethra and the anus, should be thoroughly wiped dry. Next, with the right hand, rearrange the hem of your skirt and the corners of your clothes, and holding the bucket in the right hand, leave the toilet, taking off the straw [toi-
32b let] slippers and putting on your own slippers as you pass through the entrance. Next, returning to the washstand, put the bucket back in its original place.

Then wash the hands. Taking the spoon for ash in the right hand, first scoop [some ash] onto a tile or a stone, sprinkle a few drops of water onto it with the right hand, and cleanse the soiled hand. Scrub the [fingers] on the tile or the stone, as if sharpening a rusty sword on a whetstone. Wash like this, using ash, three times. Then wash another three times, putting soil [on the stone] and sprinkling it with water. Next, take a honey locust[27] in the right hand, dip it in a small tub of water, and scrub it between the hands. Wash [the hands] thoroughly, going up to the forearms as well. Wash with care and effort, dwelling in the mind of sincerity. Three lots of ash, three lots of soil, and one honey locust, makes seven rounds altogether; that is the standard. Next, wash [the hands] in the large tub. This time skin cleansers,[28] soil, ash, and so on, are not used. Just wash with water, either cold or hot. After washing once, pour the [used] water into a small bucket, then pour some fresh water [into the tub], and wash the hands again.

[157] The *Garland Sutra* says, "When we wash the hands with water, we should pray that living beings will get excellent and fine hands, with which to receive and to retain the Buddha-Dharma."[29]

[158] To pick up the water ladle, always use your right hand. While doing this, do not noisily clatter the ladle and bucket. Do not splash water about, scatter honey locusts around, get the washstand area wet, or be generally hasty and messy. Next, wipe the hands on the common towel, or wipe them on your own towel. After wiping the hands, go under the clothes pole, 32c
in front of your gown, and take off the cord and hang it on the pole. Next, after joining hands, untie the towel, take down the gown, and put it on. Then, with the towel hanging over the left arm, apply fragrance. In the common area there is a fragrance applicator. It is fragrant wood fashioned into the shape of a treasure pot,[30] as thick as a thumb and as long as the width of four fingers. It is hung from the clothes pole with a piece of string a foot or more long, which is threaded through a hole bored in each end of the fragrant [wood]. When this is rubbed between the palms, it naturally spreads its scent to the hands. When you hang your cord on the pole, do not hang it on top of another so that cord and cord become confused and entangled. Actions like these all "purify the Buddha's land, and adorn the Buddha's kingdom," so do them carefully, and do not be hasty. Do not be in a hurry to finish, thinking that you would like to get back. Privately, you might like to consider the

principle that "we do not explain the Buddha-Dharma while in the toilet."[31] Do not keep looking into the faces of other monks who have come there. Cold water is considered better for washing when in the toilet itself; it is said that hot water gives rise to intestinal diseases. [But] there is no restriction against using warm water to wash the hands. The reason that a cauldron is provided is so that we can boil water for washing the hands. The *Shingi* says, "Late in the evening, boil water and supply oil.[32] Always ensure [a] continuous [supply of] hot and cold water, so that the minds of the monks are not disturbed." So we see that we [can] use both hot and cold water. If the inside of the toilet has become dirty, close the door, and hang up the "dirty" sign. If a bucket has been dropped [into the toilet bowl] by mistake, close the door,
33a and hang up the "fallen bucket" sign. Do not enter[33] a closet on which one of these signs is hung. If, when you are already in the toilet, [you hear] someone outside clicking the fingers, you should leave presently. The *Shingi* says, "Without washing, we must neither sit on the monks' platform, nor bow to the Three Treasures. Neither must we receive people's prostrations." The *Sutra of Three Thousand Dignified Forms* says, "If we fail to wash the anus and the urethra, we commit a *duṣkṛta,*[34] and we must not sit on a monk's pure sitting cloth[35] or bow to the Three Treasures. Even if we do bow, there is no happiness or virtue."

[162] Thus, at a place of the truth where we strive in pursuit of the truth,[36] we should consider this behavior to be foremost. How could we not bow to the Three Treasures? How could we not receive people's prostrations? And how could we not bow to others? In the place of truth of a Buddhist patriarch, this dignified behavior is always done, and people in the place of truth of a Buddhist patriarch are always equipped with this dignified behavior. It is not our own intentional effort; it is the natural expression of dignified behavior itself. It is the usual behavior of the buddhas and the everyday life of the patriarchs. It is [buddha-behavior] not only of buddhas in this world: it is buddha-behavior throughout the ten directions; it is buddha-behavior in the Pure Land and in impure lands. People of scant knowledge do not think that buddhas have dignified behavior in the toilet, and they do not think that the dignified behavior of buddhas in the *sahā* world[37] is like that of buddhas in the Pure Land. This is not learning of the Buddha's truth. Remember, purity and impurity is [exemplified by] blood dripping from a human being.

At one time it is warm, at another time it is disgusting. The buddhas have toilets, and this we should remember.

[163] Fascicle Fourteen of the *Precepts in Ten Parts*[38] says, "Śrāmaṇera Rāhula[39] spent the night in the Buddha's toilet. When the Buddha woke up, the Buddha patted Rāhula on the head with his right hand, and preached the following verse:

> You were never stricken by poverty,
> Nor have you lost wealth and nobility.[40]
> Only in order to pursue the truth, you have left home.
> You will be able to endure the hardship."

[164] Thus, there are toilet buildings in the Buddha's places of practicing the truth. And the dignified behavior done in the Buddha's toilet building is washing. That the Buddha's behavior, having been transmitted from 33b
patriarch to patriarch, still survives is a delight to those who venerate the ancients. We have been able to meet what is difficult to meet. Furthermore, the Tathāgata graciously preached the Dharma for Rāhula inside the toilet building. The toilet building was one [place of] assembly for the Buddha's turning of the Dharma wheel. The advancing and stillness[41] of that place of truth has been authentically transmitted by the Buddhist patriarchs.

[165] Fascicle Thirty-four of the *Mahāsaṃghika Precepts*[42] says, "The toilet building should not be located to the east or to the north. It should be located to the south or to the west. The same applies to the urinal."

[166] We should follow this [designation of] the favorable directions. This was the layout of all the monasteries[43] in India in the Western Heavens, and the [method of] construction in the Tathāgata's lifetime. Remember, this is not only the buddha-form followed by one buddha; it describes the places of truth, the monasteries, of the Seven Buddhas. It was never initiated; it is the dignified form of the buddhas. Before we have clarified these [dignified forms], if we hope to establish a temple and to practice the Buddha-Dharma, we will make many mistakes, we will not be equipped with the Buddha's dignified forms, and the Buddha's state of *bodhi* will not yet manifest itself before us. If we hope to build a place of practicing the truth, or to establish a temple, we should follow the Dharma-form that the Buddhist patriarchs have authentically transmitted. We should just follow the Dharma-form that has

been authentically transmitted as the right tradition. Because it is the traditional authentic transmission, its virtue has accumulated again and again. Those who are not legitimate successors to the authentic transmission of the Buddhist patriarchs do not know the body and mind of the Buddha-Dharma. Without knowing the body and mind of the Buddha-Dharma, they never clarify the buddha-actions of the Buddha's lineage. That the Buddha-Dharma of Great Master Śākyamuni Buddha has now spread widely through the ten directions is the realization of the Buddha's body and mind. The realization of the Buddha's body and mind, just in the moment, is like this.

Shōbōgenzō Senjō

Preached to the assembly at Kannondōrikōshōhōrinji in the Uji district of Yōshū,[44] on the twenty-third day of the tenth lunar month in the winter of the first year of Enō.[45]

Notes

1 Master Daikan Enō (638–713), successor of Master Daiman Kōnin.

2 Master Nangaku Ejō (677–744), successor of Master Daikan Enō. Zen Master Daie was his posthumous title.

3 *Saiten,* "Western Heavens," means India.

4 *Shinji-shōbōgenzō,* pt. 2, no. 1. See also Chapter Twenty-nine (Vol. II), *Inmo,* and Chapter Sixty-two (Vol. III), *Hensan.*

5 The *Daibikusanzenyuigikyō.*

6 *Daishōben.* In modern Japanese *daishōben* means "feces and urine," but in this chapter the words suggest the parts of the body where feces and urine emerge: the anus and the urethra. Although it is not common practice nowadays to wash around the urethra after urinating, it seems that Master Dōgen recommended us to do so.

7 It is a Buddhist tradition to sit under a tree. The Buddha is said to have realized the truth while sitting under a *bodhi* tree.

8 The *Garland Sutra* is the *Kegonkyō* in Japanese, and the *Avataṃsaka-sūtra* in Sanskrit. The sutra compares the whole universe to the realization of Vairocana Buddha. Its basic teaching is that myriad things and phenomena are the oneness of the universe, and the whole universe is myriad things and phenomena.

9 "Reverence for the old traditions" is *keiko,* lit., "consideration of the past," or "emulation of the ancients." In modern Japanese *keiko* is the term generally used for training by sumo wrestlers, martial artists, etc.

10 In Master Tendō Nyojō's quotation, "shaving the head" is *jōhatsu,* lit., "purifying the hair." In Master Dōgen's commentary, the expressions used are *teitō,* lit., "shaving the head," and *teihatsu,* lit., "shaving the hair."

11 The first quotation in this paragraph is clearly defined in the original text. But it is not totally clear where Master Dōgen's own words end and the second quotation begins.

12 Jambudvīpa is the continent south of Mount Sumeru on which, according to ancient Indian cosmology, human beings live.

13 Śāriputra was one of the Buddha's ten great disciples. There is a story in chapter 35 of the *Makasōgiritsu* (*Mahāsaṃghika Precepts*) that a non-Buddhist was converted to Buddhism on witnessing Śāriputra's method of defecating.

[14] *Juge-roji,* "beneath trees and on open ground," suggests the practice of the Buddha and the monks of his time. However, the tense of the Japanese is the present.

[15] It is not clear what was done with the remaining eleven balls of soil.

[16] A standard temple in China and Japan faces south. As you approach the temple from the south, the Buddha hall is directly in front of you, and the zazen hall is to the left (west). A toilet building located to the east would be on the far right (furthest east). In certain ages, however, the main toilet building was located to the west. See Appendix Five, Temple Layout.

[17] *Shukin.* The *shukin* is a piece of cloth, measuring one *jo* plus two *shaku* (total: 3.64 meters) in length, which is used as a towel, and also as a sash to keep up the sleeves. It is one of the eighteen articles a monk is supposed to have. The method of using the *shukin* is explained in detail in Chapter Fifty-six (Vol. III), *Senmen.*

[18] *Jōkan,* lit., "pure pole," is a bamboo or wooden pole set up horizontally at about head height.

[19] *Jikitotsu,* lit., "directly sewn." Traditionally a monk in China wore a kind of long black cotton jacket, or *hensan,* and a black skirt, or *kunzu.* By Master Dōgen's time, it was customary for the jacket and skirt to be sewn together, hence the name *jikitotsu,* or "directly sewn." The *jikitotsu* is the long black gown with wide sleeves commonly worn by priests in Japan today. A monk of Master Dōgen's time would usually have worn the following clothes: a white loincloth, white underclothes, a black jacket (*hensan*) and black skirt (*kunzu*), and/or a black gown (*jikitotsu*), and finally the *kaṣāya.* The standard form of the *kaṣāya,* or Buddhist robe, is universal (see Chapter Twelve, *Kesa-kudoku;* and Chapter Thirteen, *Den-e*), but the other clothes worn by monks have changed according to the climates and customs of different countries and different ages.

[20] *Shashu.* The left hand is curled into a fist, the fingers covering the thumb, and placed in front of the chest with the palm of the hand facing downward. The open right hand rests, palm down, on the top of the left hand.

[21] *Hensan.* See note 19.

[22] *Gasshō.* In *gasshō* the palms are brought together in front of the chest, with the tips of the fingers in line with the nostrils.

[23] Literally, "take the *banzu* and wear it on both arms." *Banzu,* lit., "binding thing," is a long cord tied round the shoulders and armpits (of the undergarment) so that the sleeves can be tucked in, leaving the arms bare.

[24] *Ho-ai,* lit., "cattail slippers." *Ho,* "cattail," is a marsh plant with long flat leaves, often used for weaving.

[25] The *Pure Criteria for Zen Monasteries.* The editing of the *Zenenshingi* was completed by Master Chōro Sōsaku in 1103. It was based on Master Hyakujō's *Koshingi* (*Old Pure Criteria*).

26 One *sun* is approximately equal to 1.2 inches.

27 Honey locusts are produced by a tall leguminous tree of the same name (*Gleditsia japonica*). They are long twisted pods containing a sweet edible pulp and seeds that resemble beans.

28 *Menyaku,* lit., "face medicines."

29 This quotation is from the old translation of the *Garland Sutra* done by Buddhabhadra in sixty fascicles between 418 and 420. A second translation was done by Śikṣānanda in eighty fascicles between 695 and 699. This is known as the new translation, but there was also a third partial translation done by Prajña in forty fascicles from 759 to 762.

30 This kind of pot has an oval body, a long neck, and a lid, often with jewels. (So the piece of fragrant wood would have been oval with tapered ends.) In certain Buddhist ceremonies, such pots were used to hold water for sprinkling on practitioners' heads.

31 The characters are in the style of a quotation from a Chinese text, though the source has not been traced.

32 Oil for lamps.

33 "Enter" is originally "ascend." The toilets were raised a little above the ground.

34 Violations of some of the two hundred and fifty precepts for monks were classed, according to their relative importance, as *duṣkṛta.* Wrongdoings in this category include, for example, failure to observe the seven methods of stopping a quarrel.

35 *Zagu* represents the Sanskrit *niṣīdana.* The *zagu* is a cloth or a mat used to do prostrations on, or to sit on.

36 "A place of the truth where we strive in pursuit of the truth" is *bendō kufu no dōjō.* Master Dōgen often used the expression *bendō kufu,* "effort in pursuit of the truth," to express zazen itself. "A place of the truth" is *dōjō,* lit., "truth-place," which represents the Sanskrit *bodhimaṇḍa,* "seat of truth." See Glossary of Sanskrit Terms.

37 The *sahā* world means the human world. See Glossary of Sanskrit Terms.

38 The *Jūjuritsu,* a sixty-one–fascicle translation of the Vinaya of the Sarvāstivāda school. It enumerates the two hundred and fifty precepts of a monk in Hinayana Buddhism, and was translated into Chinese by Puṇyatara (Hannyatara) and Kumārajīva.

39 The Sanskrit word *śrāmaṇera,* which means "novice," is a variation of *śramaṇa,* which means "monk." Rāhula was the Buddha's son from his marriage with Yaśodharā. It is said that he became a fully ordained monk when he was twenty, and that he was foremost among the ten great disciples of the Buddha in meticulous observation of the precepts.

40 Before becoming a monk, the Buddha was the heir to his father's throne, so his son Rāhula was born into the nobility.

[41] *Shinshi,* "progressing and stopping," suggests active and passive behavior, that is, real behavior in daily life.

[42] The *Makasōgiritsu,* a forty-fascicle version of the Vinaya of the Mahāsaṃghika school of Hinayana Buddhism. It was translated into Chinese by Buddhabhadra during the Eastern Jin dynasty (317–420).

[43] *Shōja* is the translation into Chinese characters of the Sanskrit *vihāra.*

[44] Corresponds to present-day Kyoto prefecture.

[45] 1239.

[Chapter Eight]

Raihai-tokuzui 33c

Prostrating to the Marrow of Attainment

Translator's Note: Raihai *means "to prostrate oneself to,"* toku *means "to get," or "to attain," and* zui *means "marrow." So* raihai-tokuzui *means prostrating oneself to attainment of the marrow, in other words, revering what has got the truth. In this chapter Master Dōgen preached to us that the value of a being must be decided according to whether or not it has got the truth. So, he said, even if it is a child, a woman, a devil, or an animal like a wild fox, if it has got the truth, we must revere it wholeheartedly. In this attitude, we can find Master Dōgen's sincere reverence of the truth, and his view of men, women, and animals.*

[169] In practicing the state of *anuttara samyaksaṃbodhi* the most difficult thing is to find a guiding teacher. Though beyond appearances such as those of a man or a woman, the guiding teacher should be a big stout fellow,[1] and should be someone ineffable.[2] He is not a person of the past and present, but may be a good counselor with the spirit of a wild fox.[3] These are the features of [someone who] has got the marrow;[4] he may be a guide and a benefactor; he is never unclear about cause and effect; he may be you, me, him, or her.[5]

[170] Having met with a guiding teacher, we should throw away myriad involvements and, without wasting a moment of time,[6] we should strive in pursuit of the truth. We should train with consciousness, we should train without consciousness, and we should train with semiconsciousness. Thus, we should learn walking on tiptoes[7] to put out a fire on our head.[8] When we behave like this, we are unharmed by abusive demons. The patriarch who cuts off an arm and gets the marrow[9] is never another, and the master who gets free of body and mind[10] is ourself already. Getting the marrow, and receiving the Dharma, invariably come from sincerity and from belief. There is no example of sincerity coming from outside, and there is no way for sincerity to emerge from within. [Sincerity] just means attaching weight to the

Dharma and thinking light of [one's own] body. It is to get free from the secular world and to make one's home the state of truth. If we attach even slightly more weight to self-regard for the body than to the Dharma, the Dharma is not transmitted to us, and we do not attain the truth. Those resolute spirits who attach [greater] weight to the Dharma are not unique, and they do not depend upon the exhortation of others, but let us take up, for the present, one or two instances. It is said that those who attach weight to the Dharma will make the body into a seat on the floor,[11] and will serve for countless *kalpa*s [whatever] is maintaining and relying upon the great Dharma, [whatever] has "got my marrow,"[12] whether it is an outdoor pillar, whether it is a stone
34a lantern, whether it is the buddhas, whether it is a wild dog, a demon or a god, a man or a woman. Bodies and minds are easily received: they are [as common] in the world as rice, flax, bamboo, and reeds. The Dharma is rarely met. Śākyamuni Buddha says, "When you meet teachers who expound the supreme state of *bodhi,* have no regard for their race or caste,[13] do not notice their looks, do not dislike their faults, and do not examine their deeds. Only because you revere their *prajñā,* let them eat hundreds and thousands of pounds of gold every day, serve them by presenting heavenly food, serve them by scattering heavenly flowers, do prostrations and venerate them three times every day, and never let anxiety or annoyance arise in your mind. When we behave like this, there is always a way to the state of *bodhi.* Since I established the mind, I have been practicing like this, and so today I have been able to attain *anuttara samyaksaṃbodhi*." This being so, we should hope that even trees and stones might preach to us,[14] and we should request that even fields and villages might preach to us.[15] We should question outdoor pillars, and we should investigate even fences and walls. There is the ancient [example of the] god Indra[16] prostrating himself to a wild dog as his master, and asking it about the Dharma; his fame as a great bodhisattva has been transmitted. [Fitness to be asked] does not rest upon the relative nobility of one's station. Nevertheless, stupid people who do not listen to the Buddha's Dharma think, "I am a senior *bhikṣu.* I cannot prostrate myself to a junior who has got the Dharma." "I have endured long training. I cannot prostrate myself to a recent student who has got the Dharma." "I sign my name with the title of master. I cannot prostrate myself to someone who does not have the title of master." "I am an Administrator of Dharma Affairs.[17] I cannot

prostrate myself to lesser monks who have got the Dharma." "I am the Chief Administrator of Monks.[18] I cannot prostrate myself to laymen and laywomen who have got the Dharma." "I am [a bodhisattva] of the three clever stages and ten sacred stages. I cannot prostrate myself to *bhikṣuṇīs* and other [women], even if they have got the Dharma." "I am of royal pedigree. I cannot prostrate myself to the family of a retainer or to the lineage of a minister, even if they have got the Dharma." Stupid people like these have heedlessly fled their father's kingdom and are wandering on the roads of foreign lands;[19] therefore, they neither see nor hear the Buddha's truth. 34b

[176] Long ago, in the Tang dynasty, Great Master Shinsai of Jōshū[20] established the mind and set off as a wayfarer.[21] In the story he says, "I shall question anyone who is superior to me, even a child of seven. And I shall teach anyone who is inferior to me, even a man of a hundred." The old man[22] is willing to prostrate himself on asking a seven-year-old about the Dharma—this is a rare example of a resolute spirit, and the working of the mind of an eternal buddha. When a *bhikṣuṇī* who has got the truth and got the Dharma manifests herself in the world,[23] *bhikṣus*[24] who seek the Dharma and learn in practice will devote themselves to her order, prostrating themselves and asking about the Dharma—this is an excellent example of learning in practice. For instance, it is like the thirsty finding drink.

[178] The Chinese Zen Master Shikan[25] is a venerable patriarch in Rinzai's lineage. Once upon a time, Rinzai sees the master coming [to visit] and holds onto him. The master says, "It is understood."[26] Rinzai lets go and says, "I will allow you to stop for a while."[27] From this point on, he has already become Rinzai's disciple. He leaves Rinzai and goes to Massan,[28] at which time Massan asks him, "Where have you come from?" The master says, "The entrance of the road." Massan says, "Why have you come here without anything on?"[29] The master has no words. He just prostrates himself, bowing as disciple to teacher. The master asks a question back to Massan: "Just what is Massan?" Massan says, "[Massan] never shows a peak."[30] The master says, "Just who is the person within the mountain?" Massan says, "It is beyond appearances such as those of a man or a woman." The master says, "Then why do you not change [your form]?" Massan says, "I am not the ghost of a wild fox. What might I change?" The master prostrates himself. Eventually he decides to work as the head of the vegetable garden and works there altogether 34c

for three years. Later, when he has manifested himself in the world,[31] he preaches to the assembly, "I got half a dipper at Old Papa Rinzai's place, and I got half a dipper at Old Mama Massan's place.[32] Making a dipper with both [halves], I have finished drinking, and, having arrived directly at the present, I am completely satisfied." Hearing these words now, I look back on the traces of those days with veneration for the past. Massan is an excellent disciple[33] of Kōan Daigu. She has power in her lifeblood, and so she has become Shikan's "Ma." Rinzai is an authentic successor of Ōbaku [Ki]un.[34] He has power in his efforts, and so he has become Shikan's "Pa." "Pa" means father, and "Ma" means mother.[35] Zen Master Shikan's prostration to and pursuit of the Dharma under the nun Massan Ryōnen are an excellent example of a resolute spirit, and integrity that students of later ages should emulate. We can say that he broke all barriers, large and small.

[180] Nun Myōshin is a disciple of Kyōzan.[36] Kyōzan, on one occasion, is choosing the Chief of the Business Office.[37] He asks around the retired officers and others on Kyōzan, "Who is the right person?" They discuss it back and forth, and eventually Kyōzan says, "Disciple [Myō]shin from the Wai River, though a woman, has the spirit of a big stout fellow.[38] She is certainly qualified to be Chief of the Business Office." All the monks agree. [So] at length Myōshin is assigned as Chief of the Business Office. The dragons and elephants in Kyōzan's order do not resent this. Though the position is in fact not so grand, the one selected for it might need to love herself. While she is posted at the business office, seventeen monks from the Shoku
35a district[39] form a group to visit teachers and seek the truth, and, intending to climb Kyōzan, they lodge at dusk at the business office. In a nighttime talk, while resting, they discuss the story of the Founding Patriarch Sōkei,[40] and the wind and the flag.[41] The words of each of the seventeen men are totally inadequate. Meanwhile, listening from the other side of the wall, the Chief of the Business Office says, "Those seventeen blind donkeys! How many straw sandals have they worn out in vain? They have never seen the Buddha-Dharma even in a dream." A temple servant present at the time overhears the Chief of the Business Office criticizing the monks and informs the seventeen monks themselves, but none of the seventeen monks resents the criticism of the Chief of the Business Office. Ashamed of their own inability to express the truth, they at once prepare themselves in the dignified form,[42]

burn incense, do prostrations, and request [her teaching]. The Chief of the Business Office (Myōshin) says, "Come up here!" The seventeen monks approach her, and while they are still walking, the Chief of the Business Office says, "This is not wind moving, this is not a flag moving, and this is not mind moving." When she teaches them like this, the seventeen monks all experience reflection. They bow to thank her and have the ceremony to become her disciples. Then they go straight back home to western Shoku. In the end, they do not climb Kyōzan. Truly the state [demonstrated] here is beyond [bodhisattvas at] the three clever and ten sacred stages;[43] it is action in the truth as transmitted by Buddhist patriarchs from authentic successor to authentic successor. Therefore, even today, when a post as master or assistant master[44] is vacated, a *bhikṣuṇī* who has got the Dharma may be requested [to fill it]. Even if a *bhikṣu* is senior in years and experience, if he has not got the Dharma, what importance does he have? A leader of monks must always rely upon clear eyes. Yet many [leaders] are drowning in the body and mind of a village bumpkin; they are so dense that they are prone to be derided even in the secular world. How much less do they deserve to be mentioned in the Buddha-Dharma? Moreover, there may be [men] who would refuse to prostrate themselves to women monks who are teachers that have received the Dharma, and who are [the men's] elder sisters, aunts, and so on.[45] Because they do not 35b
know and will not learn, they are close to animals, and far from the Buddhist patriarchs. When the sole devotion of body and mind to the Buddha-Dharma is retained deep in [a person's] consciousness, the Buddha-Dharma always has compassion for the person. Even human beings and gods, in their stupidity, have the sympathy to respond to sincerity, so how could the buddhas, in their rightness, lack the compassion to reciprocate sincerity? The sublime spirit that responds to sincerity exists even in soil, stones, sand, and pebbles. In the temples of the great kingdom of Song today, if a resident *bhikṣuṇī* is reputed to have got the Dharma, the government issues an imperial edict for her to be appointed master of a nuns' temple, and she gives formal preaching in the Dharma hall of her present temple. All the monks, from the master down, attend [the formal preaching]. They listen to the Dharma, standing on the ground, and questions are also [put by] the *bhikṣu*s, the male monks. This is a traditional standard. A person who has got the Dharma is one individual true eternal buddha here and now, and as such should not be

met as someone from the past. When that person looks at us, we meet each other in a new and singular state. When we look at that person, the mutual relation may be "today having to enter today." For example, when arhats, *pratyekabuddha*s, and [bodhisattvas at][46] the three clever and ten sacred stages come to a *bhikṣuṇī* who is retaining the transmission of the right Dharma-eye treasury, to prostrate themselves and to ask her about Dharma, she must receive these prostrations. Why should men be higher? Space is space, the four elements are the four elements,[47] the five aggregates are the five aggregates,[48] and women are also like this. As regards attainment of the truth, both [men and women] attain the truth, and we should just profoundly revere every single person who has attained the Dharma. Do not discuss man and woman. This is one of Buddhism's finest Dharma standards.

[187] In Song dynasty [China], the term "householder"[49] refers to gentlemen who have not left their families.[50] Some of them live in houses with
35c their wives, while others are single and pure, but anyway we can say that they are immensely busy in a dense forest of dusty toil.[51] Nevertheless, if one of them has clarified something, patch-robed monks[52] gather to do prostrations and to ask for the benefit [of his teaching], as to a master who had left home. We also should be like that, even toward a woman, even toward an animal. When [a person] has never seen the truths of the Buddha-Dharma even in a dream, even if he is an old *bhikṣu* of a hundred years, he cannot arrive at the level of a man or woman who has got the Dharma, so we should not venerate [such a person] but need only bow to him as junior to senior. When [a person] practices the Buddha-Dharma and speaks the Buddha-Dharma, even if a girl of seven, she is just the guiding teacher of the four groups[53] and the benevolent father of all living beings. We should serve and venerate her as we do the buddha-tathāgatas, and as it was, for example, when the dragon's daughter became a buddha.[54] This is just the time-honored form in Buddhism. Those who do not know about it, and who have not received its one-to-one transmission, are pitiful.

[188] Another case: Since the ancient past in Japan and China, there have been women emperors. The whole country is the possession of such an empress, and all the people become her subjects. This is not out of reverence for her person but out of reverence for her position. Likewise, a *bhikṣuṇī* has never been revered for her person but is revered solely for her

attainment of the Dharma. Furthermore, the virtues that accompany the four effects all belong to a *bhikṣuṇī* who has become an arhat.[55] Even [these] virtues accompany her; what human being or god could hope to surpass these virtues of the fourth effect? Gods of the triple world are all inferior to her. While being forsaken [by human beings] she is venerated by all the gods. How much less should anyone fail to venerate those who have received the transmission of the Tathāgata's right Dharma, and who have established the great will of a bodhisattva?[56] If we fail to venerate such a person it is our 36a
own wrongness. And if we fail to revere our own supreme state of *bodhi,* we are stupid people who insult the Dharma. Again, there are in our country daughters of emperors, or ministers' daughters who become queens' consorts,[57] or queens who are titled with the names of temples.[58] Some of them have shaved their head, and some of them do not shave their head. In any case, priests who [only] look like *bhikṣus*, and who crave fame and love gain, never fail to run to the house of such [a woman] and strike their head at her clogs. They are far inferior to serfs following a lord. Moreover, many of them actually become her servants for a period of years. How pitiful they are. Having been born in a minor nation in a remote land, they do not even know a bad custom like this for what it is. There was never [such ignorance] in India and China but only in our country. It is lamentable. Forcedly to shave the head and then to violate the Tathāgata's right Dharma must be called deep and heavy sin. Solely because they forget that worldly ways are dreams and illusions, flowers in space, they are bonded in slavery to women. It is lamentable. Even for the sake of a trifling secular livelihood, they act like this. Why, for the sake of the supreme *bodhi,* do they fail to venerate the venerable ones who have got the Dharma? It is because their awe for the Dharma is shallow and their will to pursue the Dharma is not pervasive. When [people] are already coveting a treasure they do not think about refusing it just because it is the treasure of a woman. When we want to get the Dharma, we must surpass such resolve. If it is so, even grass, trees, fences, and walls will bestow the right Dharma, and the heavens and the earth, myriad things and phenomena, will also impart the right Dharma. This is a truth that we must 36b
always remember. Before we seek the Dharma with this determination, even if we meet true good counselors, we will not be soaked by the benevolent water of Dharma. We should pay careful attention [to this].

[192] Furthermore, nowadays extremely stupid people look at women without having corrected the prejudice that women are objects of sexual greed. Disciples of the Buddha must not be like this. If whatever may become the object of sexual greed is to be hated, do not all men deserve to be hated too? As regards the causes and conditions of becoming tainted, a man can be the object, a woman can be the object, what is neither man nor woman can be the object, and dreams and fantasies, flowers in space, can also be the object. There have been impure acts done with a reflection on water as an object, and there have been impure acts done with the sun in the sky as an object.[59] A god can be the object, and a demon can be the object. It is impossible to count all the possible objects; they say that there are eighty-four thousand objects. Should we discard all of them? Should we not look at them? The precepts[60] say, "[Abuse of] the two male organs,[61] or the three female organs,[62] are both *pārājika,* and [the offender] may not remain in the community."[63] This being so, if we hate whatever might become the object of sexual greed, all men and women will hate each other, and we will never have any chance to attain salvation. We should examine this truth in detail. There are non-Buddhists who have no wife: even though they have no wife, they have not entered the Buddha-Dharma, and so they are [only] non-Buddhists with wrong views. There are disciples of the Buddha who, as the two classes of laypeople,[64] have a husband or a wife: even though they have a husband or a wife, they are disciples of the Buddha, and so there are no other beings equal to them in the human world or in heaven above.

[194] Even in China, there was a stupid monk who made the following
36c vow: "Through every life, in every age, I shall never look at a woman." Upon what morality is this vow based? Is it based on secular morality? Is it based on the Buddha-Dharma? Is it based on the morality of non-Buddhists? Or is it based on the morality of heavenly demons?[65] What wrong is there in a woman? What virtue is there in a man? Among bad people there are men who are bad people. Among good people there are women who are good people. Wanting to hear the Dharma, and wanting to get liberation, never depend upon whether we are a man or a woman. When they have yet to cut delusion, men and women alike have yet to cut delusion. When they cut delusion and experience the principle, there is nothing at all to choose between a man and a woman. Moreover, if [a man] has vowed never to look at a

woman, must he discard women even when vowing to save limitlessly many living beings?[66] If he discards them, he is not a bodhisattva. How much less [does he have] the Buddha's compassion. This [vow] is just a drunken utterance caused by deep intoxication on the wine of the *śrāvaka.* Neither human beings nor gods should believe this [vow] to be true. Furthermore, if we hate [others] for the wrongs they have committed in the past, we must even hate all bodhisattvas. If we hate like this, we will discard everyone, so how will we be able to realize the Buddha-Dharma? Words like those [of the monk's vow] are the deranged speech of a stupid man who does not know the Buddha-Dharma. We should feel sorry for him. If that monk's[67] vow is true, did Śākyamuni and the bodhisattvas of his time all commit wrongs?[68] And was their *bodhi*-mind less profound than the will of that monk? We should reflect [on this] quietly. We should learn in practice whether the ancestral masters who transmitted the treasury of Dharma, and the bodhisattvas of the Buddha's lifetime, had things to learn in the Buddha-Dharma without this vow. If the 37a
vow of that monk were true, not only would we fail to save women but also, when a woman who had got the Dharma manifested herself in the world and preached the Dharma for human beings and gods, we would be forbidden to come and listen to her, would we not? Anyone who did not come and listen would be not a bodhisattva, but just a non-Buddhist. When we look now at the great kingdom of Song, there are monks who seem to have been in training for a long time, [but] who have only been vainly counting the sands of the ocean[69] and rolling like surf over the ocean of life and death.[70] There are also those who, although women, have visited [good] counselors, made effort in pursuit of the truth, and thus become the guiding teachers of human beings and gods. There are [women] such as the old woman who wouldn't sell her rice cakes [to Tokusan] and threw her rice cakes away.[71] It was pitiful that although [Tokusan] was a male monk, a *bhikṣu,* he had been vainly counting the sands of the ocean of philosophy, and had never seen the Buddha-Dharma, even in a dream. In general, we should learn to understand clearly whatever circumstances we meet. If we learn only to fear and to flee [from circumstances], that is the theory and practice of a *śrāvaka* of the Small Vehicle. When we abandon the east and try to hide away in the west, the west is also not without its circumstances. Even if we think that we have escaped circumstances, unless we understand them clearly, though they may be distant

they are still circumstances, we are still not in the state of liberation, and the distant circumstances will [disturb us] more and more deeply.

[198] Again in Japan, there is one particularly laughable institution. This is either called a "sanctuary,"[72] or called a "place for practicing the truth of the Great Vehicle," where *bhikṣuṇī*s and other women are not allowed to enter. The wrong custom has long been handed down, and so people cannot recognize it for what it is. People who emulate the ancients do not rectify it, and men of wide knowledge give no thought to it. Calling it the enactment of people of authority, or terming it the legacy of men of tradition, they never
37b discuss it at all. If one laughed, a person's guts might split. Just who are the so-called people of authority? Are they sages or are they saints? Are they gods or are they devils? Are they [bodhisattvas at] the ten sacred stages or are they [bodhisattvas at] the three clever stages? Are they [bodhisattvas in] the balanced state of truth or are they [bodhisattvas in] the fine state of truth? Moreover, if old [ways] should never be reformed, should we refrain from abandoning incessant wandering through life and death? Still more, Great Master Śākyamuni is just the supreme right and balanced state of truth itself,[73] and he clarified everything that needs to be clarified, he practiced everything that needs to be practiced, and he liberated[74] all that needs to be liberated. Who today could even approach his level? Yet the Buddha's order when he was in the world included all four groups: *bhikṣu*s, *bhikṣuṇī*s, *upāsaka*s, and *upāsikā*s, it included the eight kinds of beings,[75] the thirty-seven kinds of beings, and the eighty-four thousand kinds of beings. The formation of the Buddhist order is clearly the Buddhist order itself. So what kind of order has no *bhikṣuṇī*s, has no women, and has no eight kinds of beings? We should never hope to have so-called sanctuaries which surpass in their purity the Buddhist order of the Tathāgata's lifetime, because they are the sphere of heavenly demons.[76] There are no differences in the Dharma-form of the Buddhist order, not in this world or in other directions, and not among a thousand buddhas of the three times.[77] We should know that [an order] with a different code is not a Buddhist order. "The fourth effect"[78] is the ultimate rank. Whether in the Mahayana or the Hinayana, the virtues of the ultimate rank are not differentiated. Yet many *bhikṣuṇī*s have experienced the fourth effect. [So] to what kind of place—whether it is within the triple world or in the buddha lands of the ten directions—can [a *bhikṣuṇī*] not go? Who could

stand in her path? At the same time, the fine state of truth[79] is also the supreme rank. When a woman has [thus] already become buddha, is there anything in all directions that she cannot perfectly realize? Who could aim to bar her from passing? She already has virtue that "widely illuminates the ten directions"; what meaning can a boundary have? Moreover, would goddesses be 37c
barred from passing? Would nymphs be barred from passing? Even goddesses and nymphs are beings that have not yet cut delusion; they are just aimlessly wandering ordinary beings. When they have wrong, they have; when they are without [wrong], they are without. Human women and bestial women, also, when they have wrong, they have; when they are without wrong, they are without. [But] who would stand in the way of gods or in the way of deities? [*Bhikṣuṇī*s] have attended the Buddha's order of the three times; they have learned in practice at the place of the Buddha. If [places] differ from the Buddha's place and from the Buddha's order, who can believe in them as the Buddha's Dharma? [Those who exclude women] are just very stupid fools who deceive and delude secular people. They are more stupid than a wild dog worrying that its burrow might be stolen by a human being. The Buddha's disciples, whether bodhisattvas or *śrāvaka*s, have the following ranks: first, *bhikṣu*; second, *bhikṣuṇī*; third, *upāsaka;* and fourth, *upāsikā.* These ranks are recognized both in the heavens above and in the human world, and they have long been heard. This being so, those who rank second among the Buddha's disciples are superior to sacred wheel-turning kings,[80] and superior to Śakra-devānām-indra.[81] There should never be a place where they cannot go. Still less should [*bhikṣuṇī*s] be ranked alongside kings and ministers of a minor nation in a remote land. [But] when we look at present "places of the truth" that a *bhikṣuṇī* may not enter, any rustic, boor, farmer, or old lumberjack can enter at random. Still less would any king, lord, officer, or minister be refused entry. Comparing country bumpkins and *bhikṣuṇī*s, in terms of learning of the truth or in terms of attainment of rank, who is superior and who is inferior, in conclusion? Whether discussing this according to secular rules or according to the Buddha-Dharma, [one would think that] rustics and boors should not be allowed to go where a *bhikṣuṇī* might go. [The situation in Japan] is utterly deranged; [our] inferior nation is the first to leave this stain [on its history]. How pitiful it is. 38a
When the eldest daughters of the compassionate father of the triple world

came to a small country, they found places where they were barred from going. On the other hand, fellows who live in those places called "sanctuaries" have no fear of [committing] the ten wrongs,[82] and they violate the ten important precepts[83] one after another. Is it simply that, in their world of wrongdoing, they hate people who do not do wrong? Still more, a deadly sin[84] is a serious matter indeed; those who live in sanctuaries may have committed even the deadly sins. We should just do away with such worlds of demons. We should learn the Buddha's moral teaching and should enter the Buddha's world. This naturally may be [the way] to repay the Buddha's benevolence. Have these traditionalists understood the meaning of a sanctuary, or have they[85] not? From whom have they received their transmission? Who has covered them with the seal of approval? Whatever comes into "this great world sanctified by the buddhas"—whether it is the buddhas, living beings, the earth, or space—will get free of fetters and attachments, and will return to the original state which is the wonderful Dharma of the buddhas. This being so, when living beings step once [inside] this world, they are completely covered by the Buddha's virtue. They have the virtue of refraining from immorality, and they have the virtue of becoming pure and clean. When one direction is sanctified, the whole world of Dharma is sanctified at once, and when one level is sanctified, the whole world of Dharma is sanctified. Sometimes places are sanctified using water, sometimes places are sanctified using mind, and sometimes places are sanctified using space. For every case there are traditions which have been transmitted and received, and which we should know.[86] Furthermore, when we are sanctifying an area, after sprinkling nectar[87] and finishing devotional prostrations[88]—in other words, after making the place pure—we recite the following verse:

> This world and the whole world of Dharma,
> Naturally are sanctified, pure and clean.

38b Have the traditionalists and veterans who nowadays usually proclaim sanctuaries understood this meaning, or have they not? I guess they cannot know that the whole world of Dharma is sanctified within [the act of] sanctification itself. Clearly, drunk on the wine of the *śrāvaka,* they consider a small area to be a great world. Let us hope that they will snap out of their habitual drunken delusion, and that they will not violate the wholeness of the great world of the buddhas. We should prostrate ourselves in veneration of the virtue by which [the buddhas], through acts of salvation and acceptance, cover all living beings with their influence. Who could deny that this [prostration] is the attainment of the marrow of the truth?

Shōbōgenzō Raihai-tokuzui

Written at Kannondōrikōshōhōrinji on the day of purity and brightness[89] in [the second year of] Enō.[90]

Notes

[1] *Daijōbu,* or "great stout fellow," was originally a concept in Confucianism, suggesting a man of Confucian virtue. The word was used later in Chinese Buddhism, meaning someone who has trained perfectly. In modern Japanese, *daijōbu* is commonly used as an adjective meaning "all right."

[2] *Inmonin.* Master Ungo Dōyō, quoted in Chapter Twenty-nine (Vol. II), *Inmo,* says, "If you want to attain the matter of the ineffable, you must have become someone ineffable."

[3] *Yako-zei,* or "ghost of a wild fox," often suggests criticism that a person's state is too mystical, not practical enough. But in this case, it suggests the presence of something natural and mystical.

[4] "Got the marrow" is *tokuzui.* Master Taiso Eka made three prostrations to Master Bodhidharma, and returned to his seat. Master Bodhidharma said, "You have got my marrow." The story is recorded in Chapter Forty-six (Vol. III), *Kattō.*

[5] "Him or her" is *kare,* which usually means "he" or "him," but which in this context is clearly neutral.

[6] *Sun-in,* lit., "an inch of shadow."

[7] *Gyōsoku,* lit., "holding up the feet." Legend says the Buddha naturally walked on tiptoes. To learn walking on tiptoes means to learn how to behave like the Buddha.

[8] A symbol of sincere behavior.

[9] Master Taiso Eka cut off part of his arm to show his sincerity to Master Bodhidharma (see Chapter Thirty [Vol. II], *Gyōji*), and several years later Master Bodhidharma affirmed Master Taiso Eka's state with the words "You have got my marrow."

[10] *Shinjin-datsuraku,* "getting free of body and mind," was an expression commonly used by Master Tendō Nyojō, Master Dōgen's master.

[11] A figurative expression suggesting a humble attitude.

[12] *Gozui o nyotoku seru araba,* lit., "If it has 'you-got' 'my-marrow.'" *Gozui* means Master Bodhidharma's marrow.

[13] In the Buddha's time, Indian society had four castes: *brāhmaṇa* (priests), *kṣatriya* (the ruling nobility), *vaiśya* (workers), and *śūdra* (servants). At the lowest end of the social scale were people without any caste.

[14] *Nyaku-ju nyaku-seki* alludes to a story in the *Mahāparinirvāṇa-sūtra.* A demon told a child bodhisattva the first two lines of a four-line poem: "All actions are in the state without constancy/Concrete existence is the arising and passing of *dharmas*." The demon said it was too hungry to tell the child the last two lines, so the child offered his own body as a meal for the demon if it would recite the last two lines. So the demon recited the last two lines: "After arising and passing have ceased,/The peace and quiet is pleasure itself." The child preserved the verse for posterity by writing it on some nearby trees and rocks in his own blood, before being eaten by the demon.

[15] *Nyaku-den nyaku-ri.* These words originate in the *Lotus Sutra.* See LS 3.72–74.

[16] *Tentai-shaku.* See Chapter Two, *Maka-hannya-haramitsu,* note 28.

[17] *Hōmushi.* The title is no longer in use, and the exact nature of the position is unclear. *Shi* means "government official." A monk holding this position would also have been an official in the government.

[18] *Sōjōshi.* This title has also gone out of use.

[19] Alludes to a parable in the *Shinge* ("Belief and Understanding") chapter of the *Lotus Sutra.* See LS 1.236.

[20] Master Jōshū Jūshin. A successor of Master Nansen Fugan. He also studied under Masters Ōbaku, Hōju, Enkan, and Kassan. Died in 897, at the age of one hundred and twenty. Great Master Shinsai is his posthumous title. See Chapter Thirty-five (Vol. II), *Hakujushi.*

[21] *Angya,* lit., "to go on foot," means to travel from place to place, visiting Buddhist masters, or on a pilgrimage to sacred places.

[22] It is said that Master Jōshū Jūshin was already sixty before he became a Buddhist monk.

[23] *Shusse,* lit., "manifest oneself in the world," usually means to become the master of a big temple.

[24] *Biku-sō. Biku* represents the Sanskrit word *bhikṣu,* which means a male monk. *Sō,* usually translated as "monk," is originally neutral in gender. It sometimes represents the Sanskrit word "sangha," as in the case of the Three Treasures, *buppōsō:* Buddha, Dharma, and Sangha.

[25] Master Kankei Shikan (d. 895), successor of Master Rinzai. Throughout this paragraph he is referred to as "the master."

[26] Master Rinzai wanted Master Kankei to stay in his order. Master Kankei understood Master Rinzai's intention, and agreed.

[27] *Shinji-shōbōgenzō,* pt. 3, no. 17: Master Kankei Shikan is coming to visit Master Rinzai. When Master Rinzai sees him, he holds onto him. Master Kankei says, "Understood." Master Rinzai lets go of him and says, "I will allow you to stop for a while." When Master Kankei becomes the master of his own temple, he preaches to

the assembly, "When I met Master Rinzai, there was no discussion. Arriving directly at the moment of the present, I am completely satisfied."

28 Nun-Master Massan Ryōnen, successor of Master Kōan Daigu.

29 Literally, "Why haven't you come here covering yourself?" This suggests that it is sometimes better to be polite than to give a terse "Zen" answer.

30 The proper name Massan is literally "Last Mountain" or "End Mountain."

31 *Shusse,* i.e., when he became the master of a big temple. See note 23.

32 "Papa" is *ya-ya.* "Mama" is *jō-jō.*

33 *Jinsoku,* lit., "mystical foot," is a traditional term for an excellent member of an order. The Chinese commentary *Daichidoron* (based on the *Mahāprajñāpāramitopadeśa*) explains the term *jinsoku* as follows: "Their fine abilities are difficult to fathom, so we call them mystical; they support many living beings, so we call them feet."

34 Master Ōbaku Kiun (exact dates unknown, d. between 855 and 859), successor of Master Hyakujō Ekai.

35 Master Dōgen explained the meaning of the Chinese characters *ya* and *jo* using the Japanese phonetic alphabet.

36 Master Kyōzan Ejaku (807–883), successor of Master Isan Reiyū.

37 *Kai-in.* This office was for dealing with laypeople such as government officials, merchants, and donors. The building was usually located lower down the mountain than the main temple buildings.

38 *Daijōbu.* See note 1. Suggests that she was healthy and vigorous, and had self-control.

39 In present-day Sichuan province.

40 Master Daikan Enō (638–713), successor of Master Daiman Kōnin.

41 Two monks are having a discussion. One monk says, "The flag is moving." The other monk says, "The wind is moving." Master Daikan Enō says, "The wind is not moving and the flag is not moving. You are moving mind." (*Keitokudentōroku,* chapter 5. See also Chapter Twenty-nine [Vol. II], *Inmo.*)

42 *Igi o gu su,* lit., "to prepare the dignified form," means to wear the *kaṣāya* and to take the *zagu* (prostration cloth).

43 A bodhisattva is said to pass through fifty-two stages on the road to buddhahood. The first group of ten stages is the ten stages of belief. The next three groups of ten stages are the three clever stages. The fifth group of ten stages is the ten sacred stages. The fifty-first stage is *tōkaku,* "equal enlightenment," and the fifty-second stage is *myōkaku,* "marvelous enlightenment."

44 *Hanza,* lit., "half-seat"—a reference to the story that the Buddha shared his seat with Master Mahākāśyapa.

45 Elder sister means a senior female member of one's master's order. Aunt means a senior female member of one's master's order.

46 In the *Lotus Sutra* the Buddha explains four classes of Buddhists: *śrāvaka* (lit., "auditor"), *pratyekabuddha* (lit., "individually enlightened one"), bodhisattva (lit., "enlightenment being"), and buddha. These classes were further subdivided. An arhat is at the fourth and final state of a *śrāvaka.* For further explanation, see Chapter Twenty-four (Vol. II), *Bukkyō.*

47 The four elements are earth, water, fire, and wind; representing the material world.

48 The five aggregates are form, feeling, perception, volition, and consciousness; representing the phenomenal world.

49 *Koji,* "householder," represents the Sanskrit word *gṛhapati,* which means "the master of a household." At the same time, the concept of *koji* also comes from Confucianism: a man who did not work for the imperial government, but studied Confucianism as a civilian, was called *koji.*

50 *Shukke. Shutsu* means "to get out of" or "to transcend." *Ke* means a house, a home, or a family; at the same time it suggests the web of social and economic relationships inevitably connected with family life. As a verb, *shukke* means to become a Buddhist monk; as a noun, it means a monk.

51 *Jinrō,* "dusty toil," in this context means secular work.

52 *Un-nō-ka-bei,* lit., "clouds-patches-mist-sleeves." Clouds and mist suggest the free and natural life of a Buddhist monk. Patches and sleeves suggest the Buddhist robe, and the gowns with wide sleeves usually worn by monks in China and Japan.

53 *Shishu,* the four groups of Buddhist followers: *bhikṣu*s (monks), *bhikṣuṇī*s (nuns), *upāsaka*s (laymen), and *upāsikā*s (laywomen).

54 See LS 2.224.

55 The four stages of a *śrāvaka* are as follows: *srotāpanna* (stream-enterer), *sakṛdāgāmin* (once-returner), *anāgāmin* (non-returner), and arhat (the ultimate state, which is the fourth effect). An arhat is a *śrāvaka* who has overcome all hindrances and who needs to learn nothing more. In Chapter Thirty-four (Vol. II), *Arakan,* Master Dōgen identifies arhat and buddha.

56 The will to save others before we ourselves are saved. See Chapter Sixty-nine (Vol. III), *Hotsu-mujōshin;* Chapter Seventy (Vol. III), *Hotsu-bodaishin;* and Chapter Ninety-three (Vol. IV), *Doshin.*

57 The emperor would have several wives, or queens consort. Ministers would be eager to have a daughter made a queen consort.

58 In those days Buddhism was revered highly in Japanese society. So aristocratic women liked to have a titular position in a Buddhist temple.

[59] References to old Chinese and Japanese stories. The *Kojiki* (*Record of Ancient Matters*), a book of ancient Japanese legends, tells the story of a woman who was sexually stimulated by the rays of the sun.

[60] Fascicle 1 of the *Shibunritsu* (*Vinaya in Four Divisions*).

[61] The male organ and anus.

[62] The urethra, female organ, and anus.

[63] The Sanskrit word *pārājika* expresses one of the most serious violations of the precepts, which may warrant expulsion from the monastic order.

[64] *Upāsaka* (layman) and *upāsikā* (laywoman).

[65] *Tenma* are demons in heaven who govern the world of volition and hinder Buddhism. They symbolize idealistic people. The various classes of demons are discussed in Chapter Seventy (Vol. III), *Hotsu-bodaishin.*

[66] The original words are *shujo-muhen-seigan-do,* or "living beings are limitless; I vow to save them." This is the first of *shi-gu-seigan,* the Four Universal Vows: "Living beings are countless; I vow to save them./Delusions are endless; I vow to end them./The teachings of Dharma are boundless; I vow to learn them./The Buddha's truth is supreme; I vow to realize it."

[67] "That monk" is *nanji,* or "you." Master Dōgen often uses *nanji* for the third person, when criticizing someone's wrongness.

[68] That is, by looking at women.

[69] In Master Yōka Gengaku's poem *Shōdōka* ("Song of Experiencing the Truth") there is the line "Entering the ocean and counting sands, they hinder themselves in vain." Counting the sands of the ocean symbolizes the difficulty of realizing the Dharma only by reading books.

[70] Symbolizes the life of people who do not have any meaningful goal.

[71] See Chapters Eighteen and Nineteen, *Shin-fukatoku.*

[72] *Kekkai,* lit., "bounded area," represents the Sanskrit *sīmā-bandha,* "a depository of rules of morality."

[73] *Mujō-shōtō-gaku.* These characters represent the meaning of the Sanskrit *anuttara samyaksaṃbodhi*. The Sanskrit word *bodhi* is represented by *kaku,* lit., "awakening," or "awareness"; it suggests the state experienced throughout the body and mind in zazen. *Bodhi* is usually represented by the character *dō,* lit., "Way," and it is also sometimes represented phonetically as *bodai.*

[74] *Gedatsu su. Ge* means "to solve," and *datsu* means "to get rid of." Here *gedatsu su* is used as a verb.

[75] The eight kinds of beings: *deva*s (gods), *nāga*s (dragons), *yakṣa*s (demons), *gandharva*s (celestial musicians who feed on fragrances), *asura*s (angry titans), *garuḍa*s (birds that hunt dragons), *kiṃnara*s (half horses, half men), and *mahoraga*s (serpents). These fantastic beings existed in ancient Indian legends, so they were utilized in Buddhist sutras to suggest the diversity of the Buddha's audiences. See Glossary of Sanskrit Terms and, for example, LS 2.140.

[76] *Tenma.* See note 65.

[77] *Sanze,* past, present, and future; eternity.

[78] *Shika,* arhatship, the ultimate state in Hinayana Buddhism. See note 55.

[79] The ultimate state of a bodhisattva in Mahayana Buddhism. See note 43.

[80] *Tenrinjō-ō,* from the Sanskrit *cakravarti-rāja.* In ancient Indian mythology there are four such kings who rule over the four continents surrounding Mount Sumeru. They each have a precious wheel or *cakra.*

[81] The god Indra. See note 16 and Glossary of Sanskrit Terms.

[82] There are several interpretations of the ten wrongs. One interpretation is that the ten wrongs are as follows: killing, stealing, adultery, telling lies, duplicitous speech, abusive slander, idle chatter, greed, anger, and holding wrong views.

[83] The ten important precepts, or prohibitions, are as follows: not to take life, not to steal, not to lust, not to lie, not to sell or consume liquor, not to discuss the faults of other Buddhists, not to praise oneself, not to begrudge the Dharma or one's possessions, not to get angry, and not to insult the Three Treasures. See Chapter Ninety-four (Vol. IV), *Jukai.*

[84] The five deadly sins are to kill one's father, to kill one's mother, to kill an arhat, to spill the Buddha's blood, and to disrupt the Buddhist order.

[85] "They" is originally *nanji* ("you"); see note 67.

[86] For example, it is traditional to sprinkle water over the area where a precepts ceremony is to be held.

[87] *Kanro,* lit., "sweet dew," from the Sanskrit *amṛta,* which means nectar from heaven. In this case, "nectar" means water.

[88] *Kimyō no rai,* a prostration made as a symbol of devoting one's life. In a devotional prostration, the practitioner drops five parts of the body to the ground: left knee, right knee, left elbow, right elbow, and forehead.

[89] *Sei-mei no hi.* This was the name given to the fifteenth day after the spring equinox.

[90] 1240.

[Chapter Nine]

Keisei-sanshiki

The Voices of the River Valley and the Form of the Mountains

Translator's Note: Kei *means "river valley,"* sei *means "sound" or "voice,"* san *means "mountain," and* shiki *means "form" or "color." So* keisei-sanshiki *means the voices of river valleys and the forms of mountains—that is, nature. In Buddhism, this world is the truth itself, so nature is a face of the truth. Nature is the material side of the real world, so it is always speaking the truth, and manifesting the law of the universe every day. This is why it has been said since ancient time that sounds of rivers are the preaching of Gautama Buddha and forms of mountains are the body of Gautama Buddha. In this chapter, Master Dōgen preached to us the meaning of nature in Buddhism.*

[209] In the supreme state of *bodhi,* Buddhist patriarchs who transmitted the truth and received the behavior have been many, and examples of past ancestors who reduced their bones to powder[1] cannot be denied. Learn from the ancestral patriarch who cut off his arm,[2] and do not differ by a hair's breadth [from the bodhisattva who] covered the mud.[3] When we each get rid of our husk, we are not restricted by former views and understanding, and things which have for vast *kalpa*s been unclear suddenly appear before us. In the here and now of such a moment, the self does not recognize it, no one else is conscious of it, you do not expect it, and even the eyes of Buddha do not glimpse it. How could the human intellect fathom it?

[210] In the great kingdom of Song there lived Layman Tōba, whose name was Soshoku, and who was also called Shisen.[4] He seems to have been a real dragon in the literary world,[5] and he studied the dragons and elephants of the Buddhist world.[6] He swam happily into deep depths, and floated up and down through layers of cloud.[7] Once he visited Lushan.[8] In the story he hears the sounds of a mountain stream flowing through the night, and realizes the truth. 38c
He makes the following verse, and presents it to Zen Master Jōsō:[9]

The voices of the river valley are the [Buddha's] wide and long
tongue,[10]
The form of the mountains is nothing other than his pure body.
Through the night, eighty-four thousand verses.
On another day, how can I tell them to others?

When he presents this verse to Zen Master [Jō]sō, Zen Master [Jō]sō affirms it. [Jō]sō means Zen Master Shōkaku Jōsō, a Dharma successor of Zen Master Ōryū Enan.[11] [E]nan is a Dharma successor of Zen Master Jimyō Soen.[12] Once, when Layman [Tōba] met Zen Master Butsuin Ryōgen,[13] Butsuin gave him a Dharma robe, the Buddhist precepts, and so on, and the layman always wore the Dharma robe to practice the truth. The layman presented Butsuin with a priceless jeweled belt. People of the time said, "Their behavior is beyond common folk." So the story of realizing the truth on hearing the river valley may also be of benefit to those who are later in the stream. It is a pity that, so many times, the concrete form of the teaching, preaching of Dharma by manifestation of the body,[14] seems to have leaked away. What has made [Layman Tōba] see afresh the form of the mountains and hear the voices of the river valley? A single phrase? Half a phrase? Or eighty-four thousand verses? It is a shame that sounds and forms have been hiding in the mountains and waters. But we should be glad that there are moments in which, and causes and conditions whereby, [real sounds and forms] show up in the mountains and waters. The tongue's manifestation never flags. How could the body's form exist and vanish? At the same time, should we learn that they are close when they are apparent, or should we learn that they are close when they are hidden? Should we see them as a unity, or should we see them as a half?[15] In previous springs and autumns, [Layman Tōba] has not seen or heard the mountains and waters but in moments "through the night," he is able, barely, to see and to hear the mountains and waters. Bodhisattvas who are learning the truth now should also open the gate to learning
39a [by starting] from mountains flowing and water not flowing.[16] On the day before the night during which this layman has realized the truth, he has visited Zen Master [Jō]sō and asked about stories of "the nonemotional preaching Dharma."[17] Under the words of the Zen master, the form of his somersaulting is still immature,[18] but when the voices of the river valley are heard,

waves break back upon themselves and surf crashes high into the sky. This being so, now that the voices of the river valley have surprised the layman, should we put it down to the voices of the river valley, or should we put it down to the influence of Shōkaku? I suspect that Shōkaku's words on "the nonemotional preaching Dharma" have not stopped echoing but are secretly mingling with the sounds of the mountain stream in the night. Who could empirically affirm this situation as a single gallon?[19] And who could pay homage[20] to it as the whole ocean? In conclusion, is the layman realizing the truth, or are the mountains and waters realizing the truth? How could anyone who has clear eyes not put on their eyes at once [and look] at the manifestation of the long tongue and the pure body?

[215] Another case: Zen Master Kyōgen Chikan[21] was learning the truth in the order of Zen Master Daii Daien.[22] On one occasion, Daii says, "You are sharp and bright, and you have wide understanding. Without quoting from any text or commentary, speak a phrase for me in the state you had before your parents were born."[23] Kyōgen searches several times for something to say, but he is not able. He deeply regrets the state of his body and mind, and looks through books that he has kept for years, but he is still dumbfounded. In the end, he burns all the writings he has collected over the years, and says, "A rice cake that is painted in a picture[24] cannot stave off hunger. Upon my oath, I shall not desire to understand the Buddha-Dharma in this life. I only want to be the monk who serves the morning gruel and midday meal." So saying, he spends years and months as a server of meals. "The monk who serves the morning gruel and midday meal" means one who waits upon the other monks at breakfast and the midday meal;[25] he would be like a "liveried waiter"[26] in this country. While he is thus occupied, he says to 39b
Daii, "Chikan is dull in body and mind and cannot express the truth. Would the master say something for me?" Daii says, "I would not mind saying something for you, [but if I did so,] perhaps you would bear a grudge against me later." After spending years and months in such a state, [Chikan] enters Butōzan, following the tracks of National Master Daishō,[27] and makes a thatched hut on the remains of the National Master's hermitage. He has planted bamboo and made it his friend. One day, while he is sweeping the path, a piece of tile flies up and strikes a bamboo with a crack. Hearing this sound, he suddenly realizes the great state of realization. He bathes and purifies himself,

and, facing Daiizan, he burns incense and does prostrations. Then, directing himself to [Master] Daii, he says, "Great Master Daii! If you had explained it to me before, how would this thing have been possible? The depth of your kindness surpasses that of a parent." Finally, he makes the following verse:

> At a single stroke I lost recognition.
> No longer need I practice self-discipline.
> [I am] manifesting behavior in the way of the ancients,
> Never falling into despondency.
> There is no trace anywhere:
> [The state] is dignified action beyond sound and form.
> People everywhere who have realized the truth,
> All will praise [these] supreme makings.

He presents the verse to Daii. Daii says, "This disciple is complete."[28]

[218] Another case: Zen Master Reiun Shigon[29] is a seeker of the truth for thirty years. One day, while on a ramble in the mountains, he stops for a rest at the foot of a hill and views the villages in the distance. It is spring, and the peach blossoms are in full bloom. Seeing them, he suddenly realizes the truth. He makes the following verse and presents it to Daii:

> For thirty years, a traveler in search of a sword.[30]
> How many times have leaves fallen and buds sprouted?
> After one look at the peach blossoms,
> I have arrived directly at the present and have no further doubts.

Daii says, "One who has entered by relying on external phenomena will never regress or falter."[31] This is his affirmation. What person who has entered
39c could not rely on external phenomena? What person who has entered could regress or falter? [Isan's words] are not about [Shi]gon alone. Finally, [Shigon] succeeds to the Dharma of Daii. If the form of the mountains were not the pure body, how would things like this be possible?

[220] A monk asks Zen Master Chōsha [Kei]shin,[32] "How can we make mountains, rivers, and the earth belong to ourselves?" The master says, "How can we make ourselves belong to mountains, rivers, and the earth?"[33] This says that ourselves are naturally ourselves, and even though ourselves are mountains, rivers, and the earth, we should never be restricted by belonging.

[221] Master Ekaku of Rōya, [titled] Great Master Kōshō,[34] is a distant descendant of Nangaku.[35] One day [Chōsui] Shisen,[36] a lecturer of a philosophical sect, asks him, "How does pure essentiality suddenly give rise to mountains, rivers, and the earth?" Questioned thus, the master preaches, "How does pure essentiality suddenly give rise to mountains, rivers, and the earth?"[37] Here we are told not to confuse mountains, rivers, and the earth which are just pure essentiality, with "mountains, rivers and the earth." However, because the teacher of sutras has never heard this, even in a dream, he does not know mountains, rivers, and the earth as mountains, rivers, and the earth.

[222] Remember, if it were not for the form of the mountains and the voices of the river valley, picking up a flower could not proclaim anything,[38] and the one who attained the marrow could not stand at his own place.[39] Relying on the virtue of the sounds of the river valley and the form of the mountains, "the earth and all sentient beings realize the truth simultaneously,"[40] and there are many buddhas who realize the truth on seeing the bright star. Bags of skin in this state are the wise masters of the past, whose will to pursue the Dharma was very deep. People of the present should study their traces without fail. Now also, real practitioners who have no concern for fame and gain should establish similar resolve. In [this] remote corner in recent times, people who honestly pursue the Buddha-Dharma are very rare. They are not absent, but they are difficult to meet. There are many who 40a
drift into the monkhood, and who seem to have left the secular world, but who only use Buddhism as a bridge to fame and gain. It is pitiful and lamentable that they do not regret the passing of this life[41] but vainly go about their dark and dismal business. When can they expect to become free and to attain the truth? Even if they met a true master, they might not love the real dragon.[42] My late [master, the eternal] buddha, calls such fellows "pitiful people."[43] They are like this because of the bad they have done in past ages. Though they have received a life, they have no will to pursue the Dharma for the Dharma's sake, and so, when they meet the real Dharma they doubt the real dragon, and when they meet the right Dharma they are disliked by the right Dharma. Their body, mind, bones, and flesh have never lived following the Dharma, and so they are not in mutual accord with the Dharma; they do not receive and use [in harmony] with the Dharma. Founders of sects, teachers, and disciples have continued a transmission like this for a long

time. They explain the *bodhi*-mind as if relating an old dream. How pitiful it is that, having been born on the treasure mountain, they do not know what treasure is and they do not see treasure. How much less could they [actually] get the treasure of Dharma? After they establish the *bodhi*-mind, even though they will pass through the cycle of the six states[44] or the four modes of birth,[45] the causes and conditions of that cyclical course will all become the actions and vows of the state of *bodhi.* Therefore, though they have wasted precious time in the past, as long as their present life continues they should, without delay, make the following vow: "I hope that I, together with all living beings, may hear the right Dharma through this life and through every life hereafter. If I am able to hear it, I will never doubt the right Dharma, and I will never be disbelieving. When I meet the right Dharma, I will discard secular rules
40b and receive and retain the Buddha-Dharma so that the earth and sentient beings may finally realize the truth together." If we make a vow like this, it will naturally become the cause of, and conditions for, the authentic establishment of the mind. Do not neglect, or grow weary of, this attitude of mind. In this country of Japan, a remote corner beyond the oceans, people's minds are extremely stupid. Since ancient times, no saint has ever been born [here], nor anyone wise by nature: it is needless to say, then, that real men of learning the truth are very rare. When [a person] tells people who do not know the will to the truth about the will to the truth, the good advice offends their ears, and so they do not reflect upon themselves but [only] bear resentment toward the other person. As a general rule concerning actions and vows which are the *bodhi*-mind, we should not intend to let worldly people know whether or not we have established the *bodhi*-mind, or whether or not we are practicing the truth; we should endeavor to be unknown. How much less could we boast about ourselves? Because people today rarely seek what is real, when the praises of others are available, they seem to want someone to say that their practice and understanding have become harmonized, even though there is no practice in their body and no realization in their mind. "In delusion adding to delusion"[46] describes exactly this. We should throw away this wrongmindedness immediately. When learning the truth, what is difficult to see and to hear is the attitude of mind [based in] right Dharma. This attitude of mind is what has been transmitted and received by the buddhas, buddha to buddha. It has been transmitted and received as the Buddha's brightness,

and as the Buddha's mind. From the time when the Tathāgata was in the world until today, many people have seemed to consider that our concern in learning the truth[47] is to get fame and gain. If, however, on meeting the teachings of a true master, they turn around and pursue the right Dharma, they will naturally attain the truth. We should be aware that the sickness described above might be present in the learning of the truth today. For example, among 40c
beginners and novices, and among veterans of long training, some have got the makings to receive the transmission of the truth and to pass on the behavior, and some have not got the makings. There may be some who have it in their nature to learn, in veneration of the ancients. There may also be insulting demons who will not learn. We should neither love nor resent either group. [Yet] how can we have no regret? How can we bear no resentment? Perhaps no one bears resentment because almost no one has recognized the three poisons as the three poisons.[48] Moreover, we should not forget the determination we had when we began the joyful pursuit of the Buddha's truth. That is to say, when we first establish the will, we are not seeking the Dharma out of concern for others, and, having discarded fame and gain [already], we are not seeking fame and gain: we are just singlemindedly aiming to get the truth. We are never expecting the veneration and offerings of kings and ministers. Nevertheless, such causes of and conditions for [the will to fame and gain] are present today. [Fame and gain] are not an original aim, and they are not [true] objects of pursuit. To become caught in the fetters that bind human beings and gods is [just] what we do not hope for. Foolish people, however, even those who have the will to the truth, soon forget their original resolve and mistakenly expect the offerings of human beings and gods, feeling glad that the merit of the Buddha-Dharma has come to them. If the devotions of kings and ministers are frequent, [foolish people] think, "It is the realization of my own moral way." This is one of the demons [that hinder] learning of the truth. Though we should not forget the mind of compassion, we should not rejoice [to receive devotion]. Do you remember the golden words of the Buddha, "Even while the Tathāgata is alive, there are many who have hate and envy."[49] Such is the principle that the stupid do not recognize the wise, and small animals make enemies of great saints.

[230] Further, many of the ancestral masters of the Western Heavens 41a
have been destroyed by non-Buddhists, by the two vehicles,[50] by kings, and

so on;[51] but this is never due to superiority on the part of the non-Buddhists, or lack of farsightedness on the part of the ancestral masters. After the First Patriarch[52] came from the west, he hung up his traveling stick in the Suzan Mountains,[53] but neither Bu (Ch. Wu) of the Liang dynasty nor the ruler of the Wei dynasty knew who he was.[54] At the time, there was a pair of dogs known as Bodhiruci Sanzō[55] and Precepts Teacher Kōzu. Fearing that their empty fame and false gain might be thwarted by a right person, they behaved as if looking up at the sun in the sky and trying to blot it out.[56] They are even more terrible than Devadatta,[57] who [lived when the Buddha] was in the world. How pitiful they are. The fame and profit that they[58] love so deeply is more disgusting than filth to the ancestral master. That such facts occur is not due to any imperfection in the power of the Buddha-Dharma. We should remember that there are dogs who bark at good people. Do not worry about barking dogs. Bear them no grudge. Vow to lead them and to guide them. Explain to them, "Though you are animals, you should establish the *bodhi*-mind." A wise master of the past has said, "These are just animals with human faces." But there may also be a certain kind of demon which devotes itself and serves offerings to them. A former buddha has said, "Do not get close to kings, princes, ministers, rulers, brahmans, or secular people."[59] This is truly the form of behavior that people who want to learn the Buddha's truth should not forget. [When] bodhisattvas are at the start of learning, their virtue, in accordance with their progress, will pile up.

[232] Moreover, there have been examples since ancient times of the god Indra coming to test a practitioner's resolve, or of Māra-pāpīyas[60] coming to hinder a practitioner's training. These things always happened when [the practitioner] had not got rid of the will to fame and gain. When the [spirit of] great benevolence and great compassion is profound, and when the vow
41b to widely save living beings is mature, these hindrances do not occur. There are cases when the power of practice naturally takes possession of a nation. There are cases when [a practitioner] seems to have achieved worldly fortune. At such times, reexamine the case carefully. Do not slumber on without regard to the particular case. Foolish people delight in [worldly fortune] like stupid dogs licking a dry bone. The wise and the sacred detest it as worldly people hate filth and excrement.

[233] In general, a beginner's sentimental thinking cannot imagine the Buddha's truth—[the beginner] fathoms but does not hit the target. Even though we do not fathom [the truth] as beginners, we should not deny that there is perfect realization in the ultimate state. [Still,] the inner depths[61] of the perfect state are beyond the beginner's shallow consciousness. [The beginner] must just endeavor, through concrete conduct, to tread the path of the ancient saints. At this time, in visiting teachers and seeking the truth, there are mountains to climb and oceans to cross. While we are seeking a guiding teacher, or hoping to find a [good] counselor, one comes down from the heavens or springs out from the earth.[62] At the place where we meet him, he makes sentient beings speak the truth and makes nonsentient beings[63] speak the truth, and we listen with body and listen with mind. "Listening with the ears" is everyday tea and meals, but "hearing the sound through the eyes"[64] is just the ambiguous,[65] or the undecided,[66] itself. In meeting Buddha, we meet ourselves as buddha and others as buddha, and we meet great buddhas and small buddhas. Do not be surprised by or afraid of a great buddha. Do not doubt or worry about a small buddha. The great buddhas and small buddhas referred to here are recognized, presently, as the form of the mountains and the voices of the river valley. In this the wide and long tongue exists, and eighty-four thousand verses exist; the manifestation is "far transcendent," and the insight is "unique and exceptional."[67] For this reason, secular [teachings] say "It gets higher and higher, and harder and harder."[68] And a past buddha says, "It pervades[69] the sky and pervades the meridians." Spring pines possess constant freshness, and an autumn chrysanthemum possesses sublime beauty, but they are nothing other than the direct and concrete.[70] When good counselors arrive in this field of earth,[71] they may be great masters to human beings and gods. Someone who randomly affects the forms of teaching others, without arriving in this field of earth, is a great nuisance 41c
to human beings and gods. How could [people] who do not know the spring pines, and who do not see the autumn chrysanthemum, be worth the price of their straw sandals? How could they cut out the roots?

[236] Furthermore, if the mind or the flesh grow lazy or disbelieving, we should wholeheartedly confess before the Buddha. When we do this, the power of the virtue of confessing before the Buddha saves us and makes us

pure. This virtue can promote unhindered pure belief and fortitude. Once pure belief reveals itself, both self and the external world are moved [into action], and the benefit universally covers sentient and nonsentient beings. The general intention [of the confession] is as follows:

> I pray that although my many bad actions in the past have accumulated one after another, and there are causes and conditions which are obstructing the truth, the buddhas and the patriarchs who attained the truth by following the Buddha's Way will show compassion for me, that they will cause karmic accumulations to dissolve, and that they will remove obstacles to learning the truth. May their virtue, and their gates of Dharma, vastly fill and pervade the limitless Dharma world. Let me share in their compassion. In the past, Buddhist patriarchs were [the same as] us, and in the future we may become Buddhist patriarchs. When we look up at Buddhist patriarchs, they are one Buddhist patriarch, and when we reflect upon the establishment of the mind, it is one establishment of the mind. When [the Buddhist patriarchs] radiate their compassion in all directions,[72] we can grasp favorable opportunities and we fall upon favorable opportunities. Therefore, in the words of Ryūge, "If we did not attain perfection in past lives, we should attain perfection in the present. With this life we can deliver the body that is the accumulation of past lives. The eternal buddhas, before they realized the truth, were the same as people today. After realizing the truth, people today will be eternal buddhas."

Quietly, we should master this reasoning. This is direct experience of realizing the state of buddha. When we confess like this, the mystical help
42a of the Buddhist patriarchs is invariably present. Disclosing the thoughts in our mind and the form of our body, we should confess to the Buddha. The power of confession causes the roots of wrongdoing to dissolve. This is right training of one color;[74] it is right belief in the mind and right belief in the body. At the time of right training, the voices of the river valley and the form of the river valley, the form of the mountains and the voices of the mountains, all do not begrudge their eighty-four thousand verses. When the self does not begrudge fame and gain and body and mind, the river valley and the mountains, similarly, begrudge nothing. Even though the voices of the

river valley and the form of the mountains continue throughout the night to produce, and not to produce, eighty-four thousand verses, if you have not yet understood with all your effort that river valleys and mountains are demonstrating themselves as river valleys and mountains, who could see and hear you as the voices of the river valley and the form of the mountains?

Shōbōgenzō Keisei-sanshiki

Preached to the assembly at Kannondōrikō-shōhōrinji five days after the start of the retreat in the second year of Enō.[75]

Notes

[1] Symbolizing dogged perseverance in pursuing the truth.

[2] Master Taiso Eka. See Chapter Thirty (Vol. II), *Gyōji.*

[3] In a past life as a bodhisattva, the Buddha spread his hair over a muddy puddle so that his master, Dīpaṃkara Buddha, could walk over it.

[4] The Chinese poet So Tōba (1036–1101). Tōba was the poet's pen name. *Koji* is a title used for a lay Buddhist (see Chapter Eight, *Raihai-tokuzui,* note 49). Soshoku was his formal name. He also used the name Shisen. Like Buddhist monks, men of literature in China often had many different names.

[5] *Hitsukai,* lit., "the ocean of the brush."

[6] He read the writings of excellent Buddhist masters.

[7] Master Dōgen praised his ability as a poet.

[8] A region of China famed for its beautiful scenery.

[9] Master Shōkaku Jōsō (1025–1091), successor of Master Ōryū Enan.

[10] The wide and long tongue is one of the thirty-two distinguishing marks of the Buddha.

[11] Master Ōryū Enan (1002–1069), successor of Master Sekisō Soen. He lived on Mount Ōryū and was regarded as the founder of the Ōryū sect. His posthumous title is Zen Master Fukaku.

[12] Master Jimyō (Sekisō) Soen (986–1039), successor of Master Fun'yō Zenshō.

[13] Master Butsuin Ryōgen (1032–1098). Zen Master Butsuin is his posthumous title.

[14] *Genshin-seppō,* "manifesting body and preaching Dharma." The expression derives from chapter 25 (*Kanzeon-bosatsu-fumon*) of the *Lotus Sutra,* on Bodhisattva Avalokiteśvara, who appears in different bodies in order to preach the Dharma to different beings. See LS 3.252.

[15] Should we see them (idealistically) as an inclusive whole, or should we see them (materialistically) as a concrete half?

[16] In other words, the study of nature is a gate of entry into Buddhism. *Sanryū-sui-furyū,* lit., "mountains flow, waters do not flow," expresses the relativity of nature.

[17] *Mujō-seppō,* is the title of Chapter Fifty-three (Vol. III), which contains several stories about the preaching of Dharma by the nonemotional (i.e., nature).

[18] His body did not somersault into the state of action under the master's words.

[19] *Isshō* is a measure of capacity, approximately equal to 1.8 liters.

[20] *Chōshū,* lit., "morning homage." The expression derives from the ancient custom in China of making government decisions before the emperor in the morning. In this and the preceding sentence, Master Dōgen denies the two extreme views of materialism and idealism: only seeing things as isolated and concrete, and only revering general abstractions.

[21] Master Kyōgen Chikan (d. 898), successor of Master Isan Reiyū. He originally took the precepts under Master Isan's master, Hyakujō Ekai, and later became a student of Master Isan himself. He wrote more than two hundred poems.

[22] Master Isan Reiyū (771–853), successor of Master Hyakujō Ekai. Daii (or Isan) is the name of the mountain where he lived (Daiizan). The Tang emperor Sensō gave him the posthumous title Zen Master Daien. He became a monk when he was fifteen, and became a student of Master Hyakujō when he was twenty-three. He is known as the founder of the Igyō sect.

[23] In other words, on the basis of the reality that transcends past, present, and future.

[24] See Chapter Forty (Vol. II), *Gabyō.*

[25] Monks only ate light snacks after the midday meal, so gruel for breakfast and the midday meal were the only two meals.

[26] *Baisenekisō.* The job of the *baisenekisō* was to wait on someone of high rank.

[27] Master Nan'yō Echū (d. 775), successor of the Sixth Patriarch, Master Daikan Enō. National Master Daishō was his title as the emperor's teacher. After he retired, he built a hut on Mount Butō and lived there alone.

[28] *Shinji-shōbōgenzō,* pt. 1, no. 17. The version recorded in the *Shinji-shōbōgenzō,* in Chinese characters, is slightly different from the version in this chapter.

[29] Master Reiun Shigon (dates unknown), also a successor of Master Isan Reiyū.

[30] Symbolizing something very sharp and definite, or extreme.

[31] *Shinji-shōbōgenzō,* pt. 2, no. 55.

[32] Master Chōsha Keishin (d. 868), successor of Master Nansen Fugan. At first he taught Buddhism by moving from place to place, without a temple of his own. After that he lived on Chōshazan. People at that time called him Shin Daichu or "Keishin the Tiger," because his teachings were so sharp and fast. Quoted several times in Chapter Sixty (Vol. III), *Juppō.*

[33] *Shinji-shōbōgenzō,* pt. 1, no. 16.

[34] Master Rōya Ekaku, successor of Master Fun'yō Zenshō. Great Master Kōshō is his posthumous title. Rōya is the name of a mountain and of a district.

[35] Master Nangaku Ejō (677–744). Master Rōya Ekaku belonged to the eleventh generation after Master Nangaku Ejō, who was a successor of the Sixth Patriarch, Master Daikan Enō.

[36] Chōsui Shisen (984–1038). He belonged to the Kegon sect, which is based on the study of the *Avataṃsaka-sūtra* (*Garland Sutra*). Before joining the Kegon sect, he had studied the *Śūraṃgama-sūtra.*

[37] Chōsui Shisen's question and Master Rōya's question are exactly the same. Shisen asked about the relation between abstract essence and concrete reality. The master's rhetorical question suggested that the two factors are not different. See *Shinji-shōbōgenzō,* pt. 1, no. 6.

[38] Refers to the story of the transmission between Gautama Buddha and Master Mahākāśyapa. See Chapter Sixty-eight (Vol. IV), *Udonge.*

[39] Refers to the story of the transmission between Master Bodhidharma and Master Taiso Eka, who prostrated himself three times and then stood at his own place. See Chapter Forty-six (Vol. III), *Kattō.*

[40] The Buddha's description of his realization of the truth, as quoted in several sutras, for example, the second volume of the *Shugyōhongikyō.*

[41] *Kōin,* lit., "light and shade," means passing time.

[42] Shoko was a man who loved images of dragons. Seeing that Shoko's house was full of dragons, a real dragon decided to pay him a visit. But when Shoko saw the real dragon, he was struck with horror. The story of Shoko and the real dragon is contained in the Chinese book *Sōji.*

[43] The words are originally from the *Ryogonkyō* (the Chinese translation of the *Śūraṃgama-sūtra*). They were frequently used by Master Tendō Nyojō.

[44] *Rokushu,* the six miserable states through which we pass according to the law of cause and effect: hell (symbolizing the state of suffering), hungry ghosts (symbolizing the state of greed), animals, *asura*s or angry demons, human beings, and gods.

[45] *Shishō,* the four modes of birth: from the womb, from eggs, from moisture, and from metamorphosis. In Sanskrit, they are: *jarāyuja, aṇḍaja, saṃsvedaja,* and *upapāduka.*

[46] *Mei-chū-yū-mei.* Master Dōgen used the same expression in the second paragraph of Chapter Three, *Genjō-kōan.*

[47] *Gakudō no yōjin,* as in Master Dōgen's text *Gakudōyōjinshū.*

[48] *Sandoku,* the three poisons: anger, greed, and delusion.

[49] The *Lotus Sutra, Hōsshi* ("A Teacher of the Dharma") chapter. See LS 2.152.

[50] *Nijō,* the first two of the four vehicles, which are namely: *śrāvaka*s (intellectual Buddhists), *pratyekabuddha*s (sensory Buddhists), bodhisattvas (practical Buddhists), and buddhas.

[51] The Western Heavens means India. It is said that Master Kāṇadeva, the fifteenth patriarch, was killed by non-Buddhists; Buddhamitra, the teacher of the twenty-first patriarch Vasubandhu, was defeated by non-Buddhists in a philosophical discussion; and Siṃhabhikṣu, the twenty-fourth patriarch, was executed by the king of Kaśmira (present-day Kashmir).

[52] Master Bodhidharma. The twenty-eighth patriarch in India, and the First Patriarch in China.

[53] In Chinese, Songshan. The Suzan Mountains have two main peaks. The eastern peak is called Taishitsu, and the western peak is called Shōshitsu. There were many Buddhist temples in these mountains. Shaolin (Jp. Shōrin) Temple, where Master Bodhidharma faced the wall in zazen, was on Shōshitsu Peak.

[54] Related stories are in Chapter Thirty (Vol. II), *Gyōji.*

[55] A north Indian who arrived in Luoyang in 508 and translated many Sanskrit texts into Chinese. "Sanzō" was a title given to those versed in the Tripiṭaka.

[56] They reportedly tried to poison Master Bodhidharma.

[57] Devadatta was a cousin of the Buddha who became a monk in the Buddha's order, but later turned against him and tried to destroy the Buddhist order in cooperation with King Ajātaśatru (Jp. Ajase).

[58] *Nanji* is literally "you"—an impolite form of address that Master Dōgen uses for the third person when criticizing.

[59] In the *Anrakugyō* ("Peaceful and Joyful Practice") chapter of the *Lotus Sutra,* the Buddha says to Mañjuśrī: "A bodhisattva *mahāsattva* should not get close to kings, princes, ministers, and administrators." See LS 2.244.

[60] A deadly demon or devil. See Glossary of Sanskrit Terms and Chapter Seventy (Vol. III), *Hotsu-bodaishin.*

[61] *Dō-ō,* lit., "inner sanctum."

[62] *Jū-chi-yūshutsu,* "Springing Out from the Earth," is the title of the fifteenth chapter of the *Lotus Sutra.*

[63] In general, *ujō,* "sentient beings" means, for example, birds, animals, and human beings. *Mujō,* "nonsentient beings," or "the nonemotional," means, for example, grass, trees, and stones. See Chapter Fifty-three (Vol. III), *Mujō-seppō.*

[64] References to Master Tōzan's poem, quoted in Chapter Fifty-three (Vol. III), *Mujō-seppō:* "How very wonderful! How very wonderful! The nonemotional preaching

Dharma is a mystery. If we listen with the ears, it is ultimately too difficult to understand. If we hear the sound through the eyes, we are able to know it."

65 *Kahitsu,* or "why should it necessarily be?" See Chapter Three, *Genjō-kōan,* note 11.

66 *Fuhitsu,* or "not necessarily."

67 The words "far transcendent" (*keidatsu*) and "unique and exceptional" (*dokubatsu*) are taken from Master Ungo Dōyō's preaching in the *Rentōeyō,* chapter 22: "When a single word is far transcendent, and unique and exceptional, then many words are not necessary. And many are not useful." *Datsu,* "transcendent," means to get rid of something. So *keidatsu,* or "far transcendent," suggests the state in which things are as they are, being far removed from the superfluous.

68 From the *Rongo,* the fundamental text of Confucianism. Ganen, a student of Confucius, praises Confucius (or his teaching) as follows: "When I look up at him, he gets higher and higher, and when I bore into him, he gets harder and harder."

69 "More and more" and "pervades" are originally the same character, *mi, iyo-iyo,* used in the first quotation as an adverb (*iyo-iyo*) and in the second quotation as a verb (*mi*).

70 "The direct and concrete" is *sokuze.* These two characters are explained in detail in Chapter Six, *Soku-shin-ze-butsu.*

71 *Denchi,* or "paddy field," a symbol of the concrete state.

72 *Shichitsu-hattatsu su,* lit., "make into seven paths and eight destinations."

73 Master Ryūge Kodon (835–923). A successor of Master Tōzan Ryōkai.

74 "Of one color" means pure or unadulterated.

75 1240.

[Chapter Ten]

Shoaku-makusa

Not Doing Wrongs

Translator's Note: Sho *means "many" or "miscellaneous,"* aku *means "wrong" or "bad,"* maku *means "not" or "don't," and* sa *means "to do." So* shoaku makusa *means "not doing wrong."*[1] *These words are quoted from a short poem called "The Seven Buddhas' Universal Precept":*[2] *"Don't do wrong; do right; then our minds become pure naturally; this is the teaching of the many buddhas." This poem tells us how closely the teaching of Buddhism is related to morals. In this chapter Master Dōgen teaches us the Buddhist theory of morality. Morality or ethics is, by its nature, a very practical problem. But most people are prone to forget the practical character of morality, and usually only discuss it with words or as an abstract theory. However, talking about morality is not the same as being moral. Morality is just doing right or not doing wrong. Here Master Dōgen explains real morality, quoting an interesting story about Master Chōka Dōrin and a famous Chinese poet called Haku Kyoi.*

[3] The eternal buddha says,

> Not to commit wrongs,[3]
> To practice the many kinds of right,[4]
> Naturally purifies the mind;[5]
> This is the teaching of the buddhas.[6]

This [teaching], as the universal precept of the ancestral patriarchs, the Seven Buddhas, has been authentically transmitted from former buddhas to later buddhas, and later buddhas have received its transmission from former buddhas. It is not only of the Seven Buddhas: "It is the teaching of all the buddhas." We should consider this principle and master it in practice. These words of Dharma of the Seven Buddhas always sound like words of Dharma of the Seven Buddhas. What has been transmitted and been received one-to-one is just clarification of the real situation[7] at this concrete place. This already "is the teaching of the buddhas"; it is the teaching, practice, and experience of hundreds, thousands, and tens of thousands of buddhas.

[5] In regard to the "wrongs"[8] that we are discussing now, among "rightness," "wrongness," and "indifference," there is "wrongness." Its essence[9] is just nonappearance.[10] The essence of rightness, the essence of indiffer-
42b ence, and so on are also nonappearance, are [the state] without excess,[11] and are real form. At the same time,[12] at each concrete place these three properties[13] include innumerable kinds of *dharma*s. In "wrongs," there are similarities and differences between wrong in this world and wrong in other worlds. There are similarities and differences between former times and latter times. There are similarities and differences between wrong in the heavens above and wrong in the human world. How much greater is the difference between moral wrong, moral right, and moral indifference in Buddhism and in the secular world. Right and wrong are time; time is not right or wrong. Right and wrong are the Dharma; the Dharma is not right or wrong. [When] the Dharma is in balance, wrong is in balance.[14] [When] the Dharma is in balance, right is in balance. This being so, when we learn [the supreme state of] *anuttara samyaksaṃbodhi,* when we hear the teachings, do training, and experience the fruit, it is profound, it is distant, and it is fine.

[6] We hear of this supreme state of *bodhi* "sometimes following [good] counselors and sometimes following sutras."[15] At the beginning, the sound of it is "Do not commit wrongs." If it does not sound like "Do not commit wrongs," it is not the Buddha's right Dharma; it may be the teaching of demons. Remember, [teaching] that sounds like "Do not commit wrongs" is the Buddha's right Dharma. This [teaching] "Do not commit wrongs" was not intentionally initiated, and then intentionally maintained in its present form, by the common person: when we hear teaching that has [naturally] become the preaching of *bodhi,* it sounds like this. What sounds like this is speech which is the supreme state of *bodhi* in words. It is *bodhi*-speech already, and so it speaks *bodhi.*[16] When it becomes the preaching of the supreme state of *bodhi*, and when we are changed by hearing it, we hope "not to commit wrongs," we continue enacting "not to commit wrongs," and wrongs go on not being committed; in this situation the power of practice is instantly realized. This realization is realized on the scale of the whole earth,

the whole world, the whole of time, and the whole of Dharma. And the scale of this [realization] is the scale of "not committing." For people of just this 42c reality, at the moment of just this reality[17]—even if they live at a place and come and go at a place where they could commit wrongs, even if they face circumstances in which they could commit wrongs, and even if they seem to mix with friends who do commit wrongs—wrongs can never be committed at all. The power of not committing is realized, and so wrongs cannot voice themselves as wrongs, and wrongs lack an established set of tools.[18] There is the Buddhist truth of taking up at one moment, and letting go at one moment.[19] At just this moment, the truth is known that wrong does not violate a person, and the truth is clarified that a person does not destroy wrong.[20] When we devote our whole mind to practice, and when we devote the whole body to practice, there is eighty or ninety percent realization[21] [of not committing wrongs] just before the moment, and there is the fact of not having committed just behind the brain.[22] When you practice by garnering your own body and mind, and when you practice by garnering the body and mind of "anyone,"[23] the power of practicing with the four elements and the five aggregates is realized at once;[24] but the four elements and five aggregates do not taint[25] the self. [All things,] even the four elements and five aggregates of today, carry on being practiced; and the power which the four elements and five aggregates have as practice in the present moment makes the four elements and five aggregates, as described above, into practice.[26] When we cause even the mountains, rivers, and the earth, and the sun, moon, and stars, to do practice, the mountains, rivers, and the earth, the sun, moon, and stars, in their turn, make us practice.[27] [This is] not a onetime eye; it is vigorous eyes at many times.[28] Because [those times] are moments in which the eye is present as vigorous eyes, they make the buddhas and the patriarchs practice, make them listen to the teachings, and make them experience the fruit. The buddhas and the patriarchs have never made the teachings, practice, and experience tainted, and so the teachings, practice, and experience have never hindered the buddhas and the patriarchs.[29] For this reason, when [teachings, practice, and experience] compel the Buddhist patriarchs to practice, there are no buddhas or patriarchs who flee, before the moment or after the moment, in the past, present, or future. 43a

[10] In walking, standing, sitting, and lying down through the twelve

hours,[30] we should carefully consider the fact that when living beings are becoming buddhas and becoming patriarchs, we are becoming Buddhist patriarchs, even though this [becoming] does not hinder the [state of a] Buddhist patriarch that has always belonged to us. In becoming a Buddhist patriarch, we do not destroy the living being, do not detract from it, and do not lose it; nevertheless, we have got rid of it. We cause right-and-wrong, cause-and-effect, to practice; but this does not mean disturbing, or intentionally producing, cause-and-effect. Cause-and-effect itself, at times, makes us practice. The state in which the original features of this cause-and-effect have already become conspicuous is "not committing," it is ["the state] without appearance," it is ["the state] without constancy," it is "not being unclear," and it is "not falling down"—because it is the state in which [body and mind] have fallen away.[31]

[11] When we investigate them like this, wrongs are realized as having become completely the same as "not committing." Aided by this realization, we can penetrate[32] the "not committing" of wrongs, and we can realize it decisively by sitting.[33] Just at this moment—when reality is realized as the "not committing" of wrongs at the beginning, middle, and end—wrongs do not arise from causes and conditions; they are nothing other than just "not committing."[34] Wrongs do not vanish due to causes and conditions; they are nothing other than just "not committing." If wrongs are in balance, all *dharmas* are in balance. Those who recognize that wrongs arise from causes and conditions, but do not see that these causes and conditions and they themselves are [the reality of] "not committing," are pitiful people. "The seeds of buddhahood arise from conditions" and, this being so, "conditions arise from the seeds of buddhahood." It is not that wrongs do not exist; they are nothing other than "not committing." It is not that wrongs exist; they are nothing other than not committing. Wrongs are not immaterial; they are "not committing." Wrongs are not material; they are "not committing." Wrongs are not "not committing;" they are nothing other than "not committing."[35] [Similarly,]
43b ilarly,] for example, spring pines are neither nonexistence nor existence; they are "not committing."[36] An autumn chrysanthemum is neither existence nor nonexistence; it is "not committing." The buddhas are neither existence nor nonexistence; they are "not committing." Such things as an outdoor pillar, a stone lantern, a whisk, and a staff are neither existence nor nonexistence; they

are "not committing." The self is neither existence nor nonexistence; it is "not committing." Learning in practice like this is the realized universe and it is universal realization—we consider it from the standpoint of the subject and we consider it from the standpoint of the object. When the state has become like this already, even the regret that "I have committed what was not to be committed" is also nothing other than energy arising from the effort "not to commit." But to purport, in that case, that if "not committing" is so we might deliberately commit [wrongs], is like walking north and expecting to arrive at [the southern country of] Etsu. [The relation between] "wrongs" and "not committing" is not only "a well looking at a donkey";[37] it is the well looking at the well, the donkey looking at the donkey, a human being looking at a human being, and a mountain looking at a mountain. Because there is "preaching of this principle of mutual accordance," "wrongs" are "not committing."

> The Buddha's true Dharma body[38]
> Is just like space.
> It manifests its form according to things,
> Like the moon [reflected] in water.[39]

Because "not committing" is "accordance with things," "not committing" has "manifest form." "It is just like space": it is the clapping of hands to the left and the clapping of hands to the right.[40] "It is like the moon [reflected] in water": and the water restricted by the moon.[41] Such instances of "not committing" are the realization of reality which should never be doubted at all.

[14] "Practice the many kinds of right."[42] These many kinds of right are [classed] within the three properties[43] as "rightness." Even though the many kinds of right are included in "rightness," there has never been any kind of right that is realized beforehand and that then waits for someone to do it.[44] There is none among the many kinds of right that fails to appear at the very moment of doing right. The myriad kinds of right have no set shape but they converge on the place of doing right faster than iron to a magnet,[45] and with 43c
a force stronger than the *vairambhaka* winds.[46] It is utterly impossible for the earth, mountains and rivers, the world, a nation, or even the force of accumulated karma, to hinder [this] coming together of right.[47] At the same time, the principle that recognitions differ from world to world,[48] in regard to right,

is the same [as in regard to wrong]. What can be recognized [as right] is called right, and so it is "like the manner in which the buddhas of the three times preach the Dharma." The similarity is that their preaching of Dharma when they are in the world is just temporal. Because their lifetime and body size also have continued to rely totally upon the moment, they "preach the Dharma that is without distinction."[49] So it is like the situation that right as a characteristic of devotional practice[50] and right as a characteristic of Dharma practice,[51] which are far removed from each other, are not different things. Or, for example, it is like the keeping of the precepts by a *śrāvaka* being the violation of the precepts by a bodhisattva. The many kinds of right do not arise from causes and conditions and they do not vanish due to causes and conditions. The many kinds of right are real *dharma*s, but real *dharma*s are not many kinds of right. Causes and conditions, arising and vanishing, and the many kinds of right are similar in that if they are correct at the beginning, they are correct at the end. The many kinds of right are "good doing"[52] but they are neither of the doer nor known by the doer, and they are neither of the other nor known by the other. As regards the knowing and the seeing of the self and of the other, in knowing there is the self and there is the other, and in seeing there is the self and there is the other, and thus individual vigorous eyes exist in the sun and in the moon. This state is "good doing" itself. At just this moment of "good doing" the realized universe exists but it is not "the creation of the universe," and it is not "the eternal existence of the universe." How much less could we call it "original practice"?[53] Doing right is "good doing," but it is not something that can be fathomed intellectually. "Good doing" in the present is a vigorous eye, but it is beyond intellectual consideration. [Vigorous eyes] are not realized for the purpose of considering the Dharma intellectually. Consideration by vigorous eyes is never the
44a same as consideration by other things. The many kinds of right are beyond existence and nonexistence, matter and the immaterial, and so on; they are just nothing other than "good doing." Wherever they are realized and whenever they are realized, they are, without exception, "good doing." This "good doing" inevitably includes the realization of the many kinds of right. The realization of "good doing" is the universe itself, but it is beyond arising and vanishing, and it is beyond causes and conditions. Entering, staying, leaving, and other [concrete examples of] "good doing" are also like this. At the

place where we are already performing, as "good doing," a single right among the many kinds of right, the entire Dharma, the whole body,[54] the real land, and so on are all enacted as "good doing." The cause-and-effect of this right, similarly, is the universe as the realization of "good doing." It is not that causes are before and effects are after. Rather, causes perfectly satisfy themselves and effects perfectly satisfy themselves; when causes are in balance the Dharma is in balance and when effects are in balance the Dharma is in balance. Awaited by causes, effects are felt, but it is not a matter of before and after; for the truth is present that the [moment] before and the [moment] after are balanced [as they are].

[19] The meaning of "Naturally purifies the mind" is as follows: What is "natural" is "not to commit," and what "purifies" is "not to commit." "The [concrete state"][55] is "natural," and the "mind"[56] is "natural." "The [concrete state"] is "not committing," the "mind" is "not committing." The "mind" is "good doing," what "purifies" is "good doing," "the [concrete state"] is "good doing," and what is "natural" is "good doing." Therefore it is said that "This is the teaching of the buddhas." Those who are called "buddhas" are, in some cases, like Śiva,[57] [but] there are similarities and differences even among Śivas, and at the same time not all Śivas are buddhas. [Buddhas] are, in some cases, like wheel-turning kings,[58] but not all sacred wheel-turning kings are buddhas. We should consider facts like these and learn them in practice. If we do not learn how buddhas should be, even if we seem to be fruitlessly enduring hardship, we are only ordinary beings accepting suffering; we are not practicing the Buddha's truth. "Not committing" and "good doing" are 44b
"donkey business not having gone away and horse business coming in."[59]

[20] Haku Kyoi[60] of Tang China is a lay disciple of Zen Master Bukkō Nyoman,[61] and a second-generation disciple of Zen Master Kōzei Daijaku.[62] When he was the governor of Hangzhou[63] district he practiced in the order of Zen Master Chōka Dōrin.[64] In the story, Kyoi asks, "What is the great intention of the Buddha-Dharma?"

Dōrin says, "Not to commit wrongs. To practice the many kinds of right."[65]

Kyoi says, "If it is so, even a child of three can express it!"

Dōrin says, "A child of three can speak the truth, but an old man of eighty cannot practice it."

Thus informed, Kyoi makes at once a prostration of thanks, and then leaves.

[21] Kyoi, though descended from Haku Shōgun,[66] is truly a wizard of the verse who is rare through the ages. People call him one of the twenty-four [great] men of letters. He bears the name of Mañjuśrī, or bears the name of Maitreya. Nowhere do his poetical sentiments go unheard and no one could fail to pay homage to his authority in the literary world. Nevertheless, in Buddhism he is a beginner and a late learner. Moreover, it seems that he has never seen the point of this "Not to commit wrongs. To practice the many kinds of right," even in a dream. Kyoi thinks that Dōrin is only telling him "Do not commit wrongs! Practice the many kinds of right!" through recognition of the conscious aim. Thus, he neither knows nor hears the truth that the time-honored[67] [teaching] of the "not committing" of wrongs, the "good doing" of rights, has been in Buddhism from the eternal past to the eternal present. He has not set foot in the area of the Buddha-Dharma. He does not have the power of the Buddha-Dharma. Therefore he speaks like this. Even though we caution against the intentional commitment of wrongs, and even though we encourage the deliberate practice of rights, this should be in the reality of "not committing." In general, the Buddha-Dharma is [always] the
44c same, whether it is being heard for the first time under a [good] counselor, or whether it is being experienced in the state which is the ultimate effect. This is called "correct in the beginning, correct at the end," called "the wonderful cause and the wonderful effect," and called "the Buddhist cause and the Buddhist effect." Cause-and-effect in Buddhism is beyond discussion of [theories] such as "different maturation" or "equal streams";[68] this being so, without Buddhist causes, we cannot experience the Buddhist effect. Because Dōrin speaks this truth, he possesses the Buddha-Dharma. Even if wrong upon wrong pervade the whole universe, and even if wrongs have swallowed the whole Dharma again and again, there is still salvation and liberation in "not committing." Because the many kinds of right are "right at the beginning, in the middle, and at the end,"[69] "good doing" has realized "nature, form, body, energy," and so on "as they are."[70] Kyoi has never trodden in these tracks at all, and so he says "Even a child of three could express it!" He speaks like this without actually being able to express an expression of the truth. How pitiful, Kyoi, you are. Just what are you saying? You have

never heard the customs of the Buddha, so do you or do you not know a three-year-old child? Do you or do you not know the facts of a newborn baby? Someone who knows a three-year-old child must also know the buddhas of the three times. How could someone who has never known the buddhas of the three times know a three-year-old child? Do not think that to have met face-to-face is to have known. Do not think that without meeting face-to-face one does not know. Someone who has come to know a single particle knows the whole universe, and someone who has penetrated one real *dharma* has penetrated the myriad *dharma*s. Someone who has not penetrated the myriad *dharma*s has not penetrated one real *dharma.* When students of penetration penetrate to the end, they see the myriad *dharma*s and they see single real *dharma*s; therefore, people who are learning of a single particle are inevitably learning of the whole universe. To think that a three-year-old child cannot speak the Buddha-Dharma, and to think that what a 45a
three-year-old child says must be easy, is very stupid. That is because the clarification of life,[71] and the clarification of death, are "the one great purpose"[72] of Buddhists. A master of the past[73] says, "Just at the time of your birth you had your share of the lion's roar."[74] "A share of the lion's roar" means the virtue of the Tathāgata to turn the Dharma wheel, or the turning of the Dharma wheel itself. Another master of the past[75] says, "Living-and-dying, coming-and-going, are the real human body." So to clarify the real body and to have the virtue of the lion's roar may truly be the one great matter, which can never be easy. For this reason, the clarification of the motives and actions of a three-year-old child are also the great purpose. Now there are differences between the actions and motives of the buddhas of the three times [and those of children]; this is why Kyoi, in his stupidity, has never been able to hear a three-year-old child speaking the truth, and why, not even suspecting that [a child's speaking of the truth] might exist, he talks as he does. He does not hear Dōrin's voice, which is more vivid than thunder, and so he says, "Even a child of three could express it!" as if to say that [Master Dōrin himself] has not expressed the truth in his words. Thus [Kyoi] does not hear the lion's roar of an infant, and he passes vainly by the Zen master's turning of the Dharma wheel. The Zen master, unable to contain his compassion, went on to say, "A child of three can speak the truth, but an old man of eighty cannot practice it." What he was saying is this:

A child of three has words which express the truth, and you should investigate this thoroughly. Old men of eighty say, "I cannot practice it," and you should consider this carefully. I leave you to decide whether an infant speaks the truth, but I do not leave the infant to decide. I leave
45b you to decide whether an old man can practice, but I do not leave the old man to decide.[76]

It is the fundamental principle to pursue, to preach, and to honor the Buddha-Dharma like this.

Shōbōgenzō Shoaku-makusa

Preached to the assembly at Kōshōhōrinji on the evening of the moon[77] in the [second] year of Enō.[78]

Notes

1 The meaning of *shoaku-makusa* changes in this chapter according to context. It can sometimes be interpreted as the imperative "Don't do wrong" or the ideal "not to do wrong." But sometimes it represents Master Dōgen's idea that morality is only a problem of action—the not-committing of wrong.

2 *Shichibutsu-tsūkai. Shichibutsu* refers to Śākyamuni Buddha and the six legendary buddhas who preceded him. See Chapter Fifteen, *Busso.*

3 *Shoaku-makusa,* lit., "Do not commit wrongs." *Sho* means various, miscellaneous, or all, and sometimes it simply expresses plurality. *Aku* means evil, bad, wrongdoing, or wrong. *Makusa,* "wrongs," suggests individual instances of wrongdoing as concrete facts, rather than wrong as an abstract problem. *Maku,* or *naka*[*re*], means "must not" or "don't!" *Sa,* or *tsuku*[*ru*], means to make, to produce, or to commit—it includes a suggestion of intention. It is useful to distinguish the characters *sa* and *gyō;* they both mean to do, but *sa* has more of a feeling of doing intentionally. This chapter contains the idea that, naturally, wrongdoing does not occur; i.e., without our intentional commitment, there is no wrong.

4 *Shūzen-bugyō,* lit., "devoutly practice the many kinds of good," or "good doing of the many kinds of right." *Shū* means many or many kinds of. *Zen* means good, or right. *Shūzen,* or "the many kinds of right," suggests concrete instances of right as opposed to right as an abstraction. *Bu* is a prefix denoting reverence or devotion. *Gyō,* or *okona*[*u*], means to do, to perform, to enact, or to keep moving along. *Bugyō,* or "good doing," has a feeling of doing what is natural, as opposed to intentional commitment.

5 *Jijō-go-i.* According to context, *ji* can be interpreted either as by oneself or as naturally. The interpretation here is that the verse is not a recommendation to be moral but a proclamation of the Buddha's teaching that moral conduct is just purification of the mind. Accordingly, *ji* has been translated as "naturally." *Jō* means to purify. *Go,* or *so*[*no*], means "that," suggesting something concrete and specific. *I* means intention but here the meaning is more practical: it suggests the state of the mind (and body) in action.

6 *Ze-shobutsu-kyō. Shobutsu* can be interpreted as "the buddhas" or as "all the buddhas." In Pāli, the poem is: *Sabba-pāpass akaraṇam,/kuselassūpasampada,/sacitta-pariyodapanaṃ,/etam buddhana sasanaṃ.*

7 "Clarification of the real situation" is *tsūshōsoku. Tsu* suggests penetration, clarification, opening up, running through (or universality, as in *tsukai,* universal precept). *Shōsoku* originally means exhalation and inhalation, and by extension something that is heard from someone, news, actual circumstances, the real situation.

8 *Shoaku,* as in the original poem.

9 *Shō.* In the previous sentence, "rightness" is *zenshō,* lit., "good-essence"; "wrongness" is *akushō,* lit., "bad-essence"; and "indifference" is *mukisho,* lit., "not-described-essence."

10 In this sentence Master Dōgen begins his conceptual explanation of right and wrong by introducing the idea of instantaneousness. Nonappearance (*mushō*) describes the state at the moment of the present.

11 *Murō,* lit., "without leakage," from the Sanskrit (see Glossary of Sanskrit Terms under *āsrava*), suggests the state in which things are as they are.

12 Master Dōgen is explaining right and wrong as reality. In the previous sentences he began by explaining them as inclusive concepts, in the first or conceptual phase. From here he explains them as concrete, individual, and relative facts, at the second or concrete phase.

13 Rightness, wrongness, and indifference.

14 *Hōtō-akutō,* or "Dharma in equilibrium, bad in equilibrium," suggests the balanced state in which a bad fact is seen as it is.

15 *Waku-jū-chishiki* and *waku-jū-kyōgan.* These phrases appear frequently in the *Shōbōgenzō.*

16 "*Bodhi*-speech" is *bodai-go;* "speaking *bodhi*" is *go-bodai.* Up to this sentence Master Dōgen affirms "Do not do wrong" as words of the truth. From the next sentence, he looks at the concrete reality of practice.

17 *Shōtō-inmo-ji no shōtō-inmo-nin. Shōtō,* or "exact," suggests exactly this time and place. *Shoto-inmo-ji,* or "at just this moment" is a very common expression in the *Shōbōgenzō.*

18 Master Dōgen emphasizes that if we do not do wrong, there can never be any wrong.

19 *Ichinen-ippō,* lit., "one pinch, one release." *Nen,* to twist, pinch, or grasp, symbolizes positive action. *Hō,* to release, symbolizes passive action.

20 Master Dōgen denies the idea that something exists that can be called wrong, bad, or evil outside of our own conduct.

21 *Hakkujō.* See Chapter Thirty-three (Vol. II), *Kannon.*

22 *Nōgo.* The usual expression, which appears in the last sentence of this paragraph, is *kisen-kigo,* "before the moment, after the moment." The variation *nōgo,* "behind the brain," suggests the area in which action has taken place already.

[23] *Tare,* lit., "who," suggests someone ineffable, or a person whose state cannot be described.

[24] The four elements and five aggregates symbolize all physical things and mental phenomena.

[25] *Zenna sezu,* "not tainted," expresses something as is. When we act we have to use physical things but they do not make us impure.

[26] In this sentence, Master Dōgen suggests the oneness of concrete circumstances and Buddhist practice.

[27] This sentence also suggests the mutual relation between a Buddhist practitioner and nature—in a more poetic style.

[28] The Buddhist view is not a once-and-for-all realization, but it appears vigorously at many times.

[29] "Unhindered" and "untainted" both express something as it is. Buddhist teachings, practice, and experience exist as they are. Buddhas and patriarchs live freely and independently, as they are.

[30] *Juni-ji,* lit., "twelve hours," means the twenty-four hours of a day—at that time, the day was divided into twelve periods. See Chapter Eleven, *Uji.*

[31] "Not committing" is *makusa,* as in the poem. "The state without appearance" (*mushō*) and "the state without constancy" (*mujō*) suggest concrete reality at the moment of the present from two sides—denial of momentary appearance and denial of continuous existence. "Not being unclear [about cause and effect]" (*fumai*) and "not falling down into [cause and effect]" (*furaku*) represent opposing viewpoints about the reality of cause-and-effect (see Chapter Seventy-six [Vol. IV], *Dai-shugyō;* Chapter Eighty-nine [Vol. IV], *Shinjin-inga*). "Falling away" is *datsuraku.* Master Dōgen frequently quoted Master Tendō Nyojō's words that zazen is *shinjin-datsuraku,* "the falling away of body and mind."

[32] *Kentokutetsu,* or "can see thoroughly."

[33] *Zatokudan,* or "can sit decisively." Master Dōgen often uses the word *zadan,* "sit-cut" or "sit away," to mean transcending a problem by practicing zazen (see for example, Chapter Seventy-three [Vol. IV], *Sanjushichi-bon-bodai-bunpō*). But in this case, *dan* is an adverb; "decisively."

[34] Master Dōgen denies the idea that something called wrongness manifests itself from real circumstances, as if the wrongness and the reality might be two different things. In this paragraph he emphasizes that there is no wrongness separate from the reality of our momentary action.

[35] Master Dōgen emphasized that wrong is only the problem of not doing wrong.

[36] In other words, pine trees in spring exist as they are, without any intentional activity.

37 See *Shinji-shōbōgenzō,* pt. 2, no. 25. "Master Sōsan asks Ācārya Toku, 'It is said that the Buddha's true Dharma body is just like space, and it manifests its form according to things, like the moon [reflected] in water. How do you preach this principle of mutual accordance?' Toku says, 'It is like a donkey looking into a well.' The master says, 'Your words are extremely nice words, but they only express eighty or ninety percent.' Toku says, 'What would the master say?' Master Sōsan says, 'It is like the well looking at the donkey.'" The story expresses the mutual relation between subject and object.

38 *Hōsshin,* from the Sanskrit *dharmakāya.* In this case, the Dharma body represents the spiritual or abstract face of reality, and space represents the physical or objective face of reality. The poem suggests the oneness of the two faces.

39 This verse from the *Konkōmyōkyō,* quoted in the story of Master Sōzan and Ācārya Toku, is also quoted in Chapter Forty-two (Vol. III), *Tsuki.*

40 In this sentence, space means the place where action is done.

41 The image of the moon can be compared to the individual subject, and the water which surrounds the image can be compared to objective circumstances. Water reflecting the moon symbolizes the oneness of subject and object. The moon restricting the water suggests the fact from the other side, with subject and object reversed.

42 *Shūzen-bugyō,* lit., "devoutly practice the many [kinds of] good," as in the original poem.

43 The three properties are rightness, wrongness, and indifference, as explained in the second paragraph.

44 Even though we can consider rightness abstractly, right itself can only be realized by action in the moment of the present.

45 Even though abstract rightness cannot manifest any form, in action right can manifest itself at once.

46 Very strong winds mentioned in ancient Indian legends.

47 In these opening sentences of the paragraph, Master Dōgen affirms the existence of right when realized by action. From the next sentence he explains right as something relative.

48 The usual example is water which fish see as a palace, gods see as a string of pearls, human beings see as water, and demons see as blood or pus.

49 *Mufunbetsu* [*no*] *hō* [*o*] *toku,* from the *Hōben* ("Expedient Means") chapter of the *Lotus Sutra.* "In the same manner that the buddhas of the three times/Preach the Dharma,/So now do I also/Preach the Dharma which is without distinction." (LS 1.128)

50 *Shingyō,* or "practice based on belief" suggests, for example, the devotional practice of the Pure Land sects.

51 *Hogyō,* or "practice based on the teaching of Dharma," suggests, for example, the practice of the so-called Zen sects.

52 *Bugyō,* or "devout practicing" as in the original poem.

53 *Hongyō,* "original practice," suggests practice done as our original situation, or practice done in the past, or sometimes practice done in past lives. See Chapter Seventeen, *Hokke-ten-hokke.* In this case, *hongyō* is one example of an abstract understanding of action.

54 *Zenshin.* See Chapter Seventy-one (Vol. III), *Nyorai-zenshin.*

55 "The" is *go, sono,* which means "that," suggesting the concrete, real state. See note 5.

56 "Mind" is *i,* lit., "intention." In general, human intention is opposed to the natural way, but the message of this chapter is that the mind of morality is natural.

57 Jizaiten represents the god called Śiva in Sanskrit, the god of destruction and regeneration in the Hindu triad of Brahmā (creator), Śiva, and Viṣṇu (preserver). See Glossary of Sanskrit Terms.

58 *Ten-rin-jō-ō,* from the Sanskrit *cakravarti-rāja.* Master Dōgen is urging us to come to a realistic understanding of what buddhas are.

59 Master Chōkei Eryō asks Master Reiun Shigon, "What is the Great Intention of the Buddha-Dharma?" Master Reiun says, "Donkey business being unfinished, but horse business coming in." See *Shinji-shōbōgenzō,* pt. 2, no. 56.

60 Haku Kyoi, died in in 846 at the age of seventy-six. Haku was his family name. Kyoi (lit., Sitting Easy) was one of his pen names as a poet. He was also called Haku Rakuten. It is said that he attained the truth under Master Bukkō Nyoman, after which he became the governor of several districts, visiting masters whose temples were in his district and practicing zazen.

61 Successor of Master Baso Dōitsu. Dates unknown.

62 Master Baso Dōitsu (704–788), successor of Master Nangaku Ejō. Kōzei (or Jiangxi in Chinese pronunciation) was the name of the district where Master Baso lived. Zen Master Daijaku is his posthumous title.

63 The capital of Chekiang, located at the head of Hangzhou Bay (an inlet of the East China Sea).

64 Master Chōka Dōrin, died in 824 at the age of eighty-four. He received the Dharma from Master Kinzan Kokuitsu, who belonged to a side lineage (going back to the Fourth Patriarch Daii Dōshin, but not going through Master Daikan Enō). *Chōka* means bird's nest; it is said that Master Chōka practiced zazen in, and lived in, a tree-house.

65 *Shoaku-makusa, shūzen-bugyō,* as in the original poem.

[66] Hakki, a general of the founder of the Jin dynasty (who reigned from 255 to 250 B.C.E.). The general was famed for his excellence in military strategy. In this sentence, military ability and ability as a poet are opposed.

[67] *Senko-banko,* lit., "thousand-ages old, ten-thousand ages old."

[68] The theory that moral and immoral behavior produce different results is represented by the word *ijuku,* lit., "different maturation." This expresses the moral viewpoint. The opposing theory is represented by the word *toru,* lit., "equal streams." This expresses the scientific view of cause and effect; that is, the view that is not concerned with subjective evaluation of cause and effect.

[69] *Shochūgo-zen,* from the Introductory chapter (*Jo*) of the *Lotus Sutra:* "The Dharma that they should preach is good in the beginning, middle, and end." (LS 1.40; see also Chapter Seventeen, *Hokke-ten-hokke.*)

[70] Alludes to the *Hōben* ("Expedient Means") chapter of the *Lotus Sutra.* See LS 1.68.

[71] *Sho* means both birth and life.

[72] *Ichidaiji no innen.* See Chapter Seventeen, *Hokke-ten-hokke.*

[73] The quotation is paraphrased from *Daichidoron,* the Chinese translation of the *Mahā-prajñāpāramitā-śāstra.* This treatise was largely compiled by Master Nāgārjuna.

[74] The Buddha's preaching was said to be like the roar of a lion.

[75] Master Engo Kokugon. This quotation also appears in Chapter Fifty (Vol. III), *Shohō-jissō.*

[76] A child's expression of the truth and an old man's ability to practice are just reality—they do not rely upon interpretation by the subject.

[77] The fifteenth day of the eighth lunar month, often the day of the year on which the moon is most conspicuous. Many chapters of the *Shōbōgenzō* were preached on this day.

[78] 1240.

[Chapter Eleven]

Uji

Existence-time

Translator's Note: U *means "existence" and* ji *means "time," so* uji *means "existent time," or "existence-time." In this chapter Master Dōgen teaches us the meaning of time in Buddhism. As Master Dōgen explains in other chapters, Buddhism is realism. Therefore, the view of time in Buddhism is always very realistic. Specifically, time is always related with existence and existence is always related with momentary time. So in reality, the past and the future are not existent time; the present moment is the only existent time—the point at which existence and time come together. Also, time is always related with action here and now. Action can only be realized in time, and time can only be realized in action. Thus, the view of time in Buddhism reminds us of existentialism in modern philosophy. It is very important to understand the Buddhist view of time in order to grasp the true meaning of Buddhism.*

[29] An eternal buddha[1] says,

> Sometimes[2] standing on top of the highest peak,
> Sometimes moving along the bottom of the deepest ocean.
> Sometimes three heads and eight arms,[3]
> Sometimes the sixteen-foot or eight-foot [golden body].[4]
> Sometimes a staff or a whisk,[5]
> Sometimes an outdoor pillar or a stone lantern.[6]
> Sometimes the third son of Chang or the fourth son of Li,
> Sometimes the earth and space.

[30] In this word "sometimes," time is already just existence, and all existence is time. The sixteen-foot golden body is time itself. Because it is time, it has the resplendent brightness of time. We should learn it as the twelve hours[7] of today. The three heads and eight arms are time itself. Because they are time, they are completely the same as the twelve hours of today. We can

never measure how long and distant or how short and pressing twelve hours is; at the same time, we call it "twelve hours."[8] The leaving and coming of the directions and traces [of time] are clear, and so people do not doubt it. They do not doubt it, but that does not mean they know it. The doubts which living beings, by our nature, have about every thing and every fact that we do not know, are not consistent; therefore our past history of doubt does not always exactly match our doubt now. We can say for the present, however, that doubt is nothing other than time. We put our self in order, and see [the resulting state] as the whole universe. Each individual and each object in this whole universe should be glimpsed as individual moments of time.[9] Object does not hinder object in the same way that moment of time does not
45c hinder moment of time. For this reason, there are minds which are made up in the same moment of time, and there are moments of time in which the same mind is made up. Practice, and realization of the truth, are also like this.[10] Putting the self in order, we see what it is. The truth that self is time is like this. We should learn in practice that, because of this truth, the whole earth includes myriad phenomena and hundreds of things, and each phenomenon and each thing exists in the whole earth. Such toing-and-froing is a first step [on the way] of practice. When we arrive in the field of the ineffable,[11] there is just one [concrete] thing and one [concrete] phenomenon, here and now, [beyond] understanding of phenomena and non-understanding of phenomena, and [beyond] understanding of things and non-understanding of things. Because [real existence] is only this exact moment, all moments of existence-time are the whole of time, and all existent things and all existent phenomena are time. The whole of existence, the whole universe, exists in individual moments of time.[12] Let us pause to reflect whether or not any of the whole of existence or any of the whole universe has leaked away from the present moment of time. Yet in the time of the common person who does not learn the Buddha-Dharma there are views and opinions: when he hears the words "existence-time" he thinks, "Sometimes I became [an angry demon with] three heads and eight arms, and sometimes I became the sixteen-foot or eight-foot [golden body of Buddha]. For example, it was like crossing a river or crossing a mountain. The mountain and the river may still exist, but now that I have crossed them and am living in a jeweled palace with crimson towers, the mountain and the river are [as distant] from me as

heaven is from the earth." But true reasoning is not limited to this one line [of thought]. That is to say, when I was climbing a mountain or crossing a river, I was there in that time. There must have been time in me. And I actually exist now, [so] time could not have departed. If time does not have the form of leaving and coming, the time of climbing a mountain is the present as existence-time.[13] If time does retain the form of leaving and coming, I have this present moment of existence-time, which is just existence-time itself.[14] How could that time of climbing the mountain and crossing the river 46a
fail to swallow, and fail to vomit, this time [now] in the jeweled palace with crimson towers?[15] The three heads and eight arms were time yesterday; the sixteen-foot or eight-foot [golden body] is time today. Even so, this Buddhist principle of yesterday and today is just about moments in which we go directly into the mountains and look out across a thousand or ten thousand peaks; it is not about what has passed. The three heads and eight arms pass instantly as my existence-time; though they seem to be in the distance, they are [moments of] the present. The sixteen-foot or eight-foot [golden body] also passes instantly as my existence-time; though it seems to be yonder, it is [moments of] the present. This being so, pine trees are time, and bamboos are time. We should not understand only that time flies. We should not learn that "flying" is the only ability of time. If we just left time to fly away, some gaps in it might appear. Those who fail to experience and to hear the truth of existence-time do so because they understand [time] only as having passed. To grasp the pivot and express it: all that exists throughout the whole universe is lined up in a series and at the same time is individual moments of time.[16] Because [time] is existence-time, it is my existence-time.[17] Existence-time has the virtue of passing in a series of moments.[18] That is to say, from today it passes through a series of moments to tomorrow; from today it passes through a series of moments to yesterday; from yesterday it passes through a series of moments to today; from today it passes through a series of moments to today; and from tomorrow it passes through a series of moments to tomorrow. Because passage through separate moments is a virtue of time, moments of the past and present are neither piled up one on top of another nor lined up in a row; and, for the same reason, Seigen[19] is time, Ōbaku[20] is time, and Kōzei[21] and Sekitō[22] are time.[23] Because subject-and-object already is time, practice-and-experience is moments of time. Going into the mud and going

into the water,[24] similarly, are time. The view of the common person today,
46b and the causes and conditions of [that] view, are what the common person
experiences but are not the common person's reality.[25] It is just that reality, for
the present, has made a common person into its causes and conditions. Because
he understands this time and this existence to be other than reality itself, he
deems that "the sixteen-foot golden body is beyond me." Attempts to evade
[the issue] by [thinking] "I am never the sixteen-foot golden body" are also
flashes of existence-time; they are glimpses of it by a person who has yet to
realize it in experience and to rely upon it. The [existence-time] that also causes
the horse and the sheep[26] to be as they are arranged in the world today, is a ris-
ing and falling which is something ineffable abiding in its place in the Dharma.
The rat is time, and the tiger is time; living beings are time, and buddhas are
time. This time experiences the whole universe using three heads and eight
arms, and experiences the whole universe using the sixteen-foot golden body.
To universally realize the whole universe by using the whole universe is called
"to perfectly realize."[27] Enactment of the sixteen-foot golden body[28] by using
the sixteen-foot golden body is realized as the establishment of the mind, as
training, as the state of *bodhi,* and as nirvana; that is, as existence itself, and
as time itself. It is nothing other than the perfect realization of the whole of
time as the whole of existence; there is nothing surplus at all. Because something surplus is just something surplus, even a moment of half-perfectly-real-
ized existence-time is the perfect realization of half-existence-time.[29] Even
those phases in which we seem to be blundering heedlessly are also existence.
If we leave it utterly up to existence,[30] even though [the moments] before and
after manifest heedless blundering, they abide in their place as existence-time.
Abiding in our place in the Dharma in the state of vigorous activity is just existence-time. We should not disturb it [by interpreting it] as "being without,"[31]
and we should not enforceably call it "existence." In regard to time, we strive
to comprehend only how relentlessly it is passing; we do not understand it
intellectually as what is yet to come. Even though intellectual understanding
is time, no circumstances are ever influenced by it. [Human] skin bags recognize [time] as leaving and coming; none has penetrated it as existence-time
abiding in its place: how much less could any experience time having passed
through the gate?[32] Even [among those who] are conscious of abiding in their
46c place, who can express the state of having already attained the ineffable? Even

[among those who] have been asserting for a long time that they are like this, there is none who is not still groping for the manifestation before them of the real features. If we leave [even *bodhi* and nirvana] as they are in the existence-time of the common person, even *bodhi* and nirvana are—[though] merely a form which leaves and comes—existence-time.[33]

[38] In short, without any cessation of restrictions and hindrances,[34] existence-time is realized. Celestial kings and celestial throngs, now appearing to the right and appearing to the left, are the existence-time in which we are now exerting ourselves. Elsewhere, beings of existence-time of land and sea are [also] realized through our own exertion now. The many kinds of being and the many individual beings which [live] as existence-time in darkness and in brightness, are all the realization of our own effort, and the momentary continuance of our effort. We should learn in practice that without the momentary continuance of our own effort in the present, not a single *dharma* nor a single thing could ever be realized or could ever continue from one moment to the next.[35] We should never learn that passage from one moment to the next is like the movement east and west of the wind and rain. The whole universe is neither beyond moving and changing nor beyond progressing and regressing; it is passage from one moment to the next. An example of the momentary passing of time is spring. Spring has innumerable different aspects, which we call "a passage of time."[36] We should learn in practice that the momentary passing of time continues without there being any external thing. The momentary passing of spring, for example, inevitably passes, moment by moment, through spring itself.[37] It is not that "the momentary passing of time" is spring; rather, because spring is the momentary passing of time, passing time has already realized the truth in the here and now of springtime.[38] We should study [this] in detail, returning to it and leaving it again and again. If we think, in discussing the momentary passing of time, that circumstances are [only] individual things on the outside, while something which can pass from moment to moment moves east through hundreds of thousands of worlds and through hundreds of thousands of *kalpa*s, then we are not devoting ourselves solely to Buddhist learning in practice.[39]

[40] Great Master Yakusan Kōdō,[40] the story goes, at the suggestion of Great Master Musai,[41] visits Zen Master Kōzei Daijaku.[42] He asks, "I have more or less clarified the import of the three vehicles and the twelve divisions 47a

of the teaching.[43] But just what is the ancestral master's intention in coming from the west?"[44]

Thus questioned, Zen Master Daijaku says, "Sometimes[45] I make him[46] lift an eyebrow or wink an eye, and sometimes I do not make him lift an eyebrow or wink an eye; sometimes to make him lift an eyebrow or wink an eye is right, and sometimes to make him lift an eyebrow or wink an eye is not right."

Hearing this, Yakusan realizes a great realization and says to Daijaku, "In Sekitō's order I have been like a mosquito that climbed onto an iron ox."

[42] What Daijaku says is not the same as [what] others [can say]. [His] "eyebrows" and "eyes" may be the mountains and the seas, because the mountains and the seas are [his] "eyebrows" and "eyes." In his "making himself lift [an eyebrow]," he may be looking at the mountains; and in his "making himself wink," he may be presiding over the seas. "Being right" has become familiar to "him," and "he" has been led by "the teaching."[47] Neither is "not being right" the same as "not making himself [act]," nor is "not making himself [act]" the same as "not being right."[48] All these [situations] are "existence-time." The mountains are time, and the seas are time. Without time, the mountains and the seas could not exist: we should not deny that time exists in the mountains and the seas here and now. If time decays, the mountains and the seas decay. If time is not subject to decay, the mountains and the seas are not subject to decay. In accordance with this truth the bright star appears, the Tathāgata appears, the eye appears, and picking up a flower appears,[49] and this is just time. Without time, it would not be like this.

[44] Zen Master Kishō[50] of the Shōken region is a Dharma descendant of Rinzai, and the rightful successor of Shuzan.[51] On one occasion he preaches to the assembly:

> Sometimes[52] the will is present but the words are absent,
> Sometimes the words are present but the will is absent,
> Sometimes the will and the words are both present,
> Sometimes the will and the words are both absent.[53]

[44] The will and the words are both existence-time. Presence and absence are both existence-time. The moment of presence has not finished, but the moment of absence has come—the will is the donkey and the words are the horse;[54] horses have been made into words and donkeys have been made into

will.[55] Presence is not related to having come, and absence is not related to not 47b
having come.[56] Existence-time is like this. Presence is restricted by presence itself; it is not restricted by absence.[57] Absence is restricted by absence itself; it is not restricted by presence. The will hinders the will and meets the will.[58] Words hinder words and meet words. Restriction hinders restriction and meets restriction. Restriction restricts restriction. This is time. Restriction is utilized by objective *dharmas*, but restriction that restricts objective *dharmas* has never occurred.[59] I meet with a human being, a human being meets with a human being, I meet with myself, and manifestation meets with manifestation. Without time, these [facts] could not be like this. Furthermore, "the will" is the time of the realized universe,[60] "the words" are the time of the pivot that is the ascendant state,[61] "presence" is the time of laying bare the substance,[62] and "absence" is the time of "sticking to this and parting from this."[63] We should draw distinctions, and should enact existence-time,[64] like this. Though venerable patriarchs hitherto have each spoken as they have, how could there be nothing further to say? I would like to say:

> The half-presence of will and words is existence-time,
> The half-absence of will and words is existence-time.

There should be study in experience like this.

> Making oneself[65] lift an eyebrow or wink an eye is half existence-time,
> Making oneself lift an eyebrow or wink an eye is mixed-up existence-time,
> Not making oneself lift an eyebrow or wink an eye is half existence-time,
> Not making oneself lift an eyebrow or wink an eye is mixed-up existence-time.

When we experience coming and experience leaving, and when we experience presence and experience absence, like this, that time is existence-time.

Shōbōgenzō Uji

Written at Kōshōhōrinji on the first day of winter in the first year of Ninji.[66]

Copied during the summer retreat in the [first] year of Kangen[67]—Ejō.

Notes

1 Master Yakusan Igen. *Keitokudentōroku,* chapter 18.

2 *Uji,* or *aru toki,* as in the chapter title. In this case, *uji* is an adverb, read as *a*[*ru*]*toki,* and meaning "sometimes." In the chapter title, *uji* is a compound word, "existence-time."

3 This phrase refers to the wrathful images of Buddhist guardian deities, such as Aizen-myōō, the King of Love (Skt. Rāgarāja), whose figure generally has three angry faces and six arms.

4 *Jōroku-hasshaku.* One *jō* equals ten *shaku,* and one *shaku* is slightly less than a foot. *Jōroku* suggests the sixteen-foot golden body, the idealized image of the standing Buddha. *Hasshaku* can be interpreted as representing the balanced image of the sitting Buddha.

5 *Shujō* is a staff used by Buddhist monks on their travels, and also used in Buddhist ceremonies. *Hossu* was originally a fly whisk, but its function has become ceremonial. These are concrete things that have religious meaning.

6 In China and Japan, temple roofs have long eaves supported by pillars that stand outside of the temple building itself; temple pillars and stone lanterns are thus very common objects.

7 *Jūni-ji,* lit., "twelve times." In Master Dōgen's age, a day was divided into twelve periods. Master Dōgen suggests that magnificent real time in the balanced state is not different from the ordinary time of concrete daily life.

8 When we are waiting, twenty-four hours is long, and when we are pressed for time, twenty-four hours is short. So the length of a day is relative but we measure it as "twenty-four hours."

9 "Each individual" is *zu-zu,* lit., "head-head." "Each object" is *butsu-butsu,* lit., "thing-thing." "Individual moments of time" is *ji-ji,* lit., "time-time."

10 Like the will to the truth, Buddhist practice and realization are both real existence and real time.

11 *Inmo no denchi. Inmo* means something ineffable (see Chapter Twenty-nine [Vol. II], *Inmo*). *Den* means field and *chi* means earth. *Denchi* suggests a concrete area, or real state.

[12] "Individual moments of time" is *ji-ji no ji.*

[13] "Time that does not have the form of leaving and coming" means instantaneous time, as opposed to time as a linear progression. If we see time in this way, even a continuous process—like crossing a mountain—is moments of the present.

[14] "Time that retains the form of leaving and coming" means linear time. If we see time in this way, even though the moment of the present has arrived and it will depart, it exists now. Master Dōgen's view of real time embraces both the view of time as a point and the view of time as a line, as well as the view of time as reality itself.

[15] Past time swallowing present time suggests the inclusive character of time. Past time vomiting present time suggests the independence of the past and the present.

[16] "Individual moments of time" is *ji-ji.* See notes 9 and 12.

[17] *Go-uji,* "my existence-time," emphasizes that existence-time is not only a concept but our own real life itself.

[18] *Kyōryaku* or *keireki. Kyō* or *kei* means passing through, experience, the passage of time: it represents the linear aspect of time. *Ryaku* or *reki* suggests a process through separate, successive stages; it represents the momentary aspect of time.

A note on pronunciation: In Japanese, a Chinese character is read either in its *kun-yomi* form (the native Japanese reading) or in its *on-yomi* form (imitating the Chinese pronunciation). However, the pronunciation of Chinese characters in China varied from age to age, so different readings of the *on-yomi* are possible. *Kyōryaku* approximates the pronunciation used in the Wu dynasty (222–258 C.E.). *Keireki* approximates the pronunciation used in the Han dynasty (206 B.C.E.–25 C.E.). Buddhist sutras in Japan are usually read according to the pronunciation used in the Wu dynasty.

[19] Master Seigen Gyōshi, died 740.

[20] Master Ōbaku Kiun, died between 855 and 859. A second-generation descendant of Master Baso.

[21] Master Baso Dōitsu (704–788). See note 42.

[22] Master Sekitō Kisen (700–790). A successor of Master Seigen Gyōshi. See note 41.

[23] The lives of all Buddhist masters are just moments of the present.

[24] Symbols of daily struggles.

[25] *Hō,* or Dharma.

[26] The twelve hours of the Chinese day were represented by twelve animals: rat (12:00 midnight), ox (2:00 A.M.), tiger (4:00 A.M.), rabbit (6:00 A.M.), dragon (8:00 A.M.), snake (10:00 A.M.), horse (12:00 noon), sheep (2:00 P.M.), monkey (4:00 P.M.), chicken (6:00 P.M.), dog (8:00 P.M.), and boar (10:00 P.M.). These animals were also used to represent directions, the rat indicating north, the horse south, etc.

[27] The original sentence is constructed with combinations of only three Chinese characters, *jin, kai, gu.* "The whole universe" is *jinkai; jin,* "whole," works as an adjective, and *kai,* "world," works as a noun. "Universally realize" is *kai-jin su; kai,* "universally," works as an adverb and *jin su,* "realize," works as a verb. "Perfectly realize" is *gujin su; gu,* "perfectly," works as an adverb, and *jin,* "realize," works as a verb. *Gujin* appears in the key sentence of the *Lotus Sutra* (1:68): "Buddhas alone, together with buddhas, can perfectly realize that all *dharma*s are real form."

[28] *Jōroku-konjin suru,* lit., "to sixteen-foot golden body"—a noun phrase is used as if it were a verb.

[29] *Han-uji.* Master Dōgen sometimes uses half to suggest something concrete, individual, or real, as opposed to an ideal (as in the verse in the final paragraph of this chapter).

[30] Literally, "If we leave it utterly up to him," i.e., if we let go of subjective worries. "Him" refers to existence in the previous sentence.

[31] *Mu,* "nonexistence." *U* and *mu,* "existence and nonexistence," are usually opposed. See for example, Chapter Twenty-four (Vol. II), *Busshō.*

[32] The gate suggests the dualism of illusions and their negation, or idealism and materialism.

[33] The fact that all things—even *bodhi* and nirvana—are existence-time does not change, however the fact is interpreted.

[34] *Rarō,* lit., "nets and cages." In China, silk nets (*ra*) and bamboo cages (*ro*) are used to catch and to keep small birds.

[35] "Momentary continuance" and "continue from one moment to the next" are translations of *kyōryaku.* See note 18.

[36] "The momentary passing of time" and "a passage of time" are also translations of *kyōryaku.* Spring has separate momentary aspects: the air is warm, flowers are open, birds are singing, etc. At the same time, we see it as an inclusive continuing process.

[37] When we think about "passing" we usually imagine a subject passing through an external object, but this does not apply to the passing of time, because the momentary passing of time is complete in itself.

[38] In the first clause, passing time and spring are separated; "the momentary passing of time" means the concept of the season spring, and "spring" means the concrete individual situations of spring—flowers blooming, birds singing, etc. In the second clause, Master Dōgen suggested the real springtime as the oneness of the conceptual and the concrete.

[39] Time is not a factor within the universe, it is the universe itself.

[40] Master Yakusan Igen (745–828). He became a monk at the age of seventeen and eventually succeeded Master Sekitō Kisen. Great Master Kōdō is his posthumous title.

41 Master Sekitō Kisen (700–790). He had his head shaved by Master Daikan Enō and eventually succeeded Master Seigen Gyōshi. He wrote the poem *Sandōkai* (*On Experiencing the State*), which is often recited in Sōtō sect temples. Great Master Musai is his posthumous title.

42 Master Baso Dōitsu (704–788); successor of Master Nangaku Ejō. Kōzei was the name of the district where he lived, and Daijaku is his posthumous name. The spread of Buddhism in China in the eighth century sprang from the efforts of Master Sekitō and Master Baso.

43 The three vehicles are the vehicles of the *śrāvaka, pratyekabuddha,* and bodhisattva, as outlined by the Buddha in the *Lotus Sutra.* The twelve divisions of the teachings are as follows: 1) *sūtra,* original texts, sutras; 2) *geya,* verses summarizing the prose content of sutras; 3) *vyākaraṇa,* the Buddha's affirmation that a practitioner is becoming a buddha; 4) *gāthā,* independent verses; 5) *udāna,* spontaneous preaching (usually the Buddha's preaching was prompted by questions from his followers); 6) *nidāna,* historical accounts of causes and conditions; 7) *avadāna,* parables; 8) *itivṛttaka,* stories of past occurrences (especially stories of past lives of the Buddha's disciples); 9) *jātaka,* stories of the Buddha's past lives; 10) *vaipulya,* extensions of Buddhist philosophy; 11) *adbhuta-dharma,* records of miraculous occurrences; and 12) *upadeśa,* theoretical discourses. See also Glossary of Sanskrit Terms, and Chapter Twenty-four (Vol. II), *Bukkyō.*

44 The ancestral master means Master Bodhidharma, who introduced real Buddhism to China from India. See Chapter Sixty-seven (Vol. III), *Soshi-sairai-no-i.*

45 *Arutoki,* see note 2.

46 *Kare* literally means "him" or "that one." Master Baso thought about his own behavior objectively.

47 "The teaching" is *kyō.* In Master Baso's words, *kyō* is used as an auxiliary causative verb (pronounced *seshimuru*). Master Dōgen affirmed that Master Baso's behavior was moral and that he followed the teachings. At the same time, by combining the three characters *ze, i,* and *kyō,* (right, him, and make/teaching), Master Dōgen suggested the oneness of Master Baso's words and his state.

48 Immorality is not only inaction—positive action can also be immoral. And inaction is not always immoral—to do nothing is sometimes morally right.

49 The elements of the sentence suggest real situations in the Buddha's life—it is said that he realized the truth on seeing the morning star, and that he transmitted the truth to Master Mahākāśyapa by picking up an *uḍumbara* flower. See Chapter Sixty-eight (Vol. III), *Udonge.*

50 Master Shōken Kishō, dates unknown; a successor of Master Shuzan Shōnen. Master Shōken was the fourth master in the succession from Master Rinzai, and the ninth master in the succession from Master Nangaku Ejō. It is said that he realized the truth

in the order of Master Shuzan when discussing a story about a *shippei* (bamboo stick). Shōken is in modern-day Hunan province in east central China.

51 Master Shuzan Shōnen, died in 993 at the age of sixty-eight. A successor of Master Fuketsu Enshō.

52 *Arutoki.* See note 2.

53 "Present" is *tō, ita*[*rite*], which means to arrive, or to have arrived, to be present. "Absent" is *futō, ita*[*ra*]*zu,* which means not to arrive, or not to have arrived, to be absent.

54 Master Chōkei Eryō asks Master Reiun Shigon, "What is the Great Intention of the Buddha-Dharma?" Master Reiun says, "Donkey business being unfinished, but horse business coming in." See *Shinji-shōbōgenzō,* pt. 2, no. 56.

55 The poem seems to be abstract in content, discussing only words and will, but Master Dōgen interprets that the poem is also about concrete reality.

56 Presence, or "to have arrived," and absence, or "not to have arrived," are states at the moment of the present; they do not need to be seen as the results of past processes.

57 Presence restricted by itself means real presence as it is, i.e., presence that is not restricted by worrying about absence.

58 Both expressions, "the will hinders the will" and "the will meets the will," suggest the real will as it is.

59 "Restriction" means being as it is. It is the state which real things already have, it is not something separate which can hinder real things.

60 *Genjō-kōan.* See Chapter Three, *Genjō-kōan.*

61 *Kōjō-kanrei. Kōjō,* "ascendant," describes the state which is more real than thinking and feeling. See Chapter Twenty-eight (Vol. II), *Butsu-kōjō-no-ji.*

62 *Dattai. Datsu* means to get free of, or to shed. *Tai* means the body, the substance, the concrete reality.

63 *Soku-shi-ri-shi* suggests real behavior in Buddhist life. This and the three preceding expressions can be interpreted according to four phases: a general expression of reality, the concrete state which is more real than a generalization, the clear establishment of concrete facts in reality, and real action in daily life.

64 "Enact existence-time" is *uji su—uji* is used as a verb.

65 *Kare,* as in Master Baso's words. See note 46.

66 The first day of the tenth lunar month, 1240.

67 1243.

[Chapter Twelve]

Kesa-kudoku 47c3

The Merit of the *Kaṣāya*

Translator's Note: Kesa *represents the Sanskrit word* kaṣāya, *or Buddhist robe, and* kudoku *means "virtue" or "merit." So* kesa-kudoku *means the merit of the* kaṣāya. *Being a realistic religion, Buddhism reveres our real life. In other words, Buddhism esteems our real conduct in daily life; wearing clothes and eating meals are very important parts of Buddhist life. In particular, the* kaṣāya *and* pātra, *or Buddhist bowl, are the main symbols of Buddhist life. In this chapter Master Dōgen explains and praises the merit of the* kaṣāya.

[49] The authentic transmission into China of the robe and the Dharma, which are authentically transmitted from buddha to buddha and from patriarch to patriarch, was done only by the Founding Patriarch of Sūgaku Peak.[1] The Founding Patriarch was the twenty-eighth patriarch after Śākyamuni Buddha, the transmission having passed twenty-eight times in India from rightful successor to rightful successor. The twenty-eighth patriarch went to China in person and became the First Patriarch [there]. The transmission then passed through five Chinese [masters] and reached Sōkei,[2] the thirty-third patriarch, whom we call "the Sixth Patriarch." Zen Master Daikan, the thirty-third patriarch, received the authentic transmission of this robe and Dharma on Ōbaizan[3] in the middle of the night, after which he guarded and retained [the robe] throughout his life. It is still deposited at Hōrinji on Sōkeizan. Many successive generations of emperors devoutly asked for [the robe] to be brought to the imperial court, where they served offerings and made prostrations to it, guarding it as a sacred object. The Tang dynasty[4] emperors Chūsō (Ch. Zhongzong), Shukusō (Ch. Suzong), and Taisō[5] (Ch. Daizong) frequently had [the robe] brought to the court and served offerings to it. When they requested it and when they sent it back, they would conscientiously dispatch an imperial emissary and issue an edict. Emperor Taisō once returned the

buddha robe to Sōkeizan with the following edict: "I now dispatch the great General Ryū Shūkei,[6] Pacifier of the Nation, to receive with courtesy[7] and to deliver [the robe]. I consider it to be a national treasure. Venerable priests,[8] deposit it according to the Dharma in its original temple. Let it be solemnly guarded only by monks who have intimately received the fundamental teaching. Never let it fall into neglect." Truly, better than ruling a three-thousand-great-thousandfold realm of worlds as countless as the sands of the Ganges,[9] to see and to hear and to serve offerings to the Buddha's robe as the king of a small country where the Buddha's robe is present, may be the best life among [all] good lives [lived] in life-and-death. Where, in a three-thousandfold world which has been reached by the Buddha's influence, could the *kaṣāya* not exist? At the same time, the one who passed on the authentic
48a transmission of the Buddha's *kaṣāya,* having received the face-to-face transmission from rightful successor to rightful successor, is only the ancestral patriarch of Sūgaku Peak. The Buddha's *kaṣāya* was not handed down through side lineages.[10] The transmission to Bodhisattva Bhadrapāla, a collateral descendant of the twenty-seventh patriarch,[11] duly arrived at Dharma teacher Jō,[12] but there was no authentic transmission of the Buddha's *kaṣāya.* Again, Great Master [Dōshin], the Fourth Patriarch in China,[13] delivered Zen Master Hōyū[14] of Gozusan but did not pass on the authentic transmission of the Buddha's *kaṣāya.* So even without the transmission from rightful successors, the Tathāgata's right Dharma—whose merit is never empty—confers its wide and great benefit all through thousands of ages and myriads of ages. [At the same time] those who have received the transmission from rightful successors are not to be compared with those who lack the transmission. Therefore, when human beings and gods receive and retain the *kaṣāya,* they should receive the authentic transmission transmitted between Buddhist patriarchs. In India and in China, in the ages of the right Dharma and the imitative Dharma,[15] even laypeople received and retained the *kaṣāya.* In this distant and remote land in the present degenerate age, those who shave their beard and hair and call themselves the Buddha's disciples do not receive and retain the *kaṣāya.* They have never believed, known, or clarified that they should receive and retain [the *kaṣāya*]; it is lamentable. How much less do they know of the [*kaṣāya*'s] material, color, and measurements. How much less do they know how to wear it.

[54] The *kaṣāya* has been called, since ancient time, "the clothing of liberation." It can liberate[16] us from all hindrances such as karmic hindrances, hindrances of affliction, and hindrances of retribution. If a dragon gets a single strand [of the *kaṣāya*], it escapes the three kinds of heat.[17] If a bull touches [a *kaṣāya*] with one of its horns, its sins will naturally be extinguished. When buddhas realize the truth they are always wearing the *kaṣāya.* Remember, [to wear the *kaṣāya*] is the noblest and highest virtue. Truly, we have been born in a remote land in [the age of] the latter Dharma, and we must regret this. But at the same time, how should we measure the joy of meeting the robe and the Dharma that have been transmitted from buddha to buddha, from rightful successor to rightful successor? Which [other] lineage has authentically transmitted both the robe and the Dharma of Śākyamuni in the 48b
manner of our authentic transmission? Having met them, who could fail to venerate them and to serve offerings to them? Even if, each day, we [have to] discard bodies and lives as countless as the sands of the Ganges, we should serve offerings to them. Indeed we should vow to meet them, humbly to receive them upon the head,[18] to serve offerings to them, and to venerate them in every life in every age. Between us and the country of the Buddha's birth, there are more than a hundred thousand miles of mountains and oceans, and it is too far for us to travel; nevertheless, promoted by past good conduct, we have not been shut out by the mountains and oceans, and we have not been spurned as the dullards of a remote [land]. Having met this right Dharma, we should persistently practice it day and night. Having received and retained this *kaṣāya,* we should perpetually receive it upon the head in humility and preserve it. How could this only be to have practiced merit under one buddha or two buddhas? It may be to have practiced all kinds of merit under buddhas equal to the sands of the Ganges. Even if [the people who receive and retain the *kaṣāya*] are ourselves, we should venerate them, and we should rejoice. We should heartily repay the profound benevolence of the ancestral master in transmitting the Dharma. Even animals repay kindness; so how could human beings fail to recognize kindness? If we failed to recognize kindness, we might be more stupid than animals. The merits of this buddha robe and this Buddha-Dharma were never clarified or known by anyone other than the ancestral master who transmitted the Buddha's right Dharma. If we want to follow gladly the traces of the buddhas, we should

just be glad about this [transmission]. Even after hundred thousand myriads of generations, we should esteem this authentic transmission as the authentic transmission. This [transmission] may be the Buddha-Dharma itself; the proof in due course will become evident. We should not liken [the transmission] to the dilution of milk with water. It is like a crown prince succeeding to the throne. When we want to use milk, if there is no milk other
48c than this diluted milk [described above], although it is diluted milk we should use it. Even when we do not dilute it with water, we must not use oil, we must not use lacquer, and we must not use wine. This authentic transmission may also be like that. Even a mediocre follower of an ordinary master, providing the authentic transmission is present, may be in a good situation to use milk. [But] more to the point, the authentic transmission from buddha to buddha and from patriarch to patriarch is like the succession of a crown prince. Even secular [teaching] says, "One does not wear clothing different from the official uniform of the previous reign."[19] How could disciples of the Buddha wear [robes] different from the Buddha's robe?

[58] Since the tenth year of the Eihei era,[20] during the reign of Emperor Kōmei (Ch. Mingdi) of the Later Han dynasty,[21] monks and laymen going back and forth between the Western Heavens and the Eastern Lands have followed on each other's heels without cease, but none has claimed to have met in the Western Heavens an ancestral master of the authentic transmission from buddha to buddha and from patriarch to patriarch; none has a record of the lineage of the face-to-face transmission from the Tathāgata. They have only followed teachers of sutras and commentaries, and brought back Sanskrit books of sutras and philosophy. None speaks of having met an ancestral master who is a rightful successor to the Buddha's Dharma, and none mentions that there are ancestral masters who have received the transmission of the Buddha's *kaṣāya.* Clearly, they have not entered beyond the threshold of the Buddha's Dharma. People like this have not clarified the principle of the authentic transmission by Buddhist patriarchs. When Śākyamuni Tathāgata[22] passed to Mahākāśyapa the right Dharma-eye treasury and the supreme state of *bodhi,* he transmitted them together with a *kaṣāya* received in the authentic transmission from Kāśyapa Buddha.[23] Received by rightful successor from rightful successor, [the *kaṣāya*] reached Zen Master Daikan of Sōkeizan, the thirty-third generation. The material, color, and measurements

[of the *kaṣāya*] had been transmitted intimately. Since then, the Dharma descendants of Seigen and Nangaku[24] have intimately transmitted the Dharma, wearing the Dharma of the ancestral patriarchs and keeping the Dharma of the ancestral patriarchs in order. The method of washing [the *kaṣāya*] and the method of receiving and retaining [the *kaṣāya*] cannot be known without learning in practice in the inner sanctum of the legitimate face-to-face 49a
transmission of those methods.

> [60] The *kaṣāya* is said to include three robes. They are the five-stripe robe, the seven-stripe robe, and the large robe of nine or more stripes. Excellent practitioners receive only these three robes, and do not keep other robes. To use just the three robes serves the body well enough. When we are attending to business or doing chores, and when we are going to and from the toilet, we wear the five-stripe robe. For doing good practices among the sangha, we wear the seven-stripe robe. To teach human beings and gods, and to make them devout, we should wear the large robe of nine or more stripes. Or, when we are in a private place we wear the five-stripe robe, when we go among the sangha we wear the seven-stripe robe, and when we go into a royal palace or into towns and villages we should wear the large robe. Or, when it is nice and warm we wear the five-stripe robe, when it is cold we put on the seven-stripe robe as well, and when the cold is severe we also put on the large robe. Once, in ancient times, the weather on a midwinter night was cold enough to split bamboo. As that night fell, the Tathāgata put on the five-stripe robe. As the night passed and it got colder, he put on the seven-stripe robe as well. Later on in the night, when the coldness reached a peak, he also put on the large robe. At this time, the Buddha thought, "In future ages, when the cold is beyond endurance, good sons should be able to clothe their bodies adequately with these three robes."[25]

[62] The method of wearing the *kaṣāya*: "To bare only the right shoulder"[26] is the usual method. There is a method of wearing [the *kaṣāya*] so that it goes over both shoulders, a form [followed by] the Tathāgata and veterans who are senior in years and experience: both shoulders are covered, while the chest may be either exposed or covered. [The method of] covering both

shoulders is for a large *kaṣāya* of sixty or more stripes. [Usually,] when we wear the *kaṣāya,* we wear both sides over the left arm and shoulder. The front edge goes over the left side [of the *kaṣāya*] and hangs over the [left upper] arm.[27] In the case of the large *kaṣāya,* [this] front edge passes over the left shoulder and hangs down behind the back. There are various methods of wearing the *kaṣāya* besides these; we should take time to study them and should inquire into them.

[64] For hundreds of years, through one dynasty after another—Liang,
49b Zhen, Sui, Tang, and Song[28]—many scholars of both the Great and the Small Vehicles have abandoned the work of lecturing on sutras, recognizing that it is not the ultimate, and progressed to learn the authentically transmitted Dharma of the Buddhist patriarchs; when they do so, they inevitably shed their former shabby robes and receive and retain the authentically transmitted *kaṣāya* of the Buddhist patriarchs. This is indeed the abandonment of the false and the return to the true. [In discussing] the right Dharma of the Tathāgata, [we see] the Western Heavens as the very root of the Dharma. Many teachers of human beings, past and present, have established small views based on the sentimental and parochial thinking of the common person. Because the world of buddha and the world of living beings are beyond being limited and being unlimited, the teachings, practice, and human truths of the Mahayana and the Hinayana can never fit inside the narrow thoughts of common people today. Nevertheless, [common people] in China, acting at random, have failed to see the Western Heavens as the root, and have considered their newly devised, limited, small views to be the Buddha-Dharma. Such facts should never occur. Therefore if people today who have established the mind want to receive and to retain the *kaṣāya,* they must receive and retain the *kaṣāya* of the authentic transmission. They must not receive and retain a *kaṣāya* newly created according to the idea of the moment. The *kaṣāya* of the authentic transmission means the one that has been authentically transmitted from Shaolin [Temple] and Sōkei [Mountain],[29] the one that has been received by the Tathāgata's rightful successors without missing a single generation. The *kaṣāya* worn by their Dharma children and Dharma grandchildren is the traditional *kaṣāya.* What has been newly created in China is not traditional. Now, the *kaṣāya* worn by the monks who have come from the Western Heavens, in the past and present, are all worn

as the *kaṣāya* authentically transmitted by the Buddhist patriarchs. Not one of these monks [has worn a *kaṣāya*] like the new *kaṣāya* being produced in China today by precepts scholars. Dull people believe in the *kaṣāya* of precepts scholars; those who are clear throw [such robes] away. In general, the merit of the *kaṣāya* transmitted from buddha to buddha and from patriarch to patriarch is evident and easy to believe in. Its authentic transmission has 49c
been received exactly, its original form has been handed down personally, and it exists really in the present. [The Buddhist patriarchs] have received and retained it, and succeeded to each other's Dharma, until today. The ancestral masters who have received and retained [the *kaṣāya*] are all masters and disciples who experienced the state[30] and received the transmission of Dharma. This being so, we should make [the *kaṣāya*] properly, according to the method for making the *kaṣāya* that has been authentically transmitted by the Buddhist patriarchs. This alone is the authentic tradition, and so it has long been experienced and recognized by all common and sacred beings, human beings and gods, and dragons and spirits. Having been born to meet the spread of this Dharma, if we cover our body with the *kaṣāya* only once, receiving it and retaining it for just a *kṣāṇa* or a *muhūrta,*[31] that [experience] will surely serve as a talisman to protect us[32] in the realization of the supreme state of *bodhi.* When we dye the body and mind with a single phrase or a single verse, it becomes a seed of everlasting brightness which finally leads us to the supreme state of *bodhi.* When we dye the body and mind with one real *dharma* or one good deed, it may be also like this. Mental images arise and vanish instantaneously; they are without an abode. The physical body also arises and vanishes instantaneously; it too is without an abode. Nevertheless, the merit that we practice always has its time of ripening and shedding. The *kaṣāya,* similarly, is beyond elaboration and beyond non-elaboration, it is beyond having an abode and beyond having no abode: it is that which "buddhas alone, together with buddhas, perfectly realize."[33] Nevertheless, practitioners who receive and retain [the *kaṣāya*] always accomplish the merit that is thus to be gained, and they always arrive at the ultimate. Those without past good conduct—even if they pass through one life, two lives, or countless lives—can never meet the *kaṣāya,* can never wear the *kaṣāya,* can never believe in the *kaṣāya,* and can never clearly know the *kaṣāya.* In China and Japan today, we see that there are those who have had the opportunity to clothe their body once in the

kaṣāya, and there are those who have not. [The difference] depends neither
upon high or low status nor upon stupidity or wisdom: clearly it was deter-
50a mined by past good conduct. This being so, if we have received and retained
the *kaṣāya,* we should feel glad about our past good conduct, and should not
doubt the accumulation of merit and the piling up of virtue. If we have not
got [the *kaṣāya*] yet, we should hope to get it. We should strive, without delay,
to sow the first seeds [of receiving and retaining the *kaṣāya*] in this life. Those
who are prevented by some hindrance from receiving and retaining [the *kaṣāya*]
should repent and confess before the buddha-tathāgatas and the Three Treasures of Buddha, Dharma, and Sangha. How living beings in other countries
must wish, "If only the robe and the Dharma of the Tathāgata had been authentically transmitted and were intimately present in our country, as they are in
China!" Their shame must be deep, and their sadness tinged with resentment,
that the authentic tradition has not passed into their own country. Why are we
so fortunate as to have met the Dharma in which the robe and the Dharma of
the Tathāgata, the World-honored One, have been authentically transmitted?
It is the influence of the great merit of *prajñā* nurtured in the past. In the present corrupt age of the latter Dharma, [some] are not ashamed that they themselves have no authentic transmission, and they envy others who possess the
authentic transmission. I think they may be a band of demons. Their present
possessions and abodes which are influenced by their former conduct, are not
true and real. Just to devote themselves[34] to and to venerate the authentically
transmitted Buddha-Dharma: this may be their real refuge in learning [the
state of] buddha. In sum, remember that the *kaṣāya* is the object of the buddhas' veneration and devotion. It is the body of the Buddha and the mind of
the Buddha. We call it "the clothing of liberation,"[35] "the robe of a field of
happiness,"[36] "the robe without form,"[37] "the supreme robe," "the robe of
endurance,"[38] "the robe of the Tathāgata," "the robe of great benevolence and
great compassion," "the robe that is a banner of excellence," and "the robe
of *anuttara samyaksaṃbodhi.*" We should receive and retain it like this, humbly
receiving it upon the head. Because it is like this, we should never change it
according to [our own] mind.

50b [71] As material for the robe, we use silk or cotton, according to suit-
ability. It is not always the case that cotton is pure and silk is impure. There
is no viewpoint from which to hate cotton and to prefer silk; that would be

laughable. The usual method[39] of the buddhas, in every case, is to see rags[40] as the best material. There are ten sorts and four sorts of rags; namely, burned, chewed by an ox, gnawed by rats, from clothes of dead people, and so forth.[41] "The people of the five areas of India[42] discarded rags like these in streets and fields, as if they were filth, and so they called them 'filthy rags.'[43] Practitioners picked them up, washed them and sewed them, and used them to cover the body."[44] Among those [rags] there are various kinds of silk and various kinds of cotton. We should throw away the view [that discriminates between] silk and cotton, and study rags in practice. When, in ancient times[45] [the Buddha] was washing a robe of rags in Lake Anavatapta,[46] the Dragon King praised him with a rain of flowers, and made prostrations of reverence. Some teachers of the Small Vehicle have a theory about transformed thread,[47] which also may be without foundation. People of the Great Vehicle might laugh at it. What kind [of thread] is not transformed thread? When those teachers hear of "transformation" they believe their ears, but when they see the transformation itself they doubt their eyes. Remember, in picking up rags, there may be cotton that looks like silk and there may be silk that looks like cotton. There being myriad differences in local customs it is hard to fathom [nature's] creation—eyes of flesh cannot know it. Having obtained such material, we should not discuss whether it is silk or cotton but should call it rags. Even if there are human beings or gods in heaven who have survived as rags, they are never sentient beings, they are just rags. Even if there are pine trees or chrysanthemums that have survived as rags, they are never insentient beings, they are just rags. When we believe the principle that rags are not silk or cotton, and not gold, silver, pearl, or jewel, rags are realized. Before we have got rid of views and opinions about silk and cotton, we have never seen rags even in a dream. On one occasion a monk asks the eternal 50c
buddha,[48] "Should we see the robe you received on Ōbai [Mountain] in the middle of the night as cotton, or should we see it as silk? In short, as what material should we see it?" The eternal buddha says, "It is not cotton and it is not silk." Remember, it is a profound teaching[49] of the Buddha's truth that the *kaṣāya* is beyond silk and cotton.

[74] The Venerable Śāṇavāsa[50] is third in the transmission of the Dharma treasury. He has been endowed with a robe since birth. While he is a layman this robe is a secular garment, but when he leaves home[51] it turns into a

kaṣāya. In another case, the *bhikṣuṇī* Śukra,[52] after establishing the will and being clothed in a cotton robe, has been born with a robe in every life and middle existence. On the day that she meets Śākyamuni Buddha and leaves home, the secular robe that she has had since birth changes instantly into a *kaṣāya,* as in the case of Venerable Śāṇavāsa. Clearly, the *kaṣāya* is beyond silk, cotton, and so forth. Moreover, the fact that the virtue of the Buddha-Dharma can transform body and mind and all *dharma*s is as in those examples. The truth is evident that when we leave home and receive the precepts, body and mind, object-and-subject, change at once; it is only because we are stupid that we do not know. It is not true that the usual rule[53] of the buddhas applies only to Śāṇavāsa and to Śukra but not to us; we should not doubt that benefit [accrues] in accordance with individual standing. We should consider such truths in detail and learn them in practice. The *kaṣāya* that covers the body of [the monks whom the Buddha] welcomes[54] to take the precepts is not necessarily cotton or silk: the Buddha's influence is difficult to consider. The precious pearl within the robe[55] is beyond those who count grains of sand.[56] We should clarify and should learn in practice that which has quantity and that which is without quantity, that which has form and that which is without form, in the material, color, and measurements of the *kaṣāya* of the buddhas. This is what all the ancestral masters of the Western Heavens and the Eastern Lands, past and present, learned in practice and transmitted as the authentic tradition. If someone is able to see and to hear [a master] in whom there is nothing to doubt—the authentic transmission from
51a patriarch to patriarch being evident—but fails, without reason, to receive the authentic transmission from this ancestral master, such smugness would be hard to condone. The extent of [this] stupidity might be due to unbelief. It would be to abandon the real and to pursue the false, to discard the root and to seek after branches. It would be to slight the Tathāgata. People who wish to establish the *bodhi*-mind should always receive the authentic transmission of an ancestral master. Not only have we met the Buddha-Dharma which is so difficult to meet: also, as Dharma descendants in the authentic transmission of the Buddha's *kaṣāya,* we have been able to see and to hear, to learn and to practice, and to receive and to retain [the authentic transmission of the Buddha's *kaṣāya*]. This is just to see the Tathāgata himself, it is to hear the Buddha's preaching of Dharma, it is to be illuminated by

the Buddha's brightness, it is to receive and to use what the Buddha received and used, it is to receive the one-to-one transmission of the Buddha's mind, it is to have got the Buddha's marrow, it is to be covered directly by Śākyamuni Buddha's *kaṣāya,* and it is Śākyamuni Buddha himself directly bestowing the *kaṣāya* upon us. Because we follow the Buddha, we have devoutly[57] received this *kaṣāya*.

[78] The method of washing the *kaṣāya*: Put the *kaṣāya,* unfolded, into a clean tub, then immerse the *kaṣāya* in fragrant, fully boiled hot water, and leave it to soak for about two hours.[58] Another method is to soak the *kaṣāya* in pure, fully boiled ash-water[59] and to wait for the water to cool. Nowadays we usually use [the] hot ash-water [method]. Hot ash-water is what we call *aku-no-yu* here [in Japan].[60] When the ash-water has cooled, rinse [the *kaṣāya*] again and again in clean and clear hot water. During the rinsing do not put in both hands to scrub [the *kaṣāya*] and do not tread on it. Continue until any dirt or grease has been removed. After that, mix aloes, sandalwood,[61] or other 51b
incense into some cold water and rinse [the *kaṣāya*]. Then hang it on a washing pole[62] to dry. After it is thoroughly dry, fold it and put it in a high place, burn incense and scatter petals, walk round it several times [with the *kaṣāya*] to the right,[63] and perform prostrations. After making three prostrations, six prostrations, or nine prostrations, kneel up and join the hands,[64] then hold the *kaṣāya* up with both hands, and in the mouth recite the verse [in praise of the *kaṣāya*].[65] After that stand up and put on [the *kaṣāya*] according to the method.

> [80] [66]The World-honored One addresses the great assembly: "In the ancient past when I was in the order of Buddha Jewel Treasury,[67] I was Bodhisattva Great Compassion.[68] At that time, the bodhisattva *mahāsattva* Great Compassion made the following vow before Buddha Jewel Treasury:
>
> 'World-honored One! If, after I became a buddha, there were living beings who had entered my Dharma and left home and who wore the *kaṣāya*—even if they were *bhikṣu*s, *bhikṣuṇī*s, *upāsaka*s, and *upāsikā*s[69] who had accumulated heavy sins by violating the grave prohibitions, by enacting false views, or by contemptuously disbelieving the Three Treasures—and in a single moment of consciousness the reverence arose in their mind to honor the *saṃghāṭi* robe[70] and the reverence arose in their mind to honor the World-honored One (the

Buddha) or the Dharma and the Sangha but, World-honored One, even one among those living beings could not, in [one of] the three vehicles,[71] receive affirmation,[72] and as a result regressed or went astray, it would mean that I had deceived the buddhas who are present now in the worlds of the ten directions and in countless, infinite *asaṃkheya kalpa*s, and I surely should not realize *anuttara samyaksaṃbodhi.*

'World-honored One! After I have become a buddha, if gods, dragons, and demons, and human and nonhuman beings are able to wear this *kaṣāya,* to venerate, to serve offerings to, to honor, and to praise it, as long as those people are able to see a small part of this *kaṣāya,* they will be able not to regress while within the three vehicles.

'When living beings are afflicted by hunger or thirst—whether they are wretched demons, miserable people, or living beings in the state of hungry ghosts—if they are able to obtain a piece of the *kaṣāya* even as small as four inches,[73] they will at once be able to eat and drink their fill and to accomplish quickly whatever they wish.

51c 'When living beings offend each other, causing ill will to arise and a fight to develop—or when gods, dragons, demons, *gandharva*s, *asura*s, *garuḍa*s, *kiṃnara*s, *mahoraga*s, *kumbhāṇḍa*s, *piśāca*s, and human and nonhuman beings are fighting each other—if they remember this *kaṣāya,* in due course, by virtue of the power of the *kaṣāya,* they will beget the mind of compassion, soft and flexible mind, mind free of enmity, serene mind, the regulated mind of virtue, and they will get back the state of purity.

'When people are in an armed conflict, a civil lawsuit, or a criminal action, if they retain a small piece of this *kaṣāya* as they go among these combatants, and if in order to protect themselves they serve offerings to, venerate, and honor it, these [other] people will be unable to injure, to disturb, or to make fools of them; they will always be able to beat their opponents and to come through all such difficulties.

'World-honored One! If my *kaṣāya* were unable to accomplish these five sacred merits,[75] it would mean that I had deceived the buddhas who are present now in the worlds of the ten directions and in countless, infinite *asaṃkheya kalpa*s, and in future I ought not to accomplish *anuttara samyaksaṃbodhi* or to do Buddhist works. Having lost the virtuous Dharma, I would surely be unable to destroy non-Buddhism.'

Good sons![76] At that time Tathāgata Jewel Treasury extended his golden right arm and patted the head of Bodhisattva Great Compassion, praising him with these words:

"Very good! Very good! Stout fellow! What you have said is a great and rare treasure, and is great wisdom and virtue. When you have realized *anuttara samyaksaṃbodhi,* this robe, the *kaṣāya,* will be able to accomplish these five sacred merits and to produce great benefit."

Good sons! At that time, the bodhisattva *mahāsattva* Great Compassion, after hearing the praise of that buddha, jumped endlessly for joy. Then the Buddha [again] extended his golden arm, with its hand of long, webbed fingers[77] as soft as the robe of a goddess. When he patted the [bodhisattva's] head, the [bodhisattva's] body changed at once into the youthful figure of a man of twenty. Good sons! In that order the great assembly of gods, dragons, deities, *gandharva*s, and human and nonhuman beings, with folded hands[78] venerated Bodhisattva Great Compassion; they served him offerings of all kinds of flowers; they even made music and offered that; and they also praised him in all kinds of ways, after which they abode in silence.[79]

[86] From the age when the Tathāgata was in the world until today, whenever the merits of the *kaṣāya* are quoted from the Sutra and the Vinaya[80] of bodhisattvas and *śrāvaka*s, these five sacred merits are always considered 52a
fundamental. Truly, *kaṣāya*s are the buddha robes of the buddhas of the three times. Their merits are measureless. At the same time, to get the *kaṣāya* in the Dharma of Śākyamuni Buddha may be even better than to get the *kaṣāya* in the Dharma of other buddhas. The reason, if asked, is that in the ancient past, when Śākyamuni Buddha was in the causal state[81] as the bodhisattva *mahāsattva* Great Compassion, when he offered his five hundred great vows before Buddha Jewel Treasury, he pointedly made the above vows in terms of the merits of this *kaṣāya.* Its merits may be utterly measureless and unthinkable. This being so, the authentic transmission to the present of the skin, flesh, bones, and marrow of the World-honored One, is the *kaṣāya* robe. The ancestral masters who have authentically transmitted the right Dharma-eye treasury have, without exception, authentically transmitted the *kaṣāya.* The

living beings who have received and retained this robe and humbly received it upon their heads have, without exception, attained the truth within two or three lives. Even when people have put [the *kaṣāya*] on their body for a joke or for gain, it has inevitably become the causes and conditions for their attaining the truth.

> [87] The ancestral master Nāgārjuna[82] says, "Further, in the Buddha-Dharma, people who have left family life,[83] even if they break the precepts and fall into sin, after they have expiated their sins, they can attain liberation, as the *bhikṣuṇī* Utpalavarṇā explains in the *Jātaka-sūtra:*[84] When the Buddha is in the world, this *bhikṣuṇī* attains the six mystical powers[85] and the state of an arhat.[86] She goes into the houses of nobles and constantly praises the method of leaving family life, saying to all the aristocratic ladies, 'Sisters! You should leave family life.'
>
> The noblewomen say, 'We are young and our figures are full of life and beauty. It would be difficult for us to keep the precepts. Sometimes we might break the precepts.'
>
> The *bhikṣuṇī* says, 'If you break the precepts, you break them. Just leave family life!'
>
> They ask, 'If we break the precepts we will fall into hell. Why should we want to break them?'
>
> She answers, 'If you fall into hell, you fall.'
>
> The noblewomen all laugh at this, saying, 'In hell we would have to receive retribution for our sins. Why should we want to fall [into hell]?'
>
> The *bhikṣuṇī* says, 'I remember in my own past life, once I became
> 52b a prostitute, wore all sorts of clothes, and spoke in old-fashioned language.[87] One day I put on a *bhikṣuṇī* robe as a joke, and due to this as a direct and indirect cause, at the time of Kāśyapa Buddha[88] I became a *bhikṣuṇī*. I was still proud then of my noble pedigree and fine features: vanity and arrogance arose in my mind, and I broke the precepts. Because of the wrongness of breaking the precepts I fell into hell and suffered for my various sins, but after I had suffered retribution I finally met Śākyamuni Buddha, transcended family life, and attained the six mystical powers and the truth of an arhat. Thus, I know that when we

leave family life and receive the precepts, even if we break the precepts, due to the precepts as direct and indirect causes we can attain the truth of an arhat. If I had only done bad, without the precepts as direct and indirect causes, I could not have attained the truth. In the past I fell into hell in age after age. When I got out of hell I became a bad person, and when the bad person died, I went back into hell, and there was no gain at all. Now therefore I know from experience that when we leave family life and receive the precepts, even if we break the precepts, with this as a direct and indirect cause we can attain the *bodhi*-effect.'"[89]

[90] The primary cause of this *bhikṣuṇī* Utpalavarṇā[90] attaining the truth as an arhat is just the merit of her putting the *kaṣāya* on her body for a joke; because of this merit, and no other merit, she has now attained the truth. In her second life she meets the Dharma of Kāśyapa Buddha and becomes a *bhikṣuṇī.* In her third life she meets Śākyamuni Buddha and becomes a great arhat, equipped with the three kinds of knowledge and the six powers. The three kinds of knowledge are supernatural insight, [knowing] past lives, and ending the superfluous. The six powers are the power of mystical transmutation, the power to know others' minds, the power of supernatural sight, the power of supernatural hearing, the power to know past lives, and the power to end the superfluous.[91] Truly, when she was only a wrongdoer she died and entered hell to no avail, coming out of hell and becoming a wrongdoer again. [But] when she has the precepts as direct and indirect causes, although she has broken the precepts and fallen into hell, they are the direct and indirect causes of her attaining the truth at last. Now, even someone who has worn the *kaṣāya* for a joke can attain the truth in her third life. How, then, could someone who has established pure belief, and who wears the *kaṣāya* for the 52c
sake of the supreme state of *bodhi,* fail to accomplish that merit? Still further, if we receive and retain [the *kaṣāya*] throughout our life, humbly receiving it upon the head, the merit might be universal and great beyond measure. Any human being who would like to establish the *bodhi*-mind should receive and retain the *kaṣāya,* and humbly receive it upon the head, without delay. To have met this favorable age but not to have sown a Buddhist seed would be deplorable. Having received a human body on the southern continent,[92]

having met the Dharma of Śākyamuni Buddha, and having been born to meet an ancestral master who is a perfectly legitimate successor to the Buddha-Dharma, if we idly passed up the chance to receive the *kaṣāya* which has been transmitted one-to-one and which is directly accessible, that would be deplorable. Now, in regard to the authentic transmission of the *kaṣāya,* the one authentic transmission from the ancestral master is right and traditional; other masters cannot stand shoulder to shoulder with him. Even to receive and to retain the *kaṣāya* following a master who has not received the transmission is still of very profound merit. But much more than that, if we receive and retain [the *kaṣāya*] from a true master who has quite legitimately received the face-to-face transmission, we may really be the Dharma children and the Dharma grandchildren of the Tathāgata himself, and we may actually have received the authentic transmission of the Tathāgata's skin, flesh, bones, and marrow. The *kaṣāya,* in conclusion, has been authentically transmitted by the buddhas of the three times and the ten directions, without interruption; it is what the buddhas, bodhisattvas, *śrāvaka*s, and *pratyekabuddha*s of the three times and the ten directions have, in like manner, guarded and retained.

[93] Coarse cotton cloth is the standard [material] for making the *kaṣāya.* When there is no coarse cotton cloth, we use fine cotton cloth. When there is neither coarse nor fine cotton cloth, we use plain silk. When there is neither [plain] silk nor cotton cloth, materials such as patterned cloth[93] or sheer silk may be used; [these are all] approved by the Tathāgata. For countries where there is no plain silk, cotton, patterned cloth, sheer silk, or anything of the kind, the Tathāgata also permits the leather *kaṣāya.* Generally, we should dye the *kaṣāya* blue, yellow, red, black, or purple. Whichever color
53a it is, we should make it a secondary color.[94] The Tathāgata always wore a flesh-colored *kaṣāya;* this was the color of the *kaṣāya.* The Buddha's *kaṣāya* transmitted by the First Patriarch was blue-black, and made of the cotton crepe of the Western Heavens. It is now on Sōkeizan. It was transmitted twenty-eight times in the Western Heavens and transmitted five times in China. Now the surviving disciples of the eternal buddha of Sōkei,[95] who have all received and retained the ancient customs of the Buddha's robe, are beyond other monks. Broadly, there are three kinds of robe: 1) "the robe of rags," 2) "the robe of fur," and 3) "the patched robe." "Rags" are as explained previously. In "the robe of fur," the fine [down and] hair of birds and beasts

is called "fur." "When practitioners cannot obtain rags, they pick up this [fur] and make it into the robe. 'The patched robe' describes our sewing and patching, and wearing, [cloth] that has become ragged and worn with age; we do not wear the fine clothes of the secular world."[96]

> [95] [97]The venerable monk[98] Upāli[99] asks the World-honored One, "World-honored Bhadanta![100] How many stripes does the *saṃghāṭi* robe have?"
>
> The Buddha says, "There are nine kinds. What are the nine kinds? They are [the *saṃghāṭi* robe] of nine stripes, eleven stripes, thirteen stripes, fifteen stripes, seventeen stripes, nineteen stripes, twenty-one stripes, twenty-three stripes, and twenty-five stripes. The first three of those kinds of *saṃghāṭi* robe have two long segments and one short segment [in each stripe], and we should keep [the standard] like this. The next three kinds have three long [segments] and one short, and the last three kinds have four long and one short. Anything with more [segments per] stripe than this becomes an unorthodox robe."[101]
>
> Upāli again addresses the World-honored One, "World-honored Bhadanta! How many kinds of *saṃghāṭi* robe are there?"
>
> The Buddha says, "There are three kinds: larger, medium, and smaller.[102] The larger is three cubits long by five cubits wide.[103] The smaller is two and a half cubits long by four and a half cubits wide. Anything between these two is called medium."
>
> Upāli again addresses the World-honored One: "World-honored Bhadanta! How many stripes does the *uttarasaṃghāṭi*[104] robe have?"
>
> The Buddha says, "It has only seven stripes, each with two long segments and one short segment."
>
> Upāli again addresses the World-honored One, "World-honored Bhadanta! How many kinds of seven-striped [robe] are there?"
>
> The Buddha says, "There are three kinds: larger, medium, and smaller. The larger is three cubits by five, the smaller is a half cubit shorter on each side, and anything between these two is called medium."
>
> Upāli again addresses the World-honored One: "World-honored Bhadanta! How many stripes does the *antarvāsa*[105] robe have?" 53b
>
> The Buddha says, "It has five stripes, each with one long segment and one short segment."

> Upāli again addresses the World-honored One, "How many kinds of *antarvāsa* robes are there?"
>
> The Buddha says, "There are three kinds: larger, medium, and smaller. The larger is three cubits by five. The medium and the smaller are as before."[106] The Buddha says, "There are two further kinds of *antarvāsa* robes. What are those two? The first is two cubits long by five cubits wide, and the second is two cubits long by four cubits wide."
>
> The *saṃghāṭi* is translated as "the double-layered robe," the *uttarasaṃghāṭi* is translated as "the upper robe," and the *antarvāsa* is translated as "the under robe" or as "the inner robe." At the same time, the *saṃghāṭi* robe is called "the large robe," and also called "the robe for entering royal palaces" or "the robe for preaching the Dharma." The *uttarasaṃghāṭi* is called "the seven-striped robe," or called "the middle robe" or "the robe for going among the sangha." The *antarvāsa* is called "the five-striped robe," or called "the small robe" or "the robe for practicing the truth and for doing work."

[98] We should guard and retain these three robes without fail. Among *saṃghāṭi* robes is the *kaṣāya* of sixty stripes, which also deserves to be received and retained without fail. In general, the length of a [buddha's] body depends on the span of its lifetime, which is between eighty thousand years[107] and one hundred years.[108] Some say that there are differences between eighty thousand years and one hundred years, while others say that they may be equal. We esteem the insistence that they may be equal as the authentic tradition.[109] The body measurements of buddhas and of human beings are very different: the human body can be measured, but the buddha body ultimately cannot be measured.[110] Therefore, in the present moment in which Śākyamuni Buddha puts on the *kaṣāya* of Kāśyapa Buddha,[111] [the *kaṣāya*] is not long and not wide. And in the present moment in which Maitreya Tathāgata puts on the *kaṣāya* of Śākyamuni Buddha, it is not short and not narrow. We should reflect upon clearly, decide conclusively, understand completely, and observe carefully that the buddha body is not long or short. King Brahmā,[112] though high in the world of matter, does not see the crown of the Buddha's
53c head. Maudgalyāyana,[113] having gone far into the World of the Bright Banner, does not discern the Buddha's voice: it is truly a mystery that [the

Buddha's form and voice] are the same whether seen and heard from far or near. All the merits of the Tathāgata are like this,[114] and we should keep these merits in mind.

[100] As regards [methods of] cutting out and sewing the *kaṣāya,* there is the robe of separate stripes,[115] the robe of added stripes,[116] the robe of pleated stripes,[117] and the single-sheet robe,[118] each of which is a proper method. We should receive and retain [the kind of robe] that accords with the [material] obtained. The Buddha says, "The *kaṣāya* of the buddhas of the three times is invariably backstitched." In obtaining the material, again, we consider pure material to be good, and we consider so-called filthy rags to be the purest of all. The buddhas of the three times all consider [rags] to be pure. In addition, cloth offered by devout donors is also pure. There again, [cloth] bought at a market with pure money is also pure. There are limits on the [number of] days within which the robe should be made,[119] but in the present degenerate age of the latter Dharma, in a remote country, it may be better for us to receive and to retain [the robe] by doing the cutting and sewing whenever we are promoted by belief. It is an ultimate secret of the Great Vehicle that laypeople, whether human beings or gods, receive and retain the *kaṣāya.* King Brahmā and King Śakra[120] have now both received and retained the *kaṣāya,* and these are excellent precedents in [the worlds of] volition and matter. Excellent [precedents] in the human world are beyond calculation. All lay bodhisattvas have received and retained [the *kaṣāya*]. In China, Emperor Bu[121] of the Liang dynasty and Emperor Yang[122] of the Sui dynasty[123] both received and retained the *kaṣāya.* Emperors Taisō and Shukusō both wore the *kaṣāya,* learned in practice from monks, and received and retained the bodhisattva precepts. Other people such as householders and their wives who received the *kaṣāya* and received the Buddhist precepts are excellent examples in the past and present. In Japan, when Prince Shōtoku[124] received and retained the *kaṣāya,* and lectured on such sutras as the *Lotus Sutra* and the *Śrīmālā Sutra,*[125] he experienced the miraculous omen of precious flowers raining from the heavens. From that time the Buddha-Dharma spread throughout our country. Though [Prince Shōtoku] was the regent of the whole 54a
country, he was just a guiding teacher to human beings and gods. As the Buddha's emissary, he was father and mother to many living beings. In our country today, although the materials, colors, and measurements of the *kaṣāya*

have all been misunderstood, that we can see and hear the word *kaṣāya* is due solely to the power of Prince Shōtoku. We would be in a sorry state today if, at that time, he had not destroyed the false and established the true. Later, Emperor Shōmu[126] also received and retained the *kaṣāya* and received the bodhisattva precepts. Therefore, whether we are emperors or subjects, we should receive and retain the *kaṣāya* and we should receive the bodhisattva precepts without delay. There can be no greater happiness for a human body.

[104] It has been said that "the *kaṣāya*s received and retained by laypeople are either called 'single-stitched' or called 'secular robes.' That is, they are not sewn with backstitches." It is also said that "when laypeople go to a place of [practicing] the truth, they should be equipped with the three Dharma robes, a willow twig,[127] rinsing water,[128] mealware, and a sitting cloth;[129] they should practice the same pure practices as *bhikṣu*s."[130]

[105] Such were the traditions of a master of the past.[131] However, [the tradition] that has now been received one-to-one from the Buddhist patriarchs is that the *kaṣāya*s transmitted to kings, ministers, householders,[132] and common folk, are all backstitched. An excellent precedent is that [Master Daikan Enō] had already received the authentic transmission of the Buddha's *kaṣāya* as the temple servant Ro (Ch. Lu).[133] In general, the *kaṣāya* is the banner of a disciple of the Buddha. If we have already received and retained the *kaṣāya,* we should humbly receive it upon the head every day. Placing it on the crown of the head, we join the hands and recite the following verse:

> *Daisai-gedatsu-fuku* (How great is the clothing of liberation,)
> *Musō-fukuden-e* (Formless, field of happiness, robe!)
> *Hibu-nyorai-kyō* (Devoutly wearing the Tathāgata's teaching,)
> *Kōdo-shoshujō* (Widely I will save living beings.)

After that we put it on. In the *kaṣāya,* we should feel like [our] master and should feel like a tower.[134] We also recite this verse when we humbly receive [the *kaṣāya*] on the head after washing it.

[107] The Buddha says,

> When we shave the head and wear the *kaṣāya,*
> We are protected by the buddhas.
> Each person who transcends family life
54b Is served by gods and humans.

Clearly, once we have shaved the head and put on the *kaṣāya*, we are protected by all the buddhas. Relying on this protection of the buddhas, [a person] can roundly realize the virtues of the supreme state of *bodhi*. Celestial throngs and human multitudes serve offerings to such a person.

> [135]The World-honored One says to the *bhikṣu* Wisdom-Brightness,[136] "The Dharma robe has ten excellent merits: 1) It is able to cover the body, to keep away shame, to fill us with humility and to [make us] practice good ways.[137] 2) It keeps away cold and heat, as well as mosquitoes, harmful creatures, and poisonous insects, [so that we can] practice the truth in tranquility. 3) It manifests the form of a *śramaṇa*[138] who has left family life, giving delight to those who behold it and keeping away wrong states of mind. 4) The *kaṣāya* is just the manifestation to human beings and gods of a precious flag; those who honor and venerate it are able to be born in a Brahmā heaven.[139] 5) When we wear the *kaṣāya,* we feel that it is a precious flag; it is able to extinguish sins and to produce all kinds of happiness and virtue. 6) A fundamental rule in making the *kaṣāya* is to dye it a secondary color,[140] so that it keeps us free from thoughts of the five desires,[141] and does not give rise to lust. 7) The *kaṣāya* is the pure robe of the Buddha; for it eradicates afflictions[142] forever and makes them into a fertile field. 8) When the *kaṣāya* covers the body, it extinguishes the karma of sins and promotes at every moment the practice of the ten kinds of good.[143] 9) The *kaṣāya* is like a fertile field; for it is well able to nurture the bodhisattva way. 10) The *kaṣāya* is also like a suit of armor; for it makes the poisoned arrows of affliction unable to do harm. Wisdom-Brightness! Remember, through these causes, when the buddhas of the three times, and *pratyekabuddha*s and *śrāvaka*s, and pure monks and nuns, cover the body in the *kaṣāya,* [these] three groups of sacred beings sit as one on the precious platform of liberation, take up the sword of wisdom to destroy the demons of affliction, and enter together into the many spheres of nirvana which have one taste." Then the World-honored One speaks again in verse:
>
> Bhikṣu Wisdom-Brightness, listen well!
> The traditional Buddhist robe has ten excellent merits:

Secular clothes increase taintedness from desire,
The Tathāgata's Dharma attire is not like that;
Dharma attire fends off social shame,
But fills us with the humility that produces a field of happiness.
It keeps away cold and heat, and poisonous insects;
Firming our will to the truth, it enables us to arrive at the ultimate.
It manifests [the form] of a monk and keeps away greed;
It eradicates the five views[144] and [promotes] right practice.
To look at and bow to the *kaṣāya*'s form of a precious banner,
54c And to venerate it, produces the happiness of King Brahmā.
When a disciple of the Buddha wears the robe and feels like a tower,
This produces happiness, extinguishes sins, and impresses human beings and gods.
True *śramaṇa*s, of modest appearance, showing respect,
Are not tainted in their actions by secular defilements.
The buddhas praise [the *kaṣāya*] as a fertile field,
They call it supreme in giving benefit and joy to living beings.
The mystical power of the *kaṣāya* is unthinkable,
It can cause us to practice deeds that plant the seeds of *bodhi,*[145]
It makes the sprouts of the truth grow like spring seedlings,
The wonderful effect of *bodhi* being like autumn fruit.
[The *kaṣāya*] is a true suit of armor, as hard as a diamond;
The poisoned arrows of affliction can do no harm.
I have now briefly praised the ten excellent merits,
If I had successive *kalpa*s to expound them widely, there would be no end.
If a dragon wears a single strand [of the *kaṣāya*],
It will escape [the fate of] becoming food for a *garuḍa.*[146]
If people retain this robe when crossing the ocean,
They need not fear trouble from dragonfish or demons.
When thunder roars, lightning strikes, and the sky is angry,
Someone who wears the *kaṣāya* is fearless.
If one clothed in white[147] is able personally to hold and retain [the *kaṣāya*],

All bad demons are unable to approach.
If [that person] is able to establish the will and seeks to leave home,
Shunning the world and practicing the Buddha's truth,
All the demon palaces of the ten directions will quake and tremble,
And that person will quickly experience the body of the Dharma King.[148]

[113] These ten excellent merits broadly include all the merits of the Buddha's truth. We should explicitly learn in practice the merits present in [these] long lines and [short] verses of praise, not just glancing over them and quickly putting them aside, but studying them phrase by phrase over a long period. These excellent merits are just the merits of the *kaṣāya* itself: they are not the effect of a practitioner's fierce [pursuit of] merit through perpetual training. The Buddha says, "The mystical power of the *kaṣāya* is unthinkable"; it cannot be supposed at random by the common person or sages and saints. In general, when we "quickly experience the body of the Dharma King," we are always wearing the *kaṣāya*. There has never been anyone, since ancient times, who experienced the body of the Dharma King without wearing the *kaṣāya*.

[114] The best and purest material for the robe is rags, whose merits are universally evident in the sutras, precepts, and commentaries[149] of the Great Vehicle and Small Vehicle. We should inquire into [these merits] under those who have studied them widely. At the same time, we should also be clear about other materials for the robe. [These things] have been clarified and 55a
authentically transmitted by the buddhas and the patriarchs. They are beyond lesser beings.

[115] The *Middle Āgama Sutra*[150] says:

> Furthermore, wise friends![151] Suppose there is a man whose bodily behavior is pure but whose behavior of mouth and mind is impure. If wise people see [the impurity] and feel anger they must dispel it. Wise friends! Suppose there is a man whose bodily behavior is impure but whose behavior of mouth and mind is pure. If wise people see [the impurity] and feel anger they must dispel it. How can they dispel it?

> Wise friends! They should be like a forest *bhikṣu*[152] with rags, looking among the rags for worn cloth to be thrown away, and for [cloth] soiled by feces or urine, or by tears and spit, or stained by other impurities. After inspecting [a rag, the *bhikṣu*] picks it up with the left hand and stretches it out with the right hand.[153] If there are any parts that are not soiled by feces, urine, tears, spit, or other impurities, and which are not in holes, [the *bhikṣu*] tears them off and takes them. In the same way, wise friends, if a man's bodily behavior is impure but the behavior of mouth and mind is pure, do not think about his body's impure behavior. Only be aware of his pure behavior of mouth and mind. If wise people feel anger at what they see, they must dispel it like this.

[117] This is the method by which a forest *bhikṣu* collects rags. There are four sorts of rags and ten sorts of rags. When gathering those rags, we first pick out the parts that have no holes. We should then also reject [the parts] that cannot be washed clean, being too deeply soiled with long-accumulated stains of feces and urine. We should select [those parts] that can be washed clean.

[117] The ten sorts of rags: 1) Rags chewed by an ox, 2) rags gnawed by rats, 3) rags scorched by fire, 4) rags [soiled by] menstruation, 5) rags [soiled by] childbirth, 6) rags [offered at] a shrine, 7) rags [left at] a graveyard, 8) rags [offered in] petitional prayer, 9) rags [discarded by] a king's officers,[154] 10) rags brought back from a funeral.[155] These ten sorts people throw away; they are not used in human society. We pick them up and make
55b them into the pure material of the *kaṣāya.* Rags have been praised and have been used by the buddhas of the three times. Therefore these rags are valued and defended by human beings, gods, dragons, and so on. We should pick them up to make the *kaṣāya;* they are the purest material and the ultimate purity. Nowadays in Japan there are no such rags. Even if we search, we cannot find any. It is regrettable that [this] is a minor nation in a remote land. However, we can use pure material offered by a donor, and we can use pure material donated by human beings and gods. Alternatively, we can make the *kaṣāya* from [cloth] bought at a market with earnings from a pure livelihood. Such rags and [cloth] obtained from a pure livelihood are not silk, not cotton, and not gold, silver, pearls, patterned cloth, sheer silk, brocade,

embroidery, and so on; they are just rags. These rags are neither for a humble robe nor for a beautiful garment; they are just for the Buddha-Dharma. To wear them is just to have received the authentic transmission of the skin, flesh, bones, and marrow of the buddhas of the three times, and to have received the authentic transmission of the right Dharma-eye treasury. We should never ask human beings and gods about the merit of this [transmission]. We should learn it in practice from Buddhist patriarchs.

Shōbōgenzō Kesa-kudoku

[120] During my stay in Song China, when I was making effort on the long platform, I saw that my neighbor at the end of every sitting[156] would lift up his *kaṣāya* and place it on his head; then holding the hands together in veneration, he would quietly recite a verse. The verse was:

Daisai-gedatsu-fuku (How great is the clothing of liberation,)
Musō-fukuden-e (Formless, field of happiness, robe!)
Hibu-nyorai-kyō (Devoutly wearing the Tathāgata's teaching,)
Kōdo-shoshujō (Widely I will save living beings.) 55c

At that time, there arose in me a feeling I had never before experienced. [My] body was overwhelmed with joy. The tears of gratitude secretly fell and soaked my lapels. The reason was that when I had read the Āgama sutras previously, I had noticed sentences about humbly receiving the *kaṣāya* on the head, but I had not clarified the standards for this behavior. Seeing it done now, before my very eyes, I was overjoyed. I thought to myself, "It is a pity that when I was in my homeland there was no master to teach this, and no good friend to recommend it. How could I not regret, how could I not deplore, passing so much time in vain? Now that I am seeing and hearing it, I can rejoice in past good conduct. If I had vainly stayed in my home country, how could I have sat next to this treasure of a monk,[157] who has received the transmission of, and who wears, the Buddha's robe itself?" The sadness and joy was not one-sided. A thousand myriad tears of gratitude ran down. Then I secretly vowed: "One way or another, unworthy though I am, I will become a rightful successor to the Buddha-Dharma. I will receive the authentic transmission of the right Dharma and, out of compassion for living beings in my homeland, I will cause them to see and to hear the robe and the Dharma that have been authentically transmitted by the Buddhist patriarchs." The vow I made then has not been in vain now; many bodhisattvas, in families and out of families,[158] have received and retained the *kaṣāya.* This is something to rejoice in. People who have received and retained the *kaṣāya* should humbly receive it upon the head every day and night. The merit [of this] may be especially excellent and supremely excellent. The seeing and hearing of a phrase or a verse may be as in the story of "on trees and on rocks,"[159] and the seeing and hearing may not be limited to the length and breadth of the nine states.[160] The merit of the authentic transmission of the *kaṣāya* is hardly encountered through the ten directions. To [encounter this merit] even if only for one day or for one night may be the most excellent and highest thing.

[123] In the tenth lunar month in the winter of the seventeenth year of Kajō[161] in great Song [China], two Korean[162] monks came to the city of Kei-
56a genfu.[163] One was called Chigen and one was called Keiun. This pair were always discussing the meaning of Buddhist sutras; at the same time they were also men of letters. But they had no *kaṣāya* and no *pātra,* like secular people. It was pitiful that though they had the external form of *bhikṣu*s they did not have the Dharma of *bhikṣu*s.[164] This may have been because they were from a minor nation in a remote land. When Japanese who have the external form of *bhikṣu*s travel abroad, they are likely to be the same as Chigen and such. Śākyamuni Buddha received [the *kaṣāya*] upon his head for twelve years, never setting it aside.[165] We are already his distant descendants, and we should emulate this. To turn the forehead away from prostrations idly done for fame and gain to gods, to spirits, to kings, and to retainers, and to turn instead toward the humble reception upon the head of the Buddha's robe, is joyful.

Preached to the assembly at Kannondōrikō-shōhōrinji, on the first day of winter,[166] in the first year of Ninji.[167]

Notes

1 Master Bodhidharma, the twenty-eighth patriarch in India and the First Patriarch in China, who introduced the practice of zazen from India. He lived at Shaolin Temple, one of the many Buddhist monasteries that already existed in the Songshan Mountains in the northwest of China.

2 Master Daikan Enō (638–713), successor of Master Daiman Kōnin. Sōkei is the name of the mountain where he lived.

3 Ōbai Mountain was where Master Daiman Kōnin had his Buddhist order.

4 Tang dynasty (618–907).

5 Chūsō (reigned, with an interruption of several years, 684–710) was the fourth emperor of the Tang dynasty. Emperors Shukusō (r. 756–763) and Taisō (r. 763–780) were students of Master Nan'yō Echū (d.775). See for example, Chapter Eighty (Vol. IV), *Tashintsū.*

6 Chingoku Dai Shōgun Ryū Shūkei. *Chingoku,* lit., "Pacifier of the Nation," was a title given to generals. *Dai shogun* means great general.

7 *Chōdai. Chō* means the top of the head, and *dai* means humbly to receive, so *chōdai* literally means humbly to receive something upon the head, as a sign of respect.

8 *Kei,* "you," is a term of address for lords, officials of high rank, etc.

9 *Muryō-gōga-sha.* Variations of this expression appear in many places in the *Lotus Sutra.* See, for example, LS 2.166 and 3.214.

10 *Bōshutsu. Bō,* lit., "side," describes a bystander, or something of secondary importance. *Shutsu* means to depart or to sprout. So *bōshitsu* means collateral descendants or collateral lineages. Master Dōgen revered the one line that he considered to be authentic, and so to some degree, he considered all other lineages of secondary importance. Master Dōgen's line is through Master Daikan Enō's successor, Master Seigen Gyōshi. At the same time, Master Dōgen revered Master Daikan Enō's other successors, Master Nan'yō Echū and Master Nangaku Ejō. Masters Baso Dōitsu, Nansen Fugan, Jōshū Jūshin, Hyakujō Ekai, Ōbaku Kiun, Rinzai Gigen, Isan Reiyū, Kyōgen Chikan, Kyōzan Ejaku, and Reiun Shigon were some of the descendants of Master Nangaku Ejō.

11 Master Prajñātara, successor of Master Puṇyamitra and master of Master Bodhidharma.

An image of a bodhisattva called Bhadrapāla (lit., "Good Guardian") is sometimes kept as a guardian of the temple bathhouse.

12 Jō Hōsshi, died in 414 at the age of thirty-one. *Hōsshi,* "Dharma teacher" was a title used for Buddhist priest-scholars and teachers of theory. As a layman, Jō worked as a scribe and studied the thoughts of Laozi and Zhuangzi, but after reading the *Vimalakīrti Sutra* he came to believe in Buddhism and assisted Kumārajīva in the translation of Buddhist sutras.

13 Master Daii Dōshin, died in 651. See Chapter Fifteen, *Busso.*

14 Master Gozu Hōyū, died in 657 at the age of sixty-four. He was a collateral successor of Master Daii Dōshin (whose direct successor was Master Daiman Kōnin). It is said that after living on Gozu Mountain and devoting himself to zazen, Master Hōyū was visited by Master Daii Dōshin and thereupon attained the truth.

15 Buddhist scholars divided time following the Buddha's death into three periods: 1) *shōbō,* "right Dharma," the first five hundred years during which time Buddhism flourished; 2) *zōbō,* "imitative Dharma," an intermediate period of one thousand years; and 3) *mappō,* "latter Dharma," the next ten thousand years during which Buddhism degenerates. See Glossary of Sanskrit Terms under *saddharma.*

16 *Gedatsu,* used here first as a noun and then as a verb, represents the Sanskrit word *vimukti* (setting at liberty, release, deliverance, final emancipation).

17 *Sannetsu,* the three heats, or the three kinds of burning pain. One explanation is as follows: 1) the pain of hot wind and sand being blown against the skin; 2) the pain of a violent wind that takes away jeweled clothes and jeweled ornaments; and 3) the pain of being eaten by a *garuḍa,* a dragon-eating bird.

18 *Chōdai.* See note 7.

19 This quotation appears in the *Kōkyō* (*Book of Filial Piety*), a text of Confucianism. It is quoted as an example of reverence of tradition in secular society.

20 67 C.E.

21 The Later (or Eastern) Han dynasty, 25–220 C.E. It is said that Buddhist sutras were first translated into Chinese and transmitted into China in 67 C.E.

22 *Shakamuni-nyorai. Shakamuni* is the phonetic rendering in Chinese characters of the Sanskrit Śākyamuni—sage of the Śākya clan. *Nyorai,* lit., "thus-come," represents the Sanskrit Tathāgata.

23 Kāśyapa Buddha is the sixth of the seven ancient buddhas, Śākyamuni Buddha being the seventh.

24 Master Seigen Gyōshi and Master Nangaku Ejō. See note 10.

25 This paragraph is quoted from the *Daijōgishō.*

26 *Hentan-uken.* These four characters appear in several places in the *Lotus Sutra.* See,

for example, the opening paragraph of the *Shinge* ("Belief and Understanding") chapter (LS 1.222).

27 The folded *kaṣāya* (folded lengthwise into eight) is first hung over the left shoulder, with the top of the *kaṣāya* over the front of the body (so that the single string faces the front). The two corners of the top of the *kaṣāya* are flush with each other. The left hand takes the top left-hand corner of the *kaṣāya* and the right hand takes the top right-hand corner of the *kaṣāya.* The *kaṣāya* is then opened behind the back, and the right hand brings the top right-hand corner of the *kaṣāya* under the right arm and round to the front, and then hangs it over the left shoulder and left upper arm. So "both sides" means the left and right sides of the top of the *kaṣāya,* and "the front edge" refers to the upper border of the part of the *kaṣāya* that is held in the right hand.

28 The Liang dynasty (502–556); the Zhen dynasty (557–589); the Sui dynasty (589–618), the Tang dynasty (618–907); and the Song dynasty (960–1279).

29 Master Bodhidharma lived at Shaolin Temple; Master Daikan Enō lived on Sōkei Mountain.

30 "Experienced the state" is *shōkai. Shō* means to experience; *kai* means to agree or to fit. *Shokai* means to experience the same state as the Buddha.

31 Measurements of time in India. According to one explanation, sixty-four *kṣāṇa*s pass in the clicking of the fingers, and thirty *muhūrta*s pass in a day. See Glossary of Sanskrit Terms.

32 *Goshin-fushi,* lit., "a card to guard the body." Cards bearing lucky words, called *o-mamori* in Japanese, are often sold as talismans at shrines and temples.

33 The *Lotus Sutra* says that buddhas alone, together with buddhas, can perfectly realize that all *dharma*s are real form. Master Dōgen is emphasizing that the *kaṣāya* is instantaneous and real, therefore beyond understanding.

34 *Onore* also means "our" or "ourselves." These two sentences also apply to us.

35 *Gedatsu-fuku.*

36 *Fukuden-e.*

37 *Musō-e.* The *kaṣāya* is without form in the sense that it is a simple rectangular sheet of cloth. These first three phrases all come from the verse which is recited in veneration of the *kaṣāya.* See paragraph 105 in this chapter.

38 *Ninniku-e,* lit., "enduring-humiliation robe." *Ninniku* represents the Sanskrit *kṣānti,* endurance or patience.

39 "Usual method" is *jōhō. Jō* means constant or eternal, and at the same time usual or common. *Hō* means method, or Dharma.

40 "Rags" is *funzō-e. Fun* means excrement, and *sō* (pronounced *zō*) means to sweep or "to be swept." *E* means robe, clothes, or clothing. *Funzō* represents the Sanskrit

pāṃsu-kūla, which means a dust heap or a collection of rags out of a dust heap used by Buddhist monks for their robes. *Funzō-e* has been translated either as "rags" or as "a robe of rags," according to the context.

41 The ten sorts of rags are given in paragraph 117 in this chapter. The first four of these are also known as the four sorts of rags.

42 Literally, "people of the five Indias." Ancient India is said to have been divided into five regions: east, west, central, south, and north.

43 *Funzō-e,* see note 40.

44 The section beginning with "The people of the five Indias" to here is in the style of a quotation from a Chinese text.

45 Many legends like the one referred to in this sentence appear in stories of the Buddha's past lives as a bodhisattva.

46 Lake Anavatapta was thought to be located north of the Himalayas as the source of the four great rivers of India. It was said to be the home of the king of dragons, and was called the lake where there is no suffering from heat.

47 *Keshi,* "processed thread." The process of producing silk entails boiling the cocoon while the silkworm is still alive. Some people worried that the production of silk violated the precept of not taking life in vain, and thought that silk should not be used as a material for the *kaṣāya.*

48 The eternal buddha refers to Master Daikan Enō, who received the *kaṣāya* from Master Daiman Kōnin in the middle of the night on Ōbai Mountain. See Chapter Thirty (Vol. II), *Gyōji.*

49 *Genkun,* lit., "black instruction."

50 Born about a hundred years after the death of the Buddha, Master Śāṇavāsa eventually became the third Indian patriarch, succeeding Master Ānanda. The Sanskrit word *śāṇavāsa* literally means flaxen clothes.

51 *Shukke,* lit., "leave home," means to become a monk. See Chapter Eighty-three (Vol. IV), *Shukke.*

52 *Senbyaku-bikuni. Senbyaku,* "fresh-white" represents the Sanskrit *śukra* which means bright, clear, pure, white, or spotless. Volume 8 of the *Senjūhyakuenkyō* says that the *bhikṣuṇī* (Buddhist nun) Śukra was born wearing a pure white robe that never needed washing, and that when she became a nun, the robe changed into a *kaṣāya.*

53 *Jōhō.* See note 39.

54 "Welcomed" is *zenrai,* representing the Sanskrit *svāgata,* "Welcome!" The Pāli scriptures say that the Buddha accepted his followers into the monkhood simply by saying *"Ehi bhikkhu"* ("Welcome, monk").

55 The pearl within the robe alludes to the *Gohyaku-deshi-juki* ("Affirmation of Five Hundred Disciples") chapter of the *Lotus Sutra,* which tells the story of a drunken man whose friend plants a valuable pearl in his clothes. Five hundred arhats compare themselves to the man who unknowingly carries the pearl, because they have been content with inferior wisdom instead of obtaining the buddha-wisdom (LS 2.114).

56 "Those who count grains of sand" means scholars. The original characters *sansa,* "count sand," come from the poem *Shōdōka* by Master Yōka Genkaku. He said, "They know no respite from analyzing concepts and forms; having entered the ocean, they vainly exhaust themselves by counting grains of sand."

57 The Japanese suffix translated as "devoutly" is the honorific *tatematsuru* form, invariably used by Master Dōgen to express reverence for the Buddha but usually ignored in this translation due to the lack of a suitable equivalent in English.

58 The day was divided into twelve periods. The original characters *hito-toki* indicate one such period, that is, two hours.

59 *Aku.* The ash must have been used to make the water more alkaline. In this case the word *aku* is written with the Chinese character for ash (*kai*) and the Chinese character for water, *sui,* but the word *aku* is originally Japanese, not Chinese.

60 "Hot ash-water" is *kaitō,* a Chinese word formed by the character for ash (*kai*) and the character for hot water (*tō*). *Aku-no-yu* are Japanese words written in *kana,* the phonetic Japanese alphabet. *Aku* means ash-water (see previous note) and *yu* means hot water.

61 *Sendan* is given in *Kenkyusha's New Japanese-English Dictionary* as margosa. At the same time, *sendan* originally represents the Sanskrit *candana,* sandalwood.

62 *Jōkan,* lit., "pure pole," a bamboo or wooden pole suspended horizontally at about head height. See Chapter Seven, *Senjō.*

63 An ancient Indian custom to show reverence for people or sacred objects.

64 *Koki-gasshō. Ko* means foreign and *ki* means to kneel with the hips extended, as the Chinese noticed that foreigners sometimes kneeled. Joining the hands (*gasshō*) means holding the palms together, fingers pointing upward, fingertips in front of the nostrils.

65 The verse is: *Daisai-gedatsu-fuku/musō-fukuden-e/hibu-nyorai-kyō/kōdo-shoshujō.* Loosely translated: "How great is the clothing of liberation./ Though without form it is the robe of real happiness./Wearing the Buddha's teaching,/I will save living beings everywhere." See paragraph 105.

66 The following long quotation from the *Higekyō* (in Sanskrit, *Karuṇāpuṇḍarīka-sūtra*) is originally one paragraph. It has been divided in this translation for ease of reading.

[67] *Hōzō,* from the Sanskrit *ratnagarbha.* Ratnagarbha Buddha is a legendary past buddha who appears in the *Higekyō.* He encouraged Śākyamuni Buddha and Amitābha Buddha (a symbol of eternal life) to establish the will to the truth.

[68] *Daihi,* lit., "great compassion," from the Sanskrit *mahākaruṇā.* This is another name of Bodhisattva Avalokiteśvara. See Chapter Thirty-three (Vol. II), *Kannon.*

[69] The four groups of Buddhists: monks, nuns, laymen, and laywomen.

[70] The Sanskrit root *saṃghāṭ* means to join or fasten together, suggesting the *kaṣāya* as a robe composed of miscellaneous rags. The *saṃghāṭi* robe (in Japanese, *sōgyari-e*) means the large robe.

[71] That is, as either a *śrāvaka* (intellectual Buddhist), *pratyekabuddha* (sensory Buddhist), or bodhisattva (practical Buddhist).

[72] "Affirmation" is *kibetsu,* from the Sanskrit *vyākaraṇa. Vyākaraṇa* is the Buddha's affirmation that a practitioner will become a buddha in the future. This sentence includes the first of the five sacred merits mentioned later in the paragraph. The first merit is that all who revere the *kaṣāya* and the Three Treasures can receive affirmation.

[73] Originally, four *sun.* One *sun* is slightly over an inch.

[74] Ancient Indian storytellers invented these colorful beings that later found their way into Buddhist sutras. *Gandharva*s are fragrance-devouring celestial beings, *asura*s are demons that oppose gods, *garuḍa*s are dragon-eating birds, *kiṃnara*s are half-horses, half-men, *mahoraga*s are serpents, *kumbhāṇḍa*s, lit., "having testicles like jars," are demons that feed on human energy, and *piśāca*s are demons that eat flesh.

[75] The five sacred merits are that those who wear, venerate, or retain a piece of the *kaṣāya* 1) will be able to receive affirmation, 2) will not regress, 3) will be able to satisfy hunger and thirst, and other wishes, 4) will be able to remain peaceful in hostile situations, and 5) will be protected in times of conflict.

[76] *Zen-nanshi* represents the Sanskrit word *kulaputra,* with which the Buddha commonly addressed his Buddhist audiences.

[77] Webbed fingers and toes are the fifth of the thirty-two distinguishing marks of a buddha.

[78] *Shashu.* In *shashu* the fingers of the left hand are curled round the thumb, and the left hand is placed against the chest, the left forearm being held horizontal. The right hand is placed, palm down, on the back of the left hand, the right forearm also being held horizontal.

[79] The *Higekyō,* chapter 8 (the chapter on how the bodhisattvas received their affirmation in past lives).

[80] Sutra and Vinaya are two of the three "baskets" (*piṭaka*s), or kinds of Buddhist teachings. *Vinaya* means guidance, discipline, instruction, or teaching; that is, the precepts

and related writings. The Tripiṭaka (three baskets) consists of Sutra, Vinaya (precepts), and Abhidharma (commentaries).

81 *Inchi,* "causal state," means the state that caused the Buddha to become a buddha.

82 Master Nāgārjuna was the fourteenth patriarch in India, the successor of Master Kapimala and the teacher of Master Kāṇadeva. He lived sometime around the period 150–250 C.E. This passage is a Chinese translation of the *Mahāprajñāpāramitā-śāstra,* which is thought to have been written and compiled mainly by Master Nāgārjuna himself.

83 *Shukken in,* or "people who have left home"; monks and nuns.

84 *Honshōkyō,* lit., *"Past Lives Sutra."* Legendary stories of the Buddha's past lives as a bodhisattva.

85 See explanation in the following paragraph.

86 The ultimate state of a *śrāvaka,* or intellectual Buddhist, which is identified with the state of buddha. See Chapter Thirty-four (Vol. II), *Arakan.*

87 It was the custom in Asian pleasure houses for prostitutes to use old-fashioned language. The custom remained in Japan until the end of the Edo era (1868).

88 See note 23.

89 *Daichidoron,* chapter 30. This section is also quoted near the beginning of Chapter Eighty-six (Vol. IV), *Shukke-kudoku.*

90 In the Chinese translation of the *Mahāprajñāpāramitopadeśa,* the Sanskrit name Utpalavarṇā, which means "color of the blue lotus," is represented as Ubara-ke. *Ubara* is a phonetic rendering of *utpala* (blue lotus) and *ke* means flower. Here the name is Renge-shiki, "Lotus Flower Color."

91 See Chapter Twenty-five (Vol. II), *Jinzu,* and the Glossary of Sanskrit Terms under *abhijñā.*

92 Ancient Indians imagined a universe of four continents surrounding a big mountain, with celestial beings in the north and human beings in the south. So the southern continent means the human world.

93 *Ryō, aya. Aya* has a pattern woven into a diagonal weave.

94 *E-jiki,* lit., "broken color," that is, not a bright, attractive primary color. The *kaṣāya* is not dyed a primary color.

95 Master Daikan Enō, the Sixth Patriarch in China.

96 The section beginning "When practitioners cannot obtain rags" to here is in Chinese characters only, indicating that it was quoted directly from a Chinese text.

97 From here to paragraph 98 is a passage from the *Konponissaiubuhyakuichikatsuma*

(*One Hundred and One Customs of the Mūlasarvāstivādin School*). In Chinese characters, the Sarvāstivāda school is *setsu-issai-u-bu,* "the school that preaches that all things exist." Master Dōgen esteemed their teaching especially highly. See Glossary of Sanskrit Terms and Chapter Eighty-seven (Vol. IV), *Kuyō-shubutsu.*

98 "Venerable monk" is *guju,* lit., "possessing longevity," which represents the meaning of the Sanskrit *āyuṣmat,* a term of reverence used for the Buddha's disciples. The word *āyuṣmat* literally means a vital or vigorous person, a person of long life.

99 Upāli was one of the Buddha's ten great disciples, said to be foremost in maintaining the Vinaya. Before becoming a monk he was a barber at the royal palace.

100 *Daitoku-seson,* lit., "World-honored Great Virtuous One." *Daitoku* represents the Sanskrit *bhadanta,* an epithet of the Buddha. See Glossary of Sanskrit Terms.

101 *Hanō,* lit., "broken patched-[robe]." *Nō,* "patches," suggests the Buddhist robe itself.

102 *Jō, chū, ge,* lit., "upper, middle, and lower."

103 Cubit is *chū,* lit., "elbow," representing the Sanskrit *hasta,* which means forearm or cubit. The cubit, or *nobechū* in Japanese, is the basic unit of measurement in making a *kaṣāya.* It is not a fixed distance; it is obtained by measuring the distance from the elbow to the tip of the fist, or the distance from the elbow to the tip of the middle finger, of the person who will wear the *kaṣāya.*

104 The Sanskrit *uttarasaṃghāṭi* means an upper- or outergarment. This robe would be worn for doing prostrations, listening to formal lectures, and the meeting for confession.

105 The Sanskrit *antarvāsa* means an inner- or undergarment.

106 As in the case of the *uttarasaṃghāṭi* robe, the smaller is a half cubit shorter on each side, and anything between these two is called medium.

107 It is said that Maitreya Buddha will manifest himself in this world when he is eighty thousand years old.

108 The *Fuyōkyō,* from the Sanskrit *Lalitavistara-sūtra,* says that the Buddha lived for one hundred years.

109 Master Dōgen did not deny the existence of differences in length, but at the same time he suggested that, in the phase of action, relative differences are not important.

110 The buddha body is a real state at the moment of the present, not only physical matter.

111 See note 23.

112 The creator deity in Hindu mythology.

113 Maudgalyāyana was one of the Buddha's ten great disciples. It is said that he and Śāriputra, the sons of brahmans from neighboring villages, were good friends. Maudgalyāyana was said to be foremost in mystical abilities. The World of the Bright Banner is an imaginary western realm where buddhas are living. The *Daihōshakkyō* (from

the Sanskrit *Mahāratnakūṭa-sūtra*), chapter 10, contains a story in which Maudgalyāyana goes into the World of the Bright Banner.

114 That is, the merits of the Buddha are beyond relative considerations.

115 These names are explanatory rather than accurate translations of the original Chinese characters. "The robe of separate stripes" is *katsu-setsu-e,* lit., "divided-and-cut robe"; for this robe the individual segments of each stripe are sewn together, then the stripes are sewn together, and finally the borders are sewn and fastening tapes added.

116 *Zetchō-e,* lit., "[unknown character]-leaf robe"; this is basically one large sheet of uncut cloth onto which long thin strips are sewn to create the stripes and borders.

117 *Shō-yō-e,* lit., "gathered-leaf robe"; this is again one large sheet of uncut cloth, but it is pleated to create the stripes.

118 *Man-e*—the meaning of the former character is not known; this is a single sheet of cloth with only the fastening tapes added, and sewn only around the borders.

119 The time limits were five days for the *saṃghāṭi* robe, four days for the seven-striped robe, and two days for the five-striped robe.

120 Indian legends say that King Brahmā is king of the world of volition, and King Śakra (i.e., Śakra-devānām-indra) is king of the world of matter.

121 Emperor Bu, or Wu, (464–549), reigned from 502 to 549. His conversation with Master Bodhidharma when the latter arrived in China is recorded in Chapter Thirty (Vol. II), *Gyōji.*

122 Emperor Yang (569–617), reigned from 605 to 617.

123 Taisō and Shukusō were emperors of the Tang dynasty (618–906), who lived at the time of Master Nan'yō Echū. See note 5.

124 Prince Shōtoku (573–620) was the primary organizer of the early Japanese state. He promoted Buddhism as the state religion.

125 The full name of the sutra is the *Śrīmālādevīsiṃhanāda-sūtra.* See Glossary of Sanskrit Terms.

126 Emperor Shōmu, reigned in Japan from 724 to 749.

127 The use of the willow twig to clean the teeth is explained in Chapter Fifty-six (Vol. III), *Senmen.*

128 Potable water would be kept in a small corked bottle, for drinking or for rinsing the mouth.

129 The sitting cloth, or *zagu,* is spread on the floor for formal prostrations.

130 Both quotations are from the *Makashikanhogyōdenguketsu,* a Chinese commentary on the *Makashikan,* which is a record of lectures by the Chinese Master Tendai Chigi, founder of the Tendai sect.

[131] "Master of the past" is *ko-toku,* lit., "ancient merit" or "meritorious person of the past." These words appear frequently in the *Makashikan.*

[132] "Householder" is *koji.* See Chapter Eight, *Raihai-tokuzui.*

[133] Ro was Master Daikan Enō's name before he became a monk. The story of how he worked as a temple servant in the order of Master Daiman Kōnin is related in Chapter Thirty (Vol. II), *Gyōji.*

[134] These represent the first two of the eight venerative images, or feelings, associated with wearing the *kaṣāya:* 1) feeling like a tower (because of sitting up straight), 2) feeling like the Buddha ("our master"), 3) feeling solitude and peace, 4) feeling compassion, 5) feeling veneration, 6) feeling humility, 7) feeling repentance, and 8) feeling as if one has dispelled greed, anger, and stupidity and obtained all the teachings of a monk.

[135] The following passage is from Vol. 5 of *Daijōhonshōshinchikankyō.*

[136] Chikō. The Sanskrit name of this monk is not known.

[137] "Good ways" is *zenhō,* lit., "good law." Observance of *zenhō,* or the moral rule of the universe, is the second of the three universal bodhisattva precepts (see Chapter Ninety-four [Vol. IV], *Jukai*).

[138] The Sanskrit *śramaṇa* means a striver, a mendicant, or a Buddhist monk.

[139] The first of the four *dhyāna* heavens in the world of matter is said to consist of three heavens: Brahma-pāriṣadya, Brahma-purohita, and Mahā-brahman. Beings in these heavens, having left the world of volition, are not troubled by sexual desire.

[140] *E-jiki.* See note 94.

[141] The five desires are desires associated with sight, sound, smell, taste, and touch.

[142] *Bonnō,* representing the Sanskrit *kleśa.*

[143] The ten kinds of good are abstention from the ten kinds of wrong: 1) killing, 2) stealing, 3) adultery, 4) lying, 5) two-faced speech, 6) abusive slander, 7) gossip, 8) greed, 9) anger, and 10) devotion to wrong views.

[144] *Goken,* "five views," represents the Sanskrit *pañca dṛṣṭayaḥ.* See Glossary of Sanskrit Terms.

[145] The Chinese characters *bodai, "bodhi,"* and the character *dō,* "truth," in the next line are used interchangeably.

[146] Literally, "a golden-winged king of birds," that is, a *garuḍa.* See Glossary of Sanskrit Terms.

[147] *Byaku-e,* lit., "a white robe," represents the Sanskrit *avadāta-vāsana.*

[148] Hō-ō, "Dharma King," is an epithet of the Buddha.

[149] The Tripiṭaka (three baskets) of Buddhist teachings. See note 80 and the Glossary of Sanskrit Terms.

[150] *Chūagongyō* (Skt. *Madhyamāgama;* Pāli: *Majjhima-nikāya*). The Āgama sutras relate concrete information about the behavior and speech of the Buddha and his disciples in their daily life.

[151] *Shoken,* "wise ones" or "(ladies and) gentlemen," is a term of respect used when addressing an assembly.

[152] *Arannya-biku. Arannya* represents the Sanskrit *araṇya* which means forest. A forest *bhikṣu* suggests a monk who lives a solitary life in the forest. See also Chapter Ninety (Vol. IV), *Shizen-biku.*

[153] Traditionally, the right hand is kept pure.

[154] Suggests uniforms discarded by promoted officers.

[155] *Ōkan-e,* lit., "robes of going and returning," that is, cloth used as a funeral shroud and then brought back after the ceremony.

[156] "End of sitting" is *kaijō,* lit., "release of stillness." Traditionally, the clapping of a wooden board at the end of zazen is called *shō-kaijō,* "small release of stillness," and the ringing of the bell is called *dai-kaijō,* "great release of stillness."

[157] *Sōbō,* or "sangha treasure."

[158] *Zaike-shukke,* laypeople and monks.

[159] *Nyakuju-nyakuseki,* "trees and rocks," alludes to the story of the Buddha's past life recorded in the *Mahāparinirvāṇa-sūtra.* When he was the "Child of the Himalayas" pursuing the truth in the mountains, a demon told him the first two lines of a four-line poem: "Actions are without constancy;/ Concrete existence is the arising and passing of *dharma*s." The demon said it was too hungry to tell the child the last two lines, so the child offered his own body as a meal for the demon if it would recite the last two lines. So the demon recited the last two lines: "After arising and passing have ceased,/The stillness is pleasure itself." The child preserved the verse for posterity by writing it on some nearby trees and rocks in his own blood, before being eaten by the demon.

[160] The nine states means China.

[161] 1223. The seventeenth year of the Kajō era was, in fact, 1224. However, the original sentence also identifies the year under the Chinese dating system in which characters from two separate lists are combined. These two characters—*ki, mizunoto,* the younger brother of water, or the tenth calendar sign; and *mi, hitsuji,* the sheep, or the eighth horary sign—identify the year as 1223.

[162] "Korean" is Kōrai or Kōma. At that time, the Korean peninsula was divided into three states. The state called Kōrai existed from 918 to 1353.

[163] Present-day Ningbo, in eastern China.

[164] They did not have the *kaṣāya* and *pātra.*

[165] Alludes to a story originally contained in the Āgama sutras. See Chapter Thirteen, *Den-e,* paragraph 143.

[166] The first day of winter means the first day of the tenth lunar month.

[167] 1240.

[Chapter Thirteen]

Den-e

The Transmission of the Robe

Translator's Note: Den *means "transmission" and* e *means "robe," so* den-e *means "transmission of the robe." The content of this chapter is very similar to that of the previous chapter,* Kesa-kudoku. *Furthermore, the date recorded at the end of each chapter is the same. But whereas the note at the end of* Kesa-kudoku *says "preached to the assembly at Kannondōrikōshōhōrinji," the note to this chapter says "written at Kannondōrikōshōhōrinji. . . ." It thus seems likely that* Den-e *is the draft of the lecture Master Dōgen was to give on October first, and* Kesa-kudoku *is the transcript of the lecture he gave on that day.*

[125] The authentic transmission into China of the robe and the Dharma, which are authentically transmitted from buddha to buddha,[1] was done only by the Founding Patriarch of Shaolin [Temple]. The Founding Patriarch was the twenty-eighth ancestral master after Śākyamuni Buddha. [The robe] had passed from rightful successor to rightful successor through twenty-eight generations in India, and it was personally and authentically transmitted through six generations in China; altogether it was [transmitted through] thirty-three generations in the Western Heavens and the Eastern Lands. The thirty-third patriarch, Zen Master Daikan, received the authentic transmission of this robe and Dharma on Ōbaizan in the middle of the night, and he guarded and retained [the robe] until his death.[2] It is now still deposited at Hōrinji on Sōkeizan. Many generations of emperors in succession requested 56b
that it be brought into the palace, where they served offerings to it; they guarded [the robe] as a sacred object. The Tang dynasty emperors Chūsō, Shukusō, and Taisō frequently had [the robe] brought to court and served offerings to it. Both when they requested it and when they sent it back, they would dispatch an imperial emissary and issue an edict; this is the manner in which they honored [the robe]. Emperor Taisō once returned the Buddha's

robe to Sōkeizan with the following edict: "I now dispatch the great General Ryū Shūkei, Pacifier of the Nation, to receive with courtesy and to deliver [the robe]. I consider it to be a national treasure. Venerable priests, deposit it in its original temple. Let it be solemnly guarded by monks who have intimately received the fundamental teaching. Never let it fall into neglect."

[127] Thus, the emperors of several generations each esteemed [the robe] as an important national treasure. Truly, to retain this Buddha's robe in one's country is a superlative great treasure, which surpasses even dominion over the [worlds] as countless as the sands of the Ganges in a three-thousand-great-thousandfold world. We should never compare it with Benka's gem.[3] [A gem] may become the national seal of state, but how can it become the rare jewel which transmits the Buddha's state? From the Tang dynasty[4] onward, the monks and laymen[5] who admired and bowed to [the *kaṣāya*] were all, without exception, people of great makings who believed in the Dharma. If not aided by good conduct in the past, how else would we be able to prostrate this body in admiration to the Buddha's robe which has been directly and authentically transmitted from buddha to buddha? Skin, flesh, bones, and marrow that believe in and receive [the robe] should rejoice; those that cannot believe in and receive [the robe] should feel regret—even though the situation is of their own doing—that they are not the embryos of buddhas. Even secular [teaching] says that to look at a person's behavior is just to look at that person. To have admired and to have bowed now to the Buddha's robe is just to be looking at the Buddha. We should erect hundreds, thousands, and tens of thousands of stupas and serve offerings to this buddha robe. In the heavens above and in the ocean's depths, whatever has mind
56c should value [the robe]. In the human world too, sacred wheel-turning kings[6] and others who know what is true and know what is superior should value [the robe]. It is pitiful that the people who became, in generation after generation, the rulers of the land never knew what an important treasure existed in their own country. Deluded by the teachings of Daoists, many of them abolished the Buddha-Dharma. At such times, instead of wearing the *kaṣāya,* they covered their round heads with [Daoist] caps.[7] The lectures [they listened to] were on how to extend one's lifespan and to prolong one's years. There were [emperors like this] both during the Tang dynasty and during the Song dynasty. These fellows were rulers of the nation, but they must have

been more vulgar than the common people. They should have quietly reflected that the Buddha's robe had remained and was actually present in their own country. They might even have considered that [their country] was the buddha land of the robe. [The *kaṣāya*] may surpass even [sacred] bones[8] and so on. Wheel-turning kings have bones, as do lions, human beings, *pratyekabuddha*s, and the like. But wheel-turning kings do not have the *kaṣāya,* lions do not have the *kaṣāya,* human beings do not have the *kaṣāya.* Only buddhas have the *kaṣāya.* We should believe this profoundly. Stupid people today often revere bones but fail to know the *kaṣāya.* Few know that they should guard and retain [their own *kaṣāya*]. This situation has arisen because few people have ever heard of the importance of the *kaṣāya,* and [even these few] have never heard of the authentic transmission of the Buddha-Dharma. When we attentively think back to the time when Śākyamuni was in the world, it is little more than two thousand years; many national treasures and sacred objects have been transmitted to the present for longer than this. This Buddha-Dharma and buddha robe are recent and new. The benefit of their propagation through the "fields and villages," even if there have been "fifty propagations," is wonderful.[9] The qualities of those things[10] are obvious [but] this buddha robe 57a
can never be the same as those things. Those things are not received in the authentic transmission from rightful successors, but this [robe] has been received in the authentic transmission from rightful successors. Remember, we attain the truth when listening to a four-line verse, and we attain the state of truth when listening to a single phrase. Why is it that a four-line verse and a single phrase can have such mystical effect? Because they are the Buddha-Dharma. Now, each robe and [all] nine kinds of robes[11] have been received in the authentic transmission from the Buddha-Dharma itself; [the robe] could never be inferior to a four-line verse, and could never be less effective than a single phrase of Dharma. This is why, for more than two thousand years, all followers of the Buddha—those with the makings of devotional practice and of Dharma practice—have guarded and retained the *kaṣāya* and regarded it as their body and mind. Those who are ignorant of the right Dharma of the buddhas do not worship the *kaṣāya.*

[132] Now, such beings as Śakra-devānām-indra and the Dragon King Anavatapta, though they are the celestial ruler of laymen and the king of dragons, have guarded and retained the *kaṣāya.* Yet people who shave the

head, people who call themselves disciples of the Buddha, do not know that they should receive and retain the *kaṣāya.* How much less could they know its material, color, and measurements; how much less could they know the method of wearing it; and how much less could they have seen the dignified conventions for it, even in a dream?

[133] The *kaṣāya* has been called since olden times "the clothing that wards off suffering from heat" and "the clothing of liberation." In conclusion, its merit is beyond measure. Through the merit of the *kaṣāya,* a dragon's scales can be freed from the three kinds of burning pain. When the buddhas realize the truth, they are always wearing this robe. Truly, although we were born in a remote land in [the age of] the latter Dharma, if we have the oppor-
57b tunity to choose between what has been transmitted and what has not been transmitted, we should believe in, receive, guard, and retain [the robe] whose transmission is authentic and traditional. In what lineage have both the robe and the Dharma of Śākyamuni himself been authentically transmitted, as in our authentic tradition? They exist only in Buddhism. On meeting this robe and Dharma, who could be lax in venerating them and serving offerings to them? Even if, each day, we [have to] discard bodies and lives as countless as the sands of the Ganges, we should serve offerings to them. Further, we should vow to meet [the robe] and humbly to receive it upon the head in every life in every age. We are the stupid people of a remote quarter, born with a hundred thousand or so miles of mountains and oceans separating us from the land of the Buddha's birth. Even so, if we hear this right Dharma, if we receive and retain this *kaṣāya* even for a single day or a single night, and if we master even a single phrase or a single verse, that will not only be the good fortune to have served offerings to one buddha or to two buddhas: it will be the good fortune to have served offerings and paid homage to countless hundred thousand *koṭi*s of buddhas. Even if [the servants] are ourselves, we should respect them, we should love them, and we should value them.

[135] We should heartily repay the great benevolence of the ancestral master in transmitting the Dharma.[12] Even animals repay kindness; how could human beings fail to recognize kindness? If we failed to recognize kindness, we would be inferior to animals, more stupid than animals. People other than the ancestral masters who transmit the Buddha's right Dharma have never known the merit of this buddha robe, even in a dream. How much less could

they clarify its material, color, and measurements? If we long to follow the traces of the buddhas, we should just long for this [transmission]. Even after a hundred thousand myriads of generations, the authentic reception of this authentic transmission will [still] be just the Buddha-Dharma itself. The evidence for this is clear. Even secular [teaching] says, "One does not wear clothing different from the clothing of the past king, and one does not follow laws
different from those of the past king." Buddhism is also like that. We should 57c
not wear what is different from the Dharma clothing of past buddhas. If [our clothes] were different from the Dharma clothing of past buddhas, what could we wear to practice Buddhism and to serve buddhas? Without wearing this clothing, it might be difficult to enter the Buddha's order.

[136] Since the years of the Eihei period,[13] during the reign of Emperor Kōmei of the Later Han dynasty, monks arriving in the Eastern Lands from the Western Heavens have followed on each other's heels without cease. We often hear of monks going from China to India, but it is not said that they ever met anyone who gave them the face-to-face transmission of the Buddha-Dharma. They [have] only names and forms, learned in vain from teachers of commentaries and scholars of the Tripiṭaka.[14] They have not heard the authentic tradition of the Buddha-Dharma. This is why they cannot even report that we should receive the authentic transmission of the Buddha's robe, why they never claim to have met a person who has received the authentic transmission of the Buddha's robe, and why they never mention seeing or hearing a person who has received the transmission of the robe. Clearly, they have never entered beyond the threshold of the house of Buddha. That these fellows recognize [the robe] solely as a garment, not knowing that it is in the Buddha-Dharma [an object of] honor and worship, is truly pitiful. Rightful successors to the transmission of the Buddha's Dharma treasury also transmit and receive the Buddha's robe. The principle that the ancestral masters who receive the authentic transmission of the Dharma treasury have never gone without seeing and hearing[15] the Buddha's robe is widely known among human beings and in the heavens above. This being so, the material, color, and measurements of the Buddha's *kaṣāya* have been authentically transmitted and authentically seen and heard; the great merits of the Buddha's *kaṣāya* have been authentically transmitted; and the body, mind, bones, and marrow of the Buddha's *kaṣāya* have been authentically transmitted, only

in the customs of the traditional lineage. [This authentic transmission] is not
58a known in the various schools which follow the teaching of the Āgamas.[16] The [robes] that individuals have established independently, according to the idea of the moment, are not traditional and not legitimate. When our Great Master Śākyamuni Tathāgata passed on the right Dharma-eye treasury and the supreme state of *bodhi* to Mahākāśyapa, he transmitted them together with the buddha robe. Between then and Zen Master Daikan of Sōkeizan, there were thirty-three generations, the transmission passing from rightful successor to rightful successor. The intimate experience and intimate transmission of [the robe's] material, color, and measurements have long been handed down by the lineages, and their reception and retention are evident in the present. That is to say, that which was received and retained by each of the founding patriarchs of the five sects[17] is the authentic tradition. Similarly evident are the wearing [of the robe], according to the methods of former buddhas, and the making [of the robe], according to the methods of former buddhas, which "buddhas alone, together with buddhas," through generations have transmitted and have experienced as the same state—in some cases for over fifty generations and in some cases for over forty generations—without confusion between any master and disciple. The Buddha's instruction, as authentically transmitted from rightful successor to rightful successor, is as follows:

Robe of nine stripes	three long [segments], one short [segment];[18] or four long, one short
Robe of eleven stripes	three long, one short; or four long, one short
Robe of thirteen stripes	three long, one short; or four long, one short
Robe of fifteen stripes	three long, one short
Robe of seventeen stripes	three long, one short
Robe of nineteen stripes	three long, one short
Robe of twenty-one stripes	four long, one short
Robe of twenty-three stripes	four long, one short

Robe of twenty-five stripes	four long, one short
Robe of two hundred and fifty stripes	four long, one short
Robe of eighty-four thousand stripes[19]	eight long, one short

[140] This is an abbreviated list. There are many other kinds of *kaṣāya* besides these, all of which may be the *saṃghāṭi* robe. Some receive and retain [the *kaṣāya*] as laypeople, and some receive and retain [the *kaṣāya*] 58b
as monks and nuns. To receive and to retain [the *kaṣāya*] means to wear it, not to keep it idly folded. Even if people shave off hair and beard, if they do not receive and retain the *kaṣāya,* if they hate the *kaṣāya* or fear the *kaṣāya,* they are celestial demons[20] and non-Buddhists. Zen Master Hyakujō Daichi[21] says, "Those who have not accumulated good seeds in the past detest the *kaṣāya* and hate the *kaṣāya;* they fear and hate the right Dharma."

> [142] The Buddha says, "If any living being, having entered my Dharma, commits the grave sins or falls into wrong views, but in a single moment of consciousness [this person] with reverent mind honors the *saṃghāṭi* robe, the buddhas and I will give affirmation, without fail, that this person will be able to become buddha in the three vehicles. Gods or dragons or human beings or demons, if able to revere the merit of even a small part of this person's *kaṣāya,* will at once attain the three vehicles and will neither regress nor stray. If ghosts and living beings can obtain even four inches of the *kaṣāya,* they will eat and drink their fill. When living beings offend each other and are about to fall into wrong views, if they remember the power of the *kaṣāya,* through the power of the *kaṣāya* they will duly feel compassion, and they will be able to return to the state of purity. If people on a battlefield keep a small part of this *kaṣāya*, venerating it and honoring it, they will obtain salvation."[22]

[143] Thus we have seen that the merits of the *kaṣāya* are supreme and unthinkable. When we believe in, receive, guard, and retain it, we will surely get the state of affirmation, and get the state of not regressing. Not only Śākyamuni Buddha but all the buddhas also have preached like this. Remember, the substance and form of the buddhas themselves is just the *kaṣāya.* This is why the Buddha says, "Those who are going to fall into wrong ways hate

the *saṃghāṭi* [robe]." This being so, if hateful thoughts arise when we see and hear of the *kaṣāya,* we should feel sorry that our own body is going to
58c fall into wrong ways, and we should repent and confess. Furthermore, when Śākyamuni Buddha first left the royal palace and was going to enter the mountains, a tree god, the story goes, holds up a *saṃghāṭi* robe and says to Śākyamuni Buddha, "If you receive this robe upon your head, you will escape the disturbances of demons." Then Śākyamuni Buddha accepts this robe, humbly receiving it upon his head, and for twelve years he does not set it aside even for a moment. This is the teaching of the Āgama sutras. Elsewhere it is said that the *kaṣāya* is a garment of good fortune, and that those who wear it always reach exalted rank. In general, there has never been a moment when this *saṃghāṭi* robe was not manifesting itself before us in the world. The manifestation before us of one moment is an eternal matter,[23] and eternal matters come at one moment. To obtain the *kaṣāya* is to obtain the Buddha's banner. For this reason, none of the buddha-tathāgatas has ever failed to receive and to retain the *kaṣāya.* And no person who has received and retained the *kaṣāya* has failed to become buddha.

[145] The method of wearing the *kaṣāya:* "To bare only the right shoulder" is the usual method. There is also a method of wearing [the *kaṣāya*] so that it covers both shoulders. When we wear both sides over the left arm and shoulder, we wear the front edge on the outside and the back edge on the inside.[24] This is one instance of Buddhist dignified behavior. This behavior is neither seen and heard nor transmitted and received by the various groups of *śrāvaka*s: their scriptures on the teaching of the Āgamas do not mention it at all. In general, the dignified behavior of wearing the *kaṣāya* in Buddhism has been unfailingly received and retained by the ancestral masters who received the transmission of the right Dharma and who are present before us here and now. When receiving and retaining [the *kaṣāya*], we should unfailingly receive and retain it under such an ancestral master. The traditional *kaṣāya* of the Buddhist patriarchs has been authentically transmitted from buddha to buddha without irregularity; it is the *kaṣāya* of former buddhas and
59a of later buddhas, the *kaṣāya* of ancient buddhas and of recent buddhas. When they transform[25] the state of truth, when they transform the state of buddha, when they transform the past, when they transform the present, and when they transform the future, they transmit the authentic tradition from the past

to the present, they transmit the authentic tradition from the present to the future, they transmit the authentic tradition from the present to the past, they transmit the authentic tradition from the past to the past, they transmit the authentic tradition from the present to the present, they transmit the authentic tradition from the future to the future, they transmit the authentic tradition from the future to the present, and they transmit the authentic tradition from the future to the past; and this is the authentic transmission of "buddhas alone, together with buddhas." For this reason, for several hundred years after the ancestral master came from the west, from the great Tang to the great Song [dynasties], many of those accomplished at lecturing on sutras were able to see through their own behavior; and when people of philosophical schools, of precepts, and so on entered the Buddha-Dharma, they threw away the shabby old robes that had formerly been their *kaṣāya,* and they authentically received the traditional *kaṣāya* of Buddhism. Their stories appear one after another in *Records of the Torch* such as *Den*[*tōroku*], *Kō*[*tōroku*], *Zoku*[*tōroku*], *Futōroku,* and so on.[26] When they were liberated from the small view which is limited thinking about philosophy and precepts and they revered the great truth authentically transmitted by the Buddhist patriarchs, they all became Buddhist patriarchs. People today also should learn from the ancestral masters of the past. If we would like to receive and to retain the *kaṣāya,* we should receive the authentic transmission of, and should believe in, the traditional *kaṣāya.* We should not receive and retain a fake *kaṣāya.* The traditional *kaṣāya* means the *kaṣāya* now authentically transmitted from Shaolin [Temple] and Sōkei [Mountain];[27] its reception from the Tathāgata in the transmission from rightful successor to rightful successor has never been interrupted for even a single generation. For this reason we have exactly received the practice of the truth, and we have intimately obtained, in our own hands, the Buddha's robe; and this is the reason [we should receive the authentic transmission]. The Buddha's [state of] truth is authentically transmitted in the Buddha's [state of] truth; it is not left for lazy people to receive at leisure. A secular proverb says, "Hearing a thousand times is not as good as seeing once, and seeing a thousand times is not as good as experiencing once." Reflecting on this, [we can say that] even if we see [the *kaṣāya*] a thousand times and hear of it ten thousand times, that is not as good as getting it once, and never as good as to have received the authentic transmission of the Buddha's robe. If 59b

we can doubt those who have authentic traditions, we should doubt all the more those who have never seen the authentic traditions even in a dream. To receive the authentic transmission of the Buddha's robe may be closer [in experience] than to receive and to hear Buddhist sutras. Even a thousand experiences and ten thousand attainments are not as good as one realization in experience. A Buddhist patriarch is the realization of the same state of experience; we should never rank [a Buddhist patriarch] with common followers of philosophy and precepts. In conclusion, with regard to the merits of the *kaṣāya* of the Patriarch's lineage, [we can say that] its authentic transmission has been received exactly; [that] its original configuration has been conveyed personally; and [that] it has been received and retained, together with the succession of the Dharma, without interruption until today. The authentic recipients are all ancestral masters who have experienced the same state and received the transmission of Dharma. They are superior even to [bodhisattvas at] the ten sacred stages and the three clever stages; we should serve and venerate them and should bow down to them and humbly receive them upon our heads. If this principle of the authentic transmission of the Buddha's robe is believed just once by this body and mind, that is a sign of meeting buddha, and it is the way to learn the state of buddha. [A life] in which we could not accept this Dharma would be a sad life. We should profoundly affirm that if we cover the physical body, just once, with this *kaṣāya,* it will be a talisman that protects the body and ensures realization of the state of *bodhi.* It is said that when we dye the believing mind with a single phrase or a single verse we never lack the brightness of long *kalpa*s. When we dye the body and mind with one real *dharma,* [the state] may be "also like this." Those mental images[28] are without an abode and are irrelevant to what I possess; even so, their merits are indeed as described above. The physical body is without an abode; even so, it is as described above. The *kaṣāya,* too, is without an origin and also without a destination, it is neither our own possession nor the possession of anyone else; even so, it actually abides at the place where it is retained, and it covers the person who receives and retains it. The merits acquired [by virtue of the *kaṣāya*] may also be like this. When we make the *kaṣāya,* the making is not the elaboration[29] of the common, the sacred, and the like. The import of this is not perfectly realized by [bodhisattvas at] the ten sacred or the three
59c clever [stages]. Those who have not accumulated seeds of the truth in the past

do not see the *kaṣāya,* do not hear of the *kaṣāya*, and do not know the *kaṣāya,* not in one life, not in two lives, not even if they pass countless lives. How much less could they receive and retain [the *kaṣāya*]? There are those who attain, and those who do not attain, the merit to touch [the *kaṣāya*] once with the body. Those who have attained [this merit] should rejoice. Those who have not attained it should hope to do so. Those who can never attain it should lament. All human beings and gods have seen, heard, and universally recognized that the Buddha's robe is transmitted—both inside and outside the great-thousandfold-world—only in the lineage of the Buddhist patriarchs. Clarification of the configuration of the Buddha's robe also is present only in the lineage of the patriarchs, it is not known in other lineages. Those who do not know it and [yet] do not blame themselves are stupid people. Even if they know eighty-four thousand *samādhi-dhāraṇīs*,[30] without receiving the authentic transmission of the Buddhist patriarchs' robe and Dharma, without clarifying the authentic transmission of the *kaṣāya,* they can never be the rightful successors of the buddhas. How the living beings of other regions must long to receive exactly the authentic transmission of the Buddha's robe, as it has been authentically received in China. They must be ashamed, their sorrow in their hearts must be deep, that they have not received the authentic transmission in their own country. Truly, to meet the Dharma in which the robe and the Dharma of the World-honored Tathāgata have been authentically transmitted is the result of seeds of great merit from past-nurtured *prajñā.* Now, in this corrupt age of the latter Dharma, there are many bands of demons who are not ashamed that they themselves lack the authentic transmission, and who envy the authentic transmission [of others]. Our own possessions and abodes are not our real selves. Just authentically to receive the authentic transmission; this is the direct way to learn the state of buddha.

[153] In sum, remember that the *kaṣāya* is the body of the Buddha and the mind of the Buddha. Further, it is called "the clothing of liberation," called 60a
"the robe of a field of happiness," called "the robe of endurance," called "the robe without form," called "the robe of compassion," called "the robe of the Tathāgata," and called "the robe of *anuttara samyaksaṃbodhi.*" We must receive and retain it as such. In the great kingdom of Song today, people who call themselves students of the precepts, because they are drunk on the wine of the *śrāvaka,* are neither ashamed, regretful, nor aware that they have received

the transmission of a lineage which is alien to their own clan. Having changed the *kaṣāya* that has been transmitted from the Western Heavens and handed down through the ages from Han to Tang China, they follow small thoughts. It is due to the small view that they are like that, and they should be ashamed of [their] small view. Given that they now wear a robe [based on] their own small thinking, they probably lack many [other] of the Buddhist dignified forms. Such things happen because their learning of, and reception of the transmission of, the Buddhist forms, are incomplete. The fact is evident that the body and mind of the Tathāgata has been authentically transmitted only in the lineage of the patriarchs, and it has not spread into the customs of those other lineages. If they knew only one Buddhist form in ten thousand they would never destroy the Buddha's robe. Not having clarified even [the meaning of] sentences, they have never been able to hear the fundamental.

[155] There again, to decide that coarse cotton is the only material for the robe runs deeply counter to the Buddha-Dharma; above all it ruins the buddha robe. Disciples of the Buddha should not wear [a robe made according to this rule]. Why? [Because] to uphold a view about cloth ruins the *kaṣāya*. It is pitiful that the views of the *śrāvaka* of the Small Vehicle are so tortuous. After their views about cloth have been demolished, the Buddha's robe will be realized. What I am saying about the use of silk and cotton is not the teaching of one buddha or two buddhas; it is the great Dharma of all the buddhas to see rags as the best and purest material for the robe. When, for the present,
60b ent, we list the ten sorts of rags among those [rags], they include silk, cotton, and other kinds of cloth too.[31] Must we not take rags of silk? If we are like that, we go against the Buddha's truth. If we hated silk, we would also have to hate cotton. Where is the reason to hate silk or cotton? To hate silk thread because it is produced by killing is very laughable. Is cotton not the habitat of living things? Sentiment about sentience and insentience is not liberated from the sentiment of the common and sentimental: how could it know the Buddha's *kaṣāya*? There is further speaking of nonsense by those who bring forth arguments about transformed thread.[32] This also is laughable. Which [material] is not a transformation? Those people believe the ears that hear of "transformation," but they doubt the eyes that see transformation itself. They seem to have no ears in their eyes, and no eyes in their ears. Where are their ears and eyes at the moment of the present?[33] Now remember, while we are

collecting rags, there may be cotton that looks like silk and there may be silk that looks like cotton. When we use it, we should not call it silk and we should not call it cotton; we should just call it rags. Because it is rags it is, as rags, beyond silk and beyond cotton. Even if there are human beings or gods who have survived as rags, we should not call them sentient, [but] they may be rags. Even if there are pine trees or chrysanthemums which have become rags, we should not call them insentient, [but] they may be rags. When we recognize the truth that rags are neither silk nor cotton, and that they are beyond pearls and jewels, rags are realized and we meet rags for the first time. Before views about silk and cotton have withered and fallen, we have never seen rags even in a dream. If we retain views about the cloth—even if we have spent a lifetime receiving and retaining coarse cotton cloth
as a *kaṣāya*—that is not the authentic transmission of the Buddha's robe. At 60c
the same time, the various kinds of *kaṣāya* include cotton *kaṣāya,* silk *kaṣāya,* and leather *kaṣāya:* all of these have been worn by buddhas. They have the Buddhist merits of the Buddha's robe, and they possess the fundamental principle that has been authentically transmitted without interruption. But people who are not liberated from common sentiment make light of the Buddha-Dharma; not believing the Buddha's words, they aim blindly to follow the sentiment of the common person. They must be called non-Buddhists who have attached themselves to the Buddha-Dharma; they are people who destroy the right Dharma. Some claim to have changed the buddha robe in accordance with the teaching of celestial beings. In that case, they must aspire to celestial buddhahood. Or have they become the descendants of gods? The Buddha's disciples expound the Buddha-Dharma for celestial beings; they should not ask celestial beings about the truth. It is pitiful that those who lack the authentic transmission of the Buddha-Dharma are like this. The view of the celestial multitudes and the view of the Buddha's disciples are very different in greatness, but gods come down to seek instruction in the Dharma from the Buddha's disciples. The reason is that the Buddhist view and the celestial view are very different. Discard, and do not learn, the small views of *śrāvaka*s of precepts sects. Remember that they are the Small Vehicle. The Buddha says, "One can repent for killing one's father or killing one's mother, but one cannot repent for insulting the Dharma."

[160] In general, the way of small views and foxlike suspicion is not the original intention of the Buddha. The great truth of the Buddha-Dharma is beyond the Small Vehicle. No one outside of the Patriarch's state of truth, which is transmitted with the Dharma treasury, has known of the authentic transmission of the great precepts of the buddhas. Long ago, [the story goes,] in the middle of the night on Ōbaizan, the Buddha's robe and Dharma are transmitted authentically onto the head of the Sixth Patriarch.[34] This is truly the authentic tradition for transmission of the Dharma and transmission of the robe. It is [possible] because the Fifth Patriarch knows a person.[35] Fel-
61a lows of the fourth effect and the three clever stages, as well as the likes of [bodhisattvas in] the ten sacred stages[36] and the likes of commentary teachers and sutra teachers of philosophical schools, would give the [robe and Dharma] to Jinshū;[37] they would not transmit them authentically to the Sixth Patriarch. Nevertheless, when Buddhist patriarchs select Buddhist patriarchs, they transcend the path of common sentiment, and so the Sixth Patriarch has already become the Sixth Patriarch. Remember, the truth of knowing a person and of knowing oneself, which the Buddhist patriarchs transmit from rightful successor to rightful successor, is not easily supposed. Later, a monk asks the Sixth Patriarch, "Should we see the robe you received in the middle of the night on Ōbai[zan] as cotton, or should we see it as silk, or should we see it as raw silk?[38] In short, as what material should we see it?" The Sixth Patriarch says, "It is not cotton, it is not silk, and it is not raw silk." The words of the Founding Patriarch of Sōkei are like this. Remember, the buddha robe is not silk, not cotton, and not cotton crepe. Those who, on the contrary, heedlessly recognize [the robe] as silk, as cotton, or as cotton crepe are the sort who insult the Buddha-Dharma. How could they know the Buddha's *kaṣāya*? Furthermore, there are episodes of the precepts being taken with [the Buddha's] "Welcome!" That the *kaṣāya* gained by these [monks] is utterly beyond discussion of silk and cotton is the Buddha's instruction in the Buddhist truth. In another case, the robe of Śāṇavāsa when he is a layman is a secular garment, but when he leaves family life it becomes a *kaṣāya.* We should quietly consider this fact. We should not brush it aside as if we did not see or hear it. Moreover, there is a fundamental principle which has been authentically transmitted from buddha to buddha, and from patriarch to patriarch, and which the sort who count words in sentences cannot sense and cannot fathom. Truly,

how could the thousand changes and the myriad transformations of the Buddha's truth belong in the limited area of ordinary folk? The [real state of] *samādhi* exists, and [real practices of] *dhāraṇī*[39] exist, [but] those who count grains of sand can never find [these] valuable pearls inside their clothes. We 61b
should esteem, as the right standard of the *kaṣāya* of all the buddhas, the material, color, and measurements of the present *kaṣāya* that has been received in the authentic transmission from Buddhist patriarchs. The precedents for it, in the Western Heavens and the Eastern Lands, going back to ancient times and arriving at the present, are of long standing; and people who have distinguished the right [precedents] from the wrong have already transcended the state of enlightenment. Even though outside of the Buddhism of the patriarchs there are those who claim [to have] the *kaṣāya,* no original patriarch has ever affirmed [their robes] as the twigs and leaves [of the original *kaṣāya*]; how could [their robes] germinate the seeds of good roots?[40] How much less could they bear real fruit? We now not only are seeing and hearing Buddha-Dharma that we have not met in vast *kalpa*s; we [also] have been able to see and to hear the Buddha's robe, to learn about the Buddha's robe, and to receive and to retain the Buddha's robe. This just exactly means that we are meeting the Buddha, we are hearing the voice of the Buddha, we are radiating the brightness of the Buddha, we are receiving and using the state received and used by the Buddha, we are receiving the one-to-one transmission of the mind of the Buddha, and we are getting the Buddha's marrow.

[165] For material to make the *kaṣāya* we invariably use that which is pure. Pure describes material offered by a donor of pure faith, or bought at a market, or sent by celestial beings, or donated by dragons, or donated by demons, or donated by kings and ministers, or [even] pure leather. We may use all such material. At the same time, we esteem the ten sorts of rags as pure. The ten sorts of rags are namely:

1) Rags chewed by an ox, 2) rags gnawed by rats, 3) rags scorched by fire, 4) rags [soiled by] menstruation, 5) rags [soiled by] childbirth, 6) rags [offered at] a shrine, 7) rags [left at] a graveyard, 8) rags [offered in] petitional prayer, 9) rags [discarded by] a king's officers, 10) rags brought back [from a funeral].

[166] We esteem these ten sorts as especially pure material. In secular 61c
society they throw them away, [but] in Buddhism we use them. From these

customs we can know the difference between the secular world and Buddhism. So when we want pure [material] we should look for these ten sorts. Finding them, we can know what is pure and we can intuit and affirm what is not pure. We can know mind and we can intuit and affirm body. When we obtain these ten sorts, whether they are silk or whether they are cotton, we should consider their purity and impurity. If we understand that the reason we use these rags is to idly make ourselves shabby with shabby robes, that might be extremely stupid. Rags have [always] been used in Buddhism for their splendor and beauty. In Buddhism, what makes our attire shabby is clothes which have come from impurity—[clothes of] brocade, embroidered silk, silk twill, and sheer silk, [clothes of] gold, silver, precious gems, and so on. This is the meaning of shabbiness. In general, whether in the Buddhism of this land or of other worlds, when we use pure and beautiful [cloth], it should be of these ten sorts. Not only has it transcended the limitations of purity and impurity, it also is beyond the limited sphere of the superfluous and the absence of the superfluous.[41] Do not discuss it as matter or mind. It is not connected with gain and loss. [The fact] is only that those who receive and retain the authentic transmission are Buddhist patriarchs; for when we are in the state of a Buddhist patriarch we receive the authentic transmission. To receive and to retain this [transmission] as a Buddhist patriarch does not depend on manifestation or nonmanifestation of the body, and does not depend on upholding or non-upholding of the mind, [but] the authentic transmission goes on being received. Absolutely, we should regret that in this country, Japan, monks and nuns of recent ages have, for a long time, gone without wearing the *kaṣāya;* and we should be glad that we can receive and retain [the *kaṣāya*] now. Even laymen and laywomen who receive and keep the Buddhist precepts should wear the five-stripe, seven-stripe, and nine-stripe
62a *kaṣāya*. How then could people who have left family life fail to wear [the *kaṣāya*]? It is said that [everyone] from King Brahmā and the gods of the six heavens,[42] down to secular men, secular women, and male and female slaves, should receive the Buddhist precepts and wear the *kaṣāya;* how could *bhikṣu*s and *bhikṣuṇī*s fail to wear it? It is said that even animals should receive the Buddhist precepts and wear the *kaṣāya*; how could disciples of the Buddha fail to wear the Buddha's robe? So those who want to become disciples of the Buddha, regardless of whether they are gods above, human

beings, kings of nations, or government officials, and irrespective of whether they are laypeople, monks, slaves, or animals, should receive and keep the Buddhist precepts and should receive the authentic transmission of the *kaṣāya.* This is just the direct way to enter authentically into the state of buddha.

> [170] "When washing the *kaṣāya,* you should mix miscellaneous powdered incense into the water. After drying [the *kaṣāya*] in the sun, fold it and put it in a high place, serve offerings to it of incense and flowers, and make three prostrations. Then, kneeling up, humbly receive it upon the head and, with the hands joined, render devotion by reciting the following verse:
>
> How great is the clothing of liberation,
> Formless, field of happiness, robe!
> Devoutly wearing the Tathāgata's teaching,
> Widely I will save living beings.
>
> After reciting [this verse] three times, stand up on the ground and wear [the *kaṣāya*] devoutly."[43]

[170] During my stay in Song China, making effort on the long platform, I saw that my neighbor every morning, at the time of releasing the stillness, would lift up his *kaṣāya* and place it on his head; then, holding his hands together in veneration, he would silently recite the verse. At that time, there arose in me a feeling I had never before experienced. [My] body was overfilled with joy, and tears of gratitude secretly fell and moistened the lapels of my gown. The reason was that when I had read the Āgama sutras previously, I had noticed sentences about humbly receiving the *kaṣāya* upon the head, but I had not clarified the standards for this behavior and had not understood it clearly. Seeing it done now, before my very eyes, I was overjoyed. I thought to myself, "It is a pity that when I was in my homeland there was no master to teach [me] this, and no good friend to tell [me] of it. How could I not regret, how could I not deplore, passing so much time in vain? Seeing it 62b
and hearing it now, I can rejoice in past good conduct. If I had been idly rubbing shoulders in the temples of my home country, how could I have sat shoulder-to-shoulder with this treasure of a monk who is actually wearing the Buddha's robe?" Sadness and joy were not one-sided. Tears of gratitude fell

in thousands and tens of thousands. Then I secretly vowed, "One way or another, unworthy though I am, I will receive the authentic transmission of the right traditions of the Buddha-Dharma and, out of compassion for living beings in my homeland, I will cause them to see and to hear the robe and the Dharma that have been authentically transmitted from buddha to buddha." The vow made at that time has not now been in vain; the bodhisattvas, in families and out of families, who have received and retained the *kaṣāya* are many. This is a matter in which to rejoice. People who have received and retained the *kaṣāya* should humbly receive it upon their head every day and night. The merit [of this] may be especially excellent and supremely excellent. The seeing and hearing of a phrase or a verse may be as in the story of "on trees and on rocks," [but] the merit of the authentic transmission of the *kaṣāya* is hardly encountered through the ten directions. In the tenth lunar month, in the winter of the seventeenth year of Kajō in great Song [China], two Korean[44] monks came to the city of Keigenfu. One was called Chigen, the other Keiun. Both of them were always discussing the meaning of Buddhist sutras, and they were also men of letters. But they had no *kaṣāya* and no *pātra;* they were like secular people. It was pitiful that though they had the external form of *bhikṣu*s they did not have the Dharma of *bhikṣu*s. This may have been because they were from a minor nation in a remote land. When people from our country who have the external form of *bhikṣu*s travel abroad, they are likely to be the same as those two monks. Śākyamuni Buddha himself received [the *kaṣāya*] upon his head for twelve years, never setting it aside. As already his distant descendants, we should emulate this. To turn the forehead away from pros-
62c trations idly done for fame and gain to gods, to spirits, to kings, and to retainers, and to turn it now toward the humble reception upon the head of the Buddha's robe, is a joyful and great happy event.

Shōbōgenzō Den-e

The first day of winter, in the first year of Ninji.[45]

Written at Kannondōrikōshōhōrinji
—a *śramaṇa* who entered Song [China] and received the transmission of Dharma, Dōgen.

Notes

[1] Chapter Twelve, *Kesa-kudoku,* begins *butsu-butsu so-so,* "from buddha to buddha, and from patriarch to patriarch." The difference presumably arose from Master Dōgen's feeling on the day.

[2] "Until his death" is *shōzen,* lit., "life-before." In *Kesa-kudoku* the expression is *isshō,* lit., "throughout his life." Again, the difference is incidental.

[3] Benka was a man in ancient China who found a huge gem, one foot in diameter. He offered it to three kings, but none of them valued the gem at all. In this context, Benka's gem is simply used as an example of something that is very valuable, but not on the same level as the *kaṣāya.*

[4] 619–858.

[5] "Monks and laymen" is originally "black and white," symbolizing the clothes of monks and laymen respectively.

[6] "Sacred wheel-turning kings" is *ten-rin-jō-ō,* from the Sanskrit *cakravarti-rājya.* These legendary kings were said to govern the four continents east, west, north, and south of Mount Sumeru. The king with the gold wheel rules all four continents, the king with the silver wheel rules all continents but the north, the king with the copper wheel rules the east and south, and the king with the iron wheel rules only the southern continent.

[7] *Yōkin,* lit., "leaf-cloth."

[8] *Shari* represents the Sanskrit *śarīra,* which literally means bones but which often suggests the Buddha's relics.

[9] *Nyakuden-nyakuri,* "fields and villages," and *gojū-tenden,* "fifty propagations," allude to a passage in the eighteenth chapter of the *Lotus Sutra, Zuiki-kudoku.* See LS 3.72-74.

[10] National treasures and sacred relics.

[11] The nine kinds of robe are the robes of nine stripes, eleven stripes, thirteen stripes, fifteen stripes, seventeen stripes, nineteen stripes, twenty-one stripes, twenty-three stripes, and twenty-five stripes.

[12] Refers to Master Bodhidharma's transmission of the Dharma into China.

[13] 58 to 76 C.E.

[14] *Sanzō,* lit., "three storehouses," represents the Sanskrit Tripiṭaka, or three baskets, namely: precepts (Vinaya), Sutra, and commentaries (Abhidharma).

[15] "Seeing" means knowing the concrete form, and "hearing" means understanding the principles.

[16] Many Hinayana Buddhist traditions are based on the teachings of the Āgama sutras.

[17] Master Tōzan, Master Rinzai, Master Hōgen, Master Isan, and Master Unmon. See Chapter Forty-nine, *Butsudō.*

[18] That is, three long segments and one short segment in each stripe.

[19] In Buddhist sutras, eighty-four thousand signifies a very large number.

[20] *Tenma,* celestial demons, symbolize idealistic people who disturb Buddhism.

[21] Master Hyakujō Ekai (749–814), a successor of Master Baso Dōitsu. Zen Master Daichi is his posthumous title.

[22] This is a summarized list of the five sacred merits of the *kaṣāya,* from chapter 8 of the *Higekyō* (*Karuṇāpuṇḍarīka-sūtra*). A longer enumeration of the five sacred merits, from the same sutra, appears in Chapter Twelve, *Kesa-kudoku,* paragraph 80.

[23] *Chōgō no ji,* lit., "a matter in long *kalpa*s."

[24] When the *kaṣāya* has been opened behind the back and the strings tied, and the left and right hand are holding the top corners of the *kaṣāya,* the border running vertically down from the right hand is *zento,* "the front edge," and the border running vertically down from the left hand is *koto,* "the back edge." The right hand brings the top of the "front edge" around the front of the body and over the left shoulder.

[25] "Transform" is *ke.* The character often appears in the compound *kyoke,* lit., "teach-transform," that is, to teach, to educate, or to instruct.

[26] Refers to the *Gotōroku* (*Five Records of the Torch*), compiled during the Song period (960–1297), namely: 1) *Dentōroku* or *Keitokudentōroku* (*Keitoku Era Record of the Transmission of the Torch*), completed by a monk called Dōgen in 1004, the first year of the Keitoku era. It contains the histories of one thousand seven hundred and one Buddhists, from the seven ancient buddhas to Master Hōgen Bun'eki (855–958). 2) *Kōtōroku* or *Tenshōkōtōroku* (*Tenshō Era Record of the Widely Extending Torch*), compiled by the layman Ri Junkyoku during the Tenshō era (1023–1031). 3) *Zokutōroku* (*Supplementary Record of the Torch*), completed by Master Ihaku of Bukkōku Temple in 1101, during the Kenchū-seikoku era. 4) *Rentōeyō* (*Collection of Essentials for Continuation of the Torch*), completed in 1183 and published in 1189. 5) *Futōroku* or *Kataifutōroku* (*Katai Era Record of the Universal Torch*), compiled by Master Shōju of Raian Temple during the Katai era (1201–1204).

[27] That is, from Master Bodhidharma and Master Daikan Enō.

[28] Of the believing mind described above.

[29] *Sa,* to produce, to make, or to do, sometimes represents the Sanskrit *saṃskṛta,* which describes elaboration or artificiality. *Sa* thus includes the connotation of intentional effort. See Chapter Ten, *Shoaku-makusa.* Master Dōgen describes zazen as *musa,* "without elaboration" or "unadorned," that is, natural.

[30] *Samādhi* means the balanced state, and *dhāraṇī* means a mystical formula. So *samādhi-dhāraṇīs* are mystical formulae, the incantation of which is supposed to lead the practitioner into the balanced state.

[31] The ten sorts of rags are given at the end of paragraph 165 in this chapter. The point of the classification is to determine how rags were discarded, not their original material.

[32] Some people thought that silk is the result of an artificial process, and is therefore not natural.

[33] To hear with the eyes and to see with the ears suggests inclusive intuition, as opposed to discriminating intellectual recognition and sensory perception.

[34] The story of the transmission between Master Daiman Kōnin and Master Daikan Enō is contained in Chapter Thirty (Vol. II), *Gyōji. Chōjō ni,* "on top of the head," suggests the behavior of placing the *kaṣāya* on the head in veneration.

[35] The ability to know a true person is discussed at the end of Chapter Fifty-two (Vol. III), *Bukkyō.* At the time of the transmission, Master Daikan Enō was employed as a laborer at the temple.

[36] A *śrāvaka* passes through four stages: 1) *srotāpanna* (entry into the stream), 2) *sakṛdāgāmin* (the state of being subject to one return), 3) *anāgāmin* (the state which is not subject to returning), and 4) arhat (the fourth effect, which is the ultimate state of the *śrāvaka*). A bodhisattva passes through fifty-two stages or states: ten stages of belief, thirty states classified as the three clever stages, ten sacred stages, the balanced state of truth (*tōkaku*), and finally the fine state of truth (*myōkaku*).

[37] Ācārya Jinshū was the most intelligent monk in Master Daiman Kōnin's order, accomplished at poetry and revered by emperors. See Chapter Twenty-two (Vol. II), *Kokyō.*

[38] "Raw silk" means silk that has not been dyed.

[39] Master Dōgen interpreted *dhāraṇīs* as concrete practices that have real power. See Chapter Fifty-five (Vol. III), *Darani.*

[40] *Zenkon* means good conduct as the root of happiness.

[41] *Rō* and *murō,* which represent the Sanskrit *āsrava* and *anāsrava,* suggest the presence and absence of emotional distress.

[42] *Rokuten* or *roku-yoku-ten,* are the six heavens of the world of volition, or (as in this case) the gods therein.

[43] This paragraph is in the form of a quotation from a sutra in Chinese. The content is the same as the second half of paragraph 78 on washing the *kaṣāya* in the previous chapter, *Kesa-kudoku.* But that paragraph is written in Japanese, whereas this paragraph is written in Chinese characters only.

[44] "Korean" is *sankan,* "three Koreas." In *Kesa-kudoku* the word is Kōrai, which was the name of one of the three states comprising the Korean peninsula at that time.

[45] The first day of the tenth lunar month, 1240.

[Chapter Fourteen]

Sansuigyō

The Sutra of Mountains and Water

Translator's Note: San *means "mountains,"* sui *means "water"—rivers, lakes, and so on.* Sansui *suggests natural scenery, or nature itself.* Kyō *or* gyō *means Buddhist sutras. So* Sansuigyō *means mountains and water, or nature, as Buddhist sutras. Buddhism is basically a religion of belief in the universe, and nature is the universe showing its real form. So to look at nature is to look at the Buddhist truth itself. For this reason Master Dōgen believed that nature is just Buddhist sutras. In this chapter he explains the real form of nature, giving particular emphasis to relativity in nature.*

[175] The mountains and water of the present are the realization of the words of eternal buddhas. Both [mountains and water] abide in place in the Dharma, having realized ultimate virtue. Because they are in the state before the *kalpa* of emptiness, they are vigorous activity in the present. Because they are the self before the sprouting of creation, they are real liberation. The virtues of the mountains are so high and wide that we always realize moral virtue which can ride the clouds by relying on the mountains, and we unfailingly liberate the subtle effectiveness which follows the wind by relying on the mountains.

[176] Master Kai[1] of Taiyōzan preaches to the assembly, "The Blue Mountains are constantly walking. The Stone Woman bears children by night." Mountains lack none of the virtues with which mountains should be equipped. For this reason, they are constantly abiding in stillness and constantly walking. We must painstakingly learn in practice the virtue of this walking. The walking of mountains must be like the walking of human beings; 63a
therefore, even though it does not look like human walking,[2] do not doubt the walking of the mountains. The words preached now by the Buddhist Patriarch are already pointing to "walking," and this is his attainment of the fundamental. We should pursue to the ultimate his preaching to the assembly about "constant walking": it is because [the mountains] are walking that

they are "constant."[3] The walking of the Blue Mountains is swifter than the wind, but human beings in the mountains do not sense it or know it. Being "in the mountains"[4] describes the "opening of flowers" in the "[real] world."[5] People out of the mountains never sense it and never know it—people who have no eyes to see the mountains do not sense, do not know, do not see, and do not hear this concrete fact. If we doubt the walking of the mountains, we also do not yet know our own walking. It is not that we do not have our own walking, but we do not yet know and have not yet clarified our own walking. When we know our own walking, then we will surely also know the walking of the Blue Mountains. The Blue Mountains are already beyond the sentient and beyond the insentient. The self is already beyond the sentient and beyond the insentient. We cannot doubt the present walking of the Blue Mountains. [Though] we do not know how many Dharma worlds we should use as a scale when taking in the Blue Mountains, we should investigate in detail the walking of the Blue Mountains as well as our own walking. There should be investigation both of backward steps[6] and of stepping backward.[7] We should investigate the fact that just at the moment before the sprouting of creation, and since before the King of Emptiness,[8] walking—in forward steps and backward steps—has never stopped even for an instant. If the walking ceased, the Buddhist patriarchs could not manifest themselves in reality. If there were an end to the walking, the Buddha-Dharma could not reach the present day. Forward walking never ceases, and backward walking never ceases. The moment of forward walking does not oppose backward walking, and the moment of backward walking does not oppose forward walking.[9] We call this virtue "the mountains flowing," and we call it "the flowing mountains." The Blue Mountains master in practice the act of walking and the East Mountain learns in practice the act of moving on water; therefore, this learning in practice is the mountains' learning in practice. The mountains, without changing their body and mind, with the face and eyes of mountains, have been traveling around learning in practice. Never insult them by saying that the Blue Mountains cannot walk or that the East Mountain cannot move on water. It is because of the grossness of the viewpoint of the vulgar that they doubt the phrase "the Blue Mountains are walking." It is due to the poorness of their scant experience that they are astonished at the words "flowing mountains." Now, not even fully understanding[10] the

63b

words "flowing water," they are drowned in prejudice and ignorance. This being so, they esteem as defining concepts, and esteem as lifeblood, their enumeration of the accumulated virtues [of mountains].[11] The act of walking exists, the act of flowing exists, and moments in which mountains give birth to mountain children exist. By virtue of the fact that mountains become Buddhist patriarchs, Buddhist patriarchs have manifested themselves in reality like this.[12] Though there may be eyes in which grass, trees, soil, stones, fences, and walls are realized, that moment is beyond doubt and beyond disturbance; it is not "total realization." Though moments are realized in which [the mountains] are seen to be adorned with the seven treasures, [those moments] are not "the real refuge." Though visions are realized [of the mountains] as the area in which buddhas practice the truth, [those visions] are not necessarily something to be loved. Though some have got the brains to realize a vision [of the mountains] as the unthinkable merit of the buddhas, reality is not merely this.[13] Every "realization" is an instance of object and subject. We do not esteem such ["realizations"] as the Buddhist patriarchs' action in the state of truth: they are one-sided and narrow views.[14] The moving of circumstances and the moving of mind are criticized by the Great Saint.[15] Explanations of mind and explanations of the nature[16] are not affirmed by the Buddhist patriarchs. Seeing the mind and seeing the nature[17] is the animated activity of non-Buddhists. Staying in words and staying in phrases is not the speech of liberation. There is [a state] that has got free from states like these: it is expressed "the Blue Mountains are constantly walking" and 63c
"the East Mountain moves on water." We should master it in detail.

[182] [In the words] "The Stone Woman bears children by night" time, in which the Stone Woman bears children, is called night. In general, there are male stones and female stones, and there are neither male nor female stones, whose practical function supports the heavens and supports the earth. There are heavenly stones and there are earthly stones—as the secular say, but few people know.[18] We should know the facts of childbirth: At the time of childbirth, are parent and child both transformed? How could we learn in practice only that childbirth is realized as [the parent] becoming the parent of a child? We should learn in practice, and should penetrate to the end, that the time of [the child] becoming the child of the parent is the practice-and-experience of the reality of childbirth.

[183] Great Master Unmon Kyōshin[19] says, "The East Mountain moves on water." The point realized in these words is that all mountains are an East Mountain, and every East Mountain moves on water.[20] Thus [mountains] such as the nine mountains of Mount Sumeru have been realized, and they have practiced and experienced.[21] This state is called "the East Mountain." Nevertheless, how could Unmon be liberated in the skin, flesh, bones, and marrow, the practice-and-experience, and the vigorous activity of the East Mountain.[22]

[184] At the present time in the great kingdom of Song, there is a group of unreliable[23] fellows who have now formed such a crowd that they cannot be beaten by a few real [people]. They say that the present talk of the East Mountain moving on water, and stories such as Nansen's sickle,[24] are stories beyond rational understanding. Their idea is as follows: "A story which involves images and thoughts is not a Zen story of the Buddhist patriarchs. Stories beyond rational understanding are the stories of the Buddhist patriarchs. This is why we esteem Ōbaku's use of the stick and Rinzai's shout,[25] which are beyond rational understanding and which do not involve images and thoughts, as the great realization before the sprouting of creation. The reason that the expedient means of many past masters employ tangle-cutting[26] phrases is that [those phrases] are beyond rational understanding."
64a Those fellows who speak like this have never met a true teacher and they have no eyes of learning in practice; they are small dogs who do not deserve to be discussed. For the last two or three hundred years in the land of Song there have been many such demons and shavelings [like those] in the band of six.[27] It is pitiful that the great truth of the Buddhist Patriarch is going to ruin. The understanding of these [shavelings] is inferior even to that of *śrāvaka*s of the Small Vehicle; they are more stupid than non-Buddhists. They are not laypeople, they are not monks, they are not human beings, and they are not gods; they are more stupid than animals learning the Buddha's truth. What the shavelings call "stories beyond rational understanding" are beyond rational understanding only to them;[28] the Buddhist patriarchs are not like that. Even though [rational ways] are not rationally understood by those [shavelings], we should not fail to learn in practice the Buddhist patriarchs' ways of rational understanding. If ultimately there is no rational understanding, the reasoning which those [shavelings] have now set forth also

cannot hit the target. There are many of this sort in all directions of Song China, and I have seen and heard them before my own eyes. They are pitiful. They do not know that images and thoughts are words and phrases, and they do not know that words and phrases transcend images and thoughts. When I was in China I laughed at them, but they had nothing to say for themselves and were just wordless. Their present negation of rational understanding is nothing but a false notion. Who has taught it to them? Though they lack a natural teacher, they have the non-Buddhist view of naturalism. Remember, this "The East Mountain moves on water" is the bones and marrow of the Buddhist patriarchs. Waters are realized at the foot of the East Mountain;[29] thereupon mountains ride the clouds and walk through the sky. The crowns of the waters are mountains, whose walking, upward or downward, is always "on water."[30] Because the mountains' toes can walk over all kinds of water, making the waters dance, the walking is free in all directions[31] and "practice-and-experience is not nonexistent."[32] Water is neither 64b
strong nor weak, neither wet nor dry, neither moving nor still, neither cold nor warm, neither existent nor nonexistent, neither delusion nor realization. When it is solid it is harder than a diamond; who could break it? Melted, it is softer than diluted milk; who could break it? This being so, it is impossible to doubt the real virtues that [water] possesses. For the present, we should learn in practice the moments in which it is possible to put on the eyes and look in the ten directions at the water of the ten directions. This is not learning in practice only of the time when human beings and gods see water; there is learning in practice of water seeing water.[33] Because water practices and experiences water, there is the investigation in practice of water speaking water. We should manifest in reality the path on which self encounters self. We should advance and retreat along the vigorous path on which the external world exhausts in practice the external world, and we should spring free.

[189] In general, ways of seeing mountains and water differ according to the type of being [that sees them]: There are beings which see what we call water as a string of pearls,[34] but this does not mean that they see a string of pearls as water. They probably see as their water a form that we see as something else. We see their strings of pearls as water. There are [beings] which see water as wonderful flowers; but this does not mean that they use flowers as water. Demons see water as raging flames, and see it as pus and

blood. Dragons and fish see it as a palace, and see it as a tower. Some see [water] as the seven treasures and the *maṇi* gem;[35] some see it as trees and forests and fences and walls; some see it as the pure and liberated Dharma-nature; some see it as the real human body;[36] and some see it as [the oneness of] physical form and mental nature. Human beings see it as water, the causes and conditions of death and life. Thus, what is seen does indeed differ according to the kind of being [that sees]. Now let us be wary of this. Is it that there
64c are various ways of seeing one object? Or is it that we have mistakenly assumed the various images to be one object? At the crown of effort, we should make still further effort. If the above is so, then practice-and-experience and pursuit of the truth also may not be [only] of one kind or of two kinds; and the ultimate state also may be of thousands of kinds and myriad varieties. When we keep this point in mind, although there are many kinds of water, it seems that there is no original water, and no water of many kinds. At the same time, the various waters which accord with the kinds of beings [that see water] do not depend on mind, do not depend on body, do not arise from karma, are not self-reliant, and are not reliant upon others; they have the liberated state of reliance on water itself. This being so, water is beyond earth, water, fire, wind, space, consciousness, and so on. Water is beyond blue, yellow, red, white, or black and beyond sights, sounds, smells, tastes, sensations, or properties; at the same time, as earth, water, fire, wind, space, and so on, water is naturally realized. Because the nations and palaces of the present are like this, it may be difficult to state by what and into what they are created. To assert that they hang on the circle of space and the circle of wind[37] is not true to ourselves and not true to others; it is to speculate on the basis of the suppositions of the small view. People make this assertion because they think that, without somewhere to hang, [*dharma*s] would not be able to abide.[38]

[193] The Buddha says, "All *dharma*s are ultimately liberated; they are without an abode."[39] Remember, although they are in the state of liberation, without any bonds, all *dharma*s are abiding in place.[40] Even so, when human beings look at water, the only way we see it is as flowing ceaselessly. This flowing takes many forms, each of which is an example of the human view: [Water] flows over the earth, flows through the sky, flows upward, and flows downward. It flows in a single winding brook, and it flows in the nine [great]

depths.[41] It rises up to form clouds, and it comes down to form pools. The *Bunshi*[42] says, "The way of water is to ascend to the sky, forming rain and dew, and to descend to the earth, forming rivers and streams." Now even the words of a secular person are like this. It would be most shameful for people who call themselves the descendants of the Buddhist Patriarch to be more ignorant than secular people. We can say that the way of water is beyond the recognition of water, but water is able actually to flow. Water is [also] beyond non-recognition, but water is able actually to flow. 65a

[195] "It ascends to the sky and forms rain and dew." Remember, water rises up immeasurably high into the sky above to form rain and dew. Rain and dew are of various kinds corresponding to [the various kinds of] worlds. To say that there are places not reached by water is the teaching of *śrāvaka*s of the Small Vehicle, or the wrong teaching of non-Buddhists. Water reaches into flames, it reaches into the mind and its images, into wit, and into discrimination, and it reaches into realization of the buddha-nature.[43]

[195] "It descends to the earth to form rivers and streams." Remember, when water descends to the earth, it forms rivers and streams. The vitality of rivers and streams can become sages. Common and stupid folk today assume that water is always in rivers, streams, and oceans. This is not so. Rivers and oceans are realized in water.[44] Thus, water also exists in places which are not rivers and oceans; it is just that when water descends to the earth, it takes effect as rivers and oceans. Further, we must not understand that social worlds cannot exist or that buddha lands cannot exist at a place where water has formed rivers and oceans.[45] Even inside a single drop, countless buddha lands are realized. This does not mean that there is water within buddha lands, and does not mean that there are buddha lands inside water. The place where water exists is already beyond the three times and beyond the world of Dharma. 65b
Even so, it is the universe in which water has been realized. Wherever Buddhist patriarchs go water goes, and wherever water goes Buddhist patriarchs are realized. This is why Buddhist patriarchs without exception, when taking up water, have treated it as [their] body and mind and have treated it as [their] thinking. This being so, that water rises up is not denied in any text, within [Buddhism] or without. The way of water pervades upward and downward, vertically and horizontally. At the same time, in the Buddhist sutras, "fire and wind rise upward, earth and water settle downward." There is something to

be learned in practice in this "upward" and "downward." That is, we [must] learn in practice the Buddha's teaching of "upward" and "downward," as follows: The place where earth and water go, we think of as "downward."[46] We do not think of downward as a place where earth and water go.[47] The place where fire and wind go is "upward." The "world of Dharma" should not always be related to measurements upward, downward, and in the four diagonals;[48] at the same time, the four elements, the five elements, the six elements, and so on, relying on the concrete place to which they go, just momentarily establish the four-cornered Dharma world.[49] It is not to be assumed that the Heaven of Thoughtlessness[50] is above and that the Avīci[51] Hell is below. Avīci is the whole world of Dharma, and Thoughtlessness is the whole world of Dharma. Still, when dragons and fish see water as a palace, they are probably like people looking at a palace, utterly unable to recognize that it is flowing away. If an onlooker were to explain to them, "Your palace is flowing water," the dragons and fish would likely be as startled as we were now to hear the assertion that mountains are flowing. Further, it may also be possible to maintain and to rely upon [the assertion] that there is such preaching in [every] railing, stair,
65c and outdoor pillar of a palace or a mansion. Quietly, we should have been considering this reasoning and we should go on considering it.

[199] If we are not learning the state of liberation at the face of this place, we have not become free from the body and mind of the common person, we have not perfectly realized the land of Buddhist patriarchs, and we have not perfectly realized the palaces of the common person. Although human beings now are profoundly confident that the inner content of the seas and the inner content of the rivers is water, we still do not know what dragons, fish, and other beings view as water and use as water. Do not stupidly assume that every kind of being uses as water what we view as water. When people today who are learning Buddhism want to learn about water, we should not stick blindly in only the human sphere; we should move forward and learn water in the Buddha's state of truth. We should learn in practice how we see the water that Buddhist patriarchs use. Further, we should learn in practice whether there is water or whether there is no water in the houses of Buddhist patriarchs.

[200] Mountains have been the dwelling places of great saints since beyond the past and present. All the sages and all the saints have made the

mountains into their inner sanctum and made the mountains into their body and mind; and by virtue of the sages and the saints the mountains have been realized. We tend to suppose, with respect to mountains in general, that countless great saints and great sages might be gathered there; but after we have entered the mountains there is not a single person to meet. There is only the realization of the vigorous activity of mountains. Not even the traces of our having entered remain. When we are in the secular world gazing at the moun- 66a
tains, and when we are in the mountains meeting the mountains, their heads and eyes are very different. Our notion that [the mountains] are not flowing and our view that [the mountains] are not flowing may not be the same as the view of dragons and fish.[52] While human beings and gods, in our own world, are in our element, other beings doubt this [notion and view of ours], or they may not even doubt it. This being so, we should study the phrase "mountains flow" under Buddhist patriarchs; we should not leave it open to doubt.[53] Acting once[54] is just "flowing"; acting once [more] is just "not flowing." One time round is "flowing"; one time round is "not flowing." Without this investigation in practice, it is not the right Dharma wheel of the Tathāgata. An eternal buddha[55] says, "If you want to be able not to invite the karma of incessant [hell],[56] do not insult the right Dharma wheel of the Tathāgata." We should engrave these words on skin, flesh, bones, and marrow, we should engrave them on body and mind, on object-and-subject, we should engrave them on the immaterial, and we should engrave them on matter; they are [already] engraved "on trees and on rocks"[57] and they are [already] engraved "in fields and in villages."[58] We generally say that mountains belong to a country, but [mountains] belong to people who love mountains. Mountains always love their occupiers, whereupon saints and sages, people of high virtue, enter the mountains. When saints and sages live in the mountains, because the mountains belong to these [sages and saints], trees and rocks abound and flourish, and birds and animals are mysteriously excellent. This is because the sages and saint have covered them with virtue. We should remember the fact that mountains like sages and the fact that [mountains] like saints. That many emperors have gone to the mountains to bow before sages and to question great saints is an excellent example in the past and the present. At such times, [the emperors] honor [the sages and saints] with the formalities due to a teacher, never conforming to secular norms. Imperial

authority exerts no control whatever over the mountain sages. Clearly, the mountains are beyond the human world. On Kōdō[59] [Mountain] in the bygone
66b days of Kahō,[60] the Yellow Emperor[61] visited Kōsei, crawling on his knees and kowtowing to beg [instruction]. Śākyamuni Buddha left the palace of his father, the king, to enter the mountains, but his father, the king, did not resent the mountains. The royal father did not distrust those in the mountains who would teach the prince, whose twelve years of training in the truth were mostly spent in the mountains. The revelation of [the prince's] destiny as the Dharma King also took place in the mountains. Truly, not even the wheel[-turning] kings hold sway over the mountains. Remember, the mountains are beyond the boundaries of the human world and beyond the boundaries of the heavens above; we can never know the mountains with the human intellect. If [their flowing] is not to be compared with flowing in the human world, who can doubt the flowing, the non-flowing, and the other activities of the mountains?

[205] Again, since the ancient past, there have been from time to time sages and saints who lived by the water. When they live by the water, there are those who fish fishes, those who fish human beings, and those who fish the state of truth. Each of these is in the traditional stream of those who are "in the water." Going further, there may be those who fish themselves, those who fish fishing, those who are fished by fishing, and those who are fished by the state of truth.[62] In days of old, when Master Tokujō[63] suddenly left Yakusan Mountain to live amidst the river's mind, he got the sage[64] of the Katei River. Was this not fishing fishes? Was it not fishing human beings? Was it not fishing water? Was it not fishing himself? A person who is able to meet Tokujō is Tokujō;[65] and Tokujō's "teaching people"[66] is [a human being] meeting a human being. It is not only that there is water in the world; there are worlds in the world of water. And it is not only in water that such [worlds] exist. There are worlds of sentient beings in clouds, there are worlds of sentient beings in wind, there are worlds of sentient beings in fire, there
66c are worlds of sentient beings in earth, there are worlds of sentient beings in the world of Dharma, there are worlds of sentient beings in a stalk of grass, and there are worlds of sentient beings in a staff. Wherever there are worlds of sentient beings, the world of Buddhist patriarchs inevitably exists at that place. We should carefully learn in practice the truth which is like this. In

conclusion then, water is the palace of real dragons; it is beyond flowing and falling. If we recognize it as only flowing, the word "flowing" insults water, because, for example, [the word] forces [water] to be what is other than flowing itself. Water is nothing but water's "real form as it is." Water is just the virtues of water itself; it is beyond "flowing." When we master the flow and master the non-flow of a single body of water, the perfect realization of the myriad *dharma*s is realized at once. With mountains too, there are mountains contained in treasure, there are mountains contained in marshes, there are mountains contained in space, there are mountains contained in mountains,[67] and there is learning in practice in which mountains are contained in containment.[68] An eternal buddha[69] says, "Mountains are mountains. Water is water." These words do not say that "mountains" are "mountains"; they say that mountains are mountains. This being so, we should master the mountains in practice. When we are mastering the mountains in practice, that is effort "in the mountains." Mountains and water like this naturally produce sages and produce saints.

Shōbōgenzō Sansuigyō[70]

Preached to the assembly at Kannondōrikō-shōhōrinji on the eighteenth day of the tenth lunar month in the first year of Ninji.[71]

Notes

1 Master Fuyō Dōkai (1043–1118), a Buddhist patriarch in Master Dōgen's lineage, the forty-fifth patriarch from the Buddha. Having succeeded Master Tōsu Gisei, Master Fuyō preached Buddhism on Mount Taiyō and elsewhere until he refused a title and a purple robe from the emperor and was banished. When he was eventually pardoned, he built a thatched hut on Mount Fuyō and lived there in the style of the ancient patriarchs.

2 *Gyōho,* or "going steps." In the quotation, and elsewhere in Master Dōgen's commentary the expression is *unpo,* or "transporting steps." Both expressions mean walking.

3 *Jō* means both constant and eternal. Both meanings are relevant here: action makes things balanced (for example, pedaling a bicycle) and action gives things eternal meaning.

4 *Sanchū. Chū* means "in" or "in the state of," and Master Dōgen sometimes uses the character to mean "in the state of reality." So *sanchu* means in the mountains or in the reality of the mountains.

5 *Sekairi no kekai.* This alludes to the words of Master Prajñātara, *kekai-sekai-ki,* "the opening of flowers is the occurrence of the world," suggesting that the real world itself is just the appearance of phenomena. See for example Chapter Forty-three (Vol. II), *Kūge.*

6 *Taiho.* In the *Fukanzazengi* Master Dōgen describes zazen as *taiho,* a backward step (to our original state). *Taiho* means concrete backward steps.

7 *Hotai* means stepping backward as a principle. We should not only investigate concrete backward steps (for example, by sitting in zazen, lifting weights, doing prostrations, having a bath, etc.) but also investigate the meaning of stepping backward (for example, by reading the *Shōbōgenzō,* studying the function of the autonomic nervous system, drawing inferences from trial and error in daily life, etc.).

8 Kū-ō is identified with Bhīṣmagarjitasvararāja, or King of Majestic Voice, the first buddha to appear in the *kalpa* of emptiness. See the *Lotus Sutra,* chapter 20, *Jōfugyō-bosatsu* ("Bodhisattva Never Despise").

9 Each action is done at an independent moment of the present.

10 "Fully understand" is *shichitsu-hattatsu,* lit., "pass through seven directions and arrive at eight destinations," suggesting thorough understanding from many viewpoints.

[11] Vulgar people do not value the unthinkable reality of mountains, but they esteem the characteristics of mountains which they are able to enumerate.

[12] *Kakunogotoku,* "like this," indicates what is already present here and now. *Kakunogotoku* in Chinese characters is *nyoze,* which Master Dōgen uses as an expression of reality as it is. See Chapter Seventeen, *Hokke-ten-hokke.*

[13] By denying the four views Master Dōgen emphasized the fact that reality cannot be grasped by intellectual thinking.

[14] *Ichigu no kanken,* lit., "one-corner pipe-views."

[15] "Great Saint" means the Buddha. Moving circumstances (like a pot) and moving mind (like water) is the theme of a story about Master Nansen Fugan and Master Godai Impō (see Chapter Eighty-one [Vol. IV], *Ō-saku-sendaba*). Though the words of the story and the words here are slightly different, the point is the same: that separation between subject and object can be transcended by action in the moment of the present.

[16] *Sesshin-sesshō,* or "expounding the mind and expounding the nature," is the title of Chapter Forty-eight (Vol. III), *Sesshin-sesshō.*

[17] *Kenshin-kenshō.* People in Japan who pursue enlightenment by thinking about *kōan*s (Buddhist stories) often call the enlightenment they pursue *kenshō,* "seeing the nature."

[18] Subjectively or romantically, we assign gender or other human characteristics to things in nature. Objectively or scientifically, we do not. Master Dōgen's viewpoint is beyond subjective and objective views. A Buddhist knowing of stones is more real than the romantic descriptions found, for example, in secular Chinese literature.

[19] Master Unmon Bun'en (864–949), a successor of Master Seppō Gison, who was a sixth-generation descendant of Master Seigen Gyōshi. It is said that there were never less than a thousand students in Master Unmon's order, and that in his thirty years of spreading Buddhism he produced more than ninety successors. Great Master Kyōshin is his posthumous title as founder of the Unmon sect.

[20] An East Mountain means a real mountain.

[21] Master Dōgen illustrated the principle in the previous sentence with the concrete example of Mount Sumeru and the eight mountains that surround it.

[22] Master Dōgen criticizes Master Unmon in, for example, Chapter Fifty-two (Vol. III), *Bukkyō.*

[23] "Unreliable" is *zusan,* lit., "edited by Zu [or To]." It is said that poems edited by To Moku of the Song dynasty were very irregular and unreliable. Therefore people of the time used the words "edited by Zu (or To)" to represent unreliability.

[24] Master Gan of Mount Nansen in Chishu district (Master Nansen Fugan, 748–834) is doing chores on the mountain. A monk comes by and asks the master, "Where does

Nansen's road lead?" The master holds up his sickle and says, "I got this sickle for thirty pennies." The monk says, "I didn't ask about you paying thirty pennies for the sickle. Where does Nansen's road lead?" The master says, "And now that I can use it, it is really handy." (*Shinji-shōbōgenzō,* pt. 2, no. 54). The monk wanted to know what Master Nansen considered to be the aim of his life, but he asked his question as if asking for directions. Master Nansen recommended the monk not to be conscious only of the idealistic aim but also to recognize concrete facts. The monk insisted that he also wanted to know what the real aim of our life is. Master Nansen's answer was that he was acting in reality.

25 Master Ōbaku Kiun (d. c. 855) was known for striking his disciples, including Master Rinzai Gigen (c. 815–867), to impress on them that reality is different from thinking and feeling (see for example *Shinji-shōbōgenzō,* pt. 1, no. 27). Master Rinzai used to achieve the same result by yelling *katsu!* (ibid.).

26 *Kattō,* "arrowroot and wisteria," "entanglement," or "the complicated," is the title of Chapter Forty-six (Vol. III), *Kattō.*

27 *Rokugon-tokushi.* The band of six shavelings in the Buddha's order were Nanda, Upananda, Kālodāyin, Chanda, Aśvaka, and Punarvasu. It is said that their misconduct caused the formulation of precepts. *Tokushi,* shaveling (lit., "bald child") means someone who becomes a monk in form but who has no will to the truth.

28 The original word, *nanji,* means "you." Master Dōgen usually uses this form when directing criticism at someone to whom he does not need to be polite.

29 Rivers, streams, lakes, etc. are not only an abstraction but are realized at the foot of a real mountain.

30 In other words, on the basis of reality.

31 *Shichijū-hachi-ō,* lit., "seven horizontals and eight verticals."

32 *Shushō-soku-fu-mu.* Master Nangaku Ejō's expression of practice and experience in zazen. See Chapter Seven, *Senjō;* Chapter Twenty-nine (Vol. II), *Inmo;* and Chapter Sixty-two (Vol. III), *Hensan.*

33 Master Dōgen uses the formula A sees A, A meets A, A restricts A, A succeeds A, etc., to suggest the real existence of A.

34 Alludes to the metaphor of *issui-shiken,* "one water, four views." The goddesses who are sometimes depicted floating in the sky in old Buddhist pictures see water as a string of pearls. Fish see water as a palace or as beautiful flowers. Demons hate water as pus and blood, because it puts out their fires and washes away their impurities. Human beings see water as water. See also Chapter Three, *Genjō-kōan.*

35 The Sanskrit *maṇi,* which means gem, in this case suggests the *cintāmaṇi,* a fabled gem capable of fulfilling every wish, said to be obtained from the Dragon King of the sea.

[36] *Shinjitsu-nintai,* the words of Master Chōsha Keishin. See Chapter Thirty-seven (Vol. II), *Shinjin-gakudō;* Chapter Forty-seven (Vol. III), *Sangai-yuishin;* Chapter Fifty (Vol. III), *Shohō-jissō;* Chapter Sixty-two (Vol. III), *Hensan;* and Chapter Ninety-one (Vol. IV), *Yui-butsu-yo-butsu.*

[37] In ancient Indian cosmology, the physical world is constructed of five elements, called five wheels or five circles (*pañca-maṇḍalaka* in Sanskrit): circles of earth, water, fire, wind, and space. (Interpreting the concepts more broadly: solids, liquids, combustion, gases, and space.)

[38] See also discussion of a steelyard in Chapter Thirty-eight (Vol. II), *Muchū-setsumu.*

[39] The *Daihōshakkyō,* fascicle 87.

[40] *Jū-i,* "abide in place," is short for *jūhō-i,* "abide in place in the Dharma," which appears in the second sentence of this chapter.

[41] *Kyū-en* refers to nine famous deep river pools in China.

[42] *Bunshi* is a Daoist book in ten volumes. The book is said to have been written during the Sui dynasty (581–618) but some scholars suspect that it was written later and falsely dated earlier.

[43] Examples such as the humidity of a flame, the dryness of wit, and realization in the sounds of the valley streams, negate the common-sense conception of the scope of water.

[44] Rivers and water, or entity and substance, are one.

[45] Reality (rivers and oceans) includes both the material (water), and the meaningful (human worlds, Buddhist lands).

[46] Concepts like "downward" originate with concrete facts like the location of earth and water (see Chapter Forty-two [Vol. III], *Tsuki*).

[47] We remember that "downward" is only a concept, not an actual place.

[48] *Shi-i,* or "four corners"—northwest, southwest, southeast, and northeast.

[49] *Hōgū-hokkai. Hō* suggests *shihō,* the four directions—north, south, east, and west. *Gū* suggests *shigū,* the four corners. *Hōgū-hokkai* suggests concrete reality, as opposed to "the world of Dharma" as a religious concept.

[50] *Musōten,* from the Sanskrit *asaṃjñi-sattvāḥ,* is explained as a group of heavens in the world of matter.

[51] Avīci is the Sanskrit name for the worst kind of hell.

[52] In the view of dragons and fish, mountains may be flowing.

[53] Given that even things which we take for granted are open to doubt, we should rely upon Buddhist patriarchs' teaching.

[54] *Nen-itsu,* lit., "to pick up one." *Nen* means to pinch, or to pick up; it suggests an action. *Itsu* means one.

[55] Master Yōka Genkaku, in his poem *Shōdōka.*

[56] *Mugen-jigoku,* "incessant hell," or "hell without respite," represents the Sanskrit Avīci.

[57] *Nyakuju-nyakuseki.* Alludes to the story of the Buddha's past life recorded in the *Mahāparinirvāṇa-sūtra.* See note 159 in Chapter Twelve, *Kesa-kudoku.*

[58] *Nyakuden-nyakuri.* Alludes to the *Lotus Sutra* (3.72–74). See note 9 in Chapter Thirteen, *Den-e.*

[59] The name of a mountain in modern Kansu province in China. The Daoist sage Kōsei lived in a cave on Kōdō Mountain.

[60] Kahō, lit., "Flower Fiefdom," was a legendary utopian realm.

[61] Kōtei, the Yellow Emperor, was the third of the five rulers in the legendary period of Chinese history (dates estimated as 2852–2205 B.C.E.). He visited Kōsei to ask the secret of immortality. The story is recorded in volume four of the Daoist text *Sōshi,* attributed to Zhuangzi.

[62] The action of fishing connects subject (fisherman) and object (fish), so Master Dōgen uses fishing to suggest the principle of the mutual relation between subject and object in action.

[63] Master Sensu Tokujō (dates unknown), a successor of Master Yakusan Igen (745–828). After receiving the Dharma from Master Yakusan he went to live on a river in the Katei Valley of the Shushu district, working as a boatman (*sensu* means boatman), and hoping to find among his passengers a human being with the will to the truth. Master Tokujō's brother disciple Master Dōgo Enchi (769–835) recommended Master Kassan Zenne (805–881) to go and visit Master Tokujō by the river. They had a lively conversation, at the conclusion of which Master Tokujō said that if we fish out all the river's waves (that is, if we do the impossible), we can meet the fish with the golden scales (realize our ideal) for the first time. Master Kassan covered his ears, and thus received Master Tokujō's affirmation. Finally, Master Tokujō told Master Kassan to go deep into the mountains and just teach the Dharma to one student or half a student. Master Dōgen quoted at length this story about Master Tokujō and Master Kassan in the *Shinji-shōbōgenzō,* pt. 1, no. 90.

[64] Master Kassan Zenne.

[65] In Chapter Sixty-one (Vol. III), *Kenbutsu,* Master Dōgen teaches that a person in the state of buddha is meeting buddha. In this sentence, he substitutes Tokujō for buddha.

[66] *Hito o sessuru,* lit., "to receive people." The story in the *Shinji-shōbōgenzō* says *zaike kōsen shō setsu jin,* "he received people on a boat on the Katei River."

[67] Treasure (value), marshes (nature), space (the stage of action), and mountains (reality) correspond to the four faces of reality outlined in the Buddha's Four Noble Truths.

[68] In zazen, mountains exist as they are.

[69] Master Unmon Bun'en says, "Venerable monks! Do not have delusions. The sky is the sky. The earth is the earth. Mountains are mountains. Water is water. Monks are monks. Laymen are laymen" (*Unmonkōroku,* Vol. 1).

[70] Acknowledgment is due to Professor Carl Bielefeldt of Stanford University for his exemplary translation of this chapter.

[71] 1240.

[Chapter Fifteen]

Busso 67a3

The Buddhist Patriarchs

Translator's Note: Butsu *means "buddha" or "Buddhist,"* so *means "patriarch," and therefore* busso *means Buddhist patriarchs. Master Dōgen revered buddhas of the past; he also esteemed the Buddhist transmission from buddha to buddha. Furthermore he believed in the continuity of the Buddhist order; the successive leaders of the Buddhist order held an important place in his thought. Here Master Dōgen enumerates the names of the patriarchs of the Buddhist order, and in doing so, he confirms the Buddhist tradition they maintained.*

[209] The realization of the Buddhist patriarchs[1] is [our] taking up the Buddhist patriarchs and paying homage to them. This is not of only the past, the present, and the future; and it may be ascendant even to the ascendant [reality] of buddha.[2] It is just to enumerate those who have maintained and relied upon the real features[3] of Buddhist patriarchs, to do prostrations to them, and to meet them. Making the virtue of the Buddhist patriarchs manifest and uphold itself, we have dwelled in and maintained it, and have bowed to and experienced it.

[210] (1) Great Master[4] Vipaśyin Buddha
—here[5] called Kōsetsu [Universal Preaching][6]

(2) Great Master Śikhin Buddha
—here called Ka [Fire]

(3) Great Master Viśvabhū Buddha
—here called Issaiji [All Benevolent]

(4) Great Master Krakucchanda Buddha
—here called Kinsennin [Gold Wizard]

(5) Great Master Kanakamuni Buddha
—here called Konjikisen [Golden Wizard]

(6) Great Master Kāśyapa Buddha
—here called Onkō [Drinking Brightness]

(7) Great Master Śākyamuni Buddha
—here called Nōninjakumoku [Benevolence and Serenity]

[1] Great Master Mahākāśyapa[7]

[2] Great Master Ānanda[8]

[3] Great Master Śāṇavāsa[9]

[4] Great Master Upagupta[10]

[5] Great Master Dhītika[11]

[6] Great Master Micchaka[12]

[7] Great Master Vasumitra[13]

[8] Great Master Buddhanandhi

[9] Great Master Baddhamitra

[10] Great Master Pārśva[14]

[11] Great Master Puṇyayaśas[15]

[12] Great Master Aśvaghoṣa[16]

[13] Great Master Kapimala[17]

67b [14] Great Master Nāgārjuna[18]
—also [called] Ryūju [Dragon Tree] or Ryūshō [Dragon Excellence] or Ryūmō [Dragon Might]

[15] Great Master Kāṇadeva[19]

[16] Great Master Rāhulabhadra[20]

[17] Great Master Saṃghanandi[21]

[18] Great Master Geyāśata

[19] Great Master Kumāralabdha[22]

[20] Great Master Gayata[23]

[21] Great Master Vasubandhu[24]

[22] Great Master Manura[25]

[23] Great Master Hakulenayasas[26]

[24] Great Master Siṃha[27]

[25] Great Master Vaśasuta[28]

[26] Great Master Puṇyamitra[29]

[27] Great Master Prajñātara[30]

[28] [1] Great Master Bodhidharma[31]

[29] [2] Great Master Eka[32]

[30] [3] Great Master Sōsan[33]

[31] [4] Great Master Dōshin[34]

[32] [5] Great Master Kōnin[35]

[33] [6] Great Master Enō[36]

[34] [7] Great Master Gyōshi[37]

[35] [8] Great Master Kisen[38]

[36] [9] Great Master Igen[39]

[37] [10] Great Master Donjō[40]

[38] [11] Great Master Ryōkai[41]

[39] [12] Great Master Dōyō[42]

[40] [13] Great Master Dōhi[43]

[41] [14] Great Master Kanshi[44]

[42] [15] Great Master Enkan[45] 67c

[43] [16] Great Master Kyōgen[46]

[44] [17] Great Master Gisei[47]

[45] [18] Great Master Dōkai[48]

[46] [19] Great Master Shijun[49]

[47] [20] Great Master Seiryō[50]

[48] [21] Great Master Sōkaku[51]

[49] [22] Great Master Chikan[52]

[50] [23] Great Master Nyojō[53]

[222] Dōgen, during the summer retreat of the first year of the Hōgyō era[54] of the great kingdom of Song, met and served my late master, the eternal buddha of Tendō, the Great Master. I perfectly realized the act of prostrating to, and humbly receiving upon my head, this Buddhist Patriarch; it was [the realization of] buddhas alone, together with buddhas.[55]

Shōbōgenzō Busso

Written at Kannondōrikōshōhōrinji in the Uji district of Yōshū,[56] Japan, and preached to the assembly there on the third day of the first lunar month in the second year of Ninji.[57]

Notes

1 *Busso. So,* "patriarch" or "ancestor," is originally neuter in gender. However, Master Dōgen often uses the term *so* for people of the present as well as for people of the past. Therefore, for want of a more neutral alternative, the translation "patriarch" has been preferred throughout the present volume.

2 *Butsu-kōjō.* See Chapter Twenty-eight (Vol. II), *Butsu-kōjō-no-ji.*

3 *Menmoku,* or "face and eyes."

4 "Great Master" is *daioshō.* The honorific term *oshō* was used in China to address a master directly. The corresponding term in Sanskrit is *upādhyāya* (lit., preceptor, abbot, teacher). In the recitation of the names of the Buddhist patriarchs in Japan, the word *daioshō* give a natural rhythm to the reciting. Appendix III shows the standard form of the recitation practiced in Japan.

5 China and Japan.

6 The names of the seven ancient buddhas and the first twenty-eight patriarchs (with the exception of the twelfth, Master Aśvaghoṣa) are represented by Chinese characters that transliterate the pronunciation of the original Sanskrit name. In general, sources for Sanskrit names and words are the *Zengaku-daijiten* and Sir Monier Monier-Williams's *Sanskrit-English Dictionary.* These two sources do not give Sanskrit equivalents for the names of the twentieth, twenty-second, twenty-third, and twenty-fifth patriarchs. These names were rendered into Sanskrit in Nishijima Roshi's *Gendaigo-yaku-shōbōgenzō* (*Shōbōgenzō in Modern Japanese*) relying on a variety of other sources. The names of the seven ancient buddhas and Master Nāgārjuna are given both in Chinese characters representing the Sanskrit pronunciation and in Chinese characters that have meaning.

7 One of the Buddha's ten great disciples, said to be foremost among the ten great disciples in nonattachment, and foremost at *dhūta,* the practice of austerity. He was born into a brahman family on the outskirts of Rājagṛha, and became the Buddha's disciple in the third year after the Buddha's realization of the truth. It is said that he entered the state of an arhat after only eight days. After the Buddha's death, Master Mahākāśyapa succeeded the Buddha as leader of the Buddhist order, and organized the First Council at Rājagṛha. At the First Council, in 483 B.C.E., the Pāli canon—consisting of Vinaya (precepts) and Sutra (the Buddha's discourses)—was codified so as to be passed on through recitation to future generations. One hundred years later, in 383

B.C.E., a Second Council was held to discuss revision of the Vinaya. Here two traditions emerged: the School of the Elders (Theravādins), and the members of the Great Community (Mahāsaṃghika, later to develop into the Mahayana). A Third Council was held at Patna in 253 B.C.E. under the patronage of King Aśoka. Here the existing Vinaya and Sutra were supplemented by commentaries which later become known as the Abhidharma. The Tripiṭaka (three baskets) of Vinaya, Sutra, and Abhidharma were later written on palm leaves in the monasteries of Sri Lanka in the first century B.C.E. Master Mahākāśyapa, having chosen Ānanda as his successor, retired to Kukkuṭapāda Mountain and passed away while sitting in zazen. See for example Chapter Thirty (Vol. II), *Gyōji.*

8 Also one of the Buddha's ten great disciples, foremost at remembering the Buddha's preaching. The Buddha's half brother, and only a few days younger than the Buddha himself, he served the Buddha as an attendant monk. Though a monk for forty-four years, he had not realized the truth when the Buddha died. However, he is said to have become an arhat shortly before the First Council at Rājagṛha, where he was to recall the Buddha's discourses for posterity.

9 See for example Chapter Twelve, *Kesa-kudoku.*

10 See for example Chapter Eighty-six (Vol. IV), *Shukke-kudoku;* and Chapter Ninety (Vol. IV), *Shizen-biku.*

11 A native of the ancient Indian state of Magadha. See for example Chapter Eighty-six (Vol. IV), *Shukke-kudoku.*

12 A native of central India. His name is written either as Micchaka or as Miccaka.

13 A native of the northern Indian state of Gandhāra, born at the end of the first century C.E. He is said to have organized, in the kingdom of Kaniṣka, the Fourth Council, where he compiled the *Abhidharmamahāvibhāṣa-śāstra.* See for example Chapter Seventy-seven (Vol. IV), *Kokū.*

14 A native of central India. He is also said to have presided over the Fourth Council. He was called the Side Saint, because he made a vow never to sleep like a corpse, on his back. See for example Chapter Thirty (Vol. II), *Gyōji.*

15 A native of the ancient Indian state of Kośala.

16 The Sanskrit *aśvaghoṣa* literally means "horse whinny" and in the source text the name is represented not phonetically but by the Chinese characters *memyō,* "horse whinny." A native of Śrāvastī, he was distinguished in music and in literature. His Buddhist writings include the *Buddhacarita,* a biography of the Buddha in metric form.

17 A native of the central Indian state of Magadha. It is said that at first he led a non-Buddhist group of three thousand disciples, but later he met Master Aśvaghoṣa, realized the truth, and spread the Dharma through the west of India.

[18] The three Chinese names for Master Nāgārjuna are Ryūju, Ryūshō, and Ryūmō. In each case, *ryū,* "dragon," represents the meaning of the Sanskrit *nāga.* In the case of Ryūju, the Chinese character for tree, *ju,* may represent either the sound or the meaning of the Sanskrit *arjuna,* which is the name of a tree.

Master Nāgārjuna lived in the second or third century C.E. He was born into a brahman family in southern India. When he became a monk he first studied the Hinayana canon, but later journeyed to the Himalayas and learned the teachings of the Mahayana from a venerable old *bhikṣu.* Eventually he succeeded Master Kapimala and compiled many fundamental Mahayana texts, including the *Madhyamakakārikā.* The *Mahāprajñāpāramitopadeśa* is also attributed to him. See for example, Chapter Twelve, *Kesa-kudoku;* Chapter Seventy (Vol. II), *Hotsu-bodaishin;* Chapter Eighty-five (Vol. IV), *Shime;* Chapter Eighty-nine (Vol. IV), *Shinjin-inga;* and Chapter Ninety (Vol. IV), *Shizen-biku.*

[19] Called Kāṇadeva because of his loss of an eye (the Sanskrit *kāṇa* means one-eyed). Also called Āryadeva. He lived in southern India in the third century and is said to have been killed by a non-Buddhist. See for example Chapter Twenty-two (Vol. II), *Busshō.*

[20] A native of Kapilavastu, in present-day Nepal.

[21] A native of the city of Śrāvastī, the capital of the ancient state of Kośala.

[22] See for example Chapter Eighty-four (Vol. IV), *Sanji-no-gō;* and Chapter Eighty-nine (Vol. IV), *Shinjin-inga.*

[23] A native of northern India. See for example Chapter Eighty-four (Vol. IV), *Sanji-no-gō;* and Chapter Eighty-nine (Vol. IV), *Shinjin-inga.*

[24] Born in the fifth century in Puruṣapura (close to present-day Peshawar), the capital of Gandhāra. His many works include the *Abhidharmakośa-bhāṣya.* Master Vasubandhu's brothers Asaṅga and Buddhasiṃla were also prominent Buddhist philosophers of the time. Their teaching formed the basis of the Yogācāra shool. The Yogācāra school and the Madhyamaka school of Master Nāgārjuna are seen as the two major streams of Mahayana Buddhism in India.

[25] The son of the king of Nadai (Sanskrit equivalent unknown). Became a monk at the age of thirty.

[26] Born into a brahman family. He spread the Dharma in central India.

[27] Born into a brahman family in central India. He spread the Dharma in the northern state of Kaśmīra (present-day Kashmir). It is said that he was executed by the king of Kaśmīra. See Chapter Eighty-four (Vol. IV), *Sanji-no-gō.*

[28] A native of western India.

[29] A native of southern India.

[30] Born into a brahman family in eastern India. See for example Chapter Twenty-one (Vol. II), *Kankin;* and Chapter Forty-two (Vol. III), *Kūge.*

[31] The third son of a southern Indian king. Having succeeded Master Prajñātara, he sailed to China during the reign of Emperor Bu (r. 502–549) of the Liang dynasty and became the First Buddhist Patriarch in China. He went to the Songshan Mountains in central northern China to practice zazen, and transmitted the Dharma to Master Taiso Eka. See for example Chapter Thirty (Vol. II), *Gyōji;* Chapter Forty-six (Vol. III), *Kattō;* Chapter Forty-nine (Vol. III), *Butsudō; and* Chapter Seventy-two (Vol. IV), *Zanmai-ō-zanmai.*

[32] Master Taiso Eka (Ch. Dazu Huike). See for example Chapter Thirty (Vol. II), *Gyōji;* Chapter Forty-six (Vol. III), *Kattō;* and Chapter Forty-eight (Vol. III), *Sesshin-sesshō.*

[33] Master Kanchi Sōsan (Ch. Jianzhi Sengcan). It is said that he was already in his forties when he became a disciple of Master Taiso Eka. He wrote the *Shinjinmei* (*Inscription on Believing Mind*). To escape persecution by Emperor Bu (r. 561–578) of the Northern Zhou dynasty, he secluded himself in the mountains for ten years.

[34] Master Daii Dōshin (Ch. Dayi Daoxin). Became a disciple of Master Kanchi Sōsan at the age of fourteen, and succeeded him after nine years. Died in 651.

[35] Master Daiman Kōnin (Ch. Daman Hongren) (688–761). See for example Chapter Twenty-two (Vol. II), *Busshō.*

[36] Master Daikan Enō (Ch. Dajian Huineng) (638–713). Spent eight months working as a temple servant at Master Daiman Kōnin's temple, in which time he received the master's affirmation and the authentic transmission of the Buddhist robe. After that he lived on Sōkeizan and spread Buddhism from there for forty years. Master Dōgen revered Master Daikan Enō very highly as "the Founding Patriarch" and "the eternal buddha." See for example Chapter One, *Bendōwa;* Chapter Seven, *Senjō;* Chapter Twenty-two (Vol. II), *Busshō;* Chapter Thirty (Vol. II), *Gyōji;* Chapter Forty-four (Vol. III), *Kobusshin;* and Chapter Forty-nine (Vol. III), *Butsudō.*

[37] Master Seigen Gyōshi (Ch. Qingyuan Xingsi). Died in 740. See for example Chapter Forty-nine (Vol. III), *Butsudō.*

[38] Master Sekitō Kisen (Ch. Shitou Xiqian) (700–790). Had his head shaved by the aged Master Daikan Enō, who advised him to follow Master Seigen Gyōshi. It is said that after succeeding Master Seigen, he built a hut on a rock, earning himself the nickname Sekitō (On Top of the Rock). He wrote the *Sekitōsōan-no-uta* (*Songs from Sekitō's Thatched Hut*) and the *Sandōkai* (*Experiencing the State*). See for example Chapter Forty-nine (Vol. III), *Butsudō.*

[39] Master Yakusan Igen (Ch. Yueshan Weiyan) (745–828). Having become a monk at the age of seventeen, he learned the sutras and commentaries, kept the precepts, and met Master Sekitō Kisen, at whose suggestion he also visited Master Baso Dōitsu. Eventually he became Master Sekitō's successor. See for example Chapter Twenty-seven (Vol. II), *Zazenshin.*

40 Master Ungan Donjō (Ch. Yunyan Tansheng) (782–841). Practiced for twenty years under Master Hyakujō Ekai, after whose death he became the disciple of Master Yakusan. See for example Chapter Fifty-three (Vol. III), *Mujō-seppō;* and Chapter Sixty-three (Vol. III), *Ganzei.*

41 Master Tōzan Ryōkai (Ch. Dongshan Liangjie) (807–869). Became a monk at the age of twenty-one and traveled around visiting Buddhist masters including Master Nansen Fugan and Master Isan Reiyū. At the latter's suggestion he became the disciple and later the successor of Master Ungan. He wrote the *Hōkyōzanmai* (*Samādhi, the State of a Jewel-Mirror*). See for example Chapter Forty-eight (Vol. III), *Sesshin-sesshō;* Chapter Fifty-three (Vol. III), *Mujō-seppō;* Chapter Sixty-three (Vol. III), *Ganzei;* and Chapter Sixty-six (Vol. III), *Shunjū.*

42 Master Ungo Dōyō (Ch. Yunju Daoying) (835?–902). Having succeeded Master Tōzan, he spread the Dharma from Ungozan for thirty years. It is said that his disciples always numbered at least fifteen hundred.

43 Master Dōan Dōhi (Ch. Tongan Daopi). He lived on Hōseizan in the Kōshū district, but his life history is not known.

44 Master Dōan Kanshi (Ch. Tongan Guanzhi). His life history is unclear.

45 Master Ryōzan Enkan (Ch. Liangshan Yuanguan). His life history is also unclear.

46 Master Taiyō Kyōgen (Ch. Dayang Jingxuan) (942–1027). Became a monk under a certain Master Chitsu, then traveled around learning Buddhism under various masters before becoming the disciple and eventually the successor of Master Ryōzan. When Master Taiyō was about to die, he entrusted his robe, *pātra,* etc. to Master Fuzan Hōen to give to Master Fuzan's disciple Tōsu Gisei, thus making Master Tōsu his successor. See *Shinji-shōbōgenzō,* pt. 3, no. 43.

47 Master Tōsu Gisei (Ch. Touzi Yiqing) (1032–1083). Became a monk at the age of seven. Later spent about six years in the order of Master Fuzan Hōen (a member of Master Rinzai's lineage). Receiving the portrait, shoes and other personal effects entrusted by Master Taiyō to Master Fuzan, Master Tōsu succeeded Master Taiyō as the tenth-generation descendant in the lineage of Master Seigen Gyōshi. *Goroku* in two volumes. See for example Chapter Fifty-three (Vol. III), *Mujō-seppō;* and Chapter Sixty-four (Vol. III), *Kajō.*

48 Master Fuyō Dōkai (Ch. Furong Daokai) (1043–1118). Having realized the Dharma under Master Tōsu, he preached on Taiyōzan and at other temples. The Song emperor Kisō (r. 1101–1126) bestowed on him a purple robe and the title Zen Master Jōshō, but Master Fuyō refused to accept them and was consequently banished. Later he was pardoned and built himself a thatched hut on Fuyōzan, where he lived in the ancient style. See for example Chapter Fourteen, *Sansuigyō;* and Chapter Sixty-four (Vol. III), *Kajō.*

49 Master Tanka Shijun (Ch. Danxia Zichun) (1064–1117). Having succeeded Master Fuyō, he lived on Tankazan, with such disciples as Master Wanshi Shōgaku and

Master Shinketsu Seiryō. *Goroku* in two volumes. The six-volume *Kidōshū* (*Kidō Collection*) is also a record of the words of Master Tanka Shijun. Kidō (lit., "empty hall") was probably one of Master Tanka's names.

[50] Master Shinketsu Seiryō (Ch. Zhenxie Qingliao) (1089–1151). *Goroku* in two volumes.

[51] Master Tendō Sōkaku (Ch. Tiantong Zongjue). Though he was the grandfather in Buddhism of Master Tendō Nyojō, his life history is not known clearly.

[52] Master Setchō Chikan (Ch. Xuedou Zhijian) (1105–1192). See for example Chapter Fifty-one (Vol. III), *Mitsugo.*

[53] Master Tendō Nyojō (Ch. Tiantong Rujing) (1163–1228). After realizing the Dharma in Master Chikan's order, he traveled around and taught at temples in many districts for forty years. While living at Jyōjiji, in 1224 he received an imperial edict to become the master of Keitokuzenji on Tendōzan, where he was to teach Master Dōgen. See for example Chapter Thirty (Vol. II), *Gyōji;* Chapter Fifty-nine (Vol. III), *Baike;* and Chapter Seventy-two (Vol. III), *Zanmai-ō-zanmai.*

[54] 1225.

[55] "Perfectly realize" is *gujin.* "Buddhas alone, together with buddhas" is *yui-butsu-yo-butsu.* These words are from a sentence in the *Lotus Sutra* which Master Dōgen often quoted: "Buddhas alone, together with buddhas, can perfectly realize that all *dharma*s are real form." (LS 1.684)

[56] Yōshū was the Japanese pronunciation of the name of a district in China. People of the time, looking up to China, borrowed the Chinese name, probably for the district then called Yamashiro-no-kuni. The area corresponds to present-day Kyoto prefecture.

[57] 1241.

[Chapter Sixteen]

Shisho

The Certificate of Succession

Translator's Note: Shi *means "succession" or "transmission."* Sho *means "certificate." So* shisho *means "the certificate of succession." Buddhism is not only theory but also practice or experience. Therefore it is impossible for a Buddhist disciple to attain the Buddhist truth only by reading Buddhist sutras or listening to a master's lectures. The disciple must live with a master and study the master's behavior in everyday life. After a disciple has learned the master's life and has realized the Buddhist truth in his or her own life, the master gives a certificate to the disciple, certifying the transmission of the truth from master to disciple. This certificate is called* shisho. *From a materialistic viewpoint, the certificate is only cloth and ink, and so it cannot hold religious meaning or be revered as something with religious value. But Buddhism is a realistic religion, and Buddhists find religious value in many concrete traditions. The certificate is one such traditional object that is revered by Buddhists. Therefore Master Dōgen found much value in this certificate. In this chapter he explains why the certificate is revered by Buddhists, and records his own experiences of seeing such certificates in China.*

[3] Buddhas, without exception, receive the Dharma from buddhas, buddha-to-buddha, and patriarchs, without exception, receive the Dharma from patriarchs, patriarch-to-patriarch; this is experience of the [Buddha's] state,[1] this is the one-to-one transmission, and for this reason it is "the supreme state of *bodhi*." It is impossible to certify a buddha without being a buddha, and no one becomes a buddha without receiving the certification of a buddha. Who but a buddha can esteem this state as the most honored and approve it as the supreme? When we receive the certification of a buddha, we realize the state independently, without a master,[2] and we realize the state independently, 68a
without our self.[3] For this reason, we speak of buddhas really experiencing the succession, and of patriarchs really experiencing the same state. The

import of this truth cannot be clarified by anyone other than buddhas. How could it be the thought of [bodhisattvas in] the ten states or the state of balanced awareness?[4] How much less could it be supposed by teachers of sutras, teachers of commentaries, and the like? Even if we explain it to them, they will not be able to hear it, because it is transmitted between buddhas, buddha-to-buddha.

[5] Remember, the Buddha's state of truth is the perfect realization only of buddhas, and without buddhas it has no time. The state is like, for example, stones succeeding each other as stones, jewels succeeding each other as jewels, chrysanthemums succeeding each other, and pine trees certifying each other, at which time the former chrysanthemum and the latter chrysanthemum are each real as they are, and the former pine and the latter pine are each real as they are. People who do not clarify the state like this, even if they encounter the truth authentically transmitted from buddha to buddha, cannot even suspect what kind of truth is being expressed; they do not possess the understanding that buddhas succeed each other and that patriarchs experience the same state. It is pitiful that though they appear to be the Buddha's progeny, they are not the Buddha's children, and they are not child-buddhas.

[6] Sōkei,[5] on one occasion, preaches to the assembly, "From the Seven Buddhas to Enō there are forty buddhas, and from Enō to the Seven Buddhas there are forty patriarchs."[6] This truth is clearly the fundamental teaching to which the Buddhist patriarchs have authentically succeeded. Among these "Seven Buddhas," some have appeared during the past *kalpa* of resplendence[7] and some have appeared in the present *kalpa* of the wise.[8] At the same time, to connect in a line the face-to-face transmissions of the forty patriarchs is the truth of Buddha, and is the succession of Buddha. This being so, going up from the Sixth Patriarch to the Seven Buddhas, there are forty patriarchs who are the buddha successors, and going down from the Seven Buddhas
68b dhas to the Sixth Patriarch, the forty buddhas must be the buddha successors. The truth of buddhas, and the truth of patriarchs, is like this. Without experience of the state, without being a Buddhist patriarch, we do not have the wisdom of a buddha and do not have the perfect realization of a patriarch. Without a buddha's wisdom, we lack belief in the state of buddha. Without a patriarch's perfect realization, we do not experience the same state as

a patriarch. To speak of forty patriarchs, for the present, is just to cite those who are close. Thus, the succession from buddha to buddha is profound and eternal; it is without regression or deviation and without interruption or cessation. The fundamental point is this: although Śākyamuni Buddha realizes the truth before the Seven Buddhas, it has taken him a long time to succeed to the Dharma of Kāśyapa Buddha.[9] Although he realizes the truth on the eighth day of the twelfth month, thirty years after his descent and birth, [this] is realization of the truth before the Seven Buddhas; it is the same realization of the truth shoulder-to-shoulder with, and in time with, the many buddhas; it is realization of the truth before the many buddhas; and it is realization of the truth after all the many buddhas. There is also the principle to be mastered in practice that Kāśyapa Buddha succeeds to the Dharma of Śākyamuni Buddha. Those who do not know this principle do not clarify the Buddha's state of truth. Without clarifying the Buddha's state of truth, they are not the Buddha's successors. The Buddha's successors means the Buddha's children. Śākyamuni Buddha, on one occasion, causes Ānanda to ask,[10] "Whose disciples are the buddhas of the past?" Śākyamuni Buddha says, "The buddhas of the past are the disciples of Śākyamuni Buddha." The Buddhist doctrine of all the buddhas is like this.

[9] To serve these buddhas and to accomplish the succession of Buddha is just the Buddha's truth [practiced by] every buddha. This Buddha's truth is always transmitted in the succession of the Dharma, at which time there is inevitably a certificate of succession. Without the succession of Dharma, we would be non-Buddhists of naturalism. If the Buddha's truth did not dictate the succession of Dharma, how could it have reached the present day? Therefore, in [the transmission] that is [from] buddha [to] buddha, a certifi- 68c
cate of succession, of buddha succeeding buddha, is inevitably present, and a certificate of succession, of buddha succeeding buddha, is received. As regards the concrete situation of the certificate of succession, some succeed to the Dharma on clarifying the sun, the moon, and the stars, and some succeed to the Dharma on being made to get the skin, flesh, bones, and marrow;[11] some receive a *kaṣāya;* some receive a staff; some receive a sprig of pine; some receive a whisk;[12] some receive an *uḍumbara* flower; and some receive a robe of golden brocade.[13] There have been successions with straw sandals[14] and successions with a bamboo stick.[15] When such successions of

the Dharma are received, some write a certificate of succession with blood from a finger, some write a certificate of succession with blood from a tongue, and some perform the succession of Dharma by writing [a certificate] with oil and milk; these are all certificates of succession. The one who has performed the succession and the one who has received it are both the Buddha's successors. Truly, whenever [Buddhist patriarchs] are realized as Buddhist patriarchs, the succession of the Dharma is inevitably realized. When [the succession] is realized, many Buddhist patriarchs [find that] though they did not expect it, it has come, and though they did not seek it, they have succeeded to the Dharma. Those who have the succession of Dharma are, without exception, the buddhas and the patriarchs.

[12] Since the twenty-eighth patriarch[16] came from the west, the fundamental principle has been rightly heard in the Eastern Lands that there is in Buddhism the succession of the Dharma. Before that time, we never heard it at all. [Even] in the Western Heavens, it is neither attained nor known by teachers of commentaries, Dharma teachers, and the like. It is also beyond [bodhisattvas of] the ten sacred and the three clever states. Teachers of mantric techniques who intellectually study the Tripiṭaka[17] are not able even to suspect that it exists. Deplorably, though they have received the human body which is a vessel for the state of truth, they have become uselessly entangled in the net of theory, and so they do not know the method of liberation and they do not hope for the opportunity to spring free. Therefore, we should
69a learn the state of truth in detail, and we should concentrate our resolve to realize the state in practice.

[13] Dōgen, when in Song [China], had the opportunity to bow before certificates of succession, and there were many kinds of certificate. One among them was that of the veteran master Iichi Seidō[18] who had hung his traveling staff at Tendō [Temple]. He was a man from the Etsu district, and was the former abbot of Kōfukuji. He was a native of the same area as my late master. My late master always used to say, "For familiarity with the state, ask Iichi Seidō!" One day Seidō said, "Admirable old [calligraphic] traces are prized possessions of the human world. How many of them have you seen?" Dōgen said, "I have seen few." Then Seidō said, "I have a scroll of old calligraphy in my room. It is a roster. I will let you see it, venerable brother." So saying, he fetched it, and I saw that it was a certificate of succession. It was

a certificate of the succession of Hōgen's[19] lineage, and had been obtained from among the robes and *pātra*[20] of an old veteran monk: it was not that of the venerable Iichi himself. The way it was written is as follows: "The first patriarch Mahākāśyapa realized the truth under Śākyamuni Buddha; Śākyamuni Buddha realized the truth under Kāśyapa Buddha. . . ." It was written like this. Seeing it, Dōgen decisively believed in the succession of the Dharma from rightful successor to rightful successor. [The certificate] was Dharma that I had never before seen. It was a moment in which the Buddhist patriarchs mystically respond to and protect their descendants. The feeling of gratitude was beyond endurance.

[15] The veteran monk Shūgetsu, while he was assigned to the post of head monk[21] on Tendō, showed Dōgen a certificate of succession of Unmon's lineage. The master directly above the person now receiving the certificate, and the Buddhist patriarchs of the Western Heavens and the Eastern Lands, were arranged in columns, and under those was the name of the person receiving the certificate. All the Buddhist patriarchs were directly aligned with the name of this new ancestral master. Thus, the more than forty generations from the Tathāgata all converged on the name of the new successor. For example, it was as if each of them had handed down [the Dharma] to the 69b
new patriarch. Mahākāśyapa, Ānanda, and so on, were aligned as if [they belonged to] separate lineages.[22] At that time, Dōgen asked Head Monk Shūgetsu, "Master, nowadays there are slight differences among the five sects[23] in their alignment [of names]. What is the reason? If the succession from the Western Heavens has passed from rightful successor to rightful successor, how could there be differences?" Shūgetsu said, "Even if the difference were great, we should just study that the buddhas of Unmonzan are like this. Why is Old Master Śākyamuni honored by others? He is an honored one because he realized the truth. Why is Great Master Unmon honored by others? He is an honored one because he realized the truth." Dōgen, hearing these words, had a little [clearer] understanding. Nowadays many leaders of the great temples[24] in Kōsoshō and Setsukōshō[25] are successors to the Dharma of Rinzai, Unmon, Tōzan, and so on. However, among fellows claiming to be distant descendants of Rinzai a certain wrongness is sometimes contrived; namely, they attend the order of a good counselor, and cordially request a hanging portrait and a scroll of Dharma words,[26] which they stash away as

standards of their succession to the Dharma. At the same time, there is a group of dogs who, [prowling] in the vicinity of a venerable patriarch, cordially request Dharma words, portraits, and so on, which they hoard away to excess; then, when they become senior in years, they pay money to government officials and they seek to get a temple, [but] when they are assigned as abbots they do not receive the Dharma from the master [who gave them] the Dharma words and the portrait. They receive the Dharma from fellows of fame and repute of the present generation, or from old veterans who are intimate with kings and ministers, and when they do so they have no interest in getting the Dharma but are only greedy for fame and reputation. It is deplorable that there are wrong customs like this in the corrupt age of the latter Dharma. Among people like these, not one person has ever seen or
69c heard the truth of the Buddhist patriarchs, even in a dream. In general, with respect to the granting of Dharma words, portraits, and so forth, they may be given to lecturers of doctrine and laymen and laywomen, and they may be granted to temple servants, tradesmen, and the like. This principle is clear from the records of many masters. Sometimes, when some undeserving person, out of a rash desire for evidence of succession to the Dharma, wants to get a certificate, [a master] will reluctantly take up the writing brush, though those who possess the truth hate to do so. In such a case the certificate does not follow the traditional form; [the master] just writes some brief note saying "succeeded me." The method of recent times is simply to succeed to the Dharma as soon as one attains proficiency in the order of a particular master, with that master as one's master. [That is to say, there are] people who, although they have not received certification from their former master, are occupying the long platform [of another temple] that they have visited only for entry into [the master's] room and formal preaching in the Dharma hall; [but] when they break open the great matter while staying at [this other] temple, they do not have the time to uphold the transmission of their [original] master; instead they very often take this [new] master as their master. Another matter: there was a certain Library Chief[27] Den, a distant descendant of Zen Master Butsugen, that is, Master Seion of Ryūmon.[28] This Library Chief Den also had a certificate of succession in his possession. In the early years of the Kajō era,[29] when this Library Chief Den had fallen ill, Venerable Elder[30]

Ryūzen, though a Japanese, had nursed Library Chief Den with care; so [Library Chief Den] had taken out the certificate of succession and let [Ryūzen] bow before it to thank him for his nursing work, because his labors had been unremitting. [At that time Library Chief Den] had said, "This is something hardly seen. I will let you bow before it." Eight years later, in the autumn of the sixteenth year of Kajō,[31] when Dōgen first stopped on Tendōzan, Venerable Elder Ryūzen kindly asked Library Chief Den to let Dōgen see the certificate of succession. The form of the certificate was as follows: the forty- 70a
five patriarchs from the Seven Buddhas to Rinzai were written in columns, while the masters following Rinzai formed a circle in which were transcribed the masters' original Dharma names[32] and their written seals.[33] The [name of the] new successor was written at the end, under the date. We should know that the venerable patriarchs of Rinzai's lineage have this kind of difference.

[21] My late master, the abbot of Tendō, profoundly cautioned people against bragging about succeeding to the Dharma. Truly, the order of my late master was the order of an eternal buddha, it was the revival of the monastery.[34] He himself did not wear a patterned *kaṣāya.* He had a patched Dharma robe transmitted from Zen Master Dōkai of Fuyōzan,[35] but he did not wear it [even] to ascend the seat of formal preaching in the Dharma hall. In short, he never wore a patterned Dharma robe throughout his life as an abbot. Those who had the mind and those who did not know things all praised him and honored him as a true good counselor. My late master, the eternal buddha, in formal preaching in the Dharma hall would constantly admonish monks in all directions, saying, "Recently many people who have borrowed the name of the Patriarch's truth randomly wear the Dharma robe and like [to have] long hair, and they sign their name with the title of master as a vessel of promotion. They are pitiful. Who will save them? It is lamentable that the old veterans of all directions have no will to the truth and so they do not learn the state of truth. There are few who have even seen and heard of the causes and conditions of the certificate of succession and the succession of the Dharma. Among a hundred thousand people there is not even one! This is [due to] the decline of the Patriarch's truth." He was always admonishing the old veterans of the whole country like this, but they did not resent him. In conclusion, wherever [people] are sincerely pursuing the truth they are able

70b to see and to hear that the certificate of succession exists. "To have seen and heard" may be "learning the state of truth" itself. On the Rinzai certificate of succession, first the [master] writes the name [of the successor], then writes "Disciple So-and-So served under me," or writes "has attended my order," or writes "entered my inner sanctum," or writes "succeeded me," and then lists the former patriarchs in order. [So] it also shows a trace of traditional[36] instruction about the Dharma, the point being for the successor simply to meet a true good counselor, regardless of whether the meeting is in the end or in the beginning: this is the unassailable fundamental principle.[37] Among [certificates of] the Rinzai [lineage], there are some written as described above—I saw them with my own eyes, and so I have written about them.

[24] "Library Chief Ryōha[38] is a person of the Ibu[39] district, and now he is my disciple. [I,] Tokkō,[40] served Kō[41] of Kinzan. Kinzan succeeded Gon[42] of Kassan. Gon succeeded En[43] of Yōgi. En succeeded Tan[44] of Kaie. Tan succeeded E[45] of Yōgi. E succeeded En[46] of Jimyō. En succeeded Shō[47] of Fun'yō. Shō succeeded Nen[48] of Shuzan. Nen succeeded Shō[49] of Fuketsu. Shō succeeded Gyō of Nan'in.[50] Gyō succeeded Shō[51] of Kōke. Shō was the excellent rightful successor of the founding patriarch Rinzai."[52]

[27] Zen Master Busshō Tokkō of Aikuōzan[53] wrote this and presented it to Musai [Ryō]ha. When [Musai Ryōha] was the abbot of Tendō, my brother monk[54] Chiyu secretly brought it to the Dormitory of Quiescence[55] to show to Dōgen. That was the first time I saw it, the twenty-first day of the first lunar month of the seventeenth year of the great Song era of Kajō [1224]. How overjoyed I felt! This was just the mystical response of the Buddhist patriarchs. I burned incense and did prostrations, then opened and read it. My asking for this certificate of succession to be brought out [happened as follows]: Around the seventh lunar month of the previous year [1223], in the Hall of Serene Light, Chief Officer[56] Shikō had told Dōgen about it in secret. Dōgen had asked the chief in passing, "Nowadays, what person would have one in their possession?" The chief said, "It seems that the venerable
70c abbot has one in his room. In future, if you cordially request him to bring it out, he will surely show it [to you]." Dōgen, after hearing these words, never stopped hoping, day or night. So in that year (1224), I cordially put my humble request to brother monk Chiyu. I did so with all my heart, and the request

was granted. The base on which [the certificate] was written was a lining of white silk, and the cover was red brocade. The rod was precious stone, about nine inches[57] long. [The scroll's] extent was more than seven feet.[58] It was never shown to an idle person. Dōgen thanked Chiyu at once, and then went straightway to visit the abbot, to burn incense and to bow in thanks to Master Musai. At that time Musai said, "This sort of thing is rarely able to be seen or known. Now, venerable brother, you have been able to know of it. This is just the real refuge in learning the truth." At this Dōgen's joy was uncontainable. Later, in the Hōgyō era,[59] while traveling as a cloud between Tendaizan,[60] Ganzan, and so on, Dōgen arrived at Mannenji[61] in the Heiden district. The master of the temple at that time was Master Genshi from Fukushū province. Master [Gen]shi had been assigned following the retirement of the veteran patriarch Sokan and he had completely revitalized the temple. While I was making personal salutations, we had a conversation about the traditional customs of the Buddhist patriarchs, and while quoting the story of the succession from Daii[62] to Kyōzan,[63] the veteran master said, "Have you ever seen the certificate of succession [that I have] in my room?" Dōgen said, "How might I have the chance to see it?" The veteran master himself immediately rose and, holding aloft the certificate of succession,[64] he said, "I have not shown this even to intimates, or even to those who have spent years serving as attendant monks. That is the Buddhist patriarchs' Dharma instruction. However, while staying in the city on my usual visit to the city in order to meet the governor of the district, Genshi had the following dream: An eminent monk, whom I supposed to be Zen Master Hōjō of Daibaizan,[65] appeared holding up a branch of plum blossoms and said, 'If there is a real person who 71a
has crossed the side of a ship, do not begrudge [these] blossoms.' Thus saying, he gave the plum blossoms to me. Unconsciously, Genshi dreamed of chanting, 'Even before he has stepped over the side of the ship, I would like to give him thirty strokes!' In any event, five days have not passed and I meet you, venerable brother. What is more, you have crossed over the side of a ship. And this certificate of succession is written on cloth patterned with plum blossoms. You must be what Daibai was telling me about. You match the image in the dream exactly and so I have brought out [the certificate]. Venerable brother, would you like to receive the Dharma from me? If you

desire it, I will not begrudge it." Dōgen could not contain his belief and excitement. Though he had said that I might request the certificate of succession, I only venerated and served him, burning incense and performing prostrations. Present at that time was a [monk] called Hōnei, an assistant for the burning of incense; he said that it was the first time he had seen the certificate of succession. Dōgen thought inwardly, "It would be very difficult indeed to see and to hear this sort of thing without the mystical help of the Buddhist patriarchs. Why should a stupid fellow from a remote land be so fortunate as to see it several times?" My sleeves became damp with the tears of gratitude. At that time the Vimalakīrti Room, the Great Hall,[66] and the other rooms were quiet and empty; there was no one about. This certificate of succession was written on white silk patterned with plum blossoms fallen on the ground. It was more than nine inches across, and it extended to a length of more than a fathom. The rod was of a yellow precious stone and the cover was brocade. On the way back from Tendaizan to Tendō, Dōgen lodged at the overnight quarters of Goshōji on Daibaizan. [Here] I dreamed a mystical dream in which the ancestral master Daibai came and gave me a branch of plum flowers in bloom. A patriarch's mirror is the most reliable thing there is. The blossoms on that branch were more than a foot in diameter. How could the plum blossoms not have been the flowers of the *uḍumbara*?[67] It may be that the state in a dream and the state in waking con-
71b sciousness are equally real. Dōgen, while in Song [China] and since returning to this country, has not before related [the above] to any person.

[33] Today in our lineage from Tōzan [the way] the certificate of succession is written is different from [the way] it is written in the Rinzai and other [lineages]. The founding patriarch Seigen,[68] in front of Sōkei's desk, personally drew pure blood from his finger to copy [the certificate] that the Buddhist patriarch had kept inside his robe, and [thus] he received the authentic transmission. Legend says that [the certificate] was written and transmitted using a mixture of this finger blood and blood from the finger of Sōkei. Legend says that in the case of the First Patriarch and the Second Patriarch also, a rite of mixing blood was performed.[69] We do not write such words as "My disciple" or "Served me." This is the form of the certificate of succession written and transmitted by the many buddhas and by the Seven Buddhas. So remember that Sōkei graciously mixed his own blood with the pure

blood of Seigen, and Seigen mixed his own pure blood with Sōkei's own blood, and that the founding patriarch, Master Seigen, was thus the only one to receive the direct certification—it was beyond other patriarchs. People who know this fact assert that the Buddha-Dharma was authentically transmitted only to Seigen.

[34] My late master, the eternal buddha, the great master and abbot of Tendō, preached the following: "The buddhas, without exception, have experienced the succession of the Dharma. That is to say, Śākyamuni Buddha received the Dharma from Kāśyapa Buddha, Kāśyapa Buddha received the Dharma from Kanakamuni Buddha, and Kanakamuni Buddha received the Dharma from Krakucchanda Buddha.[70] We should believe that the succession has passed like this from buddha to buddha until the present. This is the way of learning Buddhism." Then Dōgen said, "It was after Kāśyapa Buddha had entered nirvana that Śākyamuni Buddha first appeared in the world and realized the truth. Furthermore, how could the buddhas of the *kalpa* of wisdom receive the Dharma from the buddhas of the *kalpa* of resplendence?[71] 71c
What [do you think] of this principle?" My late master said, "What you have just expressed is understanding [based on] listening to theories. It is the way of [bodhisattvas at] the ten sacred stages or the three clever stages. It is not the way [transmitted by] the Buddhist patriarchs from rightful successor to rightful successor. Our way, transmitted from buddha to buddha, is not like that. We have learned that Śākyamuni Buddha definitely received the Dharma from Kāśyapa Buddha. We learn in practice that Kāśyapa Buddha entered nirvana after Śākyamuni Buddha succeeded to the Dharma. If Śākyamuni Buddha did not receive the Dharma from Kāśyapa Buddha, he might be the same as a naturalistic non-Buddhist. Who then could believe in Śākyamuni Buddha? Because the succession has passed like this from buddha to buddha, and has arrived at the present, the individual buddhas are all authentic successors, and they are neither arranged in a line nor gathered in a group. We just learn that the succession passes from buddha to buddha like this. It need not be related to the measurements of *kalpa*s and the measurements of lifetimes mentioned in the teaching of the Āgamas. If we say that [the succession] was established solely by Śākyamuni Buddha, it has existed for little over two thousand years, [so] it is not old; and the successions [number] little more than forty, [so] they might be called recent. This Buddhist succession

is not to be studied like that. We learn that Śākyamuni Buddha succeeded to the Dharma of Kāśyapa Buddha, and we learn that Kāśyapa Buddha succeeded to the Dharma of Śākyamuni Buddha. When we learn it like this, it is truly the succession of the Dharma of the buddhas and the patriarchs." Then Dōgen not only accepted, for the first time, the existence of Buddhist patriarchs' succession of the Dharma, but also got rid of an old nest.[72]

Shōbōgenzō Shisho

Written at Kannondōrikōshōhōrinji on the seventh day of the third lunar month in the second year of Japan's Ninji era,[73] by [a monk] who entered Song [China] and received the transmission of the Dharma, *śramaṇa* Dōgen.

72a The twenty-fourth day of the ninth lunar month in [the first year of] Kangen.[74] Hung our traveling staffs at old Kippōji, a thatched cottage in Yoshida district of Echizen.[75] (written seal)[76]

Notes

1 *Shōkai. Shō* means experience. *Kai* means pledge, promise, accord, or binding agreement and, by extension, the state which is exactly the same as the state of Gautama Buddha.

2 *Mushi-dokugo.* This expression appears repeatedly in the *Shōbōgenzō.*

3 *Muji-dokugo.* This is Master Dōgen's variation.

4 *Jūchi-tōgaku.* It is said that bodhisattvas pass through fifty-two stages on the way to buddhahood. The forty-first to the fiftieth stages are *jūchi,* the ten sacred stages. The fifty-first stage is *tōkaku,* or "balanced awareness," and the ultimate stage is *myōkaku,* or "subtle awareness."

5 Master Daikan Enō (638–713), successor of Master Daiman Kōnin.

6 Master Daikan Enō was the Sixth Patriarch in China, counting from Master Bodhidharma as the First Patriarch in China. He was the thirty-third patriarch, counting from the Buddha's successor, Master Mahākāśyapa as the first patriarch. And he was the fortieth patriarch counting from Vipaśyin Buddha, the first of the seven ancient buddhas.

7 *Shōgonkō.* The past age extending from the eternal past to Viśvabhū Buddha (the third of the Seven Buddhas), in which one thousand buddhas appeared.

8 *Kengō,* from the Sanskrit *bhadra-kalpa,* the age in which we are living now.

9 Kāśyapa Buddha is the sixth of the Seven Buddhas.

10 Master Ānanda is the second patriarch in India. See Chapter Fifteen, *Busso.*

11 Refers to the transmission between Master Bodhidharma and Master Taiso Eka. See Chapter Forty-six (Vol. III), *Kattō.*

12 *Hossu* (Skt. *vyajana*), a whisk usually with a long plume of white animal hair, held by a Buddhist master during a lecture or ceremony, originally used in India to clear insects from one's path.

13 Refers to the transmission between the Buddha and Master Mahākāśyapa. See Chapter Sixty-eight (Vol. III), *Udonge.*

14 For example, the succession between Master Taiyō Kyōgen and Master Tōsu Gisei (see notes to Chapter Fifteen, *Busso*).

[15] *Shippei.* A stick about three feet long, made of split bamboo, with a ceremonial handle. It is used, for example, in the ceremony to inaugurate a head monk.

[16] Master Bodhidharma, the First Patriarch in China.

[17] *Sanzō,* lit., "three storehouses," from the Sanskrit Tripiṭaka (three baskets): Sutra, Vinaya (precepts), and Abhidharma (commentaries).

[18] Seidō, lit., "west hall," is a title of respect for a veteran master who has retired from his own temple and is now living as a guest in the west hall of another temple.

[19] Master Hōgen Bun'eki (885–958), the successor of Master Rakan Keichin, who was a successor of Master Gensha Shibi.

[20] A *pātra* is a Buddhist food bowl. Robes and *pātra* symbolize the possessions of a monk.

[21] *Shuso,* lit., "head seat." The *shuso* was the leader of the main body of monks in a temple. He was the highest ranking of the six *chōshu,* or assistant officers. Ranking above them were the six *chiji,* or main officers.

[22] That is, the names of the first and second patriarchs were arranged not in a vertical line but side by side at the top of their respective columns of historical patriarchs.

[23] The Rinzai, Igyō, Sōtō, Unmon, and Hōgen sects. See Chapter Forty-nine (Vol. III), *Butsudō.*

[24] *Daisetsu. Setsu* is from the Sanskrit *kṣetra,* which means a sacred spot or district (see Glossary of Sanskrit Terms). At the same time, the character appears in Buddhist sutras in the compound *sekkan,* or "*kṣetra* pole," that is, a temple flagpole. This led Chinese scholars to interpret that *setsu* might be a transliteration of *yaṣṭi,* which means flagpole. In ancient India a flag announced Buddhist preaching and so Chinese scholars interpreted that a flagpole symbolized a place of Buddhist preaching, and hence a temple.

[25] Provinces in eastern China bordering on the Yellow Sea and the East China Sea, respectively.

[26] *Hōgo,* calligraphy containing a word or a phrase of Buddhist preaching.

[27] *Zōsu,* the monk in charge of storing sutras. The *zōsu* was one of the six *chōshu,* or assistant officers.

[28] Master Ryūmon Butsugen (d. 1120), a successor of Master Goso Hōen. He received the title Zen Master Butsugen, together with a purple robe, from the emperor. The *Goroku,* a record of his words, is in eight volumes.

[29] 1208–1224.

[30] *Jōza,* from the Sanskrit honorific *sthavira,* or in Pāli, *thera,* as in Theravāda, the School of the Elders. See Glossary of Sanskrit Terms.

[31] 1223.

[32] "Original Dharma name" is *hōki. Hō* means Dharma or Buddhist and *ki* means "the name to be avoided." After a monk had died, it was customary to avoid using the name he had used in his lifetime, and to use a posthumous title instead. While living, monks in China and Japan usually have at least two personal names, each written with two Chinese characters. One name is the *hōgō,* "Dharma title," and another name is the *hōmyō,* "Dharma name." A *hōmyō* is always a *hōki,* whereas a *hōgō* may be a name used in a monk's lifetime or it may be a posthumous name.

[33] *Kaji.* This seal was not stamped but written with a brush.

[34] *Sōrin,* lit., "clump of forest," from the Sanskrit *piṇḍavana,* meaning a large assembly of monks, or a monastery.

[35] Master Fuyō Dōkai (1043–1118), the Eighteenth Patriarch in China and a successor of Master Tōsu Gisei. See for example Chapter Fourteen, *Sansuigyō;* Chapter Twenty-nine (Vol. II), *Gyōji;* and Chapter Sixty-four (Vol. III), *Kajō.*

[36] "Traditional" is *ii kitare ru,* lit., "having been spoken."

[37] In other words, the most important matter in the transmission is the relation between master and student. This is reflected in the form of the certificate in the Rinzai sect.

[38] Master Musai Ryōha. He was the master of Keitokuji on Tendōzan when Master Dōgen arrived in China. When Master Ryōha's death was approaching, he sent a letter to Master Dōgen's future master, Master Tendō Nyojō, asking him to become the master of the temple.

[39] Present-day Fukien, a province of southeast China bordering on the Formosa Strait.

[40] Master Busshō Tokkō (1121–1203). Author of the *Sōtairoku* (*Record of Answers to an Emperor*), one volume.

[41] Master Daie Sōkō (b. 1089, d. 1163, thirty-seven years before Master Dōgen's birth). He is thought to be the founder of the so-called *kōan* Zen of the Rinzai sect, and as such was criticized by Master Dōgen several times in the *Shōbōgenzō.* See for example Chapter Seventy-five (Vol. IV), *Jishō-zanmai.*

[42] Master Engo Kokugon (1063–1135). Edited the *Hekiganroku* (*Blue Cliff Record*). Master Engo is quoted in Chapter Sixty-six (Vol. III), *Shunjū,* and Chapter Seventy-four (Vol. IV), *Tembōrin.*

[43] Master Goso Hōen (1024–1104). The *Goroku,* a record of his words, is in four volumes. He was the third patriarch of the temple on Yōgizan founded by Master Yōgi Hōe. Master Hōen is quoted in Chapter Seventy-four (Vol. IV), *Tembōrin.*

[44] Master Kaie Shutan (1025–1072). Also called Master Hakkun Shutan. (Kaie and Hakkun are both *hōgō* (Dharma titles)—see note 32).

[45] Master Yōgi Hōe (992–1049). Lived on and spread the Dharma from Yōgizan. The *Goroku* and *Kōroku,* records of his words, are in one volume each.

[46] Master Jimyō Soen (986–1039). Became a monk at the age of twenty-two.

[47] Master Fun'yō Zenshō (947–1024). The *Goroku,* a record of his words, is in three volumes.

[48] Master Shuzan Shōnen (926–993). The *Goroku,* a record of his words, is in one volume.

[49] Master Fuketsu Enshō (896?–973).

[50] Master Nan'in Egyō (d. 930?).

[51] Master Kōke Sonshō (830–888).

[52] Master Rinzai Gigen (815?–867). A successor of Master Ōbaku Kiun. The *Goroku,* a record of his words, is in one volume. His disciples included Master Kōke Sonshō, Master Sanshō Enen, and Master Kankei Shikan. See, for example, Chapter Forty-nine (Vol. III), *Butsudō.*

In this certificate, the names Ryōha and Tokkō are *hōmyō* (Dharma names) while Rinzai is a *hōgō* (Dharma title). For the other names only the first character of the *hōmyō* is written. When a master's name is written in full, the name of the master's temple or mountain often precedes the *hōmyō.* Thus E of Yōgizan is Master Yōgi Hōe, Nyojō of Tendōzan is Master Tendō Nyojō, Dōgen of Eiheiji is Master Eihei Dōgen, etc. See note 32.

[53] Aikuō means King Aśoka. In 282 a priest called Ryūsaku discovered an old stupa on this mountain, and guessed that it might be one of eighty-four thousand stupas said to have been built by King Aśoka of ancient India. So the mountain was named after King Aśoka. It later became one of the five mountains: Mount Kin, Mount Hoku, Mount Taihaku, Mount Nan, and Mount Aikuō. The government of the Song dynasty, promoting Buddhism as part of its political strategy, designated the temples on these five mountains as the most important in China.

[54] *Shō-shi-sō.* The term was used for a monk who had not passed ten summer retreats since receiving the precepts.

[55] The Dormitory of Quiescence (*ryōnen-ryō*) and the Hall of Serene Light (*jakkō-dō*) were proper names of these particular buildings on Mount Tendō.

[56] *Tsūsu,* the highest of the six temple officers. The six main officers are 1) *tsūsu,* chief officer, head of the temple office, comptroller; 2) *kansu,* prior; 3) *fūsu,* assistant prior; 4) *dōsu* or *inō,* supervisor of monks in the zazen hall, rector; 5) *tenzo,* head cook; and 6) *shisui,* caretaker.

[57] Literally, "About nine *sun.*" One *sun* is 1.193 inches.

[58] Literally, "more than seven *shaku.*" One *shaku* is ten *sun.*

[59] 1225–27.

[60] Abbreviated in the original text to Daizan. The Tendai sect takes its name from this mountain in Chekiang province in eastern China, where Master Tendai Chigi (538–597)

lived. Master Dōgen became a monk in the Tendai sect in Japan while still a teenager.

61 A temple established on Mount Tendai, at the site where Master Tendai Fugan died. Master Fugan was a successor of Master Hyakujō Ekai.

62 Master Isan Reiyū (771–853), a successor of Master Hyakujō Ekai. He had many excellent disciples such as Master Kyōzan Ejaku, Master Kyōgen Chikan, and Master Reiun Shigon. The *Goroku,* a record of his words, is in one volume.

63 Master Kyōzan Ejaku (807–883). The *Goroku,* a record of his words, is in one volume. The story of Master Kyōzan's succession is contained in the *Gotōegen,* chapter 8.

64 It is usual to place venerated things on the palms of the hands and to hold them up high.

65 Master Daibai Hōjō (752–839), a successor of Master Baso Dōitsu. He lived in seclusion on Daibaizan; see Chapter Thirty (Vol. II), *Gyōji.*

66 Proper names of these particular rooms.

67 The *uḍumbara* is a species of fig tree whose flowers form a kind of peel, so that there do not appear to be any *uḍumbara* flowers. The *uḍumbara* flower is a symbol of the transmission of Dharma. See Chapter Sixty-eight (Vol. III), *Udonge.*

68 Master Seigen Gyōshi (660–740) was one of several successors of Master Daikan Enō of Sōkei Mountain, the Sixth Patriarch in China. Master Tōzan belongs to the lineage of Master Seigen Gyōshi. Master Rinzai belongs to the lineage of another of Master Daikan Enō's successors, Master Nangaku Ejō.

69 Master Bodhidharma and Master Taiso Eka.

70 Krakucchanda Buddha, Kanakamuni Buddha, Kāśyapa Buddha, and Śākyamuni Buddha were the fourth, fifth, sixth, and seventh of the seven ancient buddhas.

71 The *kalpa* of wisdom means the present age. The *kalpa* of resplendence means the eternal past. See note 7.

72 The tense of the original Japanese sentence is the historical present. When Master Dōgen uses the historical present for a story, we generally try to use the present in translation. But in the many places in this chapter where Master Dōgen uses the historical present to describe his own experiences, and in the description of his late master, the past tense has been used in translation.

73 1241.

74 1243. The year is identified, using the Chinese dating system, by the characters *kibō. Ki* is the tenth calendar sign (the younger brother of water) and *bō* is the fourth horary sign (the rabbit). The year at the end of the chapter is usually expressed in two ways, using the Japanese dating system and the Chinese dating system (ignored in translation) as a double check. However, in this sentence the word *gannen,* "first year," was abbreviated.

[75] Corresponds to present-day Fukui prefecture.

[76] It is likely that Master Dōgen actually wrote his own seal having arrived at Kippōji, after which Master Koun Ejō, when copying Master Dōgen's original text, wrote the words *kaji,* "written seal" (see note 33).

[Chapter Seventeen]

Hokke-ten-hokke

The Flower of Dharma Turns the Flower of Dharma

Translator's Note: Hō *means "Dharma," "the law of the universe," or the universe itself.* Ke *means "flowers." So* hokke *means "the universe that is like flowers." The full title of the* Lotus Sutra, Myōhōrengekyō (Sutra of the Lotus Flower of the Wonderful Dharma), *is usually abbreviated to* Hokkekyō. *So* hokke *also suggests the wonderful universe as manifested in the* Lotus Sutra. Ten *means "to turn," or "to move." So* hokke-ten-hokke *means "the wonderful universe that is like flowers is moving the wonderful universe that is like flowers itself." This is the Buddhist view of the universe, and Master Dōgen's view. In this chapter, Master Dōgen explains this view of the universe, quoting many words from the* Lotus Sutra. *The message of the* Lotus Sutra *is "How wonderful is the universe in which we are now living!" So here Master Dōgen unfolds his view of the universe, following the theory of the* Lotus Sutra.

[39] "The content of the buddha lands of the ten directions"[1] is the "sole existence"[2] of the "Flower of Dharma."[3] Herein, "all the buddhas of the ten directions and the three times,"[4] and beings of *anuttara samyaksaṃbodhi,*[5] have [times of] turning the Flower of Dharma,[6] and have [times of] the Flower of Dharma turning.[7] This is just the state in which "original practice of the bodhisattva way"[8] neither regresses nor deviates. It is the "wisdom of the buddhas, profound and unfathomable."[9] It is the "calm and clear state of *samādhi,*"[10] which is "difficult to understand and difficult to enter."[11] As Buddha Mañjuśrī,[12] it has the "form as it is"[13] of "buddhas alone, together with buddhas,"[14] which is "the great ocean" or "the buddha land." Or as Buddha Śākyamuni,[15] it is "appearance in the world"[16] in the state of "Only I know concrete form, and the buddhas of the ten directions are also like that."[17] It is the "one time"[18] in which he "desires to cause living beings"[19]

to "disclose, to display, to realize, and to enter,"[20] [saying] "I and buddhas of the ten directions are directly able to know these things."[21] Or it is Universal Virtue,[22] "accomplishing" the Dharma Flower's turning whose "virtue is unthinkable,"[23] and "spreading throughout Jambudvīpa"[24] the "profound and eternal"[25] [truth of] *anuttara samyaksaṃbodhi*, at which time the earth is able to produce the three kinds of plants, the two kinds of shrubs, and "large and small trees,"[26] and the rain is able to moisten them. In the state in which "an object cannot be recognized,"[27] he is solely "accomplishing the total practice"[28] of the Flower of Dharma turning. While Universal Virtue's spreading [of the truth] is still unfinished, the "great order on Vulture Peak"[29] comes together. Śākyamuni experiences, as the "manifestation of light from his [circle of] white hair,"[30] the coming and going of Universal Virtue.[31] The Flower of Dharma turns when, before Śākyamuni's "Buddhist assembly is halfway through," the "consideration"[32] of Mañjuśrī "swiftly" gives "affirmation"[33] to Maitreya. Universal Virtue, the many buddhas, Mañjuśrī, and the great assembly, may all be the "*pāramitā* of knowing"[34] the Dharma
72b Flower's turning, which is "good in the beginning, middle, and end."[35] This is why [the Buddha] has "manifested himself in reality," calling "sole reliance"[36] on the "One Vehicle"[37] "the one great matter."[38] Because this manifestation in reality is itself "the one great matter," there are [the words] "buddhas alone, together with buddhas, just can perfectly realize that all *dharmas* are real form."[39] The method[40] for that is inevitably "the One Buddha Vehicle," and "buddhas alone" necessarily teach its "perfect realization" to "buddhas alone." "The many buddhas" and "the Seven Buddhas"[41] teach its "perfect realization" to each individual buddha, buddha-to-buddha, and they cause Śākyamuni Buddha to "accomplish" it.[42] [Every place from] India in the west to China in the east is "in the buddha lands of the ten directions." [For every patriarch] until the thirty-third patriarch, Zen Master Daikan,[43] [this method] is the method which is "the One Vehicle of buddhas alone," and which is just "perfect realization" itself. It is "the One Buddha Vehicle" in which "sole reliance" is decisively "the one great matter." Now it is "manifesting itself in the world."[44] It is manifesting itself at this place.[45] That the Buddhist customs of Seigen[46] have been transmitted to the present, and that Nangaku's[47] Dharma gate has been opened and preached through the world, are totally [due to] the "Tathāgata's real wisdom."[48] Truly, this [real wisdom]

is the "perfect realization of buddhas alone, together with buddhas." The Dharma Flower's turning may be preaching it[49] as the "disclosure, display, realization, and entering" of buddhas who are rightful successors, and of rightful successors of buddhas. This [real wisdom] is also called the *Sutra of the Lotus Flower of the Wonderful Dharma,*[50] and it is "the method of teaching bodhisattvas."[51] Because this [real wisdom] has been called "all *dharma*s," "Vulture Peak" exists, "space"[52] exists, the "great ocean"[53] exists, and the "great earth"[54] exists, with the Flower of Dharma as their "national land."[55] This is just "real form"; it is "reality as it is";[56] "it is the wisdom of the Buddha"; it is "the constancy of the manifestation of the world";[57] it is "the real";[58] it is "the Tathāgata's lifetime";[59] it is "the profound and unfathomable";[60] it is "the inconstancy of all actions";[61] it is "*samādhi* as [the state of] the Flower of Dharma";[62] it is "Śākyamuni Buddha"; it is "to turn the Flower of Dharma";[63] it is "the Flower of Dharma turning";[64] it is "the right Dharma-eye treasury and the fine mind of nirvana";[65] and it is "manifestation of the body to save living beings."[66] As "affirmation and becoming buddha,"[67] it is maintained and relied upon, and dwelled in and retained.

[47] To the order of Zen Master Daikan[68] at Hōrinji on Sōkeizan, in the Shōshū district of Guangdong,[69] in the great kingdom of Tang, there came a monk called Hōtatsu.[70] He boasts, "I have recited the *Lotus Sutra* three thou- 72c
sand times already."

The patriarch says, "Even if [you recite it] ten thousand times, if you do not understand the sutra, you will not be able even to recognize [your] errors."

Hōtatsu says, "The student is foolish. Until now, I have only been reading [the sutra] aloud following the characters. How could I have hoped to clarify the meaning?"

The patriarch says, "Try reciting a round [of the sutra] and I will interpret it for you."

Hōtatsu recites the sutra at once. When he reaches the "Expedient Means"[71] chapter the patriarch says, "Stop! The fundamental point of this sutra is the purpose of [the buddhas'] appearance in the world.[72] Although it expounds many metaphors, [the sutra] does not go beyond this. What is that purpose? Only the one great matter. The one great matter is just the Buddha's wisdom itself; it is to disclose, to display, to realize, and to enter [the Buddha's wisdom]. [The one great matter] is naturally the wisdom of the Buddha and someone who is equipped with the wisdom is already a buddha. You must now believe that the Buddha's wisdom is simply your own natural state of mind." He preaches again in the following verse:

> When the mind is in delusion, the Flower of Dharma turns.
> When the mind is in realization, we turn the Flower of Dharma.
> Unless we are clear about ourselves, however long we recite [the sutra],
> It will become an enemy because of its meanings.
> Without intention the mind is right.
> With intention the mind becomes wrong.
> When we transcend both with and without,
> We ride eternally in the white ox cart.[73]

Hōtatsu, on hearing this poem, addresses the patriarch again: "The sutra says that even if all in the great [order], from *śrāvaka*s to bodhisattvas, exhausted their intellect to suppose it,[74] they could not fathom the Buddha's wisdom. If you are now saying that the effort to make the common person realize his own mind is just the Buddha's wisdom, unless we are of excellent makings we can hardly help doubting and denying it. Furthermore, the sutra explains the three kinds of carts, but what kind of distinction is there between the great ox cart and the white ox cart? Please, master, bestow your
73a preaching again."

The patriarch says, "The intention of the sutra is clear. You are straying off on your own and going against it. When people of the three vehicles cannot fathom the Buddha's wisdom, the trouble is in their supposition itself. Even if together they exhaust their intellects to consider it,[75] they will only get further and further away.[76] The Buddha originally preaches only for the benefit of the common person; he does not preach for the benefit of buddhas. Some are not fit to believe this principle and withdraw from their seats;[77] they do not know that they are sitting in the white ox cart yet still searching outside the gate[78] for the three kinds of carts. The words of the sutra are clearly telling you: 'There is neither a second nor a third.'[79] Why do you not realize it? The three carts are fictitious, for they belong to the past. The One Vehicle is real, for it exists in the present. I only [wish to] make you get rid of the fiction and get back to the reality. When we get back to reality, reality is not a concept. Remember, your possessions are all treasures,[80] and they totally belong to you. How you receive and use them is up to you. [The reality of the sutra] is neither the ideas of the father nor the ideas of the children,[81] indeed it does not rely upon ideas at all; rather, it is called the *Sutra of the Flower of Dharma.* From *kalpa* to *kalpa,* from noon to night, [our] hands do not put down the sutra, and there is no time when we are not reading it." Hōtatsu, enlightened already and jumping for joy,[82] presents the following verse of praise:

> Three thousand recitations of the sutra
> With one phrase from Sōkei, forgotten.
> Before clarifying the import of [the buddhas'] appearance in the
> world,
> How can we stop recurring lives of madness?
> [The sutra] explains goat, deer, and ox as an expedient,
> [But] proclaims that beginning, middle, and end are good.
> Who knows that [even] within the burning house,
> Originally we are kings in the Dharma.

When he presents this verse, the patriarch says, "From now on, you may be called the Sutra-reading Monk."[83]

[54] The story[84] of how Zen Master Hōtatsu visited Sōkei is like this. 73b
Hereafter the Flower of Dharma began to be expounded as the Flower of Dharma turning and turning of the Dharma Flower. [Those terms] were not heard previously. Truly, the clarification of the Buddha's wisdom should always take place under a Buddhist patriarch who may be the right Dharma-eye treasury itself. [The Buddha's wisdom] cannot be known by literary scholars who vainly count sand and pebbles, as we can see again here in Hōtatsu's experience. To clarify the true meaning of the Flower of Dharma, "perfectly realize," as "only the one great purpose," that which the ancestral master "disclosed and displayed." Do not intend to study other vehicles. The present is the reality[85] as it is of the real form, the real nature, the real body, the real energy, the real causes, and the real effects of the Flower of Dharma turning.[86] This was never heard in China, and it was never present [in China], before the time of the ancestral master. "The Flower of Dharma

is turning" means "the mind is in delusion"; the mind being deluded is just the Flower of Dharma turning. Therefore, when the mind is in delusion, we are being turned by the Flower of Dharma. This means that even when mental delusion is in myriad phenomena, "form as it is"[87] is still being turned by the Flower of Dharma. This being turned is not to be rejoiced at, and it is not to be hoped for; it is not gained, and it does not come. Even so, when the Flower of Dharma is turning "there is neither a second nor a third." Because [the Flower of Dharma turning] is the "sole existence of the One Buddha Vehicle," and because it is the Flower of Dharma with "form as it is," whether it is the turner or the turned, it is "the One Buddha Vehicle," and "the one great matter."

[88]It is just moment by moment of red mind,[89] upon which we rely solely. So do not worry about the mind being deluded. Your actions are the bodhisattva way itself;[90] they are to serve the buddhas,[91] which is original practice of the bodhisattva way.[92] What you disclose, display, realize, and enter is, in every case, an instance of the Flower of Dharma turning.

[93]There is mental delusion in the burning house, there is mental delusion just at the gate itself, there is mental delusion outside the gate, there is mental delusion just in front of the gate, and there is mental delusion within
73c the gate.[94] Mental delusion has created "within the gate" and "outside the gate" and even "the gate itself," "the burning house," and so on; therefore, disclosure, display, realization, and entering may take place even on the white ox-carriage.[95] When we think of entry as "adornment"[96] on this carriage, should we hope for "open ground"[97] as the place to enter, or should we recognize "the burning house" as the place to leave?[98] Should we reach the conclusion[99] that the gate itself is merely a place of momentary passing?[100] Remember, inside the carriage, there is turning [of the Flower of Dharma] which causes us to disclose, to display, to realize, and to enter the burning house; and on the open ground there is turning which causes us to disclose, to display, to realize, and to enter the burning house.[101] There are cases in which the turning activates disclosure, display, realization, and entering through the whole gate as the gate here and now;[102] and there are cases in which the turning activates disclosure, display, realization, and entering through a single gate which is [an instance of] the universal gate.[103] There is turning which discloses, displays, realizes, and enters the universal gate

in each instance of disclosure, display, realization, and entering.[104] There are cases in which the turning activates disclosure, display, realization, and entering within the gate,[105] and there are cases in which the turning activates disclosure, display, realization, and entering outside the gate.[106] There are cases of disclosing, displaying, realizing, and entering open ground in the burning house.[107]

[108]Therefore the burning house is "beyond understanding"[109] and the open ground is "beyond knowing."[110] Who could make the turning of the wheel of the triple world[111] into a carriage and ride it as "the One Vehicle"? Who could leave and enter disclosure, display, realization, and entering as if they were a gate? If we seek the carriage from the burning house, how many times the wheel must turn! When we look upon the burning house from the open ground, how "deep in the distance"[112] it is! Should we reach the conclusion that Vulture Peak existed "in tranquility"[113] on open ground? Or should we study in action that the open ground is "balanced and even"[114] on Vulture Peak? "The place where living beings enjoy themselves"[115] has been made into "eternal presence"[116] as "my Pure Land which is immortal,"[117] and this also we must meticulously perform as "original practice."[118]

Do we realize in practice that "wholeheartedly wanting to meet Buddha"[119] is about ourselves, or do we realize in practice that it is about others? There are times when the truth is realized as an "individual body,"[120] and there are times when the truth is realized as the "whole body."[121]

"Appearance together on Vulture Peak"[122] comes from "not begrudging one's own body and life."[123] There is disclosure, display, realization, and entering in "constantly abiding here preaching the Dharma,"[124] and there is 74a
disclosure, display, realization, and entering in, "as an expedient method, manifesting nirvana."[125] In the state of "being close yet still failing to see,"[126] who could not believe in understanding of non-understanding by "wholeheartedness"?[127]

The place that is "always filled with gods and human beings"[128] is just the land of Śākyamuni Buddha and of Vairocana,[129] "the eternally peaceful and bright land"[130] itself. We who naturally belong in the "four lands"[131] are just living in "the Buddha's land" which is "real oneness."[132] When we look at "atoms"[133] that does not mean we fail to see "the world of Dharma." When we are experiencing the world of Dharma,[134] that does not mean we fail to experience atoms. When the buddhas experience the world of Dharma, they do not exclude us from the experience, which is "good at the beginning, middle, and end."

This being so, the present is the "form as it is" of the state of experience, and even "alarm, doubt, and fear"[135] are nothing other than reality as it is. With the Buddha's wisdom, this [fear] is only the difference between looking at atoms and sitting in atoms. When we are seated in the world of Dharma it is not wide, and when we are sitting in atoms, they are not confining; therefore, without maintaining and relying upon [reality as it is], we cannot sit, but when we are maintaining and relying upon [reality as it is], there is no alarm or doubt about width and confinement. This is because we have "perfectly realized" the "body" and the "energy" of the Flower of Dharma. So should we think that our own "form" and "nature" now are "originally practicing" in this world of Dharma, or should we think that they are "originally practicing" in atoms? They are without alarm and doubt, and without fear; they are simply the profound and eternal state which is original practice as the Flower of Dharma turning. This seeing atoms and seeing the world of Dharma is beyond conscious action and conscious consideration. Conscious consideration, and conscious action too, should learn Flower of Dharma consideration, and should learn Flower of Dharma action. When we hear of "disclosure, display, realization, and entering," we should understand them in terms of [the Buddha's] "desire to cause living beings."[136] In other words, that which, as the Flower of Dharma turning, discloses the Buddha's wisdom, we should learn by displaying the Buddha's wisdom. That which, as the Flower of Dharma turning, realizes the Buddha's wisdom, we should learn by entering the Buddha's wisdom. That which, as the Flower of Dharma turning, displays the Buddha's wisdom, we should learn by real-
74b izing the Buddha's wisdom. For each such instance of the Flower of Dharma turning, as disclosure, display, realizing, and entering, we can have ways of perfect realization. In sum, this wisdom-*pāramitā*[137] of the buddha-tathāgatas is the Dharma Flower's turning, which is wide, great, profound, and eternal. "Affirmation"[138] is just our own disclosure of the Buddha's wisdom; it is the Flower of Dharma's turning which is never imparted by others. This, then, is [the reality of] "When the mind is in the state of delusion, the Flower of Dharma turns."

[62] "When the mind is in the state of realization, we turn the Flower of Dharma" describes turning the Flower of Dharma. That is to say, when the Flower of Dharma has "perfectly exhausted"[139] the energy with which it turns us, the "energy as it is"[140] with which we turn ourselves will, in turn, be realized. This realization is to turn the Flower of Dharma. Though the former turning is, even now, without cease, we, reversely, are naturally turning the Flower of Dharma. Though we have not finished donkey business, horse business will still come in.[141] [Here] there exists "sole reliance on the one great purpose" as "real appearance at this place."[142] The multitudes of the thousandfold world that "spring out of the earth"[143] have long been great honored saints of the Flower of Dharma[144] but they spring out of the earth being turned by themselves and they spring out of the earth being turned by circumstances.[145] In turning the Flower of Dharma we should not only realize springing out of the earth; in turning the Flower of Dharma we should also realize springing out of space.[146] We should know with the Buddha's wisdom not only earth and space but also springing out of the Flower of Dharma itself. In general, in the time of the Flower of Dharma, inevitably, "the father is young and the son old."[147] It is neither that the son is not the son, nor that the father is not the father; we should just learn that the son is old and the father young. Do not imitate "the disbelief of the world"[148] and be surprised. [Even] the disbelief of the world is the time of the Flower of Dharma. This being so, in turning the Flower of Dharma we should realize the "one time" in which "the Buddha is living."[149] Turned by disclosure, display, realization, and entering, we spring out of the earth; and turned by the Buddha's wisdom, we spring out of the earth. At the time of this turning the Flower of Dharma, "mental realization"[150] exists as the Flower of Dharma, and the Flower of Dharma exists as mental realization.[151] For another exam- 74c
ple, the meaning of "the downward direction" is just "the inside of space."[152] This "downward," and this "space," are just the turning of the Flower of Dharma, and are just the lifetime of the Buddha. We should realize, in turning the Flower of Dharma, that the Buddha's lifetime, the Flower of Dharma, the world of Dharma, and the wholehearted state, are realized as "downward," and realized also as "space." Thus, "downward space" describes just the realization of turning the Flower of Dharma. In sum, at this moment, by turning the Flower of Dharma we can cause the three kinds of grass to exist,

and by turning the Flower of Dharma we can cause the two kinds of trees to exist. We should not expect [this] to be a state of awareness, and we should not wonder whether it is a state without awareness. When we turn ourselves and "initiate *bodhi,*"[153] that is just "the southern quarter."[154] This realization of the truth is originally present on Vulture Peak, which convenes as an order in the southern quarter. Vulture Peak is always present in our turning the Flower of Dharma. There are buddha lands of the ten directions that convene as an order in space, and this is an individual body[155] turning the Flower of Dharma. When we realize it, in turning the Flower of Dharma, as already the buddha lands of the ten directions, there is no place into which an atom could enter. There is turning the Flower of Dharma as "matter just being the immaterial,"[156] which is beyond "either disappearance or appearance."[157] There is turning the Flower of Dharma as "the immaterial just being matter,"[158] which may be "absence of life and death."[159] We cannot call it "being in the world";[160] and how could it only be in a process of "extinction"?[161] When [a person] is a "close friend"[162] to us, we are also a "close friend" to that person. We must not forget to bow to and to work for a "close friend"; therefore, we must take care to perfectly realize moments of giving "the pearl in the topknot"[163] and of giving "the pearl in the clothes."[164] There is turning the Flower of Dharma in the presence "before the Buddha" of a "treasure stupa,"[165] whose "height is five hundred *yojana*s."[166] There is turning the Flower of Dharma in the "Buddha sitting inside the stupa,"[167] whose extent is "two hundred and fifty *yojana*s." There is turning the Flower of Dharma in springing out from the earth and abiding in the earth, [in which state] mind is without restriction and matter is without restriction. There is turning the Flower of Dharma in springing out from the sky and abiding in the earth, which is restricted by the eyes and restricted by the body.[168] Vul-
75a ture Peak exists inside the stupa, and the treasure stupa exists on Vulture Peak. The treasure stupa is a treasure stupa in space, and space makes space for the treasure stupa.[169] The eternal buddha inside the stupa takes his seat alongside the buddha of Vulture Peak, and the buddha of Vulture Peak experiences the state of experience as the buddha inside the stupa.[170] When the buddha of Vulture Peak enters the state of experience inside the stupa, while object and subject on Vulture Peak [remain] just as they are, he enters into the turning of the Flower of Dharma. When the buddha inside the stupa

springs out on Vulture Peak, while still of the land of eternal buddhas, while still "long extinct,"[171] he springs out. "Springing out," and "entering into the turning," are not to be learned under common people and the two vehicles, [but] should follow turning of the Flower of Dharma. "Eternal extinction" is an ornament of real experience that adorns the state of buddha. "Inside the stupa," "before the Buddha," "the treasure stupa," and "space" are not of Vulture Peak; they are not of the world of Dharma; they are not a halfway stage; and they are not of the whole world. Nor are they concerned with only a "concrete place in the Dharma."[172] They are simply "different from thinking."[173] There is turning the Flower of Dharma either in "manifesting the body of Buddha and preaching the Dharma for others"[174] or in manifesting this body and preaching the Dharma for others. Or turning the Flower of Dharma is the manifestation of Devadatta.[175] Or there is turning the Flower of Dharma in the manifestation of "to retreat also is fine."[176] Do not always measure "the waiting, with palms held together and [faces] looking up,"[177] as "sixty minor *kalpa*s."[178] Even if the length of "wholehearted waiting"[179] is condensed into just a few countless *kalpa*s, still it will be impossible to fathom the "buddha-wisdom."[180] As how much buddha-wisdom should we see a wholehearted mind that is waiting? Do not see this turning the Flower of Dharma only as "the bodhisattva way practiced in the past."[181] Wherever the Flower of Dharma is a total order the virtue is that of turning the Flower of Dharma, [and it is expressed] as, "The Tathāgata preaches the Great Vehicle today."[182] [When] the Flower of Dharma just now is the Flower of Dharma, it is "neither sensed nor recognized,"[183] and at the same time it is "beyond knowing" and "beyond understanding."[184] This being so, "five hundred [ink]drop [*kalpa*s]"[185] are a brief thousandth [of an instant] of turning the Flower of Dharma; they are the Buddha's lifetime being proclaimed by each moment of red mind.

[70] In conclusion, in the hundreds of years since this sutra was transmitted into China, to be turned as the Flower of Dharma, very many people, here and there, have produced their commentaries and interpretations. Some, moreover, have attained the Dharma state of an eminent person by relying on this sutra. But no one has grasped the point of "the Flower of Dharma turning," or mastered the point of "turning the Flower of Dharma," in the manner of our Founding Patriarch, the eternal buddha of Sōkei. Now that 75b

we have heard these [points] and now that we have met it, we have experienced the meeting of eternal buddha with eternal buddha; how could [this] not be the land of eternal buddhas? How joyful it is! From *kalpa* to *kalpa* is the Flower of Dharma, and from noon to night is the Flower of Dharma. Because the Flower of Dharma is from *kalpa* to *kalpa,* and because the Flower of Dharma is from noon to night, even though our own body and mind grows strong and grows weak, it is just the Flower of Dharma itself. The reality that exists "as it is" is "a treasure,"[186] is "brightness,"[187] is "a seat of truth,"[188] is "wide, great, profound, and eternal,"[189] is "profound, great, and everlasting,"[190] is "mind in delusion, the Flower of Dharma turning," and is "mind in realization, turning the Flower of Dharma," which is really just the Flower of Dharma turning the Flower of Dharma.

> [72] When the mind is in the state of delusion, the Flower of Dharma turns.
> When the mind is in the state of realization, we turn the Flower of Dharma.
> If perfect realization can be like this,
> The Flower of Dharma turns the Flower of Dharma.

When we "serve offerings to it, venerate, honor, and praise it"[191] like this, the Flower of Dharma is the Flower of Dharma.

Shōbōgenzō Hokke-ten-hokke

On a day of the summer retreat in the second year of Ninji[192] I have written this and presented it to Zen person Etatsu. I am profoundly glad that he is going to leave home to practice the truth. Just to shave the head is a lovely fact in itself. To shave the head and to shave the head again: this is to be a true child of transcending family life.[193] Leaving home today is the "effects and results as they are" of the "energy as it is," which has turned the Flower of Dharma hitherto. The Flower of Dharma today will inevitably bear the Flower of Dharma's Flower of Dharma fruits. It is not Śākyamuni's Flower
75c of Dharma and it is not the buddhas' Flower of Dharma; it is the Flower of Dharma of the Flower of Dharma. Though "form" is "as it is," our habitual turning of the Flower of Dharma has been suspended in the state of "neither sensing nor recognizing." But the Flower of Dharma now is manifesting

itself afresh in the state "beyond knowing and beyond understanding." The past was exhalation and inhalation, and the present is exhalation and inhalation. This we should maintain and rely upon, as the Flower of Dharma that is "too fine to think about."[194]

Written by the founder of Kannondōrikōshōhōrinji, a *śramaṇa* who entered Song [China] and received the transmission of Dharma, Dōgen (his written seal).

The copying was completed at Hōgyōji at the beginning of spring[195] in the third year of Kagen.[196]

Notes

1 *Juppō-butsudo-chū.* See LS 1.106.

2 *Yui-i.* See LS 1.106.

3 *Hokke,* or (more freely translated) "Lotus Universe," from the title of the *Lotus Sutra.* See LS 2.156.

4 "All buddhas" is *issai-shobutsu.* "Ten directions" is *juppō.* "The three times" (past, present, and future, i.e., eternity) is *sanze.* These expressions all derive from the *Lotus Sutra.* See LS 1.90, 1.128.

5 *Anokutara-sanmyaku-sanbodai.* These characters, representing the sound of the Sanskrit *anuttara samyaksaṃbodhi,* appear frequently throughout the *Lotus Sutra.* See LS 2.156.

6 *Tenhokke. Ten* is literally "to turn," "to move," or "to change." Used here as a transitive verb, *ten* suggests 1) to turn a scroll on which the *Lotus Sutra* is written, and 2) to act in, or upon, the universe which is identified with the *Lotus Sutra.* The content of this chapter suggests that to read the *Lotus Sutra* and to realize the real universe are the same.

7 *Hokketen.* Used here as an intransitive verb, *ten* suggests 1) a scroll of the *Lotus Sutra* unrolling naturally, and 2) the activity of the universe independent of the subjective self.

8 *Hongyō-bosatsudō. Hon* means "original," and at the same time it suggests the past. *Hongyō* appears in several places in the *Lotus Sutra* referring to the practices of bodhisattvas in the eternal past. See LS 2.172, 3.20.

9 *Shobutsu-chie-shinjin-muryō.* See LS 1.66.

10 *Anshō-zanmai.* See LS 1.66.

11 *Nange-nannyū.* See LS 1.66.

12 Monjushiri. A symbol of Buddhist wisdom. In Japan the statue in the zazen hall is usually an image of Mañjuśrī. The *Lotus Sutra* describes him as springing out from the great ocean. See LS 2.212–214, 2.218.

13 *Nyozesō.* See LS 1.68.

14 *Yuibutsu-yobutsu.* See LS 1.68.

15 Shakamuni. The historical Buddha, who was born into the Śākya clan. The Sanskrit Śākyamuni means "Sage of the Śākyas." See LS 2.186–88.

16 *Shutsugen-o-se.* See LS 1.88–90.

17 *Yui-ga-chi-ze-shō, juppō-butsu-yaku-nen.* See LS 1.74.

18 *Ichiji.* See LS 1.8, and note 146.

19 *Yoku-rei-shūjō.* See LS 1.88–90.

20 *Kai-ji-go-nyu.* See LS 1.88–90.

21 *Ga-gyū-juppō-butsu, nai-nō-chi-ze-ji.* See LS 1.70.

22 Fugen, the bodhisattva called Samantabhadra in Sanskrit. The last chapter of the *Lotus Sutra* is *Fugen-bosatsu-kanpotsu* ("Encouragement of Bodhisattva Universal Virtue"). The translation into English of Chinese characters representing the names of bodhisattvas has generally followed the translation in the *Lotus Sutra.*

23 *Fukashigi no kudoku.* See LS 3.210, 3.328–30.

24 *Enbudai ni rufu se shimuru.* See LS 3.328–30. *Enbudai* represents the sound of the Sanskrit Jambudvīpa, the southern continent upon which, according to ancient Indian cosmology, human beings live.

25 *Shindai-ku-on.* See LS 3.18, 3.328–30.

26 *Daishō-shoju.* See LS 1.274.

27 *Sho-fu-nō-chi.* See LS 1.66.

28 *Jingyō-jōju.* The characters *jōju,* "accomplish," appear often in the *Lotus Sutra* (see LS 1.66, 3.328–30). *Jingyō* means "total practice" or "all-out action" (see LS 1.66). In this context *jingyō* suggests Universal Virtue's work of realizing the reality of the *Lotus Sutra;* see LS 3.326.

29 *Ryōzen no dai-e.* Vulture Peak is a natural platform on the southern slope of Mount Chatha, overlooking the Rājagṛha valley. It was so called because the silhouette of the mountain resembles a vulture. The historical Buddha often preached there. See LS 2.216, 3.30.

30 *Byakugō-kōsō.* The circle of hair, *ūrṇā* in Sanskrit, is one of the thirty-two distinguishing marks attributed to the Buddha. The *Lotus Sutra* describes many occasions when the Buddha sent forth a ray of light from between his eyebrows. See LS 1.18, 2.176.

31 The final chapter of the *Lotus Sutra*, *Fugen-bosatsu-kanpotsu,* describes Bodhisattva Universal Virtue coming from the east to Vulture Peak to hear Śākyamuni's preaching of the *Lotus Sutra,* and promising to go to any place where people read and recite the *Lotus Sutra* in order to serve and to protect them.

32 *Yuijun.* See LS 1.38, 1.52.

33 *Juki,* from the Sanskrit *vyākaraṇa.* The sixth chapter of the *Lotus Sutra* and Chapter Thirty-two (Vol. II) of the *Shōbōgenzō* have the title *Juki.* Here *juki* refers to Mañjuśrī's affirmation of Maitreya, that is, Mañjuśrī's prediction that Maitreya will become a buddha in the future. See LS 1.62.

34 *Chiken-haramitsu.* Master Dōgen picked up these characters from the *Lotus Sutra* (see LS 1.68), where they are used as a noun, and he used them as a transitive verb. *Chi* means to know and *ken* means to see. *Chiken* means knowledge or knowing. Master Dōgen sometimes uses the word *chiken* to represent the intellectual and sensory faculties (e.g., in the *Fukanzazengi:* "How could [dignified behavior] be anything other than criteria that precede knowing and seeing?"), but in this chapter and in the *Lotus Sutra, chiken* suggests the intuitive wisdom of the mind in action. *Haramitsu* is from the Sanskrit *pāramitā,* which means "gone to the opposite shore" or "accomplishment." *Chiken-haramitsu* means *prajñā,* or real wisdom experienced throughout the body and mind when the nervous system is set right in zazen (see Chapter Two, *Maka-hannya-haramitsu*).

35 *Sho-chū-kō-zen.* See LS 1.40.

36 *Yui-i.* In the *Lotus Sutra,* these characters have the meaning of "solely by [reason of. . .]." See LS 1.88–90.

37 *Ichijō,* short for *ichi-butsujō.* See LS 1.90.

38 *Ichidaiji.* See LS 1.88–90.

39 *Yuibutsu-yobutsu-nainō-gujin-shohō-jissō;* or read in Japanese, *yuibutsu-yo-butsu, sunawachi yoku hoho-jisso o gujin su.* See LS 1.68.

40 The natural method of zazen.

41 *Shichibutsu.* See LS 2.96. See also Chapter Fifteen, *Busso.*

42 *Jōju su.* See note 28.

43 Master Daikan Enō (638–713), a successor of Master Daiman Kōnin. He was the thirty-third patriarch from Master Mahākāśyapa, and the Sixth Patriarch in China. He had several excellent disciples including Master Seigen Gyōshi, Master Nangaku Ejō, and Master Nan'yō Echū.

44 *Shutsugen-o-se.* This expression appears many times in the *Lotus Sutra* with buddhas as the subject (see LS 1.88–90). Here Master Dōgen uses it with the Buddhist method, zazen, as the subject.

45 *Shutsugen-o-shi.* This is Master Dōgen's variation on the expression in the *Lotus Sutra.*

46 Master Seigen Gyōshi (660?–740). The lineages of the Sōtō, Unmon, and Hōgen sects sprang from Master Seigen's descendants.

47 Master Nangaku Ejō (677–744). His history is described in Chapter Sixty-two (Vol. III), *Hensan.* The lineages of the Rinzai and Igyō sects sprang from the descendants of Master Nangaku and his successor Master Baso Dōitsu.

48 *Nyorai* [*no*] *nyojitsu-chiken.* See LS 3.18.

49 *Hokketen su beshi.* Here *hokketen su* is used as a verb phrase—"the Dharma Flower's turning preaches."

50 *Myōhōrengekyō,* the full title of the *Lotus Sutra,* from the Sanskrit *Saddharma-puṇḍarīka-sūtra.* See LS 1.52.

51 *Kyō-bosatsu-hō.* See LS 1.52.

52 *Kokū.* See LS 2.286. See also Chapter Seventy-seven (Vol. IV), *Kokū.*

53 *Daikai.* See LS 2.212–214.

54 *Daichi.* See LS 2.196–98.

55 *Kokudo.* See LS 2.286. In this case, *kokudo* suggests a unified realm. Because the Buddha's real wisdom is identified with all things and phenomena in this world, concrete things like Vulture Peak, space, oceans, and the earth form a meaningful whole.

56 *Nyoze,* used here as a noun. See LS 1.68.

57 *Sesō-jōjū.* See LS 1.120.

58 *Nyojitsu,* as in *nyojitsu-chiken;* see LS 1.68.

59 *Nyorai-juryō,* the title of the sixteenth chapter of the *Lotus Sutra.*

60 *Shinjin-muryō.* See LS 1.66.

61 *Shogyō-mujō.* This is the first line of the four-line poem in the *Mahāparinirvāṇa-sūtra,* which a hungry demon tells the child bodhisattva Himālaya: "Actions are without constancy./Concrete existence is the arising and passing of *dharma*s./After arising and passing have ceased,/The peace and quiet is pleasure itself."

62 *Hokke-zanmai.* See LS 3.214.

63 *Tenhokke.* See note 6.

64 *Hokketen.* See note 7.

65 *Shōbōgenzō-nehan-myōshin.* The Buddha said, "I have the right Dharma-eye treasury and the fine mind of nirvana; I transmit them to Mahākāśyapa." See for example Chapter Sixty-eight (Vol. III), *Udonge.*

66 *Genshin-doshō.* See LS 3.252.

67 *Juki-sabutsu.* See for example LS 1.134, 1.322.

68 Master Daikan Enō (638–713).

69 Kōnantōro. This was the name of an administrative area (close to present-day Guangdong province) created in southeast China during the reign of the Song emperor Kinei (1068–1077).

70 Hōtatsu became a monk at the age of seven, and devoted himself to reciting the *Lotus Sutra* until meeting with Master Daikan Enō and receiving the master's affirmation.

71 *Hōben,* the second chapter of the *Lotus Sutra.*

72 *Innen-shusse.* See LS 1.88–90. *In* means direct or intrinsic causes, and *en* means indirect or external causes, connections, or conditions. At the same time, *innen* represents the Sanskrit *hetu-pratyaya,* which sometimes means "causes" or "purpose."

73 *Byakugosha.* Symbol of the state of Buddhist wisdom. See LS 1.166. The third chapter of the *Lotus Sutra*, *Hiyu* ("A Parable"), is the parable of a rich father who lures his children out of a burning house by telling them that there are three kinds of carts—goat carts, deer carts, and ox carts—for them to play with outside the gate. When the children escape the burning house, the father gives them a great cart yoked by white oxen, which is more than they had hoped for. In the same way, buddhas use expedient means to make living beings realize the Buddha's wisdom—even as they discriminate and explain the three vehicles by which *śrāvaka*s, *pratyekabuddha*s, and bodhisattvas should transcend the triple world, buddhas know that in reality there is only the One Buddha Vehicle, which is the real wisdom of zazen.

74 *Jinji-doryō.* See LS 1.72.

75 *Jinshi-gusui.* See LS 1.72.

76 *Ken-on.* See LS 1.128.

77 See LS 1.86.

78 *Monge.* See LS 1.164.

79 *Muni-yaku-musan.* See LS 1.106.

80 *Chinpō.* See LS 1.224.

81 The metaphor of father (the Buddha) and children (his followers) occurs in the parable of the burning house and in several other chapters of the *Lotus Sutra.*

82 *Yūyaku-kanki.* This expression occurs repeatedly in the *Lotus Sutra.* See LS 1.134, 1.166.

83 This is Master Daikan Enō's affirmation.

84 "Story" is *innen,* lit., "causes and conditions," in this case representing the Sanskrit *nidāna,* which means a primary cause or a historical account. See Glossary of Sanskrit Terms and note 72.

85 *Nyoze,* used as a noun. See LS 1.68.

[86] *Hokketen.* From here to the end of this long paragraph, Master Dōgen explains *hokketen,* the Flower of Dharma turning. In the following paragraph (62) he explains *tenhokke,* our turning of the Flower of Dharma.

[87] *Nyozesō.* See LS 1.68.

[88] So far in this paragraph, Master Dōgen has outlined in general terms the meaning of "the Flower of Dharma turns" (*hokketen*). This short section introduces the concrete or objective phase. The division into sub-paragraphs has been done for ease of reading; there are no divisions in the source text.

[89] *Sekishin* means "naked mind," "sincere mind," or "mind as it is."

[90] *Nanjira-shogyō, ze-bosatsudō.* See LS 1.286.

[91] *Shobutsu* [*ni*] *bugon* [*suru*], or to pay homage to the buddhas. See LS 1.300.

[92] *Hongyō-bosatsudō.* See LS 2.172, 3.20.

[93] From here Master Dōgen considers the analogy of the burning house on the basis of objective reality, as opposed to idealism. In general, the burning house symbolizes delusion; open ground symbolizes the state of realization; the gate of the house symbolizes the process leading from delusion to realization; the three carts symbolize methods of Buddhist practice; and the white ox cart symbolizes practice in the state of Buddhist wisdom, zazen.

[94] Denial of the idealistic idea that delusion exists only in the burning house.

[95] Even people who are in the state of Buddhist wisdom can experience realization by recognizing their thoughts as thoughts.

[96] *Shōkyō.* See LS 1.166.

[97] *Roji.* See LS 1.166.

[98] Denial of idealistic interpretations of entering and leaving—reality is where we are already, and so there is no area to be entered and no area to be left.

[99] *Gujin,* elsewhere translated as "perfectly realize." See LS 1.68.

[100] Denial of the idealistic view that the Buddhist process is only a means to an end.

[101] Buddhist teaching always affirms the reality of the not-ideal situation, even for those who have real wisdom and are living in the peaceful state.

[102] *Tōmon no zenmon* suggests the whole Buddhist process as this moment of the Buddhist process.

[103] *Fumon no ichimon* suggests the Buddhist process of one individual, at one time and place. The characters *ichimon* appear in the parable of the burning house. See LS 1.162. The characters *fumon* are contained in the title of the twenty-fifth chapter of the *Lotus Sutra, Kanzeon-bosatsu-fumon,* "The Universal Gate of Bodhisattva Regarder

of the Sounds of the World." *Mon* means both "gate" and "aspect," and *fu* means "universal" or "every kind of." The chapter describes how Bodhisattva Avalokiteśvara manifests himself or herself in many different guises (*fumon*), in order to save living beings. See LS 3.252, and the Glossary of Sanskrit Terms under *samantamukha.*

104 We usually think that various processes lead us to realization. This suggests, conversely, that realization leads us to realize the Buddhist process.

105 Buddhist wisdom can occur instantaneously, even before the Buddhist process is completed.

106 Buddhist wisdom can still be realized even after the process is complete.

107 We can sometimes realize the peaceful state in painful or emotional circumstances.

108 This part considers the analogy of the burning house on the practical basis of everyday life.

109 *Fue.* Master Daikan Enō said, "I do not understand the Buddha-Dharma" (*gabue buppō*). See *Shinji-shōbōgenzō,* pt. 1, no. 59.

110 *Fushiki.* Alludes to the words of Master Bodhidharma. See Chapter Thirty (Vol. II), *Gyōji,* paragraph 188; and Chapter Twenty, *Kokyō,* paragraph 162.

111 *Rinden-sangai. Rinden* represents the Sanskrit word samsara, lit., "wandering through," or "circuit of mundane existence." *Sangai,* triple world, means the world as it is divided in the minds of ordinary people; the ordinary world. The *Lotus Sutra* teaches us to see the triple world as it really is, as the triple world. See LS 3.18.

112 *Shin-on.* See LS 1.68.

113 *Anon.* Suggests an ideal situation. See LS 1.146.

114 *Heitan.* Suggests the concrete balanced state realized in practice. These characters have not been traced in the *Lotus Sutra.* An equivalent, though slightly more abstract expression, *heisho,* appears many times, often together with *anon.* See LS 1.146.

115 *Shujō-sho-yuraku.* See LS 3.32.

116 *Jōzai.* See LS 3.32.

117 *Waga-jōdo-fuki.* See LS 3.32.

118 *Hongyō,* used here as a verb. See note 8, and LS 2.172, 3.20.

119 *Isshin-yoku-kenbutsu.* See LS 3.30. See also Chapter Sixty-one (Vol. III), *Kenbutsu.*

120 *Bunshin* means "offshoot," suggesting the bodies of individual buddhas as offshoots of the Buddha. See LS 2.176.

121 *Zenshin* sometimes suggests the universe as the whole body of the Buddha (as in Chapter Seventy-one [Vol. III], *Nyorai-zenshin*). See LS 2.154.

[122] *Gushutsu-ryōjusen.* See LS 3.30.

[123] *Shinmyō o jishaku se zaru.* See LS 3.30.

[124] *Jōjū-shi-seppō.* See LS 3.30. See also Chapter Sixty-one (Vol. III), *Kenbutsu.*

[125] *Hōben-gen-nehan.* See LS 3.30.

[126] *Shi-fuken no sui-gon.* See LS 3.30.

[127] *Ishin,* lit., "one mind"; used in the *Lotus Sutra* as an adverb ("wholeheartedly"). See LS 3.30.

[128] *Tennin-jō-jūman.* See LS 3.32.

[129] Birushana. Vairocana is the Sun Buddha, not mentioned in the *Lotus Sutra* itself but mentioned in the *Kanfugenbosatsugyōhōkyō* (*Sutra of Reflection on the Practice of Dharma by Bodhisattva Universal Virtue*), which is included as the third part of the *Threefold Lotus Sutra* (LSW).

[130] *Jō-jaku-kō-do.* This sentence is related to the teaching of the Tendai sect about the four lands (see following note). The Tendai sect is based on the study of the *Lotus Sutra,* and Master Dōgen spent his teenage years as a monk of the Tendai sect at a temple on Mount Hiei in Japan.

[131] *Shido* are four lands symbolizing the four processes of Buddhist life. They are 1) *bonshō-dōgo-do,* the land where sacred beings and ordinary people live together; 2) *hōben-uyo-do,* the land of expedient methods where something still remains, that is, the land of those who are led by the Buddha's teachings but who have not yet completely realized the teaching for themselves; 3) *jippō-muge-do,* the land of real results and no hindrances, that is, the land of bodhisattvas who have realized the teaching perfectly; and 4) *jō-jaku-kō-do,* the eternally peaceful and bright land, which is the abode of those who have realized the truth.

[132] *Nyoitsu no butsudo.* See LS 3.158.

[133] *Mijin,* derived from the Sanskrit *paramāṇu,* which means an infinitesimal portion or atom. See LS 3.130.

[134] *Hokkai* means inclusive reality.

[135] *Kyōgi-fu-i.* See LS 2.156–58.

[136] *Yoku-rei-shujō.* See LS 1.88–90.

[137] *Chiken-haramitsu.* See note 34.

[138] *Juki.* See note 33.

[139] "Perfectly exhausted" is another translation of *gujin,* usually translated as "perfectly realized." See LS 1.68.

[140] *Nyozeriki.* See LS 1.68.

[141] Master Chōkei Eryō asks Master Reiun Shigon, "Just what is the Great Intent of the Buddha-Dharma?" Master Reiun says, "Donkey business being unfinished, but horse business coming in." See *Shinji-shōbōgenzō,* pt. 2, no. 56.

[142] *Shutsugen-o-shi.* See note 45.

[143] *Chi-yū.* The title of the fifteenth chapter of the *Lotus Sutra* is *Ju-chi-yūshutsu,* "Springing Out from the Earth." See LS 2.286.

[144] In the "Springing Out from the Earth" chapter, the Buddha is asked to explain why the bodhisattvas who have pursued the truth for a long time in the past have now sprung from the earth and become followers of the Buddha who has only recently realized the truth. See LS 2.318.

[145] "Circumstances" is *ta.* This can be interpreted as "circumstances" (as opposed to self), or as "others," or as "him" (the Buddha in the *Lotus Sutra;* see LS 2.286).

[146] *Kokū.* See LS 2.286. The *Threefold Lotus Sutra* says that the original Sanskrit word in this part of the *Lotus Sutra* is *ākāśa* (space, ether), which is often used as a synonym for *śūnyatā* (void). In the *Shōbōgenzō* the Chinese character *kū* includes both these meanings, that is, 1) concrete space or the sky, and 2) *śūnyatā,* i.e., the state in which there is nothing on our mind, emptiness. But *kokū* usually has a more concrete emphasis (space)—see Chapter Seventy-seven (Vol. IV), *Kokū.* In this sentence, *tenhokke su* is used as a transitive verb: "to realize . . . in turning the Flower of Dharma." Compare note 49.

[147] *Fushō-ji-shirō.* See LS 2.318.

[148] *Yo no fushin.* See LS 2.318.

[149] *Ichiji-butsu-jū,* taken from the opening words of the *Lotus Sutra.* See LS 1.8.

[150] *Shingo,* as in Master Daikan Enō's poem.

[151] In general in this paragraph Master Dōgen repeatedly suggests the synthesis of two factors: real and mental, objective and subjective, concrete and abstract, the substantial earth and the empty sky, the individual downward direction and all-inclusive space, factual Vulture Peak and the fabulous stupa, the historical Buddha and the legendary Tathāgata, and so on.

[152] The *Lotus Sutra* says *kahō-kūchū-jū,* "Down below, they live in space." See LS 2.310. Master Dōgen read the characters *kahō* and *kūchū* literally, as noun phrases: "the downward direction," and "the inside of space." He emphasized that we should realize that reality includes both the specific (the downward direction) and the inclusive (space).

[153] *Hotsu-bodai,* short for *hotsu-bodaishin,* "to establish the *bodhi*-mind." See LS 2.218.

[154] *Nanpō,* a world free of impurity. See LS 2.224.

[155] *Bunshin.* See note 120.

[156] *Shiki-soku-ze-kū.* Quoted from the *Heart Sutra.* See Chapter Two, *Maka-hannya-haramitsu.*

[157] *Nyaku-tai-nyaku-shutsu.* See LS 3.18.

[158] *Kū-soku-ze-shiki.* Also quoted from the *Heart Sutra.*

[159] *Mu-u-shōji.* See LS 3.18.

[160] *Zaise.* See LS 3.18.

[161] *Metsudo.* See LS 3.18.

[162] *Shin-yū.* See LS 2.118.

[163] *Keiju.* See LS 2.276.

[164] *Eju.* See LS 2.118.

[165] *Butsuzen ni hōtō aru.* Taken from the opening words of the eleventh chapter of the *Lotus Sutra, Ken-hōtō* ("Seeing the Treasure Stupa"). See LS 2.168.

[166] *Kō-gohyaku-yujun.* See LS 2.168. It is said that one *yojana* is equivalent to the distance an ox can pull a cart in one day—about nine miles (see Glossary of Sanskrit Terms). Master Dōgen emphasized that even a fabulous stupa has its concrete height.

[167] *Tōchū ni butsuza.* See LS 2.186–88.

[168] The *Lotus Sutra* says the stupa sprang out from the earth and abides in the sky (see LS 2.168), suggesting phenomenal realization based on the concrete. Master Dōgen considered two further cases: concrete realization which is based on the concrete (and which is therefore unrestricted realization), and concrete realization which is based on mental phenomena (and which is therefore realization restricted by the eyes and by the body).

[169] Suggests the oneness of an entity and the space that it occupies.

[170] The legendary eternal buddha called Buddha Abundant Treasures (Skt. Prabhūtaratna), and Śākyamuni Buddha who existed as a historical person on Vulture Peak, are on the same level; when we venerate them, we are venerating the same state. See LS 2.186–88.

[171] *Kumetsudo.* See LS 2.190.

[172] *Ze-hō-i.* See LS 1.120.

[173] *Hishiryō* describes the state in zazen. See for example Chapter Twenty-seven (Vol. II), *Zazenshin;* Chapter Fifty-eight (Vol. III), *Zazengi;* and the *Fukanzazengi.* The characters also appear in the *Hōben* ("Expedient Means") chapter of the *Lotus Sutra.* See LS 1.88–90.

[174] *Gen-busshin-ji-i-seppō.* See LS 3.252.

[175] Devadatta was a cousin of the Buddha and at one time the Buddha's disciple, but he later turned against the Buddha and caused a schism within the sangha. Hence Devadatta is a symbol of bad behavior. See LS 3.282–84. Nevertheless, in the chapter "Devadatta," the twelfth chapter of the *Lotus Sutra*, the Buddha gives affirmation that Devadatta will become a buddha in the future. See LS 2.208.

[176] *Tai-yaku-ke-i.* See LS 1.86–88.

[177] *Gasshō-sengō-tai,* from Śāriputra's words in the *Lotus Sutra, Hōben* chapter, describing the attitude of the Buddha's disciples waiting for him to preach the Dharma. See LS 1.80. In these sentences Master Dōgen praises the attitude of patient waiting.

[178] *Rokujū-shōkō.* See LS 1.46.

[179] *Isshin-tai.* See LS 1.64.

[180] *Fu-nō-soku-bucchi.* See LS 1.72.

[181] *Hongyō-bosatsudō.* See note 8, and LS 2.172, 3.20.

[182] *Konnichi-nyorai-setsu-daijō.* See LS 1.52.

[183] *Fukaku-fuchi.* See LS 1.160.

[184] *Fushiki, fue.* See notes 109 and 110.

[185] *Jinten,* short for *jintenkō.* See LS 2.12–214.

[186] *Chinpō.* See LS 1.224.

[187] *Kōmyō.* See LS 2.286. See also Chapter Thirty-six (Vol. II), *Kōmyō.*

[188] *Dōjō.* See LS 1.120.

[189] *Kōdai-shinnon.* See LS 1.68.

[190] *Shindai-ku-on.* See LS 3.18–20, 3.328–30.

[191] *Kuyō, kugyō, sonjū, sandan.* This phrase appears many times in the *Lotus Sutra.* See LS 1.300.

[192] 1241.

[193] *Shin* [*no*] *shukke-ji,* a true monk.

[194] *Myōnashi.* See LS 1.82.

[195] The first month of the lunar calendar.

[196] 1305.

[Chapter Eighteen]

Shin-fukatoku

Mind Cannot Be Grasped
(The Former)

Translator's Note: Shin *means "mind,"* fu *expresses negation,* ka *expresses possibility, and* toku *means "to grasp."* Shin-fukatoku, *or "mind cannot be grasped," is a quotation from the* Diamond Sutra. *On the basis of our common sense, we usually think that our mind can be grasped by our intellect, and we are prone to think that our mind must exist somewhere substantially. This belief also extends into the sphere of philosophy; René Descartes, for example, started his philosophical thinking with the premise* "Cogito ergo sum" *or "I think therefore I am." The German idealists, for example, Kant, Fichte, von Schelling, and Hegel, also based their philosophies on the existence of mind. But in Buddhism we do not have confidence in the existence of mind. Buddhism is a philosophy of action, or a philosophy of the here and now; in that philosophy, mind cannot exist independently of the external world. In other words, Buddhism says that all existence is the instantaneous contact between mind and the external world. Therefore it is difficult for us to grasp our mind independently of the external world. In short, Buddhist theory cannot support belief in the independent existence of mind. In this chapter, Master Dōgen preached that mind cannot be grasped, explaining a famous Buddhist story about a conversation between Master Tokusan Senkan and an old woman selling rice cakes.*

[75] Śākyamuni Buddha says, "Past mind cannot be grasped, present mind cannot be grasped, and future mind cannot be grasped."[1]

This is what the Buddhist Patriarch has mastered in practice. Inside cannot be grasped, it has scooped out and brought here the caves[2] of the past, present, and future. At the same time it has utilized the cave of [the Buddhist Patriarch] himself, and the meaning of "self" here is "mind cannot be grasped." The present thinking and discrimination is "mind cannot be grasped." The whole body utilizing the twelve hours is just "mind cannot be grasped."

[76] After entering the room of a Buddhist patriarch, we understand "mind cannot be grasped." Before entering the room of a Buddhist patriarch, we are without questions about, we are without assertions about, and we do not see and hear "mind cannot be grasped." Teachers of sutras and teachers of commentaries, *śrāvaka*s and *pratyekabuddha*s, have never seen it even in a dream. Evidence of this is close at hand: Zen Master Tokusan Senkan,[3] in former days, boasts that he has elucidated the *Diamond Prajñā Sutra.*[4]
76a Sometimes he calls himself "Shū, King of the *Diamond Sutra.*"[5] He is reputed to be especially well versed in the *Seiryū Commentaries,*[6] besides which he [himself] has edited texts weighing twelve *tan.*[7] It appears that there is no other lecturer to match him. [In fact,] however, he is the last in a line of literary Dharma teachers. Once, he hears that there is a supreme Buddha-Dharma, received by rightful successor from rightful successor, and angered beyond endurance he crosses mountains and rivers, carrying his sutras and commentaries with him, until he comes upon the order of Zen Master Shin of Ryūtan.[8] On the way to that order, which he intends to join, he stops for a rest. Then an old woman comes along, and she [also] stops for a rest by the side of the road.

Then Lecturer [Sen]kan asks, "What kind of person are you?"

The old woman says, "I am an old woman who sells rice cakes."

Tokusan says, "Will you sell some rice cakes to me?"

The old woman says, "Why does the master wish to buy rice cakes?"

Tokusan says, "I would like to buy rice cakes to refresh my mind."[9]

The old woman says, "What is that great load the master is carrying?"

Tokusan says, "Have you not heard? I am Shū, King of the *Diamond Sutra.* I have mastered the *Diamond Sutra.* There is no part of it that I do not understand. This [load] I am now carrying is commentaries on the *Diamond Sutra.*"

Hearing this insistence, the old woman says, "The old woman has a question. Will the master permit me [to ask] it, or not?"

Tokusan says, "I give you permission at once. You may ask whatever you like."

The old woman says, "I have heard it said in the *Diamond Sutra* that past mind cannot be grasped, present mind cannot be grasped, and future mind cannot be grasped. Which mind do you now intend somehow to refresh with rice cakes? If the master is able to say something, I will sell the rice cakes. If the master is unable to say anything, I will not sell the rice cakes." 76b

Tokusan is dumbfounded at this: he does not know how he might politely reply. The old woman just swings her sleeves[10] and leaves. In the end, she does not sell her rice cakes to Tokusan. How regrettable it is for a commentator on hundreds of scrolls [of text], a lecturer for tens of years, on merely receiving one question from a humble old woman, to be defeated at once and not even to manage a polite reply. Such things are due to the great difference between [someone] who has met a true teacher and succeeded a true teacher and heard the right Dharma, and [someone] who has never heard the right Dharma or met a true teacher. This is when Tokusan first says, "A rice cake painted in a picture cannot kill hunger." Now, so they say, he has received the Dharma from Ryūtan.

[81] When we carefully consider this story of the meeting between the old woman and Tokusan, Tokusan's lack of clarity in the past is audible [even] now. Even after meeting Ryūtan he might still be frightened of the old woman. He is just a late learner, not an eternal buddha who has transcended enlightenment. The old woman on this occasion shuts Tokusan's mouth, but it is still difficult to decide that she is really a true person.[11] The reason is that when she hears the words "mind cannot be grasped," she thinks only that mind cannot be got, or that mind cannot exist, and so she asks as she does. If Tokusan were a stout fellow, he might have the power to examine and defeat the old woman. If he had examined and defeated her already, it would also be apparent whether the old woman is in fact a true person. Tokusan has not yet become Tokusan, and so whether the old woman is a true person also is not yet apparent.

[82] That the mountain monks of the great kingdom of Song today, with their patched robes and wide sleeves,[12] idly laugh at Tokusan's inability to answer, and praise the old woman's inspired wit, might be very unreliable and stupid. For there is no absence of reasons to doubt the old woman: At the point when Tokusan is unable to say anything, why does the old woman not say to Tokusan, "Now the master is unable to say something, [so] go ahead and ask [this] old woman. The old woman will say something for the master instead." If she spoke like this, and if what she said to Tokusan after receiving his question were right in expression, it would be apparent that the old 76c

woman really was a true person. She has questions, but she is without any assertion. No one since ancient times has ever been called a true person without asserting even a single word. We can see from Tokusan's past [experience] that idle boasting is useless, from beginning to end. We can know from the example of the old woman that someone who has never expressed anything cannot be approved. Let us see if we can say something in Tokusan's place. Just as the old woman is about to question him as she does, Tokusan should tell her at once, "If you are like this, then do not sell me your rice cakes!" If Tokusan speaks like this, he might be an inspired practitioner. Tokusan might ask the old woman, "Present mind cannot be grasped, past mind cannot be grasped, and future mind cannot be grasped. Which mind do you now intend to refresh with rice cakes?" If he questions her like this, the old woman should say at once to Tokusan, "The master knows only that rice cakes cannot refresh the mind. You do not know that mind refreshes rice
77a cakes, and you do not know that mind refreshes mind." If she says this, Tokusan will surely hesitate. Just at that time, she should take three rice cakes and hand them over to Tokusan. Just as Tokusan goes to take them, the old woman should say, "Past mind cannot be grasped! Present mind cannot be grasped! Future mind cannot be grasped!" Or if Tokusan does not extend his hands to take them, she should take one of the rice cakes and strike Tokusan with it, saying, "You spiritless corpse! Do not be so dumb!" When she speaks like this if Tokusan has something to say [for himself], fine. If he has nothing to say, the old woman should speak again for Tokusan. [But] she only swings her sleeves and leaves. We cannot suppose that there is a bee in her sleeve, either. Tokusan himself does not say, "I cannot say anything. Please, old woman, speak for me." So not only does he fail to say what he should say, he also fails to ask what he should ask. It is pitiful that the old woman and Tokusan, past mind and future mind, questions and assertions, are solely in the state of "future mind cannot be grasped." Generally, even after this, Tokusan does not appear to have experienced any great enlightenment, but only the odd moment of violent behavior.[13] If he had studied under Ryūtan for a long time, the horns on his head might have touched something and broken,[14] and he might have met the moment in which the pearl [under the black dragon's] chin[15] is authentically transmitted. We see merely that his paper candle was blown out,[16] which is not enough for the transmission of the

torch.[17] This being so, monks who are learning in practice must always be diligent in practice. Those who have taken it easy are not right. Those who were diligent in practice are Buddhist patriarchs. In conclusion, "mind cannot be grasped" means cheerfully buying a painted rice cake[18] and munching it up in one mouthful.

Shōbōgenzō Shin-fukatoku 77b

Preached to the assembly at Kannondōrikō-shōhōrinji, in the Uji district of Yōshū,[19] during the summer retreat in the second year of Ninji.[20]

Notes

1 The *Kongōhannyaharamitsukyō* or the *Diamond Prajñāpāramitā Sutra,* from the Sanskrit *Vajracchedikāprajñāpāramitā-sūtra.* In Japanese the name of the sutra is usually abbreviated to *Kongōkyō* or *Diamond Sutra.*

2 *Kutsurō,* lit., "cave-cage," suggests the regulated and concrete conditions of a buddha's daily life. (This usage is also found in Chapter Seventy-nine [Vol. IV], *Ango.*) The quotation from the *Diamond Sutra* has exactly described the life of the buddhas of the past, present, and future.

3 Master Tokusan Senkan (780–865). After traveling to the south of China he met Master Ryūtan Sōshin, a third-generation descendant of Master Seigen Gyōshi. It is said that Master Tokusan received the Dharma from Master Ryūtan, and later also met Master Isan Reiyū. He lived for thirty years in the Reiyō district, then fled to Dokufuzan to escape persecution by the Tang emperor Bu (r. 841–846), who tried to abolish Buddhism. Finally, in the Daichū era (847–860), the governor of Buryō invited Master Tokusan to become the master of Kotokuzenin Temple. Master Tokusan's successors included Master Seppō Gison.

4 The most popular Chinese translation of the *Diamond Sutra* is a single-volume version by Kumārajīva. The sutra preaches that all *dharmas* are bare and without self. Many Chinese masters quoted the *Diamond Sutra* in their preaching. It was especially highly revered after the time of Master Daikan Enō.

5 Shū was Master Tokusan's family name. At the same time, the character *shū* means a complete cycle, and therefore suggests Master Tokusan's complete understanding of the *Diamond Sutra.*

6 The *Seiryū Commentaries* were written by a monk called Dōin at Seiryōji, under the orders of the Tang emperor Gensō (r. 713–755).

7 One *tan* is a hundred *kin.* One *kin* is equal to about 0.6 kilos.

8 Master Ryūtan Sōshin. A successor of Master Tennō Dōgo, who was the successor of Master Sekitō Kisen. It is said that Master Ryūtan's family sold rice cakes for a living, but his life history is not known clearly. He spent his life as a teacher in the Reiyō district.

9 "To refresh my mind" is *tenjin,* originally used not as a verb but as a noun (lit., I would like to buy a rice cake and use it as a refreshment). *Ten* means to light, as in

to light a candle. *Shin, jin* means mind. *Tenjin* means refreshments—cakes, fruit, or a cup of noodles.

10 A sign of contempt.

11 *Sono hito,* lit., "that person," or "the very person," or "a person of the fact."

12 *Un-nō-ka-bei,* lit., "clouds-patches-mist-sleeves." The words suggest the natural life and the usual clothes of a Buddhist monk, and therefore monks themselves.

13 See, for example, *Shinji-shōbōgenzō,* pt. 2, no. 45. "Tokusan preaches to an audience, 'If you ask a question, there is something wrong. If you do not ask your question, that is also a violation.' Then a monk edges forward and prostrates himself. The master strikes him at once. . . ."

14 Horns on the head can be interpreted as symbols of Master Tokusan's high opinion of himself.

15 *Ganju,* lit., "chin pearl," means the pearl that a black dragon retains under its chin. The black dragon's pearl symbolizes the truth.

16 One evening Tokusan enters Master Ryūtan's room, and stands waiting there until late at night. Master Ryūtan asks him, "Why don't you retire?" Tokusan takes his leave but then comes back saying, "It is dark outside." Master Ryūtan lights a paper candle and gives it to Master Tokusan. As soon as Tokusan touches the candle, Master Ryūtan blows it out. Then Master Tokusan has a sudden great realization and prostrates himself. The story (which suggests that a person cannot find his or her way by relying upon another person's enlightenment) is recorded in the *Shinji-shōbōgenzō,* pt. 2, no. 4, and (in a simpler version) in the *Keitokudentōroku,* chapter 15.

17 *Dentō,* "transmission of the torch," as in *Dentōroku* (*Records of Transmission of the Torch*), symbolizes the transmission of the Dharma from Buddhist patriarch to Buddhist patriarch.

18 *Gabyō;* see Chapter Forty (Vol. II), *Gabyō.*

19 Corresponds to present-day Kyoto prefecture.

20 1241.

[Chapter Nineteen]

Shin-fukatoku

Mind Cannot Be Grasped (The Latter)

Translator's Note: *The ninety-five–chapter edition of the* Shōbōgenzō *has two chapters with the same title,* Shin-fukatoku *or Mind Cannot Be Grasped. We usually discriminate between the two chapters with the words "the former," and "the latter." The contents of the two chapters are different, but the meaning of the two chapters is almost the same. Furthermore, the end of each chapter records the same date—the summer retreat in 1241. However, while the former chapter says "preached to the assembly," this chapter says "written." So it may be that the former chapter was a shorthand record of Master Dōgen's preaching, and the latter was Master Dōgen's draft of his lecture. This is only a supposition, and scholars in future may be able to find a more exact conclusion.*

[89] "Mind cannot be grasped" is the buddhas; they have maintained it and relied upon it as their own state of *anuttara samyaksaṃbodhi.*

[90] The *Diamond Sutra* says, "Past mind cannot be grasped, present mind cannot be grasped, and future mind cannot be grasped."

This is just the realized state of maintaining and relying upon "mind cannot be grasped," which is the buddhas themselves. They have maintained it and relied upon it as "triple-world mind cannot be grasped" and as "all-*dharmas* mind cannot be grasped." The state of maintenance and reliance which makes this clear is not experienced unless learned from buddhas and is not authentically transmitted unless learned from patriarchs. To learn from buddhas means to learn from the sixteen-foot body,[1] and to learn from a single stalk of grass.[2] To learn from the patriarchs means to learn from skin, flesh, bones, and marrow,[3] and to learn from a face breaking into a smile.[4] The import of this is that when we seek [the truth] under [a teacher who] has evidently received the authentic transmission of the right Dharma-eye treasury, who has received the legitimate one-to-one transmission of the state in which the mind-seal of the buddhas and the patriarchs is directly accessible, then without fail that [teacher's] bones and marrow, face and eyes, are transmitted, and we receive body, hair, and skin. Those who do not learn the Buddha's truth and who do not enter the room of a patriarch neither see nor hear nor understand this. The method of asking about it is beyond them. They have never realized the means to express it, even in a dream.

[92] Tokusan, in former days, when not a stout fellow, was an authority on the *Diamond Sutra.* People of the time called him Shū, King of the
77c *Diamond Sutra.* Of more than eight hundred scholars, he is the king. Not only is he especially well versed in the *Seiryū Commentaries,* he has also edited texts weighing twelve *tan.* There is no lecturer who stands shoulder-to-shoulder with him. In the story he hears that in the south a supreme truth has been received by rightful successor from rightful successor, and so, carrying his texts, he travels across the mountains and rivers. He takes a rest by the left of the road leading to Ryūtan, and an old woman comes by.

Tokusan asks, "What kind of person are you?"

The old woman says, "I am an old woman who sells rice cakes."

Tokusan says, "Will you sell some rice cakes to me?"

The old woman says, "What does the master want to buy them for?"

Tokusan says, "I would like to buy some rice cakes to refresh my mind."

The old woman says, "What is all that the master is carrying?"

Tokusan says, "Have you not heard? I am Shū, King of the *Diamond Sutra.* I have mastered the *Diamond Sutra.* There is no part of it that I do not understand. This [load] I am carrying is commentaries on the *Diamond Sutra.*"

Hearing this, the old woman says, "The old woman has a question. Will the master permit me [to ask] it, or not?"

Tokusan says, "I permit it. You may ask whatever you like."

She says, "I have heard it said in the *Diamond Sutra* that past mind cannot be grasped, present mind cannot be grasped, and future mind cannot be grasped. Which mind do you now intend to refresh with my rice cakes? If the master is able to say something, I will sell the rice cakes. If the master is unable to say anything, I will not sell the rice cakes."

At this, Tokusan was dumbfounded; he could not find any appropriate
78a reply. The old woman just swung her sleeves and left. In the end, she did not

sell any rice cakes to Tokusan. How regrettable it was that a commentator on hundreds of scrolls [of text], a lecturer for tens of years, on receiving one mere question from a humble old woman, promptly fell into defeat. Such things are due to the great difference between those who have received a master's transmission and those who have not received a master's transmission, between those who visit the room of a true teacher and those who do not enter the room of a true teacher. Hearing the words "cannot be grasped," [some] have simply understood that to grasp is equally impossible both for the former group and for the latter group. They totally lack the vigorous path.[5] Again, there are people who think that we say we cannot grasp it because we are endowed with it originally. Such [thinking] has by no means hit the target. This was when Tokusan first knew that rice cakes painted in a picture cannot kill hunger, and understood that for Buddhist training it is always necessary to meet a true person. He also understood that a person who has been uselessly caught up in only sutras and texts is not able to acquire real power. Eventually he visited Ryūtan and realized the way of master and disciple, after which he did indeed become a true person. Today he is not only a founding patriarch of the Unmon and Hōgen [sects],[6] [but also] a guiding teacher in the human world and in the heavens above.

[95] When we consider this story, it is evident now that Tokusan in the past was not enlightened. Even though the old woman has now shut Tokusan's mouth, it is also hard to decide that she is really a true person. In brief, it seems that hearing the words "mind cannot be grasped," she considers only that mind cannot exist, and so she asks as she does. If Tokusan were a stout fellow, he might have the power of interpretation. If he were able to 78b
interpret [the situation], it would also have become apparent whether the old woman was a true person, but because this is a time when Tokusan was not Tokusan, whether the old woman is a true person also is not known and not evident. What is more, we are not without reasons to doubt the old woman now. When Tokusan is unable to say anything, why does she not say to Tokusan, "Now the master is unable to say something, so please go ahead and ask [this] old woman. The old woman will say something for the master instead." Then, after receiving Tokusan's question, if she had something to say to Tokusan, the old woman might show some real ability. Someone who has the state of effort common to the bones and marrow and the faces and eyes

of the ancients, and [common] to the brightness and the conspicuous form of eternal buddhas, in such a situation has no trouble not only taking hold but also letting go of Tokusan, the old woman, the ungraspable, the graspable, rice cakes, and mind. The "buddha-mind" is just the three times.[7] Mind and the three times are not separated by a thousandth or a hundredth, but when they move apart and we discuss their separation, then the profound distance [between them] has [already] gone beyond eighty-four thousand.[8] If [someone] says "What is past mind?" we should say to that person "It cannot be grasped." If [someone] says "What is present mind?" we should say to that person "It cannot be grasped." If [someone] says "What is future mind?" we should say to that person "It cannot be grasped." The point here
78c is not to say that there is mind, which we provisionally call ungraspable; we are just saying for the present "It cannot be grasped." We do not say that it is impossible to grasp mind; we only say "It cannot be grasped." We do not say that it is possible to grasp mind; we only say "It cannot be grasped." Further, if [someone] says "What is the state of 'past mind cannot be grasped'?" we should say "Living and dying, coming and going." If [someone] says "What is the state of 'present mind cannot be grasped'?" we should say "Living and dying, coming and going." If [someone] says "What is the state of 'future mind cannot be grasped'?" we should say "Living and dying, coming and going." In sum, there is buddha-mind as fences, walls, tiles, and pebbles, and all the buddhas of the three times experience this as "it cannot be grasped." There are only fences, walls, tiles, and pebbles, which are the buddha-mind itself, and the buddhas experience this in the three times as "it cannot be grasped." Furthermore there is the state of "it cannot be grasped" itself, existing as mountains, rivers, and the earth. There are [times when] the state of "it cannot be grasped" as grass, trees, wind, and water, is just mind. There are also [times when] "the mind to which we should give rise while having no abode"[9] is the state of "it cannot be grasped." Still further, mind in the state of "it cannot be grasped" which is preaching eighty thousand Dharma gates through all the ages of all the buddhas of the ten directions, is like this.

[99] A further example: At the time of the National Master Daishō,[10] Daini Sanzō[11] arrived at the capital[12] from the faraway Western Heavens,[13] claiming to have attained the power to know others' minds.[14] In the story the

Tang emperor Shukusō[15] orders the National Master to examine [Sanzō]. As soon as Sanzō meets the National Master, he promptly prostrates himself and stands to the [master's] right.

At length, the National Master asks, "Have you got the power to know others' minds, or not?"

Sanzō says, "I would not be so bold [as to say]."[16]

The National Master says, "Tell me where [this] old monk is now."

Sanzō says, "Master, you are the teacher of the whole country. Why are you by the West River watching a boat race?"

The National Master, after a while, asks a second time, "Tell me where 79a
the old monk is now."

Sanzō says, "Master, you are the teacher of the whole country. Why are you on Tianjin Bridge[17] watching [someone] play with a monkey?"

The National Master asks again, "Tell me where the old monk is now."

Sanzō takes a while, but knows nothing and sees nothing. Then the National Master scolds him, saying, "You ghost of a wild fox,[18] where is your power to know others' minds?"

Sanzō has no further answer.[19]

[101] If we did not know of such an episode, that would be bad, and if we were not informed about it, we might have doubts. Buddhist patriarchs and scholars of the Tripiṭaka[20] can never be equal; they are as far apart as heaven and earth. Buddhist patriarchs have clarified the Buddha-Dharma, scholars of the Tripiṭaka have never clarified it at all. With regard to [the title] "scholar of the Tripiṭaka," indeed, there are cases of even secular people being "a scholar of the Tripiṭaka." It represents, for example, the acquisition of a place in literary culture. This being so, even if [Sanzō] has not only understood all the languages of India and China but has also accomplished the power to know others' minds as well, he has never seen the body and mind of the Buddhist truth, even in a dream. For this reason, in his audience with the National Master, who has experienced the state of the Buddhist patriarchs, [Sanzō] is seen through at once. When we learn mind in Buddhism, the myriad *dharma*s are mind itself,[21] and the triple world is mind alone.[22] It may be that mind alone is just mind alone,[23] and that concrete buddha is mind here and now.[24] Whether it is self, or whether it is the external world, we must not be mistaken about the mind of the Buddha's truth. It could never

idly flow down to the West River or wander over to Tianjin Bridge. If we want to maintain and to rely upon the body and mind of the Buddha's truth,
79b we must learn the power which is the wisdom of the Buddha's truth. That is to say, in the Buddha's truth the whole earth is mind, which does not change through arising and vanishing, and the whole Dharma is mind. We should also learn the whole of mind as the power of wisdom. Sanzō, not having seen this already, is nothing but the ghost of a wild fox. So, even the first two times, [Sanzō] never sees the mind of the National Master, and never penetrates[25] the mind of the National Master at all. He is a wild fox cub idly playing with no more than the West River, Tianjin Bridge, a boat race, and a monkey—how could he hope to see the National Master? Again, the fact is evident that [Sanzō] cannot see the place where the National Master is. He is asked three times, "Tell me where the old monk is now," but he does not listen to these words. If he could listen, he might be able to investigate [further], [but] because he does not listen, he blunders heedlessly onward. If Sanzō had learned the Buddha-Dharma, he would listen to the words of the National Master, and he might be able to see the body and mind of the National Master. Because he does not learn the Buddha-Dharma in his everyday life, even though he was born to meet a guiding teacher of the human world and the heavens above, he has passed [the opportunity] in vain. It is pitiful and it is deplorable. In general, how could a scholar of the Tripiṭaka attain to the conduct of a Buddhist patriarch and know the limits of the National Master? Needless to say, teachers of commentaries from the Western Heavens, and Indian scholars of the Tripiṭaka, could never know the conduct of the National Master at all. Kings of gods can know, and teachers of commentaries can know, what scholars of the Tripiṭaka know. How could what commentary-teachers and gods know be beyond the wisdom of [bodhisattvas at] the place of assignment; or beyond [bodhisattvas at] the ten sacred stages and the three clever stages? Gods cannot know, and [bodhisattvas at] the place of assignment[26] have never clarified, the body and mind of the National Master. Discussion of body and mind among Buddhists is like this. We should know it and believe it.

[105] The Dharma of our great teacher Śākyamuni is never akin to the
79c ghosts of wild foxes—the two vehicles, non-Buddhists, and the like. Still, venerable patriarchs through the ages have each studied this story, and their discussions have survived:

[27]A monk asks Jōshū,[28] "Why does Sanzō not see where the National Master is the third time?" Jōshū says, "He does not see because the National Master is right on Sanzō's nostrils."

Another monk asks Gensha,[29] "If [the National Master] is already on [Sanzō's] nostrils, why does [Sanzō] not see him?" Gensha says, "Simply because of being enormously close."

Kaie Tan[30] says, "If the National Master is right on Sanzō's nostrils, what difficulty could [Sanzō] have in seeing him? Above all, it has not been recognized that the National Master is inside Sanzō's eyeballs."

On another occasion, Gensha challenges[31] Sanzō with these words: "You! Say! Have you seen at all, even the first two times?" Setchō Ken[32] says, "I am defeated, I am defeated."

On still another occasion, a monk asks Kyōzan,[33] "Why is it that the third time, though Sanzō takes a while, he does not see where the National Master is?" Kyōzan says, "The first two times [the master's] mind is wandering in external circumstances; then he enters the *samādhi* of receiving and using the self,[34] and so [Sanzō] does not see him."

These five venerable patriarchs are all precise, but they have passed over the National Master's conduct: by only discussing [Sanzō's] failure to know the third time, they seem to permit that he knew the first two times. This is the ancestors' oversight, and students of later ages should know it.

[108] Kōshō's (Dōgen)[35] present doubts about the five venerable patriarchs are twofold. First, they do not know the National Master's intention in examining Sanzō. Second, they do not know the National Master's body and mind.

[109] Now the reason I say that they do not know the National Master's intention in examining Sanzō is as follows: First the National Master says, "Tell me where the old monk is just now." The intention expressed [here] is to test whether or not Sanzō has ever known the Buddha-Dharma. At this 80a
time, if Sanzō has heard the Buddha-Dharma, he would study according to the Buddha-Dharma the question "Where is the old monk just now?" Studied according to the Buddha-Dharma, the National Master's "Where is the old monk now" asks "Am I at this place?" "Am I at that place?" "Am I in the supreme state of *bodhi*?" "Am I in the *prajñāpāramitā*?" "Am I suspended in space?" "Am I standing on the earth?" "Am I in a thatched hut?"

and "Am I in the place of treasure?" Sanzō does not recognize this intention, and so he vainly offers views and opinions of the common person, the two vehicles, and the like. The National Master asks again, "Tell me where this old monk is just now." Here again Sanzō offers useless words. The National Master asks yet again, "Tell me where this old monk is just now," whereupon Sanzō takes a while but says nothing, his mind baffled. Then the National Master scolds Sanzō, saying, "You ghost of a wild fox, where is your power to know others' minds?" Thus chided, Sanzō still has nothing to say [for himself]. Having considered this episode carefully, the ancestors all think that the National Master is now scolding Sanzō because, even if [Sanzō] knows where the National Master was the first two times, he does not know the third time. That is not so. The National Master is scolding Sanzō outright for being nothing but the ghost of a wild fox and never having seen the Buddha-Dharma even in a dream. [The National Master] has never said that [Sanzō] knew the first two times but not the third time. His criticism is outright criticism of Sanzō. The National Master's idea is, first, to consider whether or not it is possible to call the Buddha-Dharma "the power to know others' minds." Further, he thinks "If we speak of 'the power
80b to know others' minds' we must take 'others' in accordance with the Buddha's truth, we must take 'mind' in accordance with the Buddha's truth, and we must take 'the power to know' in accordance with the Buddha's truth, but what this Sanzō is saying now does not accord with the Buddha's truth at all. How could it be called the Buddha-Dharma?" These are the thoughts of the National Master. The meaning of his testing is as follows: Even if [Sanzō] says something the third time, if it is like the first two times—contrary to the principles of the Buddha-Dharma and contrary to the fundamental intention of the National Master—it must be criticized. When [the National Master] asks three times, he is asking again and again whether Sanzō has been able to understand the National Master's words.

[112] The second [doubt]—that [the five venerable patriarchs] do not know the body and mind of the National Master—is namely that the body and mind of the National Master cannot be known, and cannot be penetrated,[36] by scholars of the Tripiṭaka. It is beyond the attainment of [bodhisattvas at] the ten sacred stages and the three clever stages, and it is beyond clarification by [bodhisattvas at] the place of assignment or [in] the state of

balanced awareness,[37] so how could the common person Sanzō know it? We must clearly determine [the truth of] this principle. If [people] purport that even Sanzō might know, or might attain to, the body and mind of the National Master, it is because they themselves do not know the body and mind of the National Master. If we say that people who have got the power to know others' minds can know the National Master, then can the two vehicles also know the National Master? That is impossible: people of the two vehicles can never arrive at the periphery of the National Master. Nowadays many people of the two vehicles have read the sutras of the Great Vehicle, [but] even they cannot know the body and mind of the National Master. Further, they cannot see the body and mind of the Buddha-Dharma, even in a dream. Even if they seem to read and recite the sutras of the Great Vehicle, we should clearly know that they are totally people of the Small Vehicles. In sum, the body and mind of the National Master cannot be known by people who are acquiring mystical powers or getting practice and experience. It might be difficult even 80c
for the National Master to fathom the body and mind of the National Master. Why? [Because] his conduct has long been free of the aim of becoming buddha; and so even the Buddha's eye could not glimpse it. His leaving-and-coming has far transcended the nest and cannot be restrained by nets and cages.

[114] Now I would like to examine and defeat each of the five venerable patriarchs. Jōshū says that because the National Master is right on Sanzō's nostrils, [Sanzō] does not see. What does this comment mean? Such mistakes happen when we discuss details without clarifying the substance. How could the National Master be right on Sanzō's nostrils? Sanzō has no nostrils. Moreover, although it does appear that the means are present for the National Master and Sanzō to look at each other, there is no way for them to get close to each other. Clear eyes will surely affirm [that this is so].

[38]Gensha says, "Simply because of being enormously close." Certainly, his "enormously close" can be left as it is, [but] he misses the point. What state does he describe as "enormously close"? What object does he take to be "enormously close"? Gensha has not recognized "enormous closeness," and has not experienced "enormous closeness." In regard to the Buddha-Dharma he is the farthest of the far.

Kyōzan says, "The first two times [the master's] mind is wandering in external circumstances; then he enters the *samādhi* of receiving and using the self, and so [Sanzō] does not see him." Though [Kyōzan's] acclaim as a little Śākyamuni echoes on high [even] in the Western Heavens, he is not without such wrongness. If he is saying that when [people] see each other [they] are inevitably wandering in external circumstances, then there would seem to be no instance of Buddhist patriarchs seeing each other, and he would appear not to have studied the virtues of affirmation and becoming buddha. If he is saying that Sanzō, the first two times, was really able to know the place where the National Master was, I must say that [Kyōzan] does not know the virtue of a single bristle of the National Master's hair.

81a Gensha demands, "Have you seen at all, even the first two times?" This one utterance "Have you seen at all?" seems to say what needs to be said, but it is not right because it suggests that [Sanzō's] seeing is like not seeing.[39]

Hearing the above, Zen Master Setchō Myōkaku[40] says, "I am defeated. I am defeated." When we see Gensha's words as the truth, we should speak like that; when we do not see them as the truth, we should not speak like that.

Kaie Tan says, "If the National Master is right on Sanzō's nostrils, what difficulty could [Sanzō] have in seeing him? Above all, it has not been recognized that the National Master is inside Sanzō's eyeballs." This again discusses [only] the third time. It does not criticize [Sanzō] as he should be criticized, for not seeing the first two times as well. How could [Kaie] know that the National Master is on [Sanzō's] nostrils or inside [Sanzō's] eyeballs?

[117] Every one of the five venerable patriarchs is blind to the virtue of the National Master; it is as if they have no power to discern the truth of the Buddha-Dharma. Remember, the National Master is just a buddha through all the ages. He has definitely received the authentic transmission of the Buddha's right Dharma-eye treasury. Scholars of the Tripiṭaka, teachers of commentaries, and others of the Small Vehicles, do not know the limits of the National Master at all; and the proof of that is here. "The power to know others' minds," as it is discussed in the Small Vehicles, should be called "the power to know others' ideas." To have thought that a Small Vehicle scholar of the Tripiṭaka, with the power to know others' minds, might be able to know a single bristle or half a bristle of the National Master's hair, is a mistake. We must solely learn that a Small Vehicle scholar of the Tripiṭaka is totally unable to see the situation of the virtue of the National Master. If [Sanzō] knew where the National Master was the first two times but did not

know a third time, he would possess ability which is two-thirds of the whole and he would not deserve to be criticized. If he were criticized, it would not be for a total lack [of ability]. If [the National Master] denounced such a person, who could believe in the National Master? [The National Master's] intention is to criticize Sanzō for completely lacking the body and mind of the Buddha-Dharma. The five venerable patriarchs have such incorrectness 81b
because they completely fail to recognize the conduct of the National Master. For this reason, I have now let the Buddha's teaching of "mind cannot be grasped" be heard. It is hard to believe that people who are not able to penetrate this one *dharma* could have penetrated other *dharma*s. Nevertheless, we should know that even the ancestors have [made] such mistakes that are to be seen as mistakes.

[118] On one occasion a monk asks the National Master, "What is the mind of eternal buddhas?" The National Master says, "Fences, walls, tiles, and pebbles."[41] This also is "mind cannot be grasped." On another occasion a monk asks the National Master, "What is the constant and abiding mind of the buddhas?" The National Master says, "Fortunately you have met an old monk's palace visit."[42] This also is mastery of the state of mind which "cannot be grasped." The god Indra, on another occasion, asks the National Master, "How can we be free from becoming?"[43] The National Master says, "Celestial One! You can be free from becoming by practicing the truth." The god Indra asks further, "What is the truth?" The National Master says, "Mind in the moment is the truth." The god Indra says, "What is mind in the moment?" Pointing with his finger, the National Master says, "This place is the stage of *prajñā*. That place is the net of pearls." The god Indra does prostrations.

[120] In conclusion, in the orders of the buddhas and the patriarchs, there is often discussion of the body and of the mind in the Buddha's truth. When we learn them both together in practice, the state is beyond the thinking and the perception of the common person and sages and saints. [So] we must master in practice "mind cannot be grasped."

Shōbōgenzō Shin-fukatoku

Written at Kōshōhōrinji on a day of the summer retreat in the second year of Ninji.[44]

Notes

1 The sixteen-foot golden body of the Buddha, an image of the perfect state.

2 A concrete thing.

3 Master Bodhidharma told his four disciples that they had got his skin, flesh, bones, and marrow. See Chapter Forty-six (Vol. III), *Kattō.*

4 Master Mahākāśyapa's face broke into a smile when the Buddha showed his audience an *uḍumbara* flower. See Chapter Sixty-eight (Vol. III), *Udonge.* Master Dōgen frequently used the words skin, flesh, bones, and marrow, and a face breaking into a smile as symbols of the transmission from Buddhist patriarch to Buddhist patriarch.

5 *Katsuro.* The *Fukanzazengi* contains the words *shusshin no katsuro,* "the vigorous path of getting the body out."

6 The Unmon sect traces its lineage back to Master Unmon Bun'en (864–949), a successor of Master Seppō Gison, who was a successor of Master Tokusan. The Hōgen sect traces its lineage back to Master Hōgen Bun'eki (885–958), a successor of Master Rakan Keichin, who was a successor of Master Gensha Shibi, who was a successor of Master Seppō Gison.

7 Past, present, and future; eternal existence.

8 Reality includes all things and phenomena without separation, but if we try to understand it intellectually we lose the state of reality completely.

9 *Ō-mu-shojū-ji-shō-go-shin,* or in Japanese pronunciation, *masani jusho naku shi te sono kokoro o shozu beshi,* lit., "While having no abode still we should cause the mind to arise." These words are from the *Diamond Sutra.* When Master Daikan Enō happened to hear them recited in a marketplace, he decided at once to leave home and become a monk. See Chapter Thirty (Vol. II), *Gyōji.*

10 Master Nan'yō Echū (675?–775). A successor of Master Daikan Enō. Posthumously titled by the emperor as "National Master Daishō."

11 *Sanzō* represents the meaning of the Sanskrit Tripiṭaka, the three baskets of Sutra (scriptures), Vinaya (precepts), and Abhidharma (commentaries). The title Sanzō was given to a person who was accomplished in studying the Tripiṭaka.

12 The ancient capital of modern-day Luoyang province.

[13] *Saiten* (Western Heavens): India.

[14] *Tashintsū.* See Chapter Eighty (Vol. IV), *Tashintsū.*

[15] The third son of Emperor Gensō; reigned from 756 until his death in 762; also mentioned in Chapter One, *Bendōwa,* and Chapter Eighty-six (Vol. IV), *Shukke-kudoku.*

[16] Sanzō suggested that he had the ability, but modesty forbade him from daring to say so.

[17] Tianjin is a large city and port in Hopeh province, southeast of Beijing.

[18] *Yakozei.* In Chapter Eight, *Raihai-tokuzui,* "the ghost of a wild fox" symbolizes the natural and mystical quality of a person who has got the Dharma. In this case, it refers to Sanzō's mystical pretensions.

[19] This story, together with the comments of the five venerable patriarchs, is also quoted in Chapter Eighty (Vol. IV), *Tashintsū.* In the present chapter Master Dōgen wrote the story in Japanese; in *Tashintsū* the story is quoted in Chinese characters only. The story is originally recorded in the *Keitokudentōroku,* chapter 5.

[20] "Scholars of the Tripiṭaka" is *sanzō.* See note 11.

[21] *Banpō-sokushin.*

[22] *Sangai-yuishin.* See Chapter Forty-seven (Vol. III), *Sangai-yuishin.* The two expressions in this sentence are traditional expressions.

[23] *Yuishin kore yuishin.*

[24] *Zebutsu-soku-shin.* The two expressions in this sentence are Master Dōgen's variations on traditional expressions. In Chapter Six, *Soku-shin-ze-butsu,* Master Dōgen uses the four characters *soku-shin-ze-butsu* in several different combinations. However, the combination used here, *zebutsu-soku-shin,* does not appear in Chapter Six.

[25] *Tsūzu.* The same character, as a noun, appears in the phrase *jintsū,* "mystical powers," one of which is *tashintsū,* "the power to know others' minds."

[26] *Hosho,* short for *isshō-hosho no bosatsu,* lit., "a bodhisattva at the place of assignment in one life," that is, a bodhisattva who is about to become a buddha. In the imagery of ancient India, bodhisattvas live their last lives in Tuṣita Heaven before descending to the world to become buddhas.

[27] The five following stories are contained in one paragraph in the source text.

[28] Master Jōshū Jūshin (778–897), successor of Master Nansen Fugan. See for example Chapter Thirty-five (Vol. II), *Hakujushi.*

[29] Master Gensha Shibi (835–907), successor of Master Seppō Gison. See for example Chapter Four, *Ikka-no-myōju.*

[30] Master Kaie Shutan (1025–1072), successor of Master Yōgi Hōe.

31 *Chō su* means to solicit [an opinion]. At the same time, *chō* is sometimes used interchangeably with another character pronounced *chō,* which means to chastise.

32 Master Setchō Jūken (980–1052), a successor of Master Chimon Kōso. His comment is in praise of Master Gensha's comment. Master Setchō is known for promoting the teachings of the Unmon sect (founded by Master Unmon Bun'en [864–949]). Master Setchō quoted a hundred stories, or *kōan*s, from the *Keitokudentōroku* and praised them with poems. Master Engo Kokugon (1063–1135) later based his popular commentary the *Hekiganroku* (*Blue Cliff Record*) on Master Setchō's book. Master Daie Sōkō (1089–1163), thought to be the originator of so-called *kōan* Zen, was a student of Master Engo Kokugon. After Master Setchō's death, Master Setchō's disciples compiled his works in the *Iroku* (*Bequeathed Records*), in seven volumes.

33 Master Kyōzan Ejaku (803–887). A successor of Master Isan Reiyū. The *Goroku,* a record of his words, is in one volume.

34 *Jijuyō-zanmai,* that is, the state of natural balance. See Chapter One, *Bendōwa.*

35 Kōshō. At the time, Master Dōgen was the master of Kōshōhōrinji.

36 *Tsūzu.* See note 25.

37 A bodhisattva is said to pass through fifty-two stages before becoming a buddha: ten stages of belief; then thirty states classed as the three clever stages; then ten sacred stages; then the penultimate state; and finally the ultimate state. The penultimate state is *tōkaku,* "balanced awareness." The ultimate state is *myōkaku,* "subtle awareness." The ultimate state is also called *hosho;* see note 26.

38 These five short paragraphs criticizing the five masters are contained in one paragraph in the source text.

39 Master Dōgen is concerned with the area beyond seeing and not seeing—that is, realization of the practical state.

40 Another name of Master Setchō Jūken. While still living, he was awarded the title Zen Master Myōkaku.

41 See Chapter Forty-four (Vol. III), *Kobusshin. Kobutsu* literally means "past/ancient buddhas," but in that chapter Master Dōgen says that *kobutsu* means buddhas who transcend the past and present and belong directly to eternity.

42 In other words, "Fortunately, you have met the old monk who became master of this temple." *Sandai,* "palace visit," means going to the palace to receive the emperor's permission to become the master of a temple.

43 *U-i,* from the Sanskrit *saṃskṛta.* See Glossary of Sanskrit Terms.

44 1241.

[Chapter Twenty]

Kokyō 81c3

The Eternal Mirror

Translator's Note: Ko *means "ancient" or "eternal" and* kyō *means "mirror," so* kokyō *means "the eternal mirror." And what "the eternal mirror" means is the question. In this chapter Master Dōgen quoted Master Seppō Gison's words "When a foreigner comes in front of the mirror, the mirror reflects the foreigner." From these words we can understand the eternal mirror as a symbol of some human mental faculty. The eternal mirror suggests the importance of reflection, so we can suppose that the eternal mirror is a symbol of the intuitional faculty. In Buddhist philosophy, the intuitional faculty is called* prajñā, *or real wisdom. Real wisdom in Buddhism means our human intuitional faculty on which all our decisions are based. Buddhism esteems this real wisdom more than reason or sense perception. Our real wisdom is the basis for our decisions, and our decisions decide our life, so we can say that our real wisdom decides the course of our life. For this reason, it is very natural for Master Dōgen to explain the eternal mirror. At the same time, we must find another meaning of the eternal mirror, because Master Dōgen also quoted other words of Master Seppō Gison, "Every monkey has the eternal mirror on its back." Therefore we can think that the eternal mirror means not only human real wisdom but also some intuitional faculty of animals. So we must widen the meaning of the eternal mirror, and understand it as a symbol of the intuitional faculty that both human beings and animals have. Furthermore Master Seppō Gison said, "When the world is ten feet wide, the eternal mirror is ten feet wide. When the world is one foot wide, the eternal mirror is one foot wide." These words suggest the eternal mirror is the world itself. So we can say that the eternal mirror is not only a symbol of an individual faculty but is also something universal. From ancient times Buddhists have discussed the eternal mirror. In this chapter Master Dōgen explains the meaning of the eternal mirror in Buddhism, quoting the words of ancient Buddhist masters.*

[123] What all the buddhas and all the patriarchs have received and retained, and transmitted one-to-one, is the eternal mirror. They[1] have the same view and the same face, the same image[2] and the same cast;[3] they share the same state and realize the same experience. A foreigner appears, a foreigner is reflected—one hundred and eight thousand of them. A Chinese person appears, a Chinese person is reflected—for a moment and for ten thousand years. The past appears, the past is reflected; the present appears, the present is reflected; a buddha appears, a buddha is reflected; a patriarch appears, a patriarch is reflected.

[125] The eighteenth patriarch, Venerable Geyāśata, is a man from the kingdom of Magadha in the western regions. His family name is Uzuran, his father's name is Tengai, and his mother's name is Hosho.[4] His mother once has a dream in which she sees a great god approaching her and holding a big mirror. Then she becomes pregnant. Seven days later she gives birth to the master. Even when he is newborn, the skin of the master's body is like polished lapis lazuli, and even before he is bathed, he is naturally fragrant and clean. From his childhood, he loves quietness. His words are different from those of ordinary children; since his birth, a clear and bright round mirror has naturally been living with him. "A round mirror" means a round mirror.[5] It is a matter rare through the ages. That it has lived with him does not mean that the round mirror was also born from his mother's womb.[6] The master was born from the womb, and as the master appeared from the womb the round mirror came and naturally manifested itself before the master, and became like an everyday tool. The form of this round mirror is not ordinary: when the child approaches, he seems to be holding up the round mirror before him with both hands, yet the child's face is not hidden. When the child goes away, he seems to be going with the round mirror on his back, yet the child's
82a body is not hidden. When the child sleeps, the round mirror covers him like a flowery canopy. Whenever the child sits up straight, the round mirror is there in front of him. In sum, it follows [all his] movements and demeanors, active and passive. What is more, he is able to see all Buddhist facts of the past, future, and present by looking into the round mirror. At the same time, all problems and issues of the heavens above and the human world come cloudlessly to the surface of the round mirror. For example, to see by looking in this round mirror is even more clear than to attain illumination of the

past and illumination of the present by reading sutras and texts. Nevertheless, once the child has left home and received the precepts, the round mirror never appears before him again.[7] Therefore [people of] neighboring villages and distant regions unanimously praise this as rare and wonderful. In truth, though there are few similar examples in this *sahā* world, we should not be suspicious but should be broadminded with regard to the fact that, in other worlds, families may produce such progeny. Remember, there are sutras which have changed into trees and rocks,[8] and there are [good] counselors who are spreading [the *Lotus Sutra*] in fields and in villages;[9] they too may be a round mirror. Yellow paper on a red rod[10] here and now is a round mirror. Who could think that only the master was prodigious?

[129] On an outing one day, encountering Venerable Saṃghanandi,[11] [Master Geyāśata] directly proceeds before Venerable [Saṃgha]nandi. The Venerable One asks, "[That which] you have in your hands is expressing what?"[12] We should hear "is expressing What?" not as a question,[13] and we should learn it as such in practice.

The master says:

> The great round mirror of the buddhas
> Has no flaws or blurs, within or without.
> [We] two people are able to see the same.
> [Our] minds, and [our] eyes, are completely alike.

So how could the great round mirror of the buddhas have been born together with the master? The birth of the master was the brightness of the great round mirror. Buddhas [experience] the same state and the same view in this round mirror. Buddhas are the cast image of the great round mirror. 82b
The great round mirror is neither wisdom nor reason, neither essence nor form. Though the concept of a great round mirror appears in the teachings of [bodhisattvas at] the ten sacred stages, the three clever stages, and so on, it is not the present "great round mirror of the buddhas." Because "the buddhas" may be beyond wisdom, buddhas have real wisdom, [but] we do not see real wisdom as buddhas. Practitioners should remember that to preach about wisdom is never the ultimate preaching of the Buddha's truth. Even if we feel that the great round mirror of the buddhas is already living with us, it is still a fact that we can neither touch the great round mirror in this

life nor touch it in another life; it is neither a jewel mirror nor a copper mirror, neither a mirror of flesh nor a mirror of marrow. Is [the verse] a verse spoken by the round mirror itself or a verse recited by the child? Even if it is the child who preaches this four-line verse, he has not learned it from [other] people, either by "following the sutras" or by "following [good] counselors." He holds up the round mirror and preaches like this, simply [because] to face the mirror has been the master's usual behavior since his earliest childhood. He seems to possess inherent eloquence and wisdom. Was the great round mirror born with the child, or was the child born with the great round mirror? It may also be possible that the births took place before or after [each other]. "The great round mirror" is just a virtue of "the buddhas." Saying that this mirror "has no blurs on the inside or the outside" neither describes an inside that depends on an outside, nor an outside blurred by an inside. There being no face or back, "two individuals[14] are able to see the same." Minds, and eyes, are alike. "Likeness" describes "a human being" meeting "a human being." In regard to images within, they have mind and eyes, and they are able to see the same. In regard to images without, they
82c have mind and eyes, and they are able to see the same. Object and subject which are manifest before us now are like each other within and like each other without—they are neither I nor anyone else. Such is the meeting of "two human beings," and the likeness of "two human beings." That person is called "I," and I am that person. "Minds, and eyes, are totally alike" means mind and mind are alike, eyes and eyes are alike. The likeness is of minds and of eyes; this means, for example, that the mind and the eyes of each are alike. What does it mean for mind and mind to be alike? The Third Patriarch and the Sixth Patriarch.[15] What does it mean for eyes and eyes to be alike? The eye of the truth being restricted by the eye itself.[16] The principle that the master is expressing now is like this. This is how [Master Geyāśata] first pays his respects to Venerable Saṃghanandi. Taking up his principle, we should experience in practice the faces of buddhas and the faces of patriarchs in the great round mirror, which is akin to the eternal mirror.

[134] The thirty-third patriarch, Zen Master Daikan, in former days when toiling in the Dharma order on Ōbaizan, presented the following verse to the ancestral master,[17] by writing it on the wall:[18]

In the state of *bodhi* there is originally no tree,
Neither does the clear mirror need a stand.
Originally we do not have a single thing,
Where could dust and dirt exist?

[134] So then, we must study these words. People in the world call the Founding Patriarch Daikan "the eternal buddha." Zen Master Engo[19] says, "I bow my head to the ground before Sōkei,[20] the true eternal buddha."[21] So remember [the words] with which the Founding Patriarch Daikan displays the clear mirror: "Originally we do not have a single thing, At what place could dust and dirt exist?" "The clear mirror needs no stand": this contains the lifeblood; we should strive [to understand it]. All [things in] the clear-clear state[22] are the clear mirror itself, and so we say, "When a clear head comes, a clear head will do."[23] Because [the clear mirror] is beyond "any place," it does not have "any place."[24] Still more, throughout the universe in 83a
the ten directions, does there remain one speck of dust that is not the mirror? On the mirror itself, does there remain one speck of dust that is not the mirror? Remember, the whole universe is not lands of dust;[25] and so it is the face of the eternal mirror.

[136] In the order of Zen Master Nangaku Daie[26] a monk asks, "If a mirror is cast into an image,[27] to what place does its luster return?"

The master says, "Venerable monk, to what place have the features you had before you became a monk departed?"

The monk says, "After the transformation, why does it not shine like a mirror?"

The master says, "Even though it is not shining like a mirror, it cannot delude others one bit."[28]

[137] We are not sure of what these myriad images[29] of the present are made. But if we seek to know, the evidence that they are cast from a mirror is just [here] in the words of the master. A mirror is neither of gold nor of precious stone, neither of brightness nor of an image, but that it can be instantly cast into an image is truly the ultimate investigation of a mirror.[30] "To what place does the luster return?" is the assertion that "the possibility[31] of a mirror being cast into an image" is just "the possibility of a mirror being cast into an image"; [it says,] for example, [that] an image returns to the

place of an image, and [that] casting can cast a mirror.[32] The words "Venerable monk, to what place have the features you had before you became a monk departed?" hold up a mirror to reflect [the monk's] face.[33] At this time, which momentary face[34] might be "my own face"? The master says, "Even though it is not shining like a mirror, it cannot delude others one bit." This means that it cannot shine like a mirror; and it cannot mislead others. Learn in practice that the ocean's drying can never disclose the seabed![35] Do not break out, and do not move! At the same time, learn further in practice: there is a principle of taking an image and casting a mirror. Just this moment is miscellaneous bits of utter delusion,[36] in hundred thousand myriads of shining mirror reflections.[37]

[139] Great Master Seppō Shinkaku[38] on one occasion preaches to the
83b assembly, "If you want to understand this matter,[39] my concrete state is like one face of the eternal mirror. [When] a foreigner comes, a foreigner appears. [When] a Chinese person comes, a Chinese person appears."

Then Gensha[40] steps out and asks, "If suddenly a clear mirror comes along, what then?"

The master says, "The foreigner and the Chinese person both become invisible."

Gensha says, "I am not like that."

Seppō says, "How is it in your case?"

Gensha says, "Please, master, you ask."

Seppō says, "If suddenly a clear mirror comes along, how will it be then?"

Gensha says, "Smashed into hundreds of bits and pieces!"

[141] Now the meaning of Seppō's words "this matter" should be learned in practice as "this is something ineffable."[41] Let us now try to learn Seppō's eternal mirror. In the words "Like one face of the eternal mirror. . . ," "one face" means [the mirror's] borders have been eliminated forever and it is utterly beyond inside and outside; it is the self as a pearl spinning in a bowl.[42] The present "[when] a foreigner comes, the foreigner appears" is about one individual redbeard.[43] "[When] a Chinese person comes, a Chinese person appears": although it has been said since the primordial chaos,[44] since [the reign of] Banko (Ch. Panku),[45] that this "Chinese person" was created from the three elements and five elements,[46] in Seppō's words now a Chinese person whose virtue is the eternal mirror has appeared. Because the present Chinese person

is not "a Chinese person," "the Chinese person appears." To Seppō's present words "The foreigner and the Chinese person both become invisible," he might add, "and the mirror itself also becomes invisible." Gensha's words "Smashed into hundreds of bits and pieces" mean "the truth should be expressed like that, but why, when I have just asked you to give me back a concrete fragment, did you give me back a clear mirror?"

[142] In the age of the Yellow Emperor there are twelve mirrors.[47] According to the family legend, they are gifts from the heavens. Alternately, they are said to have been given by [the sage] Kōsei of Kōdōzan.[48] The rule for using[49] the twelve mirrors is to use one mirror every hour through the twelve hours, and to use each mirror for a month through the twelve months, [and again] to use the mirrors one by one, year by year through twelve years. They say that the mirrors are Kōsei's sutras. When he transmits them to the Yellow Emperor, the twelve hours and so on are mirrors with which to illuminate the past and to illuminate the present. If the twelve hours were not 83c
mirrors, how would it be possible to illuminate the past? If the twelve hours were not mirrors, how would it be possible to illuminate the present? The twelve hours, in other words, are twelve concrete sheets [of mirror], and the twelve concrete sheets [of time] are twelve mirrors. The past and present are what the twelve hours use.[50] [The legend] suggests this principle. Even though it is a secular saying, it is in [the reality of] the twelve hours during which "the Chinese person" appears.

[144] Kenen (Ch. Xuanyuan),[51] the Yellow Emperor, crawls forward on Kōdō [Mountain] and asks Kōsei about the Way. Thereupon, Kōsei says, "Mirrors are the origin of *yin* and *yang;* they regulate the body eternally. There are naturally three mirrors: namely, the heavens, the earth, and human beings.[52] These mirrors are without sight and without hearing.[53] They will make your spirit quiet, so that your body will naturally become right. Assured of quietness and of purity, your body will not be taxed and your spirit will not be agitated. You will thus be able to live long."[54]

[145] In former times, these three mirrors are used to regulate the whole country, and to regulate the great order. One who is clear about this great order is called the ruler of the heavens and the earth. A secular [book][55] says, "The Emperor Taisō[56] has treated human beings as a mirror, and thus he fully illuminates [all problems of] peace and danger, reason and disorder." He

uses one of the three mirrors. When we hear that he treats human beings as a mirror, we think that by asking people of wide knowledge about the past and present, he has been able to know when to employ and to discharge saints and sages—as, for example, when he got Gichō (Ch. Weizheng) and got Bōgenrei (Ch. Fang Xuanling).[57] To understand it like this is not [truly to understand] the principle which asserts that Emperor Taisō sees human beings as a mirror. Seeing human beings as a mirror means seeing a mirror as a mirror, seeing oneself as a mirror, seeing the five elements[58] as a mirror, or seeing the five constant virtues[59] as a mirror. When we watch the coming and going of human beings, the coming has no traces and the going has no direction: we call this the principle of human beings as a mirror.[60] The myriad diversity of sagacity and ineptitude is akin to astrological phenomena. Truly, it may be as latitude and longitude.[61] It is the faces of people, the faces of
84a mirrors, the faces of the sun, and the faces of the moon. The vitality of the five peaks and the vitality of the four great rivers passes through the world on the way to purifying the four oceans, and this is the customary practice of the mirror itself.[62] They say that Taisō's way is to fathom the universal grid by understanding human beings. [But this] does not refer [only] to people of wide knowledge.

[147] "Japan, since the age of the gods, has had three mirrors; together with the sacred jewels and the sword they have been transmitted to the present.[63] One mirror is in the Grand Shrines of Ise,[64] one is in the Hinokuma Shrine in Kii-no-kuni,[65] and one is in the depository of the Imperial Court."[66]

[148] Thus it is clear that every nation transmits and retains a mirror. To possess the mirror is to possess the nation. People relate the legend that these three mirrors were transmitted together with the divine throne and were transmitted by the gods. Even so, the perfectly refined copper [of these mirrors] is also the transformation of *yin* and *yang*.[67] It may be that [when] the present comes, the present appears [in them], and [when] the past comes, the past appears [in them]. [Mirrors] that thus illuminate the past and present may be eternal mirrors. Seppō's point might also be expressed, "[When] a Korean comes, a Korean appears; [when] a Japanese comes, a Japanese appears." Or, "[When] a god comes, a god appears; [when] a human being comes, a human being appears." We learn appearance-and-coming like this, in practice, but we have not now recognized the substance and details of this

appearance: we only meet directly with appearance itself. We should not always learn that coming-and-appearance is [a matter of] recognition or [a matter of] understanding. Is the point here that a foreigner coming is a foreigner appearing? [No,] a foreigner coming should be an instance of a foreigner coming. A foreigner appearing should be an instance of a foreigner appearing. The coming is not for the sake of appearing. Although the eternal mirror is [just] the eternal mirror, there should be such learning in practice.

[149] Gensha steps out and asks, "What if suddenly it meets the coming of a clear mirror?"[68] We should study and clarify these words. What might be the scale of the expression of this word "clear"? In these words, the "com- 84b
ing" is not necessarily that of "a foreigner" or of "a Chinese person." This is the clear mirror, which [Gensha] says can never be realized as "a foreigner" or as "a Chinese person." Though "a clear mirror coming" is a "clear mirror coming," it never makes a duality.[69] Though there is no duality, the eternal mirror is still the eternal mirror, and the clear mirror is still the clear mirror. Testimony to the existence of [both] the eternal mirror and the clear mirror has been expressed directly in the words of Seppō and Gensha. We should see this as the Buddha's truth of essence-and-form. We should recognize that Gensha's present talk of the clear mirror coming is totally penetrating,[70] and we should recognize that it is brilliant in all aspects.[71] It may be that in his encounters with human beings, [Gensha] directly manifests [himself], and that in manifesting directness he can reach others. So should we see the clear of the clear mirror and the eternal of the eternal mirror, as the same, or should we see them as different? Is there eternity in the clear mirror, or not? Is there clarity in the eternal mirror, or not? Do not understand from the words "eternal mirror" that it must necessarily be clear. The important point is that "I am like that, and you are also like that." We should practice without delay, polishing the fact that "all the patriarchs of India were also like that."[72] An ancestral master's expression of the truth[73] says that, for the eternal mirror, there is polishing. Might the same be true for the clear mirror? What [do you say]? There must be learning in practice that widely covers the teachings of all the buddhas and all the patriarchs.

[151] Seppō's words, "The foreigner and the Chinese person both become invisible" mean that the foreigner and the Chinese person, when it is the clear mirror's moment, are "both invisible." What is the meaning of

this principle of "both being invisible"? That the foreigner and the Chinese person have already come-and-appeared does not hinder the eternal mirror, so why should they now "both be invisible"? In the case of the eternal mirror, "[when] a foreigner comes a foreigner appears," and "[when] a Chinese person comes a Chinese person appears," but "the coming of the clear mirror" is naturally "the coming of the clear mirror" itself; therefore the foreigner and the Chinese person reflected in the eternal mirror are "both invisible."[74]
84c So even in Seppō's words there is one face of the eternal mirror and one face of the clear mirror.[75] We should definitely confirm the principle that, just at the moment of "the clear mirror coming," [the clear mirror] cannot hinder the foreigner and the Chinese person reflected in the eternal mirror.[76] [Seppō's] present assertion, about the eternal mirror, that "[When] a foreigner comes a foreigner appears," and "[When] a Chinese person comes a Chinese person appears," does not say that [the foreigner and the Chinese person] come-and-appear "on the eternal mirror," does not say that they come-and-appear "in the eternal mirror," does not say that they come-and-appear "on the exterior of the eternal mirror," and does not say that they come-and-appear "in the same state as the eternal mirror." We should listen to his words. At the moment when the foreigner and the Chinese person come-and-appear, the eternal mirror is actually making the foreigner and the Chinese person come. To insist that even when "the foreigner and the Chinese person are both invisible," the mirror will remain, is to be blind to appearance and to be remiss with regard to coming. To call it absurd would not be going far enough.

[153] Then Gensha says, "I am not like that." Seppō says, "How is it in your case?" Gensha says, "Please, master, you ask." We should not idly pass over the words "Please, master, you ask" spoken now by Gensha. Without father and son having thrown themselves into the moment, how could the coming of the master's question, and the requesting of the master's question, be like this? When [someone] requests the master's question, it may be that "someone ineffable"[77] has already understood[78] decisively the state in which the question is asked. While the state of the questioner is already thundering, there is no place of escape.

[154] Seppō says, "If suddenly a clear mirror comes along, how will it be then?" This question is one eternal mirror which father and son are mastering together.

[155] Gensha says, "Smashed into hundreds of bits and pieces!" These words mean smashed into hundred thousand myriads of bits and pieces. What he calls "the moment,[79] when suddenly a clear mirror comes along," is "smashed into hundreds of bits and pieces!" That which is able to experience the state of "smashed into hundreds of bits and pieces" may be the clear mirror. When the clear mirror is made to express itself, [the expression] may be "smashed into hundreds of bits and pieces." Therefore, the place where smashed 85a
bits and pieces are dangling is the clear mirror. Do not take the narrow view that formerly there was a moment of not yet being smashed to bits and pieces and that latterly there may be a moment of no longer being smashed to bits and pieces. [The expression] is simply "smashed into hundreds of bits and pieces!" Confrontation with the hundreds of smashed bits and pieces is a solitary and steep unity.[80] This being so, does this "smashed into hundreds of bits and pieces" describe the eternal mirror, or does it describe the clear mirror?—I would like to ask further for words of transformation.[81] At the same time, it neither describes the eternal mirror nor describes the clear mirror: though [hitherto] we have been able to ask about the eternal mirror and the clear mirror, when we discuss Gensha's words, might it be that what is manifesting itself before us as only sand, pebbles, fences, and walls has become the tip of a tongue, and thus "smashed into hundreds of bits and pieces"? What form does "smashing" take? Eternal blue depths; the moon in space.

[157] Great Master Shinkaku of Seppō Mountain and Zen Master Enen of Sanshōin Temple[82] are walking along when they see a group of apes. Thereupon Seppō says, "These apes are each backed with one eternal mirror."[83]

[157] We must diligently learn these words in practice. "Ape" means monkey.[84] How are the apes that Seppō sees? We should ask questions like this, and make effort further, not noticing the passing of *kalpa*s. "Each is backed with one eternal mirror": though the eternal mirror is the face of Buddhist patriarchs, at the same time, the eternal mirror, even in the ascendant state, is the eternal mirror. That it backs each individual ape does not mean that there are big mirrors and small mirrors according to individual differences; it is "one eternal mirror." As to the meaning of "backed," for example we say that a painted image of a buddha is "backed" with what we stick behind it. When the backs of apes are backed, they are backed with the eternal mirror. "What kind of paste could have been used?"[85] To speak

85b tentatively, the backs of monkeys might be backed with the eternal mirror. Is the back of the eternal mirror backed with monkeys? The back of the eternal mirror is backed with the eternal mirror, and the backs of monkeys are backed with monkeys. The words that "each back has one face"[86] are never an empty teaching: they are the truth expressed as the truth should be expressed. So apes or eternal mirrors? Ultimately, what can we say? Are we ourselves originally apes? Or are we other than apes? Who can we ask? Whether we are apes is beyond our knowledge and beyond the knowledge of others. Whether we are ourselves is beyond [intellectual] groping.

[159] Sanshō says, "It has been nameless for successive *kalpa*s. Why would you express it as the eternal mirror?" This is a mirror, a concrete instance, with which Sanshō has certified his realization of the eternal mirror. "For successive *kalpa*s" means before a mind or a moment of consciousness has ever appeared; it means the inside of a *kalpa* not having shown its head. "Nameless" describes "the successive *kalpa*s'"sun-faces, moon-faces, and eternal mirror-faces; and describes the face of the clear mirror. When "the nameless" is really "the nameless," the "successive *kalpa*s" are never "successive *kalpa*s." Given that "the successive *kalpa*s" are not "successive *kalpa*s," Sanshō's expression cannot be an expression of the truth. Instead, "before a moment of consciousness has ever appeared" means today. We should train and polish without letting today pass in vain. Frankly, though the fame of this "nameless for successive *kalpa*s" is heard on high, it expresses the eternal mirror as what? A dragon's head with a snake's tail![87]

[161] Seppō might now say to Sanshō, "The eternal mirror! The eternal mirror!" Seppō does not say that; what he says further is, "A flaw has appeared," or in other words, "a scratch has emerged."[88] We are prone to think "how could a flaw appear on the eternal mirror?" At the same time, [in saying that] the eternal mirror has borne a flaw [Seppō] may be calling the expression "It has been nameless for successive *kalpa*s" a flaw. The eternal mirror described by "a flaw has appeared" is the total eternal mirror. Sanshō
85c has not got out of the cave of a flaw appearing on the eternal mirror, and so the understanding which he has expressed is utterly a flaw on the eternal mirror. This being so, we learn in practice that flaws appear even on the eternal mirror and that even [mirrors] on which flaws have appeared are the eternal mirror; this is learning the eternal mirror in practice.

[162] Sanshō says, "What is so deadly urgent that you are not conscious of the story?"[89] The import of these words is "why [are you in] such a deadly hurry?" We should consider in detail and learn in practice whether this "deadly emergency" is [a matter of] today or tomorrow, the self or the external world, the whole universe in ten directions or [a concrete place] inside the great kingdom of Tang?[90] As to the meaning of "story" in the words "You are not conscious of the story," there are stories that have continued to be told, there are stories that have never been told, and there are stories that have already been told completely. Now, the truths which are in "the story" are being realized. Has the story itself, for example, realized the truth together with the earth and all sentient beings?[91] It is never restored brocade.[92] Therefore it is "not conscious"; it is the "nonconsciousness" of "the man facing the royal personage";[93] it is being face-to-face without consciousness of each other. It is not that there are no stories; it is just that the concrete situation is "beyond consciousness." "Nonconsciousness" is red mind in every situation[94] and, further, not-seeing with total clarity.[95]

[163] Seppō says, "It is the old monk's mistake." Sometimes people say these words meaning "I expressed myself badly," but [the words] need not be understood like that. "The old monk" means the old man who is master in his house;[96] that is to say, [someone] who solely learns in practice the old monk himself, without learning anything else. Though he experiences a thousand changes and ten thousand transformations, heads of gods and faces of demons, what he learns in practice is just the old monk's one move.[97] Though 86a
he appears as a buddha and appears as a patriarch, at every moment and for ten thousand years, what he learns in practice is just the old monk's one move. "Mistakes" are his "abundant jobs as temple master."[98] Upon reflection, Seppō is an outstanding member[99] of [the order of] Tokusan, and Sanshō is an excellent disciple[100] of Rinzai. Neither of the two venerable patriarchs is of humble ancestry: [Seppō] is a distant descendant of Seigen and [Sanshō] is a distant descendant of Nangaku.[101] That they have been dwelling in and retaining the eternal mirror is [evidenced] as described above. They may be a criterion[102] for students of later ages.

[165] Seppō preaches to the assembly, "[If] the world is ten feet[103] wide, the eternal mirror is ten feet wide. [If] the world is one foot[104] wide, the eternal mirror is one foot wide."

At this, Gensha, pointing to the furnace, says, "Tell me then, how wide is the furnace?"

Seppō says, "As wide as the eternal mirror."

Gensha says, "The Old Master's heels have not landed on the ground."[105]

[166] He calls ten feet the world; the world is ten feet. He sees one foot as the world; the world is one foot. He describes the ten feet of the present, and describes the one foot of the present, never any other unfamiliar foot or tens of feet. When [people] study this story, they usually think of the width of the world in terms of countless and boundless three-thousand-great-thousandfold worlds or the limitless world of Dharma, but that is only like being a small self and cursorily pointing to beyond the next village. In taking up this world [here and now], we see it as ten feet. This is why Seppō says, "The width of the eternal mirror is ten feet, and the width of the world is ten feet." When we learn these ten feet [here and now], we are able to see one concrete part of "the width of the world." In other cases, when [people] hear the words "eternal mirror" they envisage a sheet of thin ice. But it is not like that.[106] The ten foot width [of the eternal mirror] is at one with the ten foot width of the world, but are the form and content [of the eternal mirror and the world] necessarily equal, and are they at one, when the world is limit-
86b less?[107] We should consider this diligently. The eternal mirror is never like a pearl. Never hold views and opinions about whether it is bright or dull, and never look at it as square or round. Even though "the whole universe in ten directions is one bright pearl,"[108] this cannot match "the eternal mirror." So the eternal mirror, regardless of the coming and the appearance of foreigners or Chinese, is every thing [that happens] through the length and breadth of [this state of] brilliance.[109] [But] it is not numerous and not large. "Width" refers to this [real] quantity; it does not mean extent. "Width" means what is expressed as two or three ordinary inches and counted, for example, in sevens and eights. In calculation of the Buddha's truth, when we calculate it in terms of great realization or nonrealization we clarify [a weight of] two pounds or three pounds; and when we calculate it in terms of buddhas and patriarchs we realize five things or ten things.[110] One unit of ten feet is the width of the eternal mirror, and the width of the eternal mirror is one thing.[111] Gensha's words, "How wide is the furnace?" are an unconcealed expression of the truth, which we should learn in practice for a thousand ages and for

ten thousand ages. To look now into the furnace is to look into [the furnace] having become a person who is "Who?"[112] When we are looking into the furnace, it is not seven feet and it is not eight feet. This [story] is not a tale of agitation and attachment; it is about the realization of a singular state in a fresh situation—[as expressed,] for example, "What is it that comes like this."[113] When the [meaning of] the words "what amount of width. . ." has come to us, the "what amount [of width]" may be different from "how [wide]" [as we have understood it] hitherto.[114] We must not doubt the fact of liberation at this concrete place. We must hear in Gensha's words the fundamental point that the furnace is beyond aspects and dimensions. Do not idly allow the one dumpling before you now to fall to the ground. Break it open! This is the effort.

[170] Seppō says, "As wide as the eternal mirror." We should quietly reflect on these words. Not wanting to say "the furnace is ten feet wide," he speaks like this. It is not true that saying ten feet would be the fit expression 86c
of the truth whereas "as wide as the eternal mirror" is an unfit expression. We should study actions that are "as wide as the eternal mirror." Many people have thought that not saying "the furnace is ten feet wide" was unfitness of expression. They should diligently consider the independence of "width"; they should reflect that the eternal mirror is a concrete thing; and they should not let action which is "reality" pass them by.[115] [Seppō] may be "manifesting behavior in the way of the ancients, never falling into despondency."[116]

[171] Gensha says, "The Old Man's heels have not landed on the ground."[117] The point here is, whether we call him "the Old Man" or whether we call him "the Old Master," that is not always Seppō himself, because Seppō may be "a [real] Old Man." As to the meaning of "heels," we should ask just where they are.[118] We should master in practice just what "heels" means. Does mastering ["heels"] in practice refer to the right Dharma-eye treasury, or to space, or to the whole ground, or to the lifeblood? How many ["heels"] are there? Is there one? Is there a half? Are there hundred thousand myriads? We should do diligent study like this. "They have not landed on the ground": what kind of thing is "the ground"?[119] We provisionally call the present earth "ground," in conformance with the view of our own kind. There are other kinds that see it, for instance, as "the Dharma gate to unthinkable salvation,"[120] and there is a kind that sees [the earth] as the buddhas'

many enactments of the truth. So in the case of the "ground" upon which heels should land, what does [Gensha] see as the "ground"? Is the "ground" the real state of being, or is it the real state of being without? Further, we should ask again and again, and we should tell ourselves and tell others, whether it is impossible for even an inch or so of what we generally call "the ground" to exist within the great order? Is heels touching the ground the right state, or is heels not landing on the ground the right state? What situation
87a leads [Gensha] to say "they have not landed on the ground?" When the earth is without an inch of soil,[121] [the words] "touching the ground" may be immature[122] and [the words] "not having landed on the ground" may be immature. This being so, "the Old Man's heels not having landed on the ground" is the [very] exhalation and inhalation of the Old Man, the [very] moment of his heels.[123]

[174] Zen Master Kōtō[124] of Kokutai-in Temple, on Kinkazan in the Bushu[125] district, the story goes, is asked by a monk, "What is the eternal mirror like before being polished?"[126]

The master says, "The eternal mirror."

The monk says, "What is it like after being polished?"

The master says, "The eternal mirror."[127]

[174] Remember, the eternal mirror under discussion now has a time of being polished, a time before being polished, and [a time] after being polished, but it is wholly the eternal mirror. This being so, when we are polishing, we are polishing the eternal mirror in its entirety. We do not polish by mixing in mercury or anything else other than the eternal mirror. This is neither polishing the self nor the self polishing; it is polishing the eternal mirror. Before being polished the eternal mirror is not dull. Even if [people] call it black, it can never be dull: it is the eternal mirror in its vivid state. In general, we polish a mirror to make it into a mirror; we polish a tile to make it into a mirror; we polish a tile to make it into a tile; and we polish a mirror to make it into a tile.[128] There are [times when] we polish without making anything; and there are [times when] it would be possible to make something, but we are unable to polish.[129] All equally are the traditional work of Buddhist patriarchs.

[175] When Baso[130] of Kōzei,[131] in former days, was learning in practice under Nangaku,[132] Nangaku on one occasion intimately transmits to Baso

the mind-seal. This is the beginning of the beginning of "polishing a tile."[133] Baso has been living at Denpōin Temple, sitting constantly in zazen for a matter of ten or so years. We can imagine what it is like in his thatched hut on a rainy night. There is no mention of him letting up on a cold floor sealed in by snow. Nangaku one day goes to Baso's hut, where Baso stands waiting. Nangaku asks, "What are you doing these days?"

Baso says, "These days Dōitsu just sits."

Nangaku says, "What is the aim of sitting in zazen?" 87b

Baso says, "The aim of sitting in zazen is to become buddha."[134]

Nangaku promptly fetches a tile and polishes it on a rock near Baso's hut.

Baso, on seeing this, asks, "What is the master doing?"

Nangaku says, "Polishing a tile."

Baso says, "What is the use of polishing a tile?"

Nangaku says, "I am polishing it into a mirror."[135]

Baso says, "How can polishing a tile make it into a mirror?"[136]

Nangaku says, "How can sitting in zazen make you into a buddha?"[137]

[178] For several hundred years, since ancient times, most people interpreting this story—great matter that it is—have thought that Nangaku was simply spurring Baso on. That is not necessarily so. The actions of great saints far transcend the states of common folk. Without the Dharma of polishing a tile, how could the great saints have any expedient method of teaching people? The power to teach people is the bones and marrow of a Buddhist patriarch. Although [Nangaku] has devised it, this [teaching method] is a common tool. [Teaching methods] other than common tools and everyday utensils are not transmitted in the house of Buddha. Further, the impression on Baso is immediate. Clearly, the virtue authentically transmitted by the Buddhist patriarchs is directness. Clearly, in truth, when polishing a tile becomes a mirror, Baso becomes buddha. When Baso becomes buddha, Baso immediately becomes Baso. When Baso becomes Baso, zazen immediately becomes zazen. This is why the making of mirrors through the polishing of tiles has been dwelled in and retained in the bones and marrow of eternal buddhas; and, this being so, the eternal mirror exists having been made from a tile. While we have been polishing this mirror—in the past also—it has never been tainted. Tiles are not dirty; we just polish a tile as a tile. In this

87c state, the virtue of making a mirror is realized, and this is just the effort of Buddhist patriarchs. If polishing a tile does not make a mirror, polishing a mirror cannot make a mirror either.[138] Who can suppose that in this "making" there is [both] "becoming" buddha and "making" a mirror?[139] Further, to express a doubt, is it possible, when polishing the eternal mirror, to mistakenly think that the polishing is making a tile? The real state at the time of polishing is, at other times, beyond comprehension. Nevertheless, because Nangaku's words must exactly express the expression of the truth, it may be, in conclusion, simply that polishing a tile makes a mirror. People today also should try taking up the tiles of the present and polishing them, and they will certainly become mirrors. If tiles did not become mirrors, people could not become buddhas. If we despise tiles as lumps of mud, then we might also despise people as lumps of mud. If people have mind, tiles must also have mind. Who can recognize that there are mirrors in which, [when] tiles come, tiles appear? And who can recognize that there are mirrors in which, [when] mirrors come, mirrors appear?

Shōbōgenzō Kokyō

Preached to the assembly at Kannondōrikō-shōhōrinji, on the ninth day of the ninth lunar month in the second year of Ninji.[140]

Notes

[1] Buddhist patriarchs and the eternal mirror.

[2] *Zō,* like the English word "image," includes two meanings: 1) a phenomenal form, and 2) a statue, that is, an image that has been cast from a mold.

[3] In Master Dōgen's time, mirrors were not made of glass; they were cast from copper and kept highly polished.

[4] Uzuran is the phonetic representation in Chinese characters of the original name. The derivation of the Chinese characters *tengai,* "celestial canopy," and *hōshō,* "exact and sacred," is uncertain.

[5] *Enkan towa enkyō nari.* Master Dōgen explained the less familiar character *kan* with the more familiar character *kyō.*

[6] *Dōshō* literally means either "lived with" or "born with." Master Dōgen clarified that the meaning here is "lived with."

[7] The implication is that after becoming a Buddhist monk he already had the criteria for behavior naturally.

[8] "Trees and rocks" alludes to the story of the young "Child of the Himalayas." See note 159 in Chapter Twelve, *Kesa-kudoku.*

[9] *Nyakuden-nyakuri ni rufu suru chishiki ari.* See LS 3.72–74. *Chishiki,* lit., knowledge or acquaintance, represents the Sanskrit *kalyāṇamitra.* See Glossary of Sanskrit Terms.

[10] Yellow paper on a red rod means a Buddhist sutra.

[11] The seventeenth patriarch in India. See Chapter Fifteen, *Busso.*

[12] Literally, "[That which] you have in your hands has the expression of what?" Master Saṃghanandi invited Master Geyāśata to express his state.

[13] "What?" suggests ineffable reality.

[14] The poem says *ryōnin,* "two people." This says *ryōko,* "two individuals," or "two concrete things"; *ko* is a counter for inanimate objects.

[15] The Third Patriarch in China was called Kanchi, "Mirror Wisdom," and the Sixth Patriarch in China was called Daikan, "Great Mirror." Both names contain the character *kan,* "mirror."

16 In other words, the Buddhist viewpoint realized as it is.

17 Master Daiman Kōnin (688–761), the thirty-second patriarch (the Fifth Patriarch in China). See Chapter Fifteen, *Busso.*

18 It was the custom at the temple for a monk who wanted to express an idea to paste up some words on the wall of the southern corridor. In the middle of one night, Ācārya Jinshū, the most intelligent member of the order, secretly took a lantern and posted up the following poem: "The body is the *bodhi* tree,/The mind is like the stand of a clear mirror./At every moment we work to wipe and polish it/To keep it free of dust and dirt." A boy from the temple recited Jinshū's poem as he passed by the temple servant's cottage where Master Daikan Enō lived and worked, pounding rice for the monks. Hearing the poem, Master Daikan Enō thought that comparing Buddhist practice to keeping a mirror clean was too intellectual or artificial, so he had someone paste up his own poem. All the monks were astonished at the excellence of the laborer's poem. The story is contained in the *Rokusodaishihōbōdangyō* (*Platform Sutra of the Sixth Patriarch's Dharma Treasure*).

19 Master Engo Kokugon (1063–1135). A successor of Master Goso Hōen and an eleventh-generation descendant of Master Rinzai. He received the title of Zen Master Bukka from the Song emperor Kisō (r. 1101–1126), and the title Zen Master Engo from the Southern Song emperor Kōsō (r. 1127–1163). His successors included Master Daie Sōkō.

20 Master Daikan Enō. Sōkei was the name of the mountain where he lived.

21 Also quoted in Chapter Forty-four (Vol. III), *Kobusshin.*

22 *Mei-mei,* lit., "clear-clear," from *mei-mei* [*taru*] *hyaku-so-to,* lit., "hundreds of weeds in the clear-clear state." These are the words of Master Chinshū Fuke, quoted in Chapter Twenty-two (Vol. II), *Busshō,* suggesting the state in which each miscellaneous concrete thing is conspicuously clear as it is. Master Chinshū Fuke was nicknamed Hōtei or "Cloth Bag" because he wandered freely from temple to temple carrying all his belongings in a sack. In Japan the fat laughing monk depicted in "Happy Buddha" statues is called Hōtei.

23 Also the words of Master Chinshū Fuke, or Hōtei, the Happy Buddha. See *Shinji-shōbōgenzō,* pt. 1 no. 22.

24 "Any place" is *izure no tokoro,* Japanese words representing the characters *doko,* "where" or "at what place," in the last line of the poem.

25 *Jinsetsu,* or "lands as numerous as dust particles."

26 Master Nangaku Ejō (677–744), a successor of Master Daikan Enō. Zen Master Daie is his posthumous title.

27 Again, it should be remembered that in those days mirrors were cast from copper which was also used to make images or statues.

28 *Shinji-shōbōgenzō,* pt. 2, no. 16.

29 *Banshō,* "myriad phenomena." Here "images" means phenomena; in the rest of this paragraph, "image" means statue. See note 2.

30 Master Dōgen praises the monk's viewpoint.

31 "Possibility" is *nyo or* [*ga*] *goto* [*ki*], translated in the story as "If. . . ."

32 The monk's question is not only abstract speculation but includes recognition of possibilities as they are, of concrete things as they are, and of the state of action that makes all things possible.

33 The monk's question was philosophical, so Master Nangaku brought the discussion back down to the monk's own experience.

34 *Men-men,* lit., "face-face."

35 Because if the sea dries up, what was formerly the seabed is now land. That the ocean's drying cannot reveal the seabed was an expression of reality in China.

36 *Man-man ten-ten,* lit., "delusion-delusion, point-point." The characters *man* and *ten* appear in Master Nangaku's words.

37 "Shining mirror reflections" is *kanshō,* lit., "mirror-shine." These characters also appear in the story ("shine like a mirror"). The last sentence suggests concrete reality which is different from abstract thinking.

38 Master Seppō Gison (822–907), a successor of Master Tokusan Senkan. Great Master Seppō Shinkaku is the title he received from Emperor Isō (r. 860–874).

39 *Kono ji,* or "the matter of this," "the state of reality."

40 Master Gensha Shibi (835–907). The *Shinji-shōbōgenzō* contains many conversations between Master Seppō and Master Gensha, of which this one is typical—with Master Seppō preaching very sincerely and Master Gensha being somewhat cynical.

41 *Ko*[*re*] *nan* [*no*] *ji* alludes to Master Daikan Enō's words, *ko*[*re*] *shimo-butsu* [*ka*] *inmorai,* "What is it that comes like this?" or "This is something [ineffable] coming like this." See Chapter Twenty-nine (Vol. II), *Inmo;* and Chapter Sixty-two (Vol. III), *Hensan.*

42 A pearl spinning in a bowl symbolizes constant movement (see for example Chapter Sixty-six [Vol. III], *Shunjū,* paragraph 135); or, in this context, busy daily life.

43 To Chinese people, redbeards were foreigners and foreigners were redbeards. See for example Chapter Seventy-six (Vol. IV), *Dai-shugyō.*

44 *Konton,* the state of chaos that existed before the forces of *yin* and *yang* had become distinct.

45 Banko appears in the Daoist book *Sangoryakuki (History of the Three* [*Elements*] *and Five* [*Elements*]). He is the emperor who ruled at the beginning of creation.

[46] The heavens, the earth, human beings; wood, fire, earth, metal, water.

[47] The Yellow Emperor (approximate dates 2697–2597 B.C.E.) was the third emperor in the legendary age of the five rulers (2852–2205 B.C.E.). Volume 8 of the Chinese book *Jibutsugenki* (*Record of the Origins of Things*), says, "According to the Yellow Emperor's confidential account, when the emperor met his mother at the royal palace, he cast twelve great mirrors, which he used one month at a time."

[48] Daoist legend says that the Yellow Emperor visited Kōsei at Kōsei's hermit's cave on Kōdōzan, to ask for the secret of immortality. See Chapter Fourteen, *Sansuigyō.*

[49] In the Far East, the use of a mirror represents the function of decision-making.

[50] The idea of past and present is subordinate to the twelve hours of today which, as the ordinary time of concrete daily life, have real substance—in Chapter Eleven, *Uji,* Master Dōgen urges us to learn real time as the twelve hours of today.

[51] Kenen is the Japanese pronunciation of the Yellow Emperor's personal name.

[52] Again it should be stressed that in the Far East a mirror means a standard. In this context, for example, the criteria of astrology, geography, and economics could be called mirrors.

[53] They are intuitional.

[54] Summarized quotation from vol. 4 of the Daoist text *Sōshi.*

[55] The *Jōkanseiyō* (*Jōkan Era* [*Treatise*] *on the Essence of Government*).

[56] The second Tang dynasty emperor (r. 627–650).

[57] Gichō and Bōgenrei were two high officials in Emperor Taisō's government.

[58] *Gogyō.* Wood, fire, earth, metal, water.

[59] *Gojō.* Paternal righteousness, maternal benevolence, friendship as an elder brother, respect as a younger brother, and filial piety.

[60] Human beings, as they are, are a criterion; in other words, reality is the criterion.

[61] Again, the point is that concrete facts are universal criteria.

[62] The five peaks are five mountains in China. The four great rivers are the Yellow River, the Yangzi River, and the Waisui and Saisui Rivers. The four oceans are the oceans of the north, south, east, and west. This part suggests Master Dōgen's optimism about the progress of human society.

[63] Refers to Japan's three sacred treasures: the mirrors, the sacred jewels, and the "grass-mowing sword."

[64] The Inner Shrine at Ise, considered the abode of Amaterasu, the Sun Goddess, still houses one of the sacred mirrors.

[65] Kii-no-kuni, present-day Wakayama prefecture, where the Hinokuma Shrine still houses the second of the three mirrors.

[66] The third of the three mirrors, called *Yata-no-kagami,* is still housed in the Imperial Palace in Tokyo. The original text is in the style of a quotation, written in Chinese characters only.

[67] It is just a physical substance.

[68] The original story is quoted in Chinese characters only. Here Master Dōgen represents Master Gensha's words in Japanese.

[69] *Nimai,* that is, two mirrors—the eternal mirror, and the clear mirror.

[70] *Shichitsū-hattatsu,* lit., "penetrating the seven directions and arriving at the eight destinations."

[71] *Hachimen-reirō.* The original meaning of *reirō* is the sound of golden bells, and hence something clear, bright, and serene.

[72] Master Daikan Enō's words to Master Nangaku Ejō. See *Shinji-shōbōgenzō,* pt. 2, no. 1, and Chapter Seven, *Senjō.*

[73] See the two stories quoted at the end of this chapter.

[74] The images of the foreigner and the Chinese person are no longer relevant.

[75] Master Seppō did not only affirm the eternal mirror—both masters affirmed both sides.

[76] The simile of the clear mirror does not deny the simile of the foreigner and Chinese person appearing in the eternal mirror. Both similes can coexist independently.

[77] *Inmonin.* See Chapter Twenty-nine (Vol. II), *Inmo.*

[78] "Has already understood" is *nyaku-e su. Nyaku* originally expresses possibility, but this usage reflects Master Dōgen's identification of what is possible and what is already there. Master Dōgen explains that *nyaku* means "already" in Chapter Twenty-two (Vol. II), *Busshō,* no. 14.

[79] *Ji, toki,* means time or moment. In Master Gensha's original question it is translated as "then."

[80] *Koshun no itsu. Itsu,* "one" or "unity," suggests reality as the one, in contrast to Master Gensha's expression which suggests reality as miscellaneous things and phenomena in their own concrete forms. *Koshun* expresses the mental aspect (solitude) and concrete aspect (steepness) of the real state.

[81] *Ichitengo,* lit., "one-turn words," i.e., words that can change a situation completely. Master Dōgen expected the answer "Both the eternal mirror and the clear mirror."

[82] Master Sanshō Enen (dates unknown), a successor of Master Rinzai.

83 See *Shinji-shōbōgenzō* pt. 3, no. 95. Also *Hekiganroku,* no. 68. In the following paragraphs, the rest of the story is quoted line by line.

84 Master Dōgen explained the relatively uncommon Chinese characters that appear in the story, *mikō,* with the familiar Japanese word *saru.*

85 The question is written in Chinese characters only, but a source earlier than Master Dōgen has not been traced.

86 Master Seppō's words are *ichimen no kokyō o hai se ri,* lit., "backed with one face of eternal mirror," with *men,* "face," used as a counter. Master Dōgen's comment suggests that all individual things have one reality in common.

87 Master Dōgen first of all affirmed Master Sanshō's words, because they say that the eternal mirror is never a concept. But in conclusion he was not impressed by Master Sanshō calling the eternal mirror "nameless for successive *kalpa*s."

88 Master Dōgen explained the meaning of the Chinese character *ka, kizu,* with the Japanese *kana* (*kizu*).

89 "Story" is *watō. Wa* means "story." *Tō,* "head," is added to make the expression more concrete. In the Rinzai sect, stories (or so-called *kōan*s) such as those recorded by Master Dōgen in the *Shinji-shōbōgenzō*, are called *watō.*

90 We should learn whether, in reality, there is anything to be hasty about.

91 The Buddha said that when he realized the truth the earth and all sentient beings realized the truth at the same time. See for example Chapter Sixty-nine (Vol. III), *Hotsumujōshin.* Master Dōgen emphasized that the story is not only abstract words, but the representation of something real.

92 The story is not to be fussed and worried over.

93 When Master Bodhidharma arrived in China from India, he was presented to Emperor Wu of the Liang dynasty. The emperor said to him, "Who is the man facing the royal personage?" Master Bodhidharma replied, "I do not know." See *Hekiganroku,* no. 1. In the Emperor Wu story, "I do not know" or "I am not conscious [of myself]" or "I do not understand [myself intellectually]" is *fushiki,* as in Master Sanshō's words. Master Sanshō's words sound like a complaint that Master Seppō is not listening to him. But Master Dōgen interpreted the word *fushiki* as ironic praise of Master Seppō's state.

94 *Jōjō no sekishin.* This is a variation on Master Dōgen's usual expression *sekishin-henpen,* or "naked mind at every moment."

95 *Meimei no fuken,* lit., "clear-clear not-seeing."

96 That is, his own master, the master of himself.

97 *Ichijaku* means one placement of a stone in a game of *go*—suggesting one action at one time and place.

98 Sanshō asks Seppō, "The golden-scaled fish that passes through the net: what does it feed on?" Seppō says, "When you have got free of the net, I will tell you." Sanshō says, "The good counselor to fifteen hundred people is not conscious of the story!" Master Seppō says, "The old monk's jobs as temple master are abundant." See *Shinji-shōbōgenzō,* pt. 1, no. 52.

99 *Ikkaku,* lit., one horn.

100 *Jinsoku,* lit., "mystical foot," from the Sanskrit *ṛddhipāda.* See the Glossary of Sanskrit Terms. See also Chapter Eight, *Raihai-tokuzui,* note 33.

101 Master Seigen Gyōshi (660–740) and Master Nangaku Ejō (677–744) were both disciples of Master Daikan Enō.

102 *Kikyō,* lit., "turtle mirror." Chinese soothsayers used to heat a turtle shell and use the positions of the cracks thus caused to divine a future course of action.

103 *Ichijō.* One *jō* is about ten feet.

104 *Issahaku.* One *shaku* is almost exactly one foot, and ten *shaku* equals one *jō.*

105 See *Shinji-shōbōgenzō,* pt. 2, no. 9.

106 Some people think about the eternal mirror too abstractly; others can only conceive it as something material.

107 In Master Seppō's example, the eternal mirror and the world are a unity within the area of ten feet. Master Dōgen asked if it would be true if the world were limitless.

108 Master Gensha's expression of the truth. See Chapter Four, *Ikka-no-myōju.*

109 *Reirō* suggests the universe itself. See note 71.

110 "Thing" is *mai,* which is used as a counter for thin flat objects such as sheets of paper, layers of clothing, mirrors, etc., and sometimes as a counter for generations of Buddhist patriarchs.

111 This sentence can be contrasted with the opening sentence of the paragraph. In this case Master Dōgen changed the final element in the sentence from *ichijō,* "one unit of ten feet," to *ichimai,* "one thing," emphasizing that the eternal mirror is concrete.

112 *Tare hito,* a person who has lost self-consciousness, a person whose state is beyond words or understanding.

113 *Ko[re] shimo-butsu [ka] inmo-rai.* Master Daikan Enō spoke these words to Master Nangaku Ejō when Master Nangaku entered his order. See also note 41.

114 Master Gensha said *hiroki koto tashō,* or *katsu-tashō.* In Chinese *tashō,* lit., "large-small," is the usual way of asking how big something is, how expensive something is, etc. However, Master Dōgen understood Master Gensha's words not only as an ordinary question, but also as a statement that the furnace was a real quantity.

[115] Master Seppō said *nyo-kokyō-katsu.* Master Dōgen considered the real meaning of each of the three elements independently. As an adverb, *nyo* means "as" or "like," but as a noun it means "real state," or "reality"—for example, in the compound *ichinyo,* "oneness" or "one reality." Here Master Dōgen repeats the character, *nyo nyo,* for emphasis: reality.

[116] The words of Master Kyōgen Chikan. See Chapter Nine, *Keisei-sanshiki.*

[117] In the story "ground" is *chi,* "ground" or "earth." "The earth" is *daichi,* "big ground" or "great earth."

[118] In general, heels are symbols of the concrete.

[119] *Chi* means "ground" or "earth"; at the same time, it means "the concrete" or "concrete state."

[120] *Fushigi-gedatsu-hōmon,* the words of Vimalakīrti, a lay student of the Buddha.

[121] When the earth is realized as it is.

[122] "Immature" is *imadashi,* lit., "not yet." This is the negative used in Master Gensha's original sentence.

[123] In this paragraph, Master Dōgen urges us to consider what each of Master Gensha's words really expresses. In conclusion, Master Gensha's words describe Master Seppō's real state, his concrete existence.

[124] Master Kokutai Kōtō, a successor of Master Gensha Shibi; dates unknown.

[125] A district in Chekiang province in east China.

[126] Because in those days mirrors were made of copper, it was natural to think of a mirror as something that needs polishing.

[127] See *Shinji-shōbōgenzō* pt. 2, no. 17.

[128] Sometimes our idealism is like polishing a mirror in order to try and make an ideal mirror, sometimes our behavior is as meaningless as trying to polish a tile into a mirror, sometimes we realize concrete things through Buddhist practice, and sometimes our action transcends idealism completely.

[129] Two examples of real situations in daily life.

[130] Master Baso Dōitsu (709–788). After receiving the Dharma from Master Nangaku Ejō, he lived on Basozan in the Jiangxi district, where he taught more than one hundred and thirty disciples, including Hyakujō Ekai, Seidō Chizō, Nansen Fugan, and Daibai Hōjō.

[131] Jiangxi, a province in southeast China.

[132] Master Nangaku Ejō (677–744).

[133] *Masen.* The words first appear in the story of Masters Nangaku and Baso in vol. 5 of the *Keitokudentōroku.* See also *Shinji-shōbōgenzō,* pt. 1, no. 8.

[134] *Sabutsu. Sa, tsukuru,* [*to*] *nasu* means to produce, to make, to become, or to act as.

[135] *Ma-sa-kyo,* or *mashi te kagami to nasu.* "Into" represents *sa,* [*to*] *nasu,* as in the preceding note.

[136] *Jōkyō,* or *kagami* [*to*] *nasu.* "Make it into" is in this case represented by the character *jō, nasu,* lit., "to accomplish," "to realize," or "to make."

[137] "Make you into a buddha" is *sabutsu,* translated previously as "to become buddha."

[138] Because polishing makes the mirror—whether the object is a tile or a mirror is not important.

[139] Making and becoming are the same character, *sa.*

[140] 1241.

[Chapter Twenty-one]

Kankin 88a3

Reading Sutras

Translator's Note: Kan *means "to read" and* kin *means "sutras." Many Buddhist sects revere reading sutras, because they think that the Buddhist truth is theory which can be understood through abstract explanation. They think that we can understand Buddhism only by reading sutras. At the same time, there are other sects who deny the value of reading sutras; they say that because Buddhist truth is not a theoretical system, we cannot attain the truth by reading sutras. Master Dōgen took the middle way on the problem: rather than deny the value of reading sutras, he said that reading sutras is one way of finding out what Buddhist practice is. He did not believe, however, that we can get the truth by reading sutras; he did not think that reciting sutras might exercise some mystical influence over religious life. In this way Master Dōgen's view on reading sutras was very realistic. However, his understanding of "reading sutras" was not limited to written sutras; he believed that the universe is a sutra. He thought that observing the world around us is like reading a sutra. So for him, grass, trees, mountains, the moon, the sun, and so forth were all Buddhist sutras. He even extended his view of reading sutras to include walking around the master's chair in the middle of the zazen hall. This viewpoint is not only Master Dōgen's; it is the viewpoint of Buddhism itself. So in this chapter, Master Dōgen explains the wider meaning of reading sutras.*

[183] The practice-and-experience of *anuttara samyaksaṃbodhi* sometimes relies on [good] counselors and sometimes relies on the sutras. "[Good] counselors"[1] means Buddhist patriarchs who are totally themselves. "Sutras" means sutras that are totally themselves. Because the self is totally a Buddhist patriarch and because the self is totally a sutra, it is like this.[2] Even though we call it self, it is not restricted by "me and you." It is vivid eyes, and a vivid fist.

[184] At the same time,[3] there is the consideration of sutras, the reading

of sutras,[4] the reciting of sutras, the copying of sutras, the receiving of sutras, and the retaining of sutras: they are all the practice-and-experience of Buddhist patriarchs. Yet it is not easy to meet the Buddha's sutras: "Throughout innumerable realms, even the name cannot be heard."[5] Among Buddhist patriarchs, "even the name cannot be heard." Amid the lifeblood, "even the name cannot be heard." Unless we are Buddhist patriarchs we do not see, hear, read, recite, or understand the meaning of sutras. After learning in practice as Buddhist patriarchs, we are barely able to learn sutras in practice. At this time the reality of hearing [sutras], retaining [sutras], receiving [sutras], preaching sutras, and so on, exists in the ears, eyes, tongue, nose, and organs of body and mind,[6] and in the places where we go, hear, and speak. The sort who "because they seek fame, preach non-Buddhist doctrines"[7] cannot practice the Buddha's sutras. The reason is that the sutras are transmitted and retained on trees and on rocks, are spread through fields and through villages, are expounded by lands of dust, and are lectured by space.

[186] Great Master Kōdō,[8] the ancestral patriarch of Yakusan Mountain, has not ascended [his seat in the Dharma] hall for a long time. The temple chief[9] says, "The monks have long been hoping for your compassionate instruction, master."

[Yaku]san says, "Strike the bell!"

The temple chief strikes the bell, and a few of the monks assemble.

[Yaku]san ascends [the seat in the Dharma] hall and passes a while. Then he gets down from the seat and goes back to the abbot's quarters. The temple chief follows behind him and says, "Just before, the master agreed
88b to preach the Dharma for the monks. Why have you not bestowed a single word upon us?"

[Yaku]san says, "For sutras there are sutra teachers. For commentaries there are commentary teachers. How could you doubt the old monk?"[10]

[188] The compassionate instruction of the ancestral patriarch is that for fists there is a fist-teacher, and for eyes there is an eye-teacher. At the same time, with due respect, I would now like to ask the ancestral patriarch this: I do not deny [your words] "how can the old monk be doubted?" but I still do not understand: the master is a teacher of What.[11]

[188] The order of the Founding Patriarch Daikan[12] is on Sōkeizan in Shōshū district. Hōtatsu,[13] a monk who recites the *Sutra of the Flower of*

Dharma,[14] comes to practice there. The Founding Patriarch preaches for Hōtatsu the following verse:

When the mind is in delusion, the Flower of Dharma turns.
When the mind is in realization, we turn the Flower of Dharma.
Unless we are clear about ourselves, however long we recite [the sutra],
It will become an enemy because of its meanings.
Without intention the mind is right.
With intention the mind becomes wrong.
When we transcend both with and without,
We ride eternally in the white ox cart.[15]

[189] So when the mind is in delusion we are turned by the Flower of Dharma; when the mind is in realization we turn the Flower of Dharma. Further, when we spring free from delusion and realization, the Flower of Dharma turns the Flower of Dharma. On hearing this verse Hōtatsu jumps for joy and praises it with the following verse:

Three thousand recitations of the sutra
With one phrase from Sōkei, forgotten.
Before clarifying the import of [the buddhas'] appearance in the world,
How can we stop recurring lives of madness?
[The sutra] explains goat, deer, and ox as an expedient,
[But] proclaims that beginning, middle, and end are good.
Who knows that [even] within the burning house,
Originally we are kings in the Dharma?

Then the Founding Patriarch says, "From now on, you will rightly be called the Sutra-reading Monk." We should know that there are sutra-reading monks in Buddhism: it is the direct teaching of the eternal buddha of Sōkei. "Reading" in this [phrase] "Sutra-reading Monk" is beyond "having ideas," "being without ideas," and so on.[16] It is "transcendence of both having and being without." The fact is only that "from *kalpa* to *kalpa* the hands never put down the sutra, and from noon to night there is no time when it is not being read."[17] The fact is only that from sutra to sutra it is never not being experienced.[18]

[191] The twenty-seventh patriarch is Venerable Prajñātara[19] of eastern India. A king of eastern India, the story goes, invites the Venerable One to a midday meal, at which time the king asks, "Everyone else recites[20] sutras. Why is it, Venerable One, that you alone do not recite?"

The patriarch says:

88c My[21] out-breath does not follow circumstances,
The in-breath does not reside in the world of aggregates.[22]
I am constantly reciting sutras like this.[23]
Hundred thousand myriad *koṭi*s of scrolls.
Never only one scroll or two scrolls.[24]

[192] The Venerable Prajñātara is a native of an eastern territory of India. He is the twenty-seventh rightful successor from Venerable Mahākāśyapa,[25] having received the authentic transmission of all the tools of the Buddha's house: he has dwelled in and retained the brains, the eyes, the fist, and the nostrils; the staff, the *pātra,* the robe and Dharma, the bones and marrow, and so on. He is our ancestral patriarch, and we are his distant descendants.[26] The words into which the Venerable One has now put his total effort [mean] not only that the out-breath does not follow circumstances, but also that circumstances do not follow the out-breath. Circumstances may be the brains and eyes, circumstances may be the whole body, circumstances may be the whole mind, but in bringing here, taking there, and bringing back here again, the state is just "not following circumstances." "Not following" means totally following; therefore it is a state of bustling and jostling. The out-breath is circumstances themselves; even so, "it does not follow circumstances." For countless *kalpa*s we have never recognized the situation of breathing out and breathing in, but just now the moment has come when we can recognize it for the first time, and so we hear "it does not reside in the world of aggregates" and "it does not follow circumstances." This is the moment when circumstances study for the first time such things as "the in-breath." This moment has never been before, and it will never be again: it exists only in the present. "The world of aggregates" means the five aggregates: matter, perception, thought, enaction, and consciousness. The reason he does not reside in these five aggregates is that he is in the world where "five aggregates" have
89a never arrived. Because he has grasped this pivotal point, the sutras he recites

are never only one or two scrolls; he is "constantly reciting hundred thousand myriad *koṭi*s of scrolls." Though we say that "hundred thousand myriad *koṭi*s of scrolls" just cites for the present an example of a large number, it is beyond only numerical quantity: it assigns the quantity of "hundred thousand myriad *koṭi*s of scrolls" to one out-breath's "not residing in the world of aggregates." At the same time, [the state] is not measured by tainted or faultless wisdom[27] and it is beyond the world of tainted and faultless *dharmas*.[28] Thus, it is beyond the calculation of wise intelligence, it is beyond the estimation of intelligent wisdom; it is beyond the consideration of non-wise intelligence, and it is beyond the reach of non-intelligent wisdom. It is the practice-and-experience of buddhas and of patriarchs, it is their skin, flesh, bones, and marrow, their eyes, fists, brains, and nostrils, and their staffs and whisks, springing out of the moment.

[196] Great Master Shinsai[29] of Kannon-in Temple in Jōshū, the story goes, is sent a donation by an old woman, who asks the Great Master to recite the whole of the sutras. The master descends from the zazen chair, goes around it once, and says to the messenger, "I have finished reciting the sutras." The messenger returns and reports this to the old woman. The old woman says, "I asked him before to recite the whole of the sutras. Why did the master only recite half the sutras?"[30]

[197] Evidently, the recitation of the whole of the sutras or half of the sutras amounts to three scrolls of sutras in the old woman's case.[31] "I have finished reciting the sutras" is the whole of Jōshū's sutra. In brief, the situation of his reciting the whole of the sutras is as follows: There is Jōshū going around the zazen chair; there is the zazen chair going around Jōshū, there is Jōshū going around Jōshū, and there is the zazen chair going around the zazen chair. At the same time, all instances of reciting the sutras are neither limited to going around a zazen chair, nor limited to a zazen chair going around.

[198] Great Master Shinshō[32] of Daizuizan in Ekishū, whose original Dharma name was Hōshin,[33] succeeded Zen Master Daian[34] of Chōkeiji. In the story, an old woman sends a donation and asks the master to recite the whole of the sutras. The master descends from his zazen chair, goes around it once, and says to the messenger, "I have already recited the whole of the sutras." The messenger returns and reports this to the old woman. The old 89b

woman says, "I asked him before to recite the whole of the sutras. Why did the master only recite half the sutras?"[35]

[199] Now, do not study that Daizui is going around the zazen chair, and do not study that the zazen chair is going around Daizui. It is not only a grouping together of fists and eyes; his making of a circle is enaction of a circle. Does the old woman have the eyes, or does she not have the eyes [to see it]? Even though she has got the expression "He only recited half the sutras" in the authentic transmission from a fist,[36] the old woman should also say, "I asked him before to recite the whole of the sutras. Why did the master only worry his soul?"[37] If she spoke like this, even by accident, she would be an old woman with eyes.

[200] [In the order] of the founding patriarch, Great Master Tōzan Gohon,[38] the story goes, there is a government official who prepares the midday meal, offers a donation, and requests the master to read and recite the whole of the sutras. The Great Master descends from his zazen chair and bows to[39] the official. The official bows to the Great Master, who leads the official once around the zazen chair, then bows to the official [again]. After a while he says to the official, "Do you understand?" The official says, "I do not understand." The Great Master says, "You and I have read and recited the whole of the sutras. How could you not understand?"

[201] That "You and I have read and recited the whole of the sutras" is evident. We do not learn that to go around the zazen chair is to read and recite the whole of the sutras, and we do not understand that to read and recite the whole of the sutras is to go around the zazen chair. All the same, we should listen to the compassionate instruction of the founding patriarch. My late master, the eternal buddha, quoted this story when, while he was residing [as master] on Tendōzan, a donor from Korea entered the mountain, made a donation for the monks to read the sutras, and requested that my late master should ascend the lecture seat. When he had quoted [the story], my late master made a big circle with his whisk and said, "Tendō today has read and recited for you the whole of the sutras." Then he threw down the whisk and descended from the seat. We should read and recite now the words spoken by the late master, never comparing them to [the
89c words of] others. Still, should we think that [Master Tendō], in reading and reciting the whole of the sutras, uses a whole eye or uses half an eye? Do

the words of the founding patriarch and the words of my late master rely on eyes or rely on tongues? How many [eyes and tongues] have they used? See if you can get to the bottom of it.

[202] The ancestral patriarch, Great Master Kōdō[40] of Yakusan Mountain, does not usually let people read sutras. One day he is reading a sutra himself. A monk asks him, "The master does not usually let others read sutras. Why then are you reading yourself?"

The master says, "I just need to shade my eyes."

The monk says, "May I copy the master?"

The master says, "If you were to read you would surely pierce holes even in ox-hide!"

[203] The words "I just need to shade my eyes" spoken now are words naturally spoken by shaded eyes[41] themselves. "Shading the eyes" describes getting rid of eyes and getting rid of sutras, it describes complete eye shading and completely shaded eyes. "Shading the eyes" means opening the eyes in the shaded state, invigorating the eyes within shade, invigorating shade within eyes, adding an extra eyelid, utilizing the eyes within shade, and eyes themselves utilizing shade. This being so, the virtue of "shading the eyes" is never [mentioned] in any [sutras] other than eye-sutras. "You would surely pierce holes even in ox hide" describes complete ox hide and a complete-hide ox, it describes utilizing the ox to become a hide.[42] This is why [possession of] the skin, flesh, bones, and marrow, and horns on the head, and nostrils, has been seen as the vigorous activity of bulls and cows.[43] In "copying the master," the ox becomes the eye—this is described as "shading the eyes." It is the eye becoming the ox.

[205] Zen Master Yafu Dōsen[44] says:

> To serve offerings to buddhas hundred million thousands of times
> is boundless happiness,
> [But] how can it compare to everyday reading of the old teachings?
> On the face of white paper characters are written in black ink.
> Open your eyes, I beg you, and look before you.[45]

[206] Remember, serving offerings to ancient buddhas and reading the old teachings may be equal in happiness and good fortune and may go beyond happiness and good fortune. "The old teachings" means characters written

in black ink on white paper, [but] who can recognize the old teachings as such? We must master just this principle.

[206] [In the order of] Great Master Kōkaku[46] of Ungozan, the story
90a goes, there is a monk who is reading a sutra in his quarters. The Great Master asks from outside the window, "*Ācārya,* what sutra is that you are reading?"

The monk replies, "The *Vimalakīrti Sutra.*"

The master says, "I am not asking you if it is the *Vimalakīrti Sutra.* That which you are reading is a What sutra."[47]

At this the monk is able to enter.[48]

[207] The Great Master's words "That which you are reading is a What sutra" mean that the "state of reading,"[49] in one line, is age-old, profound, and eternal; and it is not desirable to represent it as "reading." On the road we meet deadly snakes. This is why the question "What sutra?" has been realized. In meeting as human beings, we do not misrepresent anything. This is why [the monk replies] "The *Vimalakīrti Sutra.*" In sum, reading sutras means reading sutras with eyes into which we have drawn together all the Buddhist patriarchs. At just this moment, the Buddhist patriarchs instantly become buddha, preach Dharma, preach buddha, and do buddha-action.[50] Without this moment in reading sutras, the brains and faces of Buddhist patriarchs could never exist.[51]

[209] At present in the orders of Buddhist patriarchs, forms for the reading of sutras are many and varied: for when a donor[52] enters the mountain and requests the whole sangha to read sutras; for when the monks have been requested to read sutras regularly;[53] for when the monks read the sutras of their own volition, and so on. Besides these, there is the sutra reading by the whole sangha for a deceased monk.

[209] When a donor enters the mountain and requests the monks to read sutras, from breakfast on the day [of the reading] the hall chief[54] hangs an advance notice of the sutra reading in front of the monks' hall[55] and in all quarters. After breakfast the prostration mat is laid before the [image of the] Sacred Monk.[56] When it is time [for the reading], the bell in front of the monks' hall is struck three times, or struck once—according to the instructions of the abbot. After the sound of the bell, the head monk[57] and all the monks put on the *kaṣāya* and enter the cloud hall.[58] They go to their own

place[59] and sit facing forward. Then the abbot enters the hall, goes before the Sacred Monk, bows with joined hands, burns incense, and then sits at the [abbot's] place. Next the child helpers[60] are told to distribute the sutras. These sutras are arranged beforehand in the kitchen hall, placed in order and made ready to be given out when the time comes. The sutras are either distributed from inside the sutra box, or placed on a tray and then distributed. 90b
Once the monks have requested a sutra, they open and read it immediately. During this time, at the [right] moment, the guest supervisor[61] leads the donor into the cloud hall. The donor picks up a handheld censer just in front of the cloud hall and enters the hall holding it up with both hands. The handheld censer is [kept] in the common area by the entrance to the kitchen hall.[62] It is prepared with incense in advance, and a helper[63] is [instructed] to keep it ready in front of the cloud hall. When the donor is about to enter the hall, [the helper], upon instruction, hands [the censer] to the donor. The guest supervisor gives the orders regarding the censer. When they enter the hall, the guest supervisor leads and the donor follows, and they enter through the southern side of the front entrance to the cloud hall. The donor goes before the Sacred Monk, burns a stick of incense, and does three prostrations, holding the censer while doing the prostrations. During the prostrations the guest supervisor, hands folded,[64] stands to the north of the prostration mat, facing south but turned slightly toward the donor.[65] After the donor's prostrations, the donor turns to the right, goes to the abbot, and salutes the abbot with a deep bow, holding the censer up high with both hands. The abbot remains on the chair to receive the salutation, holding up a sutra with palms held together.[66] The donor then bows to the north. Having bowed, [the donor] begins the round of the hall from in front of the head monk. During the walk around the hall, [the donor] is led by the guest-supervisor. Having done one round of the hall and arrived [again] in front of the Sacred Monk, [the donor] faces the Sacred Monk once more and bows, holding up the censer with both hands. At this time the guest supervisor is just inside the entrance to the cloud hall, standing with hands folded to the south of the prostration mat, and facing north.[67] After saluting the Sacred Monk, the donor, following the guest supervisor, goes out to the front of the cloud hall, does one circuit of the front hall,[68] goes back inside the cloud hall proper, and performs three prostrations to the Sacred Monk. After the prostrations, [the donor] sits on a folding chair

90c to witness the sutra reading. The folding chair is set, facing south, near the pillar to the Sacred Monk's left. Or it may be set facing north near the southern pillar. When the donor is seated, the guest supervisor should turn to salute the donor, and then go to his or her own place. Sometimes we have a Sanskrit chorus while the donor is walking round the hall. The place for the Sanskrit chorus is either on the Sacred Monk's right or on the Sacred Monk's left, according to convenience. In the handheld censer, we insert and burn valuable incense like *jinko* or *sanko.*[69] This incense is supplied by the donor. While the donor is walking around the hall, the monks join palms. Next is the distribution of donations for the sutra reading. The size of the donation is at the discretion of the donor. Sometimes things such as cotton cloth or fans are distributed. The donor personally may give them out, or the main officers may give them out, or helpers may give them out. The method of distribution is as follows: [The donation] is placed in front of [each] monk, not put into the monk's hands. The monks each join hands to receive the donation as it is given out in front of them. Donations are sometimes distributed at the midday meal on the day [of the sutra reading]. If [donations] are to be distributed at lunch time, the head monk, after offering the meal,[70] strikes down the clapper[71] once again, and then the head monk gives out the donations. The donor will have written on a sheet of paper the aim to which [the sutra reading] is to be directed, and [this paper] is pasted to the pillar on the Sacred Monk's right. When reading sutras in the cloud hall, we do not read them out in a loud voice; we read them in a low voice. Or sometimes we open a sutra and only look at the characters, not reading them out in phrases but just reading the sutra [silently]. There are hundreds or thousands of scrolls provided in the common store[72] for this kind of sutra reading—mostly of the *Diamond Prajñā Sutra;* the "Universal Gate" chapter and the "Peaceful and Joyful Practice" chapter of the *Lotus Sutra;* the *Golden*
91a *Light Sutra,*[73] and so on. Each monk goes through one scroll. When the sutra reading is finished, [the child helpers] pass in front of the [monks'] seats, carrying the original tray or box, and the monks each deposit a sutra. Both when taking [the sutra] and when replacing it, we join hands. When taking, first we join hands and then we take. When replacing, first we deposit the sutra, then we join hands. After that, each person, palms together, makes the dedication in a low voice. For sutra readings in the common area,[74] the chief

officer or the prior burns incense, does prostrations, goes around the hall, and gives out the donations, all in the same way as a donor, and holds up the censer also in the same way as a donor. If one of the monks becomes a donor and requests a sutra reading by the whole of the sangha, it is the same as for a lay donor.[75] There is burning of incense, prostrations, going around the hall, distribution of donations, and so on. The guest supervisor leads, as in the case of a lay donor.

[216] There is a custom of reading sutras for the emperor's birthday. So if the celebration of the birthday of the reigning emperor is on the fifteenth day of the first lunar month, the sutra readings for the emperor's birthday begin on the fifteenth day of the twelfth lunar month. On this day there is no formal preaching in the Dharma hall. Two rows of platforms are laid out in front of [the image of] Śākyamuni Buddha in the Buddha hall. That is to say, [the rows] are laid out facing each other east and west, each running from south to north. Desks are stood in front of the east row and the west row, and on them are placed the sutras: the *Diamond Prajñā Sutra,* the *Benevolent King Sutra,* the *Lotus Sutra,* the *Supreme King Sutra,*[76] the *Golden Light Sutra,* and so on. Several monks each day are invited from among the monks in the [zazen] hall to partake in refreshments before the midday meal. Sometimes a bowl of noodles and a cup of soup are served to each monk, or sometimes six or seven dumplings with a portion of soup are served to each monk. The dumplings also are served in a bowl, [but in this case] chopsticks are provided; spoons are not provided. We do not change seats to eat, but remain at our seat for the sutra reading. The refreshments are placed on the desk that 91b
the sutras are placed on; there is no need to bring another table. While refreshments are being eaten, the sutras are left on the desk. After finishing the refreshments, each monk rises from his or her seat to [go and] rinse the mouth, then returns to the seat and resumes sutra reading immediately. Sutra reading continues from after breakfast until the time of the midday meal. When the lunch time drum sounds three times, we rise from our seats: the day's sutra reading is limited to before the midday meal. From the first day a board saying "Established as a Practice Place for Celebration of the Emperor's Birthday" is hung in front of the Buddha hall, under the eastern eaves. The board is yellow. In addition, notice of celebration of the emperor's birthday is written on a *shōji* placard,[77] which is then hung on the eastern front pillar

inside the Buddha hall. This placard [also] is yellow. The name[78] of the abbot is written on red paper or white paper; the two characters [of the name] are written on a small sheet of paper, which is pasted onto the front of the placard, beneath the date. The sutra reading continues as outlined above until the day of the imperial descent and birth, when the abbot gives formal preaching in the Dharma hall and congratulates the emperor. This is an old convention which is not obsolete even today. There is another case in which monks decide of their own accord to read sutras. Temples traditionally have a common sutra reading hall. [Monks] go to this hall to read sutras. The rules for its use are as in our present *Pure Criteria.*[79]

[219] The founding patriarch, Great Master Kōdō[80] of Yakusan Mountain, asks Śramaṇera Kō,[81] "Did you get it by reading sutras, or did you get it by requesting the benefit [of the teaching]?"[82]

Śramaṇera Kō says, "I did not get it by reading sutras, and I did not get it by requesting benefit."

The master says, "There are a lot of people who do not read sutras and who do not request benefit. Why do they not get it?"

Śramaṇera Kō says, "I do not say that they are without it. It is just that they do not dare to experience it directly."[83]

[220] In the house of the Buddhist patriarchs, some experience it directly and some do not experience it directly, but reading sutras and requesting the benefit [of the teaching] are the common tools of everyday life.

91c *Shōbōgenzō Kankin*

Preached to the assembly at Kōshōhōrinji in the Uji district of Yōshū,[84] on the fifteenth day of the ninth lunar month in the autumn of the second year of Ninji.[85]

Notes

1 *Chishiki,* short for *zen-chishiki,* from the Sanskrit *kalyāṇamitra,* or "good friend." See Glossary of Sanskrit Terms.

2 *Kakunogotoku,* "like this," describes the situation here and now.

3 In the introductory paragraph, Master Dōgen explained sutras generally, as self. This signifies a change of viewpoint to the concrete phase.

4 *Kankin,* as in the chapter title. The original meaning of *kan* is to see or to watch.

5 This sentence is in the form of a quotation from a sutra, though the source has not been located. The next two sentences Master Dōgen probably made himself, substituting "Buddhist patriarchs" and "lifeblood" for "innumerable lands," in order to emphasize the difficulty of encountering Buddhist sutras.

6 *Shinjin-jinsho,* the last two of the six sense organs. The body as a sense organ refers to the sense of touch. The mind as a sense organ is the seat of thought. Classing thought as one of six senses emphasizes that it is subordinate to real wisdom. See, for example, LS 3.122: "Though he has not yet attained faultless real wisdom, his mind-organ is pure like this."

7 The source of this quotation from a sutra has not been located.

8 Master Yakusan Igen (745–828), successor of Master Sekitō Kisen. Great Master Kōdō is Master Yakusan's posthumous title.

9 *Inshu,* or "prior," also called *kansu* and *kanin;* one of the six *chiji* or main officers in a temple. See note 54.

10 *Shinji-shōbōgenzō,* pt. 1, no. 79. Also the story is no. 7 in the *Wanshijuko.*

11 "A teacher of What" is *nan no shi,* i.e., a teacher of the ineffable, a teacher whose state and whose teaching cannot be understood intellectually.

12 Master Daikan Enō (638–713).

13 The story of Master Hōtatsu and his personal history are explained at length in Chapter Seventeen, *Hokke-ten-hokke.*

14 *Hokkekyō,* the *Lotus Sutra.* See Chapter Seventeen, *Hokke-ten-hokke.*

15 The poem is exactly the same as the one quoted in Chapter Seventeen, *Hokke-ten-hokke.*

16 "Reading" and "ideas" are the same Chinese character *nen.* In *nenkinsō,* "sutra-reading monk," *nen* is a verb, "reading," suggesting the action of reading the sutra. In the poem *nen* is a noun, "ideas." *Unen,* "having ideas," describes the presence of ideas, images, or intention, and *munen,* "being without ideas," describes the absence, or negation, of ideas, images, or intention.

17 Quotation of Master Daikan Enō's words to Hōtatsu from the *Rokusodaishihōbōdangyō* (*Platform Sutra of the Sixth Patriarch's Dharma Treasure*). The next line is Master Dōgen's addition.

18 "Sutra" and "experienced" are the same Chinese character *kyō, kin,* or *kei. Kyō* means 1) sutra, as in the title of this chapter, and 2) passing through, experience, the passage of time (see note 18 in Chapter Eleven, *Uji*). Master Dōgen identified reading sutras and experiencing reality.

19 Master Prajñātara (d. 457), was a successor of Master Puṇyamitra and the teacher of Master Bodhidharma.

20 *Tenzu* is literally "to turn," that is, to turn a scroll on which a sutra is written; see Chapter Seventeen, *Hokke-ten-hokke.*

21 *Hindō,* lit., "poor way," a humble form used by a Buddhist monk.

22 *Unkai. Un* represents the Sanskrit *skandha.* The five *skandha*s (aggregates) are matter, perception, thought, enaction, and consciousness, representing all phenomena in the world. "Circumstances" (*shu-en*) in the first line is plural, whereas "the world of aggregates" is singular, but they both suggest the world. The first two lines stress the master's independence.

23 *Nyoze-kyō* means sutras like this, sutras as they are, or sutras as reality.

24 Also quoted in Chapter Fifty-two (Vol. III), *Bukkyō.*

25 The Buddha's successor, counted as the first patriarch in India.

26 *Unson,* lit., "cloud-grandchildren," a poetic variation of the usual expression *enson,* lit., "distant grandchildren."

27 *Urō, murō-chi,* or "wisdom with excess and without excess," represents the Sanskrit terms *sāsrava-jñāna* and *anāsrava-jñāna.*

28 *Urō, murō-hō,* or "*dharma*s with excess and without excess," represents the Sanskrit terms *sāsrava-dharma* and *anāsrava-dharma.* See Glossary of Sanskrit Terms.

29 Master Jōshū Jūshin (778–897), was a successor of Master Nansen Fugan, and especially highly revered by Master Dōgen (see for example Chapter Thirty-five [Vol. II], *Hakujushi*). Great Master Shinsai is his posthumous title.

30 *Shinji-shōbōgenzō,* pt. 1, no. 24.

31 Three scrolls of sutras means sutras limited by relative consideration of numbers.

32 Master Daizui Hōshin (dates unknown), a successor of Master Chōkei Daian. The emperor sent his emissaries time and time again to invite Master Hōshin to the court, but he always declined. Great Master Shinshō is his posthumous title.

33 Hōshin is the Master's *hōki.* This means the name that was avoided after a monk's death, that is, the name a monk used in his lifetime. See notes to Chapter Sixteen, *Shisho.*

34 Master Fukushu Daian (793–883), a successor of Master Hyakujō Ekai. His posthumous title is Great Master Enju. Quoted in *Shinji-shōbōgenzō,* pt. 2, no. 57.

35 *Rentōeyō,* vol. 10.

36 A practical Buddhist master.

37 *Rōzeikon,* lit., "to play with the soul." This expression usually suggests the practice of zazen itself ("to play sport with the soul"; see for example Chapter Sixty-eight [Vol. III], *Udonge*), but in this case Master Dōgen suggested that the old woman should have said, "The master need not worry about anything!"

38 Master Tōzan Ryōkai (807–869), a successor of Master Ungan Donjō. Great Master Gohon is his posthumous title. See Chapter Fifteen, *Busso.*

39 *Iu su* means to bow the head slightly with the hands in *shashu;* see note 64. Hereafter in this chapter also, "bow" indicates this form of salutation, as opposed to a prostration.

40 Master Yakusan Igen. See note 8.

41 *Shagan,* "shaded eyes," suggests the balanced and peaceful state of action which is different from the idealistic viewpoint.

42 Interpreted simply, Master Yakusan's words mean "Reading sutras will only make your intellect sharper!" But Master Dōgen interpreted that the words also include some ironic affirmation of the monk's state—"becoming a hide" suggests realization of the concrete.

43 Oxen sometimes symbolize Buddhist practitioners. In the *Lotus Sutra,* for example, the white ox cart is the symbol of the bodhisattva way.

44 Master Yafu Dōsen. He realized the truth listening to the preaching of a head monk called Ken of Tōsai, after which he changed his name from Tekisan to Dōsen. He made commentaries on the *Diamond Sutra,* and was considered one of seventeen authorities of the age on the *Diamond Sutra.* He preached on Yafuzan during the Ryūkō era (1163–1164) of the Southern Song dynasty.

45 Quoted from Master Yafu Dōsen's commentary on the *Diamond Sutra.*

46 Master Ungo Dōyō (835?–902), a successor of Master Tōzan Ryōkai. Great Master Kōkaku is his posthumous title. See Chapter Fifteen, *Busso.*

[47] Master Ungo repeated exactly the words he had said before. He had phrased his words to sound like a simple question, but his idea was that the sutra itself was something ineffable.

[48] *Keitokudentōroku,* chapter 17.

[49] *Nentei.* In Master Ungo's words, *nentei* means "that which you are reading," but here *tei,* lit., "bottom," means "state." The latter usage occurs in the *Fukanzazengi,* in the phrase *fushiryōtei,* "the state beyond thinking."

[50] *Sabutsu su,* "become buddha," and *seppō su,* "preach Dharma," are common compounds. *Setsubutsu su,* "preach buddha," and *butsusa su,* "do buddha-action," are Master Dōgen's variations. In addition, the first three compounds are conventional verb + object compounds, but the fourth, *butsusa,* is unconventional because "to buddha" is not conventionally used as a verb. The effect is to oppose the idealism of "becoming buddha."

[51] In other words, if Buddhist sutras cannot be read intuitively, real Buddhism cannot exist—there are only abstract Buddhist patriarchs without heads and faces.

[52] *Seshu* represents the Sanskrit *dānapati.*

[53] For example, a lay sponsor bequeaths a sum of money to a monastery, and when the monks read sutras in the morning, they dedicate the reading in accordance with the wishes of that sponsor.

[54] *Dōsu* is the fourth of the six main officers. He is the main officer in charge of daily supervision of the monks. The six main officers are 1) *tsūsu,* chief officer, head of the temple office, comptroller; 2) *kansu,* prior; 3) *fūsu,* assistant prior; 4) *dōsu* or *inō,* supervisor of monks in the zazen hall, rector; 5) *tenzo,* head cook; and 6) *shishui,* caretaker.

[55] *Sōdō,* the zazen hall.

[56] *Shōsō,* the image in the center of the zazen hall, almost always of Bodhisattva Mañjuśrī in Japan. Some halls in China have an image of Hōtei, the Happy Buddha.

[57] *Shuso,* or "chief seat." One of the assistant officers below the main officers.

[58] *Undō,* another name for the zazen hall.

[59] *Hi-i,* lit., "the place of their [night]wear," i.e., the place in the zazen hall where they sleep.

[60] *Zunnan,* or "apprentices," are children or youths who generally intend to become monks in future.

[61] *Shika,* or "guest prefect," is the assistant officer in charge of supervising guests.

[62] *Inmon.* In general *in* represents the Sanskrit *saṃghārāma* or temple. In this case, however, it suggests *ku-in,* the kitchen hall.

[63] *Anja,* or temple servants, worked as helpers in the temple, not necessarily intending to become monks.

[64] *Shashu,* hands held horizontally across the chest, with left hand in a fist, thumb inside, and right hand cupped over the left.

[65] If you imagine the scene from the front entrance, the prostration mat is directly in front of you, and the donor is facing the mat, his back toward you. The guest supervisor is to the right of the mat, facing the mat but turned slightly toward the donor and you.

[66] *Gasshō,* palms together, fingertips at the level of the nostrils.

[67] Again imagining the scene from the front entrance, the donor is standing between the prostration mat and the sacred image, his back toward you. The guest supervisor is now just in front of you, to the left of the mat and facing right in order to watch the donor.

[68] *Dōzen,* lit., "hall-front," probably means the *zentan,* the smaller hall which accommodates the temple officers and others who can come and go there without disturbing the main body of monks in the zazen hall proper. Or it could indicate the area outside of the zazen hall.

[69] *Jinko* means aloes. *Sanko* was a type of incense obtained from the area of southwest China that is now Cambodia and Vietnam.

[70] *Sejiki.* The method is explained in detail in Master Dōgen's *Fushukuhanhō* (*Method of Taking Meals*).

[71] *Tsui,* a small wooden block used to beat an octagonal wooden pillar.

[72] *Jōjū,* short for *jōjū-motsu,* tools etc. available for the monks of a temple to use at any time.

[73] The *Konkōmyōkyō.* In Sanskrit, *Suvarṇaprabhāsa-sūtra.*

[74] *Jōjū-kugai.* Big temples had a communal hall for reciting sutras.

[75] In Master Dōgen's time there were monks who came from rich families and who retained their private wealth.

[76] *Saishōōkyō.* The full name of the *Golden Light Sutra* is *Konkōmyōsaishōōkyō,* "Golden Light Supreme King Sutra," from the Sanskrit *Suvarṇaprabhāsottamarāja-sūtra,* so the *Supreme King Sutra* and the *Golden Light Sutra* appear to be one and the same.

[77] A placard made of paper stuck to a wooden frame—constructed like the *shōji,* paper sliding doors, seen in Japanese houses.

[78] *Myōji* usually means surname, but in this case it means a monk's usual name. In the case of Master Dōgen, for example, it would be Dōgen.

[79] *Shingi,* "pure criteria," means a temple's rules and regulations.

[80] Master Yakusan Igen. See note 8.

[81] Kō-shami. After succeeding Master Yakusan, he built a thatched hut by the roadside and taught Buddhism to passing travelers. *Shami* represents the Sanskrit word *śramaṇera,* which means novice.

[82] *Shin-eki* means listening to the preaching of Dharma and requesting a teacher's personal instruction.

[83] *Keitokudentōroku,* chapter 14.

[84] Corresponds to present-day Kyoto prefecture.

[85] 1241.

Appendix I

Chinese Masters

Japanese	Pinyin
Baso Dōitsu	Mazu Daoyi
Bukkō Nyoman	Foguang Ruman
Busshō Tokkō	Fozhao Deguang
Butsuin Ryōgen	Foyin Liaoyuan
Chōka Dōrin	Niaowo Daolin
Chōrei (Fukushu) Shutaku	Changqing Daan
Chōsha Keishin	Changsha Jingcen
Daibai Hōjō	Damei Fachang
Daie Sōkō	Dahui Zonggao
Daii Dōshin	Dayi Daoxin
Daikan Enō	Dajian Huineng
Daiman Kōnin	Daman Hongren
Daizui Hōshin	Taisui Fazhen
Dōan Dōhi	Tongan Daopi
Dōan Kanshi	Tongan Guanzhi
Engo Kokugon	Yuanwu Keqin
Fuketsu Enshō	Fengxue Yanzhao
Fukushu (Chōkei) Daian	Chanqing Daan
Fun'yō Zenshō	Fenyang Shanzhao
Fuyō Dōkai	Furong Daokai
Gensha Shibi	Xuansha Shibei
Genshi	Yuancai
Goso Hōen	Wuzu Fayan
Gozu Hōyū	Niutou Fayong
Hōgen Bun'eki	Fayan Wenyi
Hōtatsu	Foda

Iichi	Weiyi
Isan Reiyū	Guishan Lingyou
Jimyō (Sekisō) Soen	Shishuang Chuyuan
Jōshū Jūshin	Zhaozhou Congshen
Kaie (Hakuun) Shutan	Haihui Shoudan
Kanchi Sōsan	Jianzhi Sengcan
Kankei Shikan	Guanxi Zhixian
Kōan Daigu	Gaoan Daiyu
Kōke Sonshō	Xinghua Congjiang
Kokutai Kōtō	Guotai Hongdao
Kyōgen Chikan	Xiangyan Zhixian
Kyōzan Ejaku	Yangshan Huiji
Massan Ryōnen	Moshan Liaoran
Mayoku Hōtetsu	Magu Baoche
Musai Ryōha	Wuji Liaopai
Myōshin	Miaoxin
Nan'in Egyō	Nanyuan Huiyong
Nan'yō Echū	Nanyang Huizhong
Nangaku Ejō	Nanyue Huairang
Nansen Fugan	Nanquan Puyuan
Ōbaku Kiun	Huangbo Xiyun
Ōryū Enan	Huanglong Huinan
Reiun Shigon	Lingyun Zhiqin
Rinzai Gigen	Linji Yixuan
Rōya Ekaku	Langye Huijiao
Ryōzan Enkan	Liangshan Yuanguan
Ryūge Kodon	Longya Judun
Ryūmon Butsugen	Longmen Foyan
Ryūtan Sōshin	Longtan Chongxin
Sanshō Enen	Sansheng Huiran
Seigen Gyōshi	Qingyuan Xingsi
Sekitō Kisen	Shitou Xiqian
Sensu Tokujō	Chuanzi Decheng
Seppō Gison	Xuefeng Yicun
Setchō Chikan	Xuedou Zhijian

Setchō Jūken	Xuedou Chongxian
Shinketsu Seiryō	Zhenxie Qingliao
Shōkaku (Torin) Jōsō	Donglin Changzong
Shōken Kishō	Yexian Guisheng
Shuzan Shōnen	Shoushan Shengnian
Taiso Eka	Dazu Huike
Taiyō Kyōgen	Dayang Jingxuan
Tanka Shijun	Danxia Zichun
Tendō Nyojō	Tiantong Rujing
Tendō Sōkaku	Tiantong Zongjue
Tokusan Senkan	Deshan Xuanjian
Tōsu Gisei	Touzi Yiqing
Tōzan Ryōkai	Dongshan Liangjie
Ungan Donjō	Yunyan Tansheng
Ungo Dōyō	Yunju Daoying
Unmon Bun'en	Yunmen Wenyan
Yafu Dōsen	Yefu Daochuan
Yakusan Igen	Yueshan Weiyan
Yōgi Hōe	Yangqi Fanghui

Appendix II

Fukanzazengi

Universal Guide to the Standard Method of Zazen

[*Rufubon*—The Popular Edition[1]]

Now, when we research it, the truth originally is all around: why should we rely upon practice and experience? The real vehicle exists naturally: why should we put forth great effort? Furthermore, the whole body far transcends dust and dirt: who could believe in the means of sweeping and polishing?[2] In general, we do not stray from the right state: of what use, then, are the tiptoes of training?

However, if there is a thousandth or a hundredth of a gap, the separation is as great as that between heaven and earth;[3] and if a trace of disagreement arises, we lose the mind in confusion. Proud of our understanding and richly endowed with realization, we obtain special states of insight; we attain the truth; we clarify the mind; we acquire the zeal that pierces the sky; we ramble through remote intellectual spheres, going in with the head: and yet, we have almost completely lost the vigorous road of getting the body out.

Moreover, we can [still] see the traces of the six years spent sitting up straight by the natural sage of Jetavana Park.[4] We can still hear rumors of the nine years spent facing the wall by the transmitter of the mind-seal of Shaolin [Temple].[5] The ancient saints were like that already: how could people today fail to make effort?

Therefore we should cease the intellectual work of studying sayings and chasing words. We should learn the backward step of turning light and reflecting. Body and mind will naturally fall away, and the original features will manifest themselves before us. If we want to attain the matter of the ineffable, we should practice the matter of the ineffable at once.[6]

In general, a quiet room is good for practicing [za]zen, and food and drink are taken in moderation. Cast aside all involvements. Give the myriad things a rest. Do not think of good and bad. Do not consider right and wrong. Stop the driving movement of mind, will, consciousness. Cease intellectual consideration through images, thoughts, and reflections. Do not aim to become a buddha. How could [this] be connected with sitting or lying down?[7]

We usually spread a thick mat on the place where we sit, and use a round cushion on top of that. Either sit in the full lotus posture or sit in the half lotus posture. To sit in the full lotus posture, first put the right foot on the left thigh, then put the left foot on the right thigh. To sit in the half lotus posture, just press the left foot onto the right thigh.[8]

Spread the clothing loosely and make it neat.[9] Then put the right hand above the left foot, and place the left hand on the right palm. The thumbs meet and support each other. Just make the body upright and sit up straight. Do not lean to the left, incline to the right, slouch forward, or lean backward. The ears must be aligned with the shoulders, and the nose aligned with the navel. Hold the tongue against the palate, keep the lips and teeth closed, and keep the eyes open. Breathe softly through the nose.

When the physical posture is already settled, make one complete exhalation and sway left and right. Sitting immovably in the mountain-still state, "Think about this concrete state beyond thinking." "How can the state beyond thinking be thought about?" "It is different from thinking."[10] This is just the pivot of zazen.

This sitting in zazen is not learning Zen concentration.[11] It is simply the peaceful and joyful gate of Dharma. It is the practice-and-experience which perfectly realizes the state of *bodhi.* The universe is conspicuously realized, and restrictions and hindrances[12] never reach it. To grasp this meaning is to be like a dragon that has found water, or like a tiger in its mountain stronghold. Remember, the right Dharma is naturally manifesting itself before us, and darkness and distraction[13] have dropped away already.

When we rise from sitting, we should move the body slowly and stand up calmly. We should not be hurried or violent. We see in the past that those who transcended the common and transcended the sacred, and those who died while sitting or died while standing,[14] relied totally on this power. Moreover, the changing of the moment, through the means of a finger,[15] a pole,[16] a needle, or a wooden clapper;[17] and the experience of the state,[18] through the manifestation of a whisk,[19] a fist, a staff, or a shout,[20] can never be understood by thinking and discrimination.[21] How could they be known through mystical powers or practice and experience? They may be dignified behavior beyond sound and form.[22] How could they be anything other than criteria that precede knowing and seeing?

Therefore, we do not discuss intelligence as superior and stupidity as inferior. Do not choose between clever people and dull ones. If we singlemindedly make effort [in zazen] that truly is pursuit of the truth. Practice-and-experience is naturally untainted.[23] Actions are more balanced and constant.[24]

In general, [the patriarchs] of this world and of other directions, of the Western Heavens and of the Eastern Lands, all similarly maintain the Buddha's posture, and solely indulge in the custom of our religion. They simply devote themselves to sitting, and are caught by the still state.

Although there are myriad distinctions and thousands of differences, we should just practice [za]zen and pursue the truth. Why should we abandon our own seat on the floor to come and go without purpose through the dusty borders of foreign lands?[25] If we misplace one step we pass over the moment of the present. We have already received the essential pivot[26] which is the human body: we must never pass time in vain.[27] We are maintaining and relying upon the pivotal essence[28] which is the Buddha's truth: who could wish idly to enjoy sparks [that fly] from flint? What is more, the body is like a dewdrop on a blade of grass. Life passes like a flash of lightning. Suddenly it is gone. In an instant it is lost.

I beseech you, noble friends in learning through experience, do not become so accustomed to images that you are dismayed by the real dragon.[29] Devote effort to the truth which is directly accessible and straightforward. Revere people who are beyond study and without intention.[30] Accord with the *bodhi* of the buddhas. Become a rightful successor to the *samādhi* of the patriarchs. If you practice the state like this for a long time, you will surely become the state like this itself. The treasure house will open naturally, and you will be free to receive and to use [its contents] as you like.

Fukanzazengi ends

Notes

1 There are two main versions of the *Fukanzazengi:* the *Shinpitsubon,* the Original Edition (literally, the edition written in the author's own hand), and the *Rufubon,* the Popular Edition. Master Dōgen wrote the *Shinpitsubon* shortly after returning from China to Japan in 1227. He later revised this edition before settling upon the *Rufubon.* Whereas Master Dōgen wrote the *Shōbōgenzō* itself in Japanese, he wrote the *Fukanzazengi* in Chinese characters only. It is originally one long passage; here it has been divided into paragraphs for ease of reading.

2 The words "dust and dirt" (*jinnai*) and "sweeping and polishing" (*hosshiki*) allude to a story about Master Daikan Enō and a monk called Jinshū. Jinshū compared Buddhist practice to making a mirror clean. Master Daikan Enō suggested that there is originally no impurity in the first place. (See Chapter Twenty, *Kokyō.*) Master Dōgen picked up the words of the story in these opening lines in which he expresses the fundamentally optimistic idea of Buddhist philosophy.

3 Master Dōgen picked up these words from Master Kanchi Sōsan's poem *Shinjinmei.* In this part Master Dōgen cautions us against falling into the state in which we think too much.

4 Jetavana literally means "Prince Jeta's park." This was a park purchased from Prince Jeta, a son of King Prasenajit of Kośala, by a lay disciple of the Buddha called Sudatta or Anāthapiṇḍada, and donated to the Buddha as a place for the rains retreat in Śrāvastī (northeast of present-day Lucknow).

5 *Shin-in,* "mind-seal," is an abbreviation of *butsu-shin-in,* "buddha-mind–seal." In comes from the Sanskrit word *mudrā,* which means "seal." In the *Shōbōgenzō* Master Dōgen identifies *butsu-shin-in* with the full lotus posture. Shaolin is the name of the temple where Master Bodhidharma introduced zazen into China.

6 "Matter of the ineffable" is *inmo* [*no*] *ji.* Master Tōzan preached to the assembly, "If you want to attain the matter of the ineffable, you must have become someone ineffable. Now that you are already someone ineffable, why worry about attaining the matter of the ineffable?" See Chapter Twenty-nine (Vol. II), *Inmo.*

7 Sitting and lying down represent the four kinds of behavior: sitting, standing, walking, and lying down. Master Dōgen suggested that zazen is transcendent over the ordinary actions of daily life.

8 Master Dōgen gives the left foot on the right thigh as an example. The right foot placed on the left thigh is also the correct lotus posture.

[9] Specifically this refers to the custom of not stretching the *kaṣāya* tightly across the knees.

[10] These lines come from a conversation between Master Yakusan Igen and a monk. They are discussed at length in Chapter Twenty-seven (Vol. II), *Zazenshin.*

[11] The *Sekimon-rinkanroku* relates how historians listed Master Bodhidharma alongside people who were learning Zen concentration (*shuzen*). See Chapter Thirty (Vol. II), *Gyōji,* paragraph 193. In his commentary, Master Dōgen says, "[Master Bodhidharma] sat in stillness facing the wall, but he was not learning Zen concentration."

[12] "Restrictions and hindrances" is *raro,* silk nets and bamboo cages used in China to catch birds and fish.

[13] *Konsan,* "darkness and distraction," are representative examples of unnatural or imbalanced conditions of body and mind. *Kon* represents the Sanskrit *styāna* and *san* represents *vikṣepa,* two of the many defilements listed in Sanskrit commentaries.

[14] Master Mahākāśyapa, for example, is said to have died while sitting on Kukkuṭapāda Mountain, and Master Kankei Shikan (see Chapter Eight, *Raihai-tokuzui*), is said to have died while standing up.

[15] Master Gutei used to raise one finger to answer a question that could not be answered with words.

[16] Master Ānanda realized the truth when a temple flagpole fell to the ground.

[17] *Tsui.* This is a small wooden block used to beat an octagonal wooden pillar. Bodhisattva Mañjuśrī, for example, is said to have preached the truth by using the *tsui.*

[18] *Shōkai,* literally "experience-accord," means to experience the same state as Gautama Buddha. See notes on Chapter Sixteen, *Shisho.*

[19] *Hossu,* a ceremonial whisk with a wooden handle and a plume of animal hair or other material.

[20] Master Baso Dōitsu, for example, was famous for having a very loud yell.

[21] Alludes to the *Lotus Sutra, Hōben* ("Expedient Means") chapter. See LS 1.88–90.

[22] *Shoshikino hoka no iigi.* The same characters appear in a poem by Master Kyōgen Chikan, quoted in Chapter Nine, *Keisei-sanshiki.*

[23] Alludes to a conversation between Master Daikan Enō and Master Nangaku Ejō about the oneness of practice and experience. See Chapter Seven, *Senjō.*

[24] *Byōjō. Byō, hei* means level or peaceful. *Jō* means constant. As a compound *byōjō, heijō* means normal. It appears in the phrase *byōjōshin, heijōshin,* "balanced and constant mind" or "normal mind." See Chapter Twenty-eight, *Butsu-kōjō-no-ji.*

[25] Alludes to a parable in the *Shinge* ("Belief and Understanding") chapter of the *Lotus*

Sutra about a son who wanders in poverty through foreign lands, unaware that he is the heir to his father's fortune. See LS 1.236.

[26] *Kiyō.*

[27] *Koin munashiku wataru koto nakare.* The same characters appear at the end of the verse *Sandōkai* by Master Sekitō Kisen.

[28] *Yōki.* The words *kiyō* and *yōki* feature prominently in Chapter Twenty-seven, *Zazen-shin. Ki* means mechanism or, sometimes, the state at the moment of the present. *Yō* means the main point, important part, or pivot.

[29] Refers to the story of Shoko, who loved images of dragons but who was terrified to meet a real dragon. The "real dragon" means zazen.

[30] *Zetsu-gaku-mu-i* [*no*] *hito.* Master Yōka Genkaku's poem *Shōdōka* begins with the words, "Gentlemen, do you not see? A person beyond study and without intention, who is at ease in the truth, does not try to get rid of delusion and does not want to get reality."

Appendix III

Busso

The Buddhist Patriarchs

The recitation in Japanese of the names of the Buddhist patriarchs, from the seven ancient buddhas to Master Dōgen, is as follows:

(1)	Bibashibutsu Daioshō
(2)	Shikibutsu Daioshō
(3)	Bishafubutsu Daioshō
(4)	Kurusonbutsu Daioshō
(5)	Kunagonmunibutsu Daioshō
(6)	Kashobutsu Daioshō
(7)	Shakamunibutsu Daioshō
[1]	Makakasho Daioshō
[2]	Ananda Daioshō
[3]	Shonawasu Daioshō
[4]	Ubakikuta Daioshō
[5]	Daitaka Daioshō
[6]	Mishaka Daioshō
[7]	Basumitta Daioshō
[8]	Buddanandai Daisho
[9]	Fudamitta Daioshō
[10]	Barishiba Daioshō
[11]	Funayasha Daioshō
[12]	Memyo Daioshō
[13]	Kapimara Daioshō
[14]	Nagārajuna Daioshō
[15]	Kanadaiba Daioshō
[16]	Ragorata Daioshō

[17]		Sogyanandai Daioshō
[18]		Gayashata Daioshō
[19]		Kumorata Daioshō
[20]		Shayata Daioshō
[21]		Bashubanzu Daioshō
[22]		Manura Daioshō
[23]		Kakurokuna Daioshō
[24]		Shishibodai Daioshō
[25]		Bashashita Daioshō
[26]		Funyomitta Daioshō
[27]		Hannyatara Daioshō
[28]	[1]	Bodaidaruma Daioshō
[29]	[2]	Taiso Eka Daioshō
[30]	[3]	Kanchi Sōsan Daioshō
[31]	[4]	Daii Dōshin Daioshō
[32]	[5]	Daiman Kōnin Daioshō
[33]	[6]	Daikan Enō Daioshō
[34]	[7]	Seigen Gyōshi Daioshō
[35]	[8]	Sekitō Kisen Daioshō
[36]	[9]	Yakusan Igen Daioshō
[37]	[10]	Ungan Donjō Daioshō
[38]	[11]	Tōzan Ryōkai Daioshō
[39]	[12]	Ungo Dōyō Daioshō
[40]	[13]	Dōan Dōhi Daioshō
[41]	[14]	Dōan Kanshi Daioshō
[42]	[15]	Ryōzan Enkan Daioshō
[43]	[16]	Taiyō Kyōgen Daioshō
[44]	[17]	Tōsu Gisei Daioshō
[45]	[18]	Fuyō Dōkai Daioshō
[46]	[19]	Tanka Shijun Daioshō
[47]	[20]	Shinketsu Seiryō Daioshō
[48]	[21]	Tendō Sōkaku Daioshō
[49]	[22]	Setchō Chikan Daioshō
[50]	[23]	Tendō Nyojō Daioshō
[51]	[24]	Eihei Dōgen Daioshō

Appendix IV

The *Kaṣāya*

A large *saṃghāṭi* robe made of nine vertical stripes of cloth, with two long segments and one short segment in each stripe. This style of robe is known in Japanese as the *kassetsu-e.*

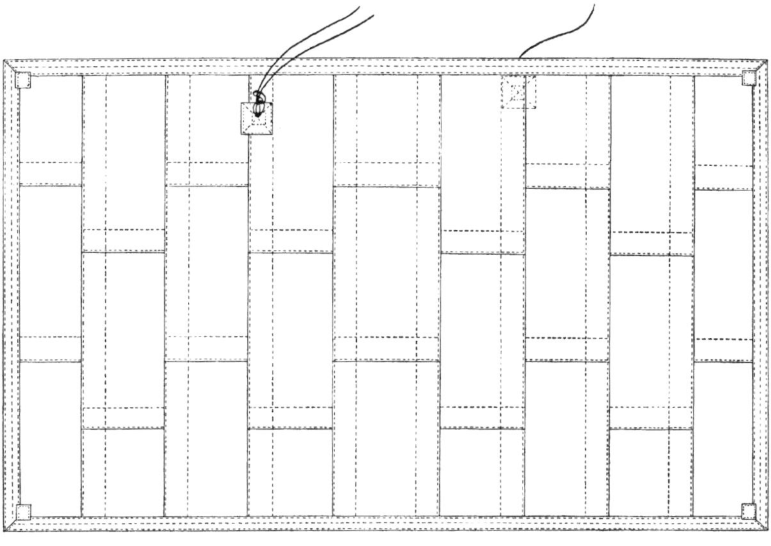

Appendix V

Traditional Temple Layout

The ground plan of the Hokuzankeitokuryōonji in modern-day Hangzhou province, together with a list of *Facilities at Major Buddhist Monasteries in the Southern Song,* upon which this appendix is based, was obtained by Nishijima Roshi several years ago at a conference of the American Academy of Religions. Unfortunately, the name of the original compiler, to whom acknowledgment is due, is not known.

The Seven Main Temple Buildings

The seven main temple buildings are the Buddha hall, the Dharma hall, the zazen hall, the kitchen hall, the gate, the bathhouse, and the toilet.

In former ages, the toilet was located to the west and was called *saichin,* "west lavatory," but later the toilet was located to the east and called *tosu,* "east office." In the original ground plan of Hokuzankeitokuryōonji both toilets, east and west, are marked as *tosu.*

The essential temple layout can be represented in brief as follows:

		(North)		
		Dharma Hall		
(West)	Zazen Hall	Buddha Hall	Kitchen Hall	(East)
	Toilet	Gate	Bathhouse	

Facilities at Major Buddhist Monasteries in the Southern Song

1. *Butsuden*	Buddha Hall
2. *Tochidō*	"Lands Hall"; Local Deities Hall
3. *Shindō*	"Trueness Hall"; Hall for Patriarchs' Images
Sodō	Patriarchs' Hall
4. *Rakandō*	Arhats Hall

5. *Shōmon*	Main Gate
6. *Suirikudō*	All Beings Hall
7. *Kannondō*	Pavilion of Regarder of the Sounds; Pavilion of Bodhisattva Avalokiteśvara
8. *Rushanaden*	Vairocana's Hall
9. *Danna*	Donors' [Hall]
10. *Hattō*	Dharma Hall; Lecture Hall
11. *Zōden*	"Storage Hall"; Sutra Library
Rinzō	"Circle Library"—alludes to a big circular table provided in the library
12. *Kankindō*	Sutra Reading Hall;
Kyōdō	Sutra Hall
13. *Shindō*	Abbot's Reception Hall;
Zen-hōjō	"Front of Abbot's Quarters";
Daikōmyō-zō	"Treasury of Great Brightness"
14. *Shūryō*	Common Quarters; Monks' Dormitories
15. *Sōdō*	Monks' Hall; Sangha Hall
Undō	Cloud Hall;
Zazendō	Zazen Hall
16. *Gosōdō*	Rear Monks' Hall
17. *Niryō*	Nuns' Quarters
18. *Hōjō*	"Ten Square Feet"; Abbot's Quarters
Dōchō	The Abbot
19. *Jisharyō*	Attendant Monks' Quarters
20. *Anjadō*	Temple Servants' Hall
Sensōdō	Novice Monks' Hall
21. *Kuge-anja-ryō*	Servants' Quarters in the Kitchen Hall
22. *Tangaryō*	Overnight Lodgings;
Unsuidō	"Clouds and Water Hall"; Transient Monks' Quarters
23. *Kaku-i*	Guest Rooms
24. *Kansu*	"Office of the Prior" (in general, *kansu* suggests the monk himself, and may thereafter suggest his quarters. However, in the present ground plan, no. 24 may be assumed to be the Prior's Office and no. 26 the Prior's Quarters)

25. *Tsusu*	Chief Officer
26. *Kansu*	Prior
27. *Fusu*	Assistant Prior
28. *Sho-chōshu-ryō*	Assistant Officers' Quarters
29. *Shika*	Guest Supervisor
30. *Yokusu*	Bath Manager
31. *Chiden*	Supervisor of the Buddha Hall
32. *Shissui*	Labor Steward
33. *Kajuryō*	Fire Chief's Quarters; Stove Chief's Quarters
34. *Inosu*	*Ino;* Supervisor of Monks in the Zazen Hall;
Dōsu	Hall Chief
35. *Shuso*	Head Monk
36. *Mōdō*	"Twilight Hall"; Quarters of Retired Main Officers
37. *Zenshiryō*	Former Officers' Quarters; Retired Officers' Quarters
38. *Sonchōryō*	Retired Abbot's Quarters;
Rōshuku	"The Old Patriarch"
39. *Ninriki*	Laborers
40. *Sanmon*	"Three Gates"—refers to the main entrance and the side entrances on either side of the main entrance;
Sanmon	"Mountain Gate"—poetically reproduces the pronunciation of *sanmon*
41. *Gai-sanmon*	"Outer Mountain Gate"; Outer Gate
42. *Chūmon*	Inner Gate
43. *Kudō*	"Pantry Hall"; Kitchen Hall; Administration Hall;
Ku-in	"Pantry Office"
44. *Kōshaku-chu*	"Fragrance-Accumulation's Office"; Kitchen
45. *Enjudō*	"Prolongation of Life Hall"; Infirmary
Nehandō	Nirvana Hall;
Shōgyōdō	"Hall of Reflection of Conduct"
46. *Jūbyōkaku*	Pavilion for the Seriously Ill
47. *Yokushitsu*	Bathhouse;
Senmyō	"Promulgation of Brightness"
48. *Senmenjo*	Washroom; Washstand;
Suige	"Water Office";
Koka	Rear Stand

49. *Tōsu*	"East Office"; Toilet;
Saichin	"West Lavatory"; Toilet
50. *Shiryō*	Urinal;
Shōkenjo	Urinal
51. *Hashinjo*	Needlework Room; Sewing Room
52. *Sen-e-jo*	Laundry
53. *Daishō*	Big Bell;
Shōrō	Bell Tower
54. *Tō*	Stupas
55. *Rōbu*	Corridors
56. *Kosō*	Stable
57. *Shōdō*	Illuminated Hall
58. *Chi*	Pond

Ground Plan of Hokuzankeitokuryōonji in Modern-day Hangzhou Province

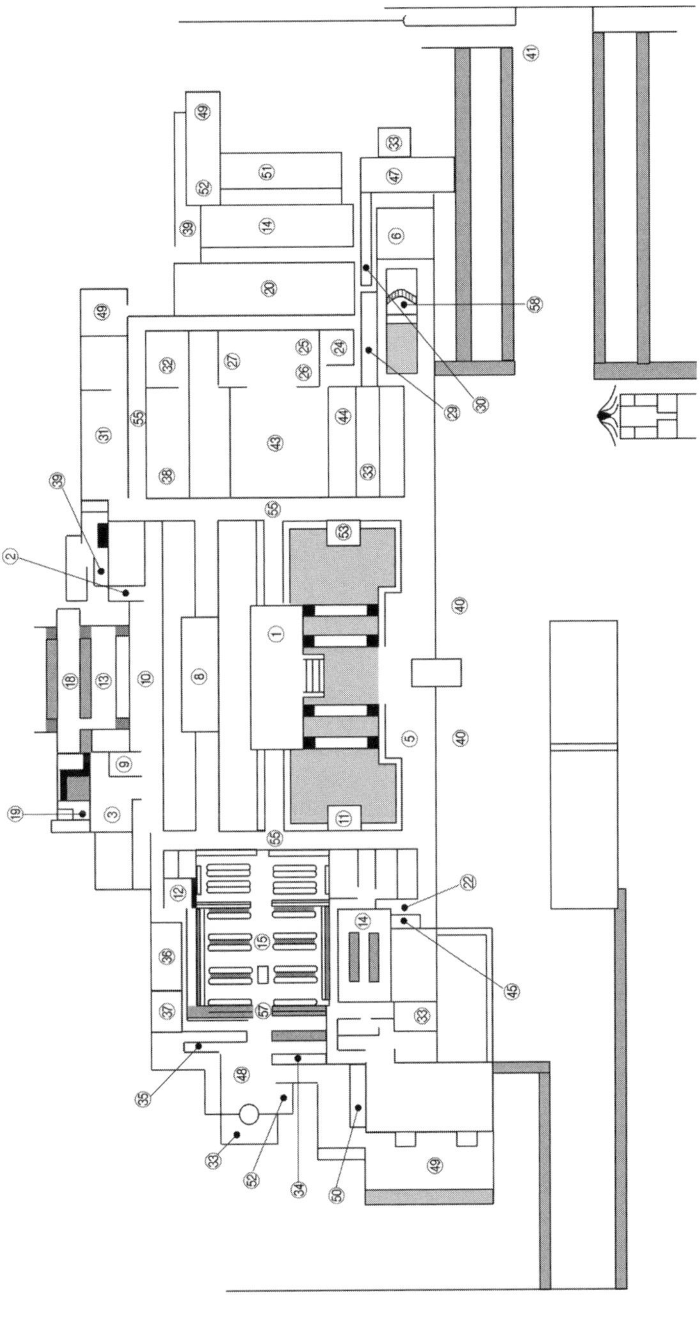

Appendix VI

Lotus Sutra References

The *Saddharmapuṇḍarīka-sūtra* (*Sutra of the Lotus Flower of the Wonderful Dharma*) was translated from Sanskrit into Chinese by Kumārajīva in 406 C.E.

The Kumārajīva translation, the *Myōhōrengekyō,* which Master Dōgen quotes in the *Shōbōgenzō* and which remains the most widely used in Japan, is reproduced in a Chinese/Japanese edition published in three parts by Iwanami Bunko. References below refer to this edition: LS 1.68 means part 1, page 68, of the Iwanami edition. The correlating citation in the *Shōbōgenzō* is indicated by the initials SBGZ followed by the chapter number(s) and paragraph number(s), in brackets, where applicable.

Kumārajīva's Chinese was rendered into English by Bunno Kato and William Soothill and published in 1930 as *The Sutra of the Lotus Flower of the Wonderful Law.* This *Sutra of the Lotus Flower of the Wonderful Law,* revised by Wilhelm Schiffer and Yoshiro Tamura, forms the core of *The Threefold Lotus Sutra* first published by Weatherhill/Kosei in 1975. The extracts that follow are basically revisions of the Weatherhill/Kosei version.

Chapter One: *Jo* (Introductory)

LS 1.8 SBGZ Chapter Seventeen; Chapter Thirty-four (Vol. II) [83]

Thus have I heard. At one time the Buddha was living at Rājagṛha. On Mount Gṛdhrakūṭa, he was with twelve thousand great *bhikṣus*. They were all arhats, having ended all excesses, being without troubles, self-possessed, realizing all bonds of existence, and liberated in mind.

LS 1.14 SBGZ Chapter Seventy-two (Vol. III) [237]

At that time [there was] Śakra-devānām-indra with his following of twenty thousand heavenly sons. . . . There were the eight dragon kings. . . each with some hundreds or thousands of followers.

LS 1.18 SBGZ Chapter Seventeen

At that time the Buddha radiated light from the circle of white hair between his eyebrows, illuminating the eastern quarter.

LS 1.26–28 SBGZ Chapter Forty (Vol. II) [216]

There are some who give alms
Of gold, silver, and coral,
Pearls and jewels,
Moonstones and agates.

LS 1.38 SBGZ Chapter Seventeen

At that time Mañjuśrī spoke to Bodhisattva Mahāsattva Maitreya and all the other great beings: "Good sons! According to my consideration, now the Buddha, the World-honored One, is going to preach the great Dharma."

LS 1.40 SBGZ Chapter Eleven [21]; Chapter Seventeen; Chapter Fifty (Vol. III) [203]

He proclaimed the right Dharma, which is good in the beginning, good in the middle, and good in the end.

LS 1.42 SBGZ Chapter Seventeen

The Dharma that they should preach is good in the beginning, middle, and end.

LS 1.42, 1.44 SBGZ Chapter Eighty-six (Vol. IV) [83]

Before the last of those [Sun Moon Light] buddhas left home, he had eight royal sons. . . . These eight princes, unrestricted in their majesty, each ruled four continents. These princes, hearing that their father had left home and attained [the truth of] *anuttara samyaksaṃbodhi,* all renounced the throne and, following him, also left home and established the mind of the Great Vehicle. They constantly practiced pure conduct, and all became teachers of Dharma. Under thousands of myriads of buddhas, they had planted many roots of goodness.

LS 1.46 SBGZ Chapter Seventeen

The listeners in that order also remained seated in one place, for sixty minor *kalpa*s, unmoving in body and mind.

LS 1.52 SBGZ Chapter Seventeen; Chapter Fifty-two (Vol. III) [21]

Therefore I consider that the Tathāgata today will preach the sutra of the Great Vehicle, which is called the Lotus Flower of the Wonderful Dharma, the method of teaching bodhisattvas, that which buddhas guard and remember.

LS 1.54 SBGZ Chapter Thirty-six (Vol. II) [126]

This light illuminated the eastern quarter
Of eighteen thousand buddha lands.

LS 1.58 SBGZ Chapter Fifty (Vol. III) [214]

When the Buddha [Sun Moon Light]
had preached this Flower of Dharma
And caused the assembly to rejoice,
Then he, on that very day,
Proclaimed to the assembly of gods and people:
"The truth that all *dharma*s are real form
Has been preached for you all. . . ."

LS 1.62 SBGZ Chapter Seventeen

This teacher of Dharma, Mystic Light,
At that time had a disciple
Whose mind was always lazy,
Who was greedily attached to fame and gain,
Who sought fame and gain tirelessly,
Who often found amusement in the homes of aristocratic families,
Who abandoned what he had learned by heart,
Forgetting everything before he had understood it clearly,
And who for these reasons
Was called Fame Seeker.
He also by practicing good works
Was able to meet countless buddhas,
To serve offerings to buddhas,
To follow them in practicing the great truth,
And to perfect the six *pāramitā*s.
Now he has seen Śākyamuni the lion.
Afterward he will become a buddha.
And will be named Maitreya.

LS 1.64

Now the Buddha radiates brightness
To help disclose the meaning of real form.
People, now you must be aware!
Hold palms together and wholeheartedly wait!

Chapter Two: *Hōben* (Expedient Means)

LS 1.66 SBGZ Chapter Seventeen

At that time the World-honored One rose calmly and clearly from *samādhi* and addressed Śāriputra: "The wisdom of the buddhas is profound and unfathomable. Their lineage of wisdom is difficult to understand and difficult to enter. All *śrāvaka*s and *pratyekabuddha*s cannot know it. Why? [Because] a buddha has experienced familiarity with countless hundred thousand myriad *koṭi*s of buddhas, and has totally practiced the unfathomable truth and reality of the buddhas; bravely persevering; [letting the buddhas'] names be universally heard; accomplishing the profound unprecedented Dharma; and preaching, as convenience permits, the meaning that is difficult to understand."

LS 1.68 SBGZ Chapter Seventeen

The Tathāgata is perfectly equipped with expediency and the *pāramitā* of wisdom. Śāriputra! The wisdom of the Tathāgata is wide, great, profound, and eternal.

LS 1.68 SBGZ Chapter Ten [21]; Chapter Seventeen; Chapter Fifty (Vol. III) [203]; Chapter Fifty-four (Vol. III) [98]; Chapter Ninety-one (Vol. IV) [71]

Buddhas alone, together with buddhas, are directly able to perfectly realize that all *dharma*s are real form. What is called "all *dharma*s" is form as it is, the nature as it is, body as it is, energy as it is, action as it is, causes as they are, conditions as they are, effects as they are, results as they are, and the ultimate state of equality of substance and detail, as it is.

LS 1.70 SBGZ Chapter Seventeen; Chapter Fifty (Vol. III) [210]

I, and buddhas in the ten directions,
Are directly able to know these things.

LS 1.72 SBGZ Chapter Seventeen

Even if the world were full

Of beings like Śāriputra
Who together exhausted their intellects to gauge it,
They could not fathom the buddha-wisdom.

LS 1.72 SBGZ recurrent phrase
As [abundant as] rice, hemp, bamboo, and reeds.

LS 1.74 SBGZ Chapter Seventeen; Chapter Sixty (Vol. III) [7]
Only I know concrete form,
And the buddhas of the ten directions
Are also like that.

LS 1.74 SBGZ Chapter Seventy-nine (Vol. IV) [169]
At that time in the great assembly, there were *śrāvaka*s, the arhat who had ended excesses, Ajñāta-Kauṇḍinya, and others, [altogether] twelve hundred people.

LS 1.80 SBGZ Chapter Seventeen
Children born of the Buddha's mouth,
Palms held together, looking up, we wait.
Please send forth the fine sound
And now preach for us [the truth] as it really is.

LS 1.82–84 SBGZ Chapter Seventeen
Stop, stop, no need to explain.
My Dharma is too fine to think about.
Arrogant people,
If they hear, will surely not believe it with respect.

LS 1.86 SBGZ Chapter One [27]; Chapter Seventeen
When he preached these words, some five thousand *bhikṣu*s, *bhikṣuṇī*s, *upāsaka*s, and *upāsikā*s in the assembly rose at once from their seats, bowed to the Buddha, and withdrew.

LS 1.86 SBGZ Chapter Twenty-three (Vol. II) [117]
The roots of wrongdoing of these fellows were deep and heavy.

LS 1.86–88 SBGZ Chapter One [11]; Chapter Sixty-eight (Vol. III)
Thereupon the Buddha addressed Śāriputra: "Now in this assembly I am

free of twigs and leaves, and only the true and real remain. Śāriputra! That arrogant people like these withdraw also is fine. Now listen well and I will preach for you." Śāriputra said, "Please do so, World-honored One, I desire joyfully to listen." The Buddha addressed Śāriputra: "Wonderful Dharma like this the buddha-tathāgatas preach only occasionally, just as the *uḍumbara* flower appears only once in an age."

LS 1.88–90 SBGZ Chapter Seventeen; *Fukanzazengi*

This Dharma cannot be understood by thinking and discrimination. Only buddhas are directly able to know it. Why? The buddhas, World-honored Ones, appear in the world only by reason of the one great purpose. Śāriputra, why do I say that the buddhas, World-honored Ones, appear in the world only by reason of the one great purpose? The buddhas, World-honored Ones, appear in the world because they desire to cause living beings to disclose the wisdom of Buddha that will make them able to become pure. They appear in the world because they desire to show living beings the wisdom of Buddha. They appear in the world because they desire to cause living beings to realize the wisdom of Buddha. They appear in the world because they desire to cause living beings to enter the state of truth which is the wisdom of Buddha. Śāriputra, this is why the buddhas appear in the world only by reason of the one great purpose.

LS 1.90 SBGZ Chapter Seventeen

Śāriputra. The Tathāgata only by means of the One Buddha Vehicle preaches the Dharma for living beings. There is no other vehicle, neither a second nor a third. Śāriputra, the Dharma of all the buddhas of the ten directions is also like this.

LS 1.98–100 SBGZ Chapter Thirty-four (Vol. II) [87], [91]

Śāriputra! If any of my disciples, calling themselves arhats or *pratyekabuddha*s, neither hear nor recognize the fact that the buddha-tathāgatas teach only bodhisattvas, they are not the Buddha's disciples, nor arhats, nor *pratyekabuddha*s. Again Śāriputra! If these *bhikṣu*s and *bhikṣuṇī*s think to themselves, "I have already attained the state of arhat; this is my last life, ultimate nirvana," and then they no longer want to pursue [the truth of] *anuttara samyaksaṃbodhi,* you should know that these are all people of lofty arrogance. Why? [Because] there is no such thing as a *bhikṣu* really attaining the state of arhat without believing this teaching.

LS 1.104 SBGZ Chapter Twenty-four (Vol. II) [177]

This my Dharma of nine divisions,
Preached as befits living beings,
Is the basis for entry into the Great Vehicle.
Therefore, I preach this sutra.

LS 1.106 SBGZ Chapter Seventeen; Chapter Twenty-nine (Vol. II) [99]; Chapter Fifty (Vol. III) [210]; Chapter Sixty (Vol. III) [4]

In the buddha lands of the ten directions,
There only exists the One-Vehicle Dharma.
There is neither a second nor a third.

LS 1.108 SBGZ Chapter Fifty (Vol. III) [213]

I, body adorned with signs,
And brightness illuminating the world,
Am honored by countless multitudes
For whom I preach the seal of real form.

LS 1.116 SBGZ Chapter Eighty-seven (Vol. IV) [150]

If people, to stupas and shrines,
To jewel images and painted images,
With flowers, incense, flags, and canopies
Reverently serve offerings;
[Or] if they cause others to make music,
To beat drums, to blow horns and conches,
[To play] panpipes, flutes, lutes, lyres,
Harps, gongs, and cymbals,
And many fine sounds such as these
They serve continually as offerings;
Or [if] with joyful hearts,
They sing the praises of the Buddha's virtue,
Even in one small sound,
They all have realized the Buddha's truth.
If people whose mind is distracted,
With even a single flower
Serve offerings to a painted [buddha] image,
They will gradually see numberless buddhas.

Again, people who do prostrations
Or who simply join palms,
Even those who raise a hand
Or slightly lower the head,
And thus serve an offering to an image
Will gradually see countless buddhas,
Will naturally realize the supreme truth,
And will widely save numberless multitudes.

LS 1.120 SBGZ Chapter Seventeen; Chapter Twenty-nine (Vol. II) [99]; Chapter Fifty (Vol. III) [215]

The Dharma abides in its place in the Dharma,
And the form of the world is constantly abiding.
Having recognized this in a place of the truth,
Guiding teachers teach it by expedient means.

LS 1.124 SBGZ Chapter Sixty-nine (Vol. III) [181]

At the time of this consideration,
The buddhas of the ten directions all appear.

LS 1.128 SBGZ Chapter Ten [14]; Chapter Seventeen; Chapter Fifty-three (Vol. III) [57]

In the same manner that the
Buddhas of the three times
Preach the Dharma,
So now do I also
Preach the Dharma that is without distinction.
The appearances of buddhas in the world
Are far apart and hard to meet,
Even when they do appear in the world,
It is still hard for this Dharma to be preached.

Chapter Three: *Hiyu* (A Parable)

LS 1.134 SBGZ Chapter Seventeen

At that time, Śāriputra, jumping for joy, stood up at once and joined together the palms of his hands.

LS 1.134 SBGZ Chapter Seventeen

In the past I heard such Dharma from the Buddha and saw bodhisattvas receiving affirmation and becoming buddhas.

LS 1.140–42

In my mind there was great alarm and doubt:
Was it not a demon acting as Buddha,
Distressing and confusing my mind?

LS 1.146 SBGZ Chapter Seventeen

The land [of Flower-Light Tathāgata] is level and straight, pure and magnificent, tranquil and prosperous.

LS 1.160 SBGZ Chapter Seventeen

Though I can leave safely through this burning gate, the children in the burning house are absorbed in their play, neither sensing nor knowing, neither alarmed nor afraid.

LS 1.162 SBGZ Chapter Seventeen

This house only has one gate; moreover, it is narrow and small. The children are young and do not yet possess knowledge; they love the places where they play. They may fall into and be burned in the fire. I must explain to them the fearfulness of this matter.

LS 1.164 SBGZ Chapter Seventeen

Many kinds of such goat carts, deer carts, and ox carts are now outside the gate to play with. Come quickly out of this burning house and I will give you all whatever you want.

LS 1.166 SBGZ Chapter Seventeen

Then the wealthy man sees that his children have got out safely and are all sitting on open ground at the crossroads, with nothing impeding them; his mind is eased and he jumps for joy. Then each of his children says to the father, "Father, please now give us those lovely playthings you promised us before; the goat carts, deer carts, and ox carts." Śāriputra! At that time the wealthy man gives to each of his children equally a great cart. The cart is high and wide, adorned with all kinds of treasures . . . and yoked by white oxen.

LS 1.176 SBGZ Chapter Seventeen

Quickly get out of the triple world and you will attain to the three vehicles, the vehicles of *śrāvaka, pratyekabuddha,* and Buddha. I now give you my guarantee of this, and in the end it will not be false. You all must solely be diligent and persevere.

LS 1.186–88 SBGZ Chapter Thirty-one (Vol. II) [8]

Whereupon the house
Suddenly catches fire.
In the four directions, all at once,
Its flames are in full blaze.

LS 1.198 SBGZ Chapter Forty-seven (Vol. III) [112]

All living beings
Are my children
[But] deeply attached to worldly pleasures
They are without wisdom. . .
The Tathāgata, already free from
The burning house of the triple world
Lives serenely in seclusion
Abiding peacefully in forests and fields.
Now this triple world
All is my possession
And the living beings in it
All are my children.

LS 1.202 SBGZ Chapter Thirty-eight (Vol. II) [175]

Riding in this precious carriage,
[We] arrive directly at the place of truth.

Chapter Four: *Shinge* (Belief and Understanding)

LS 1.222 SBGZ Chapter One [62]

Then they rose from their seats, and, arranging their garments, bared only their right shoulders.

LS 1.224 SBGZ Chapter Seventeen

Without expectation, we now suddenly are able to hear the rarely encountered

Dharma. We profoundly congratulate ourselves on having acquired a great benefit, on having got for ourselves, without seeking it, an immeasurable treasure.

LS 1.224 SBGZ Chapter Sixty-one (Vol. III) [26]; Chapter Seventy-three (Vol. IV) [66]

It is like a person who, while still a youth, leaves a father and runs away.

LS 1.236 SBGZ Chapter Twenty-five (Vol. II) [211]

This is my son begotten by me. [Since,] in a certain city he left me and ran away, he has been wandering and suffering hardship for over fifty years.

LS 1.260 SBGZ Chapter Thirty-four (Vol. II) [86]

Now we are
Truly voice-hearers,
The voice of the Buddha's truth
We cause all to hear.
Now we are
Truly arhats.

Chapter Five: *Yakusō-yu* (Parable of the Herbs)

LS 1.272 SBGZ Chapter Twenty-nine (Vol. II) [99]

The Dharma King who breaks "existence,"
Appears in the world
And according to the wants of living beings,
Preaches the Dharma in many ways. . .
The wise if they hear it,
Are able to believe and understand at once,
The unwise doubt and grieve,
Thus losing it forever.

LS 1.274 SBGZ Chapter Seventeen

Plants, shrubs, and herbs;
Large and small trees,
Grain of all kinds, and seedlings,
Sugarcane and grapevines,
Are moistened by the rain,
Without insufficiency.

Dry ground is all soaked,
Herbs and trees flourish together.

LS 1.286 SBGZ Chapter Seventeen

Your actions
Are the bodhisattva way itself.
By gradual practice and learning,
You will all become buddhas.

Chapter Six: *Juki* (Affirmation)

LS 1.300 SBGZ Chapter Seventeen

This my disciple Mahākāśyapa, in a future age, will be able to serve three hundred myriad *koṭi*s of World-honored buddhas, to make offerings to them, to revere, to honor, and to praise them, and to proclaim widely the limitless great Dharma of the buddhas.

LS 1.322 SBGZ Chapter Seventeen

My disciples,
Five hundred in number,
Perfectly equipped with dignified virtues,
All will receive affirmation,
And in a future age,
All will be able to become a buddha.

Chapter Seven: *Kejō-yu* (Parable of the Magic City)

LS 2.12–14 SBGZ Chapter Seventeen

Suppose a person, with [his or her own] power,
Grinds a three-thousand-great-thousandfold world,
And every kind of earth therein,
Entirely into ink,
And, passing through a thousand lands,
Then lets one drop fall.
Dropping them like this as [the journey] proceeds,
[The person] uses up all these specks of ink.
All the countries thus described,

Specked and unspecked alike,
Again are entirely ground to dust,
And one speck is one *kalpa*.

LS 2.30

Leaving the profound joy of the immovable state of *dhyāna*
In order to serve the Buddha.

LS 2.36

Sacred ruler, god among gods!
With the voice of a *kalaviṅka*.

LS 2.56 SBGZ Chapter One [32]

He said, "This is suffering; this the accumulation of suffering; this the cessation of suffering; this the way of cessation of suffering." And he preached extensively the law of the twelve causal connections: "Ignorance leads to action. Action leads to consciousness. Consciousness leads to name and form. Name and form lead to the six sense organs. The six sense organs lead to contact. Contact leads to feeling. Feeling leads to love. Love leads to taking. Taking leads to [new] existence. [New] existence leads to life. Life leads to aging and death; grief, sorrow, suffering, and distress. If ignorance ceases, then action ceases. If action ceases, then name and form cease. If name and form cease, then the six sense organs cease. If the six sense organs cease, then contact ceases. If contact ceases, then feeling ceases. If feeling ceases, then love ceases. If love ceases, then taking ceases. If taking ceases, then [new] existence ceases. If [new] existence ceases, then life ceases. If life ceases, then cease aging and death, grief, sorrow, suffering, and distress."

LS 2.58 SBGZ Chapter Eighty-six (Vol. IV) [83]

The sixteen royal sons, all being youths, left home and became *śramaṇera*s.

LS 2.60 SBGZ Chapter Eighty-six (Vol. IV) [83]

At that time, eight myriad *koṭi*s of people among the masses led by the sacred wheel-turning king, seeing the sixteen royal sons leave home, also sought to leave home, whereupon the king permitted them.

LS 2.62 SBGZ Chapter Eighty-six (Vol. IV) [83]

Buddha [Universal Surpassing Wisdom] preached this sutra for eight thousand *kalpa*s without cessation. When he had finished preaching this sutra, he at once entered a quiet room and remained in the immovable state of *dhyāna* for eighty-four thousand *kalpa*s. During this time the sixteen bodhisattva *śrāmaṇera*s, knowing that the Buddha had entered the room and was serenely set in *dhyāna,* each ascended a Dharma-seat and also for eighty-four thousand *kalpa*s widely preached and discriminated to the four groups the *Sutra of the* [*Lotus*] *Flower of the Wonderful Dharma.*

LS 2.66 (Ref. for *Kattō*) SBGZ Chapter Forty-six (Vol. III) [90]

Two of those *śrāmaṇera*s became buddhas in the eastern quarter, the first named Akṣobhya who lived in the Land of Joy, the second named Sumeru Peak.

Chapter Eight: *Gohyaku-deshi-juki* (Affirmation of Five Hundred Disciples)

LS 2.96 SBGZ Chapter Seventeen

*Bhikṣu*s! Pūrṇa was able to become foremost among Dharma preachers under the Seven Buddhas. Now he has also become foremost among Dharma preachers in my order. He will again be foremost among Dharma preachers under future buddhas in [this] virtuous *kalpa* (*bhadrakalpa*) and will altogether guard, maintain, assist, and proclaim the Buddha-Dharma.

LS 2.112 SBGZ Chapter Thirty-two (Vol. II) [45]

Five hundred *bhikṣu*s,
One by one, will become a buddha,
With the same title, "Universal Light,"
And one after another, they will give affirmation.

LS 2.114 SBGZ Chapter Four [105]; Chapter Twelve [74]

World-honored One! It is as if some person goes to the house of a close friend, becomes intoxicated, and lies down. Meanwhile the close friend, having to go out on official business, ties a priceless pearl within [that person's] garment as a gift, and departs.

LS 2.118 SBGZ Chapter Seventeen

It is like a poor person
Going to the house of a close friend
Whose family is very wealthy

[The friend] serves many fine dishes.
And a priceless pearl,
Ties inside [the poor one's] inner garment.

LS 2.120 SBGZ Chapter Thirty-two (Vol. II) [47]

Now, hearing from the Buddha
Of the wonderful fact of affirmation,
And of the sequential reception of affirmation,
Body and mind are full of joy.

Chapter Nine: *Ju-gaku-mugaku-nin-ki* (Affirmation of Students and People Beyond Study)

LS 2.128–30 SBGZ Chapter Seventy-three (Vol. IV) [27]

I have constantly practiced diligence, and for this reason I have already realized *anuttara samyaksaṃbodhi.*

Chapter Ten: *Hōsshi* (A Teacher of the Dharma)

LS 2.140 SBGZ Chapter Thirty-two (Vol. II) [50], [52]

At that time the World-honored One addressed eighty thousand great beings through Bodhisattva Medicine King: "Medicine King! You see among this great assembly countless gods (*deva*s), dragon kings (*nāga*s), *yakṣa*s, *gandharva*s, *asura*s, *garuḍa*s, *kiṃnara*s, *mahoraga*s, humans and nonhumans, as well as *bhikṣu*s, *bhikṣuṇī*s, *upāsaka*s, and *upāsikā*s, those who seek to be *śrāvaka*s, those who seek to be *pratyekabuddha*s, and those who seek the truth of Buddha. When such beings as these are all before the Buddha, and they hear a single verse or a single word of the *Sutra of the* [*Lotus*] *Flower of the Wonderful Dharma* and rejoice in it even for a single moment of consciousness, I give affirmation to them all: 'You will attain *anuttara samyaksaṃbodhi.*'" The Buddha addresses Medicine King: "Moreover, after the Tathāgata's extinction, if there are any people who hear even a single verse or a single word of the *Sutra of the* [*Lotus*] *Flower of the Wonderful Dharma* and rejoice in it for a single moment of consciousness, again, I give affirmation of *anuttara samyaksaṃbodhi. . . .*"

LS 2.152 SBGZ Chapter Nine [222]

This sutra, even while the Tathāgata is alive, [arouses] much hate and envy; how much more after his extinction!

LS 2.154 SBGZ Chapter Seventeen; Chapter Seventy-one (Vol. III) [221]

Medicine King! In every place where [this *Lotus Sutra*] is preached, or read, or recited, or copied, or where volumes of the sutra are kept, we should erect a stupa of the seven treasures, making it most high, wide, and ornate. [But] there is no need to place bones in it. Why? [Because] in it already there is the whole body of the Tathāgata. This stupa should be served, revered, honored, and extolled with all kinds of flowers, fragrance, strings of pearls, silk canopies, banners, flags, music, and songs of praise. If any people, being able to see this stupa, do prostrations and serve offerings to it, know that they are all close to *anuttara samyaksaṃbodhi.*

LS 2.156 SBGZ Chapter Seventeen; Chapter Fifty (Vol. III) [215]

For example, some people are parched and in need of water, for which they search by digging on a plateau. As long as they see dry earth, they know that water is still far away. Making effort unceasingly, in time they see moist earth, and then they gradually reach mud. Their minds are made up. They know that water must be near. Bodhisattvas are also like this. If they have not heard, nor understood, nor been able to practice this *Sutra of the Flower of Dharma,* we should know that they are still far from [the truth of] *anuttara samyaksaṃbodhi.*

If they are able to hear, to understand, to consider, and to practice it, we know for sure that they are close to *anuttara samyaksaṃbodhi.* Why? [Because] the *anuttara samyaksaṃbodhi* of all bodhisattvas totally belongs to this sutra. This sutra opens the door of expedient methods and reveals true and real form.

LS 2.156–58 SBGZ Chapter Seventeen

Medicine King! If a bodhisattva, on hearing this *Sutra of the Flower of Dharma,* is alarmed, doubting, or afraid, we should know that this is a bodhisattva with recently established intention. If a *śrāvaka,* on hearing this sutra, is alarmed, doubting, or afraid, we should know that this is an arrogant person.

LS 2.162

If, when they preach this sutra,
Someone abuses them with an evil mouth,
Or lays upon them swords, sticks, tiles, or stones,
Because they heed the Buddha, they will endure.

LS 2.166 SBGZ Chapter Sixty-one (Vol. III) [31]

If we are close to a teacher of the Dharma,

We at once attain the bodhisattva way.
And if we learn following this teacher,
We are able to meet buddhas [numerous] as sands of the Ganges.

Chapter Eleven: *Ken-hōtō* (Seeing the Treasure Stupa)

LS 2.168 SBGZ Chapter Seventeen

At that time, before the Buddha, a stupa of the seven treasures, five hundred *yojanas* in height, and two hundred and fifty *yojanas* in length and breadth, sprang out from the earth and abode in the sky.

LS 2.172 SBGZ Chapter Seventeen; Chapter Eighty-seven (Vol. IV) [160]

When that Buddha [Abundant Treasures] was practicing the bodhisattva way in the past, he had made a great vow: "After I have realized [the state of] Buddha and died, if in the lands of the ten directions there is any place where the *Sutra of the Flower of Dharma* is preached, my stupa shall spring up and appear before that place so that I may hear the sutra. . . ."

LS 2.176 SBGZ Chapter Seventeen

[Bodhisattva] Great Eloquence said to the Buddha, "World-honored One! We also would like to see the many buddhas who are offshoots of the World-honored One, to perform prostrations and to serve offerings to them." Then the Buddha sent forth a ray of light from [his circle of] white hair.

LS 2.186–88 SBGZ Chapter Seventeen; Chapter Fifty-one (Vol. III) [9]

Then all the assembly saw the Tathāgata Abundant Treasures sitting on the lion seat in the treasure stupa, his whole body undissipated, as if he had entered the balanced state of *dhyāna*. . . . Then the Buddha Abundant Treasures, in the treasure stupa, shared half his seat with Śākyamuni Buddha, and said, "Śākyamuni Buddha, please take this seat." Thereupon Śākyamuni Buddha entered inside the stupa, sat down on the half-seat, and sat in the full lotus posture.

LS 2.190 SBGZ Chapter Seventeen

A world-honored sacred lord,
Though long extinct
Inside the treasure stupa,
Yet comes for the Dharma.

LS 2.194 SBGZ Chapter Sixty-one (Vol. III) [44]

If they preach this sutra
Then they will meet me,
The Tathāgata Abundant Treasures,
And many transformed buddhas.

LS 2.196–98 SBGZ Chapter Seventeen

To take the great earth,
Put it on a toenail,
And ascend to Brahmā heaven:
That also is not hard.
[But] after the Buddha's death,
In a corrupt age,
To read this sutra even for a moment:
That indeed will be hard.

LS 2.198 SBGZ Chapter Twenty-three (Vol. II) [135]

After my extinction,
To keep this sutra,
And to preach it to [even] a single person:
That indeed will be hard. . .
After my extinction,
To listen to and to accept this sutra,
And to inquire into its meaning:
That indeed will be hard.

Chapter Twelve: *Daibadatta* (Devadatta)

LS 2.208 SBGZ Chapter Forty-five (Vol. III)

Through the good counsel of Devadatta, I was caused to obtain the six *pāramitā*s, kindness, compassion, joy, and detachment, the thirty-two signs, the eighty kinds of excellence, a golden complexion with purple luster, the ten powers, the four kinds of fearlessness, the four social methods, the eighteen uncommon [characteristics], the mystical abilities, and *bodhi*-powers. I realized the balanced and right state of awareness and widely saved living beings, all due to the good counsel of Devadatta.

LS 2.208 SBGZ Chapter Seventeen; Chapter Seventy-three (Vol. IV) [16]

Devadatta also, in future, after countless *kalpa*s have passed, will be able to become a buddha.

LS 2.212–214 SBGZ Chapter Seventeen

Thereupon Mañjuśrī, sitting on a thousand-petal lotus flower as big as a carriage wheel, with the bodhisattvas who accompanied him also sitting on precious lotus flowers, naturally sprang up from the great ocean, out of the palace of the Sāgara Dragon, and abided in space.

LS 2.216

[Bodhisattva Wisdom Accumulation says to Mañjuśrī:]
"Very wise, virtuous, brave, and vigorous one!
You have converted and saved countless beings.
Now this great order
And I, all already have seen
[Your] expounding of the teaching of real form,
Revelation of the One-Vehicle Dharma,
And universal guidance of living beings,
Whom you cause swiftly to realize *bodhi.*"

LS 2.218 SBGZ Chapter Seventeen

Mañjuśrī said: "I, in the sea, am constantly preaching only the *Sutra of the [Lotus] Flower of the Wonderful Dharma. . . .*"

LS 2.218 SBGZ Chapter Seventeen

Mañjuśrī said: "There is the daughter of the Dragon King Sāgara. . . . She has profoundly entered the balanced state of *dhyāna,* and penetrated all *dharma*s. In a *kṣāṇa* she established the *bodhi*-mind and attained the state of not regressing or deviating."

LS 2.218–20 SBGZ Chapter Seventy-one (Vol. III) [227]

Bodhisattva Wisdom Accumulation said, "I have seen [how] Śākyamuni Tathāgata, during countless *kalpa*s of hard practice and painful practice, accumulating merit and heaping up virtue, has pursued the bodhisattva way and has never ceased. I have observed that in the three-thousand-great-thousandfold world, there is no place even the size of a mustard seed where he has not abandoned his body and life as a bodhisattva for the sake of living beings. After acting thus, he was then able to realize the truth of *bodhi.*"

LS 2.224 SBGZ Chapter Eight [187]; Chapter Seventeen

All saw the dragon's daughter suddenly become a male, equipped with all the practices of a bodhisattva. She went at once to the southern quarter, the world which is free of impurity, [where she] sat on a precious lotus flower, realizing the balanced and right state of truth, with the thirty-two signs and the eighty kinds of excellence, and preaching the wonderful Dharma for all living beings throughout the ten directions. Then the *sahā* world of bodhisattvas, *śrāvaka*s, the eight groups of gods and dragons, and human and nonhuman beings, all seeing from afar the dragon's daughter becoming a buddha and universally preaching the Dharma for the human beings and gods in that order, rejoiced greatly in their hearts and they all bowed from afar in veneration.

Chapter Thirteen: *Kan-ji* (Exhortation to Hold Firm)
Chapter Fourteen: *Anrakugyō* (Peaceful and Joyful Practice)

LS 2.244 SBGZ Chapter Nine [230]

A bodhisattva *mahāsattva* should not get close to kings, princes, ministers, and administrators.

LS 2.258 SBGZ Chapter Fifty-six (Vol. III) [121]

[The bodhisattva] applies oil to the body,
Having bathed away dust and dirt,
And puts on a fresh and clean robe:
Totally clean within and without.

LS 2.266–68 SBGZ Chapter Fifty-six (Vol. III) [122]

Though those people neither hear, nor believe in, nor understand this sutra, when I attain [the truth of] *anuttara samyaksaṃbodhi,* wherever I am, through mystical power and through the power of wisdom, I will lead them and cause them to be able to abide in this Dharma.

LS 2.276–78 SBGZ Chapter Four [105]; Chapter Seventeen; Chapter Seventy-six (Vol. IV) [115]

If there is a brave and vigorous person,
Able to perform difficult deeds,

The king unties from inside his topknot,
The bright pearl, and this he gives. . .
It is like the king releasing from his topknot
The bright pearl, and giving it.
This sutra is honored
As supreme among all sutras,
I have always guarded it,
And not revealed it at random.
Now is just the time
To preach it for you all.

LS 2.282 SBGZ Chapter Sixty-one (Vol. III) [34]
Having profoundly entered the balanced state of *dhyāna*,
We meet the buddhas of the ten directions.

LS 2.282 SBGZ Chapter Thirty-eight (Vol. II) [187]; Chapter Sixty-nine (Vol. III) [175]; Chapter Seventy-two (Vol. III) [237]
The buddhas' bodies, golden colored,
Adorned with a hundred signs of happiness:
In the hearing of Dharma and in preaching for others,
This pleasant dream exists forever.
And in the dream-action, the king of a nation
Forsakes his palace, his followers,
And the five desires for the superior and fine,
And he goes to a place of the truth.
At the foot of a *bodhi* tree,
He sits on the lion seat,
Pursues the truth for seven days,
And attains the wisdom of the buddhas.
Having realized the supreme truth
He arises and turns the wheel of Dharma,
Preaching the Dharma to the four groups
For thousands of myriads of *koṭi*s of *kalpa*s.
He preaches the faultless wonderful Dharma
And saves countless living beings,
After which he naturally enters nirvana

Like a lamp going out when its smoke is spent.
If [anyone] in future corrupt ages
Preaches this paramount Dharma,
That person will obtain great benefit
Such as the virtuous effects [described] above.

Chapter Fifteen: *Jū-chi-yūshutsu* (Springing Out from the Earth)

LS 2.286 SBGZ Chapter Seventeen

When the Buddha had preached this, all the earth of the three-thousand-great-thousand worlds of the *sahā* world quaked and split, and from its midst countless thousand myriad *koṭi*s of bodhisattva *mahāsattva*s sprang out together. These bodhisattvas, their bodies all golden, with the thirty-two signs and measureless brightness, had previously all been below the *sahā* world, living in the space there.

LS 2.310 SBGZ Chapter Seventeen; Chapter Sixty-two (Vol. III) [62]

Ajita, you should know,
All these great bodhisattvas,
For numberless *kalpa*s,
Have practiced the Buddha's wisdom,
All of them are my converts,
I have caused them to establish
The will to the great truth,
They are my sons.
They remain in this world,
Always practicing the *dhūta* deeds,
They hope to enjoy quiet places,
Shunning the clamor of crowds,
Taking no pleasure in much explanation.
Sons like these
Are learning the method which is my truth.
They are ever diligent, day and night,
Because they want to get the Buddha's truth.
In the *sahā* world,
Down below, they live in space.

LS 2.318 SBGZ Chapter Seventeen; Chapter Forty-seven (Vol. III) [112]

It is as if a young and strong man,
Just twenty-five years old,
Indicates to others' centenarian sons,
With white hair and wrinkled faces,
[Saying], "These are my offspring,"
And the sons also saying, "This is our father"—
The father young and the sons old.
The whole world does not believe it.
So it is with the World-honored One:
He has attained the truth very recently.
All these bodhisattvas,
Are firm in will, and dauntless,
And for countless ages,
They have practiced the bodhisattva way.

Chapter Sixteen: *Nyorai-juryō* (The Tathāgata's Lifetime)

LS 3.12–14 SBGZ Chapter Seventy-one (Vol. III) [226]

Good sons! It is countless and infinite hundred thousand myriad *koṭi*s of *nayuta*s of *kalpa*s since I actually realized the state of Buddha. For instance, suppose there are five hundred thousand myriad *koṭi*s of *nayuta*s of *asaṃkheya* three-thousand-great-thousandfold worlds; let someone grind them to atoms, pass eastward through five hundred thousand myriad *koṭi*s of *nayuta*s of *asaṃkheya* countries, and then drop one atom; [suppose the person] proceeds eastward like this [until] all those atoms are used up. Good sons, what do you think? Is it possible, or not, to conceive and compute all those worlds so as to know their number?

LS 3.16 SBGZ Chapter Eighty-three (Vol. IV) [21]

Good sons! Seeing living beings who take pleasure in small things, whose virtue is scant and whose filthiness is accumulated, the Tathāgata to these people states, "In my youth I transcended family life and attained *anuttara samyak-saṃbodhi.*" And since I actually realized [the state of] Buddha, [my] eternity has been such as it is. Only to teach and transform living beings, by expedient means, so that they will enter the Buddhist truth, do I make statements like this.

LS 3.18 SBGZ Chapter Seventeen; Chapter Forty-three (Vol. III) [44]; Chapter Forty-seven (Vol. III) [110]

All that he says is real, not empty. Why? [Because] the Tathāgata knows and sees the form of the triple world as it really is, without life and death, or disappearance or appearance; without existence in the world and extinction; neither real nor void; neither thus nor otherwise. It is best to see the triple world as the triple world.

LS 3.18–20 SBGZ Chapter Seventeen; Chapter Twenty-three (Vol. II) [101]; Chapter Fifty (Vol. III) [215]; Chapter Seventy-one (Vol. III) [226]

Thus, it is very far in the distant past since I realized [the state of] Buddha. [My] lifetime is countless *asaṃkheya kalpa*s, eternally existing and not perishing. Good sons! The lifetime which I have realized by my original practice of the bodhisattva way is not even yet exhausted but will still be twice the previous number [of *kalpa*s].

LS 3.30 SBGZ Chapter Seventeen [54]; Chapter Sixty (Vol. III) [44]; Chapter Sixty-one (Vol. III) [43]

In order to save living beings,
As an expedient method I manifest nirvana,
Yet really I have not passed away,
Constantly abiding here preaching the Dharma,
I am always living at this place,
With mystical powers,
I make living beings who are upset,
Still fail to see me though I am close.
Many see that I have passed away,
And far and wide they serve offerings to my bones,
All holding romantic yearnings
And bearing thirst in their hearts.
When living beings have believed and submitted,
Being simple and straight, and flexible in mind,
And they wholeheartedly want to meet Buddha,
Without begrudging their own body and life,
Then I and many monks,
Appear together on Vulture Peak.

LS 3.32 SBGZ Chapter Seventeen; Chapter Sixty-one (Vol. III) [48]; Chapter Eighty-eight (Vol. IV) [188]

[I am] eternally present on Vulture Peak,
And in other dwelling places.
Even when living beings see, at the end of a *kalpa,*
That they are to be burned in a great fire,
This land of mine is tranquil,
Always filled with gods and human beings;
Its parks and many palaces
Are adorned with every kind of treasure;
Precious trees have abundant flowers and fruit:
It is a place where living beings enjoy themselves.
The gods strike celestial drums,
And constantly make theater and music,
Showering *mandārava* flowers
On the Buddha and the great assembly.
My Pure Land is immortal,
Yet many view it as to be burned up,
And thus entirely filled
With grief, horror, and agonies.
These living beings of many sins,
With their bad conduct as direct and indirect causes,
Even if they pass *asaṃkheya kalpa*s
Do not hear the name of the Three Treasures.
Beings who practice virtue
And who are gentle, simple, and straight,
All see my body
Existing here and preaching the Dharma.

LS 3.36 SBGZ Chapter Seventy (Vol. III) [201]

Constantly making this my thought:
"How can I make living beings
Able to enter the supreme truth,
And swiftly realize a buddha's body?"

Chapter Seventeen: *Funbetsu-kudoku* (Discrimination of Merits)

LS 3.56 SBGZ Chapter Sixty-one (Vol. III) [39]

If good sons and good daughters, hearing my preaching of the eternity of [my] lifetime, believe and understand it with a profound mind, then they will see the Buddha constantly abiding on Mount Gṛdhrakūṭa surrounded by an assembly of great bodhisattvas and many *śrāvaka*s, and preaching the Dharma. And they will see this *sahā* world with its land of lapis lazuli, level, normal, and right.

Chapter Eighteen: *Zuiki-kudoku* (The Merits of Joyful Acceptance)

LS 3.72–74 SBGZ Chapter Eight [70]; Chapter Thirteen [127]; Chapter Fourteen [200]; Chapter Twenty [125]

Then the Buddha addressed the bodhisattva *mahāsattva* Maitreya: "Ajita. If, after the Tathāgata's death, *bhikṣu*s, *bhikṣuṇī*s, *upāsaka*s, and *upāsikā*s, or other wise people, old or young, having heard this sutra and accepted it with joy, leave the Dharma order and go elsewhere to stay in monasteries or deserted places, or in cities, streets, hamlets, fields, and villages, to expound [this sutra] as they have heard it, according to their ability, to their father and mother, relatives, good friends and acquaintances; and all these people, having heard it, accept it with joy and again go on to transmit the teaching; [then] other people, having heard it, also accept it with joy and transmit the teaching, which propagates like this to the fiftieth [generation]. . . ."

LS 3.88

How much more, if we hear [the sutra] with undivided mind,
Elucidate its meaning,
And practice according to the teaching:
That happiness is beyond limit.

LS 3.90

Then the Buddha addressed the bodhisattva *mahāsattva* Ever Zealous: "If any good son or good daughter receives and retains this *Sutra of the Flower of Dharma* or reads or recites or explains or copies it, that person will obtain eight hundred merits of the eye, twelve hundred merits of the ear, eight hundred merits of the nose, twelve hundred merits of the tongue, eight hundred merits of the body, and twelve hundred merits of the mind; these merits will adorn the six organs making them all pure. . . ."

Chapter Nineteen: *Hōsshi-kudoku* (The Merits of a Teacher of the Dharma)

LS 3.122 SBGZ Chapter Twenty-one [184]

Though [he or she] has not yet attained faultless real wisdom, his or her mind-organ is pure like this.

Chapter Twenty: *Jōfugyō-bosatsu* (Bodhisattva Never Despise)

LS 3.128 SBGZ Chapter Thirty-seven (Vol. II) [161]; Chapter Fifty-two (Vol. III) [23]

In the eternal past, countless, infinite, inconceivable *asaṃkheya kalpa*s ago, there was a buddha named King of Majestic Voice.

LS 3.130 SBGZ Chapter Seventeen

The right Dharma remained in the world for a number of *kalpa*s equal to the atoms in one Jambudvīpa. The imitative Dharma remained in the world for a number of *kalpa*s equal to the atoms in four continents.

LS 3.134–36

Thus he passed many years, constantly abused, never becoming angry, always saying, "You will become buddhas." When he said these words, people would sometimes beat him with clubs, sticks, bricks, and stones. He ran away and, keeping his distance, he still called out in a loud voice, "I dare not despise you. You will all become buddhas." Because he always spoke these words, arrogant *bhikṣu*s, *bhikṣuṇī*s, *upāsaka*s, and *upāsikā*s called him "Never Despise."

Chapter Twenty-one: *Nyorai-jinriki* (The Mystical Power of the Tathāgata)

LS 3.158 SBGZ Chapter Seventeen; Chapter Twenty-five (Vol. II) [183]

Thereupon the worlds of the ten directions were realized without hindrance as one buddha land. Then the Buddha addressed Eminent Conduct and the other bodhisattvas in the great assembly: "The mystical powers of the buddhas are like this; countless, infinite, and unthinkable. . . ."

LS 3.162 SBGZ Chapter Sixty-one (Vol. III) [45]

One who is able to keep this sutra,
Is already meeting me,
And also meeting the Buddha Abundant Treasures,
And those [buddhas] who are [my] offshoots.

Chapter Twenty-two: *Zoku-rui* (The Commission)

Chapter Twenty-three: *Yaku-ō-bosatsu-honji* (The Story of Bodhisattva Medicine King)

LS 3.200 SBGZ Chapter Seventy-three (Vol. IV) [35]

As the Buddha is king of all *dharma*s, so it is also with this sutra. It is the king of sutras. Star Constellation King Flower! This sutra can save all living beings. This sutra can free all living beings from pain and suffering. This sutra can greatly benefit all living beings and fulfill their desires. Like a clear, cool pool that can satisfy all those who are thirsty; like the cold getting fire; like the naked getting clothing; like [a caravan of] merchants getting a leader; like a child getting its mother; like a crossing getting a ferry; like the infirm getting a doctor; like [those in] darkness getting a light; like the poor getting treasure; like a people getting a king; like traders getting the sea; like a torch dispelling the darkness; so it is also with this *Sutra of the Flower of Dharma.* It can free living beings from all suffering and all diseases, and can unloose all the bonds of life and death.

LS 3.210 SBGZ Chapter Seventeen

You have accomplished unthinkable virtue, being able to ask Śākyamuni Buddha such things as these, and benefiting all countless living beings.

Chapter Twenty-four: *Myo-on-bosatsu* (Bodhisattva Wonder Sound)

LS 3.214 SBGZ Chapter Seventeen

[Bodhisattva Wonder Sound] had attained *samādhi* with the form of a wonderful banner, *samādhi* as the Flower of Dharma, *samādhi* as pure virtue, *samādhi* as the sport of the Constellation King, *samādhi* as the state without involvements, *samādhi* as the wisdom-seal, *samādhi* as the state of understanding the words of all living beings, *samādhi* as the accumulation of all virtues, *samādhi* as the state of purity, *samādhi* as the playing of mystical powers, *samādhi* as the torch of wisdom, *samādhi* as the king of adornments, *samādhi* as pure brightness, *samādhi* as the pure treasury, *samādhi* as a singular state, and *samādhi* as the function of the sun. He had attained hundred thousand myriad *koṭi*s of great states of *samādhi* like these, equal to the sands of the Ganges.

Chapter Twenty-five: *Kanzeon-bosatsu-fumon* (The Universal Gate of Bodhisattva Regarder of the Sounds of the World)

LS 3.242 SBGZ Chapter Thirty-three (Vol. II)

Good son! If there are countless hundred thousand myriad *koṭi*s of living beings who, suffering from many agonies, hear of this bodhisattva Regarder of the Sounds of the World and with undivided mind call [the bodhisattva's] name, the bodhisattva Regarder of the Sounds of the World will instantly regard their cries, and all will be delivered.

LS 3.252 SBGZ Chapter Seventeen; allusions in many chapters

Good son! If living beings in any land must be saved through the body of a buddha, the bodhisattva Regarder of the Sounds of the World manifests at once the body of a buddha and preaches for them the Dharma. To those who must be saved through the body of a *pratyekabuddha,* [the bodhisattva] manifests at once the body of a *pratyekabuddha* and preaches for them the Dharma. To those who must be saved through the body of a *śrāvaka,* [the bodhisattva] manifests at once the body of a *śrāvaka* and preaches for them the Dharma. To those who must be saved through the body of King Brahmā, [the bodhisattva] manifests at once the body of King Brahmā and preaches for them the Dharma. To those who must be saved through the body of the god-king Śakra, [the bodhisattva] manifests at once the body of the god-king Śakra and preaches for them the Dharma. To those who must be saved through the body of Īśvara, [the bodhisattva] manifests at once the body of Īśvara and preaches for them the Dharma. To those who must be saved through the body of Maheśvara, [the bodhisattva] manifests at once the body of Maheśvara and preaches for them the Dharma. To those who must be saved through the body of a celestial great general, [the bodhisattva] manifests at once the body of a celestial great general and preaches for them the Dharma. To those who must be saved through the body of Vaiśravaṇa, [the bodhisattva] manifests at once the body of Vaiśravaṇa and preaches for them the Dharma. To those who must be saved through the body of a minor king, [the bodhisattva] manifests at once the body of a minor king and preaches for them the Dharma. To those who must be saved through the body of a rich man, [the bodhisattva] manifests at once the body of a rich man and preaches for them the Dharma. To those who must be saved through the body of a householder, [the bodhisattva] manifests at once the body of a householder and preaches for them the Dharma. To those who must be saved through the body of a government official, [the bodhisattva] manifests at once the body of a government official and preaches for them the Dharma. To those who must be saved through the body of a brahman, [the bodhisattva] manifests at once the body of a brahman and preaches for them the Dharma. To those who must be saved through the body of a *bhikṣu, bhikṣuṇī, upāsaka,* or *upāsikā,* [the bodhisattva] manifests at once the body of a *bhikṣu, bhikṣuṇī, upāsaka,* or *upāsikā* and preaches for them the Dharma. To those who must be saved through the body of the woman of a rich man, householder, official, or brahman, [the bodhisattva] manifests at once the body of a woman and preaches for them the Dharma. To those who must be saved through the body of a boy or a girl, [the bodhisattva] manifests at once the body of a boy or a girl and preaches for them the Dharma. To those who must be saved through the body of a god, dragon, *yakṣa, gandharva, asura, garuḍa, kiṃnara,* or *mahoraga,* a human being or a nonhuman being, [the bodhisattva], in every case, manifests at once this [body] and preaches for them the Dharma. To those who must be saved through the body of a *vajra*-holding god, [the bodhisattva] manifests at once the body of a *vajra*-holding god and preaches for them the Dharma. Infinite Thought! This bodhisattva Regarder of the Sounds of the World, accomplishing good effects like these, using all kinds of forms, roams many lands to save living beings. Therefore you all must wholeheartedly serve offerings to Bodhisattva Regarder of the Sounds of the World. This bodhisattva Regarder of the Sounds of the World, amid fear and distress, is able to give fearlessness. For this reason, in this *sahā* world, all call this [bodhisattva] "Giver of Fearlessness."

LS 3.270 SBGZ Chapter One [20]

While the Buddha preached this "Universal Gate" chapter, the eighty-four thousand living beings in the assembly all established the will to the unequaled state of equilbrium which is *anuttara samyaksaṃbodhi.*

Chapter Twenty-six: *Darani* (*Dhāraṇī*)

LS 3.282–84 SBGZ Chapter Seventeen

If anyone fails to heed our spell,

And troubles a preacher of the Dharma,
May their head be split into seven
Like an *arjaka* sprout.
Their crime is like killing a parent,
Like the sin of pressing oil,
Or cheating people with [false] weights and measures,
Or Devadatta's crime of splitting the sangha.
People who offend such a teacher of the Dharma,
Will acquire similar evil.

Chapter Twenty-seven: *Myō-shōgon-ō-honji* (The Story of King Resplendent)

LS 3.288–90 SBGZ Chapter Seventy-three (Vol. IV) [3]

These two sons possessed great mystical power, happiness, and wisdom. They had long cultivated the ways practiced by bodhisattvas; that is to say, *dāna-pāramitā, śīla-pāramitā, kṣānti-pāramitā, vīrya-pāramitā, dhyāna-pāramitā, prajñā-pāramitā,* and the expedience *pāramitā,* benevolence, compassion, charity, and the thirty-seven auxiliary *bodhi* methods—all these they had clearly realized.

LS 3.292–94 SBGZ Chapter Twenty-five (Vol. II) [186]

Thereupon the two sons, because they cared for their father, sprang up into space, to a height of seven *tāla* trees, and manifested many kinds of mystical transformation, walking, standing, sitting, and lying in space; the upper body emitting water, the lower body emitting fire [or] the lower body emitting water and the upper body emitting fire.

LS 3.302 SBGZ Chapter Eighty-six (Vol. IV) [83]

That king at once gave his kingdom to his younger brother; [then] the king together with his queen, two sons, and many followers, in the Buddha-Dharma, left home to practice the truth.

LS 3.304

These two sons of mine have already done a buddha-deed, with transformations [achieved through] mystical powers, they have changed my wrong mind, enabling me to abide peacefully in the Buddha-Dharma and to meet the World-honored One. These two sons are my friends in virtue.

LS 3.306 SBGZ Chapter Sixty-one (Vol. III) [47]

Remember, great king! A friend of virtue is the great cause which leads us to be able to meet Buddha and to establish the will to [the supreme truth of] *anuttara samyaksaṃbodhi.*

Chapter Twenty-eight: *Fugen-bosatsu-kanpotsu* (Encouragement of Bodhisattva Universal Virtue)

LS 3.326 SBGZ Chapter Seventeen

While the *Sutra of the Flower of Dharma* proceeds on its course through Jambudvīpa, anyone who receives it and retains it should reflect as follows: "This is all due to the majestic mystical power of Universal Virtue." If anyone receives and retains it, reads and recites it, rightly remembers it, understands its meaning, and practices as it preaches, we should know that this person is doing the work of Universal Virtue.

LS 3.328–30 SBGZ Chapter Seventeen

[The bodhisattva Universal Virtue said,] "World-honored One! I now by my mystical power will guard and protect this sutra. After the death of the Tathāgata, I shall cause it to spread widely throughout Jambudvīpa, and shall never let it cease to exist." Thereupon Śākyamuni Buddha praised him, saying, "How excellent, how excellent, Universal Virtue, that you are able to protect and to promote this sutra, causing peace, joy, and benefit to many living beings. You have already accomplished unthinkable virtue and profound compassion. From the long distant past, you have established the will to [the truth of] *anuttara samyaksaṃbodhi,* and have been able to make this vow of mystical power, to guard and to protect this sutra. . . ."

LS 3.330 SBGZ Chapter Sixty-one (Vol. III) [37]

Universal Virtue! If there is anyone who receives and retains, reads and recites, rightly remembers, practices, and copies this *Sutra of the Flower of Dharma,* know that this person is meeting Śākyamuni Buddha and hearing this sutra as if from the Buddha's mouth.

Glossary of Sanskrit Terms

This glossary presents brief dictionary definitions of Sanskrit terms represented in the present volume. Definitions are drawn in general from *A Sanskrit-English Dictionary* by Sir Monier Monier-Williams [MW]. Also used were *A Sanskrit Dictionary for Students* by A. A. Macdonell [MAC], the *Japanese-English Buddhist Dictionary* [JEBD], and *The Historical Buddha* [HB] by H. W. Schumann.

Chapter references, unless otherwise stated, refer to chapters of the *Shōbōgenzō*. Arrangement is according to the English alphabet.

Abhidharma ("on Dharma," prefix for names of Buddhist commentaries). Represented by *ron,* "doctrine, discussion, argument." [MW] The dogmas of Buddhist philosophy or metaphysics. *Abhi:* (a prefix to verbs and nouns, expressing) to, toward, into, over, upon. The literal meaning of *abhidharma* is therefore "that which is directed toward (or additional to) Dharma." One of the "three baskets," or Tripiṭaka (q.v.).

Abhidharmakośa-bhāṣya (name of a commentary). Represented phonetically. [MW] *Kośa:* a cask; a bucket; a box; the interior of a carriage; a storeroom; a treasury; a dictionary, lexicon, or vocabulary; a poetical collection, collection of sentences, etc. *Bhāṣya:* (q.v.): commentary. Ref: Bibliography; Chapter Eighty-seven (Vol. IV); Chapter Eighty-eight (Vol. IV).

Abhidharmamahāvibhāṣa-śāstra (name of a commentary). Represented phonetically. [MW] *Vibhāṣā:* great commentary. Ref: Bibliography; Chapter Seventy (Vol. III); Chapter Eighty-four (Vol. IV); Chapter Eighty-six (Vol. IV).

abhijñā (mystical power, supernatural faculty). Represented by *jinzū,* "mystical power." [MW] Knowing, skillful, clever; understanding, conversant with; remembrance, recollection; supernatural science or faculty of a buddha (of which five are enumerated, viz. 1) taking any form at will; 2) hearing to any distance; 3) seeing to any distance; 4) penetrating men's thoughts; 5) knowing their state and antecedents). Ref: Chapter Twelve [87]; Chapter Twenty-five (Vol. II); *Lotus Sutra,* chapter 24.

abhimāna (haughtiness). Represented by *zōjōman,* "lofty arrogance." [MW] High opinion of one's self, self-conceit, pride, haughtiness. One of the seven categories of māna (arrogance). Ref: *Lotus Sutra,* chapter 2.

ācārya. Represented phonetically. [MW] "Knowing or teaching the *ācāra* or rules (of good conduct)," a spiritual guide or teacher. Ref: Chapter Twenty-one [206].

acintya (unthinkable). Represented by *fukashigi,* "unthinkable." [MW] Inconceivable, surpassing thought. Ref: Chapter Seventeen; *Lotus Sutra,* chapter 21.

adbhuta-dharma (wonders, marvels). Represented by *kihō,* "rare occurrences, marvels" and by *mi-zō-u-hō,* "unprecedented occurrences." [MW] "A system or series of marvels or prodigies." One of the twelve divisions of the teachings. See under *aṅga.* Ref: Chapter Eleven [40].

Āgama (name of a group of sutras). Represented phonetically. [MW] A traditional doctrine or precept, collection of such doctrines, sacred work; anything handed down and fixed by tradition. Ref: Chapter Twelve; Bibliography.

aguru (aloes). Represented by *jinkō,* "aloes." [MW] The fragrant aloe wood and tree, *Aquilaria agallocha.* Ref: Chapter Twelve [78].

Ajita (epithet of Maitreya). Represented phonetically. [MW] Not conquered, unsubdued, unsurpassed, invincible, irresistible; name of Viṣṇu; Śiva; Maitreya or a future buddha. Ref: *Lotus Sutra,* chapter 15.

ākāśa (space). Represented by *kokū,* "space." [MW] A free or open space, vacuity; the ether, sky, or atmosphere. Ref: Chapter Seventeen [62]; *Lotus Sutra,* chapters 12, 15.

akṣa-sūtra (rosary). Represented by *juzu,* "counting beads," "rosary." [MW] *Akṣa:* a die for gambling; a cube; a seed of which rosaries are made; the *Eleocarpus ganitrus,* producing that seed. *Sūtra* (q.v.): a thread. Ref: Chapter Five.

Akṣobhya (name of a mythical buddha). Represented phonetically. [MW] Immovable, imperturbable; name of a buddha; name of an immense number. Ref: Chapter Forty-six (Vol. III) [90]; *Lotus Sutra,* chapter 7.

Amitābha (name of a mythical buddha). Represented phonetically. [MW] "Of unmeasured splendor," name of a *dhyāni*-buddha. Ref: Chapter Twelve [80].

amṛta (nectar). Represented by *kanro,* "sweet dew, nectar." [MW] Immortal, an immortal, a god; a goddess; a spirituous liquor; world of immortality, heaven, eternity; the nectar (conferring immortality, produced at the churning of the ocean), ambrosia. Ref: Chapter One [62]; Chapter Eight [198].

anāgāmin (the state that is not subject to returning). Represented phonetically and by *fugen-ka,* "the effect of not returning." [MW] Not coming, not arriving, not future, not subject to returning. Ref: Chapter Two.

Ānanda (name of the Buddha's half-brother and the second patriarch in India). Represented phonetically and by Keiki, "joy." [MW] Happiness, joy, enjoyment. Ref: Chapter Fifteen.

anāsrava (without excess, faultless). Represented by *muro,* "without leakage." [MW] *A* (before a vowel *an*): a prefix corresponding to the English "in" or "un," and having a negative or contrary sense. *Āsrava* (q.v.): excess, distress. Ref: Chapter Twenty-one [192].

Anāthapiṇḍada or Anāthapiṇḍika (a name of Sudatta [q.v.]). [MW] "Giver of cakes or food to the poor." Ref: *Fukanzazengi.*

Anavatapta (name of a dragon king and of a lake). Represented phonetically and by Munetsu-chi, "Lake of No Heat." [MW] Name of a serpent king; of a lake (= Rāvaṇa-hrada). Ref: Chapter Twelve [71].

aṅga (division). Represented by *bun*[*kyō*], "divisions [of the teaching]." [MW] A limb of the body; a subordinate division or department. The twelve divisions of the teaching are 1) *sūtra,* 2) *geya,* 3) *vyākaraṇa,* 4) *gāthā,* 5) *udāna,* 6) *nidāna,* 7) *avadāna,* 8) *itivṛttaka,* 9) *jātaka,* 10) *vaipulya,* 11) *adbhuta-dharma,* 12) *upadeśa* (q.v.). Ref: Chapter Eleven [40]; *Lotus Sutra,* chapter 2.

anitya (inconstant). Represented by *mujō,* "inconstant." [MW] Not everlasting, transient, occasional, incidental; irregular, unusual; unstable, uncertain. Ref: Chapter Seventeen [39]; Chapter Twenty-two (Vol. II).

añjali (salutation with joined hands). Represented by *gasshō,* "joining together of the palms." [MW] The open hands placed side by side and slightly hollowed (as if by a beggar to receive food; hence when raised to the forehead, a mark of supplication), reverence, salutation. Ref: Chapter Seventeen [62]; *Lotus Sutra,* chapter 3.

antarā-bhava (the intermediate stage of existence, middle existence). Represented by *chū-u,* "middle existence." [MW] *Antarā:* in the middle, inside, within, between; on the way. *Bhava:* coming into existence; being, state of being, existence, life. *Antarā-bhava-sattva:* the soul in its middle existence between death and regeneration. Ref: Chapter Twelve [74].

antarvāsa (inner robe). Represented phonetically and by *ge-e,* "under robe," by *nai-e,* "inner robe," by *gojō-e,* "five-stripe robe," by *shō-e,* "small robe," and by *gyōdō-samu-e,* "practice and work robe." [MW] An inner- or undergarment. Ref: Chapter Twelve [95].

anuttara samyaksaṃbodhi (the supreme right and balanced state of complete truth). Represented phonetically, and by *mujō-shōtō-kaku,* "supreme right and balanced state of truth" or by *mujō-tōshō-kaku,* "supreme balanced and right state of truth." [MW] *Anuttara:* chief, principal, best, excellent. [Supreme.] *Samyak:* in compounds for *samyañc. Samyañc:* going along with or together, turned together or in one direction, combined, united; turned toward each other, facing one another; correct, accurate, proper, true, right; uniform, same, identical. [Right and balanced.] *Sam:* a prefix expressing conjunction, union, thoroughness, intensity, completeness. [Complete.] *Bodhi:* perfect knowledge or wisdom (by which a person becomes a buddha); the illuminated or enlightened intellect. [State of truth.] Note: In the *Shōbōgenzō, bodhi* is not intellectual knowledge but a state of body and mind. Ref: Chapter One; Chapter Two; *Lotus Sutra,* chapter 1.

araṇya (forest). Represented phonetically. [MW] A foreign or distant land; a wilderness, desert, forest. Ref: Chapter Twelve [115].

arhat. Represented phonetically and by *shika,* "fourth effect." [MW] Able, allowed to; worthy, venerable, respectable; praised, celebrated; the highest rank in the Buddhist hierarchy. Ref: Chapter One [62]; Chapter Two; *Lotus Sutra,* chapter 1.

arjaka (name of a plant). Represented phonetically. [MW] The plant *Ocimum gratissimum.* LSW notes: "It is said that if one touches an *arjaka* flower its petals open and fall into seven pieces. Kern identifies the plant as *Symplocos racemosa,* while [the] Monier-Williams dictionary has *Ocinum* [sic.] *gratissimum.*" Ref: *Lotus Sutra,* chapter 26.

aśaikṣa (those beyond study). Represented by *mugaku,* "no study." [MW] "No longer a pupil," an arhat. Ref: *Lotus Sutra,* chapter 9.

asamasama (the unequaled state of equilibrium). Represented by *mutōtō,* "equality without equal." [MW] Unequaled. Ref: Chapter One [20]; *Lotus Sutra,* chapter 25.

asaṃjñi-sattvāḥ (thoughtless heaven). Represented by *musōten,* "thoughtless heaven." [MW] *Asaṃjña:* senseless; not having full consciousness. Ref: Chapter Fourteen [195].

asaṃkhyeya (innumerable). Represented phonetically. [MW] Innumerable, exceedingly numerous. Ref: Chapter Twelve [80]; *Lotus Sutra,* chapter 16.

asaṃskṛta (unadorned, without elaboration). Represented by *mui,* "without artificiality, natural." [MW] Not prepared, not consecrated; unadorned; unpolished, rude (as speech). Ref: Chapter One [11]; Chapter Twelve [64].

Aśoka (name of a great Indian emperor who ruled in the third century B.C.E.). Represented phonetically. [MW] Not causing sorrow, not feeling sorrow. Ref: Chapter Fifteen; Chapter Forty-five (Vol. III) [73]; Bibliography.

āsrava (the superfluous, excess). Represented by *ro,* "leakage." [MW] The foam on boiling rice; a door opening into water and allowing the stream to descend through it; (with Jainas) the action of the senses which impels the soul towards external objects; distress, affliction, pain. Ref: *Lotus Sutra,* chapters 1, 10.

asura (demon). Represented phonetically and by *hiten,* "anti-gods." [MW] An evil spirit, demon, ghost, opponent of the gods. Ref: Chapter Twelve [80]; *Lotus Sutra,* chapter 10.

Aśvaghoṣa (name of a Buddhist patriarch). Represented by Memyō, "Horse Whinny." [MW] *Aśva:* a horse, stallion. *Ghoṣa:* any cry or sound, roar of animals. Ref: Chapter Fifteen.

avadāna (parable). Represented by *hiyu,* "metaphor, parable." [MW] A great or glorious act, achievement (object of a legend, Buddhist literature). One of the twelve divisions of the teachings. See under *aṅga.* Ref: Chapter Eleven [40]; *Lotus Sutra,* chapter 3.

avadāta-vāsana (clothed in white; layperson). Represented by *byaku-e,* "white robe." [MW] *Avadāta:* cleansed, clean, clear; pure, blameless, excellent; of white splendor; dazzling white; white color. *Vāsana:* covering, clothing, garment, dress. Ref: Chapter Twelve [107].

Avalokiteśvara (Regarder of the Sounds of the World). Represented by Kannon, "Regarder of Sounds" and by Kanjizai, "Free in Reflection." [MW] Name of a bodhisattva worshiped by the northern Buddhists. *Avalokita:* seen, viewed, observed. Ref: Chapter Two; Chapter Thirty-three (Vol. II); *Lotus Sutra,* chapter 25.

Avataṃsaka (name of a sutra). Represented by *kegon,* "flower-solemnity." [MW] *Avataṃsa:* a garland. Ref: Chapter One [32]; Chapter Seven [141]; Bibliography.

Avīci (name of a particular hell). Represented phonetically and by *mugen-jigoku,* "incessant hell." [MW] Waveless; a particular hell. Ref: Chapter Fourteen [195].

avidyā (ignorance). Represented by *mumyō,* "ignorance, darkness." [MW] Unlearned, unwise; ignorance, illusion. Ref: Chapter Two; *Lotus Sutra,* chapter 7.

avyākṛta (indifferent, undifferentiated). Represented by *muki,* "without writing," "blank." [MW] Undeveloped, unexpounded; elementary substance from which all things were created. Ref: Chapter Ten.

āyatana (seat [of sense perception]). Represented by *sho,* "place" or *nyu,* "entry." [MW] Resting place, support, seat, place, home, house, abode; (with Buddhists) the five senses and *manas* (considered as the inner seats or *āyatana*s) and the qualities perceived by the above (the outer *āyatana*s). Ref: Chapter Two.

āyuṣmat (venerable monk). Represented by *gu-ju,* "possessing longevity" and by *chōrō,* "experienced-old" or "veteran senior." [MW] Possessed of vital power, healthy, long-lived; alive, living; old, aged; "life-possessing," often applied as a kind of honorific title (especially to royal personages and Buddhist monks). Ref: Chapter One [52]; Chapter Two.

bhadanta (virtuous one). Represented by *daitoku,* "great virtue." [MW] Term of respect applied to a Buddhist, a Buddhist mendicant. Ref: Chapter Two.

bhadrakalpa (good *kalpa*, virtuous *kalpa*). Represented by *kengō,* "*kalpa* of the wise," "*kalpa* of the sages." [MW] "The good or beautiful *kalpa,*" name of the present age. *Bhadra:* blessed, auspicious, fortunate, prosperous, happy; good, gracious, friendly, kind; excellent, fair, beautiful, lovely, pleasant, dear. *Kalpa:* eon (q.v.). Ref: *Lotus Sutra,* chapter 8.

Bhadrapāla ("Good Guardian," name of a bodhisattva). Represented phonetically. [MW] Name of a bodhisattva. *Bhadra:* good. *Pāla:* a guard, protector, keeper; an oblong pond (as "receptacle" of water?). Ref: Chapter Twelve [49].

Bhagavat. Represented phonetically and by *seson,* "World-honored One." [MW] Glorious, illustrious, divine, adorable, venerable; holy (applied to gods, demigods, and saints as a term of address; with Buddhists often prefixed to the titles of their sacred writings); "the divine or adorable one," name of a buddha or a bodhisattva. Ref: Chapter Two; *Lotus Sutra,* chapter 2.

bhikṣu (monk). Represented phonetically. [MW] A beggar, mendicant, religious mendicant; a Buddhist mendicant or monk. Ref: *Lotus Sutra,* chapter 1.

bhikṣuṇī (nun). Represented phonetically. [MW] A Buddhist female mendicant or nun. Ref: *Lotus Sutra,* chapter 2.

Bhīṣmagarjitasvararāja (name of a legendary Buddha). Represented by I-on-ō, "King of Majestic Voice" and by Kū-ō, "King of Emptiness." [MW] Name of a number of buddhas. Ref: Chapter Fourteen [176]; *Lotus Sutra,* chapter 20.

bodhi (truth, state of truth). Represented phonetically and by *dō,* "way." See *anuttara samyaksaṃbodhi.*

bodhicitta (*bodhi*-mind, the will to the truth). Represented by *bodaishin,* "*bodhi*-mind" and by *doshin,* "will to the truth." [MW] *Citta* (q.v.): intelligence, mind. Ref: Chapter Five [111]; Chapter Sixty-nine (Vol. III); Chapter Seventy (Vol. III); *Lotus Sutra,* chapter 12.

bodhimaṇḍa (place of practicing the truth, place of practice, seat of truth). Represented by *dōjō,* "truth-place," "way-place," "exercise hall," "gymnasium." [MW] Seat of wisdom (name of the seats which were said to have risen out of the earth under four successive trees where Gautama Buddha attained to perfect wisdom). *Maṇḍa:* the scum of boiled rice (or any grain); ornament, decoration. Ref: Chapter One [20]; *Lotus Sutra,* chapter 2.

bodhisattva (Buddhist practitioner). Represented phonetically. [MW] "One whose essence is perfect knowledge [*bodhi,* q.v.]." *Sattva:* being, existence, entity, reality; true essence, nature, disposition of mind, character. Ref: *Lotus Sutra.*

brahmā (moral, pure). Represented phonetically. [MW] Relating to Brahmā, holy, sacred, divine; relating to sacred knowledge. Ref: Chapter One [51]; *Lotus Sutra,* chapter 1.

Brahmā (name of the creator deity in the Hindu triad). Represented phonetically. [MW] The one impersonal universal spirit manifested as a personal creator and as the first of the triad of personal gods. Ref: Chapter Ten [19]; *Lotus Sutra,* chapters 11, 25.

brahmacarya (pure conduct). Represented by *bongyō,* "*brahma*-conduct." [MW] Study of the Veda, the state of an unmarried religious student, a state of continence and chastity; the unmarried state, continence, chastity; leading the life of an unmarried religious student, practicing chastity. *Brahma:* in compounds for *brahman* (the Veda, a sacred text, religious or spiritual knowledge; holy life). *Carya:* to be practiced or performed; driving (in a carriage); walking or roaming about; proceeding, behavior, conduct; a religious mendicant's life; practicing, peforming. Ref: Chapter One [51]; *Lotus Sutra,* chapter 1.

brahman (*brāhmaṇa*). Represented phonetically. [MW] One who has divine knowledge, a brahman (generally a priest, but often in the present day a layman although the name is strictly applicable only to one who knows and repeats the Veda). Ref: Chapter One [37]; *Lotus Sutra,* chapter 25.

buddha. Represented by *butsu, hotoke,* "buddha." [MW] Awakened, awake; conscious, intelligent, clever, wise; learned, known, understood; a wise or learned man, sage; the principal Buddha of the present age (born at Kapilavastu about the year 500 B.C.E., his father, Śuddhodana of the Śākya tribe or family, being the *rāja* of that district, and his mother, Māyādevī, being the daughter of *rāja* Suprabuddha; hence he belonged to the *kṣatriya* caste and his original name Śākyamuni or Śākyasiṃha was really his family name, while that of Gautama was taken from the race to which his family belonged). Note: In the *Shōbōgenzō*, "buddha" means not only awakened, and not only Gautama Buddha and other historical buddhas, but also the concrete state in zazen which is the same as the state of Gautama Buddha.

buddha-*śāsana* (the Buddha's teaching). Represented by *bukkyō,* "buddha-teaching." [MW] *Śāsana:* punishing; teaching, instructing, an instructor; government, dominion, rule over; an order, command, edict; a writing; any written book or work of authority, scripture; teaching, instruction, discipline, doctrine. Ref: Chapter One [68]; Chapter Twenty-four (Vol. II).

caitya (tomb). Represented by *tō,* "tower." [MW] Relating to a funeral pile or mound; a funeral monument or stupa or pyramidal column containing the ashes of deceased persons. Ref: Chapter Eighty-seven (Vol. IV) [160]; *Lotus Sutra,* chapter 10.

cakra (wheel). Represented by *rin,* "wheel." [MW] The wheel (of a carriage, of the sun's chariot, of time); a discus or sharp circular missile weapon; a number of villages, province, district; the wheel of a monarch's chariot rolling over his dominions, sovereignty, realm.

cakravarti-rāja (wheel-turning king). Represented by *ten-rin-jō,* "wheel-turning king." [MW] *Cakravartin:* rolling everywhere without obstruction; a ruler the wheels of whose chariot roll everywhere without obstruction; emperor; sovereign of the world, ruler of a *cakra* (or country described as extending from sea to sea). *Rāja:* king. Ref: Chapter Ten [19]; *Lotus Sutra,* chapter 7.

cakṣus (seeing, eyes). Represented by *gen,* "eyes." [MW] Seeing; the act of seeing; faculty of seeing, sight; the eye. Ref: Chapter Two.

caṇḍāla (outcaste). Represented phonetically. [MW] An outcaste, person of the lowest and most despised of the mixed tribes (born from a *śūdra* father and a brahman mother). Ref: Chapter Eight; Chapter Eighty-four (Vol. IV) [26].

candana (sandal[wood]). Represented phonetically. [MW] Sandal (*Sirium myrtifolium,* either the tree, wood, or the unctuous preparation of the wood held in high estimation as perfumes; hence a term for anything that is the most excellent of its kind). Ref: Chapter Twelve [78].

caṅkrama (walking about). Represented by *kinhin,* "walking about." [MW] Going about, a walk; a place for walking about. Ref: Chapter Thirty (Vol. II) [119].

cārin (practitioner). Represented phonetically and by *gyōja,* "practitioner." [MW] Following established practice. Ref: Chapter Twelve [64].

catvāro yonayaḥ (four kinds of birth). Represented by *shishō,* "four [kinds of] birth." [MW] *Catur:* four. *Yoni:* the womb; place of birth, source, origin, spring, fountain. The four are *jarāyu-ja* (birth from womb); *aṇḍa-ja* (birth from egg); *saṃsveda-ja* (birth from moisture); and *upapāduka* (metamorphosis). Ref: Chapter Nine [222].

cintāmaṇi (name of a fabulous gem). Represented by *nyo-i-ju,* "the gem of doing as one pleases." [MW] "Thought gem," a fabulous gem supposed to yield its possessor all desires. Ref: Chapter Fourteen [189].

citta (intelligence). Represented phonetically and by *shinshiki,* "mental/intellectual consciousness" or by *ryo-chi-shin,* "considering and recognizing mind." [MW] Attending, observing; thinking, reflecting, imagining, thought; intention, aim, wish; memory; intelligence, reason. One of the three kinds of mind, the others being *hṛdaya* and *vṛddha* (q.v.). Ref: Chapter One [27]; Chapter Seventy (Vol. III).

citta-manas-vijñāna (mind, will, consciousness). Represented by *shin-i-shiki,* "mind, will, consciousness." [MW] *Citta* (q.v.): thought; intelligence. *Manas* (q.v.): mind, will. *Vijñāna* (q.v.): consciousness. [JEBD] In the Hinayana, all three terms are regarded as synonyms for mind. Ref: *Fukanzazengi.*

dāna (giving). Represented phonetically and by *fuse,* "alms, charity, giving." [MW] The act of giving; giving in marriage; giving up; communicating, imparting, teaching; paying back, restoring; adding, addition; donation, gift. One of the six *pāramitā*s (q.v.). Ref: Chapter Two; Chapter Forty-five (Vol. III); *Lotus Sutra,* chapter 27.

dānapati (donor). Represented phonetically and by *seshu,* "alms-lord." [MW] "Liberality-lord," munificent person. *Dāna:* giving. *Pati:* a master, owner, possessor, lord, ruler, sovereign. Ref: Chapter Five [118].

daśa-diś (ten directions). Represented by *juppō,* "ten directions." [MW] *Diś:* quarter or region pointed at, direction, cardinal point. Ref: Chapter Sixty (Vol. III); *Lotus Sutra,* chapter 2.

deva (god). Represented by *ten,* "god." [MW] Heavenly, divine; a deity, god. Ref: *Lotus Sutra,* chapter 1.

dhāraṇī (incantation, enchantment). Represented phonetically and by *ju,* "spell, incantation." [MW] A mystical verse or charm used as a kind of prayer to assuage pain, etc. Note: in the *Shōbōgenzō, dhāraṇī* is equated with "personal salutations," i.e., prostrations, with which a practitioner asks a master for the Buddhist teaching. Ref: Chapter Two; Chapter Fifty-five (Vol. III); *Lotus Sutra,* chapter 26.

dharma (Dharma, *dharma*s, reality, method, practice, real *dharma*s, things and phenomena). Represented by *hō,* "law, method." [MW] That which is established or firm, steadfast decree, statute, ordinance, law; usage, practice, customary observance or prescribed conduct, duty; right, justice (often as a synonym of punishment); virtue, morality, religion, religious merit, good works; the law or doctrine of Buddhism; nature, character, peculiar condition or essential quality, property, mark, peculiarity.

dharmacakra (Dharma wheel). Represented by *hōrin,* "Dharma wheel." [MW] The wheel or range of the law; a particular mythical weapon; "having or turning the wheel of the law," a buddha. Ref: Chapter Three [87]; Chapter Seventy-four (Vol. IV); *Lotus Sutra,* chapter 14.

Dharmagupta (name of a Buddhist school). Represented by *hōzō-bu,* "Dharma-storage school." [MW] *Gupta:* protected, guarded, preserved; hidden, concealed, kept secret. One of the twenty Hinayana schools. Ref: Bibliography.

dharmakāya (Dharma body). Represented by *hōsshin,* "Dharma body." [MW] "Law-body," name of one of the three bodies of a buddha. Ref. Chapter Ten [11].

dhātu (elements). Represented by *dai,* "elements" or by *kai,* "spheres." [MW] Layer, stratum; constituent part, ingredient; element, primitive matter (usually reckoned as five, viz., *kha* or *ākāśa* [space], *anila* [wind], *tejas* [fire], *jala* [water], *bhū* [earth], to which Buddhists add *vijñāna* [consciousness]); a constituent element or essential ingredient of the body (distinct from the five mentioned above . . . with the southern Buddhists, *dhātu* means either the six elements; or the eighteen elementary spheres [*dhātuloka,* q.v.]). Ref: Chapter Two.

dhātuloka ([eighteen] elementary spheres). Represented by *jūhachi-kai,* "eighteen spheres." [MW] *Dhātu:* elements. *Loka:* world, sphere [q.v.]. The eighteen elementary spheres are the six *indriya*s (sense organs): 1) *cakṣur-indriya* (organ of sight, eyes), 2) *śrotrendriya* (organ of hearing, ears), 3) *ghrāṇendriya* (organ of smell, nose), 4) *jihvendriya* (the tongue as a sense organ), 5) *kāyendriya* (the body as sense organ, sense of touch), 6) *manendriya* (mind as a sense center, intelligence); the six *viṣaya*s (objects): 1) *rūpa* (forms or colors), 2) *śabda* (sounds), 3) *gandha* (smells), 4) *rasa* (tastes), 5) *sparśa* (sensations), 6) *dharma* (properties); and the six *vijñāna*s (consciousnesses): 1) *cakṣur-vijñāna* (visual consciousness), 2) *śrotra-vijñāna* (auditory consciousness), 3) *ghrāṇa-vijñāna* (olfactory consciousness), 4) *jihvā-vijñāna* (taste consciousness), 5) *kāya-vijñāna* (body consciousness), 6) *mano-vijñāna* (mind consciousness). Ref: Chapter Two.

dhūta (hard practice, austerity). Represented phonetically. [MW] *Dhūta:* morality. *Dhūtaguṇa:* ascetic practice or precept. Ref: Chapter Four; Chapter Thirty (Vol. II); *Lotus Sutra,* chapter 15.

dhyāna (*zen,* concentration, meditation). Represented phonetically by *zen* or *zen-na;* represented also by *jō-ryo,* "quiet meditation." [MW] Meditation, thought, reflection, (esp.) profound and abstract religious meditation. One of the six *pāramitā*s (q.v.). Ref: Chapter Two [71]; *Lotus Sutra,* chapters 7, 27.

dhyāni-buddha. [MW] A spiritual (not material) buddha or bodhisattva.

Dignāga (name of a logician). [JEBD] A native of southern India who lived from the end of the fifth century to the middle of the sixth, and belonged to the school of Vasubandhu. He created a new school of logic using deductive reasoning.

Dīpaṃkara (name of a buddha). Represented by Nentō-butsu, "Burning Lamp Buddha." [MW] "Light-causer," name of a mythical buddha. Ref: Chapter Nine.

duḥkha (suffering). Represented by *ku,* "suffering." [MW] Uneasy, uncomfortable, unpleasant, difficult; uneasiness, pain, sorrow, trouble, difficulty. The first of the four noble truths. Ref: Chapter Two; *Lotus Sutra,* chapter 7.

duṣkṛta (a class of sins). Represented phonetically. [MW] Wrongly or wickedly done, badly arranged or organized or applied; a particular class of sins; a wicked deed, wickedness. Ref: Chapter Seven [158].

dvādaśāṅga-pratītyasamutpāda (twelvefold chain of causation). Represented by *jūni-innen,* "twelvefold [chain of] causation," or by *jūni-rinden,* "twelvefold cycle." See *pratītyasamutpāda.* Ref: Chapter One [32]; *Lotus Sutra,* chapter 7.

dvādaśāyatanāni (twelve seats). Represented by *jūni-nyū,* "twelve entries," or *juni-sho,* "twelve places." See under *āyatana.* Ref: Chapter Two.

Ekottarāgama (name of a sutra). Represented by *Zōichiagonkyō, "Āgama Sutras Increased by One."* [MW] Name of the fourth Āgama or sacred book of the Buddhists. *Ekottara:* greater or more by one, increasing by one. *Āgama* [q.v.]: a traditional doctrine or precept. Ref: Chapter Forty-five (Vol. III); Chapter Eighty-eight (Vol. IV); Bibliography.

gandha (smell). Represented by *kō,* "fragrance, smell." [MW] Smell, odor; a fragrant substance, fragrance, scent, perfume; the mere smell of anything, small quantity. Ref: Chapter Two.

Gandhāra (place name). Represented phonetically. [JEBD] An ancient country in North India, located north of Punjab and northeast of Kashmir. The capital was Puruṣapura, present-day Peshawar. Ref. Chapter Fifteen.

gandharva (fragrance-devouring celestial musicians). Represented phonetically. [MW] *Gandha:* smell, odor; a fragrant substance, fragrance, scent, perfume. *Gandharva:* in epic poetry the *gandharva*s are the celestial musicians or heavenly singers who form the orchestra at the banquets of the gods; they follow after women and are desirous of intercourse with them; they are also feared as evil beings. Ref: *Lotus Sutra,* chapter 10.

garuḍa (king of birds, dragon-devouring bird). Represented phonetically and by *kin-shi-chō-ō,* "golden-winged king of birds." [MW] Name of a mythical bird (chief of the feathered race, enemy of the serpent race). Ref: Chapter Twelve [107]; *Lotus Sutra,* chapter 10.

gāthā (poem, independent verse). Represented phonetically and by *ge,* "verse" or by *fuju,* poetic eulogy." [MW] A song; a verse, stanza; the metrical part of a sutra. One of the twelve divisions of the teachings. See under *aṅga.* Ref: Chapter Eleven [40]; Chapter Twenty-four (Vol. II); *Lotus Sutra,* chapter 10.

geya (verse, summarizing verse). Represented by *ōju,* "adaptational eulogy," or "additional eulogy." [MW] Being sung or praised [in song]. One of the twelve divisions of the teachings. See under *aṅga.* Ref: Chapter Eleven [40]; Chapter Twenty-four (Vol. II).

ghrāṇa (nose, smelling). Represented by *bi,* "nose." [MW] Smelling, perception of odor; smell, odor; the nose. Ref: Chapter Two.

Gṛdhrakūṭa (Vulture Peak). Represented phonetically and by *jusen,* "vulture peak," *ryōzen,* "sacred mountain," or *ryōjusen,* "sacred vulture peak." [MW] "Vulture peak," name of a mountain near Rājāgṛha. Ref: Chapter Seventeen [54]; *Lotus Sutra,* chapter 1.

gṛhapati (householder). Represented by *koji,* "lay gentleman." [MW] The master of a house, householder; householder of peculiar merit. Ref: Chapter Eight [187]; *Lotus Sutra,* chapter 25.

guṇa (virtue, merit). Represented by *kudoku.* [MW] A quality, peculiarity, attribute or property; good quality, virtue, merit, excellence. Ref: Chapter Twelve [54]; *Lotus Sutra,* chapters 17, 18.

hasta (cubit). Represented by *chū,* "elbow." [MW] The forearm (a measure of length from the elbow to the tip of the middle finger = twenty-four *āngula*s or about eighteen inches). Ref: Chapter Twelve [95].

hetu-pratyaya (causes and conditions). Represented phonetically and by *innen,* "causes and conditions." [MW] *Hetu:* "impulse," motive, cause, cause of, reason for. *Pratyaya* (q.v.): a cooperating cause. Ref: Chapter One [32]; *Lotus Sutra,* chapter 2.

Himālaya (the Himalayas). Represented by *setsuzan,* "snowy mountains." [MW] "Abode of snow," the Himalaya range of mountains. Ref. Chapter Twelve; Chapter Sixty-nine (Vol. III).

Hinayana (small vehicle). Represented by *shojo,* "small vehicle." [MW] "Simpler or lesser vehicle," name of the earliest system of Buddhist doctrine (opposed to Mahayana) [q.v.]. Ref: Chapter Thirteen [155].

hṛdaya (heart). Represented by *shin,* "heart," and by *somoku-shin,* "the mind of grass and trees." [MW] The heart, soul, mind; the heart or interior of the body; the heart or center or core or essence or best or dearest or most secret part of anything. One of the three kinds of mind, the others being *citta* and *vṛddha* (q.v.). Ref: Chapter Two; Chapter Seventy (Vol. III).

indriya (sense organ). Represented by *kon,* "root." [MW] Fit for or belonging to or agreeable to Indra; power, force, the quality which belongs especially to the mighty Indra; exhibition of power, powerful act; bodily power, power of the senses; faculty of sense, sense, organ of sense; the number five as symbolical of the five senses. Ref: Chapter Two.

Īśvara ("Almighty," a name of Śiva). Represented by Jizaiten, "God of Free Will." [MW] Able to do, capable of; master, lord, prince, king, mistress, queen; God; the Supreme Being; the supreme soul (*ātman*); Śiva. Ref: Chapter Ten [19]; *Lotus Sutra,* chapter 25.

itivṛttaka (stories of past occurrences). Represented by *honji,* "past occurrences." [MW] *Iti:* in this manner, thus (in its original signification, *iti* refers to something that has been said or thought). *Vṛt:* take place, occur. One of the twelve divisions of the teachings. See under *aṅga.* Ref: Chapter Eleven [40].

Jambudvīpa (the southern continent). Represented phonetically. [MW] The central one of the seven continents surrounding the mountain Meru (India; named so either from the *jambu* trees abounding in it, or from an enormous *jambu* tree on Mount Meru visible like a standard to the whole continent). *Jambu:* rose apple tree. *Dvīpa:* an island, peninsula, sandbank; a division of the terrestrial world (either seven or four or thirteen or eighteen; they are situated around the mountain Meru, and separated from each other by distinct concentric circumambient oceans). Ref: *Lotus Sutra,* chapter 20.

jantu (living beings). Represented by *shūjō,* "living beings," and by *gunshō,* "miscellaneous beings." [MW] Child, offspring, creature, living being. Ref: *Lotus Sutra,* chapter 2.

jātaka (past lives). Represented by *honshō,* "past lives." [MW] Engendered by, born under; the story of a former birth of Gautama Buddha. One of the twelve divisions of the teachings. See under *aṅga.* Ref: Chapter Eleven [40]; Bibliography.

jāti-maraṇa (birth and death). Represented by *shōji,* "birth and death," "life and death," "living-and-dying." [MW] *Jāti:* birth, production; rebirth; the form of existence (as human, animal, etc.). *Maraṇa:* the act of dying. Ref: Chapter Nineteen [95]; Chapter Ninety-two (Vol. IV); *Lotus Sutra,* chapter 16.

Jetavana ("Jetṛi's Park," name of a grove near Śrāvasti). Represented phonetically. [MW] Jeta: in compounds for "Jetṛi" ("Victorious"), the name of a son of King Prasenajit of Kośala. *Vana:* wood, grove. Ref: *Fukanzazengi.*

jihvā (tongue). Represented by *zetsu,* "tongue." [MW] The tongue. Ref: Chapter Two.

jñāna (knowing). Represented by *chi,* "wisdom." [MW] Knowing, becoming acquainted with, knowledge, (especially) higher knowledge (derived from meditation on the one universal spirit). Ref. Chapter Twenty-one [192].

kalpa (eon). Represented phonetically. [MW] A fabulous period of time (at the end of a *kalpa* the world is annihilated). Ref: *Lotus Sutra,* chapter 1.

kalyāṇamitra (good friend, good counselor). Represented by *zen-chishiki,* "good acquaintance." [MW] A friend of virtue; a well-wishing friend; a good counselor. *Kalyāṇa:* beautiful, agreeable; illustrious, noble, generous; excellent, virtuous, good. *Mitra:* friend, companion, associate. Ref: Chapter Twenty-one [183]; *Lotus Sutra,* chapters 12, 18, 27.

kāṇa (one-eyed). Represented phonetically. [MW] One-eyed, monoculous. Ref. Chapter Fifteen.

Kaniṣka (name of a king). Represented phonetically. [JEBD] A ruler of Northern India and Central Asia. He is said to have been the third important king of the Kuśāṇa dynasty, who lived either in the latter half of the first century or the first half of the second century. He established a country called Gandhāra. Converted by Master Aśvaghoṣa, he became a great patron of Buddhism. Ref. Chapter Fifteen.

Kapilavastu (name of a city and country). [JEBD] The capital of the country of the same name. The Buddha was born at Lumbinī on the outskirts of the city. His father, Śuddhodana, was the king of the country. Ref: Chapter Fifteen.

karman (action, form of behavior). Represented by *go.* [MW] Act, action, performance, business. Ref: Chapter One [20]; Chapter Eighty-four (Vol. IV).

karuṇā (compassion). Represented by *hi,* "sadness, compassion." [MW] Mournful, miserable, lamenting; compassionate. Ref: Chapter Twelve [64]; *Lotus Sutra,* chapter 12.

Karuṇāpuṇḍarīka-sūtra (*Sutra of the Flower of Compassion*). Represented by *Higekyō,* "Flower of Compassion Sutra." [MW] *Karuṇā:* mournful, miserable, lamenting; compassionate. *Puṇḍarīka:* a lotus flower (especially a white lotus; expressive of beauty). Ref: Chapter Twelve [80]; Bibliography.

kaṣāya (robe). Represented phonetically and by *ejiki,* "broken color." [MW] Red, dull red, yellowish-red (as the garment of a Buddhist *bhikṣu*); a yellowish-red color; a dull or yellowish-red garment or robe. Ref: Chapter Twelve [107].

Kauśika. Represented phonetically. [MW] Relating to Kuśika [the father of Viśvāmitra]; name of Indra (as originally perhaps belonging to the Kuśikas [descendants of Kuśika] or friendly to them). Ref: Chapter Two.

kāya (body). Represented by *shin,* "body." [MW] The body; the trunk of a tree; the body of a lute (the whole except the wires). Ref: Chapter Two.

kiṃnara (half horse, half man). Represented phonetically. [MW] "What sort of man?", a mythical being with a human figure and the head of a horse (or with a horse's body and the head of a man; in later times reckoned among the *gandharva*s or celestial choristers, and celebrated as musicians). Ref: *Lotus Sutra,* chapter 10.

kleśa (affliction, trouble). Represented by *bonnō,* "affliction, trouble, hindrance." [MW] Pain, affliction, distress, pain from disease, anguish; wrath, anger; worldly occupation, care, trouble. Ref: Chapter Twelve [54]; *Lotus Sutra,* chapter 1.

Kośala (place name) [HB] Name of an ancient Indian kingdom situated to the north of the river Ganges and containing the cities of Śrāvasti and Vārāṇasī (present-day Benares). One of the two main kingdoms (together with Magadha [q.v.]) determining the political scene in the areas covered by the Buddha in his travels.

koṭi (tens of millions). Represented by *oku,* "hundred millions." [MW] The curved end of a bow or of claws, end or top of anything, edge or point; the highest number in the older system of numbers (viz., a crore or ten millions). Ref: *Lotus Sutra,* chapter 2.

krośa (a measure of distance). Represented phonetically. [MW] A cry, yell, shriek, shout; "the range of the voice in calling or hallooing," a measure of distance (= one-quarter *yojana;* according to others = eight thousand *hasta*s).

kṣama (confession). Represented by *sange,* "*kṣama*-repentance." [MW] Patience, forbearance, indulgence. Ref: Chapter Nine [236].

kṣāṇa (moment, instant, instantaneous). Represented phonetically. [MW] Any instantaneous point of time, instant, twinkling of an eye, moment. Ref: Chapter One [134]; Chapter Twelve [64]; *Lotus Sutra,* chapter 12.

kṣānti (patience, endurance, forbearance). Represented by *annin,* "calm endurance" or "bearing patiently." [MW] Patient waiting for anything; patience, forbearance, endurance, indulgence. One of the six *pāramitā*s (q.v.). Ref: Chapter Two; *Lotus Sutra,* chapter 27.

kṣatriya (ruling class). Represented phonetically.[MW] Governing, endowed with sovereignty; a member of the military or reigning order (which in later times constituted the second caste). Ref. Chapter Eight.

kṣaya (exhausting, end). Represented by *jin,* "exhaust." [MW] Loss, waste, wane, diminution, destruction, decay, wasting or wearing away; removal; end, termination; consumption; the destruction of the universe. Ref: *Lotus Sutra,* chapter 1.

kṣetra (countries, lands, temple). Represented phonetically and by *setsudo,* "*kṣetra*-land." [MW] Landed property, land, soil; place, region, country; a house; a town; department, sphere of action; a sacred spot or district, place of pilgrimage; an enclosed plot of ground, portion of space. Ref: Chapter One [62].

Kṣudrakāgama (name of a sutra). Represented by *Shōagonkyō,* "Small Āgama Sutra." [MW] *Kṣudraka:* small, minute. *Āgama* [q.v.]: a traditional doctrine or precept. Ref: Bibliography.

Kukkuṭapāda (name of a mountain). Represented by *keisoku,* "cock foot." [MW] "Cock-foot," name of a mountain. [JEBD] The name of a mountain in Magadha, Central India, where Mahākāśyapa died. Present-day Kurkeihar, sixteen miles northeast of Gayā. Ref. Chapter One [66]; Chapter Fifteen.

kulaputra (good sons). Represented by *zen-nanshi,* "good sons." [MW] A son of a noble family, respectable youth. *Kulaputrī:* the daughter of a good family, respectable girl. Ref: Chapter Twelve [80]; *Lotus Sutra,* chapter 1.

Kumārajīva (name of a translator). Represented phonetically. [MW] The plant *putraṃjīva.* Ref: *Lotus Sutra.*

kumbhāṇḍa (name of a class of demons). Represented phonetically. [MW] "Having testicles shaped like *kumbha,*" a class of demons. *Kumbha:* jar, pitcher, water pot. Ref: Chapter Twelve [80].

Lalitavistara-sūtra (name of a sutra). Represented by *Fuyōkyō,* "Sutra of the Diffusion of Shining [Artlessness]." [MW] Name of a sutra work giving a detailed account of the artless and natural acts in the life of the Buddha. *Lalita:* artless, innocent; beautiful. *Vistara:* spreading, extension, diffuseness. Ref: Chapter Twelve [98]; Bibliography.

loka (world). Represented by *kai,* "world, sphere." [MW] Free or open space, room, place, scope, free motion; a tract, region, district, country, province; the wide space or world (either "the universe" or "any division of it"); the earth or world of human beings; the inhabitants of the world, humankind, folk, people; ordinary life, worldly affairs. Ref: Chapter Two.

Madhyamāgama (name of a sutra). Represented by *Chūagonkyō,* "Middle Āgama Sutra." [MW] *Madhyama:* middle. *Āgama* [q.v.]: a traditional doctrine or precept. Ref: Chapter Twelve [115].

Madhyamaka (name of a school). Represented by *chūgan-ha,* "middle view school." [MW] Relating to the middle region; name of a Buddhist school. [JEBD] One of the two major Mahayana schools in India (together with the Yogācāra). The basic statement of the doctrines of this school is found in Master Nāgārjuna's *Madhyamaka-kārikā.* Ref. Chapter Fifteen.

Madhyamaka-kārikā (name of seminal work by Master Nāgārjuna). [MW] *Madhyamaka:* relating to the middle region. *Kārikā:* concise statement in verse of (especially philosophical and grammatical) doctrines. Ref. Chapter Fifteen.

Magadha (place name). [HB] An ancient state in central India stretching along the southern bank of the Ganges, with its capital at Rājagṛha. One of the two main kingdoms (together with Kośala, q.v.) determining the political scene in the central Gangetic plain in the sixth century B.C.E. It was in Magadha that the Buddha realized the truth and first turned the Dharma wheel. Ref: Chapter Twenty [125].

Mahāratnakūṭa-sūtra (name of a sutra). Represented by *Daihōshakkyō,* "Great Treasure Accumulation Sutra." [MW] *Ratna:* treasure. *Kūṭa:* a heap. Ref: Chapter Twelve; Chapter Fourteen; Chapter Eighty-four (Vol. IV); Bibliography.

Mahāsaṃghika ("Of the Great Sangha," name of a Buddhist school). Represented phonetically and by *daishubu,* "great sangha school." Together with the Theravāda school, one of the two principal schools of Hinayana Buddhism. Ref: Chapter Seven [165].

Mahāsaṃnipāta-sūtra (name of a sutra). Represented by *Daijikkyō,* "Great Aggregation Sutra." [MW] *Saṃnipāta:* falling in or down together, collapse, meeting, encounter; conjunction, aggregation, combination, mixture. Ref: Chapter Eighty-six (Vol. IV); Chapter Eighty-eight (Vol. IV); Bibliography.

mahāsattva (great being). Represented phonetically. [MW] Mahāsattva: a great creature, large animal; having a great or noble essence; noble, good (of persons); name of Gautama Buddha as heir to the throne. Mahā: great. Sattva: being. Ref: Chapter Two; *Lotus Sutra,* chapter 1.

Mahayana (Great Vehicle). Represented by *daijō,* "great vehicle." [MW] Great vehicle. Ref: Chapter Eight [198]; *Lotus Sutra,* chapter 1.

Maheśvara (name of Śiva). Represented by Daijizaiten, "Great God of Free Will." [MW] A great archer; name of Śiva (q.v.). Ref: Chapter Ten [19]; *Lotus Sutra,* chapter 25.

mahoraga (serpent). Represented phonetically. [MW] A great serpent (with Buddhists a class of demons). Ref: *Lotus Sutra,* chapter 10.

maitreya (benevolence). Represented phonetically and by *zu, ji,* "love, affection, pity." [MW] Friendly, benevolent; name of a bodhisattva and future buddha (the fifth of the present age). Ref: Chapter Twelve [64]; *Lotus Sutra,* chapter 1.

manas (mind, will). Represented by *i,* "intention." [MW] *Manas:* mind (in the widest sense as applied to all the mental powers), intellect, intelligence, understanding, perception, sense, conscience, will. Ref: Chapter Two; Chapter Ten.

maṇḍala (circle). See *pañca maṇḍalaka.*

mandārava (name of a tree and of its flowers). Represented phonetically. [MW] The coral tree. Ref: Chapter Forty-two (Vol. III); *Lotus Sutra,* chapter 16.

maṇi (jewel, gem). Represented phonetically. [MW] Jewel, gem, pearl. See also *cintāmaṇi.* Ref: Chapter Fourteen [189].

Mañjuśrī (name of a bodhisattva). Represented phonetically. [MW] Name of one of the most celebrated bodhisattvas among the northern Buddhists. Ref: Chapter Seventeen [39]; *Lotus Sutra,* chapter 12.

mantra (mantra). Represented by *shingon,* "truth-word." [MW] "Instrument of thought," speech, sacred text or speech, a prayer or song of praise; a Vedic hymn or sacrificial formula; a sacred formula addressed to any individual deity; a mystical verse or magical formula, incantation, charm, spell. Ref: Chapter One [51].

māra-pāpīyas (deadly demons, demons of death). Represented phonetically and by *shima,* "demons of death." [MW] *Māra:* the world of death, killing, the inhabitants of hell. *Pāpīyas:* worse, lower, poorer, more or most wicked or miserable; (with Buddhists) *mārah̩-pāpīyān,* the evil spirit, the devil. Ref: Chapter Nine [232]; Chapter Seventy (Vol. III) [216]; *Lotus Sutra,* chapter 3.

mārga (path, way). Represented by *dō,* "the Way." [MW] Seeking, search, tracing out, hunting; the track of a wild animal, any track, road, path, way to or through (in compounds), course (also of the wind and the stars); a way, manner, method, custom, usage; the right way, proper course. The last of the four noble truths. Ref: Chapter Two; *Lotus Sutra,* chapter 7.

Maudgalyāyana (name of a disciple of the Buddha). Represented phonetically. [MW] Name of a pupil of Gautama Buddha. Ref: Chapter Twelve [98].

moha (delusion, ignorance). Represented by *chi* or *guchi,* "foolishness." [MW] Loss of consciousness, bewilderment, perplexity, distraction, infatuation, delusion, error, folly; (in philosophy) darkness or delusion of mind; (with Buddhists) ignorance (one of the three roots of vice). Ref: Chapter Eight [194].

mudrā (seal, stamp). Represented by *in,* "seal." [MW] A seal or any instrument used for sealing or stamping, a seal ring, signet ring, any ring; any stamp or print or mark or impression; an image, sign, badge, token; name of particular positions or intertwinings of the fingers (twenty-four in number, commonly practiced in religious worship, and supposed to possess an occult meaning and magical efficacy). Ref: Chapter Nineteen [90]; Chapter Thirty-one (Vol. II); *Lotus Sutra,* chapter 2.

muhūrta (moment, short space of time). Represented phonetically. [MW] A moment, instant, any short space of time; a particular division of time, the thirtieth part of a day, a period of forty-eight minutes. Ref: Chapter Twelve [64].

muktāhāra. Represented by *yōraku,* "necklace-ornament." [MW] A string of pearls. Ref: Chapter Three [90]; *Lotus Sutra,* chapter 10.

mūla (root, fundamental). Represented by *kon,* "root." [MW] "Firmly fixed," a root; basis, foundation, cause, origin, commencement, beginning.

Mūlasarvāstivādin (name of a school). Represented by *konpon-setsu-issai-i-bu,* "Original School of the Preaching That All Things Exist." [MW] *Mūla* (q.v.): fundamental.

Sarvāstivāda (q.v.): the doctrine that all things are real. The prefix "*mūla*" was later added because many schools derived from the Sarvāstivādins. Ref: Chapter One.

nāga (dragon). Represented by *ryū,* "dragon." [MW] A snake; a serpent-demon (they are supposed to have a human face with serpentlike lower extremities; with Buddhists they are also represented as ordinary men). Ref: *Lotus Sutra,* chapter 10.

Nāgārjuna (name of a Buddhist patriarch). Represented phonetically and by *ryūju,* "dragon tree." [MW] *Nāga:* a snake; a serpent demon. *Arjuna:* the tree *Terminalia arjuna.* Ref: Chapter Twelve; Chapter Fifteen.

naraka (hell). Represented phonetically and by *jigoku,* "hell." [MW] Hell, place of torment. Ref: Chapter Twelve [87].

nayuta (numerical unit, equal to one hundred *ayuta*). Represented phonetically. [MW] *Ayuta:* "unjoined, unbounded," ten thousand, a myriad; in compounds a term of praise. Ref: *Lotus Sutra,* chapter 16.

nidāna (historical accounts [of causes and conditions]). Represented by *innen,* "causes and conditions." [MW] A band, rope, halter; a first or primary cause; original form or essence; any cause or motive; pathology. One of the twelve divisions of the teachings. See under *aṅga.* Ref: Chapter Eleven [40].

nirodha (dissolution, cessation). Represented by *metsu,* "death, destruction, annihilation." [MW] Confinement, locking up, imprisonment; enclosing, covering up; restraint, check, control, suppression, destruction; (with Buddhists) suppression or annihilation of pain. Note: in *Shōbōgenzō,* the third phase of Master Dōgen's four-phased system is negation of the intellectual views of the first two phases, namely, idealism and materialism. On that basis, *nirodha* may be interpreted not as suppression of pain but rather as dissolution of, or liberation from, the intellectual restraints of idealism and materialism. Ref: Chapter Two; *Lotus Sutra,* chapter 7.

nirvāṇa (extinction). Represented phonetically and by *jakumetsu,* "death, annihilation, extinction, nirvana." [MW] Blown or put out, extinguished (as a lamp or fire), set (as the sun), calmed, quieted, tamed, dead, deceased (lit., having the fire of life extinguished). Ref: Chapter One [45]; *Lotus Sutra,* chapter 2.

niṣīdana (sitting mat, prostration cloth). Represented by *zagu,* "sitting gear." [MW] *Niṣadana:* sitting down. Ref: Chapter Two [104].

nitya (eternal). Represented by *jōjū,* "constantly abiding," "eternal." [MW] Innate, native; continual, perpetual, eternal; constantly dwelling or engaged in, intent upon, devoted or used to; ordinary, usual, invariable; always, constantly, regularly. Ref: Chapter One [45]; Chapter Fourteen; *Lotus Sutra,* chapter 2.

pada (phrase). Represented by *ku,* "phrase." [MW] A step, pace, stride; the foot itself; a part, portion, division; a plot of ground; the foot as a measure of length; a portion of a verse, quarter or line of a stanza. Ref: Chapter One [9]; *Lotus Sutra,* chapter 10.

pāṃsu-kūla (a dust heap, rags). Represented by *funzō,* "filth-swept." [MW] A dust heap, (especially) a collection of rags out of a dust heap used by Buddhist monks for their clothing. Ref: Chapter Twelve [71].

pañca dṛṣṭayaḥ (five [wrong] views). Represented by *goken,* "five views." [MW] *Pañca:* five. *Dṛṣṭi:* seeing, viewing, beholding; view, notion; (with Buddhists) a wrong view; theory, doctrine, system. The five are *satkāya-dṛṣṭi, shinken,* the personality view; *antagrāha-dṛṣṭi, henken,* extremism; *mithyā-dṛṣṭi, jaken,* atheism; *dṛṣṭi-parāmarśa, ken ju-ken,* dogmatism; *śilavrata-parāmarśa, kaigonju-ken,* attachment to precepts and observances. Ref: Chapter Twelve [107].

pañca maṇḍalaka (five circles). Represented by *gorin,* "five circles, five wheels." [MW] *Pañca:* five. *Maṇḍala:* circular, round; a disk; anything round; a circle, globe, orb, ring, circumference, ball, wheel. Ref: Chapter Fourteen [189].

pañca viṣaya (five objects [of desire]). Represented by *goyoku,* "five desires." [MW] *Pañca:* five. *Viṣaya* (q.v.): sense object. Ref: Chapter Twelve [107].

pārājika (violation of the precepts warranting expulsion from the community). Represented phonetically. [MW] *Pāra:* far, distant, beyond, extreme, exceeding. *Aj:* to drive, propel, throw, cast. *Ka:* suffix added to nouns to express diminution, deterioration, or similarity. Ref: Chapter Eight [192].

paramāṇu (atom). Represented by *mijin,* "particle." [MW] An infinitesimal particle or atom. Ref: Chapter Seventeen [54]; *Lotus Sutra,* chapter 16.

pāramitā (an accomplishment). Represented phonetically and by *do,* which represents *do,* "to cross over" or "to have crossed over." [MW] Gone to the opposite shore; crossed, traversed, transcendent, coming or leading to the opposite shore, complete attainment, perfection in (compounds); transcendental virtue, accomplishment (there are six or ten, viz., *dāna, śīla, kṣanti, vīrya, dhyāna, prajñā,* to which are sometimes added *satya, adhiṣṭhāna, maitra,* and *upekśā*). Ref: Chapter Two; *Lotus Sutra,* chapter 27.

pariṇāma (dedication). Represented by *ekō,* "turning," "[merit]-transference," "dedication." [MW] Change, alteration, transformation into, development, evolution; ripeness, maturity; alteration of food, digestion; result, consequence, issue, end. Ref: Chapter Twenty-one [209].

parinirvāṇa (complete extinction). Represented phonetically. [MW] Completely extinguished or finished. Ref: Chapter Twenty-four (Vol. II).

parivāra (followers). Represented by *kenzoku,* "kin." [MW] Surroundings, train, suite, dependents, followers. Ref: Chapter Seventy-two (Vol. III); *Lotus Sutra,* chapter 1.

parṣad (followers). Represented by *kenzoku,* "kin." [MW] Assembly, audience, company. Ref: Chapter Seventy-two (Vol. III); *Lotus Sutra,* chapter 1.

pātra (bowl). Represented by *hatsu-u, pātra*-bowl. [MW] A drinking vessel, goblet, bowl, cup, dish, pot, plate, utensil, etc.; any vessel or receptacle. Ref: Chapter Five [122]; Chapter Seventy-eight (Vol. IV).

piṇḍavana (monastery). Represented by *sōrin,* "thicket-forest" or "clump of forest." [MW] *Piṇḍa:* any round or roundish mass. *Vana:* forest, wood, grove, thicket, quantity of lotuses or other plants growing in a thick cluster. Ref: Chapter One [65]; Chapter Five [122].

piśāca (name of a class of demons). Represented phonetically. [MW] Name of a class of demons (possibly so called either from their fondness for flesh [*piśa* for *piśita*] or from their yellowish appearance). *Piśita:* flesh which has not been cut up or prepared, any flesh or meat. Ref: Chapter Twelve [80].

Prabhūtaratna (name of a Buddha). Represented by Tahō, "Abundant Treasures." [MW] Name of a Buddha. *Prabhūta:* abundant, much, numerous. *Ratna:* a gift, present, goods, wealth, riches; a jewel, gem, treasure. Ref: Chapter Twelve [95]; *Lotus Sutra,* chapter 11.

prajñā (real wisdom). Represented phonetically and by *chiken,* "knowing," or *e,* "wisdom." [MW] Wisdom, intelligence, knowledge, discrimination, judgment; (with Buddhists) true or transcendental wisdom. One of the six *pāramitā*s (q.v.). Ref: Chapter Two; *Lotus Sutra,* chapters 2, 27.

Prasenajit (name of a king). Represented phonetically. [HB] The king of Kośala who resided in Śrāvastī (q.v.) and became a lay follower of the Buddha and supporter of the Buddhist order. Ref. *Fukanzazengi*; Chapter Fifty-nine (Vol. III).

pratītyasamutpāda (dependent origination). Represented by *engi,* "arising from conditions, origin, origination," and by *innen,* "causes and conditions." [MW] *Pratīti:* going toward, approaching; the following from anything (as a necessary result), being clear or intelligible by itself. *Samutpāda:* rise, origin, production. Ref: Chapter One [32]; *Lotus Sutra,* chapter 7.

pratyaya (cooperating cause). Represented by *en,* "relation, connection, circumstance, condition." [MW] Belief, firm conviction, trust, faith, assurance of certainty; proof, ascertainment; (with Buddhists) fundamental notion or idea; consciousness, understanding, intelligence, intellect; analysis, solution, explanation, definition; ground, basis, motive, or cause of anything; (with Buddhists) a cooperating cause; the concurrent occasion of an event as distinguished from its approximate cause.

pratyekabuddha (sensory Buddhist). Represented phonetically by *doku-kaku,* "independent realization" and by *engaku,* "realizer of conditions." [MAC] Solitary Buddha who works out his individual salvation only. Ref: *Lotus Sutra,* chapter 2.

preta (hungry ghost). Represented by *gaki,* "hungry ghost." [MW] Departed, deceased, dead, a dead person; the spirit of a dead person (especially before obsequial rites are performed), a ghost, an evil being. Ref: Chapter Twelve [80].

pṛthagjana (common person). Represented by *bonbu,* "common person." [MW] A person of lower caste or character or profession. Ref: Chapter Nineteen [11].

puṇya-kṣetra (field of virtue). Represented by *fukuden,* "field of good fortune," "field of happiness." [MW] A holy place, a place of pilgrimage; name of Buddha. *Puṇya:* auspicious, propitious, fair, pleasant, good, right, virtuous, meritorious, pure, holy, sacred; the good or right, virtue, purity, good work, meritorious act, moral or religious merit. *Kṣetra* (q.v.): place, sphere of action; plot of ground. Ref: Chapter Twelve [120]; Chapter Thirteen; Chapter Eighty-four (Vol. IV) [37].

puruṣa (human being). Represented by *nin,* "person, human being," and by *jōbu,* "stout fellow." [MW] A man, male, human being; a person; a friend; the personal and animating principle in humans and other beings, the soul or spirit. Ref: Chapter Eight [169].

Rāgarāja (King of Love). Represented by Aizenmyōō, "King with the Hue of Love." [MW] *Rāga:* the act of coloring or dyeing; color, hue, tint, dye, (especially) red color, redness; inflammation; any feeling or passion, (especially) love, affection or sympathy for, vehement desire of. *Rāja:* king. Ref: Chapter Eleven [29].

Rāhula (name of a son and disciple of the Buddha). Represented phonetically. Ref: Chapter Seven [163].

Rājagṛha (name of a city). Represented by Ōshajō, "City of Royal Palaces." [HB] Capital of the ancient Indian kingdom of Magadha, where the Buddha first realized the truth, and the site of the First Council following the Buddha's death. Ref: *Lotus Sutra,* chapter 1.

rasa (taste, flavor). Represented by *mi,* "taste." [MW] The sap or juice of plants, juice of fruit, any liquid or fluid, the best or finest part of anything; taste, flavor (as the principal quality of fluids, of which there are six original kinds); any object of taste, condiment, sauce, spice, seasoning; the tongue (as the organ of taste); taste or inclination or fondness for; the taste or character of a work. Ref: Chapter Two.

Ratnagarbha (name of a Buddha). Represented by Hōzō, "Jewel Treasury." [MW] Filled with precious stones, containing jewels, set with jewels; name of a bodhisattva. *Ratna:* a jewel, gem, treasure. *Garbha:* the womb; the inside, middle, interior of anything; an inner apartment, sleeping-room; any interior chamber, adytum or sanctuary of a temple. Ref: Chapter Twelve [80].

ṛddipāda (basis of mystical power, excellent disciple). Represented by *jin-soku,* "mystical foot." [MW] One of the four constituent parts of supernatural power. *Ṛddi:* success; accomplishment, perfection, supernatural power. *Pāda* (q.v.): foot. Ref: Chapter Eight [178]; Chapter Twenty [163].

ṛṣi (hermit, sage). Represented by *sen,* "hermit, wizard." [MW] A singer of sacred hymns, an inspired poet or sage, any person who alone or with others invokes the deities in rhythmical speech or song of a sacred character; [they] were regarded by later generations as patriarchal sages or saints, occupying the same position in Indian history as the heroes and patriarchs of other countries, and constitute a peculiar class of beings in the early mythical system; they are the authors or rather seers of the Vedic hymns. Ref: Chapter Fourteen; Chapter Fifteen.

rūpa (matter, form). Represented by *shiki,* "color, form." [MW] Any outward appearance or phenomenon or color, form, shape, figure; (with Buddhists) material form. One of the five *skandha*s (q.v.). Ref: Chapter Two.

śabda (sound). Represented by *shō,* "sound, voice." [MW] Sound, noise, voice, tone, note; a word; speech, language; the right word, correct expression. Ref: Chapter Two.

saddharma (wonderful Dharma, right Dharma). Represented by *myōhō,* "wonderful/fine/wonderful Dharma" and by *shōbō,* "right/true Dharma." [MW] The good law, true justice; (with Buddhists) designation of the Buddhist doctrines. *Sat:* being, existing; real, actual, as anyone or anything ought to be, true, good, right, beautiful, wise, venerable, honest. Ref: Chapter One [11]; Chapter Seventeen; *Lotus Sutra,* chapter 1.

saddharma-pratirūpaka ([the age of] imitation of the right Dharma). Represented by *zōbō,* "imitative Dharma." [MW] *Saddharma:* right Dharma (q.v.). *Pratirūpaka:* an image, a picture; forgery; similar, corresponding, having the appearance of anything; a quack, a charlatan. Ref: Chapter One; *Lotus Sutra,* chapter 20.

Saddharmapuṇḍarīka-sūtra (*Sutra of the Lotus Flower of the Wonderful Dharma*). Represented by *Myōhōrengekyō,* "Sutra of the Lotus Flower of the Wonderful Dharma." [MW] *Saddharma:* wonderful Dharma (q.v.). *Puṇḍarīka:* a lotus flower (especially a white lotus; expressive of beauty). Ref: Chapter Seventeen; *Lotus Sutra,* chapter 1; Bibliography.

saddharma-vipralopa ([the age of] annihilation of the right Dharma). Represented by *mappō,* "the end of the Dharma," "the latter Dharma." [MW] *Saddharma:* right Dharma (q.v.). *Vipralopa:* destruction, annihilation. Ref: Chapter One.

sādhu (good). Represented by *zenzai,* "How good!" [MW] Straight, right; leading straight to a goal, hitting the mark, unerring (as an arrow or thunderbolt); straightened, not entangled; well-disposed, kind, willing, obedient; successful, effective, efficient; peaceful, secure; powerful, excellent; fit, proper, right; good, virtuous. Ref: Chapter Twelve [80]; *Lotus Sutra,* chapter 28.

sāgara (ocean). Represented phonetically. [MW] The ocean; (plural) the sons of Sāgara (a legend asserts that the bed of the ocean was dug by the sons of Sāgara [who was a king of the solar race]). Ref: *Lotus Sutra,* chapter 12.

sahālokadhātu (the human world). Represented by *shaba-sekai,* "*sahā* world." [MW] *Sahā:* (with Buddhists) name of a division of the world. *Loka:* world. *Dhātu:* layer, stratum; part. Ref: Chapter Four; *Lotus Sutra,* chapter 12.

Śakra-devānām-indra (the god Indra). Represented phonetically and by Tentai-shaku, "the God-Emperor Śakra." [MW] *Śakra:* strong, powerful, mighty (applied to various gods, but especially to Indra). *Deva:* heavenly, divine; a deity, god; the gods as the heavenly or shining ones; name of Indra as the god of the sky and giver of rain. Indra: the god of the atmosphere and sky; the Indian Jupiter Pluvius or lord of rain (who in Vedic mythology reigns over the deity of the intermediate region or atmosphere; he fights against and conquers with his thunderbolt [*vajra*] the demons of darkness, and is in general a symbol of generous heroism; Indra was not originally lord of the gods of the sky, but his deeds were most useful to mankind, and he was therefore addressed in prayers and hymns more than any other deity; in the later mythology Indra is subordinated to the triad Brahmā, Viṣnu, and Śiva, but remained the chief of all other deities in the popular mind). Ref: Chapter Two; *Lotus Sutra,* chapter 1.

sakṛdāgāmin (the state of returning only once again). Represented phonetically and by *ichi-rai-ka,* "the effect [which is subject to] one return." [MW] "Returning only once again." Ref: Chapter Two.

Śākyamuni (name of the Buddha). Represented phonetically or by Shakuson, "Honored Śākya." [MW] *Śākya:* the Buddha's family name. *Muni:* a saint, sage, seer, ascetic, monk, devotee, hermit (especially one who has taken the vow of silence). Ref: *Lotus Sutra,* chapter 1.

samādhi (the balanced state, the state). Represented phonetically or by *jō,* "definite, fixed, constant, regular." [MW] Setting to rights, adjustment, settlement. Ref: Chapter One [11]; *Lotus Sutra,* chapters 2, 24.

Samantabhadra (name of a bodhisattva). Represented by Fugen, "Universal Wisdom" or "Universal Virtue." [MW] Wholly auspicious; name of a bodhisattva. Ref: Chapter Seventeen [39]; *Lotus Sutra,* chapter 28.

samantamukha (universal gate, all-sidedness). Represented by *fumon,* "universal gate" or "all-sidedness." [MW] *Samanta:* "having the ends together," contiguous, neighboring, adjacent; "being on every side," universal, whole, entire, all. *Mukha:* the mouth, face, countenance; a direction, quarter; the mouth or spout of a vessel, opening, aperture, entrance into or egress out of. Ref: Chapter Seventeen [54]; *Lotus Sutra,* chapter 25.

śamatha (quiet). Represented by *shi,* "ceasing, quieting." [MW] Quiet, tranquility, absence of passion. Note: *Shikan,* "quieting and reflecting," representing the Sanskrit *śamatha* and *vipaśyanā* (q.v.), is a fundamental practice of the Tendai sect. Ref: Chapter One [51].

saṃgha (sangha, the community). Represented by *sō,* "monks," and by *shū,* "the multitude." [MW] "Close contact or combination," any collection or assemblage, heap, multitude, quantity, crowd, host, number; any number of people living together for a certain purpose, a society, association, company, community; a clerical community, congregation, church; (especially) the whole community or collective body or brotherhood of monks. Ref: Chapter Two [74]; *Lotus Sutra,* chapter 26.

saṃghārāma (temple). Represented phonetically and by *in,* "temple." [MW] "Resting place for a company (of monks)," a Buddhist convent or monastery. Ref: Chapter Twenty-one [209]; Chapter Eighty-four (Vol. IV).

saṃghāṭi (large robe). Represented phonetically and by *dai-e,* "large robe." [MW] A kind of garment, a monk's robe. *Saṃghāṭa:* fitting and joining of timber, joinery. Ref: Chapter Twelve [80], [95].

saṃjñā (thinking). Represented by *sō,* "idea, thought." [MW] Agreement, mutual understanding, harmony; consciousness, clear knowledge or understanding or notion or conception. One of the five skandhas (q.v.). Ref: Chapter Two.

saṃsāra (wandering). Represented by *ruten,* "wandering, constant change," by *rinden,* "turning of the wheel," "revolving," or by *rinne,* "transmigration." [MW] Going or wandering through, undergoing transmigration; course, passage, passing through a succession of states, circuit of mundane existence, transmigration, the world, secular life, worldly illusion. Ref: Chapter Six [125]; Chapter Eight [198]; Chapter Seventeen [54].

saṃskāra (enaction, action). Represented by *gyō,* "doing, acting, carrying out." [MW] Putting together, forming well, making perfect, accomplishment, embellishment, preparation, refining, polishing, rearing; cleansing the body; forming the mind, training, education; correction, correct formation or use of a word; the faculty of memory, mental impression, or recollection; (with Buddhists) a mental conformation or creation of the mind. However, *saṃskāra* need not always be limited to the mental sphere. *Saṃskāra* is the second link in the twelvefold chain of causation, and one of the five *skandha*s (q.v.). Ref: Chapter Two; *Lotus Sutra,* chapter 7.

saṃskṛta (put together, artificial). Represented by *u-i,* "presence of becoming," "made," "artificial" (opposite of *mu-i;* see *asaṃskṛta*). [MW] Put together, constructed, well or completely formed, perfected; made ready; prepared, completed, finished; dressed, cooked; purified, consecrated; refined, adorned, ornamented, polished, highly elaborated (especially applied to highly wrought speech). Ref: Chapter One [62]; Chapter Nineteen [118].

samudaya (accumulation). Represented by *shu,* "collection, accumulation." Second of the four noble truths. Ref: Chapter One; *Lotus Sutra,* chapter 7.

Saṃyuktāgama (name of a sutra). Represented by *Zōagonkyō,* "Miscellaneous Āgama Sutra." [MW] *Sam:* conjunction expressing "conjunction." *Saṃyukta:* joined, united, connected, combined, following in regular succession. *Āgama* [q.v.]: a traditional doctrine or precept. Ref: Chapter Eighty-five (Vol. IV); Bibliography.

Śāṇavāsa (name of the third patriarch). Represented phonetically. [MW] *Śāṇa:* made of hemp or Bengal flax, hempen, flaxen, etc. *Vāsa:* a garment, dress, clothes. Ref: Chapter Twelve [74]; Chapter Fifteen.

Śāriputra (name of a disciple of the Buddha). Represented phonetically. [MW] *Śāri:* from Rūpaśārī, the name of Śāriputra's mother. *Putra:* son, child. Ref: Chapter Two; *Lotus Sutra,* chapter 2.

śarīra (bones). Represented phonetically. [MW] The body, bodily frame, solid parts of the body (pl. the bones); a dead body. Ref: Chapter Seventy-one (Vol. III); *Lotus Sutra,* chapter 10.

Sarvāstivāda (the doctrine that all is real). Represented by *setsu-issasi-u-bu,* "School that Preaches that All Things Exist." [MW] *Sarva:* all. *Asti:* existent, present. *Vāda:* speaking of or about; speech, discourse, talk, utterance, statement; a thesis, proposition, argument, doctrine. Sarvāstivāda: the doctrine that all things are real (name of one of the four divisions of the Vaibhāṣika system of Buddhism, said to have been founded by Rāhula, son of the great Buddha). Sarvāstivādin: an adherent of the above doctrine. Ref: Chapter One [45]; Chapter Eighty-seven (Vol. IV) [171].

sāsrava (having that which is superfluous, tainted). Represented by *uro,* "with leakage." [MW] (With Jainas) connected with the act called *āsrava* (q.v.). Ref. Chapter Twenty-one [192].

śāstra (commentary). Represented by *ron,* "doctrine, discussion, argument." [MW] An order, command, precept, rule; teaching, instruction, direction, advice, good counsel; any instrument of teaching, any manual or compendium of rules, any book or treatise.

satya (truth). Represented by *tai,* "clarity, enlightenment, truth," as in *shitai,* "the four [noble] truths." [MW] Truth, reality; speaking the truth, sincerity, veracity; a solemn asseveration, vow, promise, oath; demonstrated conclusion, dogma; the quality of goodness or purity or knowledge. Ref: Chapter Two.

Senika (name of a person). Represented phonetically. A non-Buddhist who questions the Buddha in the *Garland Sutra.* Ref: Chapter One [45]; Chapter Six.

śikṣā (training, learning). See *tisraḥ śikṣāḥ.*

śīla (moral conduct). Represented by *jokai,* "pure [observance of] precepts." [MW] Habit, custom, usage, natural or acquired way of living or acting, practice, conduct, disposition, tendency, character, nature; good disposition or character, moral conduct, integrity, morality, piety, virtue; a moral precept. One of the six *pāramitās* (q.v.). Ref: Chapter Two; *Lotus Sutra,* chapter 27.

sīmā-bandha (sanctuary). Represented by *kekkai,* "bounded area." [MW] A depository of rules of morality. Ref: Chapter Eight [198].

Śiva (name of the destroying deity in the Hindu triad). Represented by Jizaiten, "God of Free Will." [MW] "The Auspicious One," name of the disintegrating or destroying and reproducing deity (who constitutes the third god of the Hindu triad, the other two being Brahmā, "the creator" and Viṣṇu, "the preserver"); in the Veda the only name of the destroying deity was Rudra, "the terrible god," but in later times it became usual to give that god the euphemistic name Śiva, "the auspicious." Ref: Chapter Ten [19]; *Lotus Sutra,* chapter 25.

skandha (aggregate). Represented by *un,* "accumulations," or by *shū,* "multitudes." [MW] The shoulder; the stem or trunk of a tree; a large branch or bough; a troop, multitude, quantity, aggregate; a part, division; (with Buddhists) the five constituent elements of being (viz., *rūpa, vedanā, saṃjñā, saṃskāra,* and *vijñāna* [q.v.]). Ref: Chapter Two.

smṛti (mindfulness). Represented by *nen,* "idea, feeling, desire, attention." [MW] Remembrance, reminiscence, thinking of or upon, calling to mind, memory; the whole body of sacred tradition or what is remembered by human teachers; the whole body of codes of law as handed down memoriter or by tradition; desire, wish. Ref: Chapter Two [74]; Chapter Seventy-three (Vol. IV); *Lotus Sutra,* chapter 1 ("remember"), chapter 10 ("heed"), chapter 16 ("thought"), chapter 27 ("care for").

sparśa (touch, tangibility, sensation). Represented by *soku,* "touch." [MW] Touching, touch, sense of touch, contact; the quality of tangibility (which constitutes the skin's *viṣaya,* q.v.), any quality that is perceptible by touching any object (e.g., heat, cold, smoothness, softness, etc.); feeling, sensation. Ref: Chapter Two.

śramaṇa (striver, monk). Represented phonetically. [MW] Making effort or exertion, toiling, laboring; one who performs acts of mortification or austerity, an ascetic, monk, devotee, religious mendicant; a Buddhist monk or mendicant (also applied to Buddha himself). Ref: Chapter One [68].

śrāmaṇera (novice). Represented phonetically. [MW] (Among Buddhists) a pupil or disciple admitted to the first degree of monkhood, a novice. Ref: Chapter Seven [163]; *Lotus Sutra,* chapter 7.

śrāvaka (intellectual Buddhist). Represented by *shōmon,* "voice-hearer." [MW] Hearing, listening to; audible from afar; a pupil, disciple; a disciple of the Buddha (the disciples of the Hinayana school are sometimes so called in contradistinction to the disciples of the Mahayana school; properly only those who heard the law from the Buddha's own lips have the name *śrāvaka*). Ref: Chapter One [11]; *Lotus Sutra,* chapter 2.

Śrāvastī (name of a city). [JEBD] The capital of Kośala, sometimes treated as an independent country. It is the present-day Sāhetmātet, Gonda, India. Ref. Chapter Fifteen.

Śrīmālā (name of a district, of a queen, and of a sutra addressed to the queen). Represented phonetically. [MW] Name of a district and the town situated in it. *Śrīmālādevīsiṃhanāda-sūtra:* name of a Buddhist sutra, the *Sutra of the Lion's Roar of Queen Śrīmālā.* [JEBD] Śrīmālā: the daughter of King Prasenajit of Kośala (q.v.).

She married the king of Ayodhyā and actively engaged in the propagation of Buddhism in that country. Ref: Chapter Twelve [100].

srotāpanna (stream-enterer). Represented phonetically and by *yoru-ka,* "the effect that is to have been received beforehand into the stream." [MW] One who has entered the river (leading to nirvana). Ref: Chapter Two.

śrotra (ear, hearing). Represented by *ni,* "ear." [MW] The organ of hearing, ear, auricle; the act of hearing or listening to; conversancy with the Veda or sacred knowledge itself. Ref: Chapter Two.

sthavira (elder). Represented by *jōza,* "senior seat," and by *chōrō,* "veteran." [MW] Old, ancient, venerable; an old man; an "elder" (name of the oldest and most venerable *bhikṣu*s). Ref: Chapter Sixteen [15]; Chapter Eighty-four (Vol. IV).

stūpa (stupa, tower). Represented phonetically and by *tō,* "tower." [MW] A knot or tuft of hair, the upper part of the head, crest, top, summit; a heap or pile of earth or bricks etc., (especially) a Buddhist monument, dagoba (generally of pyramidal or domelike form and erected over sacred relics of the great Buddha or on spots consecrated as the scenes of his acts); any relic shrine or relic casket; any heap, pile, mound. Note: LSW notes that from the chapter *Hōsshi* ("A Teacher of the Dharma") onward, the *Lotus Sutra* stresses the erecting of *caitya*s (pagodas for sutras) as opposed to stupas (pagodas for relics). Master Dōgen discusses the distinction in Chapter Eighty-seven (Vol. IV). But MW does not distinguish between stupas and *caitya*s (q.v.). Ref: Chapter Seventy-one (Vol. III); Chapter Eighty-seven (Vol. IV) [160]; *Lotus Sutra,* chapter 10.

styāna (sloth). Represented phonetically and by *kon,* "darkness, stupefaction" and by *konjin,* "depression." [MW] Grown dense, coagulated; stiffened, become rigid; soft, bland; thick, bulky, gross; density, thickness; idleness, sloth, apathy. Ref: *Fukanzazengi.*

Sudatta (name of a person). [HB] A wealthy gold dealer and banker of Śrāvastī who become a lay follower of the Buddha and purchased Jetavana Park so that the Buddha and sangha could pass the rains retreat near Śrāvastī. Ref: *Fukanzazengi.*

śūdra (servant). Represented phonetically. [MW] A person of the fourth or lowest of the four original classes or castes (whose only business was to serve the three higher classes). Ref. Chapter Eight; Chapter Eighty-two (Vol. IV).

Śukra (name of a nun). Represented by Senbyaku, "Fresh-White." [MW] Bright, resplendent; clear, pure; light-colored, white; pure, spotless. Ref: Chapter Twelve [74].

Sumeru (also Meru, name of a mountain). Represented phonetically. [MW] Name of a fabulous mountain (regarded as the Olympus of Hindu mythology and said to form the central point of Jambudvīpa [q.v.]; all the planets revolve around it and it is compared to the cup or seed vessel of a lotus, the leaves of which are formed by the different *dvīpa*s). Ref: Chapter Fourteen [183]; *Lotus Sutra,* chapter 7.

śūnyatā (space, emptiness). Represented by *kū,* "space," "the sky," "emptiness." [MW] Emptiness, loneliness, desolateness; absence of mind, distraction; vacancy (of gaze); absence or want of; nothingness, nonexistence, non-reality, illusory nature of all worldly phenomena. Note: The latter set of definitions reflects idealistic thought. The philosophical meaning of *śūnyatā* that emerges in *Shōbōgenzō* is emptiness; the bare, bald, naked, raw, or transparent state, that is, the state in which reality is just as it is. At the same time, *kū* can often be interpreted as concrete space. Ref: Chapter One [45]; Chapter Two; Chapter Forty-three (Vol. III); *Lotus Sutra,* chapter 15.

Śūraṃgamasamādhinirdeśa (name of a sutra). Represented phonetically. [MW] *Śūraṃgama:* a particular *samādhi;* name of a bodhisattva. Ref: Chapter Forty-three (Vol. III); Chapter Seventy-four (Vol. IV); Bibliography.

sūtra (original texts, the sutras). Represented by *kyō,* "sutras," or by *kyōgan,* "sutras, volumes of the Sutra." [MW] A thread, yarn, string, line, cord, wire; that which like a thread runs through or holds together everything, rule, direction; a short sentence or aphoristic rule, and any work or manual consisting of strings of such rules hanging together like threads (these sutra works form manuals of teaching in ritual, philosophy, grammar, etc.; with Buddhists the term "sutra" is applied to original texts as opposed to explanatory works). One of the "three baskets," or Tripiṭaka (q.v.); and one of the twelve divisions of the teachings. See under *aṅga.*

Suvarṇaprabhāsottamarāja-sūtra (*Golden Light Sutra of the Supreme King*). Represented by *Konkōmyōsaishō-ō-kyō,* "Golden Light Supreme King Sutra." [MW] *Suvarṇa:* of a good or beautiful color, brilliant in hue, bright, golden, yellow, gold, made of gold. *Prabhāsa:* "splendor," "beauty," name of a *vasu* (one who is excellent, good, beneficient). *Uttama:* uppermost, highest, chief; most elevated; best. *Rāja:* king. Ref: Chapter Twenty-one [216]; Bibliography.

svāgata (well come, welcome). Represented by *zenrai,* "well come, welcome." [MW] Well come; welcome; a greeting, salutation. Ref: Chapter Twelve [74].

tāla (palm leaf). Represented phonetically. [MW] The palmyra tree or fan-palm (*Borassus flabelliformis*), producing a sort of spirituous liquor; considered a measure of height. Ref: *Lotus Sutra,* chapter 27.

Tathāgata ("having arrived in the state of reality," epithet of the Buddha). Represented by *nyorai,* "thus-come" or "reality-come." [MW] Being in such a state or condition, of such a quality or nature; he who comes and goes in the same way (as the buddhas who preceded him). *Tathā:* in that manner, so, thus. *Gata:* come. Ref: Chapter One [11]; *Lotus Sutra,* chapter 1.

tathatā (reality). Represented by *nyo,* "reality." [MW] True state of things, true nature. Appears, for example, in the compound *ichi-nyo,* "the oneness of reality." Ref: Chapter One [11].

tisraḥ śikṣāḥ (three kinds of training, three kinds of learning). Represented by *sangaku,* "three kinds of learning." [MW] *Tisraḥ:* three. *Śikṣā:* desire of being able to effect anything, wish to accomplish; learning, study, knowledge, art, skill in; teaching, training (held by Buddhists to be of three kinds, viz., *adhicitta-śikṣā,* training in higher thought; *adhiśīla-śikṣā,* training in higher morality; *adhiprajñā-śikṣā,* training in higher wisdom). However, in Japan the three are traditionally interpreted as *ritsu, jo, e,* "precepts, balanced state, wisdom," that is, *śīla, samādhi,* and *prajñā.* Ref: Chapter One [37].

tisro vidyāh (three kinds of knowledge). Represented by *sanmyō,* "three kinds of clarity." [MW] *Tisro:* three. *Vidyā:* knowledge, science, learning, scholarship, philosophy. Ref: Chapter Twelve [90].

Tripiṭaka (three baskets). Represented by *sanzō,* "three storehouses." [MW] The three baskets or collections of sacred writings (Sutra-*piṭaka,* Vinaya-*piṭaka,* and Abhidharma-*piṭaka* [q.v.]). Ref: Chapter Two [136].

Tuṣita (name of a celestial world). Represented phonetically. [MW] A class of celestial beings. Ref: Chapter Four [117].

udāna (spontaneous preaching). Represented by *jisetsu,* "spontaneous preaching." [MW] Breathing upwards; one of the five vital airs of the human body (that which is in the throat and rises upward); a kind of snake; joy, heart's joy (Buddhists). One of the twelve divisions of the teachings. See under *aṅga.* Ref: Chapter Eleven [40].

uḍumbara. Represented phonetically. [MW] The tree *Ficus glomerata;* the fruit of the tree. Ref: Chapter Sixty-eight (Vol. III); *Lotus Sutra,* chapter 2.

upadeśa (theoretical discourse). Represented by *rongi,* "discussion, argument." [MW] Pointing out to, reference to; specification, instruction, teaching, information, advice, prescription; name of a class of writings (Buddhist literature). One of the twelve divisions of the teachings. See under *aṅga.* Ref: Chapter Eleven [40].

upādhyāya (master). Represented by *oshō,* "master." [MW] A teacher, preceptor. Ref: Chapter Fifteen.

Upāli. Represented phonetically. [MW] Name of one of the Buddha's most eminent pupils (mentioned as the first propounder of the Buddhist law and as having been formerly a barber). Ref: Chapter Twelve [95].

upāsaka (layman). Represented phonetically. [MW] Serving, a servant; worshiping, a worshiper, follower; a Buddhist lay worshiper. Ref: *Lotus Sutra,* chapter 2.

upasaṃpadā (ordination). Represented by *gusoku-kai,* "being equipped with the precepts." [MW] The act of entering into the order of monks. *Upasaṃpad:* to come to, arrive at, reach, obtain; to bring near to, lead near to, procure, give; to receive into the order of monks, ordain. Ref: Chapter Eighty-six (Vol. IV) [69].

upāsikā (laywoman). Represented phonetically. [MW] A lay female votary of Buddha. Ref: *Lotus Sutra,* chapter 2.

upāya-kauśalya (skillful means). Represented by *zengō-hōben,* "skillful means, skillful expedient." [MW] *Upāya:* coming near, approach, arrival; that by which one reaches one's aim, a means or expedient, way, stratagem, craft, artifice. *Kauśalya:* cleverness, skillfulness, experience. Ref: *Lotus Sutra,* chapter 2.

ūrṇā (circle of hair). Represented by *byaku-gō,* "white hair." [MW] Wool, a woolen thread, thread; a circle of hair between the eyebrows. Ref: Chapter Seventeen [39]; *Lotus Sutra,* chapter 2.

utpala (blue lotus). Represented phonetically. [MW] The blossom of the blue lotus (*Nympaea caerulea*); any water lily; any flower. Ref. Chapter Twelve [90]; Chapter Forty-three (Vol. III).

Utpalavarṇā (name of a nun). Represented phonetically and by Renge-shiki, "Lotus-flower Color." Ref: Chapter Twelve [87].

uttarasaṃghāṭi (outer robe). Represented phonetically and by *jō-e,* "upper robe," *shichijō-e,* "seven-stripe robe," *chū-e,* "middle robe," and *nyū-shū-e,* "robe for going among the sangha." [MW] An upper- or outergarment. Ref: Chapter Twelve [95].

vaiḍūrya (lapis lazuli). Represented phonetically. [MW] A cat's-eye gem. Ref: Chapter Twenty [125]; *Lotus Sutra,* chapter 17.

vaipulya (extensions [of Buddhist philosophy]). Represented by *hōkō,* "square and wide" or "exact and wide." [MW] Largeness, spaciousness, breadth, thickness; a sutra of great extension, Buddhist literature. One of the twelve divisions of the teachings. See under *aṅga.* Ref: Chapter Eleven [40]; Bibliography.

vairambhaka (name of a wind) [JEBD] An all-destroying wind occurring between *kalpa*s. Ref: Chapter Ten [14].

Vairocana (Sun Buddha). Represented phonetically and by Dainichi-nyorai, "Great Sun Tathāgata." [MW] Coming from or belonging to the sun, solar; a son of the sun; name of a *dhyāni*-buddha. Ref: Chapter One [32]; Chapter Seventeen [54].

Vaiśravaṇa (a patronymic). Represented phonetically. [MW] A patronymic (especially of Kubera and Rāvana). Ref: *Lotus Sutra,* chapter 25.

vaiśya (working class). Represented phonetically. [MW] "A man who settles on the soil," a peasant, or "working man," agriculturist, person of the third class or caste (whose business was trade as well as agriculture). Ref. Chapter Eight; Chapter Eighty-two (Vol. IV).

Vajracchedikāprajñāpāramitā-sūtra (name of a sutra). Represented by *Kongōkyō,* "Diamond Sutra." [MW] *Vajra:* diamond. *Chedaka:* cutting off. Ref: Chapter Eighteen; Chapter Nineteen; Chapter Sixty-one (Vol. III); Bibliography.

Vajrasattva (Diamond Buddha). Represented by Kongō-satta, "diamond-*sattva.*" [MW] Vajrasattva: "having a soul or heart of adamant," name of a *dhyāni*-buddha. Vajra:

"the hard or mighty one," a thunderbolt (especially that of Indra; in Northern Buddhist countries it is shaped like a dumbbell and called *dorje*); a diamond (thought to be as hard as a thunderbolt or of the same substance). Ref: Chapter One [32].

vandana (worship, prostration). Represented by *raihai,* "worship," "prostration," by *keirai,* "venerative bow," and by *keishu,* "striking the head." [MW] Praise, worship, adoration; (with Buddhists) one of the seven kinds of *anuttara-pūja* or highest worship; a mark or symbol impressed on the body (with ashes, etc.); the act of praising, praise; reverence (especially obeisance to a superior by touching the feet etc.), worship, adoration. Ref: Chapter Two [74]; Chapter Eight.

vārṣika (rains retreat). Represented by *ango,* "retreat." [MW] Belonging to the rainy season, rainy; growing in the rainy season or fit for or suited to it; yearly, annual. Ref. Chapter Two [80]; Chapter Seventy-nine (Vol. IV).

vedanā (perception, feeling). Represented by *ju,* "accepting, feeling." [MW] Announcing, proclaiming; perception, knowledge; pain, torture, agony; feeling, sensation. One of the five *skandha*s (q.v.). Ref: Chapter Two.

vidyā (knowledge). See *tisro vidyāh.*

vihāra (temple). Represented by *shōja,* "spiritual building." [MW] Distribution; arrangement; walking for pleasure or amusement, wandering, roaming; sport, play, pastime, diversion, enjoyment, pleasure; a place of recreation, pleasure-ground; (with Buddhists) a monastery or temple (originally a hall where the monks met or walked about; afterward these halls were used as temples). Ref: Chapter Seven [166].

vijñāna (consciousness). Represented by *shiki,* "consciousness." [MW] The act of distinguishing or discerning, understanding, comprehending, recognizing, intelligence, knowledge; (with Buddhists) consciousness or thought faculty. One of the five *skandha*s (aggregates), one of the six *dhātu*s (elements), and one of the twelve links of the chain of causation (q.v.). Ref: Chapter Two; *Lotus Sutra,* chapter 7.

vikṣepa (distraction). Represented by *sanran* or *san,* "distraction." [MW] The act of throwing asunder or away or about, scattering, dispersion; casting, throwing, discharging; moving about, waving, shaking; letting loose, indulging; letting slip, neglecting; inattention, distraction, confusion, perplexity. Ref: *Fukanzazengi.*

Vimalakīrti (name of a lay student of the Buddha). Represented phonetically and by Jōmyō, "Pure Name." [MW] "Of spotless fame," name of a Buddhist scholar. Ref: Chapter Six [56]; Chapter Seventy-three (Vol. IV).

Vimalakīrtinirdeśa (name of a sutra). Represented by *Yuimagyō, "Vimalakīrti Sutra."* [MW] *Nīrdeśa:* pointing out, indicating, directing, order, command, instruction; description, specification, special mention, details or particulars. Ref: Chapter Thirty-two (Vol. II); Chapter Eighty-five (Vol. IV); Bibliography.

vimukti (liberation, salvation). Represented by *gedatsu,* "salvation, emancipation." [MW]

Disjunction; giving up; release, deliverance, liberation; release from the bonds of existence, final emancipation. Ref: Chapter Two [74]; Chapter Twelve; *Lotus Sutra,* chapter 25.

vinaya (discipline, precepts). Represented by *ritsu,* "rules, law, regulation." [MW] Leading, guidance, training (especially moral training), education, discipline, control, (with Buddhism) the rules of discipline for monks. One of the "three baskets," or Tripiṭaka (q.v.). Ref: Chapter Ninety-four (Vol. IV) [107]; Bibliography.

vindhyavana (monastery). Represented by *sōrin,* "thicket-forest" or "clump of forest"; see also *piṇḍavana.* [MW] A forest in the Vindhya, the name of a low range of hills connecting the northern extremities of the Western and Eastern Ghauts, and separating Hindustan proper from the Dekhan. *Vana:* forest, wood. Ref: Chapter Five [122].

vipāka-phala (maturation of effects). Represented by *ijuku-ka,* "differently maturing effects." [MW] *Vipāka:* ripe, mature; cooking, dressing; ripening, maturing (especially of the fruit of actions), effect, result, consequence. *Phala:* fruit, consequence, effect, result, retribution (good or bad), gain or loss, reward or punishment. Ref: Chapter Ten [21]; Chapter Eighty-four (Vol. IV).

vipaśyanā (insight, reflection). Represented by *kan,* "reflection." [MW] Right knowledge. *Vipaś:* to see in different places or in detail, discern, distinguish; to observe, perceive, learn, know. Ref: Chapter One [51]; Chapter Twenty-two [14]; Chapter Seventy-three (Vol. IV).

Vipaśyin (name of a Buddha). Represented phonetically and by Kōsetsu, "Universal Preaching." [MW] Name of a buddha (sometimes mentioned as the first of the seven Tathāgatas or principal buddhas, the other six being Śikhin, Viśvabhū, Krakucchanda, Kanakamuni, Kāśyapa, and Śakyasiṃha). Ref: Chapter Fifteen.

vīrya (diligence, effort, fortitude). Represented by *shōjin,* "diligence." [MW] *Vīrya:* manliness, valor, strength, power, energy; heroism, heroic deed; manly, vigor, energy, virility. *Vīrya pāramitā*: highest degree of fortitude or energy. One of the six *pāramitā*s (q.v.). Ref: Chapter Two; *Lotus Sutra,* chapter 27.

viṣaya (object). Represented by *kyō,* "boundary, sphere, circumstances" or by *kyōgai,* "boundary, environment." [MW] Sphere (of influence or activity), dominion, kingdom; scope, reach (of eyes, ears, mind etc.); an object of sense (there are five in number, the five *indriya*s or organs of sense having each their proper *viṣaya* or object, viz., 1) *śabda,* "sound," for the ear; 2) *sparśa,* "tangibility," for the skin; 3) *rūpa,* "form" or "color," for the eye; 4) *rasa,* "savor," for the tongue; 5) *gandha,* "odor," for the nose; and these five *viṣaya*s are sometimes called the *guṇa*s or "properties" of the five elements ether, air, fire, water, earth, respectively). Ref: Chapter Two.

Viṣṇu (name of the preserver god in the Hindu triad) [MW] Name of one of the principal Hindu deities (in the later mythology regarded as "the preserver"). Ref: Chapter Ten [19].

vitarka (reflection). Represented by *kaku,* "awareness." [MW] Conjecture, supposition, guess, fancy, imagination, opinion; doubt, uncertainty; reasoning, deliberation, consideration; purpose, intention. *Vitark:* to reflect. Ref: Chapter Six [129].

vṛddha (experienced). Represented phonetically and by *shakujū-shōyō-shin,* "experienced and concentrated mind." [MW] Grown, become larger or longer or stronger, increased, augmented, great, large; grown up, full-grown, advanced in years, aged, old, senior; experienced, wise, learned. One of the three kinds of mind, the others being *citta* and *hṛdaya* (q.v.). Ref: Chapter Seventy (Vol. III).

vyajana (whisk). Represented by *hossu,* "whisk." [MW] Fanning; a palm-leaf or other article used for fanning, fan, whisk. Ref: Chapter Sixteen [9]; *Fukanzazengi.*

vyākaraṇa (prediction, affirmation). Represented by *kibetsu,* "certification-discrimination," and by *juki,* "affirmation" or "giving affirmation." [MW] Separation, distinction, discrimination; explanation, detailed description; manifestation, revelation; (with Buddhists) prediction, prophecy. One of the twelve divisions of the teachings. See under *aṅga.* Ref: Chapter Eleven [40]; Chapter Thirty-two (Vol. II); *Lotus Sutra,* chapter 3.

yakṣa (demons, devils). Represented phonetically. [MW] A living supernatural being, spiritual apparition, ghost, spirit. Ref: Chapter Seventy (Vol. III) [207]; *Lotus Sutra,* chapter 10.

yaṣṭi (pole, flagpole [as symbol of Buddhist temple]). Represented phonetically. [MW] "Any support," a staff, stick, wand, rod, mace, club, cudgel; pole, pillar, perch; a flagstaff. Ref: Chapter One [61]; Chapter Sixteen [15].

Yogācāra (name of a school). [MW] The observance of yoga; a particular *samādhi;* a follower of a particular Buddhist sect or school; the disciples of that school. *Yoga:* the act of yoking, joining; a means, expedient, method; undertaking, business, work; any junction, union, combination; fitting together, fitness; exertion, endeavor, diligence. [JEBD] One of the two major Mahayana schools in India (together with the Madhyamika). Ref. Chapter Fifteen.

yojana (a measure of distance). Represented phonetically. [MW] Joining, yoking, harnessing; course, path; a stage or *yojana* (i.e., a distance traversed in one harnessing or without unyoking; especially a particular measure of distance, sometimes regarded as equal to four or five miles, but more correctly = four *krośa*s or about nine miles). Ref: Chapter Seventeen [62]; *Lotus Sutra,* chapter 11.

Bibliography

I. Main Chinese Sources Quoted by Master Dōgen in the *Shōbōgenzō*

A. Sutras

Attempts at English translations of sutra titles are provisional, and provided only for reference.

Agonkyō (Āgama sutras). In Chinese translation, there are four:

Chōagonkyō (*Long Āgama Sutra;* Pāli *Dīgha-nikāya*)

Chūagonkyō (*Middle Āgama Sutra;* Skt. *Madhyamāgama;* Pāli *Majjhima-nikāya*)

Zōagonkyō (*Miscellaneous Āgama Sutra;* Skt. *Saṃyuktāgama;* Pāli *Samyutta-nikāya*)

Zōitsuagongyō (*Āgama Sutras Increased by One;* Skt. *Ekottarāgama;* Pāli *Aṅguttara-nikāya*)

These are supplemented by the *Shōagonkyō* (*Small Āgama Sutras;* Skt. *Kṣudrakāgama;* Pāli *Khuddaka-nikāya*), a collection of all the Āgamas beside the four Āgamas. In the Pāli canon, the *Khuddaka-nikāya* is the fifth of the five Nikāyas and comprises fifteen short books.

Aikuōkyō (*Aśoka Sutra*)

Butsuhongyōjikkyō (*Sutra of Collected Past Deeds of the Buddha*)

Daibontenōmonbutsuketsugikyō (*Sutra of Questions and Answers between Mahābrahman and the Buddha*)

Daihannyakyō (*Great Prajñā Sutra*), short for *Daihannyaharamittakyō* (*Sutra of the Great Prajñāpāramitā;* Skt. *Mahāprajñāpāramitā-sūtra*)

Daihatsunehankyō (*Sutra of the Great Demise;* Skt. *Mahāparinirvāṇa-sūtra*)

Daihōkōhōkyōgyō (*Mahāvaipulya Treasure Chest Sutra*)

Daihoshakkyō (*Great Treasure Accumulation Sutra;* Skt. *Mahāratnakūṭa-sūtra*)

Daijōhonshōshinchikankyō (*Mahayana Sutra of Reflection on the Mental State in Past Lives*)

Daishūkyō (*Great Collection Sutra;* Skt. *Mahāsaṃnipāta-sūtra*)

Engakukyō (*Sutra of Round Realization*)

Fuyōkyō (*Sutra of Diffusion of Shining Artlessness;* Skt. *Lalitavistara-sūtra*)

Higekyō (*Flower of Compassion Sutra;* Skt. *Karuṇāpuṇḍarīka-sūtra*)

Hokkekyō (*Lotus Sutra, Sutra of the Flower of Dharma*), short for *Myōhōrengekyō* (*Sutra of the Lotus Flower of the Wonderful Dharma;* Skt. *Saddharmapuṇḍarīka-sūtra*)

Hōkukyō (*Sutra of Dharma Phrases*; Pāli *Dhammapada*)

Honshōkyō (*Past Lives Sutra;* Skt. *Jātaka*)

Juokyō (*Ten Kings Sutra*)

Kanfugenbosatsugyōbōkyō (*Sutra of Reflection on the Practice of Dharma by Bodhisattva Universal Virtue*)

Kegonkyō (*Garland Sutra;* Skt. *Avataṃsaka-sūtra*)

Kengukyō (*Sutra of the Wise and the Foolish*)

Keukōryōkudokukyō (*Sutra of Comparison of the Merits of Rare Occurrences*)

Kongōkyō (*Diamond Sutra*), short for *Kongōhannyaharamitsukyō* (*Sutra of the Diamond Prajñāpāramitā;* Skt. *Vajracchedikāprajñāpāramitā-sūtra*)

Konkōmyōkyō (*Golden Light Sutra*), short for *Konkōmyōsaishookyō* (*Golden Light Sutra of the Supreme King;* Skt. *Suvarṇaprabhāsottamarāja-sūtra*)

Mirokujōshōkyō (*Sutra of Maitreya's Ascent and Birth in Tuṣita Heaven*)

Mizōuinnenkyō (*Sutra of Unprecedented Episodes*)

Ninnōgyō (*Benevolent King Sutra*), short for *Ninnōhannyaharamitsugyō* (*Prajñāpāramitā Sutra of the Benevolent King*)

Senjūhyakuenkyō (*Sutra of a Hundred Collected Stories*)

Shakubukurakankyō (*Sutra of the Defeat of the Arhat*)

Shobutsuyōshūkyō (*Sutra of the Collected Essentials of the Buddhas*)

Shugyōhongikyō (*Sutra of Past Occurrences of Practice*)

Shuryōgonkyō (*Śūraṃgama Sutra;* Skt. *Śūraṃgamasamādhinirdeśa-sūtra*)

Yōrakuhongikyō (*Sutra of Past Deeds as a String of Pearls*)

Yuimagyō (*Vimalakīrti Sutra;* Skt. *Vimalakīrtinirdeśa-sūtra*)

Zuiōhongikyō (*Sutra of Auspicious Past Occurrences*)

B. Precepts

Bonmōkyō (*Pure Net Sutra*)

Daibikusanzenyuigikyō (*Sutra of Three Thousand Dignified Forms for Ordained Monks*)

Jūjuritsu (*Precepts in Ten Parts*), a sixty-one–fascicle translation of the Vinaya of the Sarvāstivādin school

Konponissaiubuhyakuichikatsuma (*One Hundred and One Customs of the Mūlasarvāstivādin School*)

Makasōgiritsu (*Precepts for the Great Sangha*), a forty-fascicle translation of the Vinaya of the Mahāsaṃghika school of Hinayana Buddhism

Shibunritsu (*Precepts in Four Divisions*), a sixty-fascicle translation of the Vinaya of the Dharmagupta school

Zenenshingi (*Pure Criteria for Zen Monasteries*)

C. Commentaries

Bosatsuchijikyō (*Sutra of Maintaining the Bodhisattva State*)

Daibibasharon (*Skt. Abhidharmamahāvibhāṣa-śāstra*)

Daichidoron (*Commentary on the Accomplishment which is Great Wisdom;* Skt. *Mahā-prajñāpāramitopadeśa*)

Daijōgishō (*Writings on the Mahayana Teachings*)

Hokkezanmaisengi (*A Humble Expression of the Form of the Samādhi of the Flower of Dharma*)

Kusharon (*Abhidharmakośa-bhāṣya*)

Makashikan (*Great Quietness and Reflection*), a record of the lectures of Master Tendai Chigi, founder of the Tendai sect

Makashikanhogyōdenguketsu (*Extensive Decisions Transmitted in Support of Great Quietness and Reflection*), a Chinese commentary on the *Makashikan* by Master Keikei Tannen

D. General Chinese Buddhist Records

Daitōsaiikiki (*Great Tang Records of Western Lands*)

Gotōroku (*Five Records of the Torch*), five independent but complementary collections compiled during the Song era (960–1279). They are represented in summary form in the *Gotōegen* (*Collection of the Fundamentals of the Five Torches*). They are:
Kataifutōroku (*Katai Era Record of the Universal Torch*)
Keitokudentōroku (*Keitoku Era Record of the Transmission of the Torch*)
Rentōeyō (*Collection of Essentials for Continuation of the Torch*)
Tenshōkotōroku (*Tensho Era Record of the Widely Extending Torch*)
Zokutōroku (*Supplementary Record of the Torch*)

Hekiganroku (*Blue Cliff Record*)

Hōenshurin (*A Forest of Pearls in the Garden of Dharma*), a kind of Buddhist encyclopedia in one hundred volumes

Kaigenshakkyōroku (*Kaigen Era Records of Śākyamuni's Teaching*)

Kosonshukugoroku (*Record of the Words of the Venerable Patriarchs of the Past*)

Rinkanroku (*Forest Record*), short for *Sekimonrinkanroku* (*Sekimon's Forest Record*)

Sōkōsōden (*Biographies of Noble Monks of the Song Era*)

Zenmonshososhigeju (*Verses and Eulogies of Ancestral Masters of the Zen Lineages*)

Zenrinhōkun (*Treasure Instruction from the Zen Forest*)

Zenshūjukorenjutsūshū (*Complete String-of-Pearls Collection of Eulogies to Past Masters of the Zen Sect*)

Zokudentōroku (*Continuation of the Record of the Transmission of the Torch*), published in China in 1635 as a sequel to the *Keitokudentōroku*

E. Records of and Independent Works by Chinese Masters

Basodōitsuzenjigoroku (*Record of the Words of Zen Master Baso Dōitsu*)

Bukkagekisetsuroku (*Record of Bukka's Attacks on Knotty Problems*); Bukka is an alias of Master Setchō Jūken

Chōreishutakuzenjigoroku (Record of the Words of Zen Master Chōrei Shutaku)

Daiefugakuzenjishūmonbuko (*War Chest of the School of Zen Master Daie Fugaku* [*Daie Sōkō*])

Daiegoroku (*Record of the Words of Daie Sōkō*)

Daiezenjitōmei (*Inscriptions on the Stupa of Zen Master Daie Sōkō*)

Engozenjigoroku (*Record of the Words of Zen Master Engo Kokugon*)

Jōshūroku (*Records of Jōshū Jūshin*)

Jūgendan (*Discussion of the Ten Kinds of Profundity*), by Master Dōan Josatsu

Hōezenjigoroku (*Record of the Words of Zen Master Yōgi Hōe*)

Hōkyōzanmai (*Samādhi, the State of a Jewel Mirror*), by Master Tōzan Ryōkai

Hōneininyūzenjigoroku (*Record of the Words of Zen Master Hōnei Ninyu*)

Hyakujōroku (*Record of Hyakujō Ekai*)

Kidōshū (*Kidō Collection*), a collection of the words of Master Tanka Shijun, compiled by Rinsen Jurin

Kōkezenjigoroku (*Record of the Words of Zen Master Kōke Sonshō*)

Nyojōoshōgoroku (*Record of the Words of Master Tendō Nyojō*)

Ōandongezenjigoroku (*Record of the Words of Zen Master Oan Donge*)

Rinzaizenjigoroku (*Record of the Words of Zen Master Rinzai Gigen*)

Rokusodaishihōbōdankyō (*Platform Sutra*), attributed to Master Daikan Enō

Sandōkai (*Experiencing the State*), by Master Sekitō Kisen

Setchōmyōkakuzenjigoroku (*Record of the Words of Zen Master Setchō Myōkaku* [*Setchō Jūken*])

Sekitōsōan-no-uta (*Songs from Sekitō's Thatched Hut*), by Master Sekitō Kisen

Shinjinmei (*Inscription on Believing Mind*), by Master Kanchi Sōsan

Shōdōka (*Song of Experiencing the Truth*), by Master Yōka Genkaku

Sōtairoku (*Record of Answers to an Emperor*), by Master Busshō Tokkō

Tōzangoroku (*Record of the Words of Tōzan Ryōkai*)

Unmonkoroku (*Broad Record of Unmon Bun'en*)

Wanshijuko (*Wanshi's Eulogies to Past Masters*), also known as the *Shoyoroku (Relaxation Record*)

Wanshikoroku (Broad Record of Wanshi Shōgaku)

Wanshizenjigoroku (*Record of the Words of Wanshi Shōgaku*)

Yafudōsenkongōkyō (*Yafu Dōsen's Diamond Sutra*)

F. Chinese Non-Buddhist and Secular Works

Confucianist:

Kōkyō (*Book of Filial Piety*)
Rongo (*Discourses of Confucius*)

Daoist:

Bunshi, from the Chinese *Wenzi,* the name of the author to whom the text is ascribed
Inzui (*Rhymes of Good Fortune*)
Kanshi, from the Chinese *Guanzi,* the name of the supposed author
Rikutō (*Six Strategies*)
Sangoryakuki (*History of the Three Elements and Five Elements*)
Shishi, from the Chinese *Shizi,* the name of the supposed author
Sōji, from the Chinese *Zhangzi,* the name of a disciple of Laozi (the ancient Chinese philosopher regarded as the founder of Daoism)

Miscellaneous:

Jibutsugenki (*Record of the Origin of Things*)
Jiruisenshu (*Collection of Matters and Examples*)
Jōkanseiyō (*Jōkan Era Treatise on the Essence of Government*)
Meihōki (*Chronicles of the Underworld*)
Taiheikōki (*Widely Extending Record of the Taihei Era*)

II. Other Works by Master Dōgen

Eiheikōroku (*Broad Record of Eihei*)

Eiheishingi (*Pure Criteria of Eihei*), including: *Bendōhō* (*Methods of Pursuing the Truth*), *Fushukuhanhō* (*The Method of Taking Meals*), *Tenzokyōkun* (*Instructions for the Cook*), etc.

Fukanzazengi (*Universal Guide to the Standard Method of Zazen*)

Gakudōyōjinshū (*Collection of Concerns in Learning the Truth*)

Hōgyōki (*Hōgyō Era Record*)

Shinji-shōbōgenzō (*Right Dharma-eye Treasury, in Original Chinese Characters*)

III. Japanese References

Akiyama, Hanji. *Dōgen-no-kenkyu.* Tokyo: Iwanami Shoten, 1935.

Eto, Soku-o. *Shōbōgenzō-ji-i.* Tokyo: Iwanami Shoten, 1965.

Hakuju, Ui, ed. *Bukkyo-jiten.* Tokyo: Daito Shuppansha, 1935.

Hashida, Kunihiko. *Shōbōgenzō-shaku-i.* 4 vols. Tokyo: Sankibo Busshorin, 1939–1950.

Hokkekyō. Tokyo: Iwanami Shoten, 1964–1967.

Jinbo, Nyoten, and Bunei Ando, eds. *Shōbōgenzō-chukai-zensho.* 10 vols. Tokyo: Shobo Genzo Chukai Zensho Kankokai, 1965–1968.

—. *Zengaku-jiten.* Kyoto: Heirakuji Shoten, 1976.

Jingde chuan deng lu (*Keitokudentōroku*). Taibei: Zhenshan mei chu ban she, 1967.

Kindaichi, Kyosuke, ed. *Jikai.* Tokyo: Sanseido, 1970.

Morohashi, Tetsuji. *Dai-kanwa-jiten.* 13 vols. Tokyo: Taishukan Shoten, 1955–1960.

Mujaku, Kosen. *Shobo Genzo Shoten-zoku-cho.* Tokyo: Komeisha, 1896.

Nakajima, Kenzo, ed. *Sogo-rekishi-nenpyo.* Tokyo: Nitchi Shuppan, 1951.

Nakamura, Hajime, ed. *Bukkyogo-daijiten.* 3 vols. Tokyo: Tokyo Shoseki, 1975.

—. *Shin-bukkyo-jiten.* Tokyo: Seishin Shobo, 1962.

Nishiari, Bokuzan. *Shōbōgenzō-keiteki.* Tokyo: Daihorinkaku, 1979–1980.

Nishijima, Gudo. *Gendaigoyakushōbōgenzō (Shōbōgenzō in Modern Japanese*). Twelve volumes plus a one-volume appendix. Tokyo: Kanazawa Bunko, 1970–1981.

—. *Shōbōgenzōteishoroku* (*Record of Lectures on Shōbōgenzō*). Thirty-four volumes. Tokyo: Kanazawa Bunko, 1982–1986.

Okubo, Doshu. *Dōgen-zenji-den-no-kenkyu.* Tokyo: Chikuma Shobo, 1966.

Oyanagi, Shigeta. *Shinshu-kanwa-daijiten.* Tokyo: Hakubunkan, 1937.

Satomi, Ton. *Dōgen-zenji-no-hanashi.* Tokyo: Iwanami Shoten, 1953.

Sawaki, Kodo. *Sawaki-kodo-zenshu.* 19 vols. Tokyo: Daihorinkaku, 1962–1967.

Shōbōgenzō. Commentaries by Minoru Nishio, Genryu Kagamishima, Tokugen Sakai, and Yaoko Mizuno. Tokyo: Iwanami Shoten, n.d.

Taishō-shinshū-daizōkyō. Tokyo: Taishō Issaikyō Kankōkai, 1924–1932.

Tetsugaku-jiten. Tokyo: Hibonsha, 1971.

Tetsugaku-shojiten. Tokyo: Iwanami Shoten, 1938.

Watsuji, Tetsuro. *Watsuji-tetsuro-zenshu.* Vols. 4, 5. Tokyo: Iwanami Shoten, 1961–1963.

Zengaku-daijiten. Edited by scholars of Komazawa University. Tokyo: Taishukan Shoten, 1985.

Zokuzokyō. Collection of Buddhist sutras not included in the *Taishō-shinshū-daizōkyō.* Taibei: Xin Wen Feng chu ban gong si, 1976–1977.

III. English References

Japanese-English Buddhist Dictionary. Tokyo: Daito Shuppansha, 1979.

Macdonell, A. A. *A Practical Sanskrit Dictionary.* London: Oxford University Press, 1954–1958.

Masuda, Koh, ed. *Kenkyusha's New Japanese-English Dictionary.* Tokyo: Kenkyusha, 1974.

Monier-Williams, Sir Monier. *A Sanskrit-English Dictionary.* Oxford: Oxford University Press, 1899.

Nelson, Andrew. *Japanese-English Character Dictionary.* Rutland, VT: Charles Tuttle, 1974.

Schiffer, Wilhelm, and Yoshiro Tamura. *The Threefold Lotus Sutra.* New York: Weatherhill, 1975. A revised version of *The Sutra of the Lotus Flower of the Wonderful Law* (1930) by Bunno Kato and William Soothill.

Schumann, H. W. *The Historical Buddha.* New York: Arkana, 1989.

Spahn, Mark, and Wolfgang Hadamitzky. *Japanese Character Dictionary.* Tokyo: Nichigai Asssociates, 1989.

Index

A

Abhidharma 189, 214, 240, 258, 309
Abhidharmakośa-bhāṣya 241
Abhidharmamahāvibhāṣa-śāstra 240
Abundant Treasures 286, 397, 398, 408
Āgama(s) 181, 193, 194, 200, 202, 211, 214, 255
Aikuō. *See* Aśoka, King
Aikuōzan (*see also* Mount Aikuō) 252
Aizenmyōō 151
Ajase. *See* Ajātaśatru
Ajātaśatru 124
Ajita (*see also* Mañjuśrī) 402, 406
Ajñāta-Kauṇḍinya 385
Akṣobhya 394
Amaterasu 334
American Academy of Religions 375
Amitābha 188
anāgāmin 38, 106, 215
Ānanda 19, 29, 186, 236, 240, 247, 249, 257, 368
Anāthapiṇḍada. *See* Sudatta
Anavatapta 197
anuttara samyaksaṃbodhi 23, 32, 35, 38, 89, 90, 107, 128, 164, 168, 169, 205, 263, 264, 277, 297, 341, 382, 386, 395, 396, 400, 403, 410, 412
A Record of the Origins of Things. See Jibutsugenki
arhat(s) 10, 26, 29, 32, 34, 38, 94, 95, 106, 108, 170, 171, 187, 215, 239, 240, 375, 381, 385, 386, 391
arjaka 441
Āryadeva. *See* Kāṇadeva
Asaṅga 241
Aśoka, King 240, 260
asura(s) 108
Aśvaghoṣa 236, 239, 240
Aśvaka 231
Avalokiteśvara (*see also* Giver of Fearlessness; Great Compassion; Regarder of the Sounds of the World) 31, 35, 37, 52, 56, 121, 188, 283, 376
Avataṃsaka-sūtra (*see also Garland Sutra*) 26, 28, 85, 123
Avīci Hell 224, 232, 233

B

Banko 318, 333
barbarian(s) 20, 29
Baso Dōitsu 47, 141, 152, 154, 155, 183, 214, 242, 261, 280, 328–29, 338, 339, 359, 368
Basozan 338
Beijing 310
Benevolent King Sutra 351
Benka 196, 213
Bequeathed Records. See Iroku
Bhadrapāla 158, 184
bhikṣu(s) (*see also* monk) xvii, 20, 32, 38, 53, 90, 91, 93, 94, 95, 97, 98, 99, 104, 106, 167, 176, 177, 180, 182, 210, 212, 241, 381, 385, 386, 394, 395, 406, 407, 410
  forest 180, 193

bhikṣuṇī(s) (*see also* nun) 91, 93, 94, 95, 98, 99, 106, 166, 167, 170, 171, 186, 210, 385, 386, 395, 406, 407, 410
Bhīṣmagarjitasvararāja. *See* King of Majestic Voice; Kū-ō
Bi, Bizuda (*see also* Gensha Shibi) 49, 55
Bielefeldt, Carl 234
Birushana. *See* Vairocana
Blue Cliff Record. See Hekiganroku
Blue Mountains 217–19
Bō, Minister 16
bodhi xviii, 3, 8, 10, 11, 15, 23, 25, 32, 33, 35, 38, 69, 83, 90, 95, 107, 109, 114, 128, 138, 146, 147, 153, 160, 163, 171, 177, 178, 192, 200, 204, 245, 272, 303, 317, 364, 365, 399, 400, 410
  -effect 171
  -mind 65, 97, 114, 116, 166, 171
  -powers 398
  -speech 128, 138
Bodhidharma 4, 11, 12, 24, 28, 49, 55, 103, 123, 124, 154, 183, 185, 191, 213, 214, 237, 257, 258, 261, 283, 309, 336, 354, 367, 368
bodhimaṇḍa 87
Bodhiruci 116
bodhisattva(s) 11, 25, 27, 35, 38, 39, 56, 90, 91, 93, 94, 95, 97, 98, 99, 104, 105, 106, 108, 109, 110, 116, 121, 123, 132, 154, 169, 172, 182, 184, 186, 188, 189, 204, 208, 212, 215, 246, 248, 255, 257, 265, 266, 277, 278, 280, 281, 284, 285, 302, 304, 310, 311, 315, 383, 386, 389, 394, 396, 399, 400, 402, 403, 406, 407, 409–10, 411, 412
  mahāsattva(s) 33, 34, 124, 167, 169, 400, 402, 406
  precepts 175, 176, 192
  way 177, 263, 268, 273, 355, 392, 397, 399, 403, 404
bodhi tree 6, 85, 332
body(ies), of the Buddha, buddha(s), Tathāgata 56, 62, 84, 109, 110, 131, 140, 164, 174, 190, 205, 273, 283, 401, 405
  eight-foot golden 143, 144, 145
  sixteen-foot golden 68, 72, 143, 144, 145, 146, 151, 153, 297, 309
Bōgenrei 320, 334
Book of Filial Piety. See Kōkyō
Brahmā 141, 174, 175, 178, 191, 210
Brahmā heaven 177, 398
Brahma-pāriṣadya heaven 192
Brahma-purohita heaven 192
brahman(s) 11, 28, 116, 190, 239, 241, 242, 410
Bu, Emperor (r. 502–549) 116, 191, 242
Bu, Emperor (r. 561–578) 242
Bu, Emperor (r. 841–846) 295
Buddha (*see also* Gautama; Śākyamuni) xv, 6, 7, 8, 10, 11, 20, 22, 24, 25, 26, 28, 30, 32, 33, 38, 39, 56, 60, 71, 81, 83, 85, 86, 87, 99, 100, 103, 105, 106, 108, 109, 115, 116, 117, 118, 121, 123, 124, 135, 154, 159, 161, 165, 166, 167, 169, 170, 173–74, 175, 176, 179, 186, 187, 188, 189, 190, 191, 192, 193, 196, 197, 198, 199, 200, 201, 202, 207, 208, 209, 213, 222, 229, 230, 234, 239, 240, 246, 247, 257, 264, 266, 268, 269, 270, 271, 272, 273, 278, 280, 281, 283, 285, 287, 305, 309, 329, 336, 338, 342, 344, 367, 381, 382, 384, 385, 386, 387, 389, 390, 393, 394, 395, 396, 397, 402, 404, 405, 406, 407, 408, 411
  affirmation 154, 188, 287
  body (*see also* body, of the Buddha) 56, 84, 110, 131, 140, 144, 164, 205, 273, 283, 309
  brightness 114, 167, 209

death 29, 184, 186, 239, 398
Dharma (*see also* Buddha-Dharma) 9, 11, 12, 14, 90, 99, 128, 159, 160, 198, 199, 306
disciple(s) 10, 15, 39, 85, 87, 96, 99, 154, 158, 160, 176, 178, 190, 198, 206, 207, 210, 239, 240, 287, 367, 386
image 72, 151
influence 6, 7, 158, 166
kaṣāya, robe (see also *kaṣāya;* robe) 158, 160, 166, 172, 176, 177, 181, 182, 195–96, 197, 199, 203–212
land (*see also* buddha land) 81, 269
lineage 4, 84
marrow 167, 209
mind 5, 84, 115, 164, 167, 205, 209
mind–seal 13, 24
name 5, 63
order 29, 98, 99, 124, 199, 231
past life, lives 154, 186, 189, 193, 233
posture xvi, 5, 10, 365
preaching 15, 42, 76, 142, 154, 166, 240
-seal 16, 24
state 10, 17, 83, 185, 196, 209, 224, 245, 246, 247, 397, 403, 404
successor(s) 247, 248, 257, 354
teaching(s) 21, 22, 71, 100, 137, 187, 224, 284
thirty-two marks (*see also* thirty-two marks) 121, 278
truth 9, 17, 41, 42, 44, 60, 82, 91, 107, 115, 116, 117, 133, 165, 179, 203, 206, 209, 220, 224, 246, 247, 298, 301, 302, 304, 307, 315, 321, 326, 365, 387, 391, 395
Way 18, 49, 118
wide and long tongue 110, 121
wisdom 265, 266, 267, 270, 271, 280, 281, 386, 402
buddha(s) 3, 5, 6, 7, 8, 9, 10, 12, 14, 17, 18, 19, 23, 26, 34, 38, 41, 51, 52, 59, 65, 66, 67, 68, 69, 70, 72, 75, 82, 83, 90, 93, 94, 99, 100, 101, 106, 113, 114, 116, 117, 118, 123, 127, 128, 129, 130, 133, 137, 139, 141, 146, 153, 154, 157, 159, 160, 162, 163, 164, 165, 166, 167, 168, 169, 172, 174, 176, 177, 178, 179, 185, 188, 189, 190, 195, 196, 197, 198, 199, 200, 201, 203, 204, 205, 206, 207, 208, 212, 213, 219, 229, 233, 235, 238, 244, 245–46, 247, 248, 249, 254, 255, 256, 257, 263, 264, 265, 266, 267, 268, 270, 272, 274, 277, 279, 281, 282, 283, 287, 295, 297, 298, 300, 301, 305, 306, 307, 310, 311, 314, 315, 316, 321, 325, 326, 327, 329, 330, 339, 343, 345, 347, 348, 356, 364, 365, 382, 383, 385, 386, 387, 388, 389, 392, 394, 397, 394, 400, 407, 408
-action(s), deed, behavior 82, 84, 348, 356, 411
body 174, 190, 401, 404, 409
eternal 33, 51, 62, 68, 77, 91, 93, 113, 127, 143, 165, 172, 186, 217, 225, 227, 238, 242, 251, 255, 271, 273, 274, 286, 291, 300, 307, 317, 329, 343, 346
five 9, 26
image 63, 323, 387
kaṣāya, robe(s) (see also *kaṣāya;* robe) 158, 159, 166, 169, 175, 196, 197, 198, 200, 206, 207, 208, 209
-mind 68, 300, 367
of the ten directions 263, 264, 300, 401
of the three times 35, 98, 132, 135, 140, 169, 175, 177, 180, 181, 300, 172
past 117, 188, 199, 235, 311
samādhi 8, 9
seven ancient (*see also* Seven Buddhas) 25–26, 184, 214, 239, 257, 261, 371

buddha(s) (*continued*)
state 6, 8, 9, 21, 26, 41, 118, 164, 189, 204, 205, 211, 233, 246, 273
thirty-two marks (*see also* thirty-two marks) 188
transformed 398
-wisdom, wisdom of 7, 15, 187, 273, 384, 385, 401
Buddhabhadra 87, 88
buddha-bhagavat(s) 34
Buddhacarita 240
Buddha-Dharma 4–5, 6, 7, 8, 10, 11, 12, 13, 15, 16, 17, 18, 19, 20, 21, 22, 25, 41, 42, 44, 76, 81, 82, 83, 84, 92, 93, 94, 96, 97, 99, 111, 113, 114, 115, 116, 133, 134, 135, 136, 141, 144, 155, 159, 160, 162, 164, 166, 170, 172, 175, 181, 182, 196, 197, 199, 203, 206, 207, 208, 209, 212, 218, 255, 283, 285, 290, 301, 302, 303, 304, 305, 306, 307, 394, 411
Buddha, Dharma, and Sangha (*see also* Three Treasures) xv, 32, 104, 164, 168
Buddha hall 86, 351, 352, 375, 377
buddhahood 105, 130, 207, 257
buddha land(s) 22, 98, 197, 223, 263, 264, 272, 383, 387, 407
Buddhamitra 124, 236
Buddhanandhi 236
buddha-nature 10, 67, 223
Buddhasiṃla 241
buddha-tathāgata(s) (*see also* Tathāgata) 3, 6, 14, 94, 164, 202, 386
Buddhism xv, xvi, 23, 31, 39, 41, 65, 71, 75, 85, 94, 103, 106, 107, 109, 113, 121, 122, 127, 128, 134, 143, 154, 157, 184, 191, 198, 199, 202, 203, 209, 210, 214, 217, 223, 224, 229, 230, 242, 243, 244, 245, 248, 255, 259, 284, 295, 301, 313, 341, 343, 356, 358
esoteric 26, 28
Hinayana 29, 87, 88, 108
Mahayana 25, 108, 241
Theravāda 40
Vajrayana 26
Buddhist(s) xv, xvi, 6, 9, 11, 12, 15, 16, 25, 27, 31, 38, 45, 47, 73, 75, 76, 87, 108, 109, 121, 123, 127, 134, 135, 139, 145, 151, 155, 169, 171, 184, 186, 188, 202, 206, 207, 230, 231, 232, 235, 240, 241, 242, 245, 247, 255, 259, 264, 284, 289, 299, 302, 313, 314
bowl (*see also pātra*) 64, 157, 258
four groups of 106, 108
intellectual (*see also śrāvaka*) 123, 188, 189
learning 26, 247
master(s) 29, 104, 121, 152, 243, 257, 313, 355
method 25, 279
monastery(ies) 375
monk(s) 30, 38, 56, , 104, 106, 121, 151, 186, 192, 296, 331, 354
order 63, 98, 108, 124, 183, 235, 239
patriarch(s) xvi, 10, 12, 13, 16, 22, 28, 34, 59, 62, 68, 75, 77, 82, 83, 84, 93, 109, 118, 129, 130, 158, 160, 162, 163, 176, 181, 182, 202, 203, 204, 205, 208, 209, 210, 218, 219, 220, 221, 223, 224, 225, 226, 229, 232, 235, 239, 246, 248, 249, 250, 252, 253, 254, 255, 256, 267, 290, 293, 296, 301, 302, 306, 309, 323, 328, 329, 330, 331, 337, 341, 342, 348, 352, 353, 356, 371–72
philosophy, theory xv, 71, 154, 313, 367
practical (*see also* bodhisattva) 123, 188
practice 10, 139, 151, 282, 332, 338, 341, 367

practitioner(s) 39, 56, 139, 355
preaching 25, 38, 258
precepts 110, 175, 210, 211
process 282, 283
robe (*see also kaṣāya;* robe) 29, 86, 106, 157, 177, 190, 242
sensory (*see also pratyekabuddha*) 123, 188
sutra(s) 108, 152, 182, 184, 188, 204, 212, 214, 217, 223, 245, 258, 331, 341, 353, 356
teaching(s) 39, 47, 56, 139, 188, 193, 282
temple(s), monasteries 27, 106, 124, 183
tradition 85, 214, 235
truth 16, 129, 208, 217, 245, 301, 341, 403
view 139, 143, 207, 263, 332
wisdom 277, 281, 282, 283
Buddhist Patriarch (*see also* Buddha; Bodhidharma) 16, 28, 76, 217, 220, 223, 238, 242, 289
Bukka. *See* Engo Kokugon
Bukkō Nyoman 133, 141, 359
Bukkōku Temple 214
Bunka era xvii
Bunshi 223, 232
burning house, parable of 267, 268–69, 281, 282, 283, 343, 389, 390
Buryō 295
Bushu district 328
Busshō Tokkō 252, 259, 359
Butōzan (*see also* Mount Butō) 111
Butsuin Ryōgen 110, 121, 359

C

Cambodia 357
cart(s), three 266, 281, 282, 389
deer 281, 389
goat 281, 389
white ox 266, 281, 282, 343, 355, 389
Chanda 231
Chang 143
Changqing Daan. *See* Chōrei Shutaku
Changsha Jingcen. *See* Chōsha Keishin
Chanqing Daan. *See* Fukushu Daian
Chekiang province 4, 141, 260, 338
Chigen 182, 212
Chikan (*see also* Setchō Chikan) 238, 244
Chikō (*see also* Wisdom-Brightness) 192
Child of the Himalayas (*see also* Himālaya) 193, 331
Chimon Kōso 311
China xvi, 4, 5, 11, 13, 14, 16, 17, 19, 20, 22, 23, 24, 26, 28, 29, 41, 55, 56, 59, 61, 63, 64, 65, 71, 86, 94, 95, 96, 106, 121, 122, 124, 133, 151, 152, 153, 154, 155, 157, 158, 162, 163, 164, 172, 175, 181, 182, 183, 184, 189, 191, 193, 194, 195, 199, 205, 206, 211, 212, 213, 221, 232, 233, 239, 242, 244, 245, 248, 254, 256, 257, 158, 258, 259, 260, 261, 264, 267, 273, 275, 279, 281, 295, 301, 331, 332, 333, 334, 336, 338, 356, 357, 367, 368
Chinese xviii, 24, 29, 71, 91, 103, 121, 127, 152, 157, 187, 191, 193, 233, 258, 261, 295, 314, 318–19, 321, 322, 326, 333, 335, 337, 359
book(s), commentary(ies), literature, sutra(s), text(s), translation(s) xviii, xix, 105, 123, 142, 186, 189, 191, 230, 295, 334
language xvii, xviii, xix, xx, 27, 37, 38, 39, 47, 48, 71, 87, 88, 105, 107, 122, 124, 141, 152, 153, 184, 187, 189, 190, 191, 192, 216, 230, 239, 240, 241, 244, 259, 278, 285, 310, 331, 335, 336, 337, 354, 367, 381
Chinshū Fuke (*see also* Hōtei) 332
Chinzei 45

Chishu district 230
Chitsu 243
Chiyu 252, 253
Chōka Dōrin 127, 133, 141, 359
Chōkei Daian (*see also* Fukushu Daian) 355, 359
Chōkei Eryō 141, 155, 285
Chōkeji 345
Chōrei Shutaku 73, 359
Chōro Sōsaku 27, 86
Chōsha Keishin 112, 122, 232, 359
Chōshazan 122
Chōsui Shisen 113, 123
Chūagongyō. See Middle Āgama Sutra
Chuanzi Decheng. *See* Sensu Tokujō
Chūsō, Emperor 157, 183, 195
cintāmaṇi (*see also maṇi*) 231
Collection of Concerns in Learning the Truth. See Gakudōyōjinshū
Collection of Essentials for Continuation of the Torch. See Rentōeyō
conduct 16, 28, 65, 117, 137, 138, 157, 164, 302, 303, 305, 307, 382
  four forms of 11, 12, 38, 367
  past good 159, 163, 164, 181, 196, 211, 215
  ten kinds of bad 39
  three forms of xvi, 5, 25
Confucian, Confucianism 103, 106, 125, 184
Confucius 125
Constellation King 408

D

Dahui Zonggao. *See* Daie Sōkō
Daian (*see also* Fukushu Daian) 345
Daibai Hōjō 253, 254, 261, 338, 359
Daibaizan 253, 254, 261
Daibikusanzenyuigikyō (*see also Sutra of Three Thousand Dignified Forms for Ordained Monks*) 85
Daibyakuhō Mountain (*see also* Tendōzan) 4, 24
Daichi (*see also* Hyakujō Ekai) 201, 214
Daichidoron 105, 142, 189
Daichū era 295
Daie (*see also* Nangaku Ejō) 75, 85, 317, 332
Daien. *See* Isan Reiyū
Daie Sōkō 259, 311, 332, 359
Daihannyakyō (*see also Heart Sutra*) 38, 39
Daihōshakkyō 190–91, 232
Daii Daien (*see also* Isan Reiyū) 111–112, 122, 253
Daii Dōshin 141, 184, 242, 359, 372
Daiizan 112, 122
Daijaku (*see also* Baso Dōitsu; Kōzei Daijaku) 148, 154
Daijōgishō 184
Daijōhonshōshinchikankyō 192
Daikan Enō (*see also* Sixth Patriarch) 5, 12, 24, 27, 28, 29, 71, 85, 105, 122, 123, 141, 154, 157, 160, 176, 183, 185, 186, 189, 192, 195, 200, 214, 215, 242, 257, 261, 264, 265, 279, 280, 281, 283, 285, 295, 309, 316, 317, 331, 332, 333, 335, 337, 342, 353, 354, 359, 367, 368, 372
Daiman Kōnin 85, 105, 183, 184, 186, 192, 215, 242, 257, 279, 332, 359, 372
Daini Sanzō 300
Daishō (*see also* Nan'yō Echū) 67, 68, 71, 111, 122, 300, 309
Daizan (*see also* Daibaizan) 260
Daizong. *See* Taisō
Daizui Hōshin 346, 355, 359
Daizuizan 345
Dajian Huineng. *See* Daikan Enō
Daman Hongren. *See* Daiman Kōnin
Damei Fachang. *See* Daibai Hōjō
Danxia Zichun. *See* Tanka Shijun

Daoism, Daoist(s) 196, 232, 233, 333, 334
Dayang Jingxuan. *See* Taiyō Kyōgen
Dayi Daoxin. *See* Daii Dōshin
Dazu Huike. *See* Taiso Eka
demon(s) (*see also asura; yakṣa*) 25, 47, 50, 51, 53, 57, 71, 89, 90, 96, 98, 100, 104, 107, 108, 115, 116, 123, 124, 128, 140, 144, 164, 168, 177, 178, 179, 188, 193, 201, 202, 205, 209, 214, 220, 221, 231, 280, 325, 389
Den 250–51
Denpōin Temple 329
Dentōroku (*see also Keitokudentōroku*) 203, 214, 296
Descartes, René 289
Deshan Xuanjian. *See* Tokusan Senkan
deva(s) (*see also* god) 25, 108, 395
Devadatta 116, 124, 273, 287, 398, 399, 411
dhāraṇī(s) 209, 215
 samādhi- 205, 215
dharma(s) xvii, 6, 7, 15, 17, 23, 28, 32, 34, 35, 37, 38, 41, 42, 43, 44, 47, 66, 68, 72, 76, 104, 128, 130, 132, 135, 147, 149, 153, 163, 166, 185, 193, 204, 222, 227, 244, 264, 265, 280, 295, 297, 301, 307, 345, 354, 383, 384, 399, 408
Dharma (*see also* Buddha-Dharma; Buddha, Dharma, and Sangha; right Dharma-eye treasury) xv, xvii, xx, 3, 4–5, 6, 7, 8, 9, 10, 11, 13, 14 15, 18, 19, 23, 26, 29, 41, 42, 43, 50, 52, 53, 68, 75, 76, 77, 83, 89, 90, 91, 92, 93, 94, 95, 96, 97, 99, 100, 107, 108, 110, 111, 112, 113, 114, 115, 121, 123, 124, 127, 128, 129, 132, 133, 134, 138, 140, 141, 142, 146, 152, 157, 158, 159, 160, 161, 162, 163, 164, 166, 167, 169, 171, 172, 174, 178, 182, 185, 195, 196, 197, 198, 199, 201, 204, 205, 206, 207, 208, 212, 217, 232, 233, 240, 241, 242, 243, 244, 245, 247, 248, 249, 250, 251, 252, 253, 255, 256, 259, 263, 267, 269, 273, 287, 291, 295, 302, 310, 316, 329, 338, 342, 343, 344, 348, 356, 358, 382, 384, 385, 386, 387, 388, 389, 391, 392, 394, 397, 399, 400, 401, 402, 404, 405, 406, 409, 410, 411
 body 131, 140
 children 162, 172
 descendant(s) 148, 161, 166
 -form 83, 98
 gate(s) 12, 118, 264, 300, 327, 364
 imitative 18, 29, 158, 184, 407
 latter 18, 29, 159, 164, 175, 184, 198, 205, 250
 name(s) 49, 55, 251, 259, 260, 345
 of nine divisions 387
 order 406
 practice(s) 75, 132, 197
 right 4, 11, 12, 18, 20, 21, 29, 77, 95, 113, 114, 115, 128, 158, 159, 162, 181, 184, 197, 198, 201, 202, 207, 225, 291, 364, 382, 407
 robe 78, 110, 176, 177, 251
 succession, successor 110, 204, 247–48, 249, 250, 251, 255, 256
 teacher(s) 9, 184, 248, 290, 382, 383, 396
 title(s) 259, 260
 transmission 13, 22, 163, 165, 204, 208, 212, 213, 256, 261, 275, 296
 treasury 97, 165, 199, 208
 wheel 6, 10, 25, 32, 38, 42, 83, 135, 225, 401
 world(s), world of xv, 5, 6, 15, 100, 118, 218, 223, 224, 226, 232, 269–70, 273, 326

Dharma Flower (*see also* Flower of Dharma) 264, 265, 267, 270, 280
Dharma hall 93, 250, 251, 342, 351, 352, 375, 376
Dharma King (*see also* Buddha) 179, 192, 226, 391
Dharma-nature 23, 222
Dhītika 236
dhūta (*see also* practice, ascetic) 49, 55, 239, 402
dhyāna (*see also* meditation) 11, 27, 38, 393, 394, 397, 398, 401
Diamond Buddha. *See* Vajrasattva
Diamond Sutra 289, 290, 295, 297, 298, 309, 350, 351, 355
Dīpaṃkara 121
Dōan Dōhi 243, 359, 372
Dōan Kanshi 243, 359, 372
Dōgen (compiler of the *Keitokudentōroku*) 214
Dōgen (*see also* Eihei Dōgen) xv, xvi, xvii, xviii, xix, xx, 22, 23, 24, 26, 27, 28, 30, 31, 37, 38, 39, 41, 49, 57, 59, 62, 63, 65, 71, 75, 85, 86, 87, 89, 103, 105, 106, 107, 109, 121, 122, 123, 124, 127, 137, 138, 139, 140, 141, 143, 151, 152, 153, 154, 155, 157, 183, 185, 187, 190, 195, 212, 213, 215, 217, 229, 230, 231, 233, 235, 238, 239, 242, 244, 245, 248–49, 251, 252–54, 255, 256, 257, 259, 260, 261, 262, 263, 275, 279, 282, 284, 285, 286, 287, 289, 297, 303, 309, 310, 311, 313, 331, 333, 334, 335, 336, 337, 338, 341, 353, 354, 355, 356, 357, 367, 368, 371, 381
Dōgo Enchi 233
Dōhi (*see also* Dōan Dōhi) 237
Dōin 295
Dōkai (*see also* Fuyō Dōkai) 238, 251
Dokufuzan 295
Donglin Changzong. *See* Shōkaku Jōsō
Dongshan Liangjie. *See* Tōzan Ryōkai
Donjō (*see also* Ungan Donjō) 237
Dōrin (*see also* Chōka Dōrin) 133–34, 135
Dormitory of Quiescence 252, 260
Dōshin (*see also* Daii Dōshin) 158, 237
Dōyō (*see also* Ungo Dōyō) 237
dragon(s) (*see also* *nāga*) 52, 57, 67, 92, 94, 108, 109, 113, 123, 152, 159, 163, 168, 169, 178, 180, 184, 186, 188, 197, 198, 201, 209, 222, 224, 225, 227, 232, 241, 292, 296, 324, 364, 365, 369, 381, 395, 399, 400, 410
Dragon King 165, 197, 231, 399
Dragon Sea 21
duṣkṛta 82, 87

E

E (*see also* Yōgi Hōe) 252, 260
East China Sea 24, 141, 258
Eastern Han dynasty. *See* Later Han dynasty
Eastern Jin dynasty 88
Eastern Lands (*see also* China) 5, 8, 15, 16, 24, 49, 55, 160, 166, 195, 199, 209, 248, 249, 365
East Mountain 218, 219, 220, 221, 230
Echizen 256
Echū (*see also* Nan'yō Echū) 14, 67
Edo era 189
eight destinations 125, 229, 335
eighteen realms 32, 37
Eighteenth Patriarch (*see also* Fuyō Dōkai) 259
eight kinds of beings 98, 108
Eihei Dōgen (*see also* Dōgen) 260, 372
Eihei era, period 160, 199
Eiheiji xvii, 260
Eisai 4, 24
Ejō (*see also* Koun Ejō) 53, 149

Eka (*see also* Taiso Eka) 4, 237
Ekaku. *See* Rōya Ekaku
Ekishū 345
elements
five 224, 232, 318, 320
four 69, 94, 106, 129, 139, 224
six 38, 224
three 318
Eminent Conduct 407
En (*see also* Goso Hōen; Jimyō Soen) 252
Enen (*see also* Sanshō Enen) 323
Engo Kokugon 142, 259, 311, 317, 332, 359
Enju. *See* Fukushu Daian
Enkan (*see also* Ryōzan Enkan) 104, 237
Enō (year of) 70, 84, 101, 119, 136
Enō (*see also* Daikan Enō) 237, 246
esoteric Buddhism 26, 28
Esshū 53
Etatsu 274
Etsu district 9, 34, 131, 248
Ever Zealous 406
expedience, expediency, expedient means, methods 220, 267, 269, 281, 284, 329, 343, 384, 388, 396, 403, 404, 411

F

Facilities at Major Buddhist Monasteries in the Southern Song 375
Fame Seeker 383
Fang. *See* Bō, Minister
Fang Xuanling. *See* Bōgenrei
Far East 334
Fayan Wenyi. *See* Hōgen Bun'eki
Feng. *See* Hyō, Minister
Fengxue Yanzhao. *See* Fuketsu Enshō
Fenyang Shanzao. *See* Fun'yō Zenshō
Fichte, Johann Gottlieb 289
Fifth Patriarch (*see also* Daiman Kōnin) 208, 332
First Council 239
First Patriarch (*see also* Bodhidharma) 24, 116, 124, 157, 172, 183, 242, 254, 257, 258
five aggregates 31, 35, 69, 94, 106, 129, 139, 344, 354
five peaks 320, 334
Five Records of the Torch. See Gotōroku
five sects 200, 249
Flower of Dharma (*see also Lotus Sutra*) 9, 263, 264, 266, 267–68, 270–75, 282, 285, 343, 383, 408
Flower-Light 389
Foda. *See* Hōtatsu
Foguang Ruman. *See* Bukkō Nyoman
Formosa Strait 259
Founding Patriarch (*see also* Bodhidharma) 77, 157, 195
Founding Patriarch (*see also* Daikan Enō) 12, 92, 208, 242, 273, 317, 342, 343
four continents 108, 189, 213, 382, 407
four *dhyāna* heavens 39, 192
four elements 69, 94, 106, 129, 139, 224
four great rivers 186, 320, 334
four groups of followers 94, 98, 106, 188, 394, 401
four lands 269, 284
four modes of birth 114, 123
Four Noble Truths xvi, xvii, 37, 234
four oceans, seas 17, 320, 334
Fourth Council 240
fourth effect (*see also* arhat) 20, 26, 29, 95, 98, 106, 208, 215
Fourth Patriarch (*see also* Daii Dōshin) 141, 158
Four Universal Vows 107
four views 230, 231
Foyin Liaoyuan. *See* Butsuin Ryōgen
Fozhao Daguang. *See* Busshō Tokkō
Fugen. *See* Universal Virtue
Fukaku. *See* Ōryū Enan

Fukanzazengi 21, 23, 27, 30, 56, 63, 229, 279, 286, 309, 356, 363–65, 367, 386
Rufubon ("Popular Edition") 30, 363, 367
Shinpitsubon ("Original Edition") 30, 367
Fuketsu Enshō 155, 252, 260, 359
Fukien 259
Fukui prefecture xvii, 40, 57, 262
Fukushu Daian (*see also* Chōkei Daian) 355, 359
Fukushū province 253
Fun'yō Zenshō 121, 122, 252, 260, 359
Furong Daokai. *See* Fuyō Dōkai
Fushukuhanhō 357
Futōroku (*see also Kataifutōroku*) 203, 214
Fuyō Dōkai 229, 243, 259, 359, 372
Fuyōkyō 190
Fuyōzan (*see also* Mount Fuyō) 243, 251
Fuzan Hōen 243
Fuzhou province 49

G

Gakudōyōjinshū 26, 123
Gan. *See* Nansen Fugan
Gandhāra 240, 241
gandharva(s) 108, 188, 395, 410
Ganen 125
Ganges River 7, 158, 159, 196, 198, 397, 409
Ganzan 253
Gaoan Daiyu. *See* Kōan Daigu
Garland Sutra 9, 26, 28, 76, 81, 85, 87, 123
garuḍa(s) 108, 168, 178, 184, 188, 192, 395, 410
gasshō 86, 187, 357
gate(s) 4, 7, 12, 16, 110, 118, 121, 146, 364
authentic 3, 7, 8
universal 268
Gautama (*see also* Buddha; Śākyamuni) xv, xvii, 109, 123, 257, 368
Gayata 237
Gendaigo-yaku-shōbōgenzō xvii, 239
Genroku era 3
Gensha Shibi 49–50, 51, 53, 55, 56, 57, 258, 303, 305, 306, 309, 310, 311, 318–19, 321, 322–23, 326–28, 333, 335, 337, 338, 359
Genshazan 49
Genshi 253, 359
Gensō, Emperor 295, 310
German idealists 289
Geyāśata 236, 314, 315, 316, 331
Gichō 320, 334
Gisei (*see also* Tōsu Gisei) 238
Giver of Fearlessness (*see also* Avalokiteśvara) 410
god(s) 5, 7, 16, 17, 20, 25, 27, 33, 39, 43, 47, 57, 71, 77, 90, 93, 95, 96, 97, 98, 99, 108, 115, 116, 117, 123, 140, 141, 158, 161, 163, 165, 168, 169, 175, 176, 177, 178, 180, 181, 182, 188, 201, 202, 205, 207, 210, 212, 215, 220, 221, 225, 269, 302, 307, 314, 320, 325, 393, 395, 400, 405, 409, 410
Godai Impō 230
goddess(es) 99, 169, 231
Gohon (*see also* Tōzan Ryōkai) 346, 355
Golden Light Sutra 350, 351, 357
Gon (*see also* Engo Kokugon) 252
Goshōji 254
Goso Hōen 48, 258, 259, 332, 359
Gotōroku 214
Gotōegen 261
Gozu Hōyū 184, 359
Gozu Mountain, Gozusan 158, 184
Gṛdhrakūṭa (*see also* Mount Gṛdhrakūṭa; Vulture Peak) 24

Great Community (*see also* Mahāsaṃghika) 240
Great Compassion (*see also* Avalokiteśvara) 167, 169
Great Eloquence 397
Great Hall 254
Great Saint (*see also* Buddha) 219, 230
Great Vehicle (*see also* Mahayana) 8, 9, 18, 98, 162, 165, 175, 179, 273, 305, 382, 383, 387
Great Wisdom Sutra. See Mahāprajñāpāramitā-sūtra
Guangdong 265, 281
Guanxi Zhixian. *See* Kankei Shikan
Guishan Lingyou. *See* Isan Reiyū
Guotai Hongdao. *See* Kokutai Kōtō
Gutei 368
Gyō (*see also* Nan'in Egyō) 252
Gyōshi (see also Seigen Gyōshi) 5, 237

H

Haihui Shoudan. *See* Kaie Shutan
Hakkun Shutan. *See* Kaie Shutan
Haku Kyoi 127, 133–34, 141
Hakulenayasas 237
Haku Shōgun 134
Hakuyō Hōjun 63
Hall of Serene Light 252, 260
Han dynasty 152
Hangyō Kōzen xvii, 3
Hangzhou Bay 141
Hangzhou province 133, 375, 379
Hannyatara. *See* Puṇyatara
Happy Buddha. *See* Hōtei
Heart Sutra 25, 31, 35, 37, 38, 39, 47, 286
Heaven of Thoughtlessness 224
Hegel, Georg Wilhelm Friedrich xv, 289
Heiden district 253
Hekiganroku 259, 311, 336
Higekyō 187, 188, 214
Himālaya (*see also* Child of the Himalayas) 280
Himalayas 186, 193, 241
Hinayana (*see also* Small Vehicle) 29, 87, 88, 98, 108, 162, 214, 241
Hinokuma Shrine 320, 335
History of the Three Elements and Five Elements. See Sangoryakuki
Hōgen Bun'eki 18–19, 29, 214, 249, 258, 309, 359
Hōgen sect 5, 24, 29, 258, 279, 299, 309
Hōgyō era 238, 253
Hōgyōji 275
Hōjō (*see also* Daibai Hōjō) 253
Hōju 104
Hokuzankeitokuryōonji 375, 379
Hōkyōzanmai 243
Hōnei 254
Honjō 28
Honshōkyō 189
Hopeh province 310
Hōrinji 157, 195, 265
Hōseizan 243
Hōshin (*see also* Daizui Hōshin) 345, 355
Hosho 314
Hōtatsu 265–66, 267, 281, 342–43, 353, 354, 359
Hōtei (*see also* Chinshū Fuke) 332, 356
Hōtetsu (*see also* Mayoku Hōtetsu) 44
householder(s) 94, 106, 175, 176, 192, 410
Hōyū (*see also* Gozu Hōyū) 158, 184
Huangbo Xiyun. *See* Ōbaku Kiun
Huanglong Huinan. *See* Ōryū Enan
Hunan province 155
Hyakujō Ekai 86, 105, 122, 183, 201, 214, 243, 261, 338, 355
Hyō, Minister 17

I

Ibu district 252

Igen (*see also* Yakusan Igen) 237
Igyō sect 5, 24, 122, 258, 280
Ihaku 214
Iichi 248–49, 360
Imperial Court 320
Imperial Palace 335
India, Indian xvi, 11, 19, 20, 24, 28, 29, 47, 55, 63, 65, 75, 83, 85, 95, 103, 124, 154, 157, 158, 165, 183, 185, 186, 187, 188, 189, 195, 199, 240, 241, 242, 257, 258, 260, 264, 301, 302, 310, 321, 331, 336, 344, 354
  cosmology 85, 232, 278
  legends, mythology 108, 140, 191
Indra (*see also* Śakra-devānām-indra) 33, 39, 90, 108, 116, 307
Infinite Thought 410
Inscription on Believing Mind. See Shinjinmei
Iroku 311
Isan Reiyū 73, 105, 112, 122, 183, 214, 243, 261, 295, 311, 360
Ise, Grand Shrines, Inner Shrine 320, 334
Isō, Emperor 333
Issaiji. *See* Viśvabhū
Īśvara 409

J

Jambudvīpa 77, 85, 264, 278, 407
Japan 24, 26, 28, 30, 59, 63, 86, 94, 98, 99, 106, 114, 151, 152, 163, 167, 175, 180, 189, 191, 210, 230, 238, 239, 256, 259, 261, 277, 279, 284, 320, 332, 334, 356, 381
Japanese xviii, 26, 106, 107, 182, 191, 251, 261, 320, 357
  language xvii, xviii, xix, 27, 29, 39, 63, 85, 86, 103, 105, 107, 152, 185, 187, 188, 190, 216, 244, 261, 279, 295, 309, 310, 332, 334, 335, 336, 367, 371, 373
Jeta, Prince 367
Jetavana Park 363, 367
Jewel Treasury (*see also* Ratnagarbha) 167, 169
Jiangxi district, province 141, 338
Jianzhi Sengcan. *See* Kanchi Sōsan
Jibutsugenki 334
Jimyō Soen (*see also* Sekisō Soen) 110, 121, 252, 260, 360
Jinshū 208, 215, 332, 367
Jō 158, 184
Jōkan Era Treatise on the Essence of Government. See Jōkanseiyo
Jōkanseiyō 334
Jōmyō. *See* Vimalakīrti
Jōshū Jūshin 91, 104, 183, 303, 305, 310, 345, 354, 360
Jōshō. *See* Fuyō Dōkai
Jōsō (*see also* Shōkaku Jōsō) 109, 110
Jō Zenji. *See* Tendō Nyojō
Jūjuritsu (*see also Precepts in Ten Parts*) 87
Junsō, Emperor 16, 28
Jyōjiji 244

K

Ka. *See* Śikhin
Kagen era 275
Kahō 226, 233
Kai (*see also* Fuyō Dōkai) 217
Kaie Shutan 252, 259, 303, 306, 310, 360
Kajō era 182, 193, 212, 250, 251, 252
kalaviṅka 393
Kālodāyin 231
kalpa(s) 9, 26, 66, 69, 90, 109, 147, 204, 209, 214, 255, 267, 273, 274, 323, 324, 343, 344, 393, 394, 399, 401, 402, 403, 404, 405, 407
  asaṃkheya 168, 404, 405, 407
  bhadra- 257, 394

of emptiness 217, 229
inkdrop 273
of resplendence 246, 255, 261
sixty minor 273, 382
successive 178, 324, 336
of wisdom, of the wise 246, 255, 261
Kāṇadeva 124, 189, 236, 241
Kanakamuni 25, 235, 255, 261
Kanbun era 3
Kanchi Sōsan 242, 331, 360, 367, 372
Kanfugenbosatsugyōhōkyō 284
Kangen era 34, 53, 149, 256
Kaniṣka 240
Kanjizai. *See* Avalokiteśvara
Kankei Shikan 104–105, 260, 360, 368
Kanki 22
Kannondōri-in Temple 34
Kannondōrikōshōgokokuji 62
Kannondōrikōshōhōrinji 53, 59, 70, 84, 101, 119, 182, 195, 212, 227, 238, 256, 275, 293, 330
Kannon-in Temple 75, 345
Kanshi (*see also* Dōan Kanshi) 237
Kansu province 233
Kant, Immanuel 289
Kantsū era 49
Kapilavastu 241
Kapimala 189, 236, 241
karma, karmic 56, 118, 131, 159, 177, 222, 225
Karoku era 21, 30
Karuṇāpuṇḍarīka-sūtra. See Higekyō
kaṣāya (*see also* robe) 20, 29, 78, 80, 86, 105, 157, 158–72, 174–82, 185, 186, 188, 189, 190, 192, 194, 196, 197–98, 201–207, 208–209, 210–212, 213, 214, 215, 216, 247, 251, 348, 368, 373
five-stripe 210
merit(s) of 157, 163, 169, 179, 198, 199, 201, 204, 214
nine-stripe, of nine stripes 78, 210, 373
seven-stripe, of seven stripes 78, 210
of sixty stripes 162, 174
Kashmir 124, 241
Kaśmira. *See* Kashmir
Kassan 252
Kassan Zenne 104, 233
Kāśyapa 25, 160, 170, 171, 174, 184, 236, 247, 249, 255, 256, 257, 261
Katai era 214
Katai Era Record of the Universal Torch. See Kataifutōroku
Kataifutōroku (*see also Futōroku*) 214
Katei era 53
Katei River, Valley 226, 233
Kato, Bunno 381
Kauśika (*see also* Indra) 33, 39
Kegonkyō (*see also Garland Sutra*) 26, 28, 85
Kegon sect 26, 123
Keigenfu 182, 212
Keitokudentōroku 28, 105, 151, 214, 296, 310, 311, 339, 356, 358
Keitoku era 214
Keitoku Era Record of the Transmission of the Torch. See Keitokudentōroku
Keitokuji 259
Keitokuzenji 244
Keiun 182, 212
Ken 355
Kenchō era 45
Kenchū-seikoku era 214
Kenen (*see also* Yellow Emperor) 319, 334
Kenkyusha's New Japanese-English Dictionary 187
Kennin Temple 4
Kidō Collection. See Kidōshū
Kidōshū 244
Kii-no-kuni 320, 335
kiṃnara(s) 108, 168, 188, 395, 410
Kinei, Emperor 281

King of Emptiness (*see also* Kū-ō) 218
King of Love. *See* Aizenmyōō
King of Majestic Voice (*see also* Kū-ō) 229, 407
Kinkazan 328
Kinmei, Emperor 21
Kinsennin. *See* Krakucchanda
Kinzan Kokuitsu 141, 252
Kippōji, Kippō Temple 34, 53, 256, 262
Kisen (*see also* Sekitō Kisen) 237
Kishō (*see also* Shōken Kishō) 148
Kisō, Emperor 243, 332
Kō (*see also* Daie Sōkō) 252
kōan(s) 41, 72, 230, 259, 311, 336
Kōan Daigu 92, 105, 360
Kōdō (*see also* Yakusan Igen) 147, 153, 342, 347, 352, 353
Kōdō Mountain, Kōdōzan 226, 233, 319, 334
Kōfukuji 248
Kojiki 107
Kōkaku (*see also* Ungo Dōyō) 348, 355
Kōke Sonshō 252, 260, 360
Kokutai-in Temple 328
Kokutai Kōtō 338, 360
Kōkyō 184
Kōma. *See* Korea
Kōmei, Emperor 160, 199
Kōnantōro (*see also* Guangdong; Shōshū district) 281
Kongōhannyaharamitsukyō. See Diamond Sutra
Kongōkyō. See Diamond Sutra
Kōnin (*see also* Daiman Kōnin) 237
Konjikisen. *See* Kanakamuni
Konkōmyōkyō (*see also Golden Light Sutra*) 140, 357
Konkōmyōsaishōōkyō. See Golden Light Sutra
Konponissaiubuhyakuichikatsuma 189
Kōrai (*see also* Korea) 182, 216
Korea, Korean 182, 193, 212, 216, 320, 346
Kośala 240, 241, 367
Kōsei 226, 233, 319, 334
Kōsetsu. *See* Vipaśyin
Kō-shami (*see also* Śrāmaṇera Kō) 358
Koshingi 86
Kōshō (*see also* Dōgen) 303, 311
Kōshō (*see also* Rōya Ekaku) 113, 122
Kōshōhōrinji 136, 149, 307, 311, 352
Kōshū district 243
Kōsō, Emperor 332
Kōsoshō 249
Kōtei (*see also* Yellow Emperor) 233
Kōtō (*see also* Kokutai Kōtō) 328
Kotokuzenin Temple 295
Kōtōroku (*see also Tenshōkōtōroku*) 203, 214
Koun Ejō (*see also* Ejō) 262
Kōzei Daijaku (*see also* Baso Dōitsu) 133, 141, 145, 147, 154, 328
Kōzu 116
Krakucchanda 25, 235, 255, 261
Kūkai 26
Kukkuṭapāda Mountain 240, 368
Kumārajīva 87, 184, 295, 381
Kumāralabdha 236
kumbhāṇḍa(s) 168, 188
Kū-ō (*see also* King of Emptiness; King of Majestic Voice) 229
Kyōgen (*see also* Taiyō Kyōgen) 237
Kyōgen Chikan 111, 122, 183, 259, 261, 338, 360, 368
Kyōshin (*see also* Unmon Bun'en) 220, 230
Kyoto 3, 57, 59, 73, 88, 244, 296, 358
Kyōzan (mountain, temple) 92, 93
Kyōzan Ejaku 73, 92, 105, 183, 253, 261, 303, 305–306, 311, 360
Kyushu 48

L

Lake Anavatapta 165, 186
Lalitavistara-sūtra. See Fuyōkyō
Land of Joy 394
Langye Huijiao. *See* Rōya Ekaku
Laozi 184
Later Han dynasty 5, 160, 199, 204
lay 121, 338, 351, 360
  bodhisattva 175
  disciple 45, 133, 367
layman, laymen (*see also upāsaka*) 11, 16, 29, 49, 55, 91, 106, 107, 110, 111, 160, 165, 184, 188, 196, 197, 208, 210, 213, 214, 234, 250
laypeople, layperson 16, 20, 61, 71, 96, 105, 158, 175, 176, 193, 201, 211, 220
laywoman, laywomen (*see also upāsikā*) 16, 91, 106, 107, 188, 210, 250
Li 143
Li. *See* Ri, Minister
Liang dynasty 116, 162, 175, 185, 242, 336
Liangshan Yuanguan. *See* Ryōzan Enkan
lineage(s) 4, 10, 15, 26, 28, 84, 91, 141, 158, 159, 160, 183, 198, 200, 204, 205, 206, 243, 249, 254, 261, 279, 280, 384
  Dōgen 24, 229
  five 4, 5, 19
  Hōgen 249, 279, 309
  Rinzai 4, 91, 242, 251, 252, 254
  Sōtō 279
  Unmon 249, 279, 309
Lingyun Zhiqin. *See* Reiun Shigon
Linji Yixuan. *See* Rinzai Gigen
lion seat 397, 401
Longmen Fayan. *See* Ryūmon Butsugen
Long River 45, 48
Longtan Chongxin. *See* Ryūtan Sōshin
Longya Judun. *See* Ryūge Kodon
Lotus Sutra xviii, xx, 23, 25, 26, 27, 38, 56, 63, 72, 104, 106, 153, 154, 175, 183, 184, 185, 233, 244, 263, 265, 277, 278, 279, 280, 281, 283, 284, 285, 286, 287, 315, 351, 353, 355, 368–69, 381, 396–412
  Anrakugyō ("Peaceful and Joyful Practice") chapter 27, 124, 350, 400–402
  Daibadatta ("Devadatta") chapter 287, 398–400
  Darani (*Dhāraṇī*) chapter 410–11
  Fugen-bosatsu-kanpotsu ("Encouragement of Bodhisattva Universal Virtue") chapter 278, 412
  Funbetsu-kudoku ("Discriminatin of Merits) chapter 406–407
  Gohyaku-deshi-juki ("Affirmation of Five Hundred Disciples") chapter 187, 394–95
  Hiyu ("A Parable") chapter 281, 398–90
  Hōben ("Expedient Means") chapter 140, 142, 265, 281, 286, 287, 368, 384–88
  Hōsshi ("A Teacher of the Dharma") chapter 123, 395–97
  Hōsshi-kudoku ("The Merits of a Teacher of the Dharma") chapter 407
  Jo ("Introductory") chapter 142, 381–84
  Jōfugyō-bosatsu ("Bodhisattva Never Despise") chapter 229, 407
  Jū-chi-yūshutsu ("Springing Out from the Earth") chapter 124, 285, 402–403
  Ju-gaku-mugaku-nin-ki ("Affirmation of Students and People Beyond Study") chapter 395
  Juki ("Affirmation") chapter 279, 392

Lotus Sutra (*continued*)
Kan-ji ("Exhortation to Hold Firm") chapter 400
Kanzeon-bosatsu-fumon ("The Universal Gate of Bodhisattva Regarder of the Sounds of the World") chapter 37, 56, 121, 282–83, 350, 409–10
Kejō-yu ("Parable of the Magic City") chapter 392–94
Ken-hōtō ("Seeing the Treasure Stupa") chapter 286, 397–98
Myo-on-bosatsu ("Bodhisattva Wonderful Sound") chapter 408–409
Myō-shōgun-ō-honji ("The Story of King Resplendent") chapter 411–12
Nyorai-jinriki ("The Mystical Power of the Tathāgata") chapter 407–408
Nyorai-juryō ("The Tathāgata's Lifetime") chapter 280, 403–405
Shinge ("Belief and Understanding") chapter 104, 185, 368, 390–91
Yaku-ō-bosatsu-honji ("The Story of Bodhisattva Medicine King") chapter 408
Yakusō-yu ("Parable of the Herbs") chapter 391–92
Zoku-rui ("The Commission") chapter 408
Zuiki-kudoku ("The Merits of Joyful Acceptance") chapter 213, 406
Lu. *See* Ro
Lucknow 367
Luetchford, Michael and Yoko xx
Luoyang 124, 309
Lushan 109

M

Madhyamāgama. See Middle Āgama Sutra
Madhyamaka-kārikā 241
Madhyamaka school 241
Magadha 30, 240, 314
Magu Baoche. *See* Mayoku Hōtetsu
Mahā-brahman heaven 192
Mahākāśyapa 4, 11, 12, 24, 29, 30, 105, 123, 154, 160, 200, 236, 239, 240, 249, 257, 279, 280, 309, 344, 368, 392
Mahāparinirvāṇa-sūtra 104, 193, 233, 280
mahāprajñāpāramitā (*see also prajñāpāramitā*) 31, 35
Mahāprajñāpāramitāhṛdaya-sūtra (*see also Heart Sutra*) 31, 35
Mahāprajñāpāramitā-śāstra 142, 189
Mahāprajñāpāramitā-sūtra xix, 39
Mahāprajñāpāramitopadeśa 105, 189, 241
Mahāratnakūṭa-sutra. See Daihōshakkyō
Mahāsaṃghika Precepts (*see also Makasōgiritsu*) 83, 85
Mahāsaṃghika school 88, 240
mahāsattva(s) 33, 34, 39, 124, 167, 169, 400, 402, 406
Mahayana (*see also* Great Vehicle) 25, 98, 108, 162, 240, 241
Maheśvara 409
mahoraga(s) 108, 168, 188, 395
Maitreya (*see also* Ajita) 52, 56, 134, 174, 190, 264, 279, 382, 383, 406
Majjhima-nikāya. See Middle Āgama Sutra
Makashikan 191, 192
Makashikanhogyōdenguketsu 191
Makasōgiritsu (*see also Mahāsaṃghika Precepts*) 85, 88
mandala 26
mandārava flowers 405
maṇi (*see also cintāmaṇi*) 222, 231
Mañjuśrī (*see also* Ajita) 124, 134, 263, 264, 277, 279, 356, 368, 382, 399
Mannenji 253
mantra, mantric 16, 28, 35, 248

Manura 237
mappō. See Dharma, latter
Māra-pāpīyas 116
Marx, Karl xv
Massan Ryōnen 91–92, 105, 360
Master Dogen's Shobogenzo xx
Maudgalyāyana 174, 190, 191
Mayoku Hōtetsu (*see also* Hōtetsu) 360
Mayokuzan 44
Mazu Daoyi. *See* Baso Dōitsu
Medicine King 395, 396
meditation (*see also dhyāna*) 27, 32, 38
  four states of 34
merit(s) 7, 9, 115, 157, 158, 159, 163, 164, 169, 171, 172, 175, 179, 181, 182, 188. 191, 192, 204, 205, 212, 219, 399, 406–407
  five sacred 168, 169, 188, 214
  of the *kaṣāya,* robe 157, 159, 163, 169, 171, 177, 178, 179, 182, 198, 199, 201, 204, 205, 207, 212
  ten excellent 177, 179
Method of Taking Meals. See Fushuku-hanhō
Miaoxin. *See* Myōshin
Micchaka 236, 240
Middle Āgama Sutra 179
middle way xv
Milky Way. *See* Long River
mind-seal 13, 24, 298, 329, 363, 367
Mingdi. *See* Kōmei
Monier Monier-Williams, Sir xvii, 239
Monjushiri. *See* Mañjuśrī
monk(s), monkhood (*see also bhikṣu*) xvii, xix, 11, 13, 18, 20, 29, 30, 38, 44, 47, 49, 50, 51, 55, 56, 61, 63, 64, 67, 77, 78, 79, 82, 86, 87, 91, 92–93, 94, 96, 97, 104, 105, 106, 107, 111, 112, 113, 121, 122, 124, 151, 153, 158, 160, 162, 163, 165, 166, 172, 175, 177, 178, 181, 182, 186, 188, 189, 190, 192, 193, 196, 199, 201, 208, 210, 211, 212, 213, 214, 215, 220, 230–31, 234, 240, 241, 242, 243, 249, 251, 252, 253, 254, 256, 258, 259, 260, 261, 265, 281, 284, 287, 293, 295, 296, 301, 302, 303–304, 307, 309, 311, 317, 318, 325, 328, 331, 332, 333, 337, 342, 343, 346, 347, 348, 349, 350, 351, 352, 354, 367, 368, 376, 377
  attendant 34, 240, 253, 376
  hall 61 64, 348, 376
  head 63, 249, 258, 348, 349, 350, 355, 377
  mountain 291
  venerable 33, 39, 173, 190, 234, 317, 318
Moshan Liaoran. *See* Massan Ryōnen
Mount Aikuō (*see also* Aikuōzan) 260
Mount Butō (*see also* Butōzan) 122
Mount Chatha 278
Mount Fuyō (*see also* Fuyōzan) 229
Mount Gṛdhrakūṭa (*see also* Gṛdhrakūṭa) 381, 406
Mount Hiei 24, 284
Mount Hoku 260
Mount Kin 260
Mount Nan 260
Mount Nansen 230
Mount Ōryū 121
Mount Sumeru 85, 108, 213, 220, 230
Mount Taihaku 260
Mount Taiyō (*see also* Taiyōzan) 229
Mount Tendai (*see also* Tendaizan) 261
Mount Tendō (*see also* Tendōzan) 260
Musai (*see also* Sekitō Kisen) 147, 154
Musai Ryōha 252, 253, 259, 360
Myōhōrengekyō (*see also Lotus Sutra*) 263, 280, 381
Myōkaku (*see also* Setchō Jūken) 306, 311

Myōshin 92–93, 360
Myōzen 4, 23–24
mystic, mystical 5, 6, 7, 35, 103, 105, 118, 171, 190, 197, 215, 252, 254, 310, 337, 341, 398, 411
  powers 34, 40, 170, 178, 179, 305, 310, 365, 400, 404, 407, 408, 411, 412
Mystic Light 383

N

Nadai 241
nāga(s) (*see also* dragon) 241, 395
Nāgārjuna 170, 236
Nakamae, Tadashi xx
Nanda 231
Nangaku Ejō 5, 24, 27, 85, 113, 123, 141, 161, 154, 183, 184, 231, 261, 264, 279, 280, 317, 325, 328–29, 330, 332, 333, 335, 337, 338, 339, 360, 368
Nangakuzan 75
Nan'in Egyō 252, 260, 360
Nanquan Puyuan. *See* Nansen Fugan
Nansen Fugan 104, 122, 183, 220, 230–31, 243, 310, 338, 354, 360
Nantai River 49
Nanyang Huizhong. *See* Nan'yo Echū
Nan'yō Echū 28, 71, 122, 183, 191, 279, 309, 360
Nanyuan Huiyong. *See* Nan'in Egyō
Nanyue Huairang. *See* Nangaku Ejō
National Master (*see also* Nan'yō Echū) 14, 28, 67, 68, 71, 111, 122, 300–307, 309
Nen (*see also* Shuzan Shōnen) 252
Nepal 241
Never Despise 407
Niaowo Daolin. *See* Chōka Dōrin
Ningbo 194
Ninji era 149, 182, 212, 227, 238, 256, 274, 293, 307, 330, 352
nirvana 15, 28, 35, 69, 146, 147, 153, 177, 255, 269, 386, 401, 404
  fine mind of 11, 265, 280
  hall 377
Nishijima, Gudo Wafu xv, xvii, xviii, xx, 239
Niutou Fayong. *See* Gozu Hōyū
non-Buddhism, non-Buddhist(s), 12, 14, 16, 65, 67, 68, 76, 77, 85, 96, 97, 115, 116, 124, 169, 201, 207, 219, 220, 221, 223, 240, 241, 247, 255, 302, 342
Nōninjakumoku. *See* Śākyamuni
non-returner. *See anāgāmin*
Northern Zhou dynasty 242
novice(s) 87, 115, 238, 376
nun(s) (*see also bhikṣuṇī*) 92, 93, 105, 106, 177, 186, 188, 189, 201, 210, 376
Nyojō (*see also* Tendō Nyojō) 4, 238, 260
Nyojōoshōgoroku 39

O

Ōbai Mountain, Ōbaizan 157, 165, 183, 186, 195, 208, 316
Ōbaku Kiun 71, 92, 104, 105, 145, 152, 183, 220, 231, 260, 360
Old Pure Criteria. See Koshingi
once-returner. *See sakṛdāgāmin*
One Hundred and One Customs of the Mūlasarvāstivādin School. See Konponissaiubuhyakuichikatsuma
One Vehicle 264, 266, 269, 386, 387, 399
On Experiencing the State. See Sandōkai
Onkō. *See* Kāśyapa
Ōryū Enan 110, 121, 360
Ōryū sect 121

P

Pāli 137, 193, 258
  canon, scriptures 71, 186, 239
Panku. *See* Banko
pārājika 96, 107

pāramitā(s) 27, 31, 279
dāna 27, 411
dhyāna 11, 27, 411
expedience 411
of knowing 264
kṣānti 27, 411
prajñā (*see also prajñāpāramitā*) 27, 411
śīla 27, 411
six 11, 27, 38, 63, 383, 398
vīrya 27, 411
wisdom-, of wisdom (*see also prajñā-pāramitā*) 38, 270, 384
Pārśva 236
Past Lives Sutra. See Honshōkyō
Patna 240
pātra (*see also* Buddhist, bowl) 62, 64, 157, 182, 194, 212, 243, 249, 258, 344
patriarch(s) 4, 5, 8, 11, 12, 14, 16, 51, 59, 65, 82, 83, 89, 118, 129, 130, 139, 157, 160, 163, 166, 179, 200, 208, 209, 213, 235, 239, 245, 246–47, 248, 249, 251, 252, 253, 254, 256, 258, 259, 264, 265, 266, 267, 297, 298, 299, 307, 314, 316, 317, 321, 325, 326, 337, 344, 345, 346, 347, 352, 365, 375, 377
ancestral 109, 127, 158, 161, 342, 344, 347
ancient 18, 69, 229
Buddhist 10, 12, 13, 16, 22, 28, 34, 59, 62, 68, 75, 77, 82, 83, 84, 93, 109, 118, 130, 158, 160, 162, 163, 176, 181, 182, 202, 203, 204, 205, 208, 209, 210, 218, 219, 220, 221, 223, 224, 225, 226, 229, 232, 235, 239, 246, 248, 249, 250, 252, 253, 254, 255, 256, 267, 290, 293, 296, 301, 302, 306, 309, 323, 328, 329, 330, 331, 341, 342, 348, 352, 353, 356, 371–72
eighteenth (*see also* Geyāśata) 314
fifteenth (*see also* Kāṇadeva) 124
first (*see also* Mahākāśyapa) 24, 249, 257, 258, 354
fourteenth (*see also* Nāgārjuna) 189
lineage of 205, 206
second (*see also* Ānanda) 29, 257, 258
seventeenth (*see also* Saṃghanandi) 331
third (*see also* Śāṇavāsa) 186
thirty-second (*see also* Daiman Kōnin) 332
thirty-third (*see also* Daikan Enō) 157, 195, 257, 264, 279, 316
twelfth (*see also* Aśvaghoṣa) 239
twentieth (*see also* Gayata) 239
twenty-eighth (*see also* Bodhidharma) 24, 124, 157, 183, 248
twenty-fifth (*see also* Vaśasuta) 239
twenty-first (*see also* Vasubandhu) 124
twenty-fourth (*see also* Siṃhabhikṣu) 124
twenty-second (*see also* Manura) 239
twenty-seventh (*see also* Prajñātara) 158, 344
venerable 76, 91, 149, 250, 251, 302, 303, 304, 305, 306, 307, 310, 325
Patriarch (*see also* Buddha) 16, 17
Peshawar 241
piśāca(s) 168, 188
Platform Sutra (*see also Rokusodaishi-hōbōdangyō*) 67
Platform Sutra of the Sixth Patriarch's Dharma Treasure. See Rokusodaishi-hōbōdangyō
power(s) 7, 21, 50, 92, 129, 176, 215, 291, 299, 302, 304, 306, 329, 364, 392
bodhi- 398
of the Buddha-Dharma 116, 134
of confession 117, 118
of the *kaṣāya* 168, 178, 189, 201

power(s) (*continued*)
mystical 171, 179, 305, 310, 365, 400, 404, 407, 408, 411, 412
of practice 116, 128
ten 398
to know others' minds 171, 300, 301, 304, 305, 306, 310
of wisdom 302, 400
Prabhūtaratna. *See* Abundant Treasures
practice(s) 4, 5, 6, 7, 8, 9, 10, 12, 13, 16, 17, 19, 21, 25, 28, 41, 43, 51, 60, 61, 65, 68, 75, 76, 77, 86, 91, 97, 99, 114, 127, 128, 129, 131, 133, 134, 138, 141, 142, 144, 147, 161, 162, 165, 166, 175, 176, 177, 178, 179, 181, 217, 218, 219, 220, 221, 224, 225, 226, 227, 245, 247, 248, 255, 269, 277, 282, 283, 289, 293, 307, 315, 316, 318, 320, 321, 323, 324, 325, 326, 327, 328, 342, 400
ascetic, of austerity, hard (*see also dhūta*) 55, 239, 399
Buddhist 10, 56, 139, 151, 282, 332, 338, 341, 367
devotional 132, 140, 197
of *dhāraṇī* 209, 215
Dharma 75, 132, 141, 197
gradual 8, 392
instantaneous 8
mantra 16, 28
original 7, 76, 132, 141, 263, 268, 269, 270, 404
power of 116, 128
quiet-reflection 16, 28
subtle 12, 13
total 264, 278
of the truth 59, 61, 203
of zazen 3, 11, 12, 27, 28, 31, 39, 55, 183, 355
practice and experience 6, 12, 13, 17, 41, 44, 69, 75, 145, 219, 220, 222, 231, 305, 341, 342, 345, 363, 364, 365, 368
prajñā (*see also* wisdom) xvii, 4, 6, 21, 27, 31, 32, 33, 34, 35, 37, 38, 39, 90, 164, 205, 279, 307, 313
Prajña 87
prajñāpāramitā (*see also mahāprajñāpāramitā; pāramitā*, wisdom) 31, 32, 33, 34, 35, 303
Prajñātara 183, 229, 237, 242, 344, 354
Prasenajit, King 367
pratyekabuddha(s) 27, 38, 94, 106, 123, 154, 172, 177, 188, 197, 281, 290, 384, 386, 390, 395, 409
precepts 16, 27, 32, 38, 39, 62, 87, 96, 107, 110, 122, 132, 163, 166, 170, 171, 175, 179, 186, 188, 203, 204, 205, 207, 208, 210, 211, 214, 231, 239, 242, 258, 260, 309, 315
bodhisattva 175, 176, 192
ceremony 108
ten important 100, 108
two hundred and fifty 87
universal 127, 138, 192
Precepts in Ten Parts (*see also Jūjuritsu*) 83
Punarvasu 231
Puṇyamitra 183, 237, 354
Puṇyatara 87
Puṇyayaśas 236
Pure Criteria for Zen Monasteries (*see also Zenenshingi*) 27, 86, 352
Pure Land 82, 269, 405
Pure Land sects 140
Pūrṇa 394
Puruṣapura 241

Q

Qingyuan Xingsi. *See* Seigen Gyōshi

R

Rāgarāja. *See* Aizenmyōō
Rāhula 83, 87
Rāhulabhadra 236
Raian Temple 214
Rājagṛha 239, 240, 278, 381
Rakan Keichin 29, 258, 309
Ratnagarbha 188
Record of Ancient Matters. See Kojiki
Record of Answers to an Emperor. See Sōtairoku
Record of the Origin of Things. See Jibutsugenki
Record of the Words of Master Tendō Nyojō. See Nyojōoshogōroku
Records of the Torch (*see also Gotōroku*) 203
Records of Transmission of the Torch. See Dentōroku
Regarder of the Sounds of the World (*see also* Avalokiteśvara) 409–410
Reiun Shigon 112, 122, 141, 155, 183, 261, 285, 360
Reiyō district 295
Rekinin 62
Rentōeyō 125, 214, 355
Ri, Minister 16
Ri Junkyoku 214
right Dharma-eye treasury xx, 11, 52, 94, 160, 169, 181, 200, 265, 267, 280, 297, 306, 327
Rinzai Gigen 71, 91–92, 104–105, 148, 154, 183, 214, 220, 231, 243, 249, 251, 252, 260, 261, 325, 332, 335, 360
Rinzai lineage, sect 4, 5, 24, 71, 91, 251, 252, 254, 288, 259, 280, 336
Ro (*see also* Daikan Enō) 176
robe(s) (*see also kaṣāya*) 21, 29, 50, 78, 86, 94, 106, 110, 157–66, 169–70, 172–82, 185-86, 187, 190, 191, 192, 193, 195–212, 229, 242, 243, 247, 249, 251, 254, 258, 291, 344, 373, 400
  antarvāsa 173–74, 190
  five-stripe 161, 173, 174, 191
  nine-stripe 161, 173, 200, 213, 373
  saṃghāṭi 167, 173, 174, 188, 191, 201–202, 373
  seven-stripe 161, 173, 174, 191
  uttarasaṃghāṭi 173, 174, 190
Rokusodaishihōbōdangyō 71, 332
Rongo 125
Rōya Ekaku 113, 123, 360
Ryogonkyō. See Śūraṃgama-sūtra
Ryōha (*see also* Musai Ryōha) 252, 259, 260
Ryōkai (*see also* Tōzan Ryōkai) 237
Ryōnenryō Dormitory 23
Ryōzan Enkan 243, 360, 372
Ryūge Kodon 30, 118, 125, 360
Ryūge Mountain 21, 30
Ryūju (*see also* Nāgārjuna) 236, 241
Ryūkō era 355
Ryūmō (*see also* Nāgārjuna) 236, 241
Ryūmon Butsugen 250, 258, 360
Ryūsaku 260
Ryūshō (*see also* Nāgārjuna) 236, 241
Ryū Shūkei 158, 183, 196
Ryūtan Sōshin 72, 290, 291, 292, 295, 296, 298, 299, 360
Ryūzen 251

S

Sacred Monk, image of 348, 349, 350
Saddharmapuṇḍarīka-sūtra (*see also Lotus Sutra; Sutra of the Lotus Flower of the Wonderful Dharma*) 280, 381
Sāgara 399
sahā world 49, 55, 82, 87, 315, 400, 402, 406, 410
Saichō 26
Saishōōkyō. See Supreme King Sutra

Saisui River 334
Śakra (*see also* Śakra-devānām-indra) 175, 191, 409
Śakra-devānām-indra (*see also* Indra; Śakra) 39, 99, 191, 197, 381
sakṛdāgāmin 38, 106, 215
Śākya clan 184, 278
Śākyamuni 4, 7, 12, 17, 18, 19, 20, 25, 26, 32, 34, 70, 84, 90, 97, 98, 137, 157, 159, 160, 166, 167, 169, 170, 171, 172, 174, 182, 184, 188, 195, 197, 198, 200, 201, 202, 212, 226, 236, 247, 249, 255, 256, 261, 263, 264, 265, 269, 274, 278, 286, 289, 302, 306, 351, 383, 397, 399, 408, 412
samādhi(s) xvi, xvii, 3, 5, 8, 9, 23, 209, 215, 263, 265, 365, 384, 408–409
-*dhāraṇī*(s) 205, 215
of receiving and using the self 3, 5, 8, 303, 305–306
Samādhi, the State of a Jewel-Mirror. See Hōkyōzanmai
Samantabhadra. *See* Universal Virtue
śamatha 28
Saṃghanandi 236, 315, 316, 331
Śāṇavāsa 165–66, 186, 208, 236
Sandōkai 154, 242, 369
sangha xv, 50, 60, 104, 161, 174, 193, 287, 348, 351, 376, 411
Sangoryakuki 333
Sansheng Huiran. *See* Sanshō Enen
Sanshō Enen 260, 324, 325, 335, 336, 337, 360
Sanshōin Temple 323
Sanskrit xvii, xviii, 23, 25, 26, 27, 28, 29, 30, 31, 37, 38, 39, 47, 55, 63, 64, 73, 85, 87, 88, 104, 106, 107, 108, 123, 124, 138, 140, 141, 154, 157, 160, 184, 185, 186, 187, 188, 189, 190, 191, 192, 193, 213, 214, 215, 231, 232, 233, 239, 240, 241, 257, 258, 259, 277, 278, 279, 280, 281, 283, 284, 285, 286, 295, 311, 331, 337, 350, 353, 354, 356, 357, 358, 364, 381
Sanskrit-English Dictionary xviii, 239
Sanzō 300–302, 303–307, 309, 310
Śāriputra 34, 35, 39, 77, 85, 190, 287, 384, 385, 386, 388, 389
Sarvāstivāda school 28, 87, 190
Schiffer, Wilhelm 381
School of the Elders (*see also* Theravāda) 240, 258
Second Council 240
Second Patriarch (*see also* Taiso Eka) 24, 49, 55, 254
secular 11, 29, 47, 49, 76, 77, 90, 93, 95, 96, 99, 106, 113, 114, 116, 117, 128, 160, 165, 166, 173, 176, 178, 182, 184, 196, 199, 203, 208, 209, 210, 212, 219, 223, 225, 230, 300, 319
Seidō Chizō 338
Seigen Gyōshi 5, 24, 145, 152, 154, 161, 183, 184, 230, 242, 243, 254–55, 261, 264, 279, 295, 325, 337, 360, 372
Seihō 18
Seion (*see also* Ryūmon Butsugen) 250
Seiryō (*see also* Shinketsu Seiryō) 238
Seiryōji 295
Seiryū Commentaries 290, 295, 298
Sekimon-rinkanroku 368
Sekisō Soen (*see also* Jimyō Soen) 121
Sekitō Kisen 145, 148, 152, 153, 154, 242, 295, 353, 360, 369, 372
Sekitōsōan-no-uta 242
Senika 14, 28, 65, 67, 68
Senjūhyakuenkyō 186
Senshi. *See* Tendō Nyojō
Sensō, Emperor 122
Sensu Tokujō 233, 360
Seppō Gison 49–50, 55, 230, 295, 309, 310, 313, 318–19, 320, 321–26, 327, 333, 335, 336, 337, 338, 360

Seppō Mountain, Seppōzan 49, 323
Setchō Chikan 24, 244, 360, 372
Setchō Jūken 303, 306, 311, 361
Setsukōshō 249
Seven Buddhas (*see also* buddhas, seven ancient) 9, 25–26, 83, 127, 246, 247, 251, 254, 257, 264, 394
Seventh Patriarch (*see also* Seigen Gyōshi) 24
Sha. *See* Gensha Shibi
Shakamuni. *See* Śākyamuni
Shaolin Temple xix, 11, 27, 124, 162, 183, 185, 195, 203, 363, 367
shashu 63, 86, 188, 355, 357
Shibi. *See* Gensha Shibi
Shibi county 53
Shibunritsu 107
Shikō 252
Shin Daichu. *See* Chōsha Keishin
Shijun (*see also* Tanka Shijun) 238
Shikan (*see also* Kankei Shikan) 91, 92
Shin (*see also* Ryūtan Sōshin) 290
Shingi (see also *Zenenshingi*) 82
Shingon sect 9, 26, 28
Shinjinmei 242, 367
Shinji-shōbōgenzō 27, 47, 55, 57, 73, 85, 104, 122, 123, 140, 141, 155, 231, 233, 243, 283, 285, 296, 332, 333, 335, 336, 337, 338, 339, 353, 354, 355
Shinkaku (*see also* Seppō Gison) 49, 55, 318, 323, 333
Shinketsu Seiryō 244, 361, 372
Shinsai (*see also* Jōshū Jūshin) 91, 104, 345, 354
Shinshō (*see also* Daizui Hōshin) 345, 355
Shintō, Shintōist(s) 10, 26
Shisen. *See* Tōba
Shishuang Chuyuan. *See* Jimyō Soen
shiso. *See* succession, certificate of
Shitou Xiqian. *See* Sekitō Kisen
Shō (*see also* Fuketsu Enshō; Fun'yo Zenshō; Kōke Sonshō) 252
shōbō. *See* Dharma, right
Shōbōgenzō xv–xx, 3, 22, 23, 24, 34, 38, 41, 45, 48, 53, 55, 56, 59, 70, 84, 101, 119, 136, 138, 142, 149, 181, 212, 227, 229, 238, 256, 257, 259, 274, 279, 285, 293, 307, 330, 352, 367, 381
  Chapter One, *Bendōwa* xvi, xvii, xviii, 3–29, 38, 71, 242, 310, 311, 385, 390, 393, 410
  Chapter Two, *Maka-hannya-haramitsu* xix, 24, 25, 31–39, 47, 104, 279
  Chapter Three, *Genjō-kōan* 40–48, 72, 123, 125, 155, 231
  Chapter Four, *Ikka-no-myōjo* 27, 49–57, 310, 337, 394, 400
  Chapter Five, *Jū-undō-shiki* 58–64
  Chapter Six, *Soku-shin-ze-butsu* 26, 28, 65–73, 125, 310
  Chapter Seven, *Senjō* 75–88, 187, 231, 242, 335, 368
  Chapter Eight, *Raihai-tokuzui* 89–108, 121, 192, 310, 337, 368, 400, 406
  Chapter Nine, *Keisei-sanshiki* 29, 109–125, 338, 368, 395, 400
  Chapter Ten, *Shoaku-makusa* xviii, 127–42, 215, 384, 388
  Chapter Eleven, *Uji* 139, 143–55, 334, 354, 382
  Chapter Twelve, *Kesa-kudoku* 29, 86, 157–94, 213, 214, 233, 240, 241, 331, 394
  Chapter Thirteen, *Den-e* 86, 194, 195–216, 233, 406
  Chapter Fourteen, *Sansuigyō* 217–34, 243, 259, 334, 406
  Chapter Fifteen, *Busso* 25, 28, 137, 184, 235–44, 257, 279, 331, 332, 355
  Chapter Sixteen, *Shisho* 55, 245–62, 355, 368

Shōbōgenzō (*continued*)
Chapter Seventeen, *Hokke-ten-hokke* xvii, xix, 27, 141, 142, 230, 263–87, 353, 354, 381, 382, 383, 384, 385, 386, 387, 388, 389, 390, 391, 392, 394, 396, 397, 398, 399, 400, 402, 403, 404, 405, 407, 408, 409, 410, 412
Chapter Eighteen, *Shin-fukatoku (The Former)* 28, 72, 107, 289–96
Chapter Nineteen, *Shin-fukatoku (The Latter)* 28, 107, 297–311
Chapter Twenty, *Kokyō* 283, 313–39, 367, 406
Chapter Twenty-one, *Kankin* xvii, 63, 64, 242, 341–58
Chapter Twenty-two (Vol. II), *Busshō* 37, 39, 56, 57, 215, 241, 242, 332, 335
Chapter Twenty-three (Vol. II), *Gyō-butsu-yuigi* 385, 398, 404
Chapter Twenty-four (Vol. II), *Bukkyō* 27, 38, 106, 153, 154, 387, 408
Chapter Twenty-five (Vol. II), *Jinzū* 40, 189, 391, 407, 408, 411
Chapter Twenty-six (Vol. II), *Daigo* 47
Chapter Twenty-seven (Vol. II), *Zazen-shin* 242, 286, 368, 369
Chapter Twenty-eight (Vol. II), *Butsu-kōjō-no-ji* 155, 239, 368
Chapter Twenty-nine (Vol. II), *Inmo* 27, 28, 57, 85, 103, 105, 151, 231, 259, 333, 335, 367, 387, 388, 391
Chapter Thirty (Vol. II), *Gyōji* 55, 103, 121, 124, 186, 191, 192, 215, 240, 242, 244, 261, 283, 309, 368
Chapter Thirty-one (Vol. II), *Kai-in-zanmai* 390
Chapter Thirty-two (Vol. II), *Juki* 279, 394, 395
Chapter Thirty-three (Vol. II), *Kannon* 37, 56, 138, 188, 409
Chapter Thirty-four (Vol. II), *Arakan* 26, 106, 189, 381, 386, 391
Chapter Thirty-five (Vol. II), *Haku-jushi* 104, 310, 354
Chapter Thirty-six (Vol. II), *Kōmyō* 287, 383
Chapter Thirty-seven (Vol. II), *Shinjin-gakudō* 232, 407
Chapter Thirty-eight (Vol. II), *Muchū-setsumu* 232, 390, 401
Chapter Forty (Vol. II), *Gabyō* 122, 296, 382
Chapter Forty-two (Vol. III), *Tsuki* 30, 140, 232, 242
Chapter Forty-three (Vol. III), *Kūge* 27, 122, 229, 404
Chapter Forty-four (Vol. III), *Kobusshin* 28, 242, 311, 332
Chapter Forty-five (Vol. III), *Bodai-satta-shishōbō* 38, 398
Chapter Forty-six (Vol. III), *Kattō* 25, 103, 123, 231, 242, 257, 309, 394
Chapter Forty-seven (Vol. III), *Sangai-yuishin* 71, 72, 232, 310, 390, 403, 404
Chapter Forty-eight (Vol. III), *Sesshin-sesshō* 230, 242, 243
Chapter Forty-nine (Vol. III), *Butsudō* 24, 71, 214, 242, 258, 260
Chapter Fifty (Vol. III), *Shohō-jissō* 142, 232, 382, 383, 384, 387, 388, 396, 404
Chapter Fifty-one (Vol. III), *Mitsugo* 244, 397
Chapter Fifty-two (Vol. III), *Bukkyō* xix, 215, 230, 354, 383, 407
Chapter Fifty-three (Vol. III), *Mujō-seppō* 124, 243, 388

Chapter Fifty-four (Vol. III), *Hosshō* 384
Chapter Fifty-five (Vol. III), *Darani* 215
Chapter Fifty-six (Vol. III), *Senmen* 86, 191, 400
Chapter Fifty-eight (Vol. III), *Zazengi* 286
Chapter Fifty-nine (Vol. III), *Baike* 244
Chapter Sixty (Vol. III), *Juppō* 122, 385, 387, 404
Chapter Sixty-one (Vol. III), *Kenbutsu* 233, 283, 284, 391, 396, 398, 401, 404, 405, 406, 408, 411, 412
Chapter Sixty-two (Vol. III), *Hensan* 27, 55, 85, 231, 232, 280, 333, 402
Chapter Sixty-three (Vol. III), *Ganzei* 243
Chapter Sixty-four (Vol. III), *Kajō* 243, 259
Chapter Sixty-six (Vol. III), *Shunjū* 243, 259, 333
Chapter Sixty-seven (Vol. III), *Soshi-sarai-no-ji* 154
Chapter Sixty-eight (Vol. III), *Udonge* 123, 154, 257, 261, 280, 309, 355, 385
Chapter Sixty-nine (Vol. III), *Hotsu-mujōshin* 106, 336, 388, 401
Chapter Seventy (Vol. III), *Hotsu-bodai-shin* xviii, 106, 107, 124, 241, 405
Chapter Seventy-one (Vol. III), *Nyorai-zenshin* 56, 141, 283, 396, 399, 403, 404
Chapter Seventy-two (Vol. III), *Zanmai-ō-zanmai* 24, 242, 244, 381, 401
Chapter Seventy-three (Vol. IV), *San-jūshichi-bon-bodai-bunpō* 139, 391, 395, 399, 408, 411
Chapter Seventy-four (Vol. IV), *Ten-bōrin* 25, 38, 259
Chapter Seventy-five (Vol. IV), *Jishō-zanmai* 259
Chapter Seventy-six (Vol. IV), *Dai-shugyō* 57, 139, 333, 400
Chapter Seventy-seven (Vol. IV), *Kokū* 39, 240, 280, 285
Chapter Seventy-eight (Vol. IV), *Hatsu-u* 64
Chapter Seventy-nine (Vol. IV), *Ango* 295, 385
Chapter Eighty (Vol. IV), *Tashintsū* 183, 310
Chapter Eighty-one (Vol. IV), *Ō-saku-sendaba* 230
Chapter Eighty-three (Vol. IV), *Shukke* 186, 403
Chapter Eighty-four (Vol. IV), *Sanji-no-gō* 241
Chapter Eighty-five (Vol. IV), *Shime* 241
Chapter Eighty-six (Vol. IV), *Shukke-kudoku* 189, 240, 310, 382, 393, 411
Chapter Eighty-seven (Vol. IV), *Kuyō-shōbutsu* 190, 387, 397
Chapter Eighty-eight (Vol. IV), *Kie-sanbō* 405
Chapter Eighty-nine (Vol. IV), *Shinjin-inga* 139, 241
Chapter Ninety (Vol. IV), *Shizen-biku* 39, 193, 240, 241
Chapter Ninety-one (Vol. IV), *Yui-butsu-yo-butsu* 232, 384
Chapter Ninety-two (Vol. IV), *Shōji* 28
Chapter Ninety-three (Vol. IV), *Dōshin* 106
Chapter Ninety-four (Vol. IV), *Jukai* 108, 192
ninety-five–chapter edition xvii, 3, 59, 297
seventy-five–chapter edition 41, 59

Shōbōgenzō in Modern Japanese. See Gendaigo-yaku-shōbōgenzō
Shōdōka 107, 187, 233, 369
Shōjō era 4, 24
Shojū 214
Shōkaku Jōsō 110–111, 121, 361
Shōken Kishō 154, 361
Shōken region 148, 155
Shoko 123, 369
Shoku district 92, 93
Shōmu, Emperor 176, 191
Shōrinji, Shōrin Temple. *See* Shaolin Temple
Shō River 51, 56
Shōshitsu Peak 27, 124
Shōshū district 265, 342
Shōtoku, Prince 175–76, 191
Shoushan Shengnian. *See* Shuzan Shōnen
Shū (*see also* Tokusan Senkan) 290, 295, 298
Shūgetsu 249
Shugyōhongikyō 123
Shūitsu (*see also* Gensha Shibi) 49, 55
Shukusō, Emperor 157, 175, 183, 191, 195, 301
Shushu district 233
Shuzan Shōnen 148, 154, 155, 255, 260, 361
Sichuan province 105
Side Saint (*see also* Pārśva) 240
Śikhin 25, 235
Śikṣānanda 87
śīla (*see also pāramitā;* precepts) 27, 38
Siṃha 237
Siṃhabhikṣu 124
six *pāramitās*. *See pāramitā*(s), six
six states of existence, rebirth 6, 53, 57, 66, 71, 114
Sixth Patriarch (*see also* Daikan Enō) 5, 19, 24, 71, 75, 122, 123, 124, 157, 189, 208, 246, 257, 261, 279, 316, 331
Small Vehicle (*see also* Hinayana) 97, 162, 223, 305, 306
Sōji 123
Sōkaku (*see also* Tendō Sōkaku) 165, 179, 206, 207, 208, 220, 238
Sōkei (*see also* Daikan Enō) 157, 172, 183, 208, 246, 254, 255, 267, 273, 317, 332, 343
Sōkei (*see also* Nan'yō Echū) 68, 92
Sōkei Mountain, Sōkeizan 157, 158, 160, 162, 172, 183, 185, 195, 196, 200, 203, 242, 261, 265, 332, 342
Sokkō 18–19, 29
Song dynasty (*see also* Southern Song dynasty) 4, 5, 13, 17, 22, 49, 68, 71, 76, 93, 94, 97, 109, 162, 181, 182, 185, 196, 203, 205, 211, 212, 214, 220, 221, 230, 238, 243, 248, 252, 254, 256, 260, 275, 281, 291, 332, 355
"Song of Experiencing the Truth." *See Shōdōka*
Songs from Sekitō's Thatched Hut. See Sekitōsoan-no-uta
Songshan Mountains (*see also* Suzan Mountains) 11, 27, 124, 183, 242
Soothill, William 381
Sōsan (*see also* Kanchi Sosan) 140, 237
Sōshi 233, 334
Soshoku. *See* Tōba
Sōtairoku 259
So Tōba. *See* Tōba
Sōtō sect 5, 24, 154, 258, 279
Southern Song dynasty (*see also* Song dynasty) 332, 355, 375
śramaṇa (*see also* monk) 22, 62, 87, 177, 178, 192, 212, 256, 275
śrāmaṇera(s) (*see also* novice) 87, 358, 393, 394
Śrāmaṇera Kō (*see also* Kō-shami) 352
śrāvaka(s) xvii, 26, 27, 38, 97, 99, 100, 106, 124, 132, 154, 169, 172, 177,

188, 189, 202, 205, 206, 207, 215, 220, 223, 266, 281, 290, 384, 385, 390, 395, 396, 400, 406, 409
four stages of 38, 106, 215
Śrāvastī 240, 241, 367
Sri Lanka 71, 240
Śrīmālā Sutra, Śrīmālādevīsiṃhanāda-sūtra 175, 191
srotāpanna 38, 106, 215
stage(s) 6, 13, 105, 152, 234, 273, 307
fifty-two 105, 215, 257, 311
four, of *śrāvaka*s 38, 106, 215
myōkaku 105, 215, 257, 311
ten, of belief 105, 215, 311
ten sacred 91, 93, 94, 98, 105, 204, 208, 215, 255, 257, 302, 304, 311, 315
three clever 91, 93, 94, 98, 105, 204, 208, 215, 255, 302, 304, 311, 315
tōkaku 105, 215, 257, 311
Stanford University 234
Star Constellation King Flower 408
Stone Woman 217, 219
stream-enterer. *See srotāpanna*
stupa(s) 196, 260, 272, 273, 285, 286, 378, 387
treasure, of seven treasures 272, 273, 396, 397
Subhūti 33, 39
succession(s) (*see also* transmission) 51, 154, 160, 195, 204, 245, 246, 247–48, 249, 250, 251, 252, 253, 255–56, 257, 261
certificate of 245, 247–49, 250, 251–52, 253, 254
Sudatta 367
Sūgaku Peak 157, 158
Sui dynasty 162, 175, 185, 232
Śukra 166, 186
Sumeru Peak 394
Sun Buddha. *See* Vairocana
Sun Goddess. *See* Amaterasu
Sun Moon Light 382, 383
śūnyatā 28, 37, 285
Śūnyatā school 28
Supplementary Record of the Torch. See Zokutōroku
Supreme King Sutra (*see also Golden Light Sutra*) 351, 357
Śūraṃgama-sūtra 123
sutra(s) xviii, xix, 4, 5, 8, 18, 31, 37, 38, 50, 76, 85, 108, 113, 123, 128, 152, 154, 160, 162, 169, 175, 179, 182, 184, 188, 189, 191, 203, 204, 208, 212, 214, 216, 217, 223, 239, 240, 246, 258, 265, 266, 267, 273, 290, 295, 299, 309, 315, 316, 319, 331, 341, 342, 343, 345, 346, 347, 348, 349, 350, 351, 353, 354, 356, 357, 376, 383, 387, 393, 394, 395, 396, 397, 398, 400, 401, 406, 408, 412
Āgama 181, 193, 194, 202, 211, 214, 242
reading 5, 8, 61, 63, 245, 265, 305, 315, 341–42, 343, 346, 347, 348, 350, 351, 352, 354, 355, 356, 376
Sutra of Reflection on the Practice of Dharma by Bodhisattva Universal Virtue. See Kanfugenbosatsugyohokyō
Sutra of the Flower of Dharma (*see also Lotus Sutra*) 26, 267, 342–43, 396, 397, 406, 408, 412
Sutra of the Lotus Flower of the Wonderful Dharma (*see also Lotus Sutra*) 263, 265, 381, 383, 394, 395, 399
Sutra of the Lotus Flower of the Wonderful Law, The 381
Sutra of Three Thousand Dignified Forms for Ordained Monks 75, 82
Sutra-reading Monk (*see also* Hōtatsu) 267, 343
Suvarṇaprabhāsa-sūtra. See Golden Light Sutra

Suvarṇaprabhāsottamarāja-sūtra. See Golden Light Sutra; Supreme King Sutra
Suzan Mountains (*see also* Songshan Mountains) 116, 124
Suzong. *See* Shukusō

T

Taishitsu Peak 27, 124
Taisō, Emperor 16, 28, 157, 175, 183, 191, 195, 319–20, 334
Taiso Eka 24, 55, 103, 121, 123, 242, 257, 261, 361, 372
Taisui Fazhen. *See* Daizui Hōshin
Taiyō Kyōgen 243, 257, 361, 372
Taiyōzan (*see also* Mount Taiyō) 217, 243
tāla tree 411
Tamura, Yoshiro 381
Tan (*see also* Kaie Shutan) 252, 306
Tang dynasty 13, 14, 28, 49, 67, 71, 91, 122, 133, 157, 162, 183, 185, 191, 195, 196, 203, 206, 265, 295, 301, 325, 334
Tanka Shijun 243–44, 361, 372
Tankazan 243
Tan River 51, 56
tathāgata(s) (*see also* buddha-tathāgata) 7, 23, 34
Tathāgata xvii, 8, 11, 21, 83, 95, 98, 115, 135, 148, 158, 160, 161, 162, 164, 166, 169, 172, 175, 176, 178, 181, 184, 203, 205, 206, 211, 225, 249, 264, 265, 273, 285, 383, 384, 386, 390, 395, 396, 403, 404, 406, 412
Tekisan. *See* Yafu Dōsen
Tendai Chigi 26, 191, 260
Tendai Fugan 261
Tendai sect 24, 26, 28, 191, 260, 261, 284
Tendaizan (*see also* Mount Tendai) 253, 254
Tendō Nyojō (*see also* Nyojō) 24, 27, 30, 85, 103, 123, 139, 238, 244, 259, 260, 346, 361, 372
Tendō Sōkaku (*see also* Sōkaku) 244, 361, 372
Tendō Temple 248, 249, 251, 252, 254, 255
Tendōzan (*see also* Mount Tendō) 23, 24, 244, 251, 259, 260, 346
Tengai 314
Tennō Dōgo 295
Tenpuku era 34, 45
Tenshō era 214
Tenshō Era Record of the Widely Extending Torch. See Tenshōkōtōroku
Tenshōkōtōroku (*see also Kōtōroku*) 214
Theravāda, Theravādin(s) 40, 240, 258
Third Patriarch (*see also* Kanchi Sōsan) 316, 331
thirty-two marks 121, 188, 278
three baskets. *See* Tripiṭaka
three carts, parable of (*see also* carts, three) 266, 281, 282, 389
Threefold Lotus Sutra 284, 285, 381
three kinds of burning pain, heat 159, 184, 198
three kinds of training 11, 39
three mirrors 319–20, 334, 335
three poisons 115, 123
three properties 128, 131, 140
three (miserable) states, of existence 6, 25
Three Treasures (*see also* Buddha, Dharma, and Sangha) 82, 104, 108, 164, 167, 188, 405
three worlds (*see also* worlds, three, triple) 66, 71
Tianjin, Tianjin Bridge 301, 302, 310
Tiantong Rujing. *See* Tendō Nyojō
Tiantong Zongjue. *See* Tendō Sōkaku
Tōba 109, 110, 121

Tokkō (*see also* Busshō Tokkō) 252, 260
Toku 140
Tokujō (*see also* Sensu Tokujō) 226, 233
Tokusan Senkan 55, 72, 289, 290, 295, 333, 361
Tokyo 335
To Moku 230
Tongan Daopi. *See* Dōan Dōhi
Tongan Guanzhi. *See* Dōan Kanshi
Tōsai 355
Tōsu Gisei 229, 243, 257, 259, 361, 372
Touzi Yiqing. *See* Tōsu Gisei
Tōzan Ryōkai (*see also* Ryōkai) 30, 125, 214, 243, 249, 254, 261, 346, 355, 361, 367, 372
transmission (*see also* succession) 9, 10, 11, 13, 22, 24, 26, 59, 94, 95, 100, 113, 115, 123, 127, 157, 158, 160, 163, 165, 172, 181, 195, 199, 200, 202, 203, 204, 206, 208, 210, 212, 213, 215, 235, 245, 247, 250, 256, 257, 259, 261, 275, 292, 296, 299, 309
  authentic 4, 5, 8, 9, 10, 16, 44, 76, 84, 157, 159, 160, 162, 163, 164, 166, 169, 172, 181, 182, 195, 197, 198, 199–200, 203–204, 205, 207, 208, 209, 210, 211, 212, 242, 254, 297, 306, 344
  face-to-face 158, 160, 161, 172, 199, 246
  one-to-one 3, 11, 12, 94, 167, 209, 245, 298
Tripiṭaka 124, 189, 193, 199, 214, 240, 248, 258, 301, 302, 304, 306, 309, 310
Tuṣita Heaven 310
twelve divisions of the teachings 147–48, 154
twelve causal conditions, twelvefold cycle 10, 27, 393
twelve entrances 32, 37

U

uḍumbara flower 154, 247, 254, 261, 309, 386
Uji district 53, 70, 84, 238, 243, 293, 352, 355
Ungan Donjō 243, 355, 361, 372
Ungo Dōyō 57, 103, 125, 243, 355, 356, 361, 372
Ungozan 243, 348
Universal Guide to the Standard Practice of Zazen. See Fukanzazengi
Universal Light 394
Universal Surpassing Wisdom 393
Universal Virtue 264, 278, 412
Unmon Bun'en 214, 220, 230, 234, 249, 309, 311, 361
Unmonkōroku 234
Unmon sect 5, 24, 230, 258, 279, 299, 309, 311
Unmonzan 249
Upagupta 236
Upāli 173–74, 190
Upananda 231
upāsaka(s) (*see also* layman) 98, 99, 106, 107, 167, 385, 395, 406, 407, 410
upāsikā(s) (*see also* laywoman) 98, 99, 106, 107, 167, 85, 395, 406, 407, 410
Utpalavarṇā 170, 171, 189
Uzuran 314, 331

V

Vairocana 9, 26, 85, 269, 284, 376
Vaiśravaṇa 409
vajra 410
Vajracchedikāprajñāpāramitā-sūtra. See Diamond Sutra
Vajrasattva 9, 26
Vajrayana 26
Vaśasuta 237
Vasubandhu 124, 237, 241

Vasumitra 236
vehicle(s) (*see also* Great Vehicle; One Vehicle; Small Vehicle) 154, 267, 363, 390
five 10, 27
four 124
three 10, 27, 147, 154, 168, 201, 266, 281, 390
two 68, 115, 273, 302, 304, 305
Vietnam 357
Vimalakīrti 67, 71, 338
Vimalakīrtinirdeśa-sūtra. *See Vimalakīrti Sutra*
Vimalakīrti Room 254
Vimalakīrti Sutra 71, 184, 348
Vinaya 87, 88, 169, 188, 189, 190, 214, 239, 240, 258
Vinaya in Four Divisions. *See Shibun-ritsu*
vipaśyanā 28
Vipaśyin 25, 235, 257
Viśvabhū 25, 235, 257
von Schelling, Friedrich Wilhelm 289
Vulture Peak (*see also* Gṛdhrakūṭa) 4, 8, 11, 22, 24, 264, 265, 269, 272–73, 278, 280, 285, 286, 404, 405

W

Wai River 92
Waisui River 334
Wakayama prefecture 335
Wanshijuko 353
Wanshi Shōgaku 243
Way, the 18, 32, 49, 107, 118, 319
Wei dynasty 116
Weiyi. *See* Iichi
Weizheng. *See* Gichō
Western Heavens (*see also* India) 5, 8, 15, 16, 24, 50, 55, 83, 85, 115, 124, 160, 162, 166, 172, 195, 199, 206, 209, 248, 249, 300, 302, 306, 310, 365
Western philosophy xv
West River 301, 302
wheel-turning king(s) 99, 133, 196, 197, 213, 393
wisdom (*see also prajñā*) 20, 21, 24, 27, 31, 32, 33, 35, 38, 39, 164, 169, 177, 246, 264, 265, 266, 277, 279, 281, 282, 283, 302, 313, 315, 316, 345, 353, 354, 384, 400, 407, 408, 411
Buddha, buddha-, of the buddhas 7, 15, 187, 246, 263, 265, 266, 267, 270, 271, 273, 280, 281, 384, 385, 386, 401, 402
complete, perfect 16, 23
inferior 8, 187
kalpa of 255, 261
-*pāramitā, pāramitā* of 270, 384
-seal 408
Wisdom Accumulation 399
Wisdom-Brightness (*see also* Chikō) 177, 178
Wonder Sound 408
world(s) 7, 9, 11, 17, 20, 25, 29, 34, 43, 47, 49, 63, 69, 82, 90, 91, 92, 97, 98, 100, 104, 109, 115, 116, 128, 129, 131, 132, 146, 147, 153, 162, 168, 169, 170, 179, 190, 196, 197, 202, 210, 218, 223, 226, 229, 255, 263, 264, 265, 267, 271, 272, 273, 280, 283, 285, 310, 313, 315, 317, 320, 325, 326, 337, 341, 343, 344, 345, 354, 386, 387, 388, 391, 400, 402, 403, 404, 407
of aggregates 344, 345, 354
Buddha's, of the buddhas 100, 101, 162
of demons 25, 100
Dharma, of the Dharma xv, 5, 6, 15, 100, 118, 218, 223, 224, 232, 269–70, 271, 273, 326
external 7, 39, 42, 118, 221, 289, 301, 325
of gods 25

great-thousandfold, thousandfold, three-thousandfold 20, 59, 63, 158, 196, 205, 271, 326, 392, 399, 402, 403
human, of human beings 25, 55, 69, 87, 96, 99, 128, 175, 189, 196, 226, 232, 248, 299, 302, 314
of hungry ghosts 25
of the immaterial 71
literary 109, 134
material, physical 106, 232
of matter 40, 71, 174, 175, 191, 192, 232
sahā 49, 82, 87, 315, 400, 402, 406, 410
secular 29, 47, 76, 90, 93, 113, 128, 173, 210, 225
spirit 14
three, triple 25, 66, 69, 71, 72, 95, 98, 99, 269, 280, 283, 297, 301, 390, 404
of volition 71, 107, 175, 191, 192, 215
World-honored One (*see also* Buddha) 33, 76, 164, 167, 168, 169, 173, 174, 177, 190, 382, 384, 386, 394, 395, 397, 403, 411
worldly 17, 20, 60, 95, 114, 116
World of the Bright Banner 174, 190–91
Wu dynasty 152
Wu, Emperor (*see also* Bu) 191, 336
Wuji Liaopai. *See* Musai Ryōha
Wuzu Fayan. *See* Goso Hōen

X

Xiangyan Zhixian. *See* Kyōgen Chikan
Xinghua Congjiang. *See* Kōke Sonshō
Xuansha Shibei. *See* Gensha Shibi
Xuanyuan. *See* Kenen
Xuedou Chongxian. *See* Setchō Jūken
Xuedou Zhijian. *See* Setchō Chikan
Xuefeng Yicun. *See* Seppō Gison

Y

Yafu Dōsen 347, 355, 361
Yafuzan 355
yakṣa(s) (*see also* demon) 108, 395, 410
Yakusan Igen (*see also* Kōdō) 52, 147–48, 151, 153, 233, 242, 243, 342, 353, 355, 358, 361, 368, 372
Yakusan Mountain 226, 342, 347, 352
Yamashiro-no-kuni (*see also* Yōshū) 244
Yang, Emperor 175, 191
Yangqi Fanghui. *See* Yōgi Hōe
Yangshan Huiji. *See* Kyōzan Ejaku
Yangzi River 334
Yaśodharā 87
Yefu Daochuan. *See* Yafu Dōsen
Yellow Emperor (*see also* Kōtei) 226, 233, 319, 334
Yellow River 334
Yellow Sea 258
Yexian Guisheng. *See* Shōken Kishō
yin and *yang* 10, 26, 319, 320, 333
Yogācāra school 241
Yōgi Hōe 252, 259, 260
Yōgizan 259, 260
Yōka Genkaku 107, 187, 233, 369
Yō Kōshu 45
Yōmei, Emperor 21
Yoshida district 53, 256
Yōshu 53, 70, 84, 238, 293, 310, 352
Yōshū 244
Yuancai. *See* Genshi
Yuanwu Keqin. *See* Engo Kokugon
Yueshan Weiyan. *See* Yakusan Igen
Yunju Daoying. *See* Ungo Dōyō
Yunmen Wenyan. *See* Unmon Bun'en
Yunyan Tansheng. *See* Ungan Donjō

Z

zazen xviii, 3, 6, 7–8, 9, 10, 11, 12, 13, 16, 17, 18, 19, 20, 21, 23, 25, 28, 31, 39,

zazen (*continued*)
55, 56, 61, 87, 107, 124, 139, 141, 183, 184, 193, 215, 229, 231, 234, 240, 242, 279, 281, 282, 286, 329, 355, 364, 365, 367, 369
chair 345, 346
hall(s) 13, 59, 63, 64, 86, 260, 277, 341, 351, 356, 357, 376, 377
sect (*see also* Zen, sect) 27
Zen 16, 60, 105, 220, 274
concentration (*see also* zazen) 364, 368
kōan 259, 310
master(s) xix, 18, 19, 110, 135
monastery(ies) 4, 13
sect(s) 11, 26, 141
Zenenshingi 27, 79
Zengaku-daijiten 239
Zengen. *See* Subhūti
Zenkō. *See* Myōzen
Zhaozhou Congshen. *See* Jōshū Jūshin
Zhen dynasty 162, 185
Zhenxie Qingliao. *See* Shinketsu Seiryō
Zhongzong. *See* Chūsō
Zhuangzi 184, 233
zōbō. *See* Dharma, imitative
Zokudentōroku 63
Zokutōroku 203, 214
Zu. *See* To Moku

BDK English Tripiṭaka (First Series)

Abbreviations

Ch.:	Chinese
Skt.:	Sanskrit
Jp.:	Japanese
Eng.:	Published title

	Title	**Taishō No.**
Ch.	Changahanjing (長阿含經)	1
Skt.	Dīrghāgama	
Ch.	Zhongahanjing (中阿含經)	26
Skt.	Madhyamāgama	
Ch.	Dachengbenshengxindiguanjing (大乘本生心地觀經)	159
Ch.	Fosuoxingzan (佛所行讚)	192
Skt.	Buddhacarita	
Ch.	Zabaocangjing (雜寶藏經)	203
Eng.	*The Storehouse of Sundry Valuables* (1994)	
Ch.	Fajupiyujing (法句譬喩經)	211
Eng.	*The Scriptural Text: Verses of the Doctrine, with Parables* (1999)	
Ch.	Xiaopinbanruoboluomijing (小品般若波羅蜜經)	227
Skt.	Aṣṭasāhasrikā-prajñāpāramitā-sūtra	
Ch.	Jingangbanruoboluomijing (金剛般若波羅蜜經)	235
Skt.	Vajracchedikā-prajñāpāramitā-sūtra	
Ch.	Daluojingangbukongzhenshisanmoyejing (大樂金剛不空眞實三麼耶經)	243
Skt.	Adhyardhaśatikā-prajñāpāramitā-sūtra	
Ch.	Renwangbanruoboluomijing (仁王般若波羅蜜經)	245
Skt.	Kāruṇikārājā-prajñāpāramitā-sūtra (?)	

Title		Taishō No.
Ch.	Banruoboluomiduoxingjing (般若波羅蜜多心經)	251
Skt.	Prajñāpāramitāhṛdaya-sūtra	
Ch.	Miaofalianhuajing (妙法蓮華經)	262
Skt.	Saddharmapuṇḍarīka-sūtra	
Eng.	*The Lotus Sutra* (Revised Second Edition, 2007)	
Ch.	Wuliangyijing (無量義經)	276
Ch.	Guanpuxianpusaxingfajing (觀普賢菩薩行法經)	277
Ch.	Dafangguangfohuayanjing (大方廣佛華嚴經)	278
Skt.	Avataṃsaka-sūtra	
Ch.	Shengmanshizihouyichengdafangbianfangguangjing (勝鬘師子吼一乘大方便方廣經)	353
Skt.	Śrīmālādevīsiṃhanāda-sūtra	
Eng.	*The Sutra of Queen Śrīmālā of the Lion's Roar* (2004)	
Ch.	Wuliangshoujing (無量壽經)	360
Skt.	Sukhāvatīvyūha	
Eng.	*The Larger Sutra on Amitāyus* (in *The Three Pure Land Sutras,* Revised Second Edition, 2003)	
Ch.	Guanwuliangshoufojing (觀無量壽佛經)	365
Skt.	Amitāyurdhyāna-sūtra	
Eng.	*The Sutra on Contemplation of Amitāyus* (in *The Three Pure Land Sutras,* Revised Second Edition, 2003)	
Ch.	Amituojing (阿彌陀經)	366
Skt.	Sukhāvatīvyūha	
Eng.	*The Smaller Sutra on Amitāyus* (in *The Three Pure Land Sutras,* Revised Second Edition, 2003)	
Ch.	Dabanniepanjing (大般涅槃經)	374
Skt.	Mahāparinirvāṇa-sūtra	
Ch.	Fochuiboniepanlüeshuojiaojiejing (佛垂般涅槃略説教誡經)	389
Eng.	*The Bequeathed Teaching Sutra* (in *Apocryphal Scriptures,* 2005)	
Ch.	Dicangpusabenyuanjing (地藏菩薩本願經)	412
Skt.	Kṣitigarbhapraṇidhāna-sūtra (?)	
Ch.	Banzhousanmeijing (般舟三昧經)	418
Skt.	Pratyutpannabuddhasammukhāvasthitasamādhi-sūtra	
Eng.	*The Pratyutpanna Samādhi Sutra* (1998)	

Title		**Taishō No.**
Ch.	Yaoshiliuliguangrulaibenyuangongdejing (藥師琉璃光如來本願功德經)	450
Skt.	Bhaiṣajyaguruvaiḍūryaprabhāsapūrvapraṇidhānaviśeṣavistara	
Ch.	Milexiashengchengfojing (彌勒下生成佛經)	454
Skt.	Maitreyavyākaraṇa (?)	
Ch.	Wenshushiliwenjing (文殊師利問經)	468
Skt.	Mañjuśrīparipṛcchā (?)	
Ch.	Weimojiesuoshuojing (維摩詰所說經)	475
Skt.	Vimalakīrtinirdeśa-sūtra	
Eng.	*The Vimalakīrti Sutra* (2004)	
Ch.	Yueshangnüjing (月上女經)	480
Skt.	Candrottarādārikāparipṛcchā	
Ch.	Zuochansanmeijing (坐禪三昧經)	614
Ch.	Damoduoluochanjing (達磨多羅禪經)	618
Ch.	Yuedengsanmeijing (月燈三昧經)	639
Skt.	Samādhirājacandrapradīpa-sūtra	
Ch.	Shoulengyansanmeijing (首楞嚴三昧經)	642
Skt.	Śūraṅgamasamādhi-sūtra	
Eng.	*The Śūraṅgama Samādhi Sutra* (1998)	
Ch.	Jinguangmingzuishengwangjing (金光明最勝王經)	665
Skt.	Suvarṇaprabhāsa-sūtra	
Ch.	Rulengqiejing (入楞伽經)	671
Skt.	Laṅkāvatāra-sūtra	
Ch.	Jieshenmijing (解深密經)	676
Skt.	Saṃdhinirmocana-sūtra	
Eng.	*The Scripture on the Explication of Underlying Meaning* (2000)	
Ch.	Yulanpenjing (盂蘭盆經)	685
Skt.	Ullambana-sūtra (?)	
Eng.	*The Ullambana Sutra* (in *Apocryphal Scriptures,* 2005)	
Ch.	Sishierzhangjing (四十二章經)	784
Eng.	*The Sutra of Forty-two Sections* (in *Apocryphal Scriptures,* 2005)	
Ch.	Dafangguangyuanjuexiuduoluoliaoyijing (大方廣圓覺修多羅了義經)	842
Eng.	*The Sutra of Perfect Enlightenment* (in *Apocryphal Scriptures,* 2005)	

Title		**Taishō No.**
Ch.	Dabiluzhenachengfoshenbianjiachijing (大毘盧遮那成佛神變加持經)	848
Skt.	Mahāvairocanābhisambodhivikurvitādhiṣṭhānavaipulyasūtrendra-rājanāmadharmaparyāya	
Eng.	*The Vairocanābhisaṃbodhi Sutra* (2005)	
Ch.	Jinggangdingyiqierulaizhenshishedachengxianzhengdajiao-wangjing (金剛頂一切如來眞實攝大乘現證大教王經)	865
Skt.	Sarvatathāgatatattvasaṃgrahamahāyānābhisamayamahākalparāja	
Eng.	*The Adamantine Pinnacle Sutra* (in *Two Esoteric Sutras,* 2001)	
Ch.	Suxidijieluojing (蘇悉地羯囉經)	893
Skt.	Susiddhikaramahātantrasādhanopāyika-paṭala	
Eng.	*The Susiddhikara Sutra* (in *Two Esoteric Sutras,* 2001)	
Ch.	Modengqiejing (摩登伽經)	1300
Skt.	Mātaṅgī-sūtra (?)	
Ch.	Mohesengqilü (摩訶僧祇律)	1425
Skt.	Mahāsāṃghika-vinaya (?)	
Ch.	Sifenlü (四分律)	1428
Skt.	Dharmaguptaka-vinaya (?)	
Ch.	Shanjianlüpiposha (善見律毘婆沙)	1462
Pāli	Samantapāsādikā	
Ch.	Fanwangjing (梵網經)	1484
Skt.	Brahmajāla-sūtra (?)	
Ch.	Youposaijiejing (優婆塞戒經)	1488
Skt.	Upāsakaśīla-sūtra (?)	
Eng.	*The Sutra on Upāsaka Precepts* (1994)	
Ch.	Miaofalianhuajingyoubotishe (妙法蓮華經憂波提舍)	1519
Skt.	Saddharmapuṇḍarīka-upadeśa	
Ch.	Shih-chu-pi-p'o-sha-lun (十住毘婆沙論)	1521
Skt.	Daśabhūmika-vibhāṣā (?)	
Ch.	Fodijinglun (佛地經論)	1530
Skt.	Buddhabhūmisūtra-śāstra (?)	
Eng.	*The Interpretation of the Buddha Land* (2002)	
Ch.	Apidamojushelun (阿毘達磨俱舍論)	1558
Skt.	Abhidharmakośa-bhāṣya	

Title		Taishō No.
Ch.	Zhonglun (中論)	1564
Skt.	Madhyamaka-śāstra	
Ch.	Yüqieshidilun (瑜伽師地論)	1579
Skt.	Yogācārabhūmi	
Ch.	Chengweishilun (成唯識論)	1585
Eng.	*Demonstration of Consciousness Only* (in *Three Texts on Consciousness Only,* 1999)	
Ch.	Weishisanshilunsong (唯識三十論頌)	1586
Skt.	Triṃśikā	
Eng.	*The Thirty Verses on Consciousness Only* (in *Three Texts on Consciousness Only,* 1999)	
Ch.	Weishihershilun (唯識二十論)	1590
Skt.	Viṃśatikā	
Eng.	*The Treatise in Twenty Verses on Consciousness Only* (in *Three Texts on Consciousness Only,* 1999)	
Ch.	Shedachenglun (攝大乘論)	1593
Skt.	Mahāyānasaṃgraha	
Eng.	*The Summary of the Great Vehicle* (Revised Second Edition, 2003)	
Ch.	Bianzhongbianlun (辯中邊論)	1600
Skt.	Madhyāntavibhāga	
Ch.	Dachengzhuangyanjinglun (大乘莊嚴經論)	1604
Skt.	Mahāyānasūtrālaṃkāra	
Ch.	Dachengchengyelun (大乘成業論)	1609
Skt.	Karmasiddhiprakaraṇa	
Ch.	Jiujingyichengbaoxinglun (究竟一乘寶性論)	1611
Skt.	Ratnagotravibhāgamahāyānottaratantra-śāstra	
Ch.	Yinmingruzhenglilun (因明入正理論)	1630
Skt.	Nyāyapraveśa	
Ch.	Dachengjipusaxuelun (大乘集菩薩學論)	1636
Skt.	Śikṣāsamuccaya	
Ch.	Jingangzhenlun (金剛針論)	1642
Skt.	Vajrasūcī	
Ch.	Zhangsuozhilun (彰所知論)	1645
Eng.	*The Treatise on the Elucidation of the Knowable* (2004)	

Title		Taishō No.
Ch.	Putixingjing (菩提行經)	1662
Skt.	Bodhicaryāvatāra	
Ch.	Jingangdingyuqiezhongfaanouduoluosanmiaosanputixinlun (金剛頂瑜伽中發阿耨多羅三藐三菩提心論)	1665
Ch.	Dachengqixinlun (大乘起信論)	1666
Skt.	Mahāyānaśraddhotpāda-śāstra (?)	
Eng.	*The Awakening of Faith* (2005)	
Ch.	Shimoheyanlun (釋摩訶衍論)	1668
Ch.	Naxianbiqiujing (那先比丘經)	1670
Pāli	Milindapañhā	
Ch.	Banruoboluomiduoxinjingyuzan (般若波羅蜜多心經幽賛)	1710
Eng.	*A Comprehensive Commentary on the Heart Sutra (Prajñāpāramitā-hṛdaya-sūtra)* (2001)	
Ch.	Miaofalianhuajingxuanyi (妙法蓮華經玄義)	1716
Ch.	Guanwuliangshoufojingshu (觀無量壽佛經疏)	1753
Ch.	Sanlunxuanyi (三論玄義)	1852
Ch.	Dachengxuanlun (大乘玄論)	1853
Ch.	Zhaolun (肇論)	1858
Ch.	Huayanyichengjiaoyifenqizhang (華嚴一乘教義分齊章)	1866
Ch.	Yuanrenlun (原人論)	1886
Ch.	Mohezhiguan (摩訶止觀)	1911
Ch.	Xiuxizhiguanzuochanfayao (修習止觀坐禪法要)	1915
Ch.	Tiantaisijiaoyi (天台四教儀)	1931
Ch.	Guoqingbailu (國清百録)	1934
Ch.	Zhenzhoulinjihuizhaochanshiwulu (鎭州臨濟慧照禪師語録)	1985
Eng.	*The Recorded Sayings of Linji* (in *Three Chan Classics,* 1999)	
Ch.	Foguoyuanwuchanshibiyanlu (佛果圜悟禪師碧巖録)	2003
Eng.	*The Blue Cliff Record* (1998)	
Ch.	Wumenguan (無門關)	2005
Eng.	*Wumen's Gate* (in *Three Chan Classics,* 1999)	

Title		**Taishō No.**
Ch.	Liuzudashifabaotanjing (六祖大師法寶壇經)	2008
Eng.	*The Platform Sutra of the Sixth Patriarch* (2000)	
Ch.	Xinxinming (信心銘)	2010
Eng.	*The Faith-Mind Maxim* (in *Three Chan Classics,* 1999)	
Ch.	Huangboshanduanjichanshichuanxinfayao (黃檗山斷際禪師傳心法要)	2012A
Eng.	*Essentials of the Transmission of Mind* (in *Zen Texts,* 2005)	
Ch.	Yongjiazhengdaoge (永嘉證道歌)	2014
Ch.	Chixiubaizhangqinggui (勅修百丈清規)	2025
Eng.	*The Baizhang Zen Monastic Regulations* (2007)	
Ch.	Yibuzonglunlun (異部宗輪論)	2031
Skt.	Samayabhedoparacanacakra	
Eng.	*The Cycle of the Formation of the Schismatic Doctrines* (2004)	
Ch.	Ayuwangjing (阿育王經)	2043
Skt.	Aśokāvadāna	
Eng.	*The Biographical Scripture of King Aśoka* (1993)	
Ch.	Mamingpusachuan (馬鳴菩薩傳)	2046
Eng.	*The Life of Aśvaghoṣa Bodhisattva* (in *Lives of Great Monks and Nuns,* 2002)	
Ch.	Longshupusachuan (龍樹菩薩傳)	2047
Eng.	*The Life of Nāgārjuna Bodhisattva* (in *Lives of Great Monks and Nuns,* 2002)	
Ch.	Posoupandoufashichuan (婆藪槃豆法師傳)	2049
Eng.	*Biography of Dharma Master Vasubandhu* (in *Lives of Great Monks and Nuns,* 2002)	
Ch.	Datangdaciensisancangfashichuan (大唐大慈恩寺三藏法師傳)	2053
Eng.	*A Biography of the Tripiṭaka Master of the Great Ci'en Monastery of the Great Tang Dynasty* (1995)	
Ch.	Gaosengchuan (高僧傳)	2059
Ch.	Biqiunichuan (比丘尼傳)	2063
Eng.	*Biographies of Buddhist Nuns* (in *Lives of Great Monks and Nuns,* 2002)	

Title		Taishō No.
Ch.	Gaosengfaxianchuan (高僧法顯傳)	2085
Eng.	*The Journey of the Eminent Monk Faxian* (in *Lives of Great Monks and Nuns,* 2002)	
Ch.	Datangxiyuji (大唐西域記)	2087
Eng.	*The Great Tang Dynasty Record of the Western Regions* (1996)	
Ch.	Youfangjichao: Tangdaheshangdongzhengchuan (遊方記抄: 唐大和上東征傳)	2089-(7)
Ch.	Hongmingji (弘明集)	2102
Ch.	Fayuanzhulin (法苑珠林)	2122
Ch.	Nanhaijiguineifachuan (南海寄歸内法傳)	2125
Eng.	*Buddhist Monastic Traditions of Southern Asia* (2000)	
Ch.	Fanyuzaming (梵語雑名)	2135
Jp.	Shōmangyōgisho (勝鬘經義疏)	2185
Jp.	Yuimakyōgisho (維摩經義疏)	2186
Jp.	Hokkegisho (法華義疏)	2187
Jp.	Hannyashingyōhiken (般若心經秘鍵)	2203
Jp.	Daijōhossōkenjinshō (大乘法相研神章)	2309
Jp.	Kan-jin-kaku-mu-shō (觀心覺夢鈔)	2312
Jp.	Risshūkōyō (律宗綱要)	2348
Eng.	*The Essentials of the Vinaya Tradition* (1995)	
Jp.	Tendaihokkeshūgishū (天台法華宗義集)	2366
Eng.	*The Collected Teachings of the Tendai Lotus School* (1995)	
Jp.	Kenkairon (顯戒論)	2376
Jp.	Sangegakushōshiki (山家學生式)	2377
Jp.	Hizōhōyaku (秘藏寶鑰)	2426
Eng.	*The Precious Key to the Secret Treasury* (in *Shingon Texts*, 2004)	
Jp.	Benkenmitsunikyōron (辨顯密二教論)	2427
Eng.	*On the Differences between the Exoteric and Esoteric Teachings* (in *Shingon Texts*, 2004)	

Title		**Taishō No.**
Jp.	Sokushinjōbutsugi (即身成佛義)	2428
Eng.	*The Meaning of Becoming a Buddha in This Very Body* (in *Shingon Texts*, 2004)	
Jp.	Shōjijissōgi (聲字實相義)	2429
Eng.	*The Meanings of Sound, Sign, and Reality* (in *Shingon Texts*, 2004)	
Jp.	Unjigi (吽字義)	2430
Eng.	*The Meanings of the Word Hūṃ* (in *Shingon Texts*, 2004)	
Jp.	Gorinkujimyōhimitsushaku (五輪九字明秘密釋)	2514
Eng.	*The Illuminating Secret Commentary on the Five Cakras and the Nine Syllables* (in *Shingon Texts*, 2004)	
Jp.	Mitsugoninhotsurosangemon (密嚴院發露懺悔文)	2527
Eng.	*The Mitsugonin Confession* (in *Shingon Texts,* 2004)	
Jp.	Kōzengokokuron (興禪護國論)	2543
Eng.	*A Treatise on Letting Zen Flourish to Protect the State* (in *Zen Texts,* 2005)	
Jp.	Fukanzazengi (普勧坐禪儀)	2580
Eng.	*A Universal Recommendation for True Zazen* (in *Zen Texts,* 2005)	
Jp.	Shōbōgenzō (正法眼藏)	2582
Eng.	*Shōbōgenzō: The True Dharma-eye Treasury* (Volume I, 2007)	
Jp.	Zazenyōjinki (坐禪用心記)	2586
Eng.	*Advice on the Practice of Zazen* (in *Zen Texts,* 2005)	
Jp.	Senchakuhongannenbutsushū (選擇本願念佛集)	2608
Eng.	*Senchaku Hongan Nembutsu Shū: A Collection of Passages on the Nembutsu Chosen in the Original Vow* (1997)	
Jp.	Kenjōdoshinjitsukyōgyōshōmonrui (顯淨土眞實教行証文類)	2646
Eng.	*Kyōgyōshinshō: On Teaching, Practice, Faith, and Enlightenment* (2003)	
Jp.	Tannishō (歎異抄)	2661
Eng.	*Tannishō: Passages Deploring Deviations of Faith* (1996)	
Jp.	Rennyoshōninofumi (蓮如上人御文)	2668
Eng.	*Rennyo Shōnin Ofumi: The Letters of Rennyo* (1996)	

Title		Taishō No.
Jp.	Ōjōyōshū (往生要集)	2682
Jp. Eng.	Risshōankokuron (立正安國論) *Risshōankokuron or The Treatise on the Establishment of the Orthodox Teaching and the Peace of the Nation* (in *Two Nichiren Texts,* 2003)	2688
Jp. Eng.	Kaimokushō (開目抄) *Kaimokushō or Liberation from Blindness* (2000)	2689
Jp. Eng.	Kanjinhonzonshō (觀心本尊抄) *Kanjinhonzonshō or The Most Venerable One Revealed by Introspecting Our Minds for the First Time at the Beginning of the Fifth of the Five Five Hundred-year Ages* (in *Two Nichiren Texts,* 2003)	2692
Ch. Eng.	Fumuenzhongjing (父母恩重經) *The Sutra on the Profundity of Filial Love* (in *Apocryphal Scriptures,* 2005)	2887
Jp. Eng.	Hasshūkōyō (八宗綱要) *The Essentials of the Eight Traditions* (1994)	extracanonical
Jp.	Sangōshīki (三教指帰)	extracanonical
Jp. Eng.	Mappōtōmyōki (末法燈明記) *The Candle of the Latter Dharma* (1994)	extracanonical
Jp.	Jūshichijōkenpō (十七條憲法)	extracanonical